PRINCIPLES AND PRACTICES OF LIGHT CONSTRUCTION

Sixth Edition

Ronald C. Smith

Ted L. Honkala
Southern Alberta Institute of Technology

Malcolm W. Sharp
MacNel Consulting Ltd.

Upper Saddle River, New Jersey
Columbus, Ohio

Library of Congress Cataloging in Publication Data

Smith, Ronald C.
Principles and Practices of Light Construction/Ronald C. Smith, Ted L. Honkala, Malcolm W. Sharp—6th ed.
p. cm.
Includes index.
ISBN 0-13-049662-6
1. Building. 2. Carpentry. I. Honkala, T.L. II. Sharp, Malcolm W. III. Title.

TH145.S577 2004
690—dc21 2003049826

Editor in Chief: Stephen Helba
Executive Editor: Ed Francis
Development Editor: Linda Cupp
Production Editor: Holly Shufeldt
Project Management: Preparé, Inc.
Design Coordinator: Diane Ernsberger
Cover Designer: Thomas Mack
Cover art: Corbis
Production Manager: Matt Ottenweller
Marketing Manager: Mark Marsden

This book was set in Times Ten by Preparé, Inc. It was printed and bound by Courier/Kendallville, Inc. The cover was printed by The Lehigh Press, Inc.

Pearson Education Ltd.
Pearson Education Singapore, Pte. Ltd.
Pearson Education Canada, Ltd.
Pearson Education—Japan
Pearson Education Australia, Pty. Limited
Pearson Education North Asia Ltd.
Pearson Educación de Mexico, S.A. de C.V.
Pearson Education Malaysia, Pte. Ltd.

10 9 8 7 6 5 4 3 2 1

ISBN 0-13-049662-6

PREFACE

As this is the sixth edition of *Principles and Practices of Light Construction*, we ascertain that it has been serving an important role in the light construction industry for many years. Since its publication in 1963 there have been numerous advances made, not only in building practices but also in materials, equipment processes, and design. Keeping abreast of these advances is a challenging task for all of us.

There has been a continual increase in the demand for new buildings, regardless of where you live. The pressures of increasing populations, urban expansion and renewal, the attractiveness of rural living, and a focus on different lifestyles all contribute to the demand.

We all learn from our experiences. From those experiences new ideas and methods evolve. The building industry is no exception. New materials, improved labor-saving techniques, better processes, and better trained personnel all make a difference in the way the construction industry has evolved. Prefabrication, molded products, plastics, vinyl components, composition materials, metals, and modifications in glass products all have required changes in the way we build. The increased demand for oil and gas along with higher prices has also led consumers to seek more energy-efficient buildings, and, with the introduction of sophisticated electronic systems in buildings, has necessitated changes.

The intent of this book is to provide a tool for people involved in the construction of "light" buildings to enable them to become better informed about current practices, methods, and materials. This book is written for those who are practitioners, or those intending to be practitioners, those who are involved in a peripheral way with buildings, and those who are novices interested in becoming knowledgeable about light construction, regardless of their reasons.

Acknowledgment must be given to Ronald Smith, a longtime colleague of mine who created the first edition. His knowledge and skills as a competent practitioner and instructor allowed him to put together a much-needed book on the subject. Likewise, Ted Honkala, who co-authored with Ronald Smith, was also a colleague of mine. I have the greatest respect for his competence in the construction field and in his ability to put forth his experiences in a manner that allows others to reap untold benefits. Both of these people have set the groundwork for an exceptional book that made my job of editing and updating it much easier.

I also want to thank all those who have contributed their expertise, illustrations, and other materials that make the book as current as possible. Without their help and cooperation, this book would not have been possible. In addition, particular thanks are due to David L. Batie, East Carolina University; Eugene H. Wright, University of Nebraska–Lincoln; D. Perry Achor, Purdue University; and Robert Pyle, North Carolina A & T State University, for their assistance with the sixth edition text review.

Malcolm W. Sharp

CONTENTS

4

5

6

7

THE CEILING AND ROOF FRAME *199*

8

STAIR BUILDING *249*

9

EXTERIOR FINISHING *273*

10

11

Chapter 1

TOOLS AND EQUIPMENT

OBJECTIVES

Here is what you will be able to do when you complete each component of this chapter:

1. Identify and determine uses of common hand and power tools used in the construction of buildings.
2. Describe how to care for tools.
3. Identify common construction equipment.

Regardless of trade or occupation, tools are an integral part of the job. Granted, they have evolved, but they remain essential. Hand tools are necessary for a multitude of tasks even though electrical or pneumatic tools have replaced many of the operations, resulting in increased efficiency. New hand and power tools continue to be developed as a result of new materials and processes.

A successful practitioner must have a wide variety of hand and power tools, in order to perform many different operations required in the course of daily activities in the construction industry. Competence in their proper use is mandatory, and it is with this purpose this chapter deals with the identification and explanation for their intended use. Skill in performing operations will have to be achieved through experience and guidance from others. It is strongly recommended that this textbook be used in conjunction with a comprehensive hands-on component.

HAND TOOLS

Hand tools may be divided into the following groups, based on the type of work done with them:

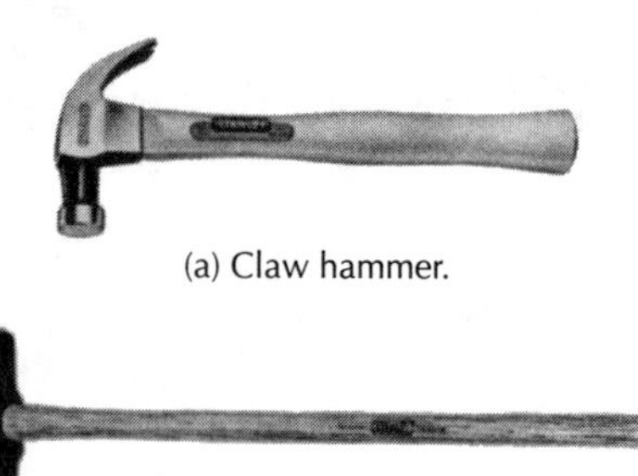
(a) Claw hammer.

(b) Sledge hammer.

FIGURE 1-1 Hammers.

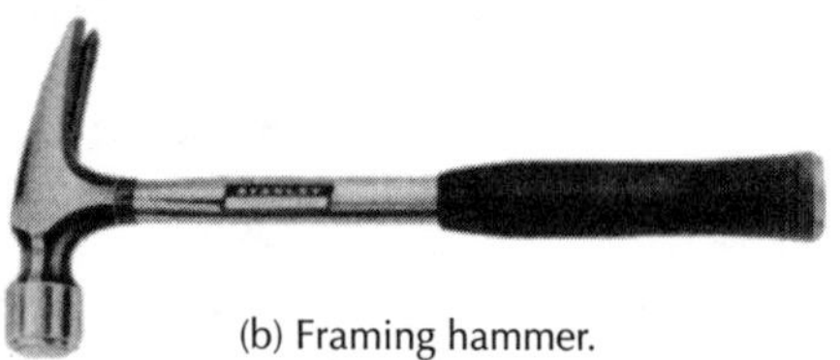
(a) Nailing hammer, steel handle.

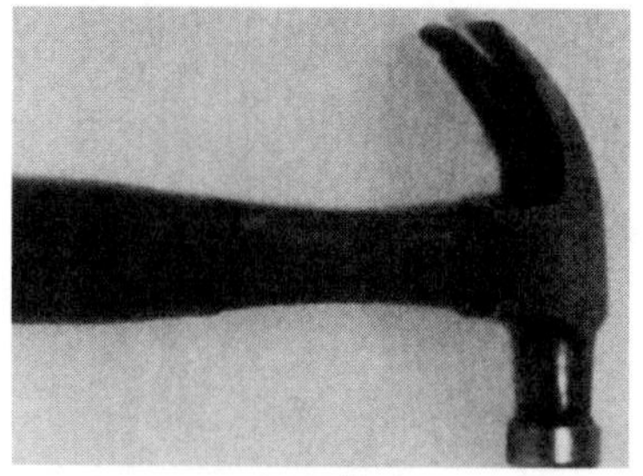
(b) Framing hammer.

FIGURE 1-2 Hammer claws.

(a) Belled.

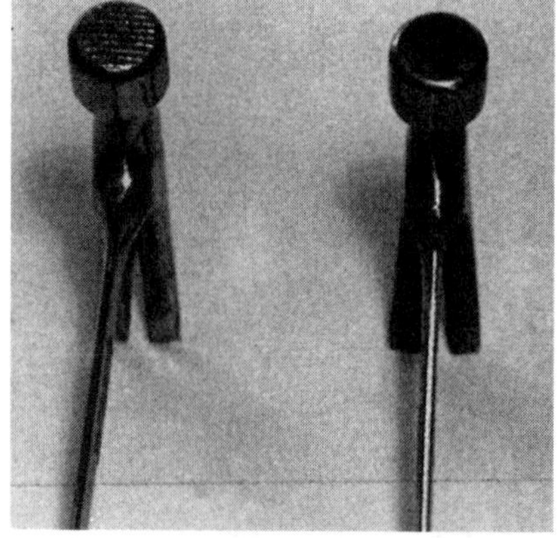
(b) Knurled and plain.

FIGURE 1-3 Hammer faces.

1. Assembling tools
2. Boring tools
3. Cutting tools
4. Holding tools
5. Layout and marking tools
6. Leveling and plumbing tools
7. Measuring tools
8. Sharpening tools
9. Smoothing tools
10. Wrecking tools.

On occasion there may be a tool that belongs in more than one of these groups.

Assembling Tools

Hammers. Hammers are classified according to the type of work done with them. Two of the most common classifications are sledgehammers [see Fig. 1-1(b)] and claw hammers [see Fig. 1-1(a)]. Claw hammers are used for driving nails while sledgehammers are used for driving stakes into the ground, or possibly for demolition work.

Claw hammers are made with either curved claws for nail pulling or straight claws for ripping and wrecking work [see Fig. 1-2(a) and 1-2(b)]. The ripping claw hammer is called a *framing hammer* and is typically used by those involved in framing work. The curved claw hammer is typically used for finishing or general work. The face of a nail hammer may be belled (convex surface), plane (flat surface), or knurled (checkered) (see Fig. 1-3). The weight of a hammer is usually 13 oz (370 g) for light finish work, 16–20 oz (455–570 g) for general work, and 22–28 oz (625–800 g) for framing work. Choose the hammer best suited for the job to be done.

Hammer handles may be made of wood, steel, graphite, or fiberglass. The wooden-handled hammer has more give or spring than the other types, but steel, graphite, and fiberglass handles are stronger and less likely to break. The grips on these handles are available in leather, plastic, or vinyl materials

Claw hammers should never be used for purposes other than driving or pulling regular nails. When using a hammer to pull nails, use a block placed between the hammer and the surface next to the nail to increase the leverage (see Fig. 1-4), or if very hard to pull, use a wrecking bar (see Fig. 1-52).

When using a hammer, grip the handle near the end so the entire length of the handle provides leverage. Holding the handle near the head provides very little power behind the swing. Hold the handle firmly, use short strokes to start the nail, and then drive it home with longer strokes. When driving small nails with short strokes, use

FIGURE 1-4 Block to assist pulling.

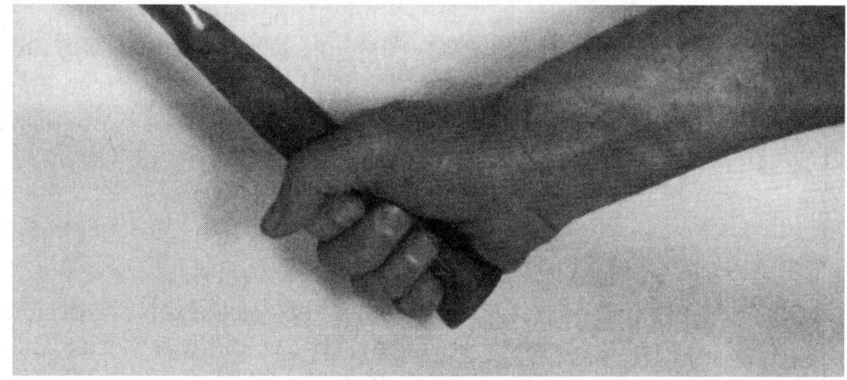

FIGURE 1-5 Hammer grip.

only your wrist and forearm in the swing. Long nails, such as those used in framing, need the force of your entire arm to drive them easily (see Fig. 1-5).

Screwdrivers. Screwdrivers are most common in three types: *flat blade*, for use with slotted screws; *Robertson*, for use with Robertson head screws, that have a square pocket in the head; and *Phillips*, for use with Phillips head screws, that have an indented cross in the head (see Fig. 1-6).

The blades of flat blade screwdrivers are made in a number of widths and thickness to accommodate the various sizes of screws (see Fig. 1-7). Some of these screwdrivers, called stubbies, have a very short blade and handle for use in hard-to-get-at places (see Fig. 1-8).

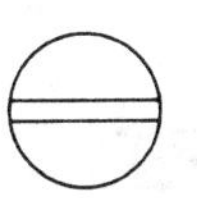

Slotted head

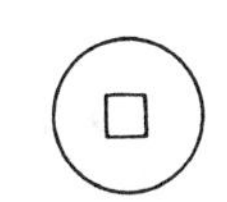

Robertson head

Phillips head

FIGURE 1-6 Screw head types.

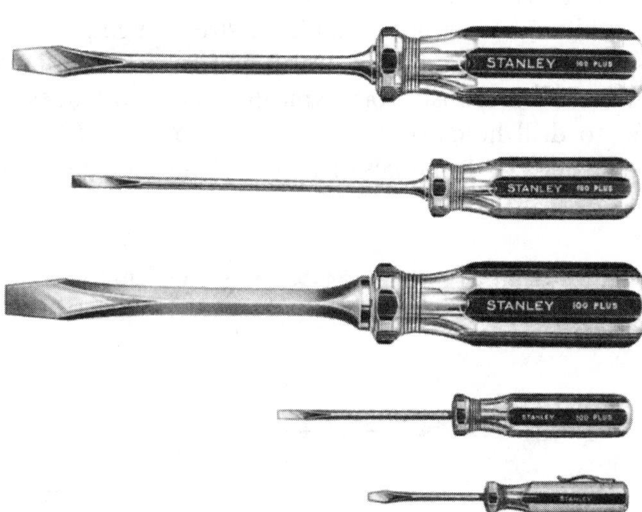

FIGURE 1-7 Plain-handled screwdrivers.

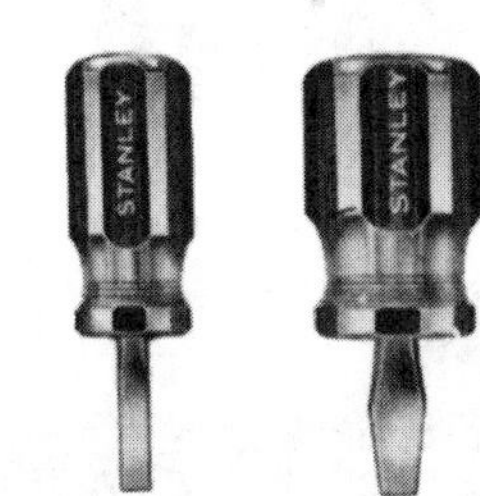

(a) Flat blade.

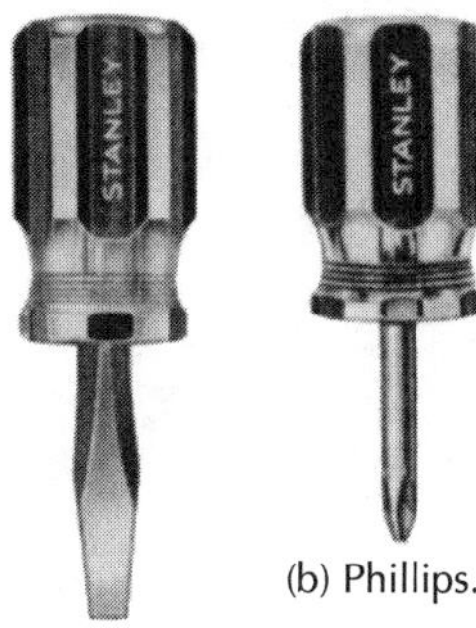

(b) Phillips.

FIGURE 1-8 "Stubby" screwdrivers.

FIGURE 1-9 Robertson screwdriver.

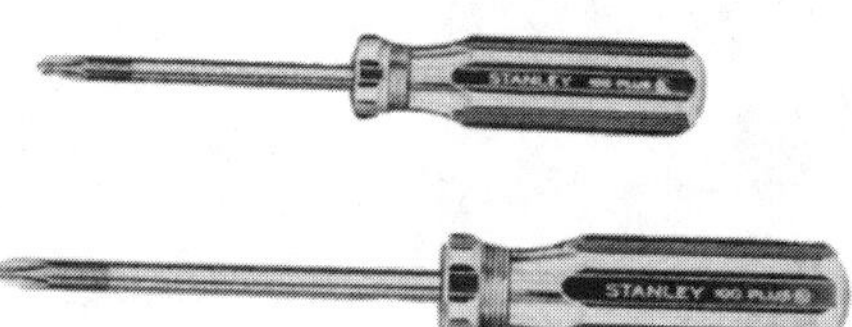

FIGURE 1-10 Phillips screwdrivers.

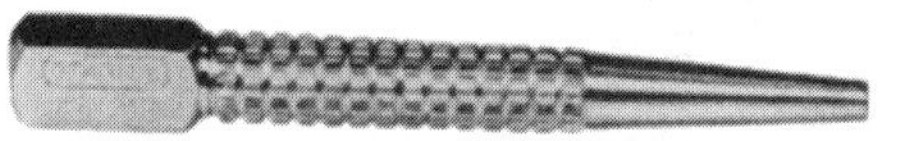

FIGURE 1-11 Nail set.

(a) Hand tacker.

(b) Hammer type stapler.

FIGURE 1-12

Robertson and Phillips screwdrivers are made in a variety of lengths with four tip sizes—Nos. 0, 1, 2, and 3—to fit the standard sizes of screw sockets (see Figs. 1-9 and 1-10). These types of openings in the screw sockets distribute the force more equally than a slotted screw.

There are also screwdrivers available with interchangeable blades where the blades are stored in the handle.

Nail Sets. Nail sets are designed to drive finishing nail heads below the surface of the material. The diameter of the tip is the size, ranging from $\frac{1}{16}$ in. (1.5 mm) to $\frac{3}{16}$ in. (5 mm). The shank is usually knurled for better grip (see Fig. 1-11).

Staplers. Staplers perform a variety of operations, such as attaching building paper, vapor barrier, ceiling tile, and roofing materials (see Fig. 1-12). The hand tackers are spring-loaded for driving the staple, while the hammer type requires it to be swung like a hammer.

Boring Tools

Today's trades rarely use hand boring tools, but there are occasions when they are used and you should be able to recognize them. Included in this group of tools are ones that cut holes in wood—*bits*—as well as tools that hold and turn them—*bit braces*.

Wood Bits. Wood bits are used with a bit brace and are made in several styles; two of the more common ones are illustrated in Fig. 1-13, a solid center auger bit and an expansive bit. Both have square ends for insertion into the chuck of a bit brace.

Auger bits are commonly made in sizes ranging from $\frac{1}{4}$ in. to $1\frac{1}{4}$ in. (6–31 mm) in diameter, increasing in size by increments of $\frac{1}{16}$ in. (1.5 mm). Expansive bits typically have two blades, one that can be set to drill holes of 1 in. (25 mm) to $1\frac{1}{2}$ in. (38 mm), and one that can be set to drill holes of $1\frac{1}{2}$ in. (38 mm) to 3 in. (75 mm).

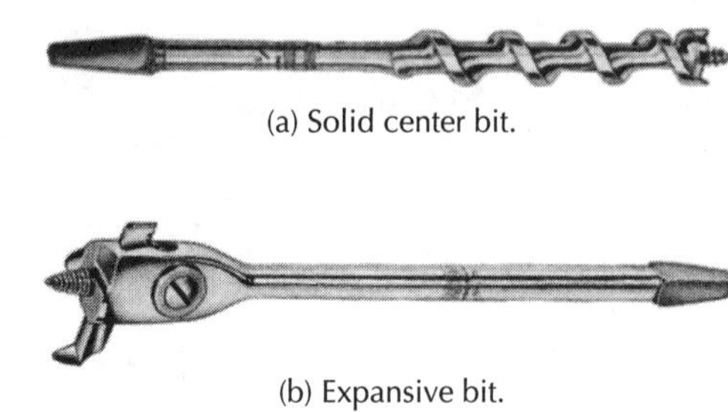

(a) Solid center bit.

(b) Expansive bit.

FIGURE 1-13 Wood bits.

Bit Brace. Figure 1-14 illustrates a standard bit brace that is capable of holding both square-end auger bits and expansive bits. The type shown is a *ratchet* brace. Ratchet braces can be set to drive in one direction (clockwise or anticlockwise rotation) or locked to turn in both directions. When set to rotate in a clockwise direction, as in a confined space, a full rotation of the handle is not necessary to drill a hole.

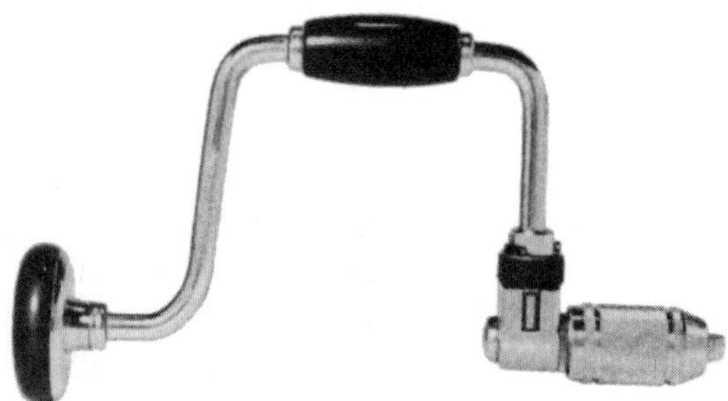

FIGURE 1-14 Hand brace with box ratchet.
(Courtesy Stanley Tools)

Cutting Tools

Cutting tools include *saws*, *chisels*, *axes*, *snips*, and *knives*. In each of these major categories there are a number of styles or varieties, each adapted for a specific purpose.

Saws. Included in this category are *handsaws, backsaws, compass saws, coping saws, utility saws*, and *hacksaws*.

Handsaws. Two types of handsaws are made: one designed to cut across the fibers of wood—*crosscut saw*—and the other designed to cut along the fibers—a *ripsaw*. The main difference between them is the method of shaping and sharpening the teeth.

Crosscut saws have teeth with the cutting edge sloped forward and filed at an angle so that each tooth, as it is drawn across the wood, severs the fibers like a knife. They are used for cutting across the wood fibers. Ripsaw teeth have the front shaped nearly at right angles to the blade that results in each tooth cutting the fibers much like a chisel would cut. They are used for cutting parallel to the wood fibers (See Fig. 1-15).

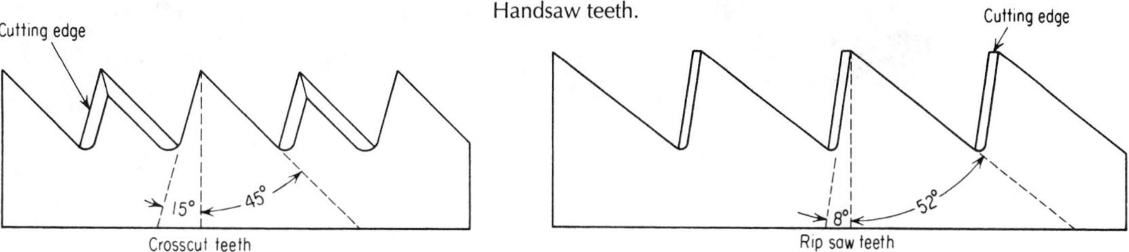

FIGURE 1-15 Handsaw teeth.

FIGURE 1-16 Full tapered saw blade.
(Courtesy of Kennametal Inc.)

Some of these saws have a tapered blade (thicker at the cutting edge than at the back of the blade), and some require the teeth to be slightly bent alternately left and right to prevent "binding" in the saw "kerf" (see Fig. 1-16). Typically, crosscut saws are made in lengths of 26 in. (660 mm) and 20 in. (510 mm) although other lengths are available. The 20-in. (510 mm) saw is often called a *panel* saw.

All handsaws are identified by the number of teeth or *points* per inch (25 mm) and will vary from $5\frac{1}{2}$ to 13, depending on the type. The closer the teeth are together the finer or smoother the cut will be (see Fig. 1-17). Some saws are available with the tips of the teeth hardened through a heat-treating process. These saws retain their sharpness much longer than the other types but are more difficult to re-sharpen (see Fig. 1-18).

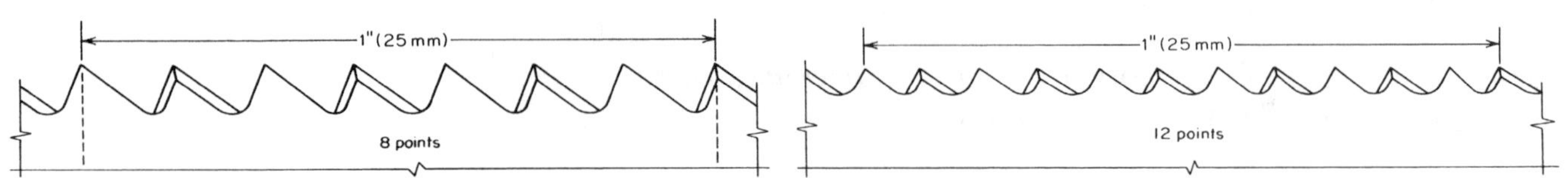

Fine and coarse saw teeth.

FIGURE 1-17 Fine and coarse saw teeth.

FIGURE 1-18 Hardened tipped tooth saw.

FIGURE 1-19 Short saw.

A specially sharpened crosscut saw is available where the teeth are longer and narrower making the saw capable of cutting on both the down as well as the up stroke. This can result in an increased cutting speed of up to 50% (see Fig. 1-19).

Backsaws. Backsaws are made with a stiff rib along the back of the blade and are intended for smoother cuts because of more teeth per inch (TPI). Several styles are available, including the *standard* backsaw, 12 in. to 14 in. (300–350 mm) with 12 to 15 TPI [see Fig. 1-20(a)]. Another type of backsaw is the *dovetail* saw that is 10 in. (250 mm) long with 16 TPI [see Fig. 1-20(b)]. Cabinetmakers prefer this type, as the cuts are smoother.

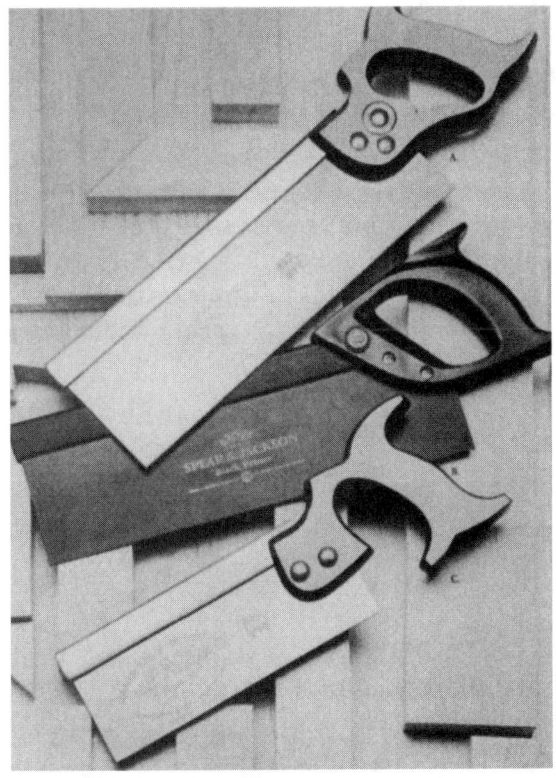

(a) Standard backsaws.

(b) Dovetail saw.

FIGURE 1-20 Specialty saws.

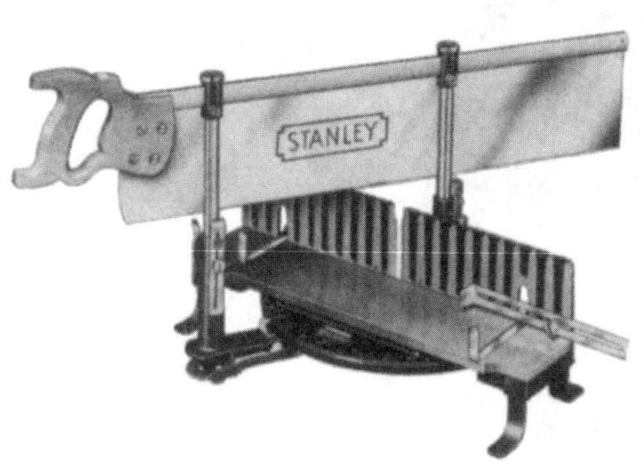

FIGURE 1-21 Miter saw and frame.
(Courtesy Stanley Tools)

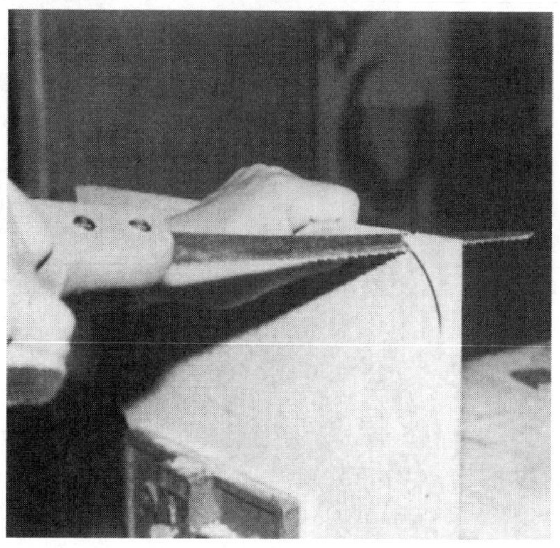

FIGURE 1-22 Compass saw in use.

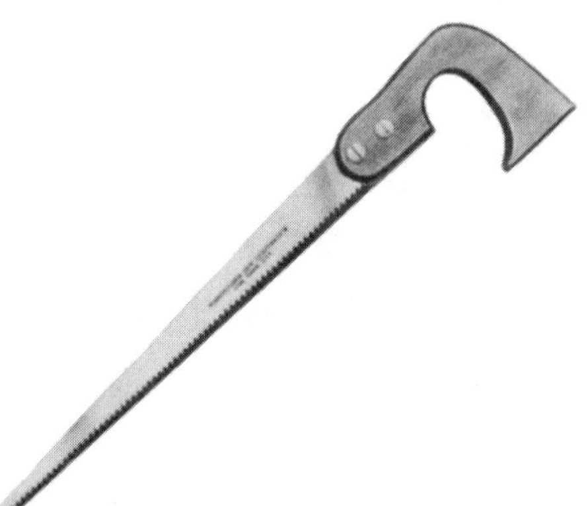

FIGURE 1-23 Compass saw.

Miter saws are rarely used in the construction industry anymore, but they are still manufactured for use, primarily by hobbyists. They are also a type of backsaw but are much longer. They are designed to fit in a frame to guide the saw while making cuts. The frame allows the saw to cut on various angles from 90° to up to 45° left or right (see Fig. 1-21).

Compass Saws. Compass saws are made with narrow, tapered blades and teeth designed to cut either along or across the wood grain (see Figs. 1-22 and 1-23). They are used for cutting circles or curves.

Coping Saws. Coping saws consist of a bow frame fitted with a very small, thin blade and are used for cutting curved shapes (see Fig. 1-24). They are very useful for interior finishing work such as for making *coped* joints in moldings, casing, and baseboard.

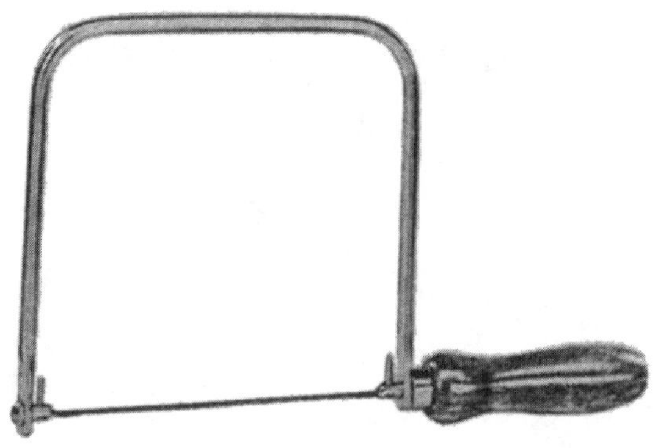

FIGURE 1-24 Coping saw.
(Courtesy Stanley Tools)

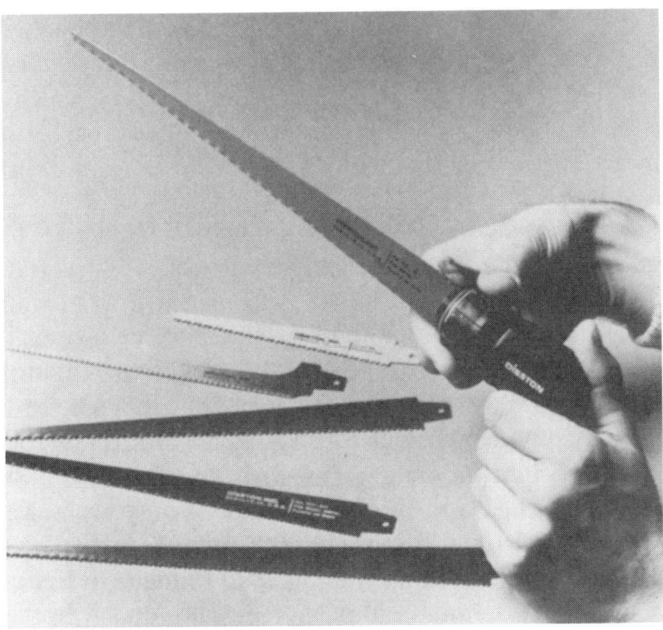

FIGURE 1-25 Utility saw with detachable handle.

Utility Saw. A utility saw consists of a thin, hardened blade with small teeth, useful for cutting hard materials such as metal or plastic laminates or gypsum board which tends to dull normal saw teeth. The utility saw shown in Fig. 1-25 has several blades that can be inserted into the handle that can also be rotated into any position.

Wallboard Saw. These saws are designed for cutting gypsum board, particularly for electrical boxes or plumbing pipes (see Fig. 1-26). The point of the blade is sharpened to allow the blade to be driven into the gypsum board for ease in starting the cut.

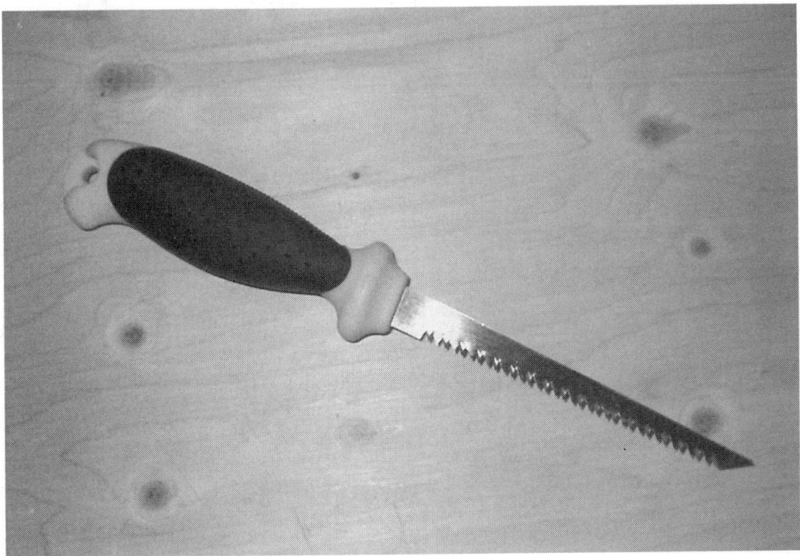

FIGURE 1-26 Wallboard saw.

FIGURE 1-27 Hacksaw.
(Courtesy Stanley Tools)

Hacksaw. A hacksaw is used for cutting metal. Most saws will adjust to take a 10-in. (240-mm) to 12-in. (300-mm) blade (see Fig. 1-27). The number of TPI varies from 18 to 32, the selection of which will depend on the thickness of the metal, as a minimum of two teeth should be in contact at all times for an efficient cut.

How to Use a Handsaw. First draw a line on the material to be cut. To begin the cut, rest the blade on the edge of the material, on the waste side of the cutting line. Steady the blade with your thumb [see Fig. 1-28(a)] and slowly draw the saw toward you several times to form a slight groove. Then use long, easy strokes with light pressure on the downward stroke. For a crosscut saw, try to keep the blade at an angle of 45° to the material, as this will allow the saw to cut efficiently [see Fig. 1-28(b)]. For a ripsaw, an angle of 60° is the most efficient [see Fig. 1-28(c)]. Be sure to place your body in a position where you can see the cutting line. The saw, the forearm, and the shoulder should form a straight line at right angles to the material. Be sure to support the material properly, either on sawhorses, a low flat surface, or in a vise [see Figs. 1-28(d) and 1-28(e)]. As you near the end of the cut, support the piece being cut off to prevent it splintering the underside of the material.

(a) Guiding blade with thumb.

(b) Cross-cut saw angle (45°).

(c) Ripping saw angle (60°).

(d) Supporting work with sawhorses.

(e) Holding work in a vise.

FIGURE 1-28 Using a handsaw.

Because handsaw teeth need to be sharp to cut efficiently, take care in handling and storing them. Do not let the teeth come in contact with any metal surface.

Chisels. Chisels are divided into two main classifications, depending on whether they are used to cut wood (wood chisels) or other material such as metal or concrete (cold chisels). Figure 1-29 illustrates these typical chisels.

Wood chisels range from $\frac{1}{4}$ in. to 2 in. (6–50 mm). Figure 1-30 illustrates a common set, $\frac{1}{4}$, $\frac{1}{2}$, $\frac{3}{4}$, and 1 in. Most of these chisels are equipped with plastic handles and care should be taken not to damage them. If possible, a wooden or plastic mallet should be used to tap these chisels (see Fig. 1-31).

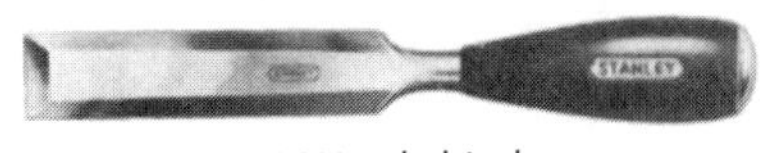

(a) Wood chisel.

(b) Cold chisel.

FIGURE 1-29 Chisel types.

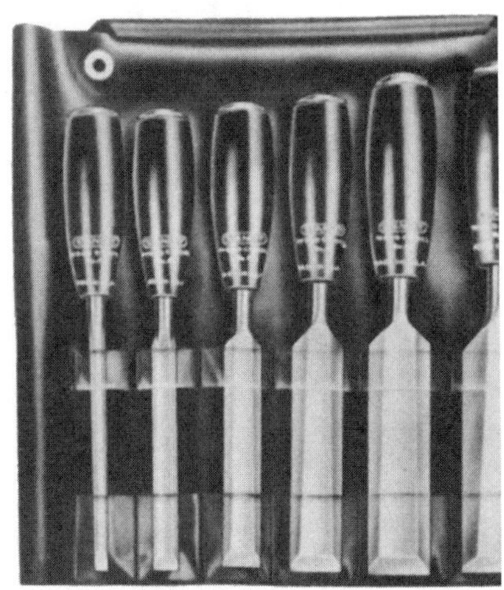

FIGURE 1-30 Chisel set.
(Courtesy Stanley Tools)

FIGURE 1-31 Using mallet on head of chisel.

There are a wide variety of cold chisels available, each suited for a particular use. Some are designed for cutting brick while others are suited for cutting or punching metal or concrete.

Axes. In some types of construction an ax is useful, depending on the size, shape, and weight. Several types are shown in Fig. 1-32. A *bench* ax or *hatchet* can be used for sharpening wooden stakes (Fig. 1-32(a). Many workers that frame buildings prefer a *framing hatchet* to drive nails (Fig. 1-32(b). *Shingling hatchets* are used to apply shingles and are equipped with an adjustable pin to gauge the amount of shingle exposure [see Fig. 1-32(c)].

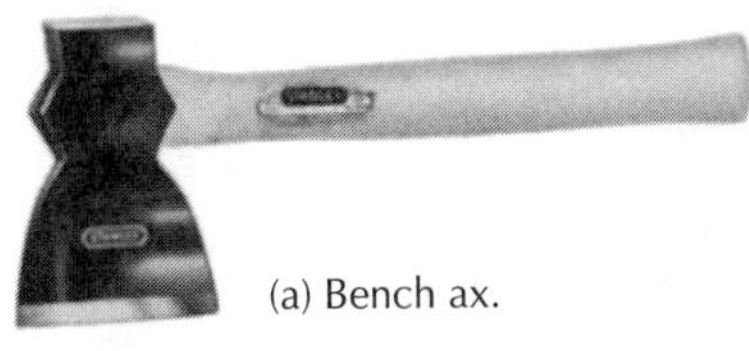

(a) Bench ax.

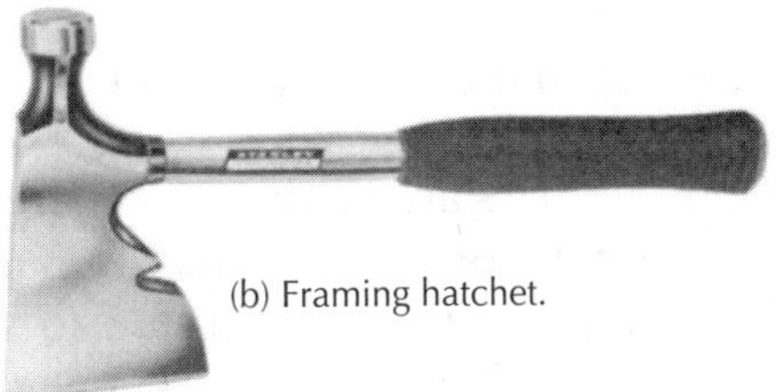

(b) Framing hatchet.

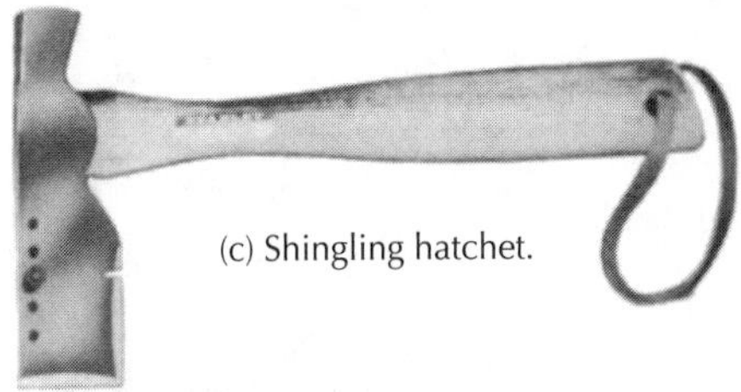

(c) Shingling hatchet.

FIGURE 1-32 Hatchets.
(Courtesy Stanley Tools)

Snips. Snips are specifically designed for cutting thin sheet metal, though they can be useful in cutting other materials [see Fig. 1-33(a)]. The snips illustrated in Fig. 1-33(b) are suited for cutting small circles, either for left or right cutting, and are also available for straight cuts.

(a) Tin snips. (Courtesy Stanley Tools)

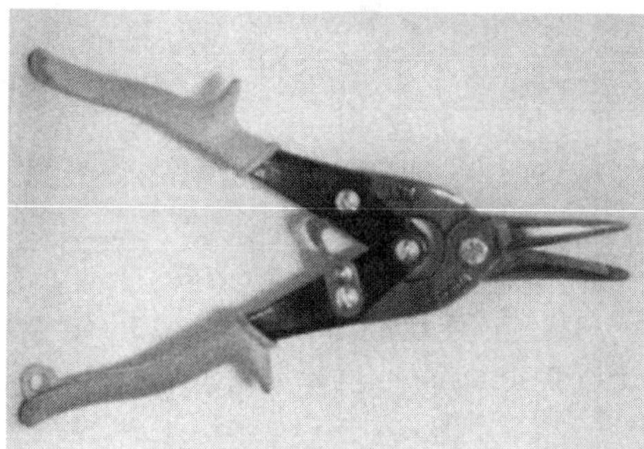

(b) Aviation snips.

FIGURE 1-33 Metal-cutting tools.

Knives. Utility knives are excellent tools for cutting thin veneers, sheathing paper, polyethylene, and gypsum board [see Fig. 1-34(a) and 1-34(b)]. The hooked blade knife is particularly suited for cutting asphalt shingles. There are many different types of utility knives and each is designed for a specific purpose.

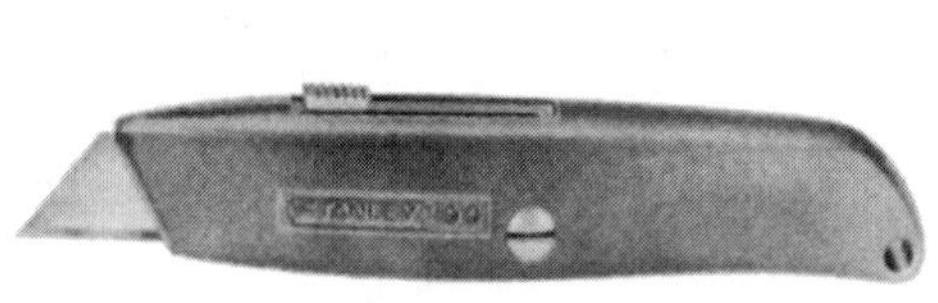

(a) Utility knife.

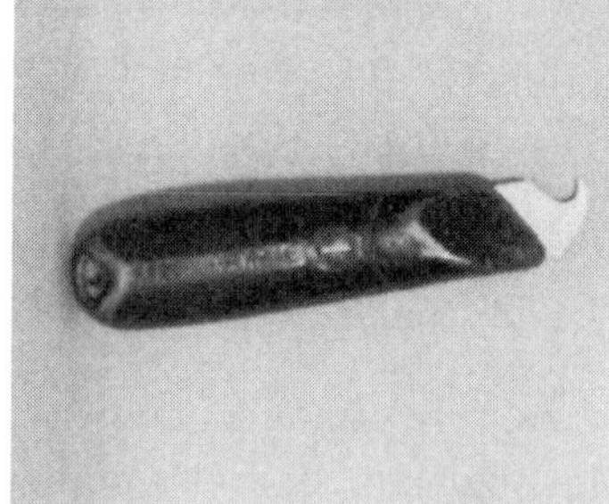

(b) Utility knife with a hooked blade.

FIGURE 1-34 Knives.
(Courtesy Stanley Tools)

Holding Tools

Included in this group are *pliers*, *clamps*, and *vises*.

Pliers. Pliers are made in a variety of sizes, shapes, and styles. Some common types are *adjustable*, *side cutting*, and *locking*. The adjustable pliers can be adjusted to fit different sizes or thickness of material while side-cutting pliers can be used for cutting wire. The vise grip is excellent for holding material on which adjustable pliers may slip (see Figs. 1-35 and 1-36).

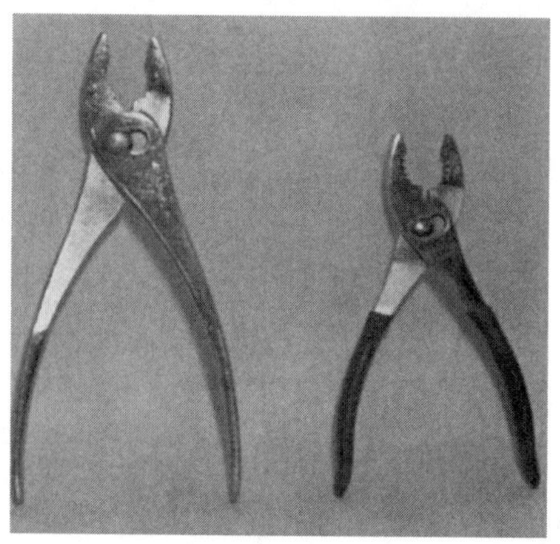

FIGURE 1-35 Adjustable pliers.

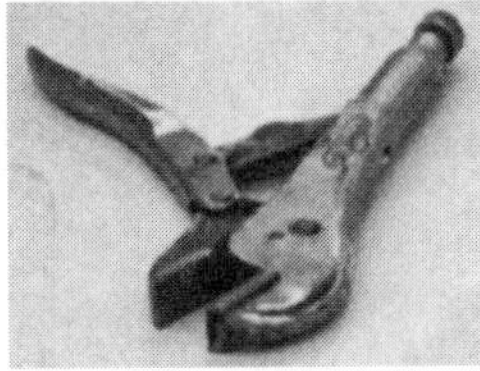

(a) Vise grip.

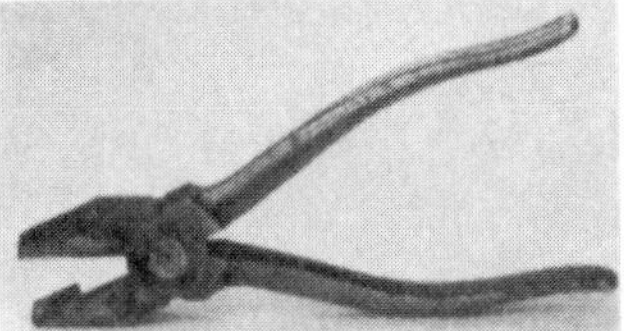

(b) Sidecutting pliers.

FIGURE 1-36 Pliers.

C-clamps. C-clamps are so named because of their shape. Various sizes are available typically ranging from 3 in. to 16 in. (75–400 mm) (see Fig. 1-37).

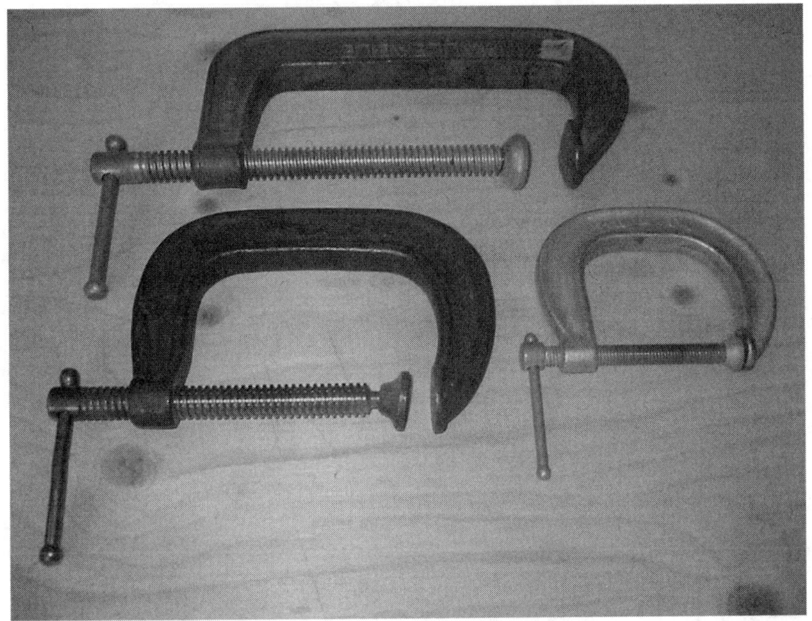

FIGURE 1-37 C-clamps.

Bar and Pipe Clamps. These clamps consist of a screw head and a movable tail block mounted on a pipe that can be any suitable length. They are most useful for clamping pieces of wood during gluing operations [see Fig. 1-38(a)].

Two examples of adjustable bar clamps are shown in Figs. 1-38(b) and 1-38(c). The size of these clamps is dependent on the opening width between the moveable screw head and the fixed tail block. These clamps have a greater "reaching" distance than pipe clamps.

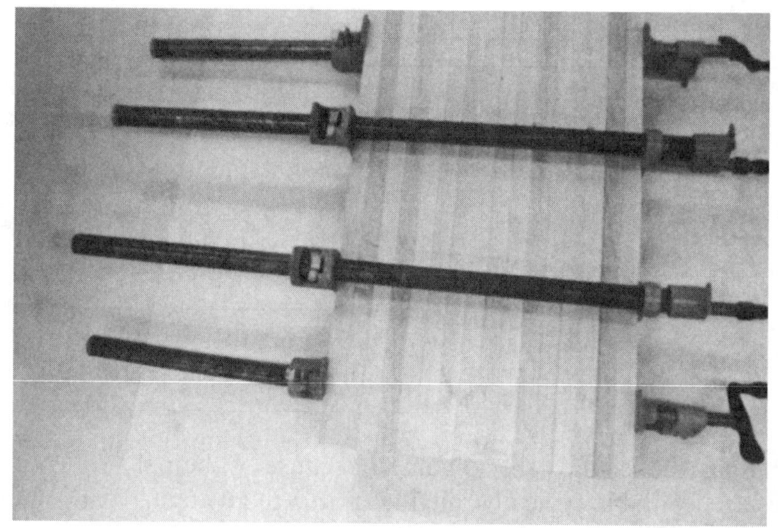
(a) Pipe clamps.

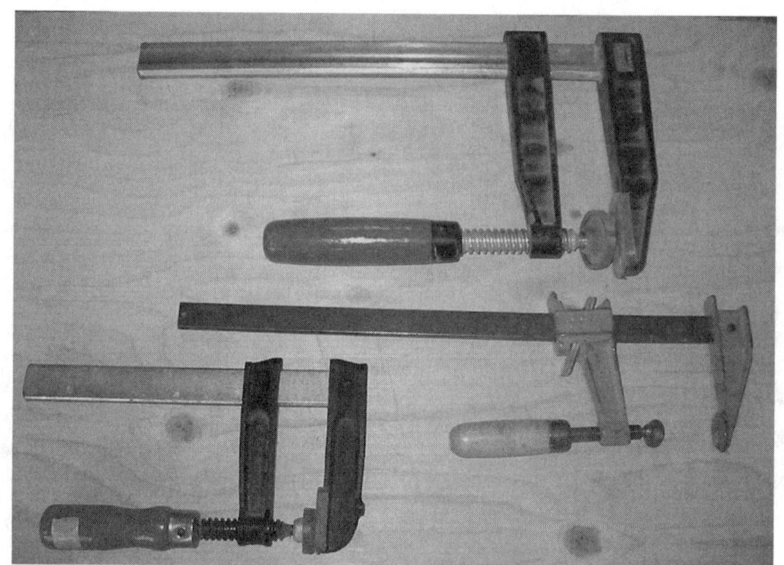
(b) Adjustable bar clamps.

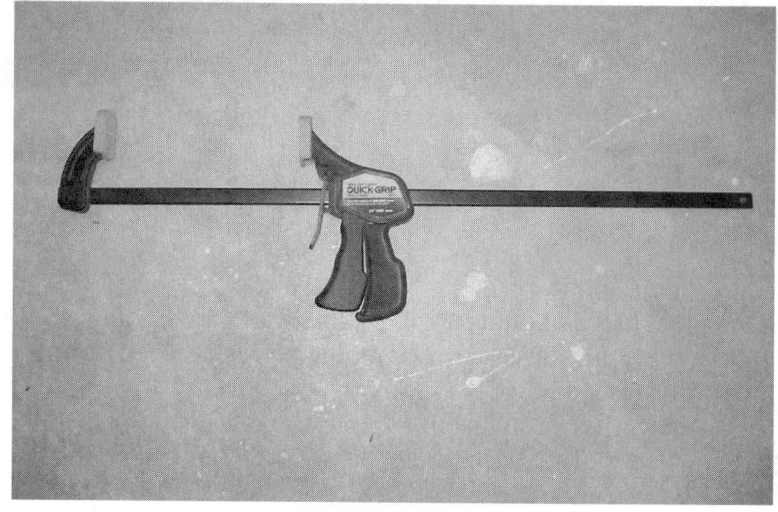

(c) Quick grip clamp.

FIGURE 1-38 Types of clamps.

Woodworkers' Vise. This is a small, sturdy vise that may be clamped to a bench or sawhorse to hold work. It is particularly useful on a sawhorse to hold a door or window sash being worked upon (see Fig. 1-39).

FIGURE 1-39 Woodworker's vise in use.

Layout and Marking Tools

This group includes the *framing square*, the *combination square*, and the *quick square*. Another included in this group is the *chalk line*.

Framing Square. The standard framing square is a basic layout tool, and one of good quality is capable of providing a variety of information necessary for roof framing and other layout operations. It has a 24-in. (600-mm) blade, is 2 in. (51 mm) wide, and has a 16-in. (400-mm) tongue, $1\frac{1}{2}$ in. (38 mm) wide (see Fig. 1-40). These squares are available with marks in inches and fractions of an inch, or in the metric system marked in millimeters.

Besides being used as a guide for establishing 90° angles, the framing square is especially useful for laying out the location of studs on wall plates and the cut angles for rafters. Tables on the square also assist in determining the lengths of rafters. A further explanation of how a framing square is used is provided in the chapters dealing with roof framing and stair building.

FIGURE 1-40 Framing square.

Combination Square. This tool is a versatile one and, as its name implies, can be used for several operations. The blade has a slot machined into it that allows the head to slide along it and be locked in any position (see Fig. 1-41). One edge of the head is at 90° to the blade, and the opposite edge of the head is at 45° to the blade. Some manufacturers include a spirit bubble for use in limited plumbing and leveling operations.

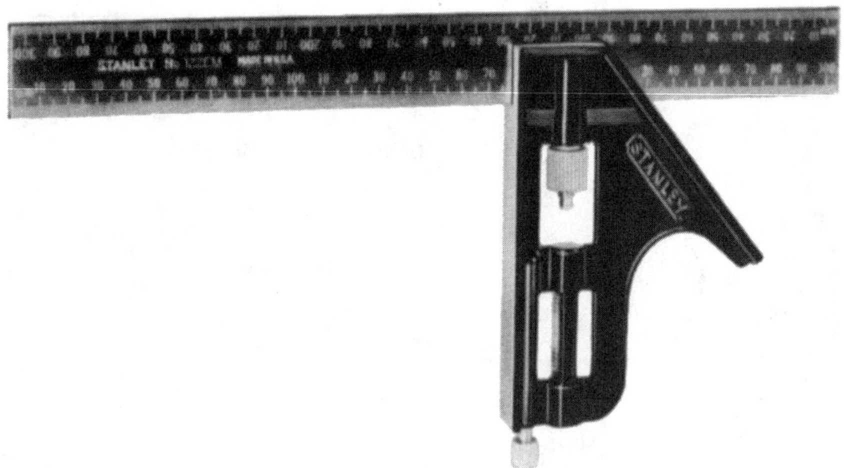

FIGURE 1-41 Combination square.

Quick or Speed Square. This tool is designed to provide a quick and repeatable means of laying out various angles, such as for the cuts for many types of rafters (see Fig. 1-42). This versatile layout tool features a movable locking arm to established various angles and can be used as a power saw guide, protractor, rafter square, or combination square.

FIGURE 1-42 Quick or speed square.

Chalk Line. A chalk line is an easy way to mark long lines, particularly in framing operations. The chalk-coated line is stretched between two previously established points and then lifted near the midpoint and allowed to "snap" onto the material being marked (see Fig. 1-43). This will leave a distinct line on the material. A special reel re-chalks the line each time it is wound into the case (see Fig. 1-44).

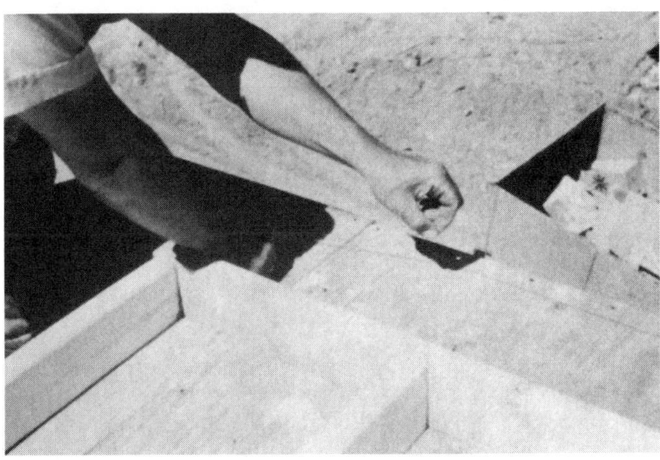

FIGURE 1-43 Chalk line in use.

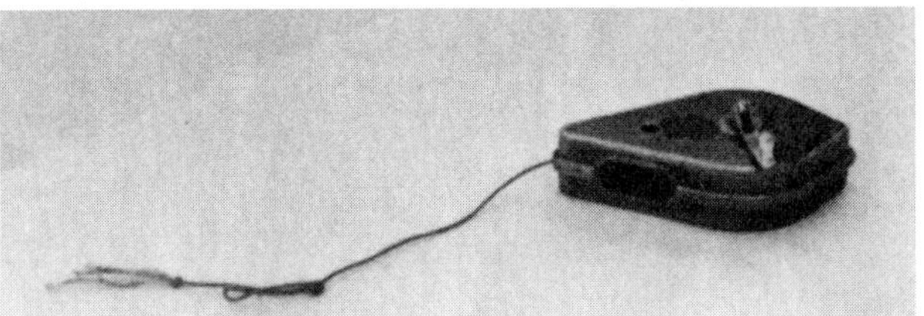

FIGURE 1-44 Chalk line.

Leveling and Plumbing Tools

These tools are used to establish a level (horizontal) surface or a plumb (vertical) surface on components of a structure being erected. In this category are the *carpenter's level*, *line level*, *plumb bob*, and *builder's level*.

Carpenter's Level. This tool can be used for both leveling and plumbing operations. The body can be made of wood, aluminum, or magnesium and is machined on the top and bottom surfaces for accuracy. Typically these tools contain three or more bubble vials to indicate a level or plumb surface (see Fig. 1-45). Various lengths of spirit levels are available, ranging from 18 in. (450 mm) to 96 in. (2400 mm). As these tools must be accurate, they must be handled with care.

FIGURE 1-45 Spirit level.
(Courtesy Stanley Tools)

Line Level. A line level is a very short version of the spirit level and is equipped with hooks to hold it on a line (see Fig. 1-46). It is used by stretching a line, with the spirit level attached, between two points to determine if they are level with one another.

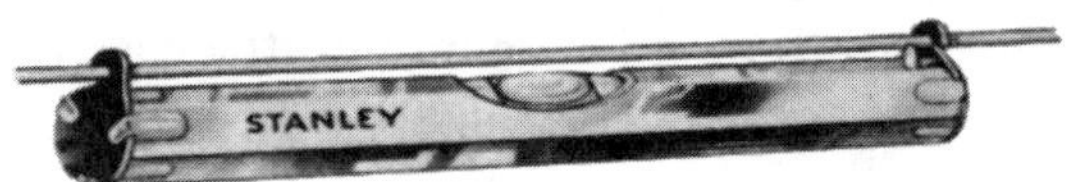

FIGURE 1-46 Line level.
(Courtesy Stanley Tools)

Plumb Bob. The plumb bob is an ancient but useful tool. It consists of a cone-shaped piece of steel or brass that hangs point down from a cord attached to the center of the top (see Fig. 1-47). It is suspended from a point above and allowed to cease swinging to indicate a point directly below.

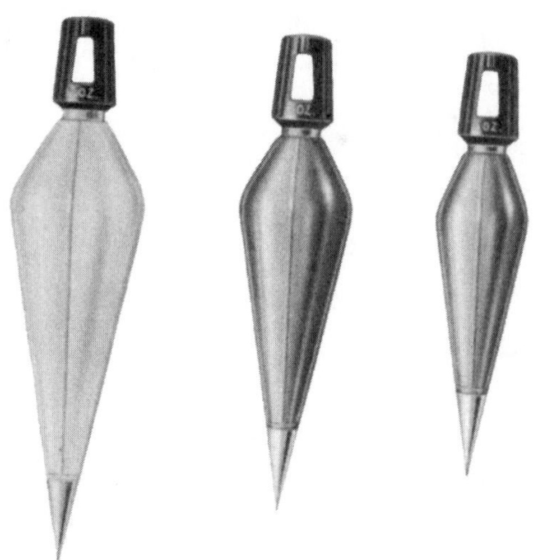

FIGURE 1-47 Plumb bobs.
(Courtesy Stanley Tools)

Builder's Level. A builder's level is an expensive instrument consisting of a telescoping tube through which to sight, on a level line, from one point to another. It is used in leveling operations for building layouts. This tool is further discussed in Chapter 3.

Measuring Tools

These tools, as the name implies, are used to measure distances as well as an aid in laying out locations along the length. Two common ones are the spring-loaded tape rule and the rolled tape. Tape rules vary in lengths up to 30 ft (9 000 mm) or longer and are available with markings in inches and fractions of an inch as well as in millimeters [see Fig. 1-48(a)]. Rolled tapes are much longer versions and are available up to 100 ft (30 000 mm) or longer [see Fig. 1-48(b)].

(a) Pocket tape measure.

(b) Rolled steel tape.

FIGURE 1-48 Steel tapes.

Sharpening Tools

Tools in this category are used to sharpen woodworking tools. Included in this group are various *files* and various *sharpening stones.*

Files. There are triangular files for sharpening handsaws, flat files used for jointing handsaws or general metal filing, and round files used for sharpening chain saws. There are also half-round files and auger bit files available. Some of these files are shown in Fig. 1-49.

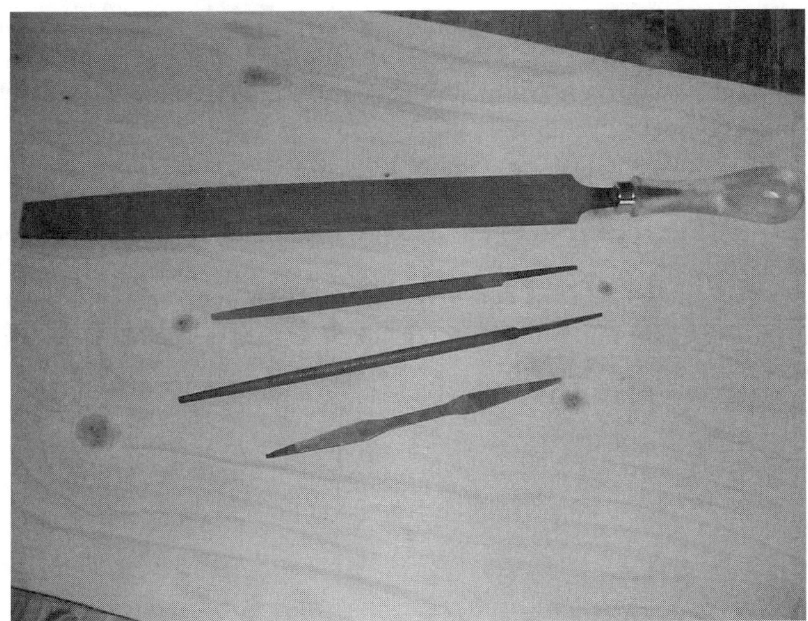

FIGURE 1-49 Assorted files.

Sharpening Stones. Although there are numerous stones shaped or manufactured for use in sharpening tools, the one most commonly used for sharpening knives and plane blades is called a slip stone.

There are different grits available, and when using them for sharpening tools light oil is used as a lubricant (see Fig. 1-50). Electrically operated emery stones are circular and are used for grinding operations including sharpening axes.

FIGURE 1-50 Sharpening stones.

Smoothing Tools

There are only two main types of tools that will be discussed in this group: *planes* and *sandpaper*. The purpose of each is to produce a smooth surface, and each has a specific use. Planes and scrapers work on flat surfaces, rasps are generally used on irregular surfaces, and sandpaper is used for final smoothing operations.

Planes. Surfacing planes are made in several sizes, both in width as well as length. A common one is a *block* plane that is a small, light, one-handed tool 6 in. to 7 in. (150–180 mm) long [see Fig. 1-51(a)]. It is used for surfacing small areas.

Another common one is the *smooth* plane, sometimes called a *bench* plane, available from $9\frac{1}{4}$ in. to $10\frac{1}{4}$ in. (235–260 mm) long [see Fig. 1-51(b)]. These planes are used on intermediate-sized areas and joint work.

The *jack* plane is probably the most common one and is 14 in. to 15 in. (355–380 mm) long [see Fig. 1-51(c)]. It is used for general smoothing operations.

(a) Block plane.

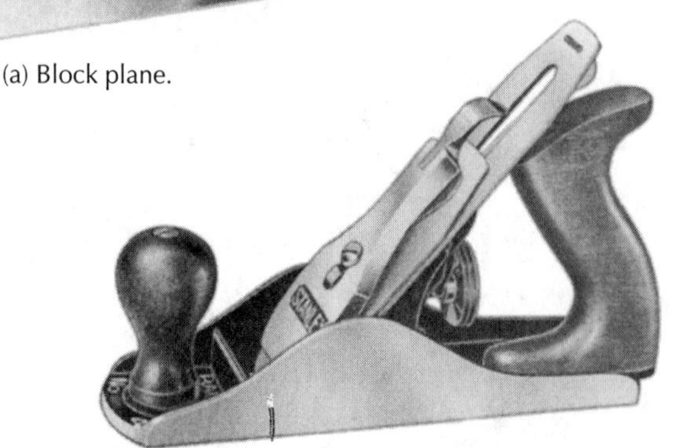

(b) Smooth plane.

(c) Jack plane.

FIGURE 1-51 Surfacing planes.

There are many more specialty planes available, some of which are *fore* planes, *jointer* planes, *nose* planes, *trimming* planes, *rabbet* planes, and *router* planes.

Sandpaper. Sandpaper, or abrasive paper, is made with abrasive particles (grit) glued to a paper backing. Silicone carbide, zinc stearate, aluminum oxide, and garnet are the common materials used. The size of the grit will determine the smoothness of the finished surface. For example, a 60 grit will cut faster than a 100 grit, but will leave the surface rougher. Sandpaper is used in finishing operations just prior to the application of finishing materials.

Wrecking Tools

Although not intended to actually "wreck" things, these tools are used to dismantle structures or parts of structures. Dismantling concrete forms is one example of where they are used.

Rip Claw Hammer. The claws on this style of hammer are made for ripping or prying (see Fig. 1-2).

Pry Bar. A pry bar is a relatively thin body with the ends sharpened like a chisel for ease in inserting into cracks between materials, such as for removing baseboards [see Fig. 1-52(b)]. The body may be tempered steel or forged high carbon steel that is heat treated.

Ripping Bar. A ripping bar, sometimes called a "goose neck," is used for both pulling nails and for prying. Several lengths are available, ranging from 12 in. to 36 in. (300–900 mm) [see Fig. 1-52(a) and (c)].

Nail Claw. Nail claws, sometimes called a cat's paw, are used with a hammer to pull nails that are flush with a surface. The hammer is used to drive the "claw" end into the wood and under the head of the nail and then the nail claw is used to pry the nail above the surface at which time a ripping bar or claw hammer can be used to extract the nail. One type is shown in Fig. 1-52(d).

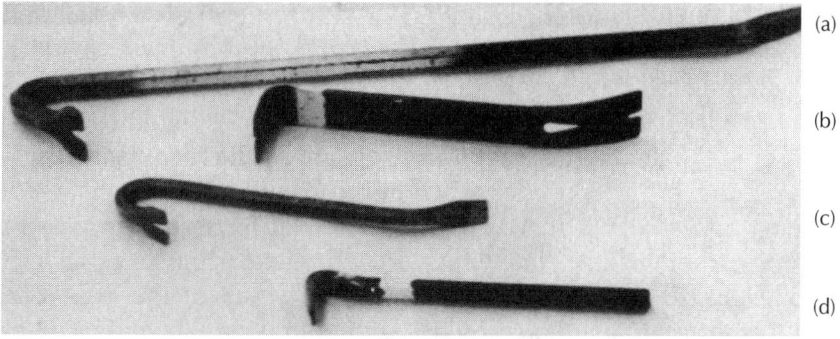

FIGURE 1-52 Wrecking bars.

Nail Puller. A nail puller is made for one purpose only—pulling nails (see Fig. 1-53). The long handle has a moveable sleeve that can be used to drive the pair of jaws into the wood and below the head of a nail. By pulling the handle toward the curved lever arm, the nail can then be pulled above the surface to allow a wrecking bar to be used to pull the nail.

FIGURE 1-53 Nail puller.

Power Tools

Power-operated tools continue to be developed to increase productivity, accuracy, and consistency. They do not entirely replace hand tools, but when used in conjunction, they lighten the workload that would otherwise be required. At the same time, there is an increased safety concern and because of this it is imperative that the operators observe the detailed instructions provided by the manufacturers.

Most of the tools described in this chapter are handheld while being operated, but there are also some stationary power tools that warrant being identified. Most are operated using electricity, but some utilize compressed air or gasoline. Some of these handheld power tools are manufactured to be operated with rechargeable batteries and are thus called *cordless* tools.

Hand Electric Saw. This tool, being quite versatile, may be used almost anywhere that a handsaw could be used. It will both crosscut and rip material, depending on the type of blade used. A wide variety of saw blades are available and include blades specifically designed for crosscutting, ripping, or combination blades that are more versatile for both crosscut and ripping work. Other types include plywood blades, masonry blades, and metal-cutting blades. The size of a hand electric saw is determined by the maximum diameter blade it can hold, generally ranging from 6 in. to 10 in. (150–250 mm) (see Fig. 1-54). These saws are generally used "freehand" so the accuracy of the cut is determined by the skill of the operator (see Fig. 1-55). A spring-loaded guard keeps the blade covered until the saw is in use.

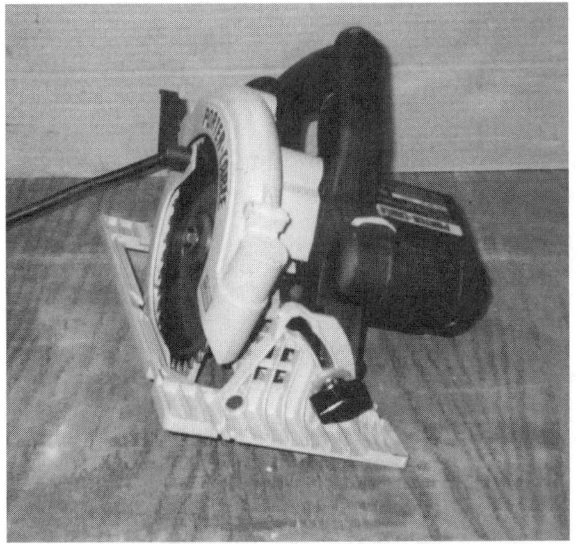

(a)

(b)

FIGURE 1-54 Hand electric saws.

FIGURE 1-55 Saw in use.

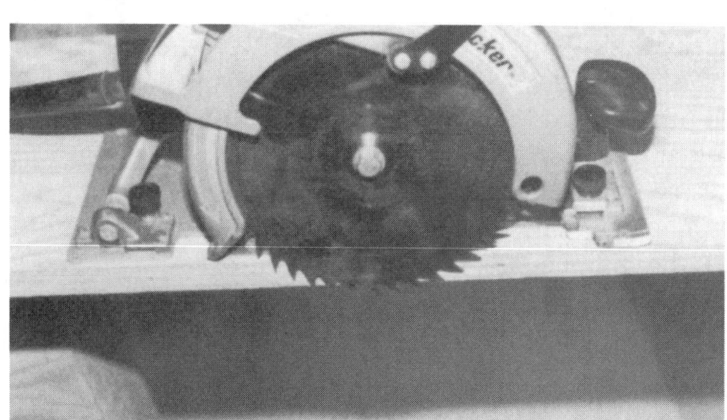
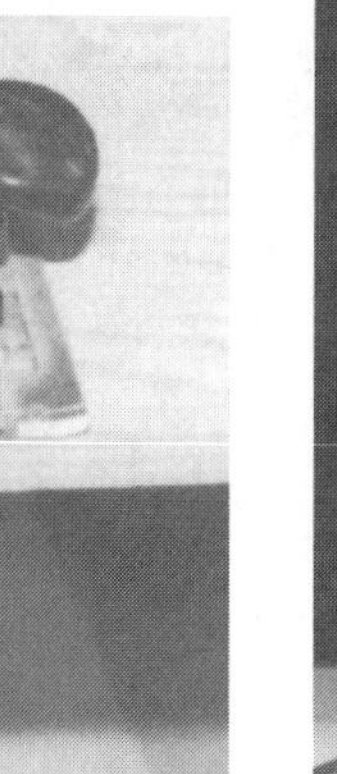

FIGURE 1-56 Depth of saw blade.

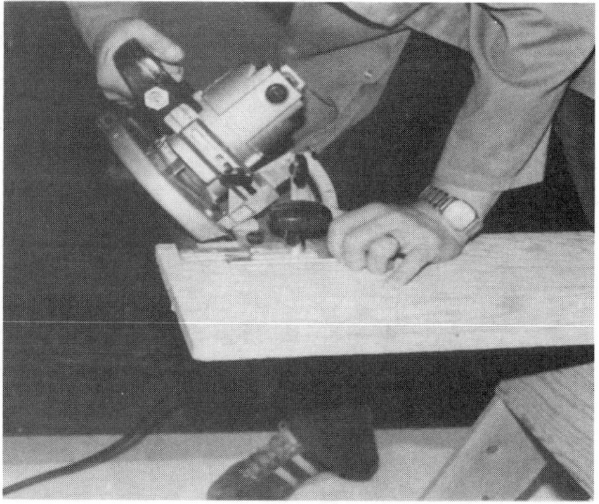

FIGURE 1-57 Bevel cut.

Raising or lowering the base of the saw adjusts the depth of cut. The proper depth is equal to the thickness of material plus a full tooth protruding through the work (see Fig. 1-56). The base can also be set to cut on an angle (see Fig. 1-57). There are situations where it is desired to start a cut other than at the edge of the material. In this case a plunge cut can be made (see Fig. 1-58), where the front edge of the base is in contact with the material prior to starting the cut. In this operation the spring-loaded guard must be held partly open to allow the blade to come into contact with the material.

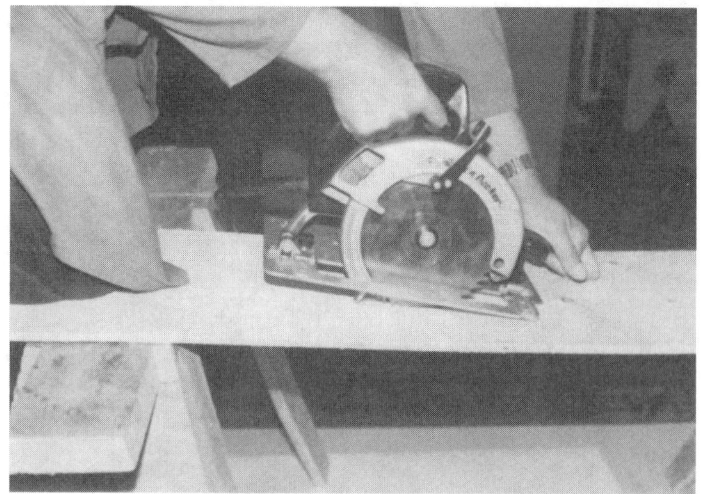

FIGURE 1-58 Plunge cut.

There are many different types of blades available for hand electric saws, as shown in Fig. 1-59. A chisel combination blade is most commonly used, as it cuts equally well for crosscutting and rip-

FIGURE 1-59 Circular saw blade types.

ping operations. Some operators prefer carbide-tipped blades, as they stay sharp longer than steel blades.

Electric Sanders. There are many types of hand electric sanders manufactured, each designed for a specific use. Figure 1-60(a) illustrates a belt sander for which belts of various degrees of fineness are available. When using a belt sander it is very important to keep the belt flat on the surface being sanded and kept constantly on the move in a forward and backward motion to avoid leaving deep depressions on the surface being sanded. Only the weight of the sander is required to do the work. The material must be supported so that it doesn't move during the sanding operation.

Figure 1-60(b) illustrates two types of orbital sanders that are designed primarily for finish sanding, although various grades of abrasive paper can be used with them. The base of these sanders operates by sanding in a very small circular pattern, and only the weight of the sander is required to do the work.

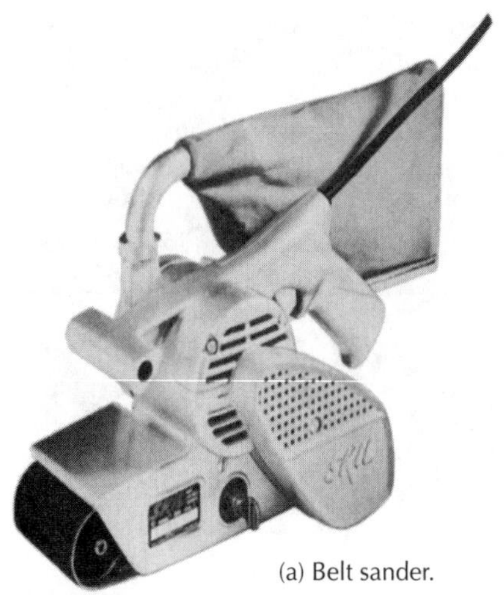

(a) Belt sander.

(b) Orbital sander.

FIGURE 1-60 Electric sanders.

Electric Drills. Hand electric drills are designed to hold straight-shanked bits and are available in several sizes, depending on the maximum diameter shank that can be held in the chuck of the drill. Figure 1-61(a) illustrates a type that can be operated with one hand and will take bits with a shank up to 3/8 in. (10 mm). Some of these drills have a variable speed control switch or trigger as well as a reversing option.

Figure 1-61(b) illustrates a specially designed drill for driving screws into gypsum board. A special chuck holds a screwdriver bit, and a sleeve can be adjusted to set the screw being driven to slightly below the surface of the board. Again, it is designed with a variable speed trigger and can be reversed.

Another type of drill utilizes a rechargeable battery [see Fig. 1-61(c)]. Without the need for electrical cords, this drill can be used where electrical power sources are not available.

(a) Electric drill 3/8 in. (10 mm)

(b) Multi-use electric drill.

(c) Cordless drill

(d) Electric drill [1/2 in. (13 mm)].

FIGURE 1-61 Electric drills.

Figure 1-61(d) illustrates a larger drill that is operated with both hands. The chuck will hold bits with a shank up to $\frac{1}{2}$ in. (13 mm), and, because of the design, more pressure can be exerted. Care must be exercised, as the motor can exert considerable torque on the bit; this can have the tendency to twist the drill out of your hands.

Electric drills utilize a variety of bits [see Fig. 1-62(a–e)]. Twist bits are most common and, depending on their type, can be used to drill into metal or softer material, such as wood. Auger bits similar to those used with a brace are suitable for use in wood and can drill deep holes. Speed bore (spade) bits and spur bits are designed to drill holes in wood or similar material. And, there are a number of specialties bits available, such as screwdriver, masonry, and spur edged.

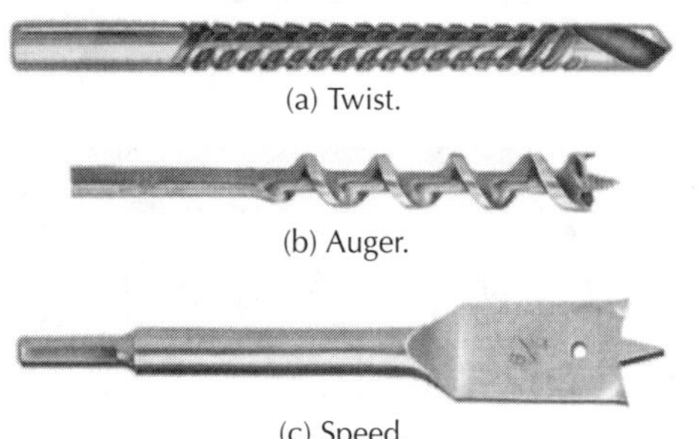

(a) Twist.

(b) Auger.

(c) Speed.

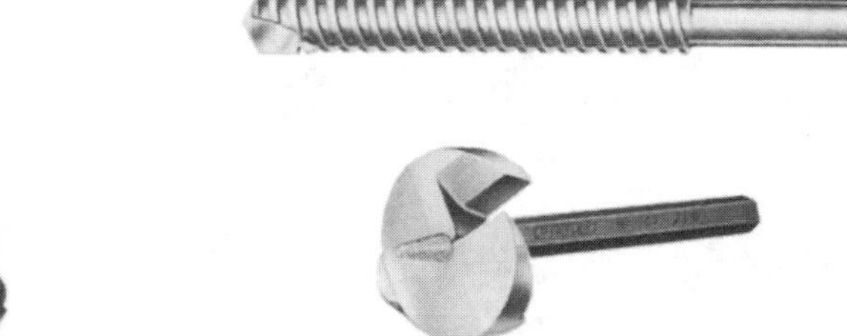

(d) Spur.

(e) Speciality bits.

FIGURE 1-62 Electric drill bits.

Routers. Electric routers consist of a motor fitted with a special chuck to hold a straight-shank bit and rotate at a very high RPM (see Fig. 1-63). They are very versatile in that, depending on the bit, they can perform dado and rabbet cuts, as well as cut a variety of profiles on the edge of material, such as bull nose, ogee, and flutes. Bits are available in high-speed steel as well as carbide tipped (see Fig. 1-64).

(a) Electric router.

(b) Plastic laminate trimmer.

FIGURE 1-63 Routers.

FIGURE 1-64 Router bits.
(Courtesy Stanley Tools)

Saber Saw. Saber saws can do the work of a crosscut or rip saw, band saw, keyhole saw, hacksaw, or jigsaw (see Fig. 1-65). Blades cut through material with a fast up–down motion, and the saw allows straight or angled cuts. A variety of blades are available for cutting different materials (see Fig. 1-66).

FIGURE 1-65 Saber saw.

POINTS PER 1 IN. (25 mm)	BLADE DESCRIPTION AND RECOMMENDED USE
 10	Taper ground, clean cuts in paneling, formica, plastic and related materials.
 10	Scroll cutting for wood, plywood, masonite and plastic, up to 5 mm thick.
 12	Taper ground for smooth, clean finish cuts in wood, plywood, plastic and hardboard.
 6	Coarse tooth for extra fast cuts in wood, plywood and hardboard. Extra long.
 8	Flush cutting for wood and plastic.
18	Metal cutting for non-ferrous metals up to 1/4"(6.5 mm) thick.
24	Metal cutting for non-ferrous metals up to 1/8"(3 mm) thick.
36	Metal cutting for non-ferrous metals up to 1/16"(1.5 mm) thick.
 8, 12, 18	General purpose assortment for wood: coarse, medium and fine.
 8	Coarse tooth wood cutting for heavy, fast cuts.
 18	Fine tooth wood cutting for smooth cuts in wood, plywood, plastic and counter top materials.

FIGURE 1-66 Saber saw blades.

Circles are easily cut either freehand or by utilizing a guide (see Fig. 1-67). Plunge cuts are achieved by tipping the tool forward with the base resting on the material and the end of the blade just clearing the surface. Turn the saw on and slowly lower the blade into the material until it penetrates through (see Fig. 1-68).

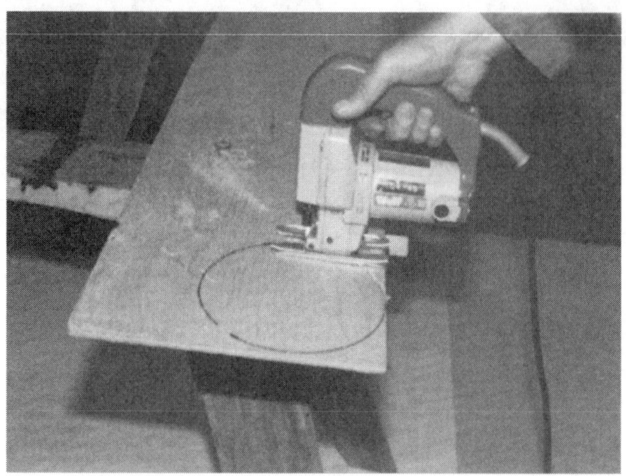

FIGURE 1-67 Cutting a circle with a saber saw.

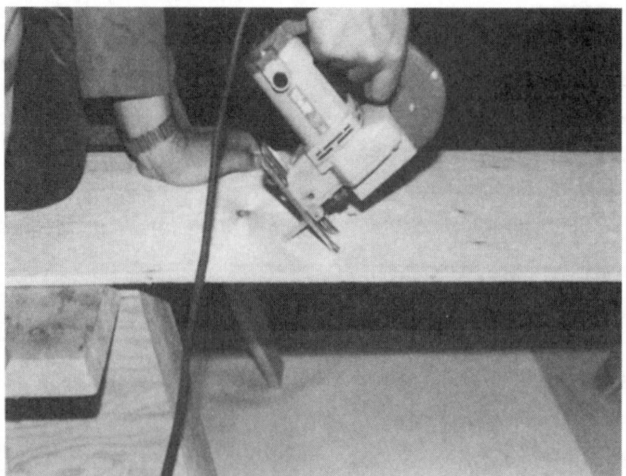

FIGURE 1-68 Plunge cut.

Reciprocating Saw. The reciprocating saw is similar to the saber saw (see Fig. 1-69). Because of the shape, this saw is particularly useful in confined spaces and utilizes longer blades than those used in a saber saw.

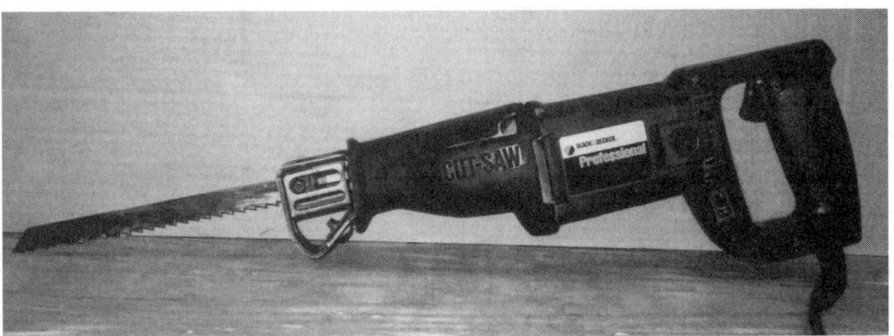

FIGURE 1-69 Reciprocating saw.

Electric Plane. There are several different electric planes available, but the most common type is used for jointing an edge (see Fig. 1-70). A typical use is for jointing the edge of a door to fit into a doorjamb. The fence can be tilted to allow the plane to cut a bevel.

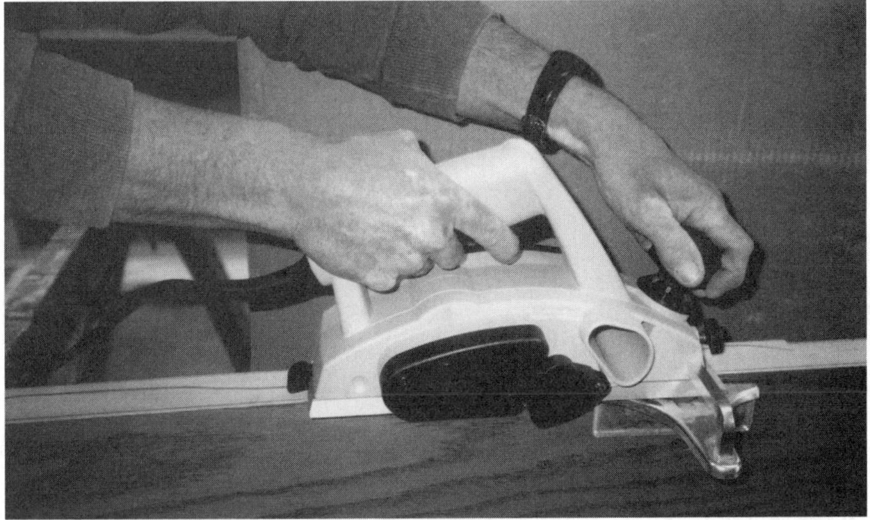

FIGURE 1-70 Electric plane.

Electric Plate Cutter. The electric plate, or wafer cutter, cuts a slot in wood into which a wafer-shaped spline is inserted for use in making a joint. The spline is made of compressed wood and is available in three sizes, 0, 10, and 20. When glue is used at the joint, the spline expands to provide a secure connection. This tool is typically used in the fabrication of cabinets (see Fig. 1-71).

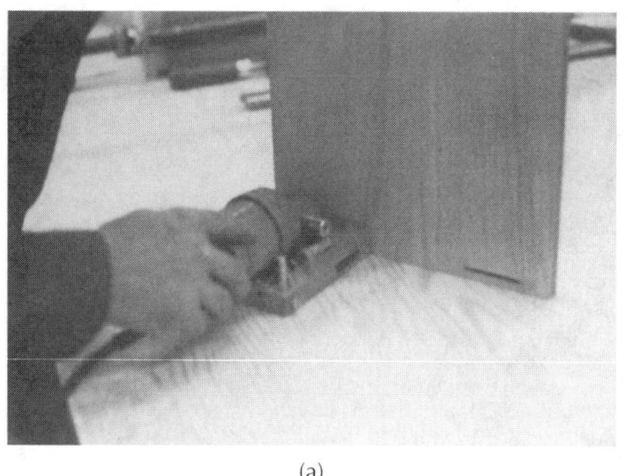

(a)

(b)

(c)

(d) Plate cutter.

FIGURE 1-71 Using an electric plate cutter to make a corner connection.

Hammer Drill. Hammer drills operate not only in a rotary direction, but also in a very fast reciprocating direction. They are used to penetrate such material as concrete or stone (see Fig. 1-72). Some of these tools are capable of being adjusted to just hammer without the rotary action and consequently utilize special bits or chisels.

(a)

(b)

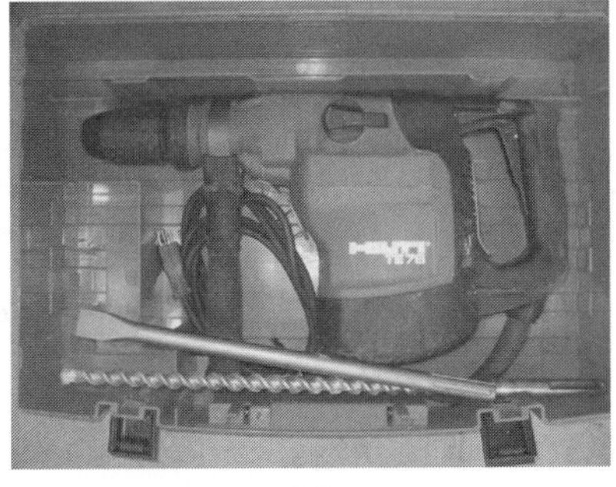

(c)

FIGURE 1-72 Hammer drills.

Power Screwdriver. There are a variety of cordless screwdrivers available allowing the tool to be operated in areas where there is no external source of electrical power available. One example is shown in Fig. 1-73.

FIGURE 1-73 Battery operated power screwdriver (cordless screwdriver).

Radial Arm Saw. The radial arm saw gets its name because the motor and saw are suspended on a horizontal arm that allows a variety of movement. The saw can travel along the arm, pivot on the arm, or be rotated into a horizontal position, and the arm itself can turn either left or right from the column on which it is attached (see Fig. 1-74).

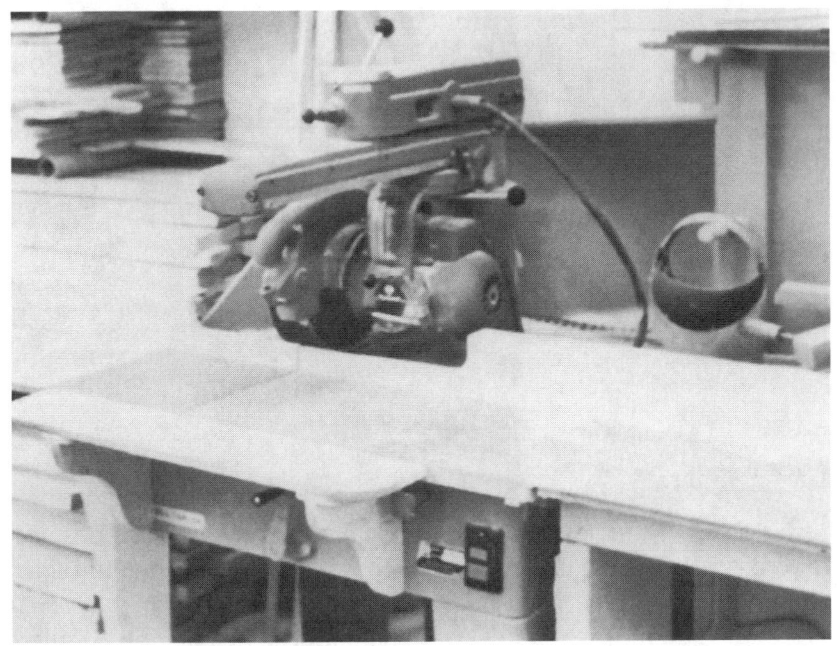

FIGURE 1-74 Radial arm saw.

The versatility of the tool is illustrated in Figs. 1-75(a)–(d), which shows it being used for ripping, mitering, and crosscutting. When crosscutting, mitering, or making dado cuts, the work is held firmly on the table and against the fence, and the saw is pulled through the work. Care should be taken to prevent the saw from cutting across the material too quickly. For ripping, the saw head is rotated parallel to the fence and locked into position. Material is then fed into the blade in an opposite direction to the blade rotation [see Fig. 1-75(b)].

(a) Miter cutting.

(b) Ripping.

(c) Compound miter.

(d) Crosscutting.

FIGURE 1-75 Using a radial arm saw.

Miter Saw. Miter saws, sometimes called chop saws, are designed for crosscutting such material as wood, plastic, and soft metal such as aluminum. One type pivots vertically on an arm at the rear as the saw blade and motor is pulled into the material in a downward direction [see Fig. 1-76(a)]. Another type operates with a sliding arm, and the motor and blade are pulled into the material horizontally, like a radial arm saw [see Fig. 1-76(b)]. Both these saws pivot horizontally left and right up to 45° and are well suited for cutting moldings to length. Some types of sliding arm saws are capable of compound bevel cuts.

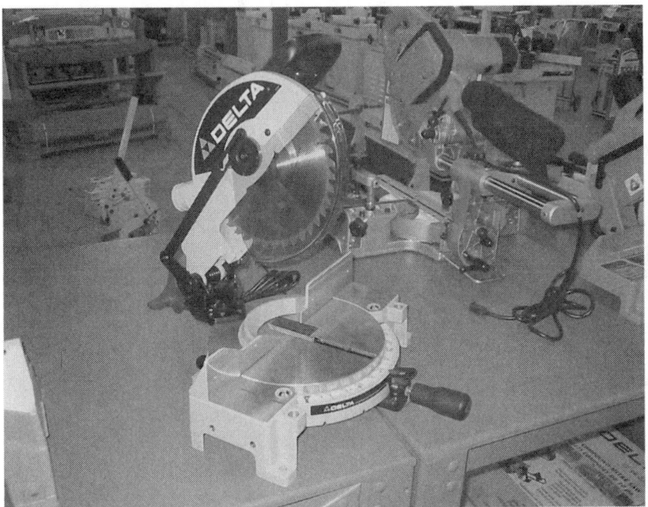

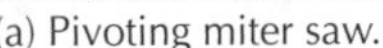
(a) Pivoting miter saw.

(b) Sliding miter saw.

FIGURE 1-76 Miter saws.

Table Saw. This saw is primarily used for cabinetmaking but is also used for a variety of other finishing operations. It can be used for crosscutting, ripping, making miter cuts, and dado cuts. The size of the saw depends on the diameter of the saw blade recommended. Typical sizes are 8 in. to 12 in. (200–300 mm). The example shown in Fig. 1-77 is a cabinet model, while others are mounted on an open stand.

FIGURE 1-77 Table saw.

There are a number of different saw blades available, including those with carbide tipped teeth (see Fig. 1-78). It is important to use only those blades with the proper size arbor hole for the particular saw.

(a) Rip and cross-cut blades.

(b) Plywood and combination blades.

(c) Hardened tip and carbide tip blades.

FIGURE 1-78 Saw blades.

Jointer. Jointers are generally used for jointing the edge of material but can also be used for surfacing a relatively narrow board. Some additional uses are for cutting bevels, tapers, and rabbets. The size of a jointer is dependent on the length of knives on the cutter head. Care should be taken to keep your hands well away from the area directly above the cutter head, and the use of a wood push stick is recommended [see Fig. 1-79(a)].

Fig. 1-79(b) is an example of a combination jointer and thickness planer. A thickness planer is used to surface material to a uniform thickness. As with the jointer, the size is dependent on the length of the knives on the cutter head.

(a) Jointer.

(b) Combination jointer-thickness planer.

FIGURE 1-79 Surfacing tools.

Gasoline-Powered Tools

Some tools are available utilizing small gasoline engines. These include *chain saws*, *soil compactors*, and *air compressors* to provide compressed air for *paint sprayers* and a number of different *pneumatic tools*. There are also gasoline-powered generators suitable for providing a portable electrical power source for those power tools listed above.

Chain Saw. Chain saws are used for cutting heavy timbers, posts, and for cutting trees in the logging industry. Their size is dependent on the length of the bar on which the chain runs. The one illustrated in Fig. 1-80 is a 14-in. (350-mm) saw.

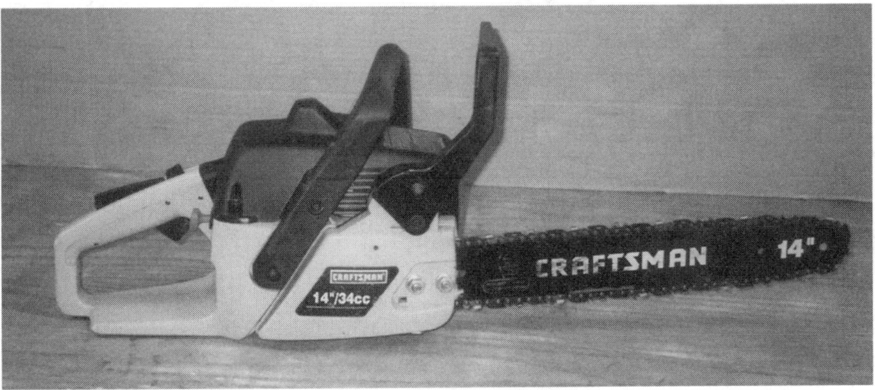

FIGURE 1-80 Gas-powered chain saw.

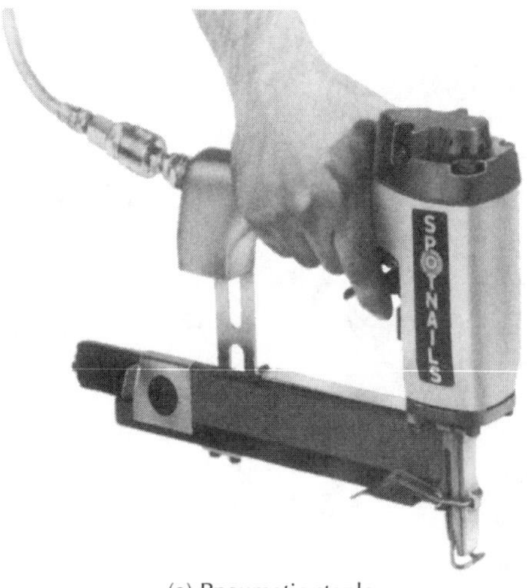

(a) Pneumatic stapler.
(Courtesy Spotnails Inc.)

Pneumatic Tools. Pneumatic tools are *staplers*, *nailers*, brad *tackers*, *drills*, and *sanders*. Compressed air can be provided with either gasoline-powered engines or those utilizing electrical power.

Staplers are designed to drive staples for fastening paneling, building paper, siding, and shingles [see Fig. 1-81(a)]. A wide variety of staplers are available for driving staples of various crowns and leg lengths.

Nailers are designed to drive various lengths and styles of nails [see Fig. 1-81(b)]. Framing crews generally use nailers for securing studs to plates as well as for attaching panels to the studs. Brad tackers are smaller and lighter versions of nailers and are used to drive small finishing nails, mostly for finishing work.

Pneumatic drills can take the place of electric drills, as the same kinds of bits can be used in them [see Fig. 1-81(c)].

Compressors are available to operate either with electric power or with a gasoline engine [see Fig. 1-81(d) and 1-81(e)].

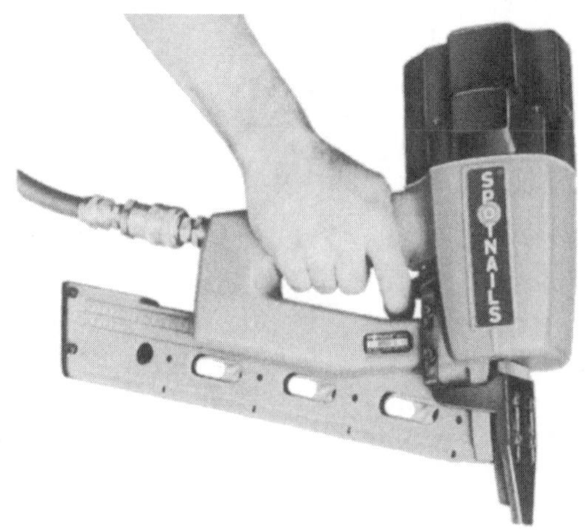

(b) Pneumatic nailer.
(Courtesy Spotnails Inc.)

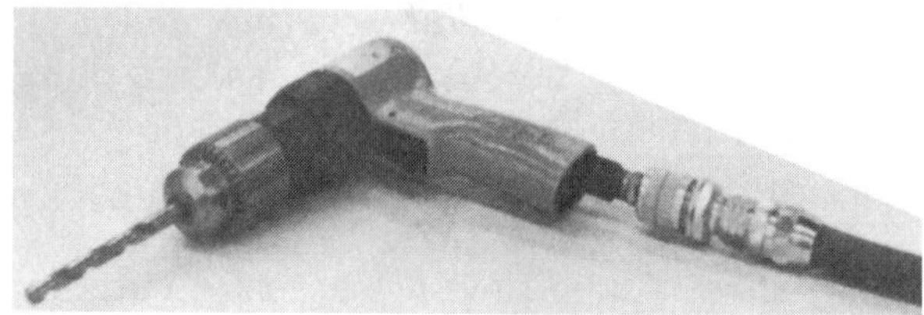

(c) Pneumatic drill.

(d) Electric compressor.

(e) Gas compressor.

FIGURE 1-81 Air-operated tools.

Powder-Actuated Tools

In many situations, it is necessary to attach some object or material to concrete, masonry, or steel surfaces. Not only is a special fastener necessary—one that is hard enough to penetrate the surface without bending—but also special power is required to drive the fastener. Tools designed to do such a job use an explosive charge contained in a small cartridge similar to a .22-caliber cartridge. There are different energy levels available, the selection dependent on the length of fastener and the hardness of the material. The color of the cartridge, gray, brown, green, yellow, red, and purple denotes the energy level from low to high, and are available in either copper or nickel casings—the nickel casings being a higher energy level. By this means, several types of pins and threaded fasteners can be driven into these hard materials (see Fig. 1-82).

There are many different manufacturers of powder-actuated tools, and one example is shown in Fig. 1-83(a). When using these tools it is very important to protect your head, eyes, and ears using a hard hat, safety glasses or shield, and earmuffs [see Figs. 1-83(b) and 1-83(c)], as required by the manufacturer and OSHA or OHS.

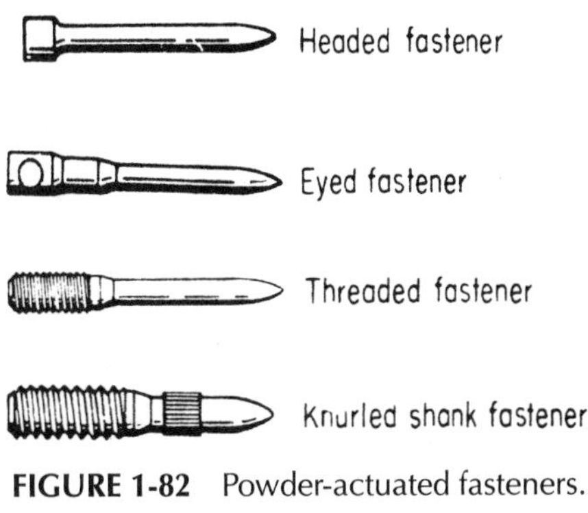

FIGURE 1-82 Powder-actuated fasteners.

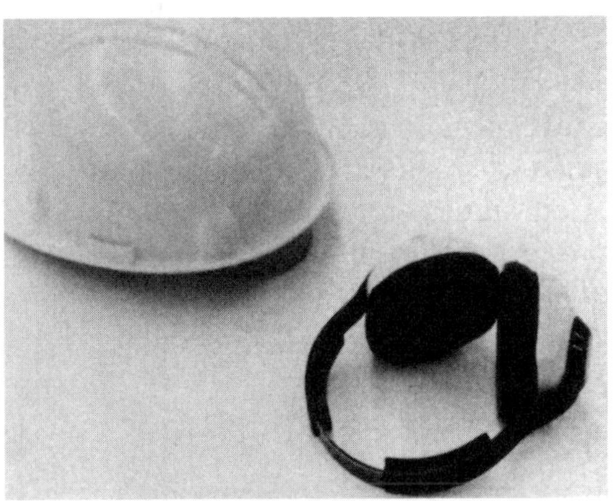

(b) Hard hat and muffs.

(a) Powder actuated tool.

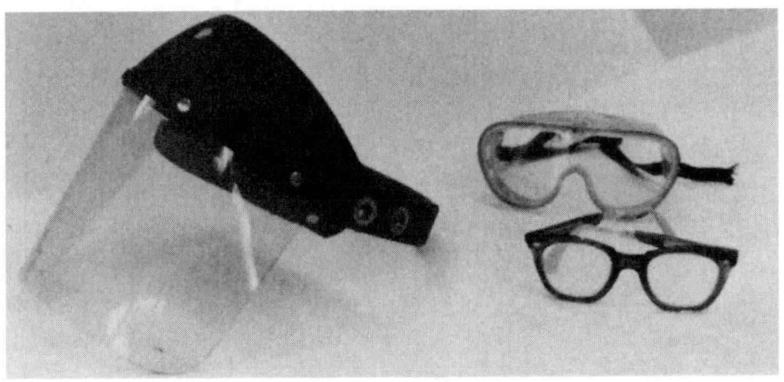

(c) Shield and safety glasses.

FIGURE 1-83 Powder-actuated tool safety.

It should be noted here that operators of powder-actuated tools may have to be trained and licensed to do the work, and you should check with local authorities regarding regulations that are in force.

Care of Tools

The success that one achieves with one's tools depends to a great extent on the care one takes of them. No tool, no matter how expensive, will give good service unless it is given the proper attention. Tools must be kept sharp and in good repair and must be protected against the weather and against rough usage. Dull tools are dangerous to the operator and others, and will not achieve the desired results on the material being worked.

Sharpening Tools

While all cutting tools must be kept sharp, the ones that will probably need the most careful and constant attention are plane blades, chisels, and saws.

Plane Blade. When sharpening a plane blade the first step is to shape the cutting edge, either square or slightly crowned, depending on how it is to be used. A crowned edge is preferable for dressing a flat surface, and a straight edge is preferable for straightening an edge. In both cases the cutting edge should be square with the blade length as shown in Fig. 1-84.

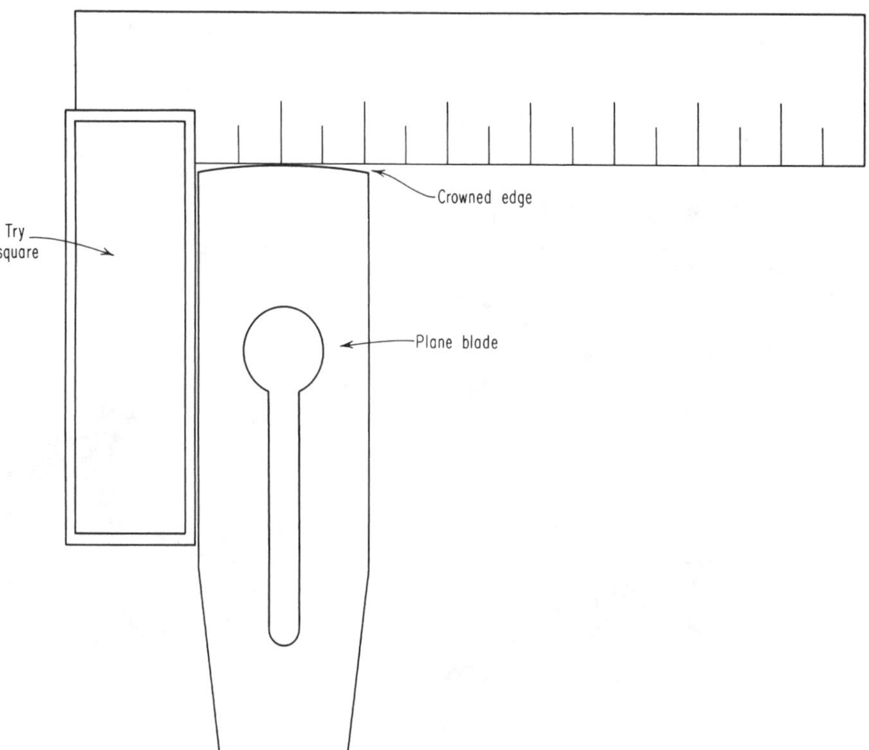

FIGURE 1-84 Testing shape of blade edge.

Plane blades are ground on a grinder at an angle of 25° for most general work. A simple gauge can be made to check the angle of the bevel (see Fig. 1-85). Move the blade back and forth across the face of the grinding wheel using very light pressure to avoid overheating the cutting edge. If the cutting edge turns to a dark color, it has been overheated and has lost its temper and will have to be completely ground off.

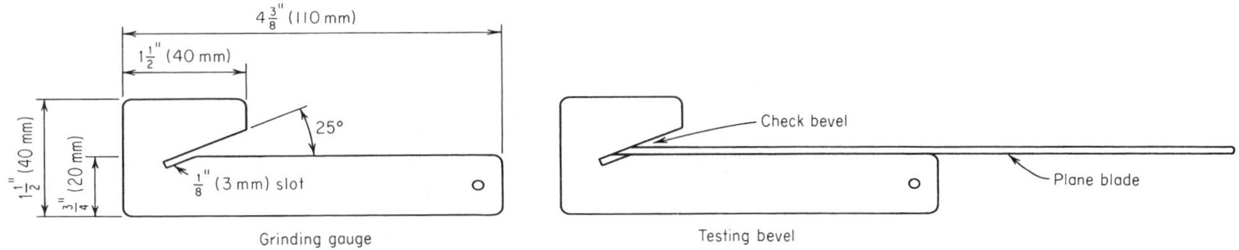

FIGURE 1-85 Grinding gauge.

Check the grinding angle frequently and make sure the entire cutting edge has been ground sharp (the edge will appear slightly jagged, and there will be a burr on the back of the blade).

The next step is to whet the blade on an oilstone. Oilstones are available in different grades of coarseness, either manufactured or in natural stone, such as an Arkansas stone. A few drops of lubricant (light oil manufactured for this purpose or made by combining equal parts of a light machine oil and solvent) is applied to the stone to prevent the stone from being clogged with metal particles. Set the bevel edge flat on the stone and then slightly raise the heel as shown in Fig. 1-86. Slide the blade back and forth along the stone a few times maintaining the same angle, and then turn the blade over so that it is perfectly flat on the stone and slide it back and forth a few times to remove the burr. Repeat the procedure until you have a very sharp edge. If desired, a finer Arkansas stone can be used to repeat the operation for an improved sharpness.

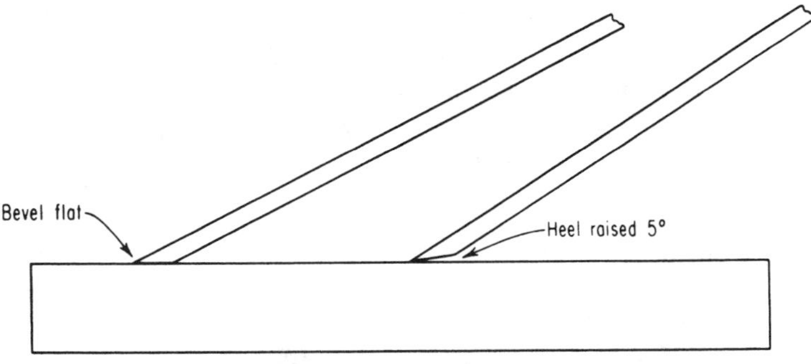

FIGURE 1-86 Whetting a blade.

The final step is *stropping* the edge on a piece of leather to remove any remnants of the burr.

Chisel. The same procedure is used to sharpen a chisel as used for a plane blade. However, the cutting edge of a chisel is always square with the length.

Handsaw. Well-shaped, sharp teeth are required to ensure that saws cut efficiently. Take care when selecting a sharpening shop to make sure that you get the quality of sharpening needed for fine workmanship. Always check your newly sharpened saws to see that a good job was done. One way is to sight down the length of the blade to check that the teeth on both sides are of equal size. If they are, the "V" shape you see on a crosscut saw will be down the center of the blade (see Fig. 1-87). If it is not, then the teeth on one side will be larger than on the other side and the saw will tend to pull toward that side, preventing a straight cut. Any "kinks" in the blade should be pointed out to the sharpener so that it can be straightened.

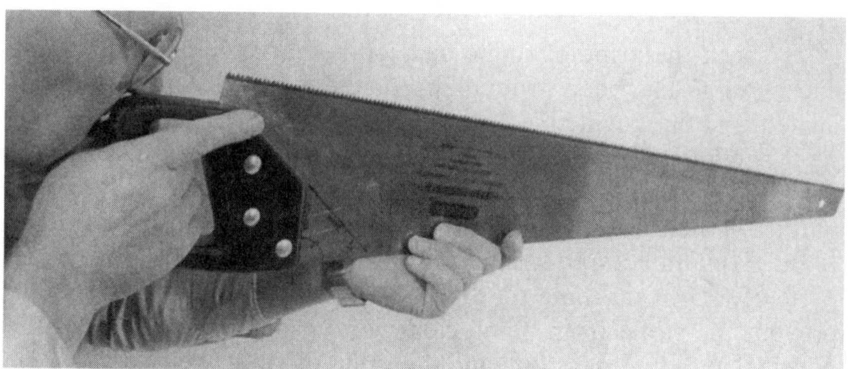

FIGURE 1-87 Sighting a crosscut saw.

Storing Tools

Proper storage of your tools will contribute considerably to the life of them. Sharp-edge tools such as saws and chisels should be so placed that the edges do not become damaged from contact with other tools. Some chisels come with a plastic tip that can be removed to use them. Likewise, some saws come with a plastic cap. If storing these tools in a toolbox, compartments designed for each will provide the necessary protection. If you take care of all your tools, you will be rewarded with longer use and better results.

Handling Tools

Equally important as the sharpness of your tools is how you handle them. Dropping a tool on the floor, whether of concrete, wood, or dirt, can damage it. Don't place tools where they can slip or fall.

Planes should never be placed with the bed in contact with a surface—always place them on their side. Don't allow a large variety of tools to be stacked around your work area. When you are finished with one tool for a while, put it away where it will not be damaged.

Care in handling power tools is also very important, not only from the standpoint of possible damage to the tool, but also from the possible danger to you or others. Knowing the proper way to use these tools is very important; any careless or improper use could result in a serious injury.

Keep your hand tools dry, clean, and well maintained. Develop a pride in your tools—in their appearance and condition—and you will find that you will do a better job, that tool replacement will be less costly, and that you will be looked upon as a competent and professional person.

CONSTRUCTION EQUIPMENT

During the course of the construction of light buildings, a variety of equipment, other than hand and power tools, is often employed. Some of the typical equipment you will see on job sites are earth-moving, concrete, soil-breaking, and soil-compaction equipment. Other equipment you might encounter is for soil testing, but this equipment is generally used for heavy buildings or, in the case of a new residential development, an overall investigation of the soil to ensure there are no unforeseen problems that might be discovered during the construction of light buildings.

FIGURE 1-88 Trac hoe.

Earth-Moving Equipment. Earth-moving equipment includes such machines as the *bulldozer* and the *backhoe* or *trac hoe* (see Fig. 1-88 and Chapter 4), used for excavating or trenching, and a *front-end loader* (see Fig. 1-89). A smaller version of a front-end loader is com-

FIGURE 1-89 Front-end loader.

monly called a *bobcat* (see Fig. 1-90). This type of equipment can be used for moving as well as loading soil.

FIGURE 1-90 Tractor with bucket for moving earth (Bobcat).

FIGURE 1-91

Concrete Equipment. Small concrete jobs can be handled with a *portable mixer* (Fig. 1-91) where the concrete ingredients are mixed on site. However, with most concrete jobs a transit-mix truck usually delivers concrete from a central plant. Figure 1-92 illustrates one type.

FIGURE 1-92 Transit mix truck.

When concrete is delivered to a job site, there is often a need to place it using wheelbarrows, power buggies, a concrete pump [see Figs. 1-93(a) and 1-93(b)], or a lifting bucket (see Fig. 1-94). Figure 1-93(a) illustrates the extended reach of the pump arm, and Fig. 1-93(b) illustrates the concrete being placed in a foundation wall. Once placed, the concrete usually has to be consolidated using an *internal vibrator* (see Fig. 1-95). A number of tools are used in

(a) Concrete pump truck.

(b) Placing concrete in forms.

FIGURE 1-93

FIGURE 1-94 Lifting bucket.

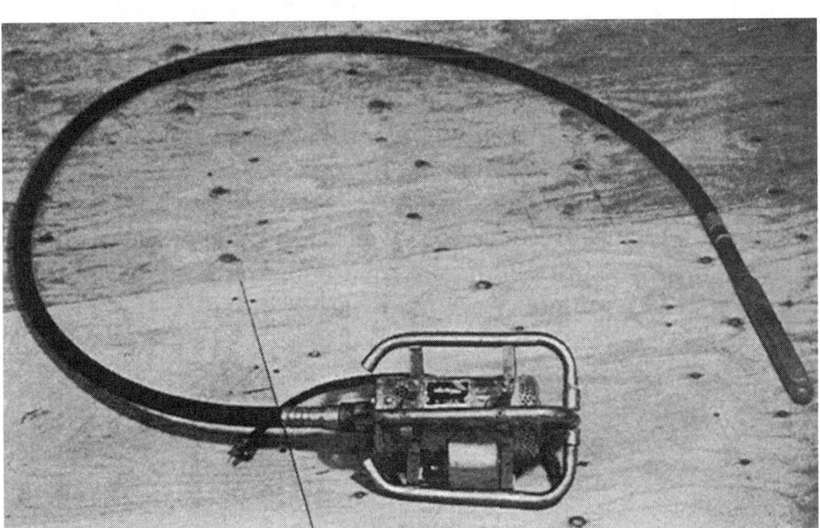

FIGURE 1-95 Concrete internal vibrator.

finishing freshly placed concrete surfaces, including a *bull float* (see Fig. 1-96), a *hand trowel* and *edger*, and a *power trowel*, such as that illustrated in Fig. 1-97.

FIGURE 1-96 Bullfloat.

FIGURE 1-97 Concrete power trowel.

Soil Breaking and Compaction Equipment. At some sites, it may be necessary to break up the surface of compacted soil or concrete. A *jackhammer* can be used (see Fig. 1-98) for this purpose. When soil must be compacted, a *rammer* can be used (see Fig. 1-99) for small areas such as trenches. A *plate vibrator*, as shown in Fig. 1-100, can be used for large areas such as in preparation for the placement of a concrete slab. For very large areas, vibratory rollers may be used, as shown in Fig. 1-101.

FIGURE 1-98 Jackhammer in use.
(Courtesy Wacker Corp.)

FIGURE 1-99 Rammer compacting backfill.
(Courtesy Wacker Corp.)

FIGURE 1-100 Vibro-compactor or flat-plate compactor at work.
(Courtesy Wacker Corp.)

FIGURE 1-101 Vibratory roller.

REVIEW QUESTIONS

1-1. What style of hammer would carpenters use to frame a residential building?

1-2. What is recommended for driving long nails into framing materials?

1-3. How many tip sizes of Phillips screwdrivers are available?

1-4. Which tool is used to drive a finishing nail below the surface of the material?

1-5. What saw has been designed for cutting an opening in gyproc for an electrical outlet?

1-6. If you need to ensure that a wall is perfectly vertical, what hand tool would be best suited?

1-7. What part on a hand electric saw is a safety device?

1-8. How is the hand electric saw adjusted to cut a bevel?

1-9. What type of shank is required for bits to fit into an electric drill?

1-10. What type of hand electric saw causes the blade to cut with an up and down motion?

1-11. What is the difference between an electric drill and an electric hammer drill?

1-12. How do you operate a radial arm saw to crosscut material?

1-13. If you wanted to make a compound miter cut, what type of miter saw would be best suited?

1-14. How is the size of a table saw determined?

1-15. What type of tool is used to drive nails during framing operations using compressed air?

1-16. What type of equipment would be suitable for excavating a small trench?

1-17. What equipment is used to load soil onto a truck?

1-18. What is the purpose of having concrete delivered to a job site by a transit-mix truck?

1-19. What is the intended purpose of a bull float?

1-20. What equipment is useful in compacting soil around a buried pipe?

Chapter 2

SCAFFOLDS

OBJECTIVES

Here is what you will be able to do when you complete each component of this chapter:

1. Differentiate between the various types of scaffolds used in the construction industry.
2. Identify safety organizations governing the use of scaffolds.

As construction progresses, *scaffolding* or *staging* is required to reach work areas beyond the normal reach of workers standing on the ground or floor. This necessitates some form of supporting framework suitable to safely accommodate the required activities. Many different types of scaffolds are available, some of which are very specific in how and where they should be used.

A definition of a scaffold can be found in many different references. Dictionaries, various governmental agencies, and the Scaffold Industry Association all have descriptions for scaffolds, but there is a common premise that, in essence, defines scaffolds as elevated work platforms. To quote the Scaffold Industry Association: "A temporary elevated or suspended work unit and its supporting structure used for supporting worker(s) or materials, or both." The Federal Occupational Safety and Health Administration (OSHA) describe a scaffold as: "Any temporary elevated platform and its supporting structure used for supporting workers, or materials, or both." And the Canadian Standards Association (CSA) describes a scaffold as: "Any temporary elevated platform and its supporting structure for supporting workers, or worker's equipment and materials."

As you can see, the definition is quite broad and could include almost anything that provides an elevated platform. However, the aspect of safety must be the key consideration in any type of scaffold. The intention of this chapter is to introduce some of the more common types of scaffolds and their components along with an emphasis on safety, as there is an increasing rate of serious accidents, even death, resulting from the improper erection or use of scaffolds. The scope of the material is limited to typical scaffolds used in residential construction.

TYPES OF SCAFFOLDS

Wood Scaffolds

Although there are a few instances in which wood scaffolds built on the job site are used, their use has diminished over the past few years. The main problem with them is that they are often not properly designed and assembled, which could result in accidents. Further, they take a lot of material that must be assembled and later dismantled, which takes time and results in having to dispose of used material. Consequently you will find various manufactured scaffolds on most job sites.

Frame Scaffolds

There are a variety of frame scaffolds produced by scaffold manufacturers. In fact, most manufacturers have a number of different frame styles, sizes, and capacities available. In comparison with other stationary scaffolds, frame scaffolds are the least versatile of other stationary scaffolds but their ease of erection, availability of various components, and minimum level of required erection expertise make them popular for many scaffold applications. These scaffolds are well suited for square and rectangular structures where there is easy access and the foundation is relatively level.

Frame scaffolds are a welded assembly of tubular members. They are joined together with crossbraces, coupling pins (connectors with retainer pins), bases, brackets, and guardrail systems. The upper horizontal welded member of the frame provides support for a working platform, and there is automatic spacing between the frames by use of the crossbraces. An example of a basic scaffold unit is shown in Fig. 2-1.

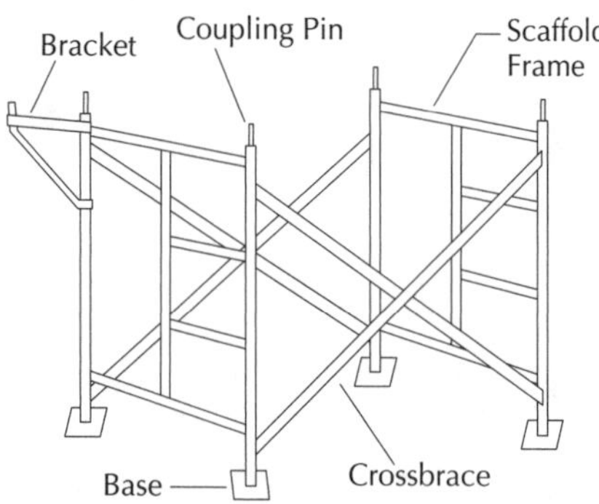

FIGURE 2-1 Basic scaffold unit. (Courtesy Southern Alberta Institute of Technology and Scaffold Industry Association)

Frame scaffolds are typically made from steel, although aluminum and fiberglass frames are available from certain manufacturers. The frames can be any width and height depending on the manufacturer, although the most common widths are 3 ft (1 m) and 5 ft (1.5 m) while the most common heights are 5 ft (1.5 m) and approximately 6 ft–7 in. (1.98 m). Figure 2-2 illustrates several of the more common styles.

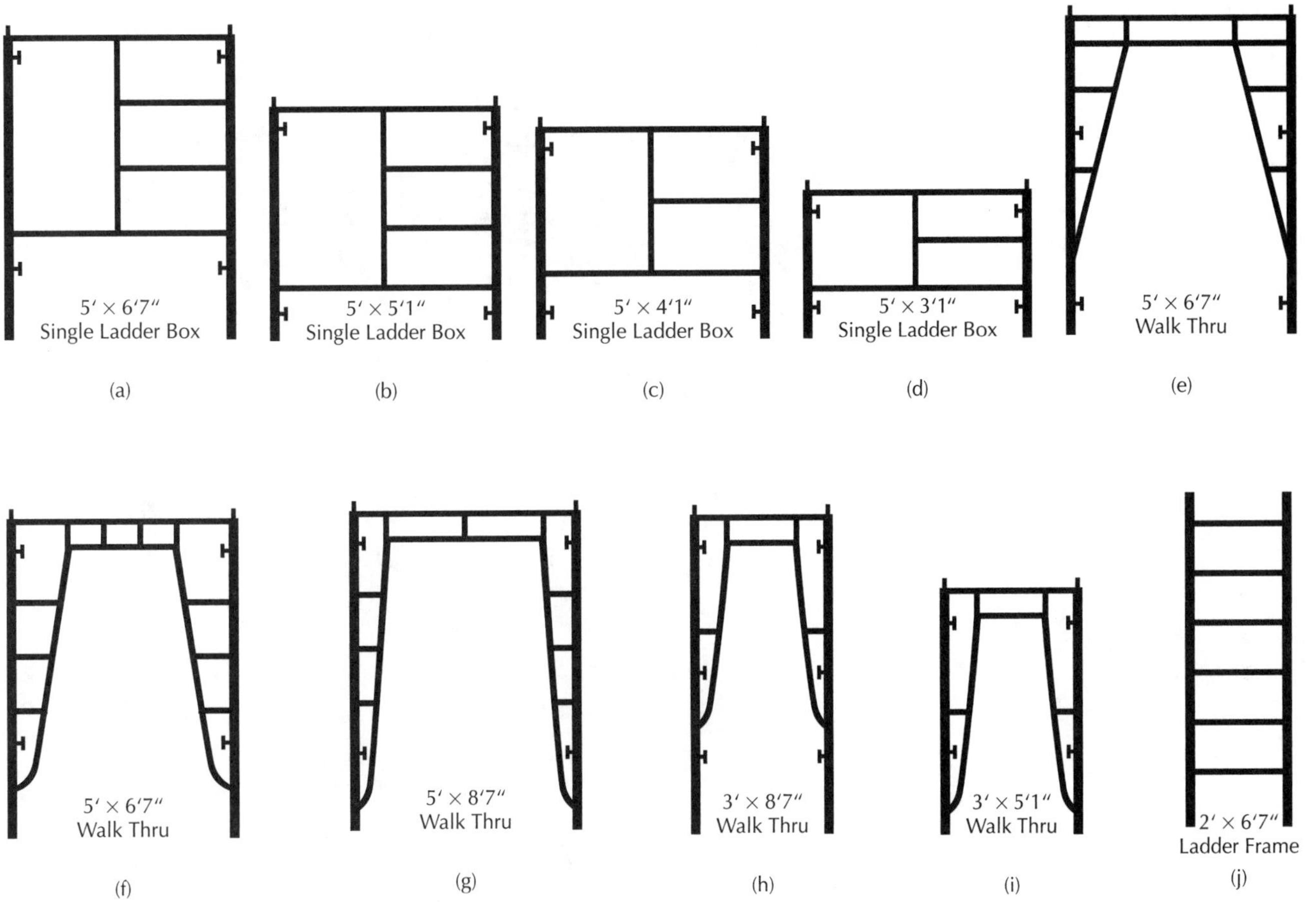

5′ × 6′7″
Single Ladder Box
(a)
5′ × 5′1″
Single Ladder Box
(b)
5′ × 4′1″
Single Ladder Box
(c)
5′ × 3′1″
Single Ladder Box
(d)
5′ × 6′7″
Walk Thru
(e)
5′ × 6′7″
Walk Thru
(f)
5′ × 8′7″
Walk Thru
(g)
3′ × 8′7″
Walk Thru
(h)
3′ × 5′1″
Walk Thru
(i)
2′ × 6′7″
Ladder Frame
(j)

FIGURE 2-2 Frame scaffold styles.
(Courtesy Southern Alberta Institute of Technology and Scaffold Industry Association)

One of the more important components of any scaffold is the base plate. Base plates are required to support each leg of the frame to distribute the load of the scaffold over a wide area. Several types are available with some of the more common ones shown in Fig. 2-3. When a scaffold is built on uneven surfaces, either the screwjack or extension base plate should be used.

Base Plate
Extension
Base Plate
Screwjack
with
Base Plate

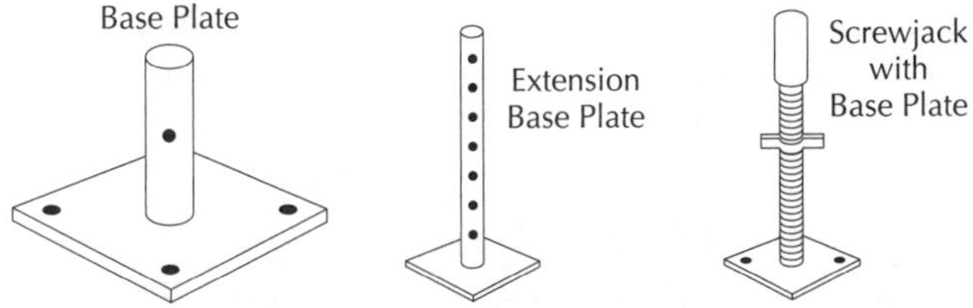

FIGURE 2-3 Base plates.
(Courtesy Southern Alberta Institute of Technology and Scaffold Industry Association)

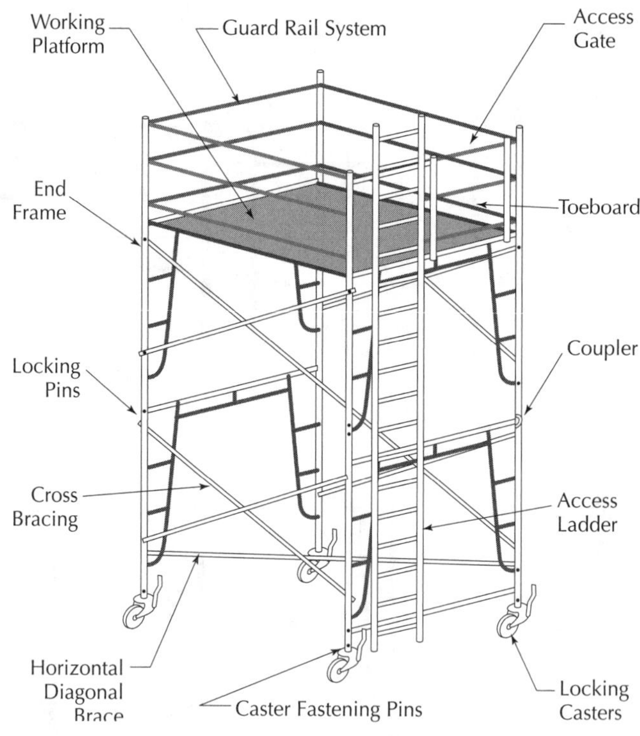

FIGURE 2-4 Mobile scaffold.
(Courtesy Scaffold Industry Association)

An example of a mobile frame scaffold tower is shown in Fig. 2-4. Notice that there is a full working platform complete with toeboard and guardrail system for worker safety, as well as a ladder for safe access to the platform. Also, there is a horizontal diagonal brace at the bottom to prevent the scaffold from wracking. The casters are of a type that can be locked to prevent any movement while the scaffold is being used.

Tube and Coupler Scaffolds (Tube and Clamp)

Tube and coupler scaffolds are assembled using several 2-in. (48-mm) diameter tubes of various lengths, clamped together to make a rigid structure that can be used multiple times as long as they have not been damaged. They are particularly useful for jobs that require irregular shapes, as they are very versatile. In many cases tube and coupler scaffolding is used in combination with frame scaffolds. Both steel and aluminum tubes are available, but they must not be mixed on the same job, as they behave differently under the same loads. An example of this type of scaffold is shown in Fig. 2-5.

Notice the safety features built into this example.

The vertical tubes or posts are located where they are required, and horizontal tubes, called runners or ledgers, are used to hold them in a vertical position. The horizontal tubes, called *bearers* or *transoms*, are used to support the platforms and the associated loads.

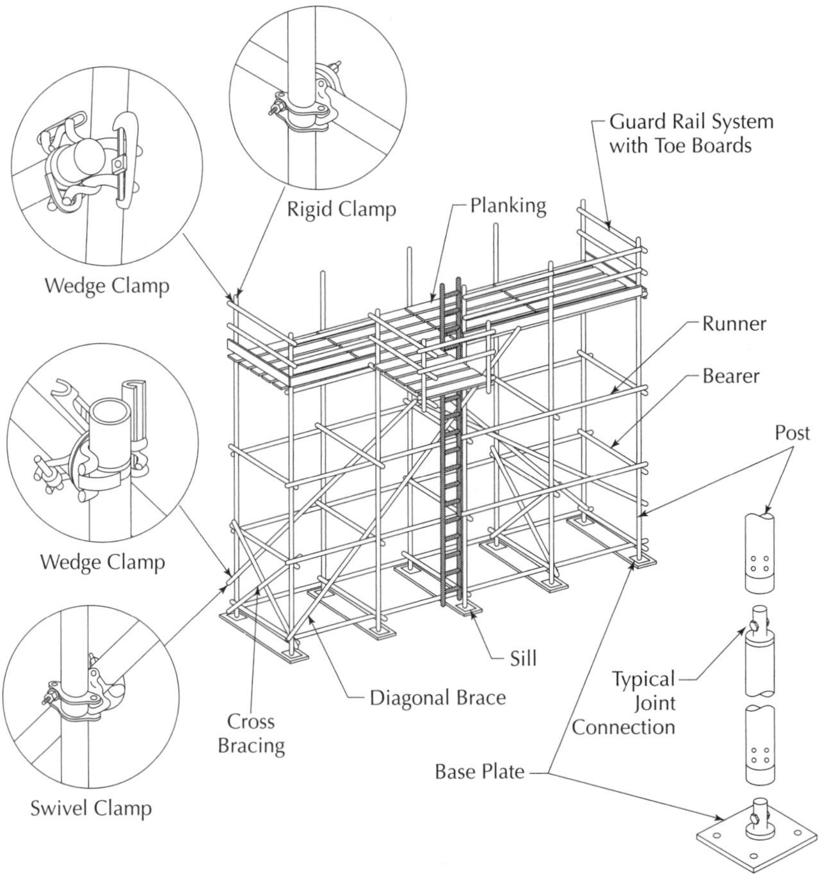

FIGURE 2-5 Tube and Coupler scaffold.
(Courtesy Scaffold Industry Association)

Diagonal tubes located on the face of the scaffold are called *sway braces* and ensure that the scaffold remains plumb, while diagonal tubes located between the inner and outer posts are called *transverse* or *cross bracing*. Plain braces are the tubes located horizontally in a diagonal direction at the base and various other levels to keep the scaffold square. Various couplers are used to join the tubes and are also shown in Fig. 2-5.

It should be noted here that tube and coupler scaffolds require considerable expertise in their erection. Improper connections or improperly placed, and improperly located posts, bearers, runners and bracing can result in the scaffold failing, thus causing injury to workers. Training in the proper erection of these scaffolds is highly recommended!

System Scaffolds

System scaffolds are similar to tube and coupler scaffolds in that they are assembled using individual tubes of steel or aluminum. The difference between them is the method of connecting the various parts. The posts have special connectors welded to them at fixed intervals, and the runners and bearers are made in specific lengths and have fittings at each end for attachment to the post connectors. Figures 2-6, 2-7, and 2-8 illustrate how the components are assembled.

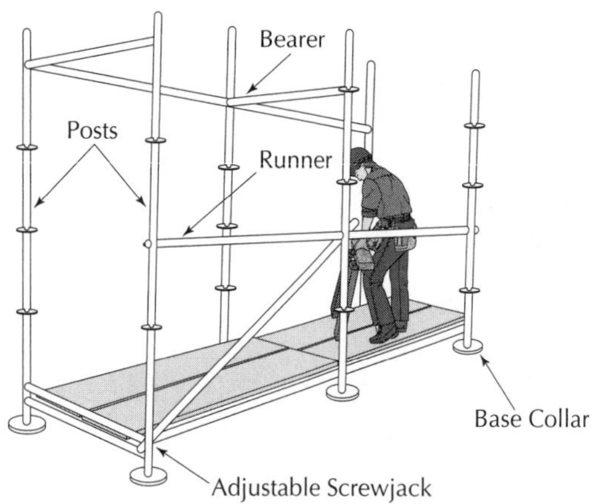

FIGURE 2-6 System scaffold.
(Courtesy Southern Alberta Institute of Technology and Scaffold Industry Association)

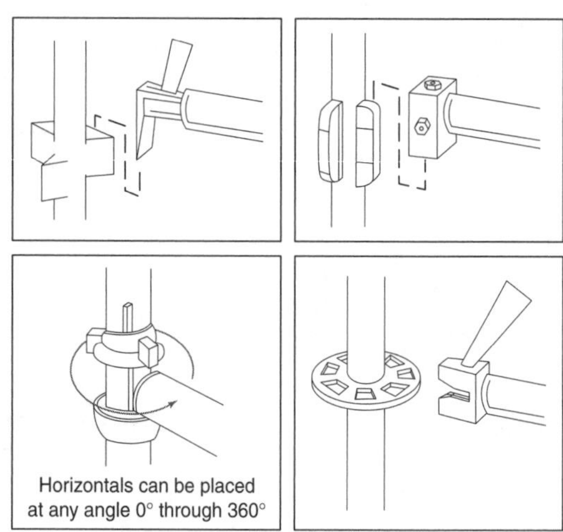

FIGURE 2-7 System scaffold.
(Courtesy Southern Alberta Institute of Technology and Scaffold Industry Association)

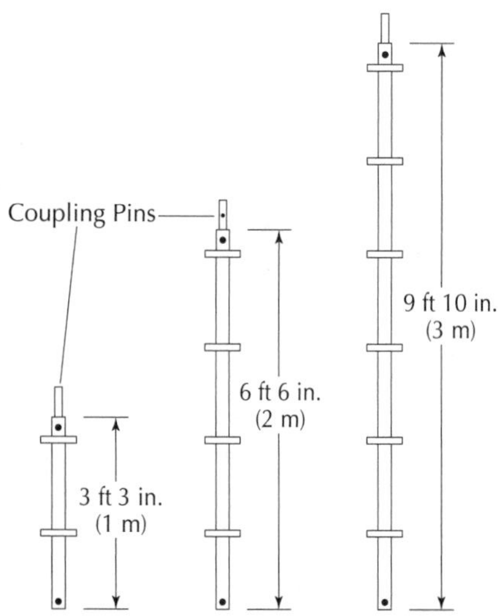

FIGURE 2-8 System scaffold.
(Courtesy Southern Alberta Institute of Technology and Scaffold Industry Association)

Platforms

Various types of scaffold platforms can be used, but the most important aspect is that it must be capable of supporting the load that will be imposed on it. The American National Standards Institute (ANSI) has developed a chart that assists scaffold designers, erectors, and users in recognizing the various products and their corresponding limitations. For example, the chart makes reference to a one-person, two-person, and three-person load. The term "person" refers to a standard accepted weight of 250 lb (113.4 kg) that includes, along with the person, the weight of materials and equipment. Regardless, careful selection of platform materials is critical to the safety of workers.

Some examples of suitable platform materials are identified next.

Sawn wood planks are the most common and usually are 2-in. × 10-in. dressed planks (actual size is $1\frac{1}{2} \times 9\frac{1}{4}$ in.) (38 mm × 238 mm). In the United States, planks suitable for scaffold platforms must be stamped for that purpose (see Fig. 2-9).

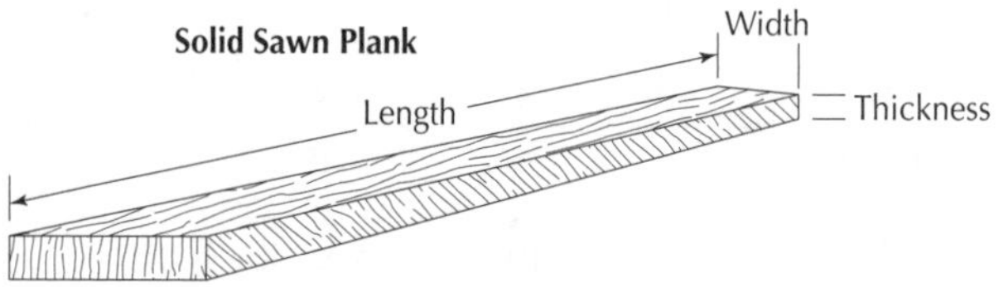

FIGURE 2-9 Wood plank platform.
(Courtesy Southern Alberta Institute of Technology and Scaffold Industry Association)

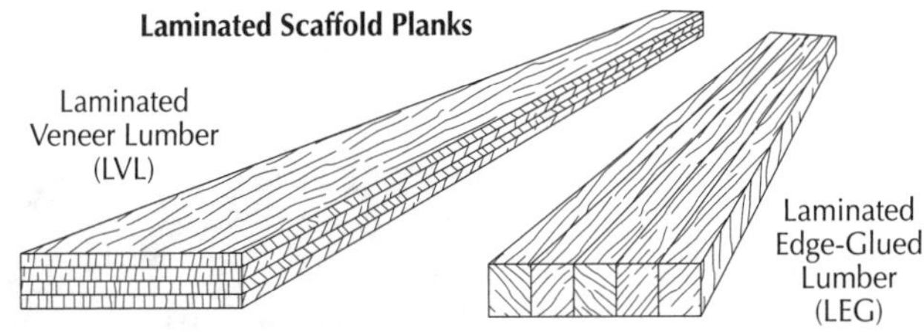

FIGURE 2-10 Laminated platform planks.
(Courtesy Southern Alberta Institute of Technology and Scaffold Industry Association)

Two other types of wood planks are laminated veneer planks and laminated edge-glued planks (Fig. 2-10). Unlike sawn lumber, laminated scaffold planks are tested and rated by the manufacturer.

Scaffold decks are manufactured modules that are usually 19 in. (483 mm) wide, although other sizes are also available. This type of unit is equipped with end hooks to secure them to scaffold bearers (see Fig. 2-11). The most common material is aluminum. Some have aluminum side-rails supporting a plywood deck, while others are entirely aluminum.

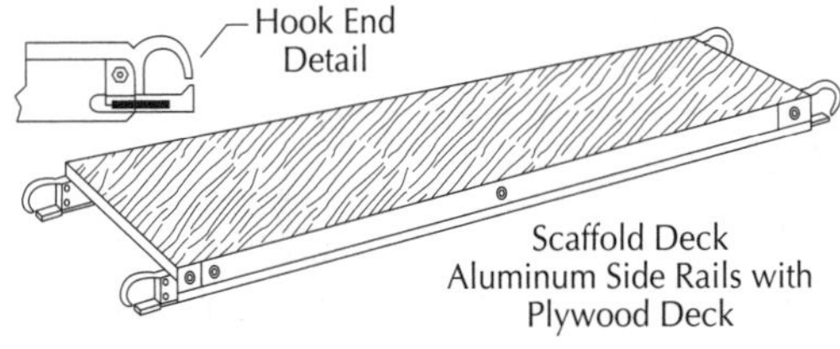

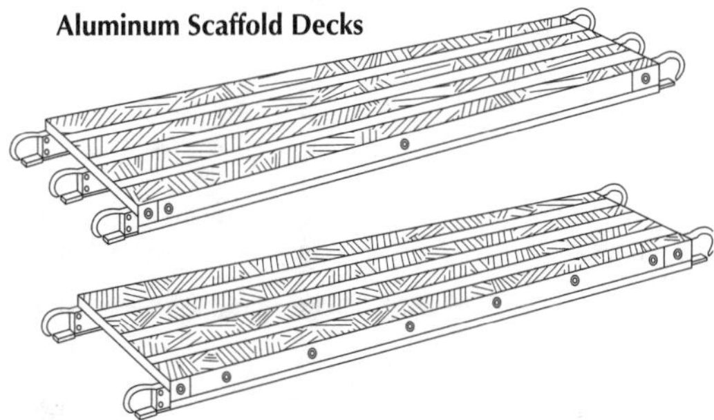

FIGURE 2-11 Aluminum scaffold decks.
(Courtesy Southern Alberta Institute of Technology and Scaffold Industry Association)

Carpenter Bracket

These special metal brackets are secured to wood wall studs to provide a support for a platform and guardrail system. They are easily erected and dismantled and can be transported from job to job easily because of their size. Figure 2-12(a) illustrates how they are secured.

Another type is a roof bracket where it is fastened with nails into rafters or trusses between layers of shingles. In this way roofers will have a narrow platform from which to apply shingles [see Fig. 2-12(b)].

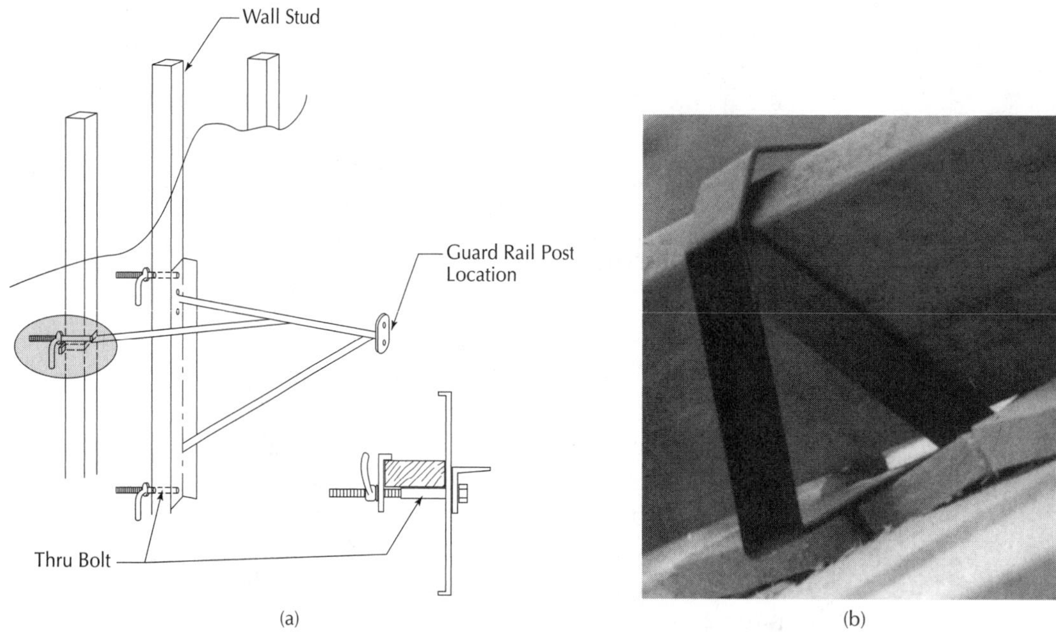

FIGURE 2-12 Carpenter bracket.
(Courtesy Scaffold Industry Association)

FIGURE 2-12 Roof bracket.

Pump Jack Scaffold

Pump jack scaffolds, sometimes called climbing or adjustable scaffolds, make use of a vertical post of wood or metal on which a platform is secured. The platform can be raised or lowered by the use of a jacking system, as illustrated in Fig. 2-13.

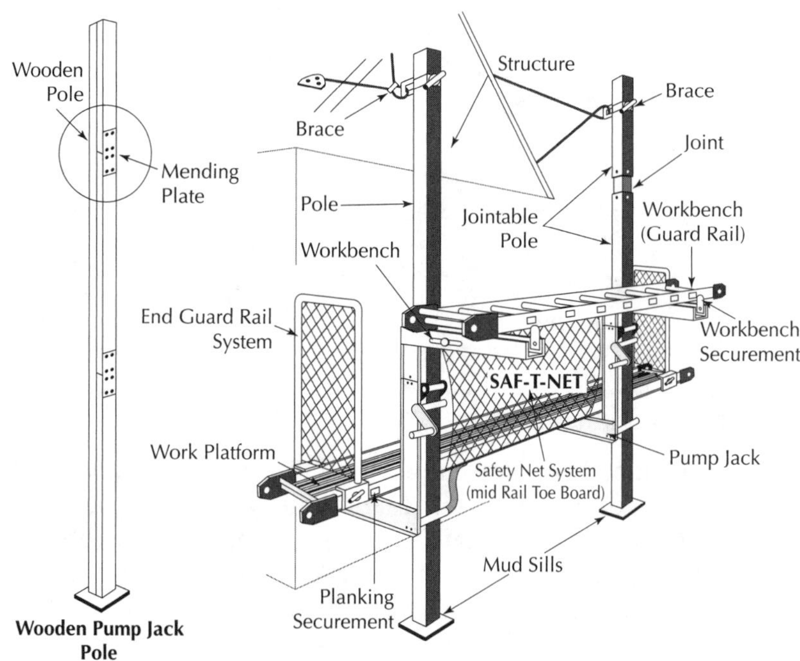

FIGURE 2-13 Pump Jack scaffold.
(Courtesy Scaffold Industry Association)

Ladder Jack Scaffold

Ladder jacks are often used by siding applicators and are especially convenient, as they do not need fastening to the wall. This allows for placing finishing materials with little or no interference with the material being applied [see Fig. 2-14(a)]. It should be noted here that the second highest rung on a ladder is the highest allowable location for the platform.

Brackets are available for placement on either the outside of the ladder or on the inside, as shown in Fig. 2-14(b).

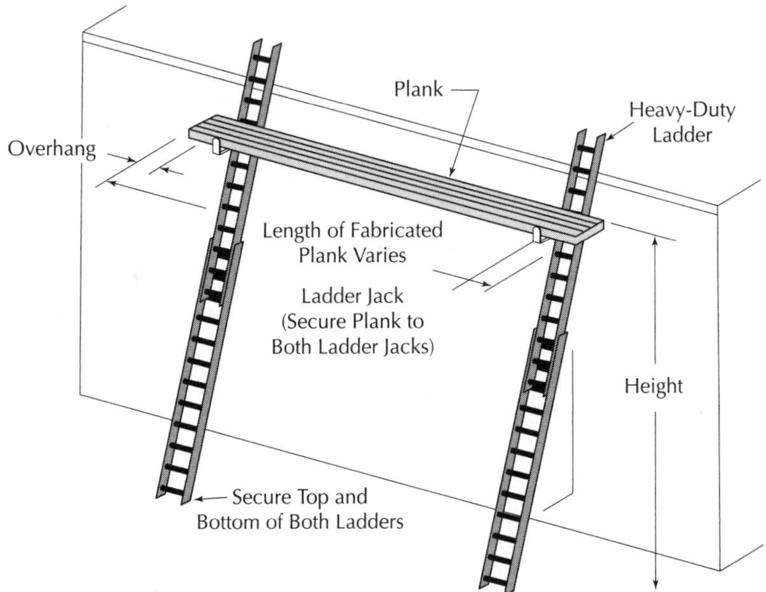

(a) Ladder jack scaffold (Courtesy Scaffold Industry Association)

(b) Ladder jack scaffold (inner placement).

FIGURE 2-14

Stepladder Scaffold

Two stepladders joined with a work platform are often suitable for jobs that do not require a high scaffold. This scaffold is easily erected and dismantled and is particularly suitable for small jobs, especially where it is set up inside a building (see Fig. 2-15). Note that, as said before, the highest location of the platform can only be on the second highest rung.

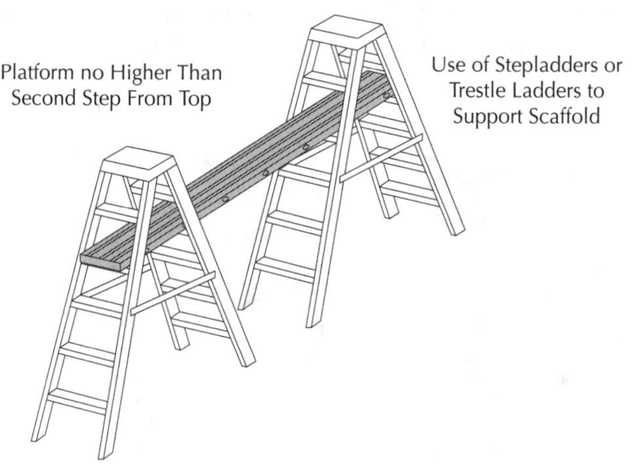

FIGURE 2-15 Stepladder scaffold.
(Courtesy Scaffold Industry Association)

FIGURE 2-16 Aerial platform (bucket, truck-mounted).
(Courtesy Scaffold Industry Association)

Aerial Platforms

Aerial platforms are often found on work sites, and there are a wide variety of types. One type is a vehicle-mounted aerial platform that uses a telescoping boom to raise, lower, and position a one- or two-person basket (see Fig. 2-16). These are often used for relatively small jobs that can be completed quickly without the need to erect more elaborate scaffolds.

Another vehicle-mounted type uses a large platform that is raised and lowered using a scissor lifting system (see Fig. 2-17). With a large platform several workers along with limited material can be lifted to the work area.

There are also many types of independent aerial platforms available, some of which have a motorized base and some with hand-operated mechanical or hydraulic lifting devices. The illustration in Fig. 2-18 is a motorized type equipped with supporting pads for stability. It should be noted that these boom lifts are limited as to the loads they can support, which is also tied to the amount of horizontal projection. **Also, it is imperative that workers not be on the platform during any movement of the base.**

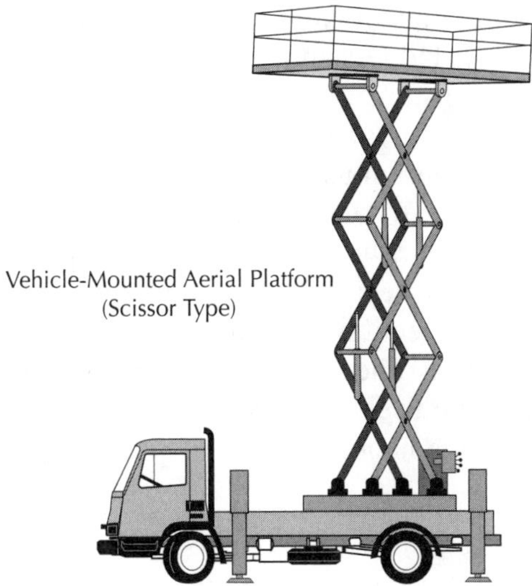

FIGURE 2-17 Aerial platform (truck-mounted).
(Courtesy Scaffold Industry Association)

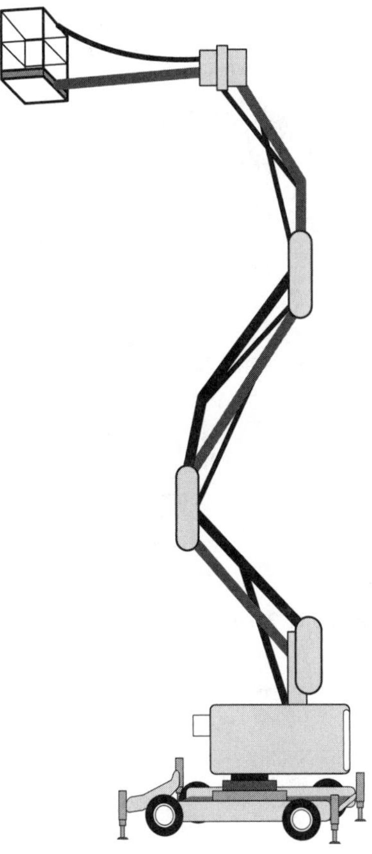

FIGURE 2-18 Aerial platform (bucket, mobile unit).
(Courtesy Scaffold Industry Association)

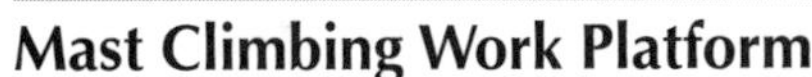

Mast Climbing Work Platform

There are several types of mast climbing scaffolds, as illustrated in Fig. 2-19. These are similar to the pump jack scaffolds but are much larger and more capable of supporting several workers along with materials. Some have a single mast while others utilize several masts. Bricklayers often use this scaffold while erecting masonry walls.

Ladders

Obviously, various ladders are used on work sites. Several types are available, manufactured from either wood or aluminum or a combination of both. *Stepladders* range from 4 to 18 ft (1.2–6 m). *Extension ladders* are available up to 32 ft (10 m) and should be of the heavy duty type on construction sites (see Fig. 2-20). Lighter ladders are not suitable because they may not be capable of supporting continuous use and the loads expected of them.

There are a few safety considerations when selecting and using ladders. It is a requirement that portable ladder rungs be positioned not less than 10 in. (250 mm) and not more than 14 in. (360 mm) apart (center to center) and have rungs that are corrugated, knurled, dimpled, or coated with skid-resistant material to minimize slipping. Stepladders are allowed to have the steps not less than 8 in. (200 mm) and not more than 12 in. (300 mm) apart. Wood ladders are not allowed to have any opaque coating, as this could potentially cover up any defect such as decay.

When using ladders it is very important that they do not have any defects; are free of oil, grease, or other slipping hazards; and are

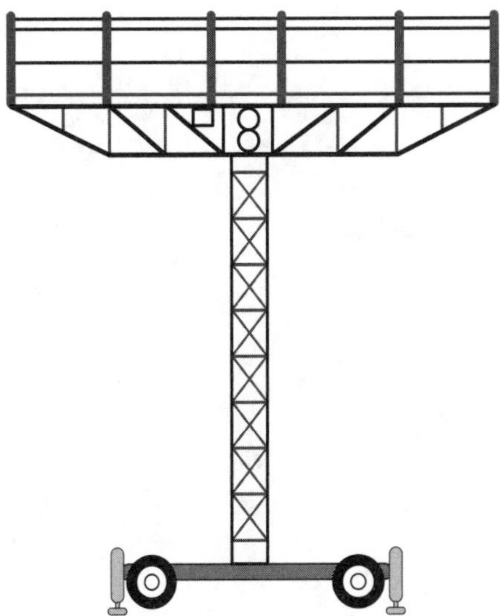

FIGURE 2-19 Mast climbing scaffold.
(Courtesy Scaffold Industry Association)

not loaded beyond the maximum manufacturer's rated capacity. Non-self-supporting ladders must be positioned on an angle such that the horizontal distance from the top support to the foot is approximately one-quarter of the working length of the ladder (see Fig. 2-21). These ladders must extend at least 3 ft (1 m) above the upper landing surface to which the ladder is used to gain access. When placed in an area where they could be displaced by workplace activities, they must be secured to prevent accidental displacement, or barricaded for protection. The area around the top and bottom must be kept clear of other material. And, when ascending or descending a ladder the user must face the ladder while grasping the rungs with at least one hand.

FIGURE 2-20 Heavy duty aluminum ladders.

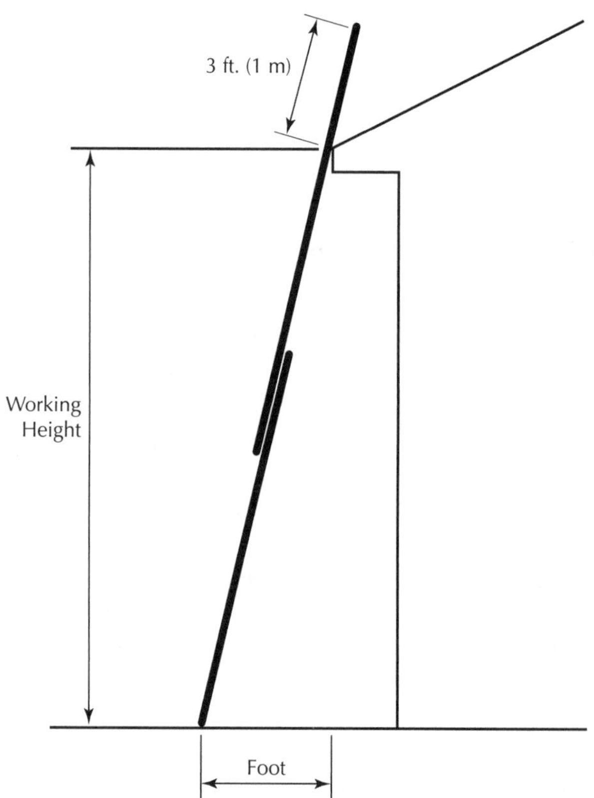

FIGURE 2-21 Ladder positioning.

FIGURE 2-22 Forklift hoist.

Materials Hoist

Some type of equipment is required to lift materials that are to be applied to a building and normally some type of hoist will be used. For relatively low lifts, a *forklift* mounted on a tractor or one that is specifically designed for that purpose is used (see Fig. 2-22).

For higher lifts and heavy loads, a truck-mounted crane is often used (see Fig. 2-23).

Another type of lift is a stationary hoist, some of which are capable of a horizontal swing to lower the material being lifted onto a platform or roof deck. This type of lift uses either an electric or gas-powered motor and hoist mechanism to lift materials onto a roof or scaffold (see Fig. 2-24). Another type utilizes a hand-operated crank.

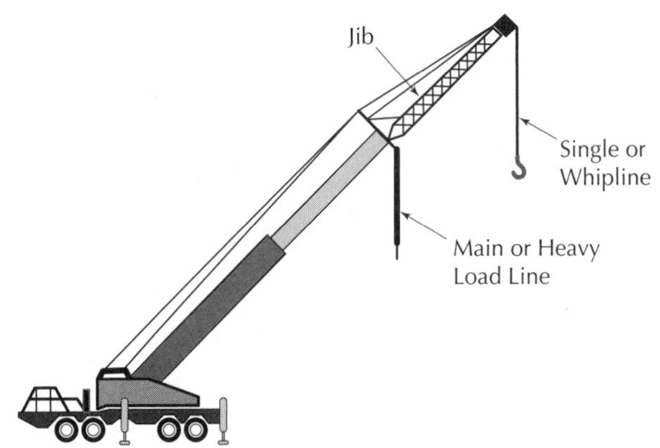

FIGURE 2-23 Truck-mounted crane.
(Courtesy Southern Alberta Institute of Technology and Scaffold Industry Association)

Hydraulic swing hoist.

FIGURE 2-24 Roof-mounted stationary hoist.

SAFE USE OF SCAFFOLDS

Workers erecting and using scaffolds must follow certain codes and regulations that are established to ensure their safety while on a job. Both workers and employers are responsible for ensuring that the requirements are fulfilled. In Canada, the Occupational Health and Safety Act (OHS) sets out certain regulations, and the Canadian Standards Association (CSA) establishes the standards that must be followed. In the United States the Occupational Safety and Health Administration (OSHA) sets out the primary regulation governing scaffolds, and several states have their own Occupational Safety and Health Regulations. In addition, the Uniform Building Code affects the design and use of scaffolds, while interested industry groups, such as the Scaffold Industry Association, have established certain standards.

An accident resulting from improperly designed or improper use of scaffolds is very serious and that is why these regulations, codes, and standards have been established. Far too many workers and even the public have been injured, which has resulted in the need for fines or other punishable measures to be put in place. OSHA Regulations are the basic rules governing scaffolds and are very comprehensive, covering all the different situations where scaffolds are used; they can be quite confusing. However, the Construction Standard, 29 CFR 1926.450-454, is the regulation most appropriate to the construction industry.

In Canada there is no single Occupational Health and Safety Act governing all of Canada, as each province has created its own regulations. There are differences in the regulations from province to province, but each act covers the same concepts regarding worker safety.

Regardless of where scaffolds are erected and used, it is the responsibility of both the workers and their employers to become conversant with the regulations, codes, and standards that apply and to conform to the requirements.

Acknowledgments

Much of the text and diagrams included in this chapter have been provided through both the Southern Alberta Institute of Technology and the Scaffold Industry Association. Through the partnership between these two organizations extensive training courses have been developed for those that erect scaffolds and those that use scaffolds. It is highly recommended that a person erecting or using scaffolds take training for the sake of safety.

REVIEW QUESTIONS

2-1. What are the unique characteristics of frame scaffolds?

2-2. Why is it important that base plates be used with scaffolds?

2-3. How are tube and coupler scaffolds assembled?

2-4. What is the unique characteristic of system scaffolds?

2-5. In the United States what type of sawn wood plank is suitable for a scaffold platform?

2-6. How are carpenter brackets secured to a wall?

2-7. How are ladder jack scaffolds assembled?

2-8. What is an aerial platform?

2-9. How much of a portable ladder must extend above a platform or roof to which it is leaning against for the purpose of access?

2-10. What organization in Canada sets out scaffold regulations?

2-11. What organization in the United States sets out the basic scaffold regulations?

Chapter 3

THE BUILDING SITE

OBJECTIVES

Here is what you will be able to do when you complete each component of this chapter:

1. Identify the requirements for a site investigation.
2. Determine what is required for soil investigation.
3. Describe typical services that are provided or needed for buildings.
4. Identify what zoning restrictions means.
5. Define site layout.
6. Identify common leveling instruments and how they are used.

SITE INVESTIGATION

The erection of a building, large or small, necessitates a good deal of prior study and planning, both in connection with the building itself and with the site on which it will be built.

This study, commonly referred to as *site investigation*, will vary widely as to method and degree, depending on the type, size, and proposed use of the building to be constructed. Planners in the light construction industry will likely be most interested in surface aspects of the site and the subsoil at relatively shallow depths. On the other hand, planners of large, heavy buildings are usually interested in the nature of the subsoil at considerable depth and are concerned with the surface chiefly from the standpoint of site area and adjacent buildings.

Site Investigation in Light Construction

In many instances, land developers will conduct site investigation over large areas and do all the preparatory work so that residential or light commercial builders will not have to duplicate their efforts. In these situations, land developers will likely remove all unnecessary trees, shrubs, and topsoil. They will determine subsurface conditions and make that data available to the builders. All services such as main water and sewer lines, electrical lines, and natural gas lines will have been put in place ready for builders to connect from each piece of property. Likewise, all roads will have been laid out and the confines of each piece of property will have been located. Local government agencies will have to approve this process even before work actually takes place.

In these situations, builders or owners need only select and purchase the piece of property on which they choose to build. In some instances, there will be restrictions on height, area and appearance of the building.

In situations where "raw" land is available for building, surface aspects of the site that must be considered are:

1. Presence or absence of trees and shrubs;
2. Contours of the site;
3. Elevation of the site in relation to the surrounding area;
4. The size, shape, and proximity of surrounding buildings;
5. Perk testing (soil testing for permeability);
6. Environmental review (impact on the environment).

Particularly in the case of planning for residential construction, the presence of trees and their size often influence the design of the building and may also influence the type of equipment needed to clear the site. In some cases, it may be deemed necessary to remove all the trees, while in others trees may influence the overall design or positioning of the building.

The designer must determine whether the site is flat, rolling, or is sloped, as these factors can also influence the design of the building. For example, a slope or small hill may enable the building design to include entrances at different levels. Other considerations might include the necessity of introducing fill soil to change the existing elevation, particularly if the site is low in comparison to the surrounding land. Finally, care must be taken to ensure that water runoff will not cause damage to adjoining property. This may require may require swales to direct the water away.

Another consideration may be the overall design in relation to existing buildings. For example, a tall, narrow building in the midst of a group of low, rambling ones would probably look out of place. Marketing, aesthetics, and function of the house type and style are important considerations.

SOIL INVESTIGATION

Soil investigation, carried out in connection with light construction projects, will consist of tests to determine the kinds of soil to a depth of twice the building depth below the surface, the level of the water table in the soil, and any unusual soil characteristics. Where frost is a problem, the depth of penetration must also be determined (often available from the local government). In some areas where surface foundations are employed this investigation need not be as comprehensive as in those areas where below grade foundations are the norm.

The type of soil present will indicate the bearing strength and will help determine the excavating equipment best suited for the job. Depending on the type of soil, the excavated material will either have to be removed from the site and replaced with other soil or stored to be used for backfilling and landscaping. Some very fine clay soils expand substantially when subjected to moisture penetration, and care must be taken when these are encountered at the foundation level of a building. If the area is subject to frost, the type of soil will determine how serious a problem it may be.

In the case of below grade foundations, the level of the water table—the natural water level in the soil—will determine whether particular precautions must be taken, such as the installation of weeping tile or sump holes fitted with a pump. It may also influence the waterproofing techniques used on the exterior of the foundation walls.

Testing for the presence of a number of aggressive chemical substances, particularly sulfates of calcium, sodium, or magnesium, in the groundwater or soil is important in the study of soils on building sites. When there are appreciable amounts of these sulfates that can come into contact with concrete or masonry, the sulfates react chemically with hydrated lime and hydrated calcium aluminates in the cement paste. This causes considerable expansion in the paste, resulting in corrosion and disintegration of the concrete.

To prevent this deterioration, concrete that will be in contact with these sulfates should be made using cement that has a low content of calcium aluminate. If the soil contains over 0.10% sulfates or the water contains over 150-ppm (parts per million) water-soluble sulfate, sulfate-resistant cement should be used.

Penetration of the soil by frost may have serious consequences under certain conditions. When moisture is present in any of several fine-grained soils, freezing may result in the formation of ice lenses and consequent heaving of the soil. Under these conditions, building codes will require the footings to be placed below the frost line. Possible alternatives are to eliminate the soil moisture by draining it away or to replace the soil with one that is not affected by frost action, such as gravel or coarse sand.

In some situations, particularly in heavy construction work, the method of soil testing commonly used is through boring. Machine augers may be used to bring soil to the surface for analysis in a *disturbed* condition (see Fig. 3-1). Disturbed samples are generally used for soil grain size analysis, to determine the specific gravity of the soil, and for compaction testing. For determining other properties of soils such as strength and permeability, it is necessary to obtain an *undisturbed* sample. The most common method for

FIGURE 3-1 Soil test operation.

obtaining an undisturbed sample is to push a thin *Shelby tube* into the soil, thereby trapping the sample inside the tube (see Fig. 3-2).

Where subsurface foundations are to be constructed, a danger that must be considered is the presence of underground watercourses or springs. Without special equipment, this situation is very difficult to detect. These watercourses normally flow underground to some natural outlet, but if the soil is disturbed and the natural outlets dammed off, often difficulties result. Water begins to collect underground, the hydrostatic pressure builds up, and eventually the water must break out somewhere. This could occur under a basement floor and the pressure could break through the floor. If there is the slightest hint of an underground water flow, drainage tile must be installed.

AVAILABLE SERVICES

Are services such as electricity, sewer, water, gas, and telephone available? The answer will affect plans and preparations for the building. If a main sewer line is already installed, it will be necessary to know its depth in order to ensure that there is a sewer line drop

(a)

(b)

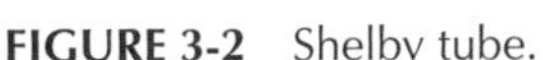

FIGURE 3-2 Shelby tube.

from the building to the main line. Often local governments will establish the maximum depth of foundations to accommodate sewer connections.

If no main sewer line is available, plans must be made to provide for a private sewage disposal system. In this case, local governments and codes will dictate the requirements, and special permits will have to be acquired.

The location of the water connection must be considered in order to accommodate its installation. If there is a locally supplied source, its location near the property involved can be obtained from the local government. If the property involved is located where there is no source, then provisions must be made to drill a well or to obtain access to another source.

The availability of electricity will certainly have an effect on the actual construction work. In new areas that have been pre-prepared for buildings and where services have been installed, this will not be a problem, provided the service has been installed adjacent to the property involved. In this case it will be necessary to apply to the utility company to have it connected to a temporary service. If it is not available at the time of commencement of construction, a portable generator will likely have to be employed (see Figure 3-3).

If natural gas or other form of heating service is available, knowing where it is located is important so that provisions can be made for its connection. In some locations, electricity may be the source of heat and provisions for the appropriate service will have to be made.

FIGURE 3-3 Portable electric generator.

ZONING RESTRICTIONS

Most urban areas have zoning laws that restrict specified areas to certain uses. They may be industrial, business, local commercial, multiple-family dwelling, or single-family dwelling areas. In addition, a building in a particular area may be required to have a specified minimum main floor area. Regulations stipulate how far back from the front property line the building must be (setback) and the minimum distance it must be away from the side property line (side yard). Often minimum lot areas and the maximum area of the lot a building may cover are defined. The setback for garages, whether front-drive or lane-drive, is specified in many cases. Always check with the local zoning office of your municipality.

In some areas there are services such as electrical, sewer, water, natural gas, and telephone lines that may infringe on a particular property. In this case the municipality will designate this as an easement called a Public Utility Easement. If an easement adjoins a property there can be no building placed on it, but the surface can be used as part of the yard. In other cases the easement may be fenced for restricted access.

These regulations will vary to some degree from municipality to municipality. However, the basic reasons for these restrictions are the same, namely, the preservation of certain standards and the protection of the citizens. Therefore, it is quite essential that developers and builders be familiar with local regulations to ensure compliance.

SITE LAYOUT

When the design work for a building has been completed, plans are drawn to indicate in detail how the building is to be constructed. In most cases a *site plan* is included to show the exact location of the building on the property. If no site plan is required, more freedom of location may be possible, but still subject to the local or regional building regulations. These plans typically require the approval of local building officials and are generally submitted at the time of application for a building permit.

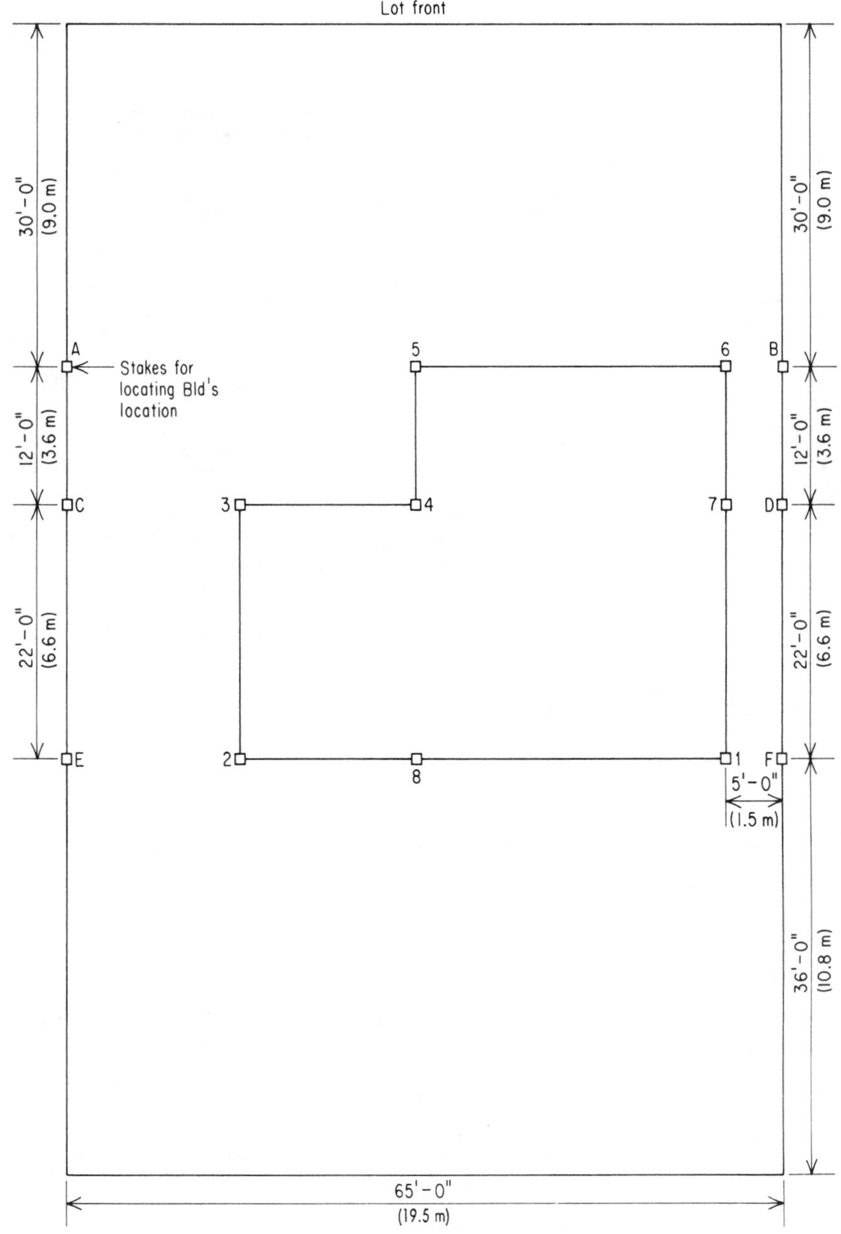

FIGURE 3-4 Lot layout.

Once a building permit has been issued, the builder must first lay out the position of the building on the site. In some areas it is necessary to employ a registered land surveyor to accomplish this. Typically, wooden stakes are positioned at the corners of the building. However, because in most situations a certain amount of soil will have to be removed, the corner stakes must be placed in a setback position so that they will remain in place during and after any excavation work. In many situations these stakes are set along the property lines (see Fig. 3-4). The distance to the building corners will be indicated on the stakes. The amount of excavation or "cut" will also show on these stakes (see Fig. 3-5). After the completion of excavation the actual corners of the building are located. The footings or surface slab can be located from these stakes.

(a)

(b)

FIGURE 3-5 Building stakes.

In some cases, for larger buildings, an alternate method using batter boards is sometimes used (see Fig. 3-6). Batter boards are positioned well outside the actual building location to avoid them being disturbed during any excavation work. When the excavation work has been completed, building lines are stretched between batter boards, and each intersection of two building lines represents a point on the building. These points can be established in the excavation by dropping a plumb bob from the line intersections.

When batter boards first are placed, accurate positions for the building lines must be established. This is usually done through the use of leveling instruments (see Figs. 3-7, 3-8, and 3-9). A saw kerf slot is cut or a nail is driven into the top of the horizontal bar of the batter board to locate the position of the building lines.

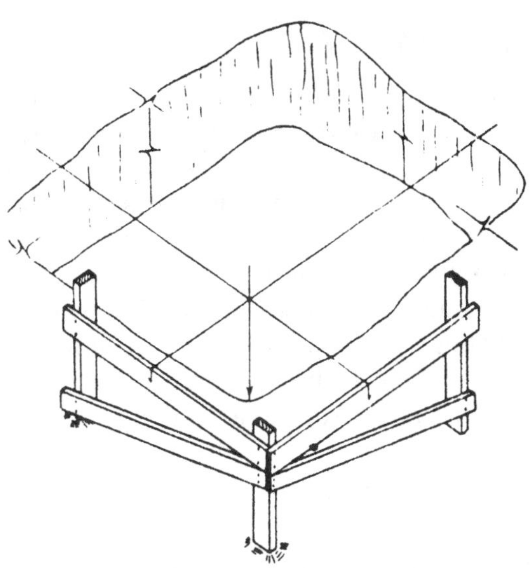

FIGURE 3-6 Locating building corner in excavation from batter boards.

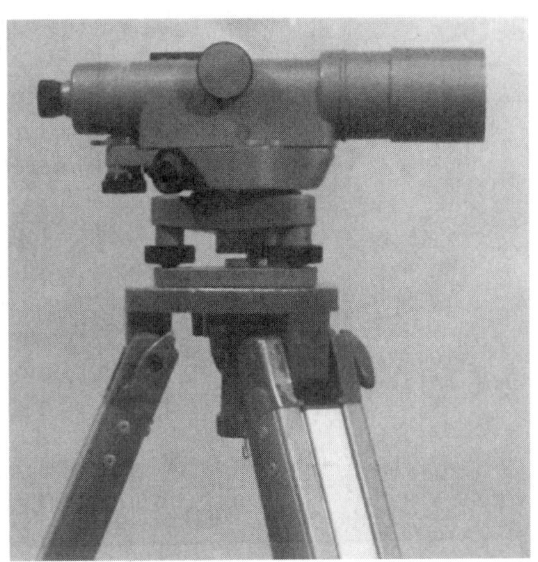

FIGURE 3-7 Builder's level.

FIGURE 3-8 Transit level.

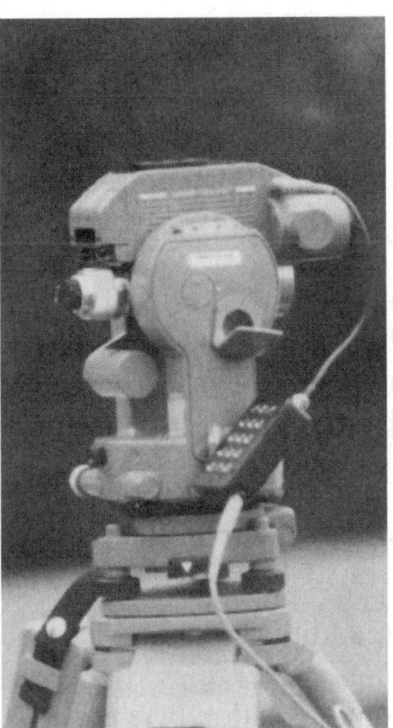

(a)

(b)

FIGURE 3-9 Transit level equipped with EDM. (Electronic Distance Measuring equipment).

LEVELING INSTRUMENTS

A *leveling instrument* is usually employed to lay out a building site. The basic types of levels used are the *builder's level* (see Fig. 3-7) and a *transit-level* (see Figs. 3-8 and 3-9). A *laser level*, as illustrated in Fig. 3-17, is very effective in determining levels on a construction site.

The builder's level turns in a horizontal plane only, while the transit level turns in both horizontal and vertical planes, making it much more versatile. Some instruments are leveled by means of either three or four leveling screws, while others are automatic—they simply require a small bubble to be centered in a circular dial by means of a single adjustment in order to level them.

Builder's Level

The leveling instrument illustrated in Fig. 3-7 consists of a *telescope tube* containing an *objective lens* in front that can be focused by means of a *focusing knob* on the side. The telescope is mounted in a *frame* and has attached to it a *bubble tube* very similar to a small spirit level. The telescope and bubble tube are leveled by means of the *leveling screws*, turned against a *leveling head*. The screws are adjusted until the bubble is centered in the dial, regardless of the direction in which the instrument points.

At the rear end of the telescope, there is an *eyepiece* that contains a small lens and an *eyepiece ring* that can be turned to focus the lens. A pair of *cross hairs* is mounted in front of the eyepiece lens, and they are brought into sharp focus by the adjustment of the eyepiece ring.

At the bottom of the frame, there is a *graduated horizontal circle* and a *vernier scale*, used to read horizontal angles accurately. The instrument may be held in any horizontal position by tightening a *horizontal motion clamp screw*. It can then be brought into fine adjustment by a *horizontal motion tangent screw*.

Some automatic levels are equipped with a *compensator* that allows accurate level readings even if the base is slightly off level. This allows the instrument to be set up without the precision required of an instrument with leveling screws. However, there are limits to the degree of off level that the instrument is capable of compensating.

Transit Level

In addition to being capable of turning in a horizontal direction, a transit level telescope is pivoted in the frame and held in the horizontal position by a *locking lever*. When it is unlocked, the telescope may be tilted through a vertical arc and held in a tilted position by a *vertical motion clamp screw*. The *vertical motion tangent screw* can then make a fine adjustment to the position.

Attached to the telescope is a *graduated vertical arc* that moves as the telescope is tilted. Fixed to the frame is a *vertical vernier scale*, used to read the degree of tilt accurately.

The entire instrument is carried on a *centering head* that sits in a circular opening in the leveling head and allows lateral movement of the instrument within the confines of the opening when the leveling screws are loosened slightly. With some instruments a *plumb bob* is hung from the underside of the centering head and this lateral movement aids in the final centering of the instrument over a pin or reference point. Other instruments use an *optical plummet* (a visual sighting arrangement) to center over a point.

As mentioned before, automatic transit levels are also available.

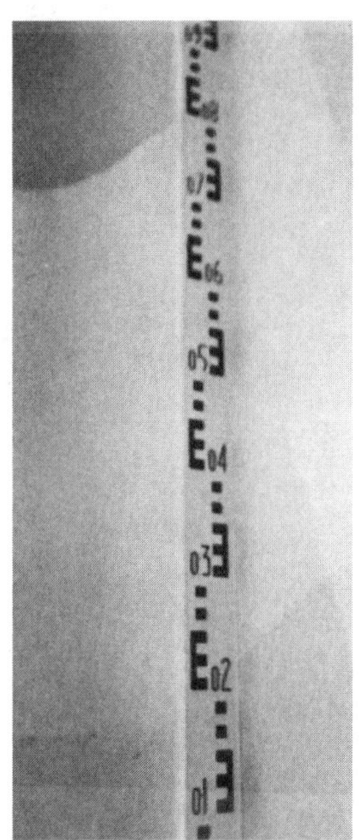

FIGURE 3-10 Metric leveling rod.

Care of Instruments

Leveling instruments have numerous delicate parts that can easily be damaged, resulting in inaccurate measurements. Therefore, it is important that you avoid sudden shocks, jolts, or bumps to the instrument. The threads and bearing surfaces must be kept clean and lightly oiled to ensure smooth adjustments can be made. Whenever the instrument is not in use, it should be kept in the case where it is cushioned against any damage. When placed in the case, the leveling screws and clamps should be tightened just enough to prevent motion when the case is moved. However, these parts should not be overtightened. When lifting the instrument out of the case, grasp the base or frame of the instrument, not the telescope.

When moving the instrument and tripod from point to point, first loosen the leveling screws and clamps slightly, fold the tripod legs together, grasp the frame of the instrument and carry the unit under your arm.

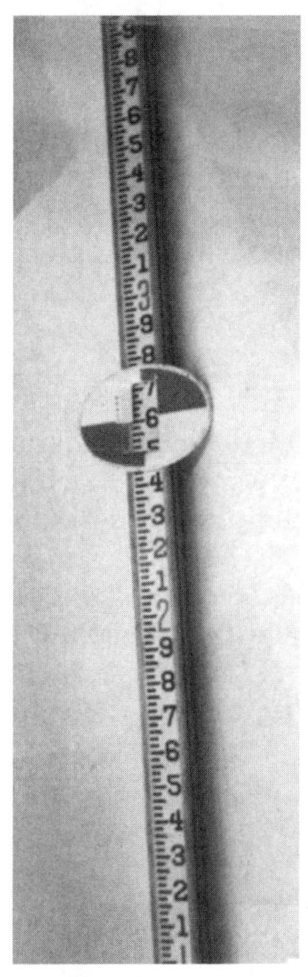

FIGURE 3-11 Target rod.

LEVELING OPERATIONS

Once the instrument is leveled, it is ready for use, and a *leveling rod* or thin pole is required to establish levels. Commercial leveling rods are usually made in two or more sections that can be fitted together, and are marked off in feet, and either in inches and eighths of an inch or subdivided by the decimal system. They are also available in the metric system (see Fig. 3-10).

Some rods are equipped with a sliding *target* (see Fig. 3-11), which is adjusted until the horizontal line coincides with the horizontal cross hair in the instrument, and then locked in position. The reading is then taken at the horizontal line. To take a level sight on a rod with target, proceed as follows:

1. Have a colleague (rodman) hold a leveling rod with target at a convenient distance away from the leveled instrument. The rodman should

- Ensure that the base of the rod is clean and the point on which the rod will be placed is clean.
- Place the rod on the point, standing directly behind facing the instrument with the graduations facing the instrument and the right side up.
- Hold as vertical as possible—the rod should stand by itself briefly if it is vertical.

2. The instrumentman should aim the telescope at the rod by sighting along the top, and then
    - Sight through the eyepiece and adjust the focus by turning the focusing knob. Adjust the instrument until the rod is centered as closely as possible. Tighten the horizontal motion clamp screw and adjust the instrument with the horizontal motion tangent screw until the vertical cross hair is centered on the rod.
    - Have the rodman adjust the target up or down until the horizontal cross hair coincides with the horizontal line on the target. The reading on the rod can now be noted.

If, for example, you want to know the difference of elevation between two points, and the rodman has placed the rod on a *benchmark* (BM) with a known elevation of 100 ft (30.48 m), then the procedure would be:

1. Set up your instrument about halfway between the two points, A and B.
2. Sight the instrument on the rod positioned over the BM (Point A) and record the reading, for example, 3.625 ft (1.105 m). This is called a back sight (BS).
3. This reading is the horizontal height above the known elevation and is called the *height of instrument* (HI). In this example the HI would be 100 + 3.625 = 103.625 ft (30 + 1.105 = 31.105 m).
4. Turn the instrument to sight on Point B and have the rodman position the rod directly over that point. This is called a fore sight (FS).
5. Record the rod reading.
6. Suppose the rod reading is 4.746 ft (1.447 m). Since the rod reading at the BS was 3.625 ft (1.105 m) and the rod reading at the FS is 4.765 ft (1.447 m), then Point B is lower than Point A by 4.746 − 3.625 = 1.121 ft (0.342 m) and would have an elevation of 100 − 1.121 ft (30.138 m).

It should be noted that a *benchmark* is a fixed reference point that is known and recorded as to the exact height above sea level. A *datum point* is a temporary reference point, and its elevation is usually determined in relation to a benchmark.

Use of a Transit Level to Establish Building Lines

A transit level is useful for setting a number of points in a straight line—piers for a pier foundation or for resetting building lines at the bottom of an excavation. The setting of these points can be achieved with a builder's level, but a transit level is much more convenient, especially when a difference in elevation is involved.

Set the instrument directly over the reference point and level the instrument. Release the telescope level lock and swing the instrument in the desired direction and align the cross hair on the desired stake. Tighten the horizontal circle clamp to prevent it from moving in a horizontal direction. Moving the telescope up or down will allow you to set stakes in a straight line (see Fig. 3-12). This same process will easily establish a line at the bottom of an excavation from reference points outside the excavation (see Fig. 3-13).

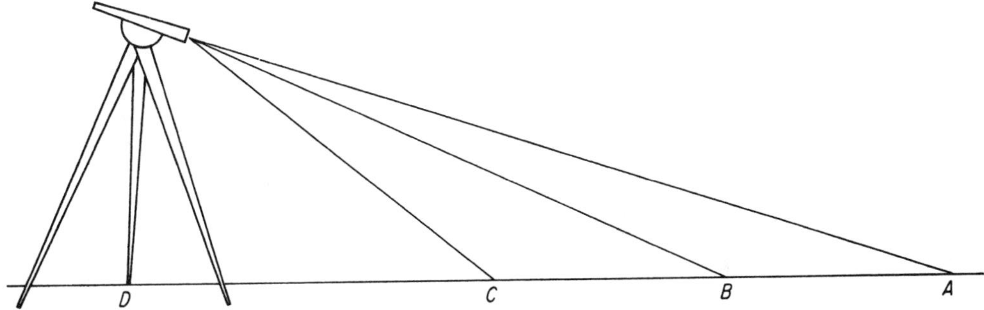

FIGURE 3-12 Using a transit to establish a straight line.

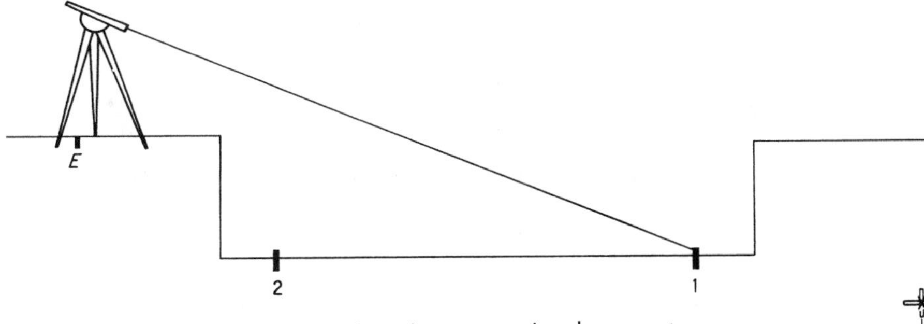

FIGURE 3-13 Locating corners in a basement.

Using an Instrument to Turn a Horizontal Angle

To lay out an angle with a builder's level, set the instrument directly over the required point (station A). This point is commonly marked with a nail driven into the top of a stake. Turn the instrument and sight on station B (see Fig. 3-14) and set the horizontal circle to zero to align with zero on the vernier scale. Swing the instrument to the required angle to locate station C, and clamp the horizontal circle.

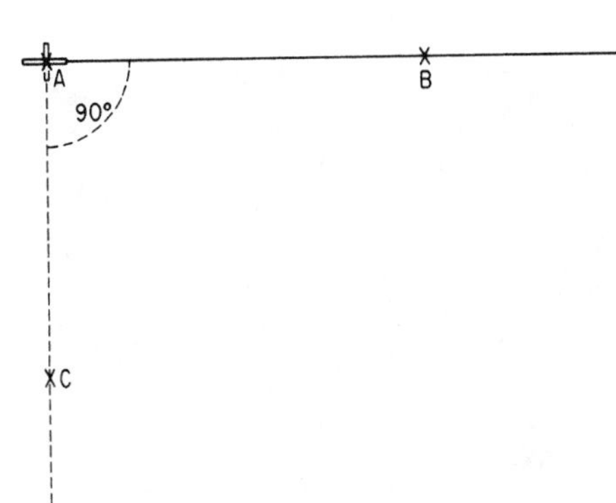

FIGURE 3-14 Turning a 90° angle with a transit or a level.

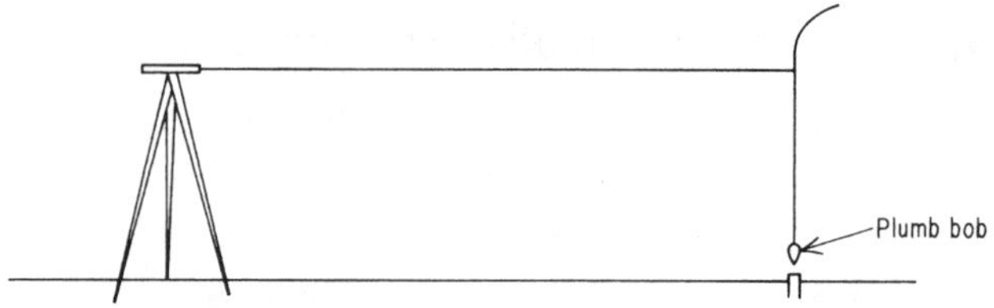

FIGURE 3-15 Dropping line of sight to ground when using a builder's level.

Because the builder's level will only turn in a horizontal direction, the line of sight must be dropped with a plumb line to the position below where a stake can be driven into the ground (see Fig. 3-15). This dropping is unnecessary when a transit level is used as it can be turned on a vertical plane.

Right angles can be established without the use of an instrument by using the right-angle method illustrated in Fig. 3-16. Once the layout is complete, work can progress on the building foundation.

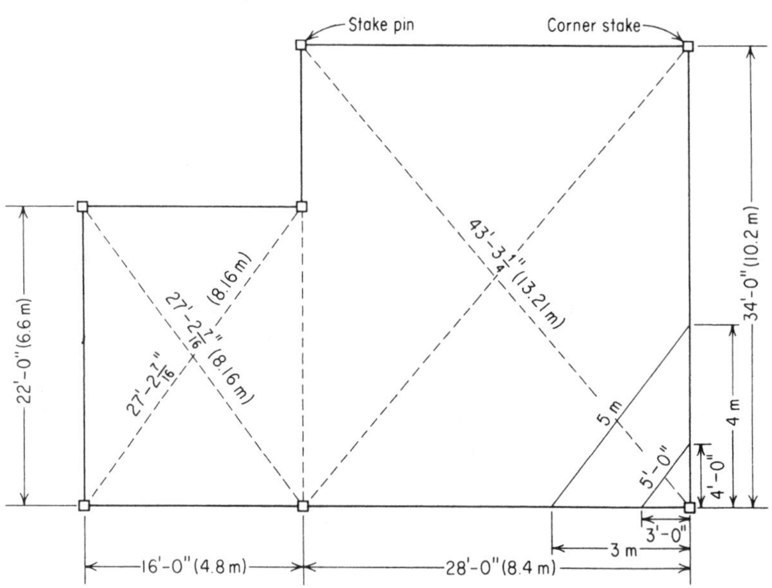

FIGURE 3-16 Checking diagonals.

Laser Level

FIGURE 3-17 Laser level.

The laser level is a one-person measurement system. It self-levels when set on a horizontal surface or when set on a tripod allowing the worker the freedom to move around the construction site to establish levels at any point. The range of the laser is much greater than the normal builder's or transit level. The instrument emits a narrow beam of light that can be used for accurate references for elevation work and as a vertical reference for line and plumb control. The level rotates the beam in a level plane, and workers can measure elevations from this beam using a laser rod or a tape measure to, for example, level concrete forms (see Fig. 3-17). The laser level's accuracy is especially effective on a warm day since atmospheric refraction doesn't affect the beam as it does with the line of sight of a standard builder's or transit level.

REVIEW QUESTIONS

3–1. Give two reasons for site inspection of the raw land being selected for a residential building before plans are drawn.

3–2. What are three results of soil investigation?

3–3. From what source would a builder determine the maximum depth of a subsurface foundation?

3–4. What is the reason for the stakes for the corners of a building to be set back from the finished building corners?

3–5. What is the main difference between a builder's level and a transit level?

3–6. Explain the process of using a builder's level to determine the difference of elevation between two points.

3–7. How does a transit level equipped with a compensator assist in making accurate readings?

3–8. How is it recommended to lift a leveling instrument out of its case?

3–9. How should a leveling instrument be carried from one point on a building site to another?

3–10. What is the difference between a benchmark and a datum point?

Chapter 4

THE FOUNDATION

OBJECTIVES

Here is what you will be able to do when you complete each component of this chapter:

1. Identify the different types of foundations.
2. Evaluate the qualities of a good foundation.
3. Describe how below-grade concrete foundations are built.
4. Recognize acceptable floor frame anchoring options.
5. Describe how to accommodate window and door openings in foundation walls.
6. Identify the process of erecting a concrete block foundation.
7. Recognize the requirements for a good surface and slab-on-ground foundation.
8. Identify pier foundations.
9. Identify how wood foundations are constructed.
10. Describe how concrete should be placed.

The foundation is the supporting base upon which the superstructure of a building is built; it anchors the building to the earth and transfers the loads of that building to the soil beneath. It is therefore of the utmost importance that the foundation be strong, accurately built to size, plumb and level, and of such dimensions that its loads are spread over an area of undisturbed soil large enough to support them safely. Any errors made in the size, shape, or strength of the foundation may lead not only to construction difficulties but may also contribute to instability and future movement.

A building falling into the category of light construction may be constructed on any one of a number of types of foundation, depending on its size, use, location, the prevailing climatic conditions, and the type of soil in the area.

FOUNDATION TYPES

The types of foundation most commonly used include *concrete full basement foundation, concrete surface foundation, slab-on-ground foundation, pier foundation*, and *preserved wood foundation*.

FOUNDATION EXCAVATION

Regardless of the type of foundation to be used, some soil removal will be necessary, the amount depending on the type of foundation, type of soil, depth of frost penetration, soil drainage conditions, and the proposed use of the building.

For a full concrete or preserved wood basement foundation, the excavation may be of considerable depth, while for a slab-on-ground, relatively little earth removal may be required. For a surface, pier, or slab foundation, the excavating may be confined to holes or trenches.

In any case, the topsoil and vegetable matter must be removed because of the danger of future settlement and odors due to decay. In localities in which termites occur, all stumps, roots, and other wood debris must be removed to a minimum depth of 18 in. (450 mm) in unexcavated areas under a building, such as crawl spaces.

National or local building codes specify the *minimum depths* of foundations based on the type of soil encountered and on whether or not the foundation will contain an enclosed heated space. In general, for rock or soils with good drainage, there is no depth limit, but for soils with poor drainage and where there will be no heated space, the minimum depth will normally be 4 ft, 0 in. (1200 mm) or the depth of frost penetration, whichever is greater. The local building authority establishes the depth of frost penetration in a particular area. As described in Chapter 3, the depth to be excavated is determined from a reference point of known elevation.

The first step in carrying out an excavation, as described in Chapter 3, is to stake out the area to be excavated. This will include not only the area covered by the building, but also enough extra space that workers can move about outside the foundation forms (see Fig. 4-1). The deeper the excavation, the more necessary it is to allow outside working room. Generally, 2 ft, 0 in. to 3 ft, 0 in. (600 – 900 mm) on all sides will be sufficient. However, the required clearance falls under OSHA (CSA) regulations and should be verified.

The type of soil involved will also have an influence on the excavation limits. If it is firm, well packed, and has good cohesive qualities, it may be possible to excavate and leave perpendicular earth

FIGURE 4-1 Excavation space around foundation forms.

walls standing at the outlined limits. However, if the soil is granular or if it becomes loose as it dries out, it will be necessary to *slope the sides* of the excavation, up to about 45°, depending on the type of soil, thus increasing the excavation limits. In some cases it might be necessary to temporarily *shore* the sides, but this is usually when the excavation is very deep.

If the soil is very loose and sloping the excavation is not an option, it may be necessary to drive cribbing into the ground around the perimeter of the area and excavate inside it. This type of cribbing may be interlocking sheet piling or wooden or steel piles behind which some type of sheathing is placed as the excavating proceeds.

Another problem involved is the disposal of the earth from the excavation. If the topsoil is good loam, it may be required for landscaping on the site after construction, in which case it should be stripped and piled by itself. The remainder of the earth must be disposed of according to circumstances. If some of it is required for backfilling, it should be piled at the site, out of the way of construction. If space does not permit storage, excavation machinery should be used that will allow direct loading onto trucks for removal (see Fig. 4-2). In locations where a land developer has prepared the building site for multiple lot sites, the topsoil is usually stripped from the entire site and stored close by for later dispersion.

FIGURE 4-2 Track hoe and truck removing excess soil.

EXCAVATING PROCEDURES

The type of machinery used to do the excavating work will depend on the area and depth of the excavation, the type of soil involved, and the available space outside the excavation.

Shallow excavations may be dug with a *bulldozer blade* provided there is room around the excavation to deposit the soil or another machine to load it onto trucks. Deeper excavations may be carried out with a front-end loader on a tracked or rubber-tired tractor (see Figs. 4-2 and 4-3).

Another excellent machine for excavating, particularly for light construction, is a *power shovel, trac hoe,* or *backhoe* (see Fig. 4-4). It can dig either shallow or deep excavations with straight, vertical walls and a level floor.

Power trenchers are very useful for perimeter foundations that will enclose crawl spaces or with slab on grade when the soil is stable enough to resist caving. This is especially suited to shallow foundations.

Foundation Construction

When the excavation has been completed, the work of constructing the footings and foundation can begin. For foundations involving cast-in-place concrete, forms have to be built. For others, gravel must

FIGURE 4-3 Front-end loader.

FIGURE 4-4 Trac hoe (back hoe).

be laid and compacted. In each case, the building lines must be established on the excavation floor with a transit or by dropping a plumb from lines strung on batter boards as described in Chapter 3 (see Fig. 4-5).

FIGURE 4-5 Batter boards.

CONCRETE FULL BASEMENT FOUNDATION

In some areas a *full basement* concrete foundation is one of the most common types used in residential construction because of the extra usable space provided. It consists of walls of cast-in-place concrete or concrete block, usually 8 in. (200 mm) thick and of such a height that there will be at least 7 ft, 10 in. (2350 mm) of headroom. The walls usually encompass an area of the same dimensions as the main floor plan of the building and also enclose a basement floor of livable space.

The walls are supported on *continuous footings* wide enough that the building loads are supported safely by the soil beneath them [see Fig. 4-6 and Fig. 4-20]. Interior loads are carried on one or more bearing walls or on *beams* that are supported on posts located on individual *post (or column) footings*.

FIGURE 4-6 Concrete basement.

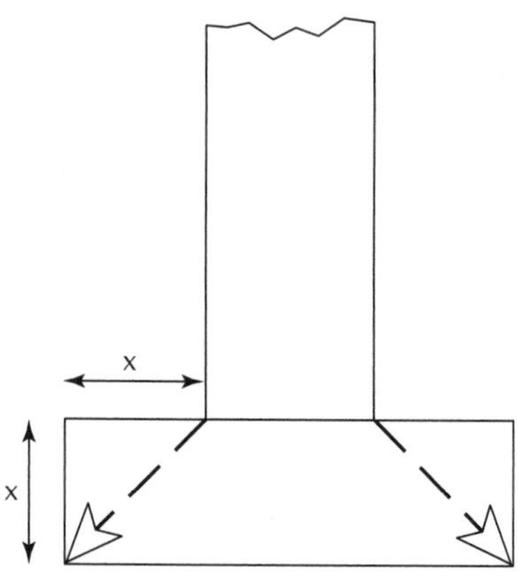

FIGURE 4-7 Concrete shear angle.

Footing Forms

Forms for the continuous perimeter footings and the interior post footings are the first requirement in the construction of a full basement foundation.

Minimum footing widths for buildings are available in building codes and will depend on the thickness of foundation wall, the loads that will be imposed on them (such as the number of floors being supported), and the type of soil on which they are placed. The thickness of the footing must not be less than the projection beyond the supported element (see Fig. 4-7), except where the footing is suitably reinforced and, in any case, must not be less than 4 in. (100 mm). However, if the foundation is being placed on solid rock, no footings may be required. Regardless, all footings must rest on undisturbed soil or rock.

The type and thickness of material required for footing forms will depend on their size and on whether they are to be constructed above or below ground level (see Figs. 4-8 and 4-9). If they are to be set above the ground level, they should be built using $1\frac{1}{2}$ in. (38 mm) lumber to withstand the pressure of the freshly placed concrete. Footings below ground level may be made from lighter material.

In some areas it may be practical to dig a shallow trench for these footings and place the concrete without the need for any additional forms. In this case, the soil must be a cohesive type that will allow the trench sides to remain relatively vertical while the concrete is placed [see Figs. 4-8(d) and (e)].

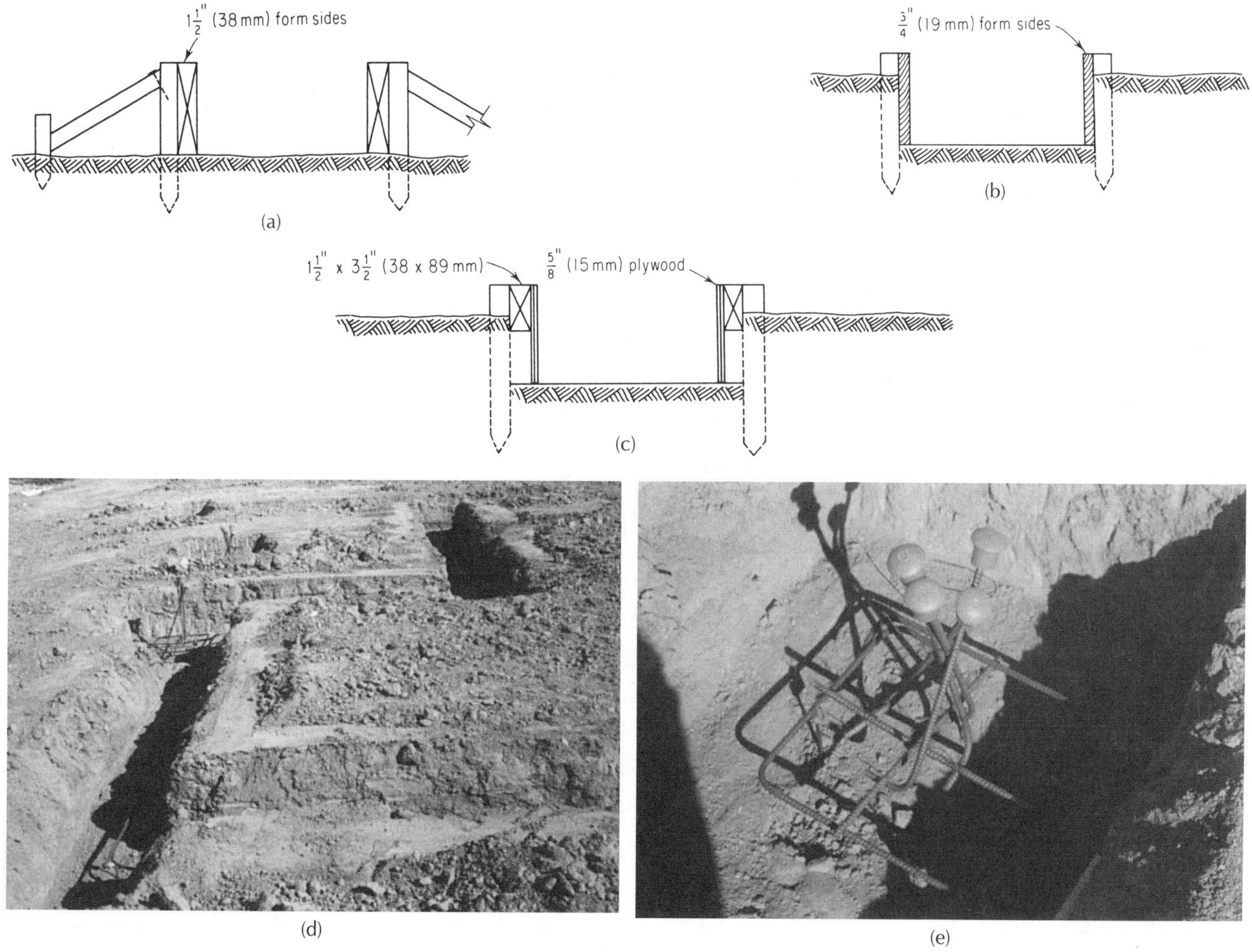

$1\frac{1}{2}''$ (38 mm) form sides

(a)

$\frac{3}{4}''$ (19 mm) form sides

(b)

$1\frac{1}{2}''$ x $3\frac{1}{2}''$ (38 x 89 mm)

$\frac{5}{8}''$ (15 mm) plywood

(c)

(d)

(e)

FIGURE 4-8 Footing forms.

FIGURE 4-9 Footing forms with laser level used for leveling.

To lay out and construct footing forms above grade level, proceed as illustrated in Figs. 4-10 through 4-13. These forms can be leveled using a builder's level, a spirit level, or a line level. Forms constructed of 1-in. (25-mm) boards should be held with stakes placed 2–3 ft (600–1000 mm) apart. When 2-in. (38-mm) material is used, the stake spacing may be increased as can be seen in Fig. 4-9.

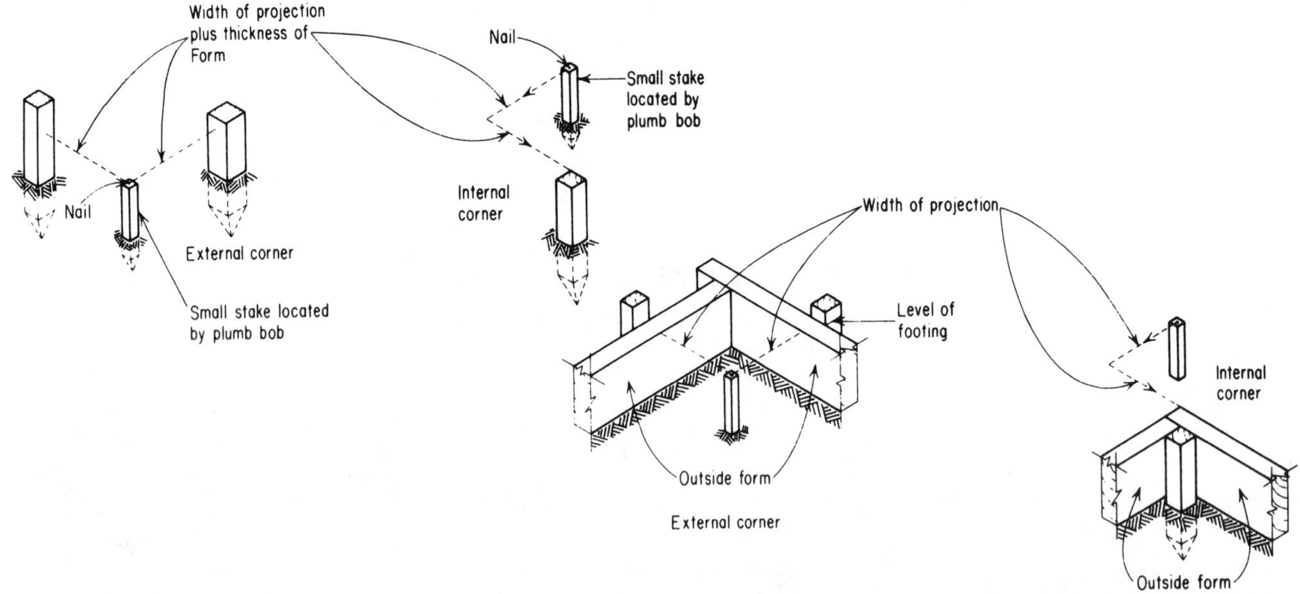

FIGURE 4-10 Layout of footing form corner stakes.

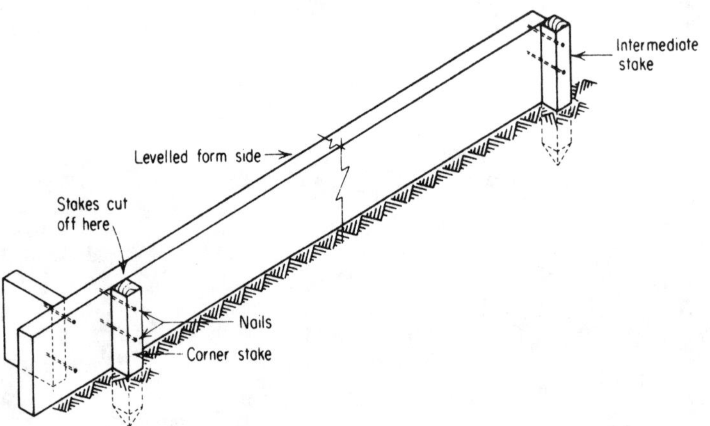

FIGURE 4-11 Footing outside form.

Footing-to-Wall Ties

Most concrete walls are poured directly onto the footing with no special keying. However, when walls are subjected to high lateral pressure, some means should be provided to tie the wall to the footing. One method is to insert short pieces of reinforcing into the concrete

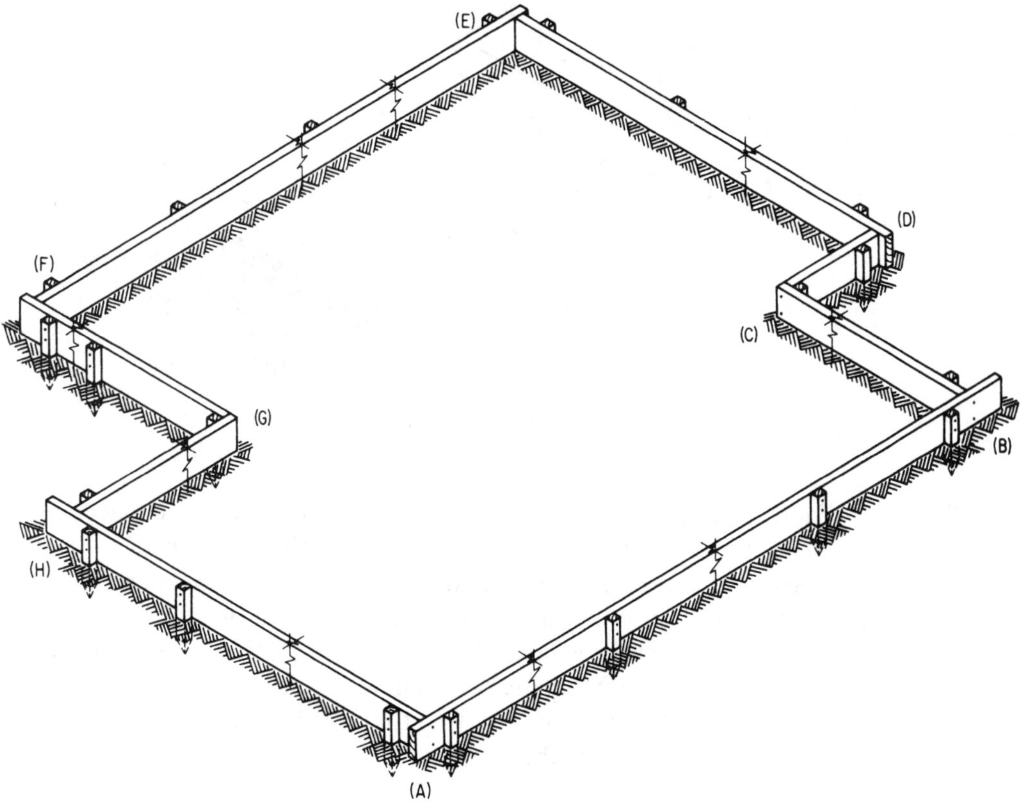

FIGURE 4-12 Footing outside forms in place.

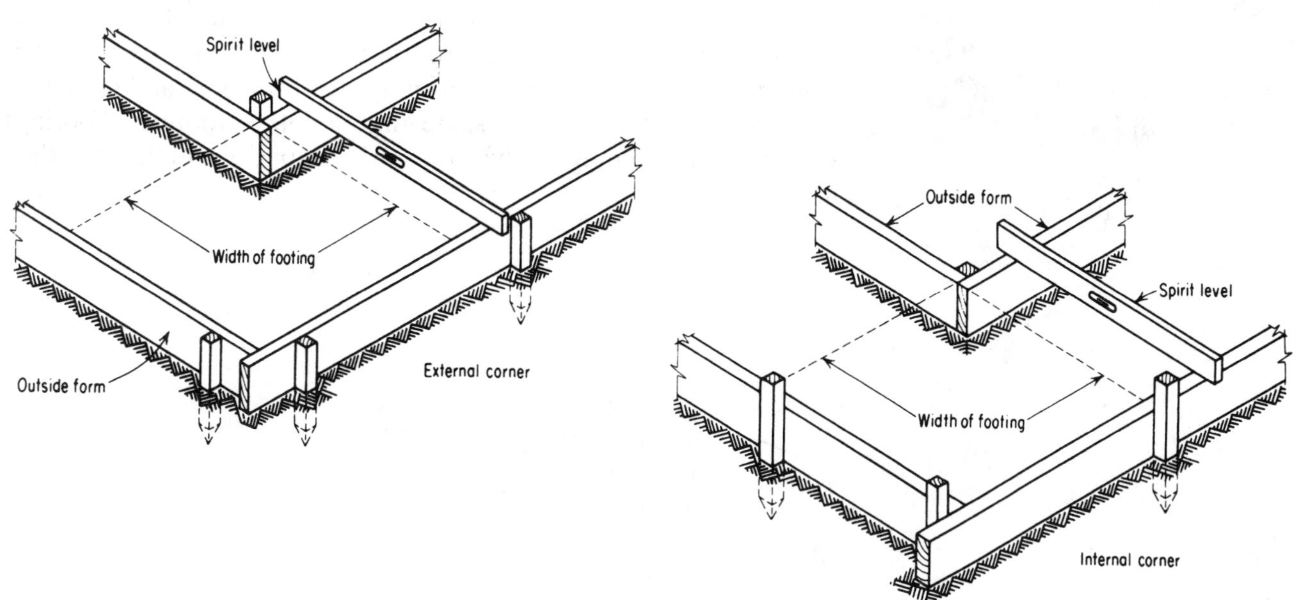

FIGURE 4-13 Inside form set and leveled.

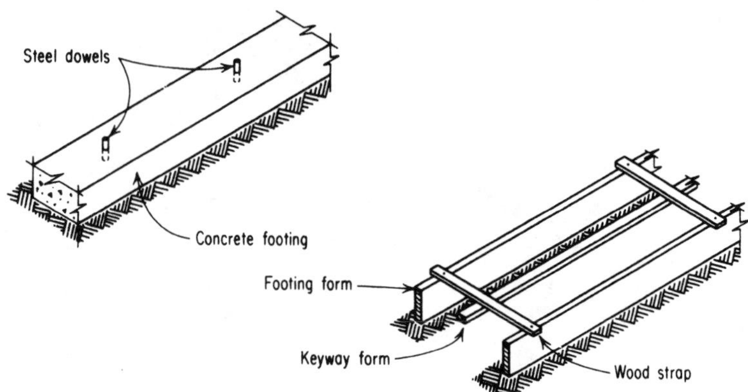

FIGURE 4-14 Footing-to wall ties.

footing during pouring to provide a tie. These dowels are placed along the centerline at intervals of 4 ft, 0 in. projecting 3 to 4 in. (75–100 mm) above the footing. Another method involves setting a tapered wooden keyway form into the top of the footing (see Fig. 4-14).

If the keyway is coated with a thick coating of asphalt before the wall is cast, it will provide a barrier against penetration of moisture between the wall and footing that will be particularly effective if there is a high water table.

FIGURE 4-15 Strip and post (independent) footings.

Post or Isolated Footings

Isolated footings, usually square in plan view, are required for the posts that will support main floor beams (see Fig. 4–9 and 4-15). The minimum required area for these footings is available from codes, but the depth will normally be a minimum of 6 in. (150 mm) for unreinforced footings. If the column is to be of wood, a layer of polyethylene should be wrapped around the bottom end to protect it from moisture (see Fig. 4-16). Footings for fireplaces and chimneys are normally placed at the same time as other footings. Footings vary in size depending on the soil-bearing capacity and the load they must carry.

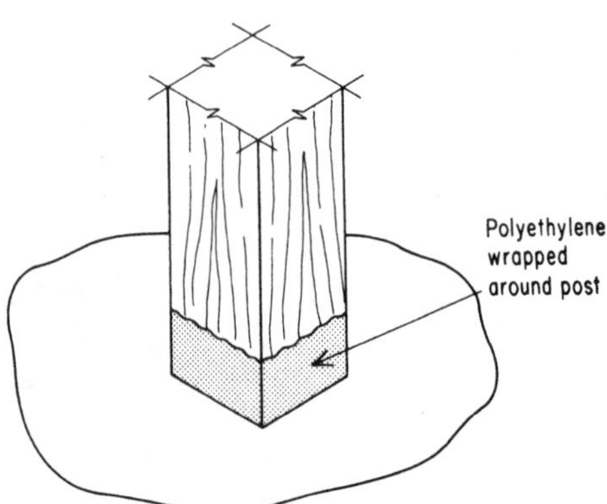

FIGURE 4-16 Polyethylene around base of wood post.

In Fig. 4-17(a) there have been concrete footings placed without any restraining forms. In this case there is to be an attached garage to the residence and all footings have been placed below the depth of frost penetration. Considerable fill will be required inside the foundation walls so concrete piers or posts will be placed on these footings [see Fig. 4-17(b) to support the concrete floor (notice the reinforcing bar in the post footings)]. Also, in this particular situation, there has been a trench dug across where the garage will be placed for the installation of underground services, such as sewer and water, and a concrete pier was cast under the strip footing to provide support across the trench [see Fig. 4-17(c)]. This was necessary because all footings must bear on undisturbed soil.

(a)

(b)

(c)

FIGURE 4-17 (a) Independent footings without forms; (b) Pier support for concrete garage floor; (c) Foundation support across excavation.

Bearing Wall or T-Footing

Where a wood-framed floor system is to be supported on a perimeter foundation there is usually a need for a center beam or bearing wall. Beams are generally supported on posts that are in turn supported on post footings. However, if a *bearing wall* is used, which is normally made of a 2 × 6 in.(38 × 140 mm) wood frame (see Chapter 5 for framing details), it must be supported on a continuous footing, similar in dimensions to the outside wall footings but with a raised center portion to keep the bottom of the bearing wall plate above the level of the basement floor [see Fig. 4-18(a)].

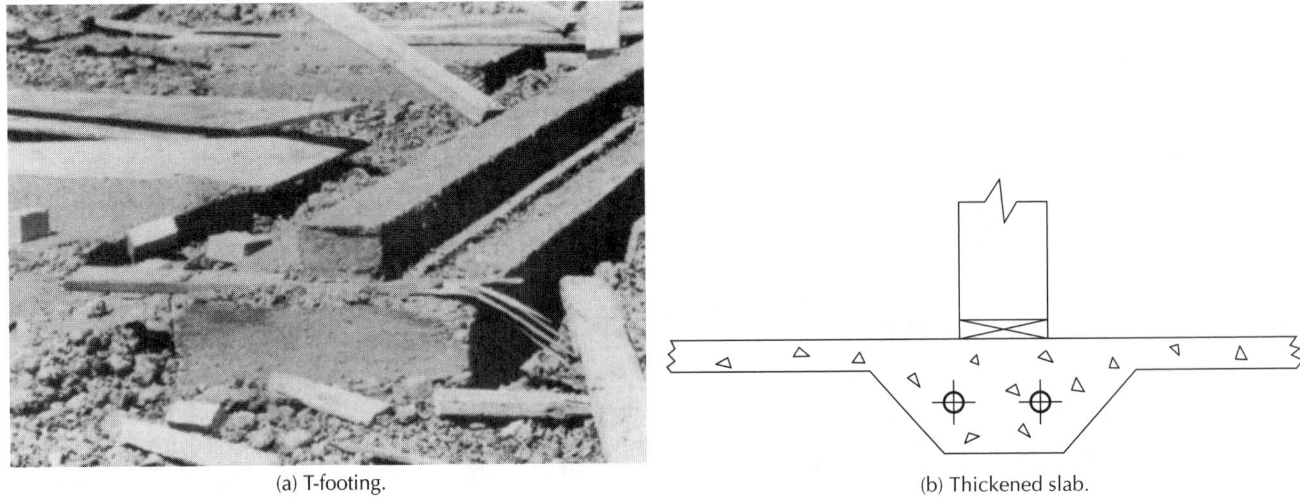

(a) T-footing.

(b) Thickened slab.

FIGURE 4-18

The bottom part of the form is similar to that used for perimeter footings, while the center section is formed by suspending a narrow form the same width as the bearing wall (see Fig. 4-19).

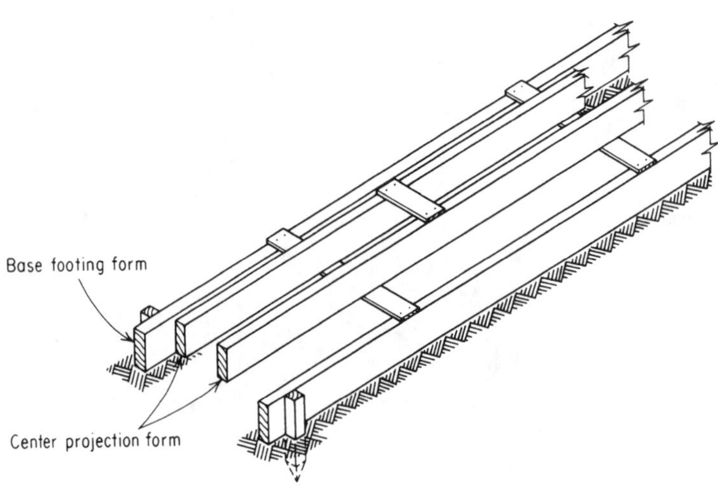

FIGURE 4-19 T-footing form.

This forming method is very expensive and time-consuming; and another method that is acceptable in some areas is to cast the floor with a thickened portion under the bearing wall location as shown in Fig. 4-18(b).

Stepped Footings

Stepped footings are used on steeply sloping lots and where an attached garage is placed above the basement level (see Fig. 4-15). There is generally a requirement that the vertical part of the step be placed at the same time as the footing unless steel reinforcing is used. The bottom of the footing should be set level on undisturbed soil below the frost line. The vertical thickness of the step should be a minimum of 6 in. (150 mm) and the same width as the footing. The vertical portion of the step should not exceed 2 ft (600 mm), and the horizontal portion for each step should not be less than 2 ft (600 mm). In very steep slopes or while building on rock, special footings may be required [see Figs. 4-20(a) and 4-20(b)].

(a)

(b)

FIGURE 4-20 (a) Step footings; (b) Step footings and foundation wall over.

In residential construction, loads are seldom heavy enough that reinforcement is necessary in the footings. But other types of light construction may require reinforced footings, and, in such cases, the reinforcement should be in the form of *deformed rods* with hooked ends, placed *across the width* of the footing. There should be about 3 in. (75 mm) of concrete below the reinforcement, and the ends of the hooks should not be closer than 1 in. (25 mm) to the side form (see Fig. 4-21). Post footings are reinforced in the same manner, except that in some cases two layers of bars may be placed to run at right angles to one another—*two-way reinforcement.*

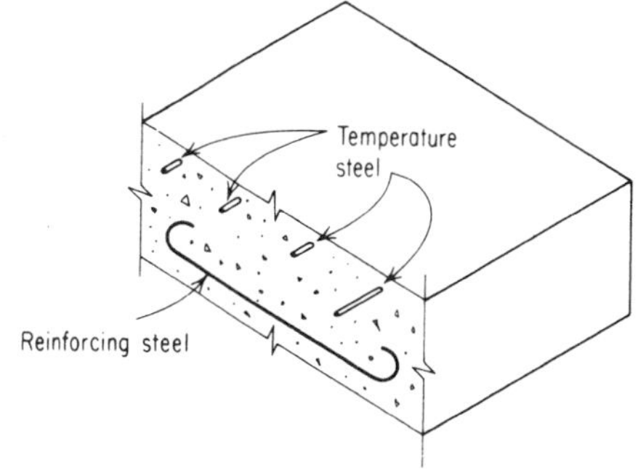

FIGURE 4-21 Reinforced footing.

Wall Forms

When the footing concrete has hardened and at least partially cured, the forms are removed, and the job is ready for the erection of wall forms. There are many methods of building them; here we discuss a few of the well-known ones.

Wall forms all contain the same basic features, although they may vary as to the details of construction and hardware required. The main component is the *sheathing,* which will give the concrete its desired shape. The sheathing is stiffened and aligned by horizontal *walers*, which, in turn, are supported by *bracing*. The two sides of the form are fastened together by a system of *ties* and are held at their proper spacing by *spreaders*. Figure 4-22 displays several different form ties while Fig. 4-23 shows one type in use.

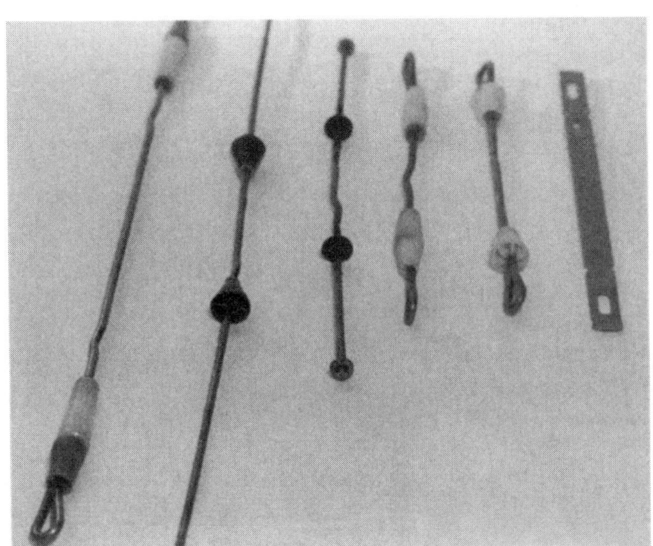

FIGURE 4-22 Typical form ties.

FIGURE 4-23 Form mock-up.

A commonly used forming system involves the use of $\frac{3}{4}$-in.(19-mm)) *plywood panels without any framework, ties* with loops or slots in their ends, and *metal bars* which are inserted through the tie ends on the outside of the forms to act as *walers* to align the forms [see Figs. 4-24(a) and 4-24(b)]. Panels are held together at the corner by a vertical rod running through a series of metal straps with looped ends, which are bolted along the panel edge, as illustrated in Fig. 4-24(a). An alternate method of tying the corners is to use a metal angle nailed to the panel edges as shown in Fig. 4-24(b).

The erection of a wall form by this method is quite simple. First, the plywood panels are slotted to receive the tie ends. The number of ties required depends on the rate of concrete placement and the air temperature, but commonly accepted tie spacing for a 4-ft (1200-mm) rate of placement at 70°F (21°C) are as follows:

(a) Corner rod.

(b) Corner angle.

FIGURE 4-24

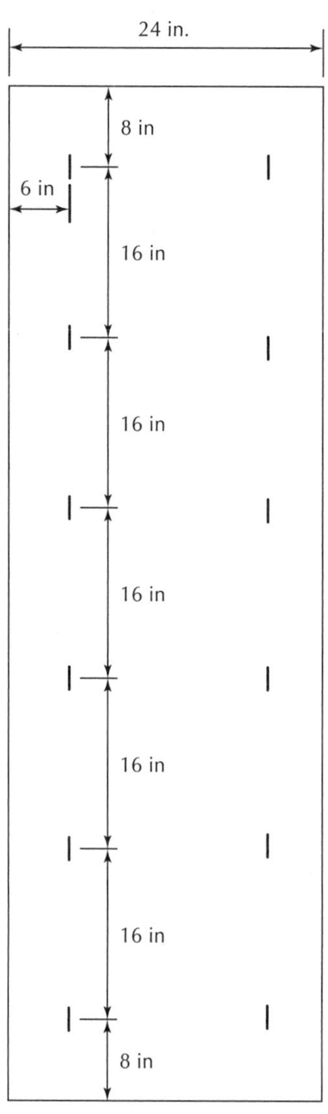

FIGURE 4-25 Location of tie holes in a form.

For a 2 ft × 8 ft (600 × 2400 mm) panel, the end slots are cut 8 in. (200 mm) from the top and bottom of the panel and 6 in. (150 mm) from the edges. A series of tie cuts are located between the top and bottom cuts at 16 in. (400 mm) o.c. (on center) (see Fig. 4-25).

For a 4 ft × 8 ft (1200 × 2400 mm) panel, the *three* end slots are spaced 16 in. (400 mm) o.c., 8 in. (200 mm) from top, bottom, and edges. The rest of the slots are cut in the same manner as shown in Fig. 4-25. All panels are treated with oil or other form coating to prevent concrete from adhering to them.

The first step in erecting the panels is to determine the location of the inside face of the foundation wall on the perimeter footings. This will be the position of the concrete after it has been placed. Then, the panels are erected as follows:

1. Snap a chalk line on the footing $\frac{3}{4}$ in.(19 mm) inside the foundation wall line to allow for the thickness of the panels.
2. Nail a 2 × 4 plate to the footing on that line with concrete nails (see Fig. 4-26).
3. Hinge the inside corner panels together with a rod and stand them in place (see Fig. 4-27).
4. Nail them to the plate with 2-in. (50-mm) nails and plumb and brace them temporarily.
5. Set all the panels between the corners in place and nail two 2 × 4 (38 × 89 mm) members to them horizontally, one at the top and one at the center (see Fig. 4-28) to align the panels.
6. Place the ties in the slots and insert the rods or bars as shown in Fig. 4-29.
7. Put outside corners together and set them in place, using temporary wooden spreaders to maintain proper spacing.

FIGURE 4-26 Plate fastened to footing.

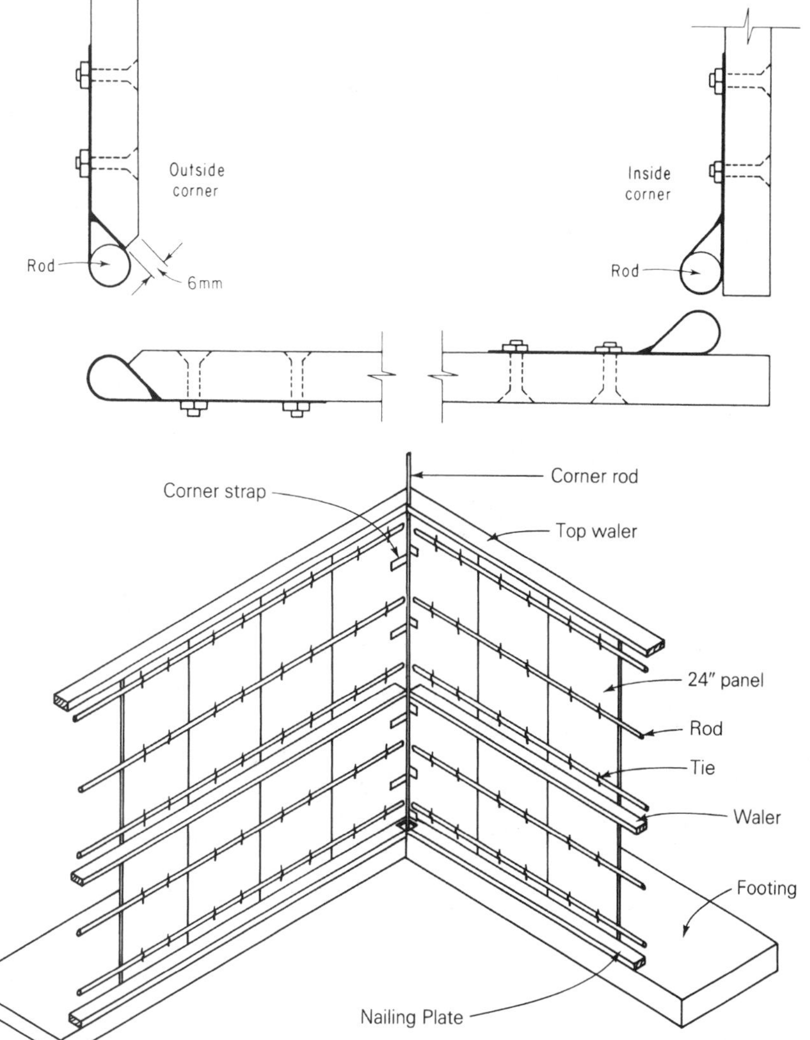

FIGURE 4-27 Corner straps for plywood forms.

FIGURE 4-28 Inner form panels and walers installed.

FIGURE 4-29 Waler bars placed in tie ends.

8. Place the remainder of the outside panels, guiding the tie ends through the slots as each is erected.
9. Insert the rods or bars through the tie ends.
10. Finally, align the outside form and brace it as required from the two single walers to ensure that the form is plumb and will not be distorted during the placement of the concrete.

In a cast-in-place floor system where the floor joists are cast into the concrete, the inside forms are set and firmly held in position first (see Fig. 4-30). The outside forms are a little longer to allow fastening to the outside of the floor frame (see Fig. 4-31).

FIGURE 4-30 Inside forms set for cast-in-place system.

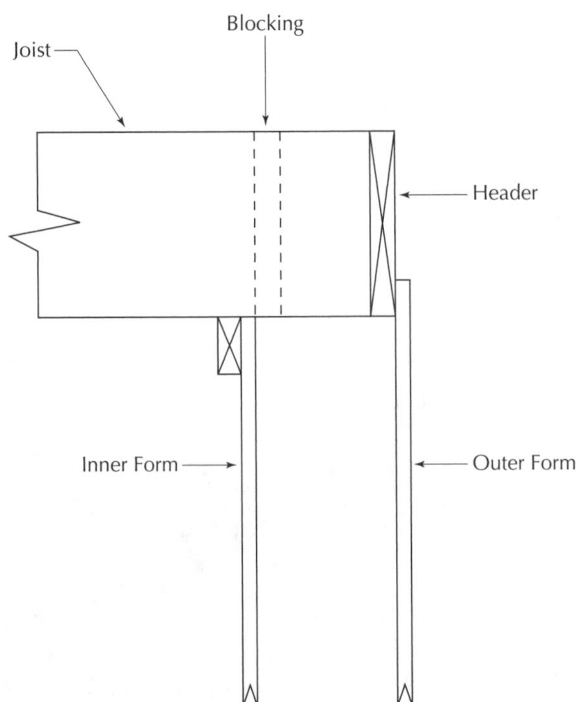

FIGURE 4-31 Forming for cast-in-place floor joists.

When a straighter wall is required, a system of wall forms using 2 × 4 walers is recommended (see Fig. 4-32). Strongbacks give vertical stiffness to the forms. This system is more rigid and will not deflect as much due to the concrete pressure. The bottom waler is fastened to the footing as shown in Fig. 4-33. Figure 4-34 illustrates the tie system used to support the walers and how overlapping the walers and using vertical members support corners.

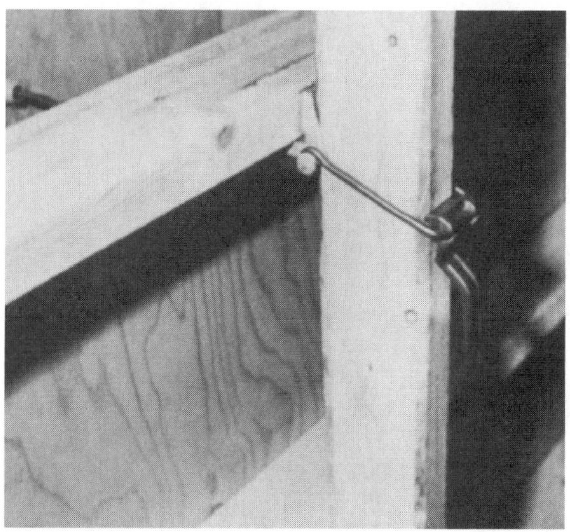

FIGURE 4-32 Single waler system with vertical strongback.

FIGURE 4-33 Fastening bottom waler (single waler system).

(a) Corner support.

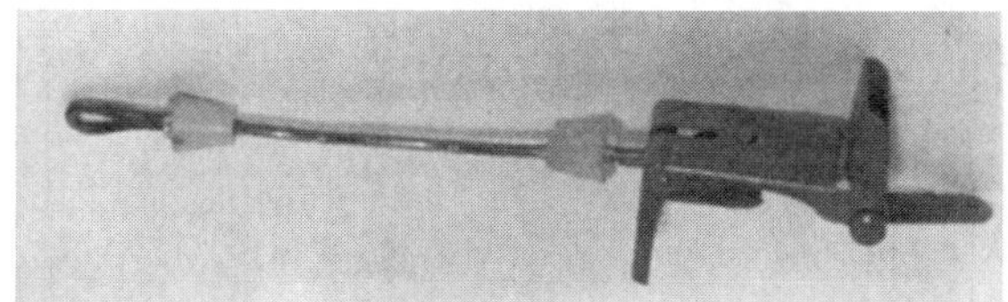

(b) Waler bracket and tie.

FIGURE 4-34 Single waler system.

Figure 4-35 illustrates the use of double walers to provide even more support to the forms, particularly for high walls and where the rate of concrete placement is high.

FIGURE 4-35 Double waler system.

Beam Pocket Form

In designs in which the floor frame is to be built on top of the foundation walls (box sill), it is necessary to provide a pocket in two opposite foundation walls in which the ends of the center beam may rest [see Fig. 4-36(b)]. It is formed by a box, wide enough to allow for an air space around the end of the beam [see Fig. 4-36(a)] and deep

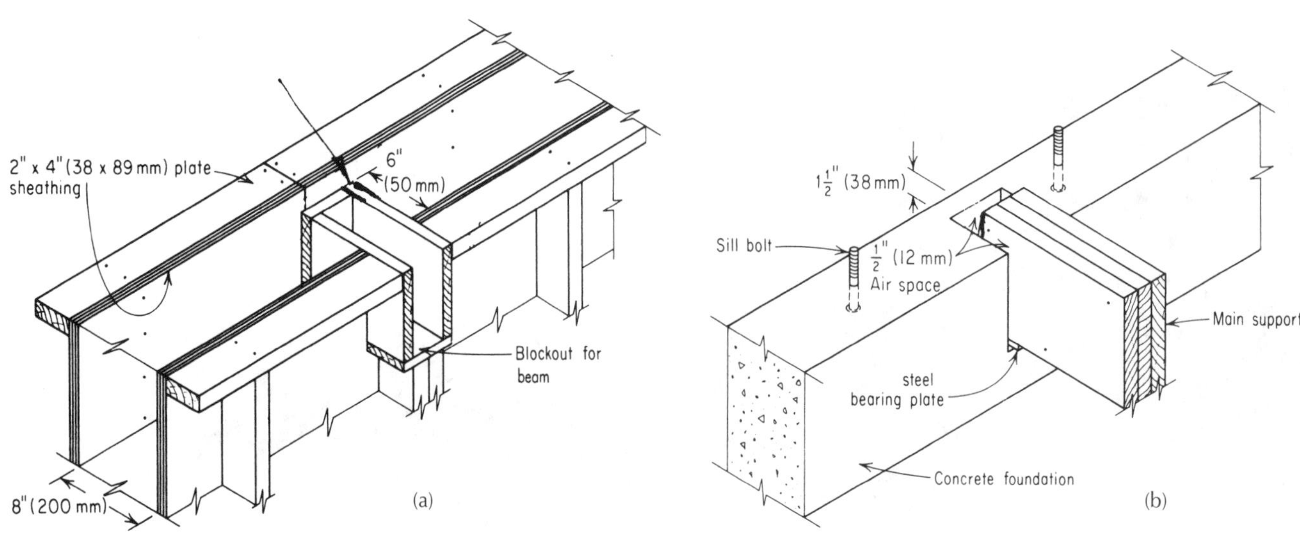

FIGURE 4-36 Beam pocket in concrete foundation.

enough to allow for a bearing plate under the end of the beam. When a sill plate is to be anchored on top of the wall, the top of the beam must be $1\frac{1}{2}$ in. (38 mm) above the top of the foundation wall.

Sill Plate Bolts (Wood Floor Frame)

In cases where box sill construction is used, the floor frame must be anchored to the foundation walls. One method being used is to build a "ladder" using 2 × 4's (38 × 89 mm) placed between the concrete forms before the concrete is cast (see Fig. 4-35). Another method is to bolt a 2 × 6-ft (38 × 140-mm) *sill plate* to the top of the foundation and nailing the floor frame to it. The anchors are $\frac{1}{2}$-in.(12.7-mm) bolts, spaced approximately 4 ft (1200 mm) o.c., set into the concrete [see Fig. 4-36(b)] to hold the sill plate in position. They may be set after the concrete has been placed but before it has hardened, or they may be suspended by wood straps nailed across the top of the form before concrete is placed, as shown in Fig. 4-37.

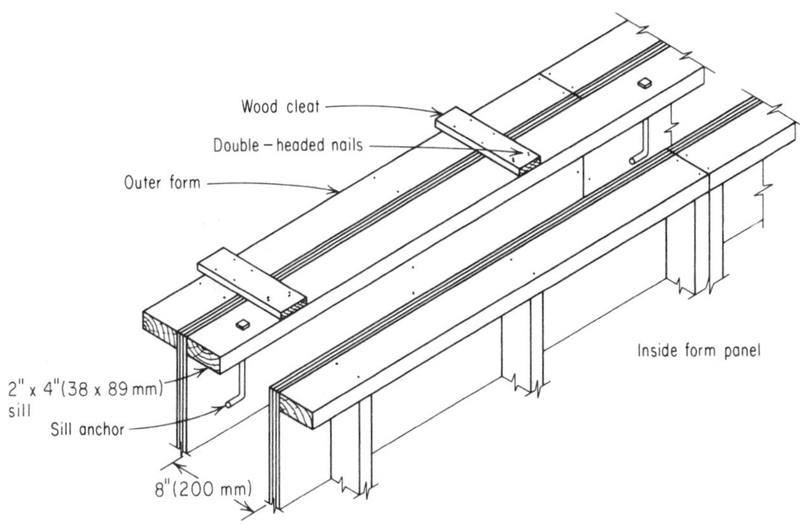

FIGURE 4-37 Sill plate anchoring.

Several different methods are used for setting a sill plate in a foundation wall. If the building is to have conventional wood siding or similar finish, a 2 × 4-ft (38 × 89-mm) sill plate is set into the top *outside* edge of the wall form and held in place by anchor bolts, as illustrated in Fig. 4-37. Anchor bolts are suspended from the sill, to be cast into the concrete.

If the foundation wall is to support brick veneer exterior finish, the sill plate is cast into the top *inside* edge of the wall (see Fig. 4-38).

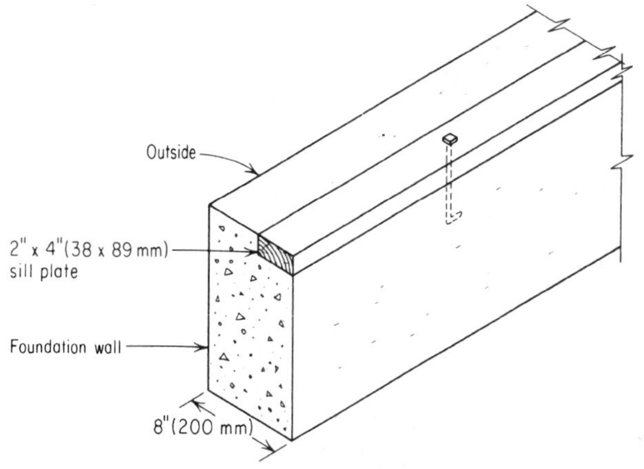

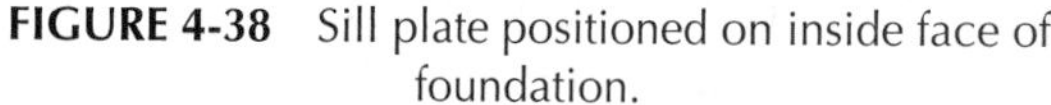
FIGURE 4-38 Sill plate positioned on inside face of foundation.

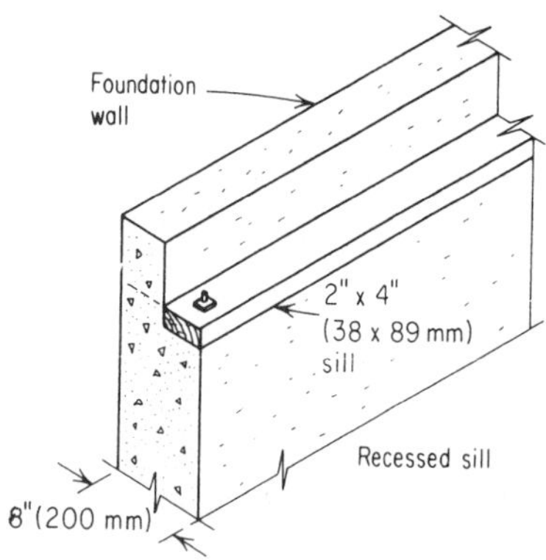

FIGURE 4-39 Recessed sill plate.

When steel joists are to be used, the design may call for the top of steel joists to be flush with the top of the foundation. The sill plate must then be *recessed* below the top of the wall by the depth of the joists (see Fig. 4-39).

"Cast-in" Wood Floor Frame

Another method of anchoring the floor frame to the foundation is the *cast-in joist* system. Instead of resting on top of the foundation, the ends of the floor joists and the beam-ends are treated and embedded in the concrete (see Fig. 4-40).

As a result, the beam and floor joists must be set in place before concrete is placed. The procedure is as follows:

1. Treat the ends of the beam and one end of each joist with a wood preservative.
2. Cut notches in two opposite inside wall forms, the width and depth of the beam, and nail a support block at the bottom of each notch and install the beam (see Fig. 4-40).
3. Lay out the joists so that one end rests on the center beam and the other on the wall forms.
4. Lay out the header joists according to the specified joist centers and nail the joists to them at these locations (see Fig. 4-41).
5. Position the joist assembly so that the outer face of the header joists is flush with the inner face of the outside form (see Fig. 4-31).
6. Nail *blocking* flush with the inner face of the form sheathing (see Fig. 4–31).

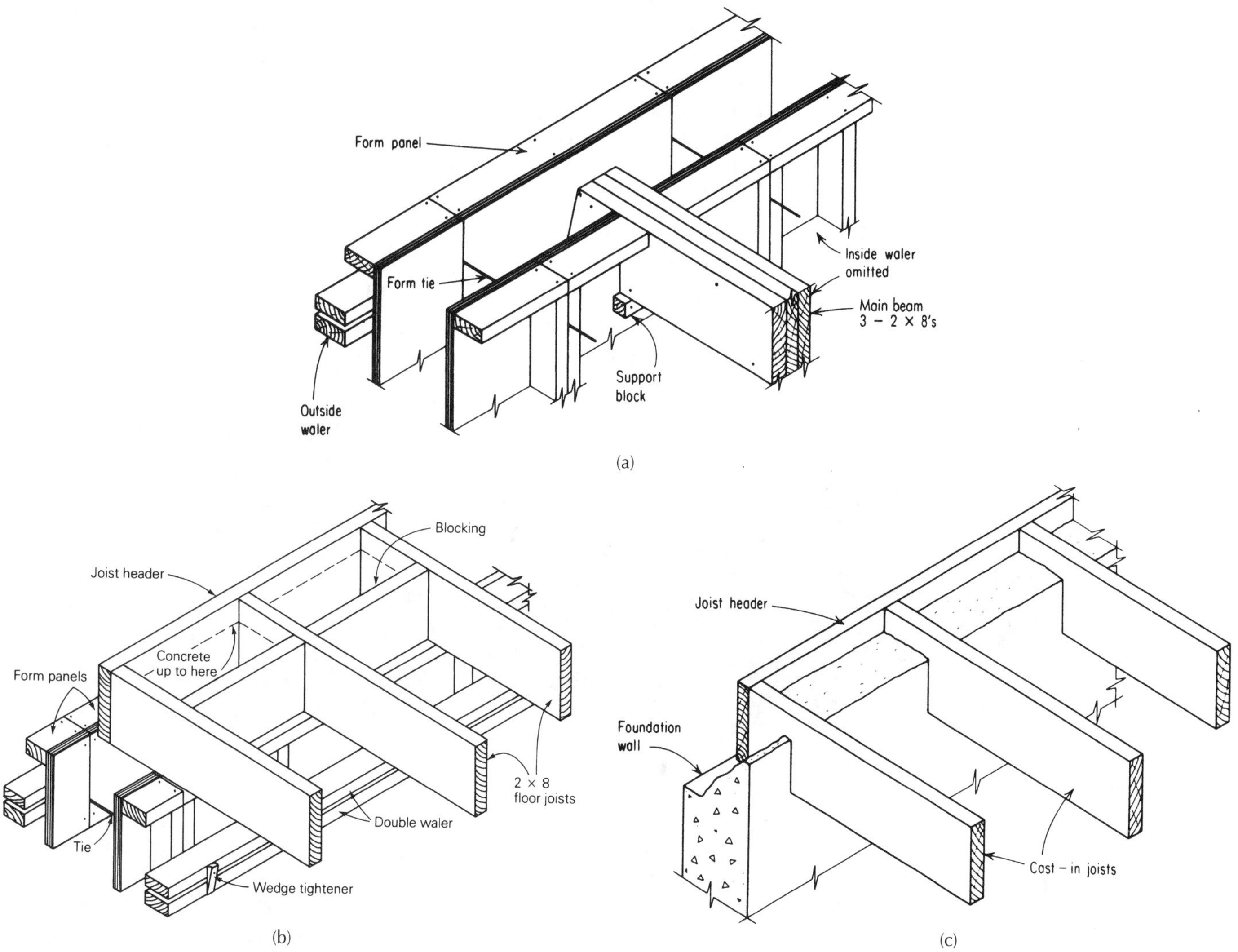

FIGURE 4-40 "Cast-in-place" floor system.

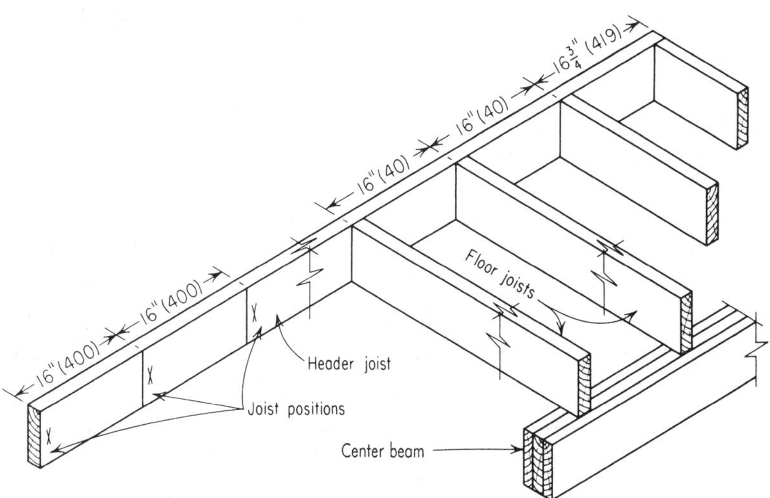

FIGURE 4-41 Header joist laid out with joists partially assembled.

Door and Window Openings

Openings for doors and windows may be blocked out in two ways. One method is to secure the door or window *frame* into the form in its correct position. Wood frames must be made to coincide with the wall thickness (see Fig. 4-42). Metal frames are produced to fit any wall thickness. Wood frames should have nails driven part way into the outside surface so that the nail heads will be cast into the concrete, or be manufactured with grooves so they will not be able to move after the concrete has set. Wood frames must also be suitably braced so that the pressure of the concrete will not change their shape during placing.

(a)

(b)

FIGURE 4-42 Window frame set into forms.

Another method of forming openings is to set *rough bucks* into the form. A rough buck is a frame made from 2-in. (38-mm) material with *outside dimensions* equal to those of the frame to be used. *Wedge-shaped nailers* are nailed to the outside of the buck as illustrated in Fig. 4-43. After the concrete is placed and hardened and the forms removed, the rough buck is also removed, leaving the key embedded in the concrete. The door or window frame is then inserted into the opening and held in place by nailing it to the nailer.

CONCRETE BLOCK FOUNDATION WALLS

Concrete block is the name given to a type of masonry unit made from a mixture of expanded shale or clay, some fine aggregate and cement, with or without color added. A great variety of blocks are available, in a wide range of types, shapes, and sizes, each for a specific purpose. Figure 4-45 illustrates some common shapes used in basement construction. Concrete block is mainly used for foundations or for exterior walls in light construction. Regardless of the use to which blocks are to be put, a basic requirement for good results, both from the standpoint of structural stability and good appearance, is good mortar that binds the blocks together.

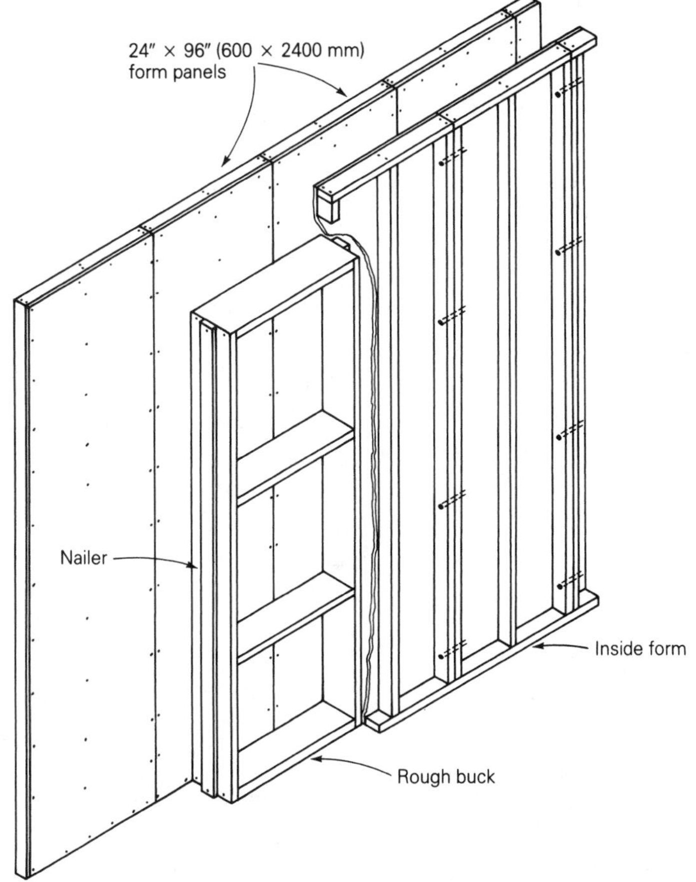

FIGURE 4-43 Rough buck for door secured in forms.

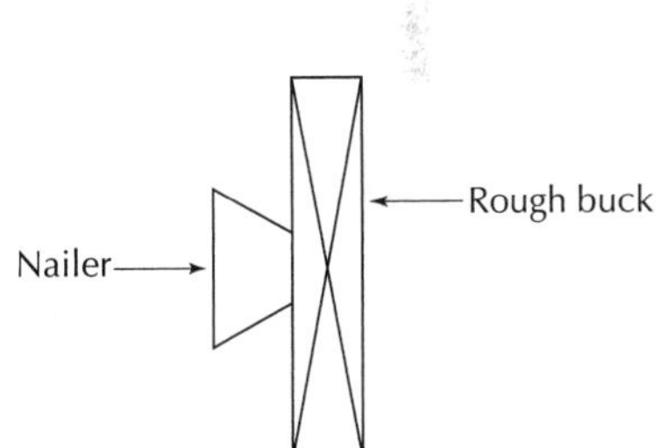

FIGURE 4-44 Anchoring rough buck in concrete.

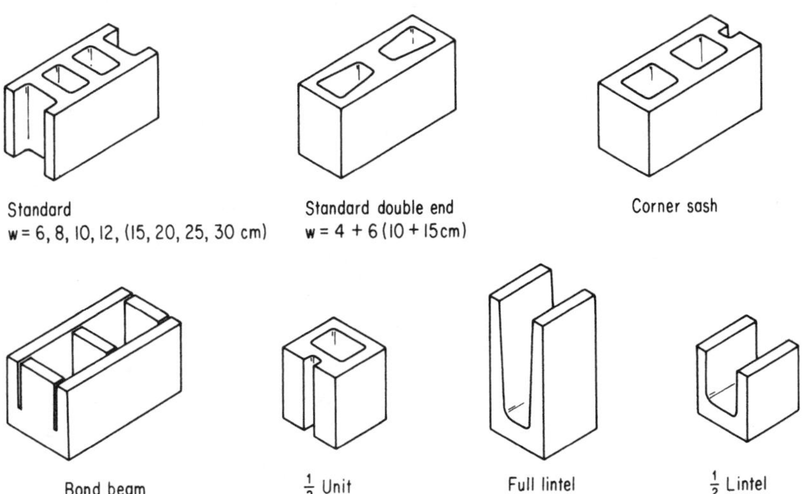

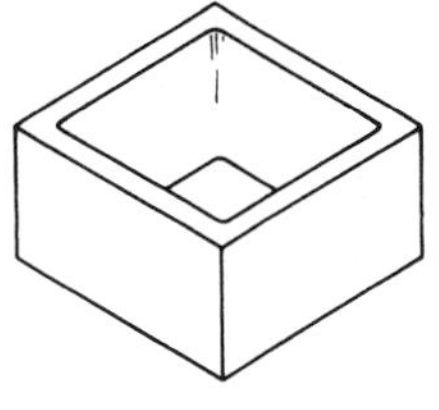

FIGURE 4-45 Typical block shapes.

Mortar

Mortar serves a number of purposes, the main one being to *join the masonry units together* into a strong, well-knit structure. In addition, mortar is required to *produce tight seals between units*; to *bond to steel reinforcement, metal ties,* and *anchor bolts*; to *provide a bed* which will accommodate variations in the size of units; and to *provide an architectural effect* by the various treatments given to mortar joints in exposed walls.

Masonry mortar is composed of one or more *cementitious materials* (normal Portland cement, masonry cement, and hydrated lime); clean, well-graded *masonry sand*; and enough *water* to produce a plastic, workable mixture. In addition, *admixtures* (accelerators, retarders, and water-reducing agents) may be added for a special purpose.

A number of mortar types are recognized in industry, based on strength and composed of varying amounts of cement and hydrated lime, by volume. Table 4-1 indicates the types and the proportions of ingredients in each case.

To obtain good workability and allow the development of the maximum strength possible, mortar ingredients must be thoroughly mixed. Whenever possible, the mixing should be done by machine, except when only a small quantity of mortar is required.

Mixing time should be from 3 to 5 minutes after all ingredients have been added. A shorter mixing time may result in poor-quality mortar, while a longer mixing time may adversely affect the air content of mortars made with air-entraining cements.

If the mortar becomes stiff because of water evaporation, it may be *retempered* by the addition of a little water and thorough remixing. However, if the stiffness is due to partial hydration, the material should be discarded. Generally, mortar should be used within 2 hours after the original mixing if the temperature is above 80°F (26°C) or within 3 hours if the temperature is below that point.

TABLE 4-1: Mortar types by cement and lime proportions.

		Parts by volume		
Specification	*Mortar type*	*Portland cement*	*Masonry cement*	*Hydrated lime or lime putty*
	M	1	1	—
		1	—	$\frac{1}{4}$
	S	$\frac{1}{2}$	1	—
		1	—	Over $\frac{1}{4}$ to $\frac{1}{2}$
For plain masonry	N	—	1	—

Note: The total aggregate will not be less than two and one quarter or more than three and one half times the total volume of cementitious material.

Two methods are used for applying mortar to concrete masonry units. One is to apply the mortar to the two long edges only. This is known as *face-shell bedding* (see Fig. 4-46). The other is to apply mortar to the cross webs as well as the face shells, and this is known as *full mortar bedding* (see Fig. 4-47).

FIGURE 4-46 Face shell bedding.

FIGURE 4-47 Full mortar bedding.

Laying Blocks

The first step in laying blocks is to locate accurately the positions of the corners of the building on the footings and to establish the line of the outside of the wall. This can be done by taking the dimensions from the plans and snapping chalk lines on the footing to indicate the corners and building lines. Then the first course may be laid without mortar to ascertain what spacing is required between blocks (see Fig. 4-48), although, in general, that spacing should be $\frac{3}{8}$ in. (10 mm) in order to maintain a 16-in. (400-mm) module, center to center of mortar joints.

Next, the blocks are removed, and a full bead of mortar long enough to accommodate at least three blocks is spread. The corner

FIGURE 4-48 Test lay-up for spacing.

block is then placed on the mortar, making sure that it is positioned to the *foundation line*, and it is *plumb* and *level*. The ends of the face shells of the second block is *buttered* and is placed in its final position by setting it down into the mortar bed while at the same time pressing it against the previously laid block to ensure a tight vertical joint (see Fig. 4-49).

(a)

(b)

FIGURE 4-49 Full mortar bed for first course.

FIGURE 4-50 Mortar on block ends.

At this point, the ends of several blocks are buttered, as shown in Fig. 4-50, so that they can be laid up in quick succession. After several blocks have been laid each way, a straight-edge and level is used to make sure that the blocks are *aligned,* brought to the *correct level*, and *plumb*, as illustrated in Fig. 4-51.

(a)

(b)

(c)

FIGURE 4-51 Block aligning, leveling, and plumbing.

After the first course is laid, the corners are built up as shown in Fig. 4-52. A tape measure is used to ensure that the bedding joints are maintained at the same thickness for each course, so that the corners of the foundation will remain level with one another. A straight-edge and level are used frequently to make sure that the corners are plumb and level (see Fig. 4-53).

FIGURE 4-52 Building up corners.

FIGURE 4-53 Plumbing and leveling corners.

When the corners have been built up, the walls are completed between them. To do so, a string is run from corner to corner, along the top edge of the course to be laid (see Fig. 4-54). A *string holder* is attached to each corner and adjusted so that the string is at the correct height—level with the top of each course. The string is then drawn as tight as possible to provide a horizontal guide for the blocks in the course.

The bed joint mortar is then laid, and the ends of enough blocks buttered to complete the course. Each block is set and carefully tapped down until it comes to the string (see Fig. 4-54).

The final block in each course is the *closure* block. All the edges of the opening are buttered as well as the four vertical edges of the closure block. It is set carefully into place (see Fig. 4-55) such that the mortar is pressed firmly into the joint. Finally, any extruded mortar is removed that appears on both the exterior and interior faces of the wall.

After the mortar is set hard enough that it can just be dented by the thumb nail, the joint may be *tooled*—shaped and compacted. Figure 4-56 illustrates the tooling of a concave joint.

FIGURE 4-54 Line from corner to corner.

FIGURE 4-55 Closure block set in place.

FIGURE 4-56 Concave mortar joint.

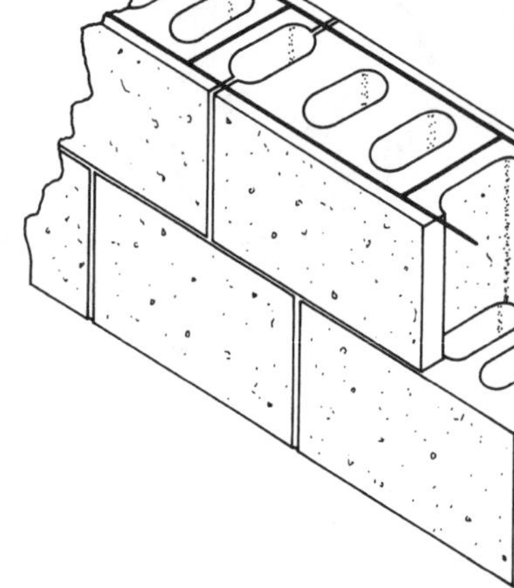

FIGURE 4-57 Horizontal joint reinforcing.

Joint reinforcing is usually placed in the bed joint of every second or third row in a block wall to provide a tie between the units in the wall. This reinforcing is usually galvanized sections of welded wire, generally of the truss or ladder type (see Fig. 4-57).

National and local building codes should be consulted regarding the placement of reinforcing. For example, in some areas where the earth pressures may be excessive, such as in expansive clay soils, it may be necessary to include vertical reinforcement placed in the block cores and filled with concrete.

Plate Anchored to Block Wall

When a wooden plate is to be fastened to the top of a block wall, anchor bolts are used. They should be $\frac{1}{2}$ in.(12 mm) in diameter, 18 in. (450 mm) long, and not more than 4 ft (1.2 m) apart. Lay a piece of metal lath over the cell in which the bolt will be set, two courses below the top of the wall, as shown in Fig. 4-58. When the wall is complete, fill the cell with concrete and set the bolt in place so that at least 2 in. (50 mm) project above the wall.

FIGURE 4-58 Setting anchor bolts in block wall.

Lintels

A horizontal member that is supported on each end must span window and door openings in block walls. Such a member is called a *lintel*, and it may be provided by two different methods. One is to use a precast concrete lintel, designed for the span, with its ends resting on the block at each side of the opening (see Fig. 4-59). The other method involves the use of *lintel blocks* that are laid across the top of the opening and filled with reinforced concrete. Lintel blocks must be supported until the concrete has hardened, and this may be done in one of two ways. One is to set the window frame in place and use it to support the blocks, and the other is to provide a temporary support, which will be removed when the concrete has reached its design strength.

FIGURE 4-59 Precast lintel in place.

Watertight Block Walls

To ensure that block walls below grade will be watertight, they must be parged and sealed. Parging consists of applying two $\frac{1}{4}$-in.(6-mm) coats of plaster, using the same mortar that was used for laying the blocks (see Fig. 4-60). The wall must be dampened before applying the plaster in order to get sufficient bond. The first coat should extend at least from 6 in. (150 mm) above the grade line down to the footing. When it is partially set up, the surface is roughened with a wire brush and then allowed to harden for at least 24 hours. Before the second coat is applied, the wall should be dampened again and the plaster kept damp for 48 hours so the desired impermeability can be achieved.

(a)

(b)

(c)

FIGURE 4-60 Parging block wall.

In poorly drained soils, the plaster should be covered with two coats of asphalt waterproofing, brushed or sprayed on the surface (see Fig. 4-61). In some instances a waterproof membrane is used for even greater resistance to water infiltration (see Fig. 4-62).

In heavy, wet soils the wall may be further protected by laying a line of drainage tile or plastic hose, that is 4 in. (100 mm) in diameter, around the outside of the footing to prevent a buildup of moisture in the area. Figure 4-62 displays a layer of coarse gravel placed over the drainage tile to prevent silt infiltrating the tile or hose preventing proper drainage.

FIGURE 4-61 Waterproofing sealant below grade.

FIGURE 4-62 Waterproofing membrane and gravel over weeping hose.

Pilasters

A pilaster is a type of *column*, incorporated into a block wall for the purpose of providing additional lateral support and/or providing a larger bearing surface for the ends of beams that must be supported on the wall. In concrete block construction the pilaster is formed by means of a *pilaster block,* one of which is illustrated in Fig. 4-45. Pilaster blocks may be filled with reinforced concrete to give them additional strength.

CONCRETE SURFACE FOUNDATION

A surface foundation also consists of concrete or block walls, but they extend into the earth only far enough to reach below the topsoil or below the frost line in areas where frost penetration is a problem. Surface foundations are especially popular in regions where there is little exposure to freezing temperatures since this type of foundation is less expensive than a full basement. The crawl space can be either a heated area or ventilated if unheated. Forms for a concrete surface foundation are the same as those for a full basement, except the wall forms are not as high. Masonry surface foundation walls are built in the same way as full masonry basements.

Heated Crawl Space

Although local building codes should be consulted, all crawl spaces must be at least 1 ft (300 mm) high. However, in localities where termites are known to occur the minimum clearance between structural wood elements and the ground must be at least 18 in. (450 mm). When equipment installed in the crawl space requires servicing, this clearance must be at least 2 ft (600 mm) high for an area within 3 ft (900 mm) around the equipment. In some cases this area is enlarged to provide storage space for the building. This space is usually accessed from the interior of the building. Intermediate floor supports are provided by pouring strip T-footings in the interior of the excavation (see Fig. 4-63).

A short bearing wall is built on this footing to support the underside of the floor frame (see Fig. 4-64).

FIGURE 4-63 Concrete surface foundation.

FIGURE 4-64 Bearing wall supporting floor frame.

To control heat loss or gain, rigid insulation is applied on the interior or exterior of the foundation wall and may be placed under the concrete floor if used. In areas affected by termites, the insulation should be placed on the inside. Termite barriers, as illustrated in Fig. 4-65, are usually placed on the outside of the wall at the base of the floor frame to provide protection from the insects.

Stepping the top of the foundation wall (see Fig. 4-66) provides additional protection to the floor frame.

If a concrete floor is cast in the crawl space, a moisture barrier (polyethylene) may be placed under the concrete slab to ensure a

FIGURE 4-65 Termite barrier.

FIGURE 4-66 Ledge for floor joists.

FIGURE 4-67 Post footings.

dry floor. Instead of building bearing walls, another method of providing support for the floor frame is to pour several post footings in the excavation and set posts and beams to support the floor system (see Fig. 4-67).

Ventilated (Unheated) Crawl Space

In an unheated crawl space the method used to build the foundation is the same as for a heated crawl space. The only differences are to control heat loss or gain in which case only the floor above the crawl space is insulated and no insulation is put under the concrete slab or on the foundation walls. The insulation between the joists can be supported with a covering such as an air barrier house wrap, preventing the wind from stripping the heat out of the insulation. The crawl space must be ventilated to prevent deterioration of the framing members, and local codes specify the amount of ventilation required. Because the working conditions are somewhat restrictive the actual installation of insulation can be difficult and time consuming. In general, unheated crawl spaces are not recommended in colder regions because of water and sewer pipes that could freeze.

SLAB-ON-GRADE FOUNDATION

Many residential buildings and utility buildings do not have basements. This is very common in southern regions where it is not necessary to excavate to reach a frost line. Two types of concrete floor construction are the *combined slab and foundation* and the *independent concrete slab and foundation walls.*

Combined Slab and Foundation

The combined slab and foundation consists of a shallow perimeter footing or beam that is placed at the same time as the concrete floor slab. This type of foundation is especially useful in southern regions where frost penetration is not a problem and where good predictable ground conditions exist [see Fig. 4-68(a)]. The footing is reinforced, and the bottom of the footing should be at least 12 in. (300 mm) below grade line. Figure 4-68(b) illustrates this type of foundation where insulation is installed to control heat loss or gain.

This thickening of the slab may also occur under interior load-bearing walls. The outside edge of the slab can be stepped as illustrated in Fig. 4-69 to provide not only a support for a brick veneer, but also protection from water penetration.

(a) Slab-on-ground foundation.

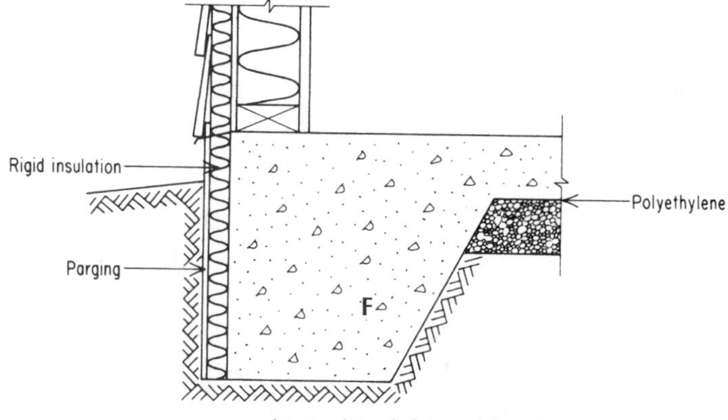

(b) Combined slab and foundation.

FIGURE 4-68

FIGURE 4-69 Stepped edge on slab.

FIGURE 4-70 Insulated edge of slab.

Fig. 4-70 illustrates a type of insulation that has been placed around the outside edge of the slab. Rigid insulation may also be placed under the entire surface of the slab for added control.

Independent Concrete Slab and Foundation Walls

An independent slab-on-ground foundation consists of perimeter footings and stub walls surrounding a reinforced concrete slab cast directly on compacted granular material. The walls must extend down to solid undisturbed soil and below frost level in areas where frost can affect the foundation (see Fig. 4-71). However, in areas of deep frost penetration, it may be impractical to extend the footings to below the frost line, and instead the footing is placed on a well-drained gravel pad at least 4 in. (100 mm) in depth. In all cases the concrete slab must be no less than 3 in. (75 mm) thick, although in most cases it is 4 in. (100 mm) thick.

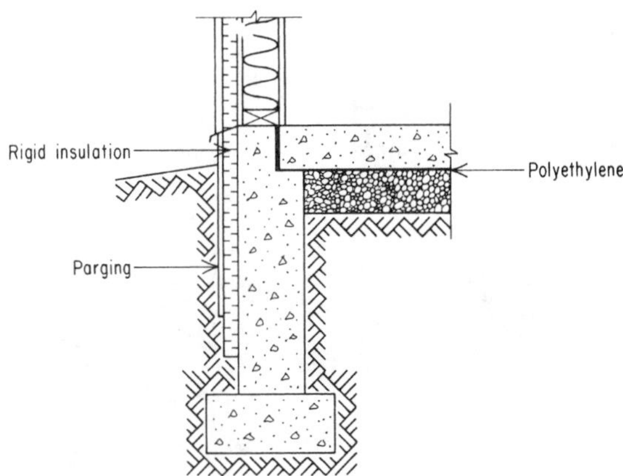

FIGURE 4-71 Independent slab and foundation wall.

FIGURE 4-72 Connection at top of foundation wall.

Walls may be cast-in-place concrete or concrete blocks and, in many cases, may not exceed 16–32 in. (400–800 mm) in height. If concrete walls are specified, forms for them will be similar to those for other concrete walls except for the height. Cast-in plates at the top of the wall are easily fastened inside the form prior to casting, providing a base connection for framed walls (see Fig. 4-72).

A ledge may be formed in the wall to receive the slab and provide additional support. Inserting slab reinforcing into the concrete wall will also provide support (see Fig. 4-73). Placing piers inside the perimeter walls will give the slab additional support (see Fig. 4-74). Continuing the reinforcing from the piers into the slab will provide a positive tie.

When the walls are complete, the earth within them is leveled and compacted. A layer of gravel is added and compacted to a level within 3–4 in. (75–100 mm) from desired finished elevation of the concrete slab. A power-driven compactor, similar to that shown in Fig. 4-75, usually carries out compaction.

FIGURE 4-73 Reinforcing inserted into concrete wall.

FIGURE 4-74 Pier supports for concrete slab.

FIGURE 4-75 Power compactor at work.
(Courtesy Wacker Corporation)

Two very important considerations with this type of foundation are *moisture control* and *insulation*, and Figs. 4-68 and 4-71 illustrate typical slab constructions with these two factors in mind.

A continuous waterproof membrane is laid over the entire compacted gravel surface to prevent the migration of moisture into the slab from below. Six-mil polyethylene is often used for this membrane. A strip of rigid insulation at least 2 in. (50 mm) thick is applied to the outer exposed wall surface with asphalt adhesive. Then rigid insulation is laid on the entire surface. This insulation may only be placed around the perimeter or may be eliminated in warmer regions. Where it is used on exterior surfaces, it should be covered with a $\frac{1}{2}$ in. (12 mm) of cement parging on wire lath. Finally, welded wire mesh or $\frac{3}{8}$ in. (10-mm) steel placed 24 in. (600 mm) o.c. in both directions is placed over the whole surface, and then concrete is placed to encompass the reinforcing.

PIER FOUNDATION

A pier foundation is one in which the building is constructed on a number of beams, with each supported by several *piers* or posts of pressure-treated wood, masonry, or concrete. Each post rests on an individual concrete footing or is used without a footing when the soil has sufficient bearing capacity [see Fig. 4-76(a) and 4-76(b)]. Pier footings should always be placed below the frost line or placed on well-drained gravel pads.

Forms for pier footings are usually built in individual excavations, square in plan, and may be *rectangular* or *stepped.* The footing area is based on the amount of load carried by each one and the type of soil on which it rests. The construction of these footing forms is illustrated in Fig. 4-77(a) and 4-77(b).

(a) Pier foundation.

(b) Post footing.

FIGURE 4-76

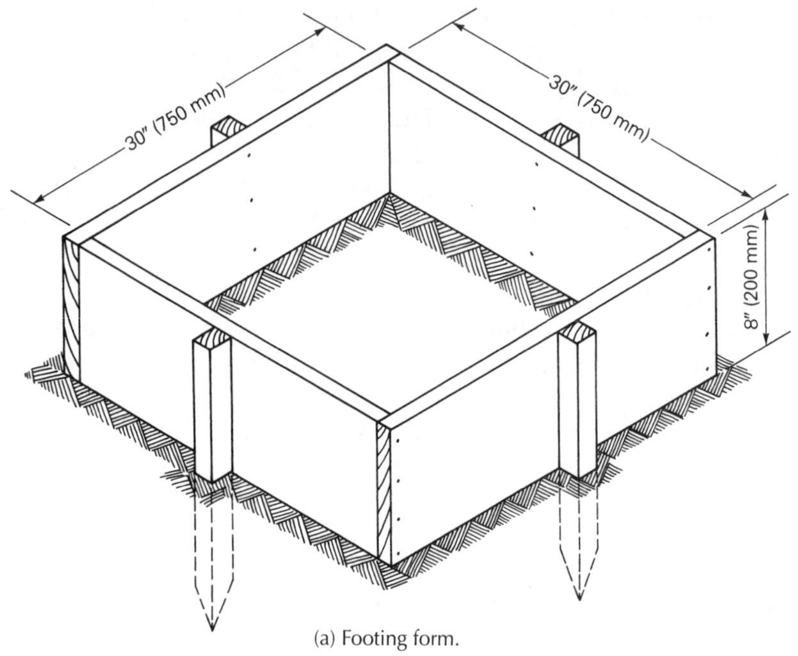

(a) Footing form.

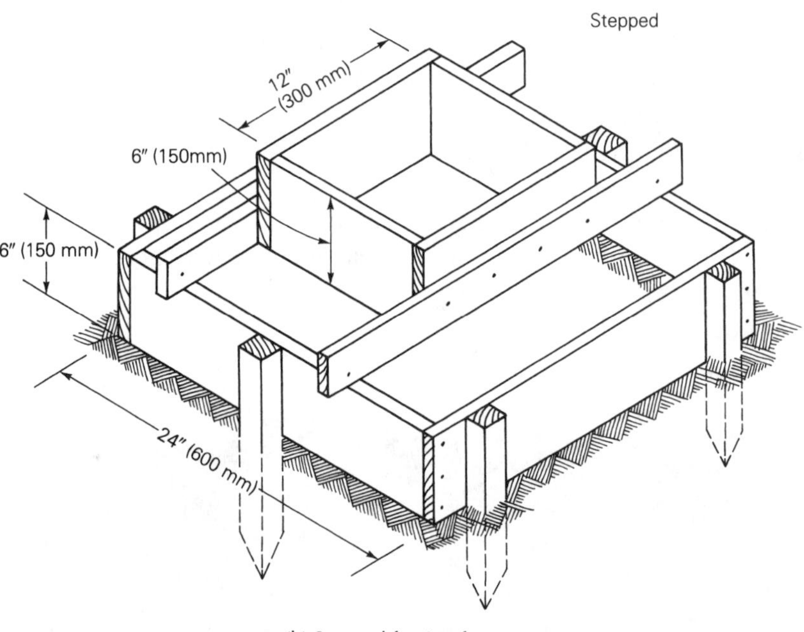

(b) Stepped footing form.

FIGURE 4-77 Independent footings.

FIGURE 4-78 Base plate for post.

Footings that are to support wooden piers should have a base plate set in the center of the top surface to anchor the pier in place (see Fig. 4-78). Mortar is sufficient to anchor a masonry pier to the footing.

PRESERVED WOOD FOUNDATION

A preserved wood foundation (also called a permanent wood foundation) is a complete *wood-frame foundation* system, built with preservative-treated lumber and intended for buildings falling into the light construction category. In this system all wood exposed to decay hazard is pressure-treated with chemical preservatives that permanently impregnate the wood cells to the degree that makes the wood resistant to attack by decay organisms and termites. **Note: this system is not universally accepted in all areas; you must consult local regulations.**

It can be built as a *full basement* foundation (see Fig. 4-79) with a *concrete slab floor, wood sleeper floor,* or *suspended wood floor* or as a *surface* foundation (see Fig. 4-80).

(a) Preserved wood foundation with pressure-treated plank footings. (Courtesy of Forest Industries of B.C.)

(b) Preserved wood foundation with concrete footings.

FIGURE 4-79 Preserved wood foundation exterior walls.

FIGURE 4-80 Surface foundation.

Site Preparation

After the excavation has been completed to the desired level, service and drain lines and a sump, if necessary, are installed, the trenches are backfilled and compacted. In some localities the sump pit may be replaced by a 4-in. (100-mm) perforated, vertical standpipe, at least 24 in. (600 mm) high, surrounded by 16 in. (400 mm) of washed, coarse gravel. The standpipe should extend through the floor and be capped by a cleanout plug. No drainage system is required for unexcavated crawl spaces if the final grade inside the crawl space is equal to or higher than the grade outside.

Next, 5 in. (125 mm) of clean gravel is laid on undisturbed soil over an area extending 12 in. (300 mm) beyond the dimensions of the building and leveled. The gravel under all *footing plates* is compacted at least 12 in. (300 mm) beyond the edges of the plates to provide good bearing for loads.

(a)

(b)

FIGURE 4-81 Continuous wood footings.

Footings

Continuous wood footings, consisting of the *wood footing plates* and the *compacted gravel bed* beneath them are the most practical and economical for this type of foundation, because they eliminate the building of forms and placement of concrete (see Fig. 4-81).

Wood footing plates are placed directly on the level, compacted gravel bed, butted together at end joints and wall intersections. The treated lumber can be ordered in specified lengths to suit the footing layout, and members may extend beyond the line of the wall at corners to avoid the cutting of plates wherever possible. However, if members must be cut, the exposed ends must be thoroughly saturated with wood preservative.

In some cases specially constructed wood footings are installed to support heavy loads as illustrated in Fig. 4-82(a) and 4-82(b).

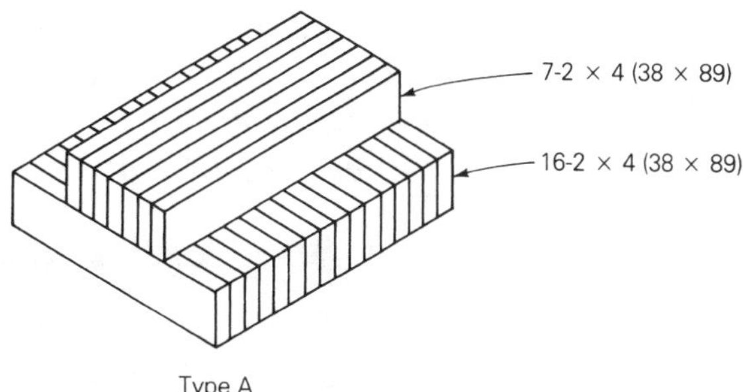

Type A

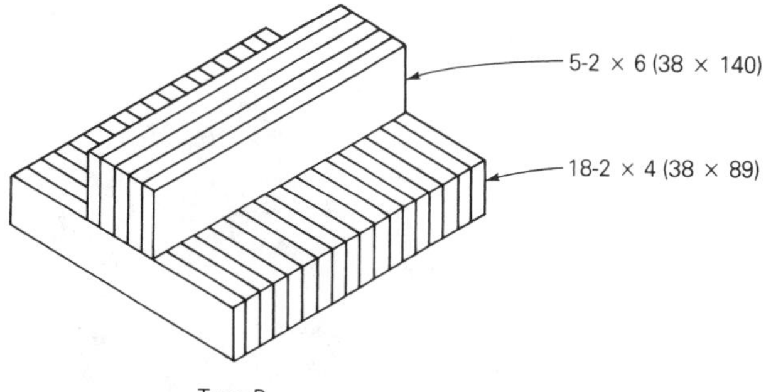

Type B

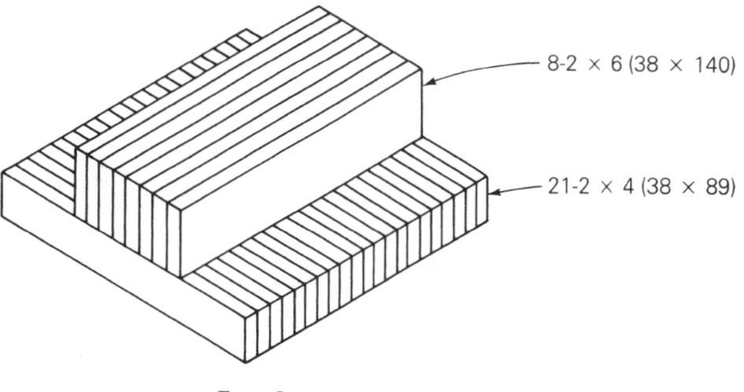

Type C

(a) Alternative post footings.

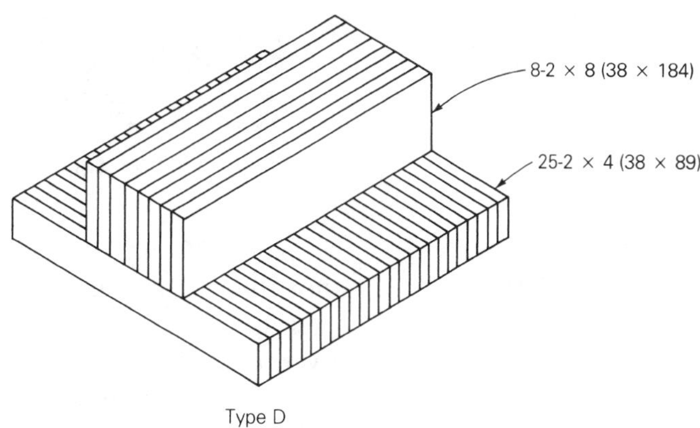

Type D

(b) Wood post footings.

FIGURE 4-82 Independent footings.

Concrete footings can be used under wood foundation walls instead of wood footings. They are more convenient on sloped lots, where stepped footings are necessary (Fig. 4-83). They can be placed on a gravel bed or directly on undisturbed soil. When they are placed on undisturbed soil, drainage should be provided through the footing, as illustrated in Fig. 4-84. The size of concrete footings supporting exterior walls will be determined by local codes.

FIGURE 4-83 Foundation wall framing.

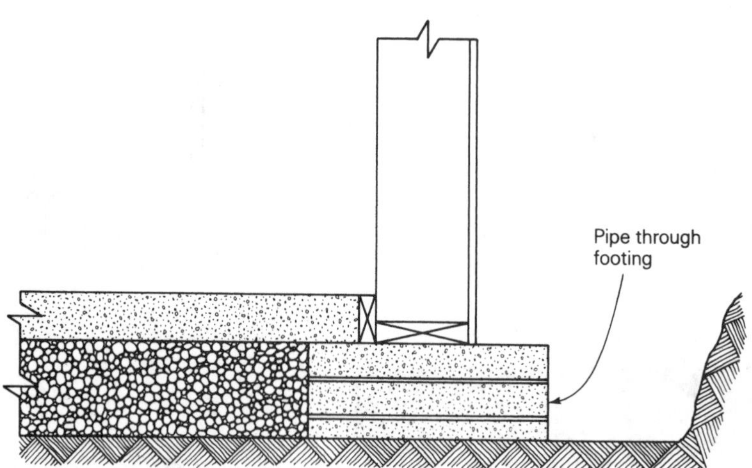

FIGURE 4-84 Concrete footing on undisturbed soil.

When a beam and posts are used to support the interior loads rather than a bearing wall, post footings may be either concrete or preservative-treated wood. Concrete footings are similar to those in conventional foundations, and Fig. 4-82 illustrates the construction of wood post footings for various loading conditions. Post footings may be set on undisturbed soil below the gravel bed to avoid the top of the footings interfering with the basement floor.

Foundation Walls

Wood foundation walls, consisting of a *frame* made up of *studs* with *single top and bottom plate, sheathed with plywood* and all treated with preservative, may be prefabricated in sections in a shop or completely assembled on site. Where plywood sheets are applied horizontally, *blocking* is required between studs at the plywood joint (see Fig. 4-85). In addition, all plywood joints are caulked with sealant. Double top plates are required where the floor joists are offset more than 2 in. (50 mm) from the foundation studs.

(a) Positioning prefabricated foundation walls.

(b) Horizontal blocking behind plywood joints.

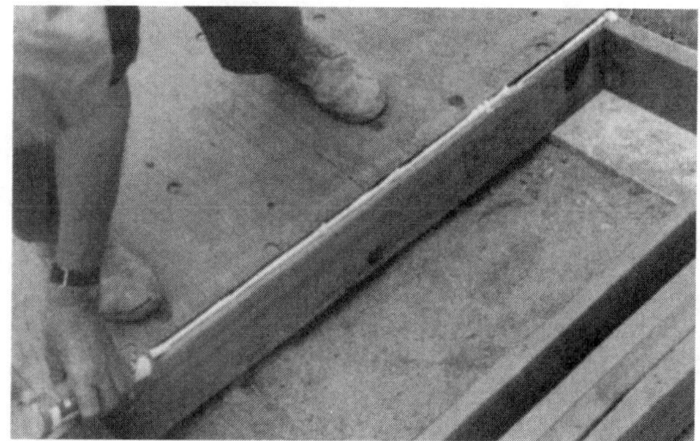

(c) Sealant applied at plywood joints.

FIGURE 4-85 Assembly of foundation walls.

For full basement construction, walls are 8 ft (2.4 m) high for slab and sleeper floors and 10 ft (3.0 m) high for suspended wood floors. The size and spacing of studs depend on the *building loads, species* and *grade of lumber,* and the *height of backfill,* which in turn depends on the depth of the excavation. The thickness of plywood used for sheathing depends on the *direction of face grain* (that is, whether the face grain is parallel or perpendicular to the studs), the *stud spacing*, and the *height of the backfill.*

Most governing authorities require that (1) size and spacing of members in a pressure-treated wood *foundation* are determined by using engineering principles, (2) the foundation be inspected by a *professional engineer* or a *registered architect*, and the plans and specifications are stamped by a *registered engineer or architect.*

Plywood may be fastened to the frame with hot dipped galvanized nails or corrosion resistant staples, minimum length 2 in. (50 mm). Nails and staples are spaced 6 in. (150 mm) o.c. along outside edges and 12 in. (300 mm) o.c. along intermediate supports. Framing and fastening requirements for openings in wall panels for windows or landings of split-level entrances are given in Fig. 4-86.

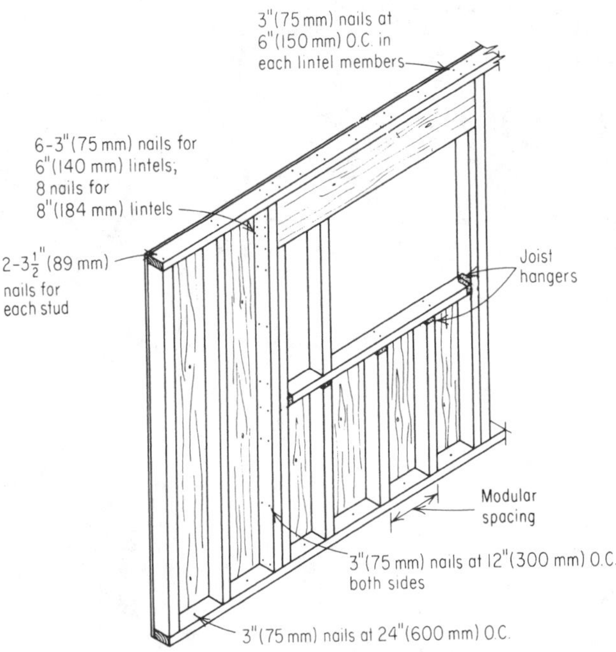

FIGURE 4-86 Nailing requirements at openings in preserved wood foundation wall.

FIGURE 4-87 Polyethylene membrane.

All joints between plywood panels below grade are sealed by pressing the plywood edge into a bead of sealant. The exterior of the foundation walls below grade is also covered with a 6-mil polyethylene membrane, extending from a minimum of 3 in. (75 mm) above the finished grade line to the bottom of the footing plate, where it should be cut off. The membrane *should not* extend under the gravel pad or under the footing plate (see Fig. 4-87).

The polyethylene is cemented to the sheathing at the top edge by a 6-in. (150-mm) band of adhesive (see Fig. 4-88). It is also protected at the grade level by a 12 in. wide (300 mm wide) strip of treated plywood, set with its top edge at least 3 in. (75 mm) above the

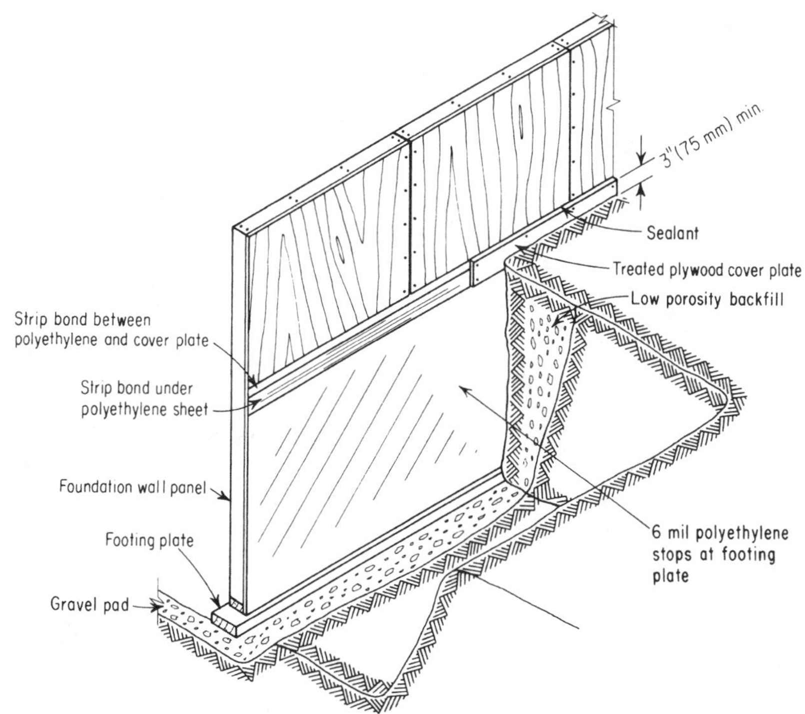

FIGURE 4-88 Polyethylene membrane on exterior of preserved wood foundation wall.

finished grade line. A strip of sealant about 3 in. (75 mm) wide is applied to the top inside face of the plywood before it is nailed to the foundation wall.

The polyethylene sheet exterior protection is not required if all surfaces below grade are coated with two coats of bituminous dampproofing material applied by brush or spray.

Concrete Slab Floors

Concrete slab floors used in conjunction with wood foundations are similar to those used for conventional basement floors. Basically, they consist of a minimum 3–4-in. (75–100-mm) concrete slab, placed over a 4-in. (100 mm) gravel bed, with a 6-mil polyethylene moisture barrier between concrete and gravel.

To transmit lateral soil loads from the wall into the slab, the top edge of the floor slab must butt directly against the bottom ends of the wall studs. This may be done by fastening a continuous, treated wooden strip along the lower edge of the foundation wall (see Fig. 4-89) wide enough that distance "d" will be from 1 to 2 in. (25–45 mm), depending on stud spacing and depth of backfill. This strip can be used as a screed to level the concrete slab and will remain in place after the concrete has hardened.

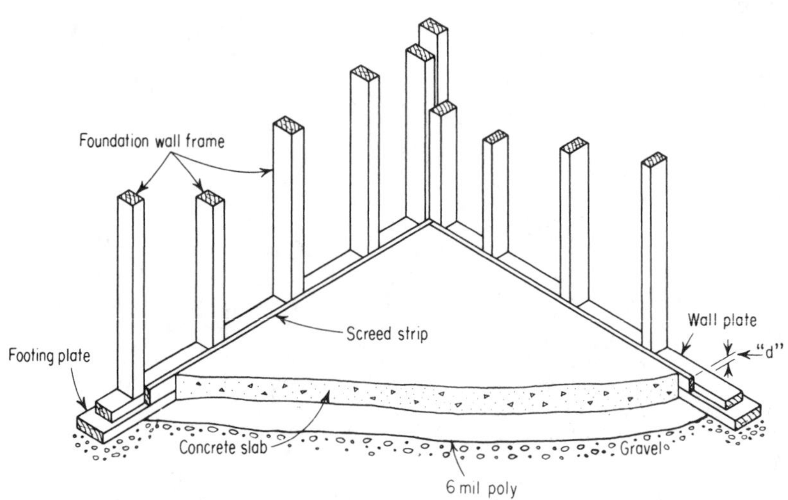

FIGURE 4-89 Concrete slab floor in wood foundation basement.

Wood Sleeper Floors

Wood sleeper floors (see Fig. 4-90) are damp-proofed by laying 6-mil, 4-ft-wide (1200-mm-wide) strips of polyethylene, overlapped 4 in. (100 mm) at the joints, not a continuous membrane, over the leveled gravel bed.

The 2 × 4 in. (38 × 89 mm) treated wood *sleepers* are placed on the polyethylene cover at a spacing of from 4 to 6 ft (1200–1800 mm), depending on the depth of the floor joists to be used. Floor joists, 2 × 4 in. (38 × 89 mm) or larger, are placed to span between the footing plates and the sleepers with at least $1\frac{1}{2}$-in. (38-mm) bearing on the footing plate. To achieve this, it may be necessary to use wider footing plates than the design requires.

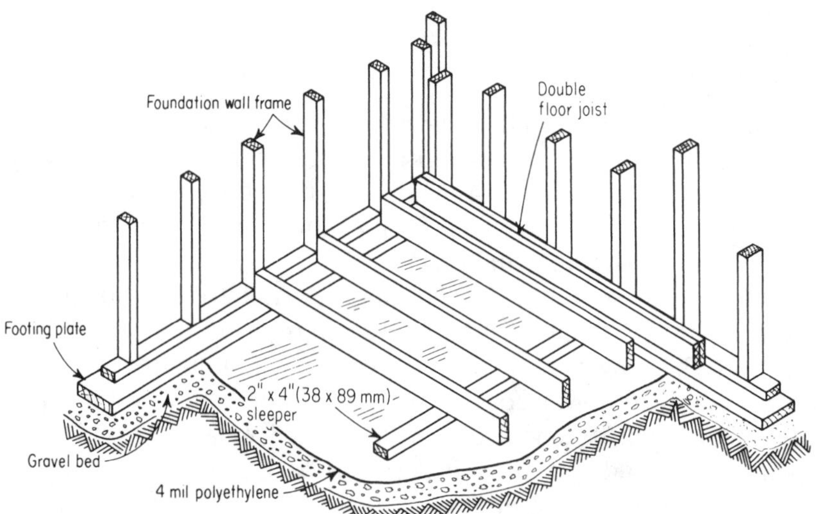

FIGURE 4-90 Wood floor frame on wood sleepers.

Joists are placed in line with foundation wall studs (see Fig. 4-90) and butt inline over the sleeper supports. They are toe-nailed to the sleepers and to the wall studs with at least two 3-in. (75-mm) nails at each junction.

Plywood subflooring is installed over the floor joists and acts as a diaphragm to resist lateral earth loads. For the thickness of plywood required, refer to local codes. Generally, when the supports are placed 16 in. (400 mm) o. c., $\frac{5}{8}$-in. (15.5-mm) plywood and waferboard is required. If the supports are further apart, greater thickness is required.

To ensure the proper transfer of lateral soil loads from the *end* walls to the floor frame and plywood subfloor, it is necessary to provide additional nailing and, in some cases, additional framing. Figure 4-91 illustrates this additional support.

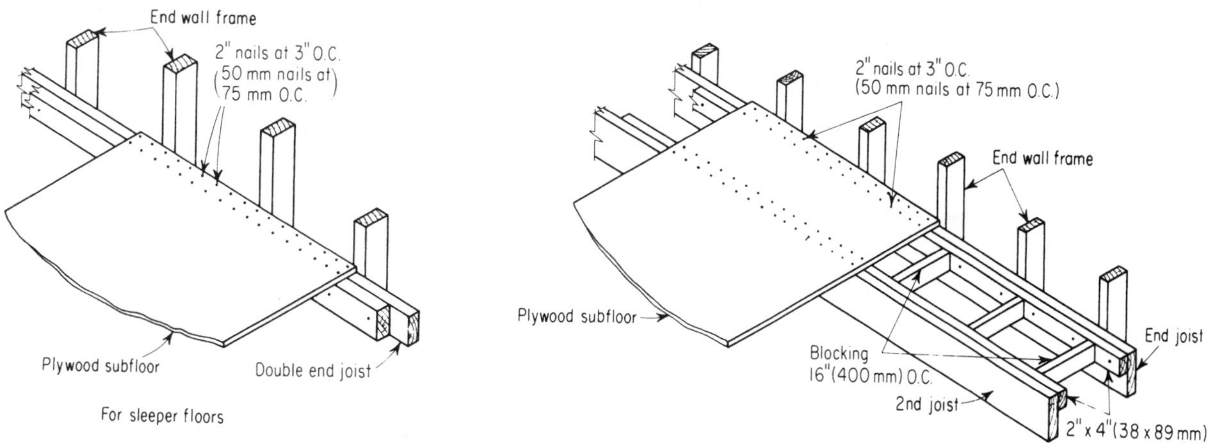

FIGURE 4-91 Sleeper and suspended floors end nailing and reinforced framing.

Suspended Wood Floors

Joists for a suspended wood floor are supported above the gravel base on a continuous 2 × 4 in. (38 × 89 mm) *ledger* on the foundation walls and by a low bearing wall for intermediate support (see Fig. 4-92).

Joists are placed directly in line with the foundation wall studs and must be butted in line over the bearing wall to provide continuous lateral support to the foundation walls (see Fig. 4-92). Plywood subflooring is applied over the joists and nailed as required in the same manner as for sleeper floors.

CONCRETE PLACING

Regardless of the care spent in building forms, the final test of the strength and durability of the foundation being built will lie in the quality of the concrete used. That quality will depend on a number of factors, all of major importance. They include the following:

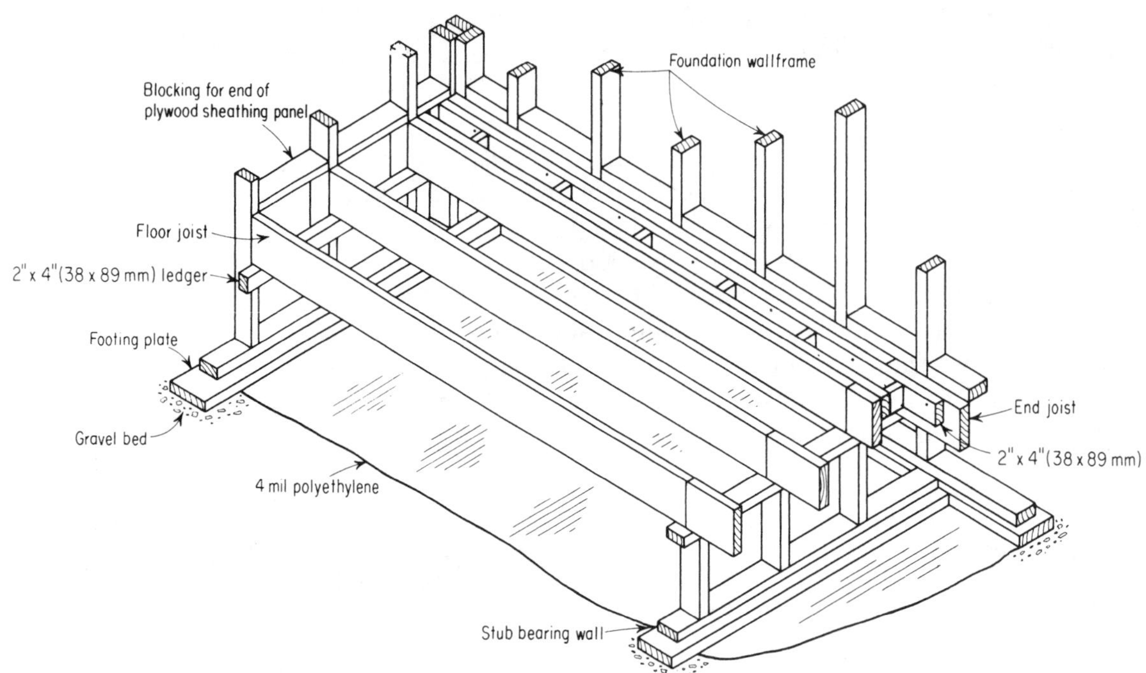

FIGURE 4-92 Suspended wood floor.

1. Clean and well-graded aggregate and properly proportioned fine and coarse aggregate.
2. Clean water; water fit for human consumption is the best test.
3. The amount of water used in the mix per unit of cement is a matter of primary importance. This ratio to a large extent controls the strength of the concrete. The less water used, within limits, the stronger the concrete, and, conversely, the more water used, the less strength will be achieved. The ratio, expressed in pounds (kilograms) of water per pound (kilogram) of cement, will ordinarily vary from 0.40 to 0.70 lb/lb (kg/kg).
4. A decision regarding whether or not *entrained air* is included in the mix. Entrained air consists of thousands of tiny, stable bubbles of air that are introduced into the fresh concrete to improve the *flow ability* of the mix. Air entrainment does, however, result in some reduction in compressive strength.

Table 4-2 indicates the probable compressive strength that will be achieved, using a number of different water/cement ratios, both with and without entrained air.

The concrete may be mixed on the job, delivered ready-mixed from a concrete mixing plant, or delivered from a batching plant, mixed in transit. No matter which method is used, great care must be taken in placing the concrete in these forms:

1. Concrete should not be allowed to drop freely more than 48 in. (1200 mm). If the height of the form is greater than that, some type of chute is required so that the concrete may be conducted to at least within 48 in. (1200 mm) of the bottom.
2. Concrete should be placed in such a way that it will drop straight down, not bounce from one form face to the other.
3. Place in even layers around the form—don't try to place all in one spot and allow the concrete to flow to its final position.
4. Start placing at the corners and work toward the center of the form. All of these precautions will help prevent *segregation*, that is, the separation of the aggregates from the water-cement paste.

TABLE 4-2: Compressive strengths of concrete for various water/cement ratios.

Water/cement ratio [lb/lb (kg/kg) of cement]	*Probable compressive strength after 28 days [psi (MPa)]*	
	Non-air-entrained	*Air-entrained*
0.40	5800 (40)	4800 (33)
0.50	4800 (33)	3650 (25)
0.60	3900 (27)	2750 (19)
0.70	3050 (21)	1750 (12)

The placement of concrete can be improved by the use of a labor saving concrete pump. The hose from the truck at one location can be easily moved over the entire site, reducing the placement time. Special ramps and chutes are not needed to place concrete on a sloped or uneven site (see Fig. 4-93).

Concrete can best be consolidated in the form by vibration. This may be done either internally or externally. An internal vibrator (see Fig. 4-94) is inserted into the concrete and operated until consolidation has taken place. An external vibrator is operated against

FIGURE 4-93 Concrete pump.

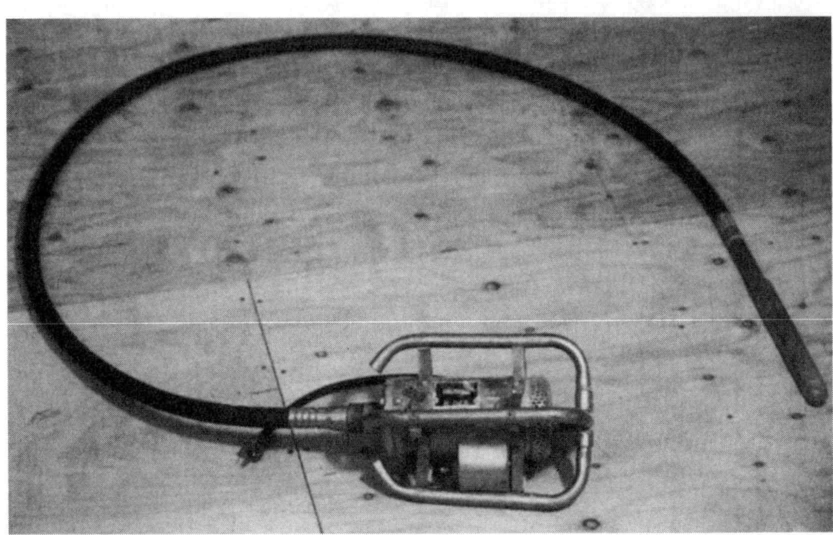

FIGURE 4-94 Concrete vibrator.

the outside of the form. Care must be taken not to over-vibrate, because excess paste will be brought to the top or out to the face of the forms, causing segregation. Careful consolidation of the concrete is necessary to ensure that *honeycombing* does not occur. Honeycombing occurs when the large aggregates in the concrete are exposed without the finer aggregates completely surrounding them. This results in a porous foundation allowing moisture to penetrate through the foundation wall, makes it weaker, and is obviously unsightly.

Proper curing of the concrete, that is, allowing it to gain its rated strength, is very important. Temperature and moisture conditions control the curing. Concrete cures best at a temperature of about 70°F (21°C) and cures very slowly below 40°F (5°C). Moist conditions are required for good curing. If the concrete is allowed to dry out soon after it is placed, it cannot be expected to gain the strength required of it. Keep the concrete warm and moist for as long as possible.

One means of keeping the concrete moist is to leave the forms in place. However, if it is necessary to remove the forms early in the curing process, care must be taken not to damage the green concrete.

There are occasions when it is necessary to use concrete made with other than normal cement. If the land on which the foundation will rest contains alkali salts, concrete made with normal Portland cement will set and cure poorly. In such cases, it is wise to specify alkali-resistant cement, which will produce concrete that will set and cure under alkaline conditions. Sometimes it may be necessary to have the concrete set and cure more quickly than is normally the case. If this is so, special cement, called *high-early-strength cement*, should be used in making the concrete. Concrete so made will cure much more rapidly in its early stages than that made with normal cement.

BASEMENT FLOOR

The concrete basement floor is placed in one layer after the proper base preparations have been completed. First a minimum 4-in. (100-mm) layer of packed gravel is placed under the floor. A 6-mil polyethylene membrane may then be laid over the gravel, initially to prevent the loss of water from the concrete to the base and eventually to prevent the migration of moisture upward through the slab. The level of the slab is established by measuring down from the underside of the joists or by placing screeds around the outside of the slab. A *screed* is simply a guide strip, the top of which represents the level of the finished floor. Stakes or screeds may be placed in the middle of the floor to establish the level at the middle of the floor (see Fig. 4-95).

The concrete is placed either with a concrete pump or by chute (see Fig. 4-96). It is then compacted and leveled with a straight edge

FIGURE 4-95 Stakes to establish concrete floor level.

FIGURE 4-96 Placing concrete by chute.

(a) Leveling with a straight edge.

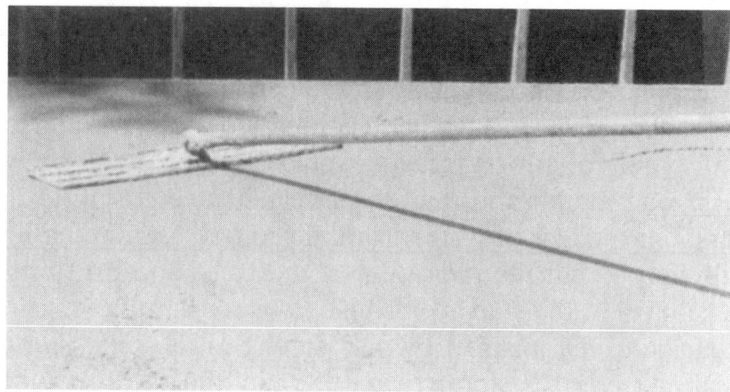

(b) Bullfloating.

FIGURE 4-97 Leveling fresh concrete.

and trued with a bullfloat, eliminating the ridges and filling the surface voids [see Fig. 4-97(a)]. Bullfloating should immediately follow the screeding and must be completed before any bleed water is present on the surface [see Fig. 4-97(b)].

Machine floating is not done until the concrete has stiffened. This floating will depress the larger aggregates slightly below the surface, remove the imperfections, and compact the mortar at the surface in preparation for finishing. The final compaction and smoothing are achieved by steel troweling with a hand- or a power-driven trowel (see Fig. 1-97).

Concrete Joints and Reinforcement

The joint between floor and wall may require some special consideration. Since the floor is probably placed after the wall concrete has hardened, there is little bond between them, and eventually shrinkage will produce a crack around the perimeter. This crack may be a source of trouble if moisture collects under the footings, because the water will find its way up through the joint. Such an occurrence may be prevented by sealing the joint with an asphalt caulking compound (see Fig. 4-98).

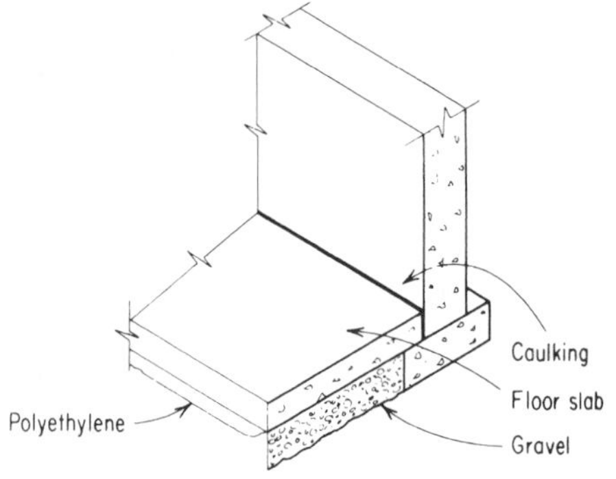

FIGURE 4-98 Floor to wall joint.

The need for reinforcement will depend on the size of the floor and its use. Residential floors do not usually require reinforcing, but larger ones may. Reinforcing may be done for two reasons, one being to give the concrete greater strength in bending and the other to control contraction and expansion of the top surface due to temperature changes. In the first case the reinforcement will be rod (see Fig. 4-95) or heavy wire mesh placed near the bottom of the slab. In the second it will be light wire mesh placed close to the top surface (see Fig. 4-99).

FIGURE 4-99 Reinforcing mesh

CONCRETE STEPS

Entrance steps must be attached to the foundation wall by means of reinforcing placed during wall construction or bolts fastened through the wall after construction. The foundation for the step can be piers or a wall resting on a footing when needed [see Fig. 4-100(a)] or concrete or metal brackets fastened to the wall [see Figs. 4-100(b) and 4-100(c)]. Steps may be included and poured as part of the platform

(a) Foundation wall.

(c) Metal bracket attached fo foundation wall.

(b) Concrete bracket attached to foundation wall.

FIGURE 4-100 Entrance step support.

FIGURE 4-101 Step forms.

(see Fig. 4-101). When the steps are over 3 ft (1 m) wide, 2-in. (38-mm) material should be used for the risers, and additional support should be added when the width is over 6 ft (2 m), as shown in Fig. 4-101.

The risers of the steps should be set at an angle of about 10° to provide a nosing. The bottom edge of the riser should be beveled to permit troweling of the entire surface of the step (see Fig. 4-102).

Precast platforms and steps are commonly used, particularly where custom work is not required (see Fig. 4-100) and are supported on concrete brackets.

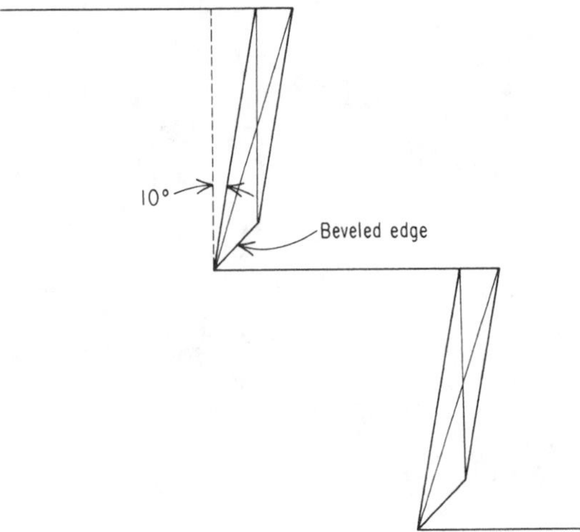

FIGURE 4-102 Placement of the riser form.

SIDEWALKS AND DRIVEWAYS

Sidewalks and driveways are not usually poured until after construction of the building is complete. In some areas the slab may be poured directly in contact with the soil. If the base is subjected to moisture and frost action, a gravel base is advised. Concrete thickness can also be reduced from 4 in. (100 mm) to $3\frac{1}{2}$ in. (90 mm) when put down on a 4-in. (100-mm) gravel base.

The forms for the slab should be set so that there is a drainage slope of at least 1:60. Reinforcing of deformed steel or welded wire mesh is commonly used to keep the floating slab together and to minimize cracking (see Fig. 4-103). Expansion joints are used when the slab comes in contact with a garage slab, curb, or public sidewalk or every 20 ft (6 m). Control joints act as a stress relief to limit uncontrolled cracking.

FIGURE 4-103 Deformed steel in slab.

Construction joints usually form the edges of each day's work. They are located to conform to the slab-jointing pattern and constructed to function as and to align with control or expansion joints (see Fig. 4-104). For sidewalks, the distance between joints should be equal to the width of the slab. Form sides are usually 2 × 4s (38 × 89) or 2 × 6s (38 × 150) so the edges can be kept straight (see Fig. 4-105).

Edges and expansion joints should be rounded with an edger. A jointing tool is commonly used to establish a control joint as well. The surface of the slab can be troweled, or when extra traction is required, a fine brush finish is used.

Interlocking paving stones may be used for sidewalks and driveways. Numerous different shapes are available in a variety of colors (see Fig. 4-106). The unique geometric shape of the paving stones provides a completely interlocking surface that will transfer individual loads to adjacent stones, allowing the surface to move like a mesh. The flexibility of the system makes repairing the surface an easy procedure.

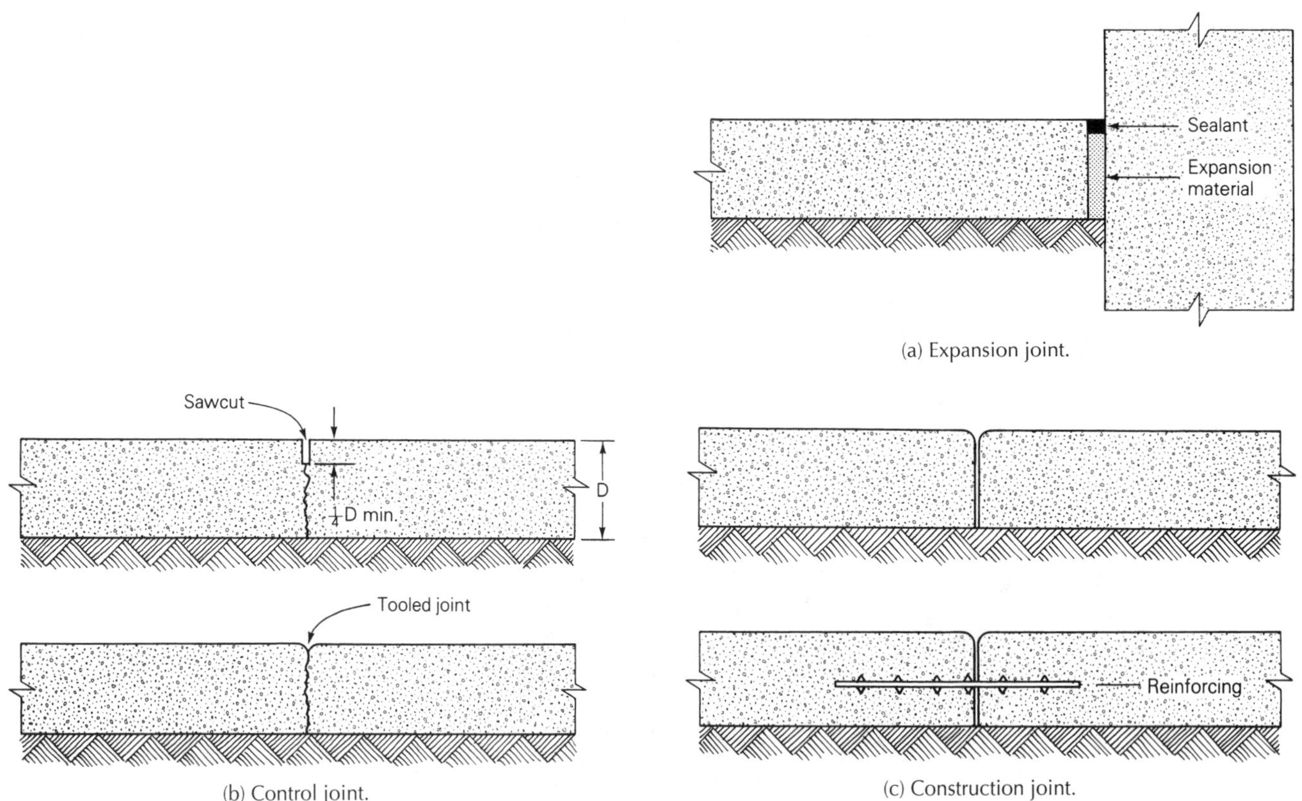

(a) Expansion joint.

(b) Control joint.

(c) Construction joint.

FIGURE 4-104 Joints in a concrete slab.

FIGURE 4-105 Sidewalk form.

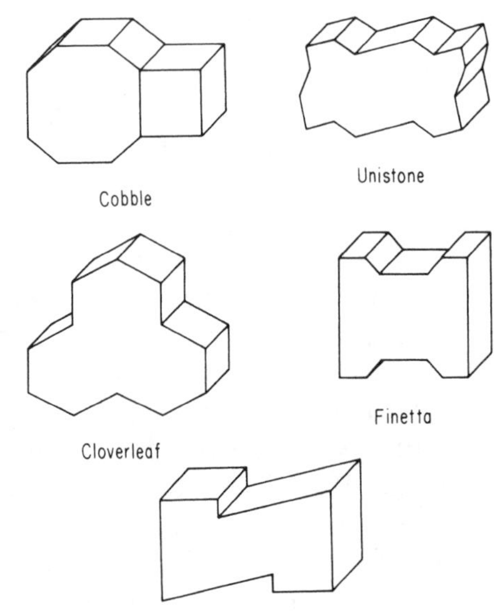

FIGURE 4-106 Paving stone shapes.

TABLE 4-3: Minimum subgrade thickness

	Walk or patio	*Driveway*
CBR of greater than 8% (well-compacted rocky round, gravel, sandy loam, or sand with a small amount of silt)	Not required	Not required
CBR of 4–8% (sand, loam, and stiff clay not subject to moisture)	Not required	3 in. (75 mm)
CBR of less than 4% (wet clays or soils which may easily deform when wet or subject to car traffic)	3 in. (75 mm)	5 in. (125 mm)

Interlocking concrete paving consists of a layer of *concrete pavers*, a *sand bedding layer*, and a compacted *subgrade* and is held in place by solid *curbs*. The thickness of the pavers can vary from $2\frac{3}{8}$ in. (60 mm) to 4 in. (100 mm) depending on the type of traffic. The herringbone pattern provides the best locking effect, though other patterns are also used (see Fig. 4-107). The subgrade should be level, and the thickness depends on ground conditions and use of the area. The strength of the soil is measured in terms of the California bearing ratio (CBR). The minimum recommended subgrade thickness is given in Table 4-3.

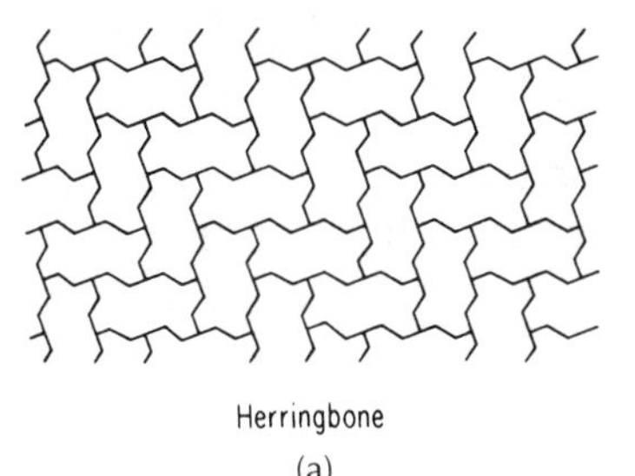

(a)

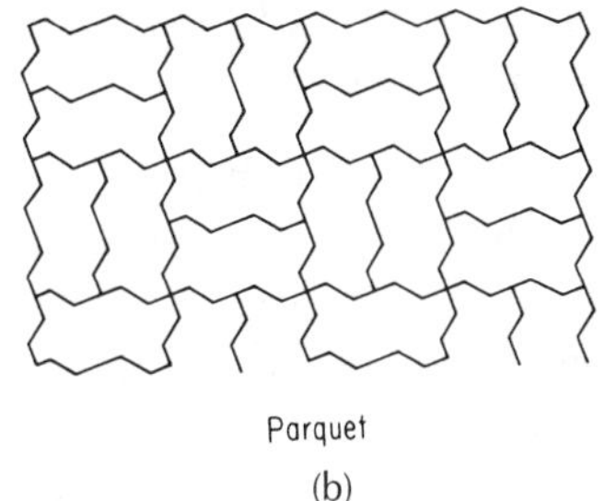

(b)

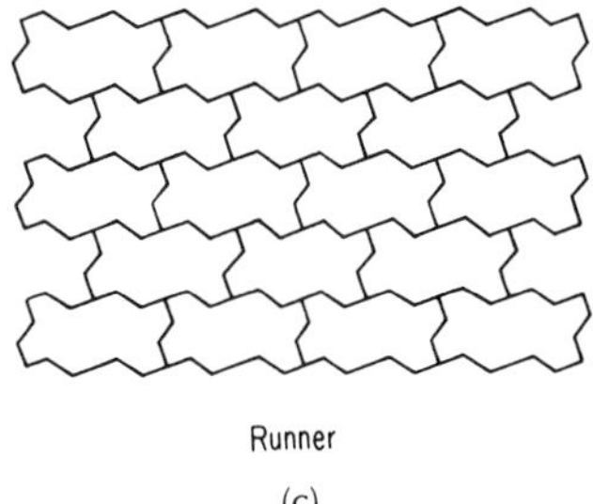

(c)

FIGURE 4-107 Paving stone patterns.

The sand-bedding layer should consist of well-graded concrete sand. Uniformity of the layer is important to achieve a good-quality surface. This layer should not be over $1\frac{1}{2}$-in. (40-mm) thick after compaction and should not be used for leveling low spots (see Fig. 4-108).

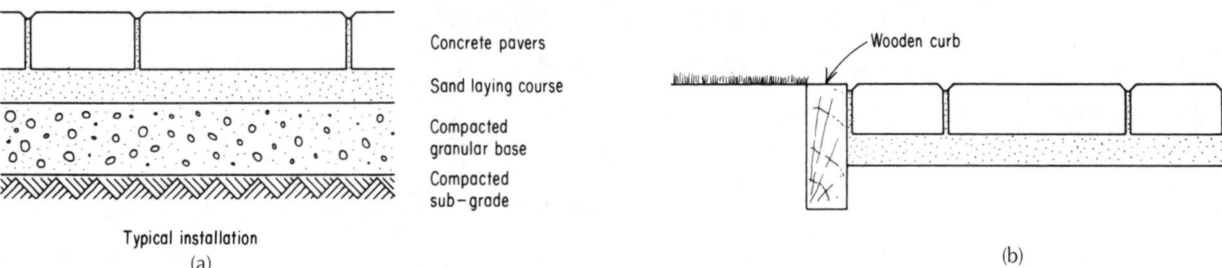

FIGURE 4-108 Concrete paving stone structure.

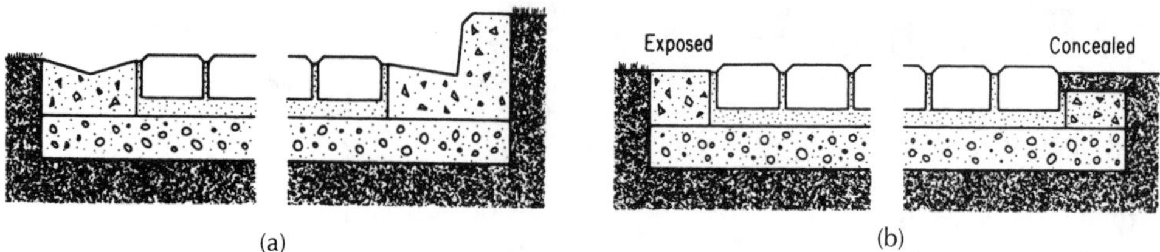

FIGURE 4-109 Edge restraints.

Solid curbs are needed around the perimeter to prevent moving and slipping of the stones. Curbs can be made of concrete, pressure-treated wood, lawn, compacted earth, or an existing building (see Fig. 4-109).

Construction procedures should conform to the following steps:

1. Ground should be cut out and shaped for area needed and then compacted.
2. Subgrade should be spread to the required level and compacted.
3. Edge restraint can be placed before or after placing of stones.
4. Sand is spread and screeded to a level that will result in proper level after compaction.
5. Lay stones starting from a straight-edge and a corner directly onto screeded sand in the pattern selected. Joints between stones should not exceed $\frac{1}{8}$ in. (3 mm), and the surface should have a 2% slope to provide drainage.
6. Vibrate stones with a plate vibrator to final level.
7. Spread dry sand over surface and brush into joints to complete the interlock.

Now that the concrete work and foundation are complete, the job is ready for the erection of the superstructure. If it has been carefully planned and carried out, the completion of the remainder of the building will be easier, with fewer chances of errors as work continues.

REVIEW QUESTIONS

4–1. What is the general purpose of a building foundation?

4–2. Outline the essential difference between a full basement foundation and a surface foundation.

4–3. What are the reasons for removal of all vegetable matter before the placement of foundations?

4–4. How does a gravel pad under a slab foundation compensate for the fact that the foundation is not below the frost line?

4–5. Why is it necessary, in many cases, to make the excavation larger than the size of the foundation?

4–6. When would it be necessary to use cribbing in an excavation?

4–7. If there is expected to be a high lateral load on a foundation wall, what is recommended for joining the footing and wall?

4–8. What is the purpose of a T-footing?

4–9. What is the name of the part of a concrete wall form that aligns the forms and provides stiffness?

4–10. For what purpose is a beam pocket formed in a concrete foundation wall?

4–11. What is the function of a sill plate?

4–12. What is a "rough buck"?

4–13. How are concrete block foundations aligned on a footing?

4–14. Must all crawl spaces be ventilated?

4–15. How are slabs-on-ground formed?

4–16. What is a "pier" foundation?

4–17. What type of support is acceptable for wood foundation footings?

4–18. How does the amount of water used in the mixing of concrete affect the final product?

4–19. What mechanical device is used to consolidate concrete in a wall form?

4–20. What mechanical device is used for the final compaction and smoothing of a concrete slab?

Chapter 5

THE FLOOR FRAME

OBJECTIVES

Here is what you will be able to do when you complete each component of this chapter:

1. Identify floor frame posts, beams, bearing walls, sills, joists, headers, trimmers, bridging, and subfloor.
2. Describe how the floor frame is assembled.

COMPONENT PARTS

After the foundation is completed, the next logical step in the construction of a building is the erection of the floor frame. This, as the name implies, is the part of the structure that carries the floor and interior walls, along with its supporting members. This floor frame consists of *bearing posts*, the beam which they support, the *floor joists* carried by the beam and foundation walls, the *bridging* between the joists, and the *subfloor*; sometimes a *bearing wall* will replace posts and beam. When the box sill or ladder type of construction is used, a sill plate or ladder becomes one of the components of the floor frame.

POST AND BEAMS

Posts and beams are fundamental structural components of the floor frame. When a beam is located along the center of the building, the beam will support approximately half the total load of the building and transmit this load to the foundation walls and footings.

Posts

The bearing posts may be made of either steel or wood. Wooden ones are sometimes one solid piece of timber but more often are built up of three or four pieces of $1\frac{1}{2}$-in. (38-mm) material laminated

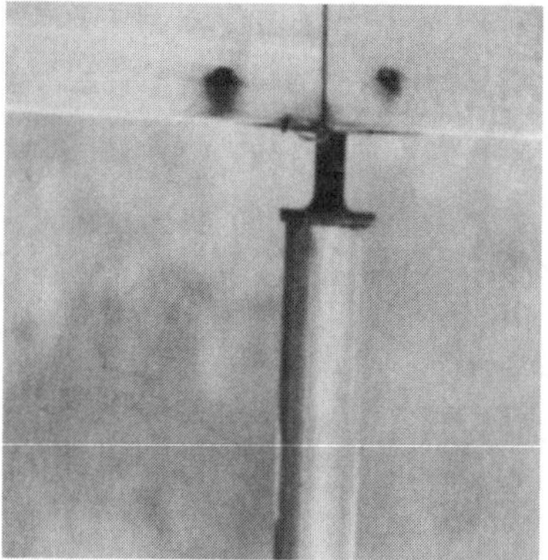

(a) Round steel adjustable post.

FIGURE 5-1

FIGURE 5-1 (b) Square steel adjustable post.

together. The cross-sectional area depends on the load to be carried, but usually 6 × 6(140 × 140 mm) will prove ample. One factor governing the size will be the width of the beam. One dimension of the post should be equal to that width in order to provide full bearing.

A steel post, round or square, will be smaller in cross section as a wood post. It must be capped with a steel plate to provide a suitable bearing area and will include an internal thread so that a short, heavy stem may be threaded into it [see Figs. 5-1(a) and 5-1(b)]. These posts are also equipped with holes through which a rod can be inserted at various elevations so that the post can be adjusted in length. This is a decided advantage, because the post can be adjusted to the exact length required on installation, and later if the beam shrinks in its depth, the post can be lengthened by adjusting the top threaded rod to take up the shrinkage.

The location of these posts depends on the total floor load and the size of the beam. Local building codes determine this spacing.

Beams

Beams may be made of wood or steel, but a wood beam has been most popular for light construction. In some cases it is built up of a number of $1\frac{1}{2}$-in. (38-mm) material laminated together, although it may be one solid piece of timber. When the beam is laminated, care must be taken in its construction. Pieces may be nailed, bolted, or factory-manufactured by gluing thin layers of wood together, the latter method providing the most rigid unit [see Fig. 5-2(a)]. Another type of beam is manufactured by gluing strands of wood together under pressure [see Fig. 5-2(d)]. Both types of manufactured beams can be purchased at various lengths and are fully engineered to support designated loads.

When assembling a built-up beam, rarely will it be possible to find pieces long enough to reach from one end of the beam to the other, and consequently pieces must be end-jointed, usually with butt joints. Individual laminations must be selected or cut to such a length that the joints will occur directly over posts [see Fig. 5-2(b)]. When this is not possible, some codes will allow joints within 6 in. (150 mm) of the quarter point in the span [see Fig. 5-2(c)]. If nails are

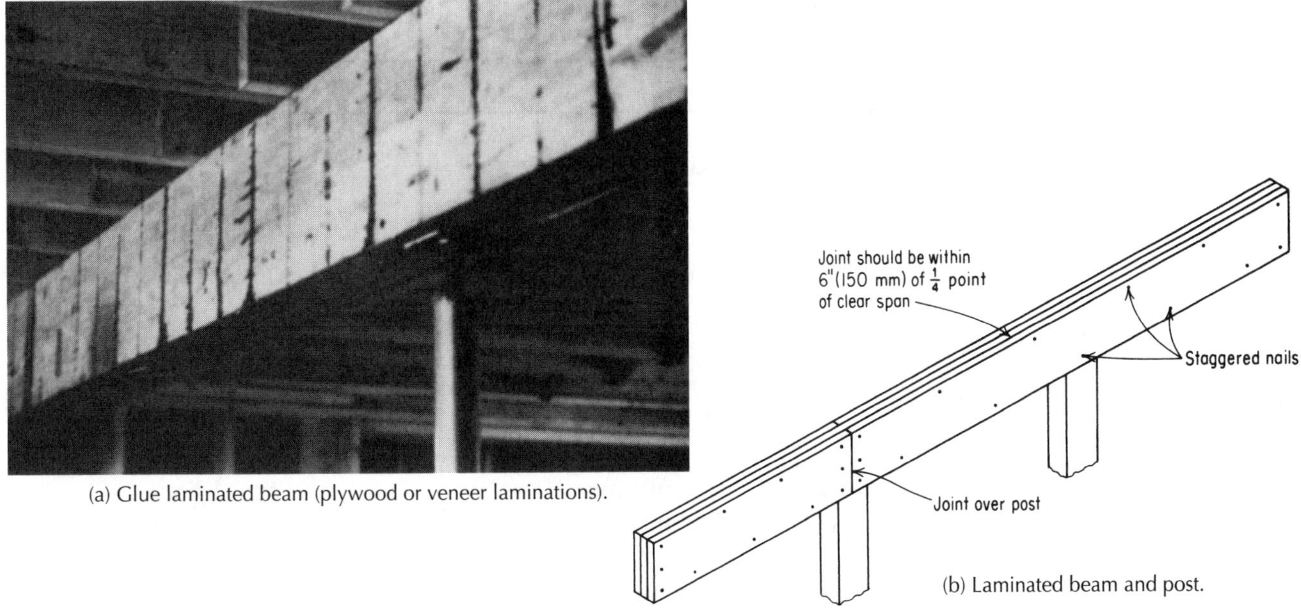

(a) Glue laminated beam (plywood or veneer laminations).

(b) Laminated beam and post.

(d) Parallel strand beam.

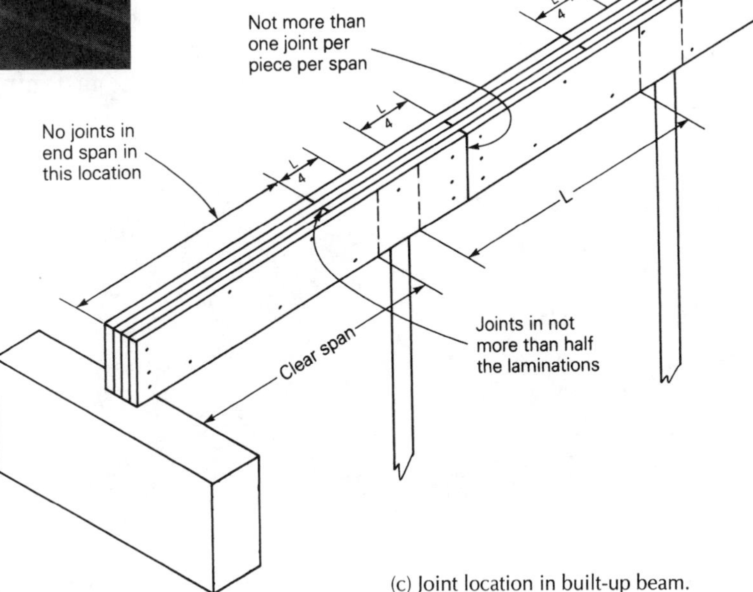

(c) Joint location in built-up beam.

FIGURE 5-2

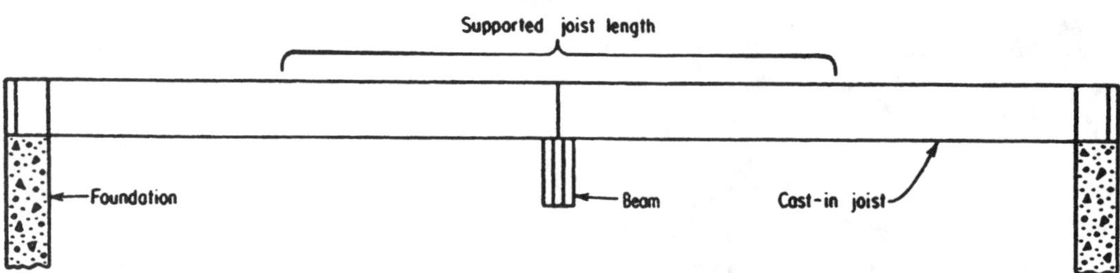

FIGURE 5-3 Supported joist length.

used in laminating, they should be spaced not more than 16 in. (450 mm) apart in double rows, one near the top and one near the bottom of the beam, as illustrated in Fig. 5-2(b)]. In some cases an extra row of nails may be necessary along the centerline.

The size of the beam depends on the load it must support, the species and grade of lumber, and the spacing of the posts. The load is determined by the *supported joist length* that is defined as being one-half the width of the building, or one half the span of joists on each side of the beam (see Fig. 5-3). Using these factors, the maximum allowable *clear span* (measurement from face of support to face of support) of the beam or, in other words, the maximum allowable spacing of posts, is determined. Local building code tables give the maximum allowable free spans for wooden beams that support one or more floors.

Steel Beam

A steel beam for light construction may be a *standard* or *wide flange rolled shape* (see Fig. 5-4).

Several depths of rolled shapes are commonly used, the number of supports (posts) required being determined by the imposed load. If the joists rest on top of the beam, a wood plate is generally used to facilitate fastening the joist ends to the beam, and the height

(a) Steel beam.

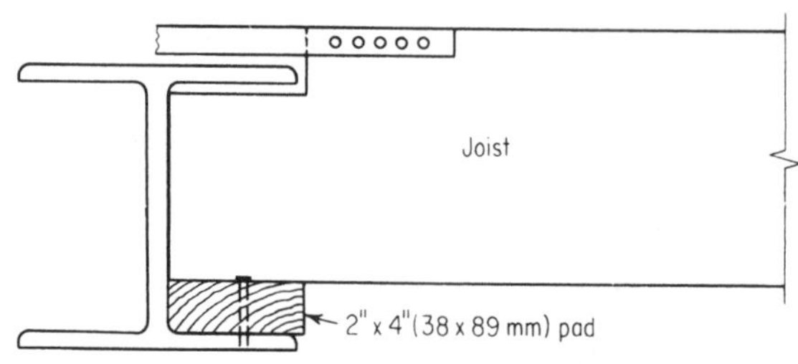

(b) Steel beam supporting joist ends.

FIGURE 5-4

(c) Steel beam and post.

FIGURE 5-4

of the beam must be regulated accordingly [see Fig. 5-4(a)]. Another method is to have the joist ends carried by the bottom flange of the beam, as illustrated in Fig. 5-4(b). In the latter case, the joists must be joined over the beam using 2 × 2 (38 × 38) lumber at least 2 ft (600 mm) in length.

BEARING WALLS

Bearing walls can be used in place of posts and beams. As discussed in Chapter 4, a continuous footing is required to support these walls. The material must be 2 × 6 (38 × 140 mm), minimum, with top and bottom plates and studs spaced not more than 16 in. (400 mm) o.c. (see Fig. 5-5). At the midpoint between top and bottom, blocks must be fitted snugly between the studs, staggered if required, to facilitate nailing, as illustrated in Fig. 5-5. If the wall is covered with finishing material, this blocking is not required. The double top plate must be level with the top of the sill plate or with the bottom edge of the joists, depending on how the floor joists join the exterior foundation walls.

When an opening occurs in the bearing wall, it must be framed with a lintel across the top (see Fig. 5-5) to comply with local building codes. Often it is made with two 2 × 8 (38 × 184 mm) members, if the opening is not more than 4 ft (1200 mm) wide.

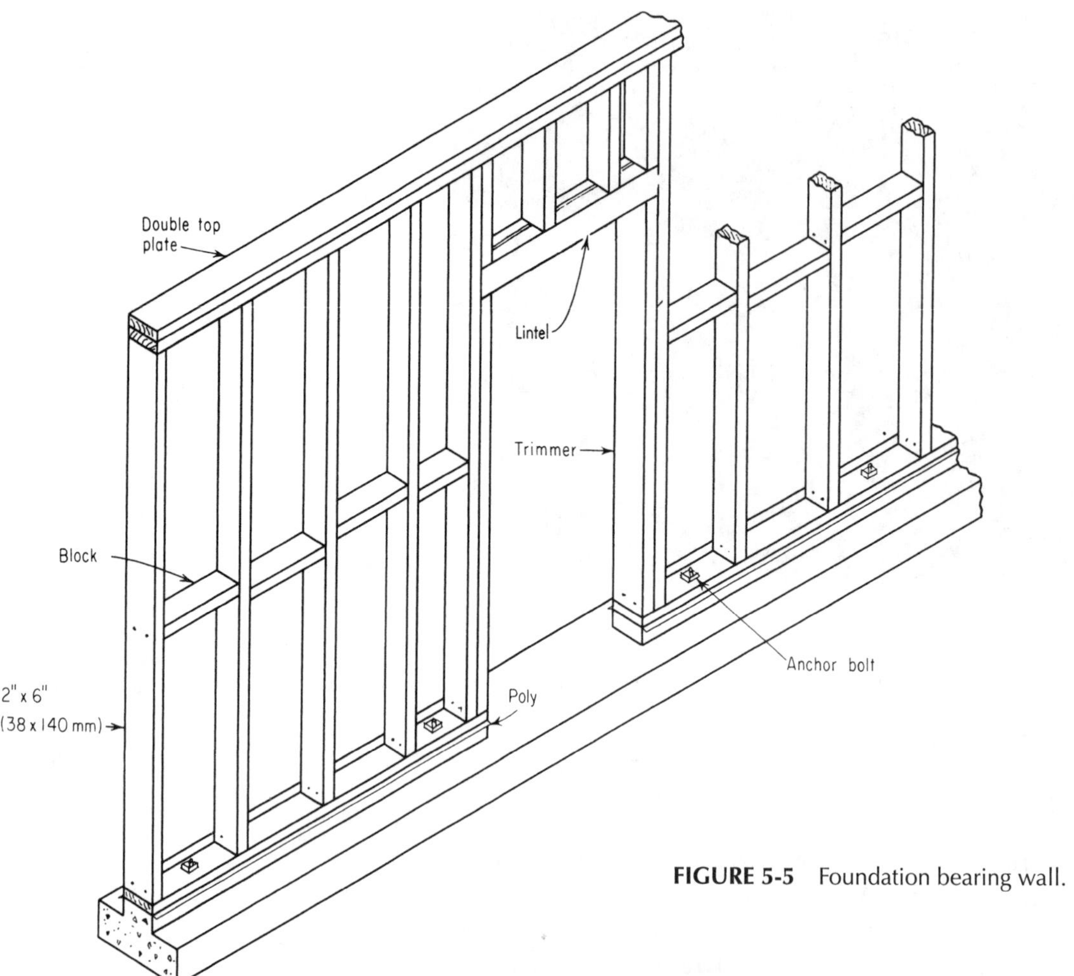

FIGURE 5-5 Foundation bearing wall.

FOUNDATION WALL-FLOOR FRAME CONNECTION

When a concrete foundation wall is used, a wood sill is either anchored to or cast into the foundation wall to provide a nailing surface for the floor joists. The sill plate is anchored to the top of wall by casting anchor bolts [see Fig. 5-6(a)] or metal nailing straps [see Fig. 5-6(b)] into the concrete. A sill gasket is placed under the sill plate to seal the junction between the wood and concrete (see Fig. 5-7). This method is also used when the foundation wall is constructed with concrete blocks.

Another way to provide a good connection is to cast a wood ladder into the top of the foundation wall, as illustrated in Fig. 5-8. In some areas floor joists are embedded into the top of the foundation wall providing a strong connection as discussed in Chapter 4.

JOISTS

Floor joists are the members that span from foundation wall to beam or in some cases from wall to wall or beam to beam, and that transfer building loads to those support members. Joists may be wood or

(a) Sill plate anchored with anchor bolts.

(b) Metal straps for anchoring sill plate.

FIGURE 5-6

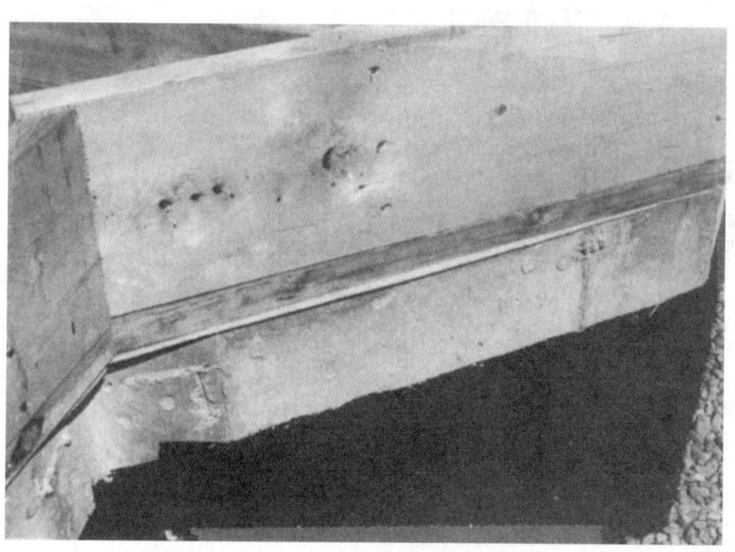

FIGURE 5-7 Sill gasket.

FIGURE 5-8 Ladder-type sill plate.

FIGURE 5-9 Solid wood joists.

steel. Wood joists have been widely used, particularly in residential construction (see Fig. 5-9), but manufactured wood joists are quite popular as they are lighter, available in various lengths, and maintain their straightness better with less deflection than solid wood joists [see Fig. 5-10(a)]. When manufactured joists are used the header is usually a 1-in. (25-mm) thick member of the same material as the joist web [see Fig. 5-10(b)]. Steel joists are also used in some areas, particularly for long spans (see Fig. 5-11).

Manufactured joists are available in a wide variety of sizes and shapes. Some advantages for using these joists include long spans with minimum intermediate support, and minimal deflection to keep floors stiff with little or no "squeaks." They can be erected much faster than solid lumber joists. Manufacturers will provide span data for their joists that have been designed by professional engineers to comply with building codes.

(b) Manufactured joists.

(a) Prefabricated wood joists.

FIGURE 5-10

FIGURE 5-11 Steel joists.

Wood Joists

Wood joists consist of 2-in. (38-mm) material, varying in widths from 6 to 12 in. (140–286 mm), depending on their load, length, spacing, and the species and grade of lumber. Common spacing is 12, 16, and 24 in. (300, 400, and 600 mm) o.c. Building codes give maximum spans for floor joists for residential construction based on lumber species and grade, and joist spacing.

For buildings other than residential, with heavier loads, a structural engineer must design the size of joists.

Joist Framing

Two systems are used for assembling joists—the *cast-in* system, previously described in Chapter 4, and the *box sill* system, in which the whole assembly is mounted on top of the foundation wall, secured to a plate or ladder sill. Most floor systems utilize the boxed sill, particularly when manufactured joists are being used.

In the box system, joists are held in position at the foundation wall by the *header joists*, sometimes called *rim joists*, running at right angles to the regular joists and bearing on the sill plate (see Fig. 5-12). At the inner end, the joists may be carried *on top* of the beam, or, where more headroom is needed under the beam, supported by joist hangers [see Figs. 5-13(a) and 5-13(b)]. When using solid lumber joists, care must be taken to allow for shrinkage of the material when a joist hanger supports them. The top edge of the joists must be above the beam level, or differential shrinkage will cause an uneven floor (see Fig. 5-14).

Where non-load-bearing partitions are to be placed parallel with the floor joists, they must bear on joists or on blocking between the joists. This blocking should be a minimum of 2 × 4 (38 × 89 mm)

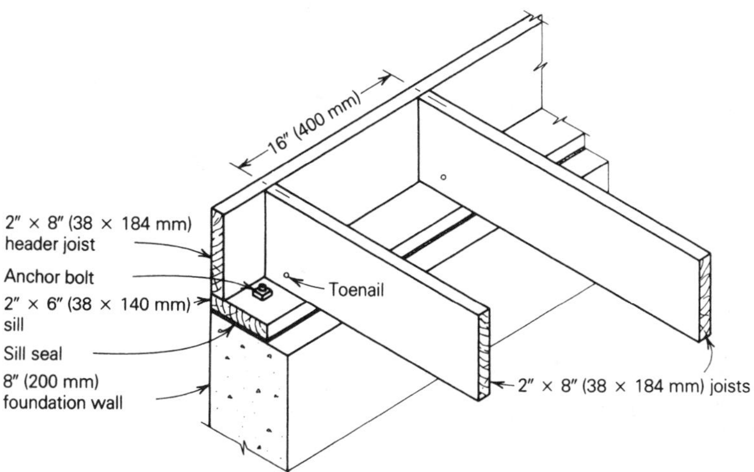

FIGURE 5-12 Joist framing at foundation wall.

(a) Lapped.

(b) Butted joist with hangers.

FIGURE 5-13

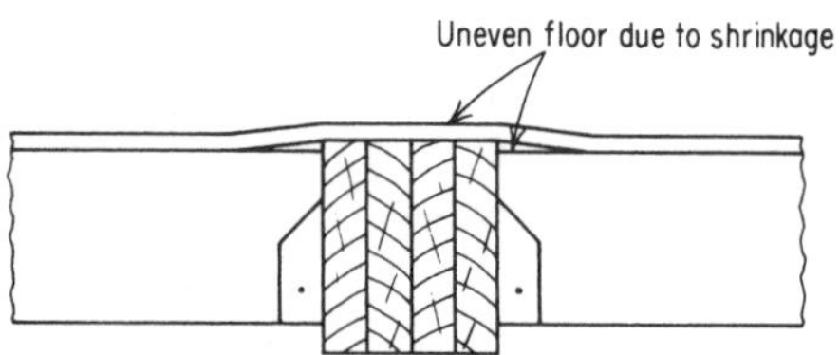

FIGURE 5-14 Differential shrinkage.

lumber that is spaced not more than 4 ft, 0 in. (1.2 m) on center. However, often the same size of joist material is used for this blocking (see Fig. 5-15). Interior non-load-bearing walls placed at right angles to the joists are not limited as to their location.

Beams or loadbearing walls must support loadbearing partitions that are parallel to the joists. Loadbearing partitions at right angles to the floor joists must be located not more than 3 ft (1 m) from the joist support when the wall does not support an upper floor and not more than 2 ft (600 mm) when the wall supports one or more upper floors unless floor joists have been designed to carry the concentrated loads as prescribed by building codes.

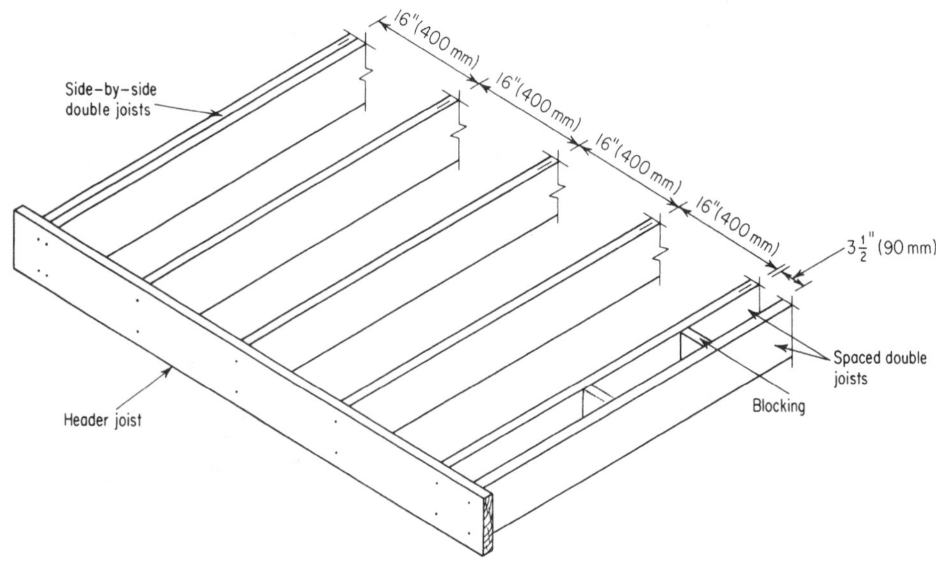

FIGURE 5-15 Partition support.

Openings in the floor frame for a stairwell or where a chimney or fireplace comes through the floor must be framed in the proper way. Trimmer joists are doubled if they support header joists more than 32 in. (800 mm) long. Header joists longer than 48 in. (1.2 m) should also be doubled. Trimmer joists that support header joists more than 6 ft (2 m) long and header joists that are more than 10 ft, 8 in. (3.2 m) long should be designed according to accepted engineering practice. Joist hangers are used to support long joist headers and tail joists (see Fig. 5-16). Most codes require that a chimney opening be at least 2 in. (50 mm) larger on all sides than the dimensions of the chimney and that the framing be kept back 4 in. (100 mm) from the back of a fireplace. See Chapter 8 for stairwell opening calculations.

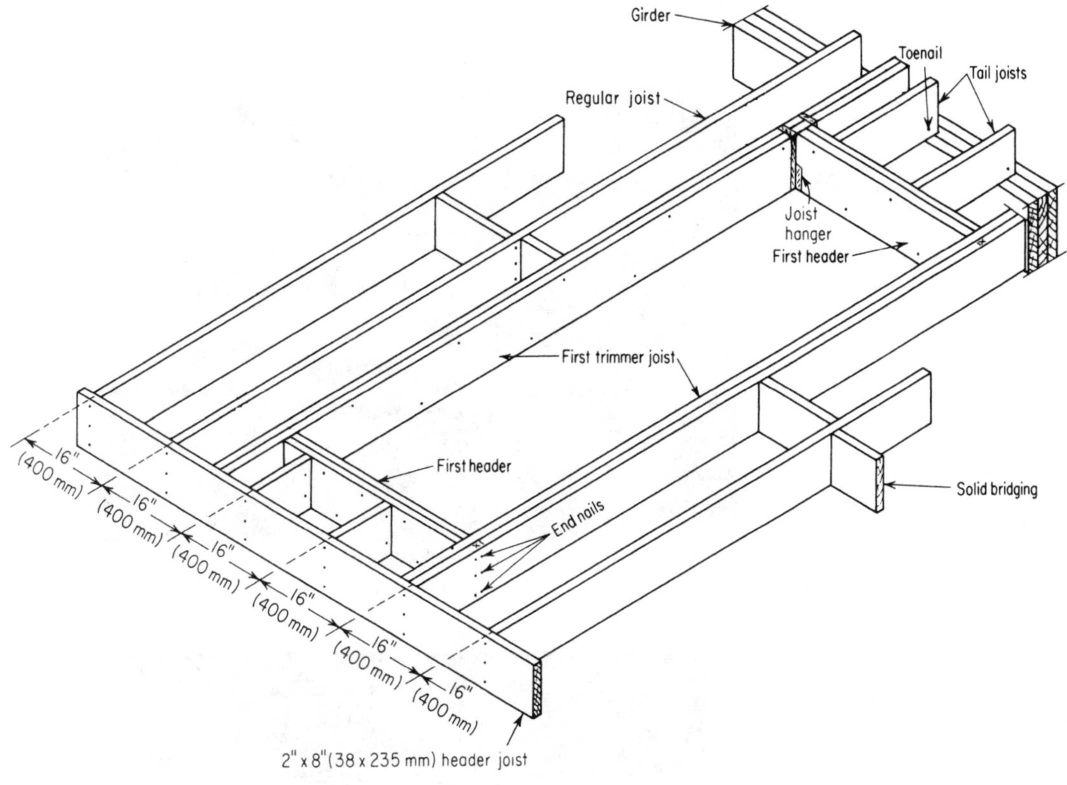

FIGURE 5-16 Stairwell opening.

Bridging

It is important that joists be prevented from twisting after they are in place and, unless board type *ceiling* finish is installed on the underside, restraint must be provided, both at end supports and at intervals not exceeding 7 ft (2.1 m) between supports. At the end supports, the restraint is provided by toenailing the joists to the supports and by end nailing through the header joist.

Bridging provides the intermediate restraint, and may be in the form of *solid blocking* between joists, *cross bridging*, or *wood strapping*. The solid blocking will be pieces of $1\frac{1}{2}$-in. (38-mm) material or manufactured joist material the same depth as the joists and may be *offset* one-half their thickness to facilitate end nailing (see Fig. 5-16), or blocks of 2 × 4(38 × 89 mm) nailed into the lower edge of the joists [see Fig. 5-17(a)]. Cross bridging is made from 2 × 2-(38 × 38-mm) [see Fig. 5-17(b)], 2 × 4-(38 × 89-mm) [see Fig. 5-17(c)], or 1 × 3-(19 × 64-mm) material. Continuous wood strapping nailed to the underside of the joists or blocking between is the easiest way to provide intermediate joist restraint. The use of bridging or a combination of bridging and strapping allows an increase in the maximum span permitted with some sizes of floor joists, as bridging helps to transfer loads from one joist to another. Check your local code restrictions for spans in your area.

(a) Block bridging.

(b) 2 × 2 cross bridging.

FIGURE 5-17

Joist Assembly

Setting the joists in their proper location, nailing them securely in place, and providing the extra framing necessary for concentrated loads and frame rigidity are very important steps in the framing of a building. The following procedure is typical for solid wood joists, but it will be similar for manufactured joists although the manufacturer will generally provide advice and drawings when necessary.

Joist Layout

1. Study the plans to check the location and centers of the joists. Note where they are to be doubled and if the doubling will be side-by-side or separated.
2. Select straight header joists and mark them off according to the plans. Be sure that joints in the header joist occur at the center of a regular joist (see Fig. 5-18). Note that if joists are to be *lapped* at the beam, the header joist lay-off on the two opposite sides of the building will have to be offset from one another by the thickness of the joists. Where joists are to be supported on beams or bearing walls, the location marks for the joists must correspond to the header joists.
3. Check for the number of full-length regular joists required, square one end and cut them to length, unless they are to be lapped.
4. For box sill construction, toenail the header joists in place on the sill plate.
5. Where joist hangers are to be used, nail them in place on the beam, in line with the header joist layout.
6. Position all the regular joists on one side of the building. Set them in position *with the crown up*, and *end nail* into them through the header joist.
7. Repeat with the regular joists on the opposite side and if joists lap at the beam, nail the two together along the lap.
8. Check the plans for the location of floor openings and mark on the joist header the location of the trimmer joists. Set only one trimmer on each side of the opening to allow the opening header to be end nailed in place.

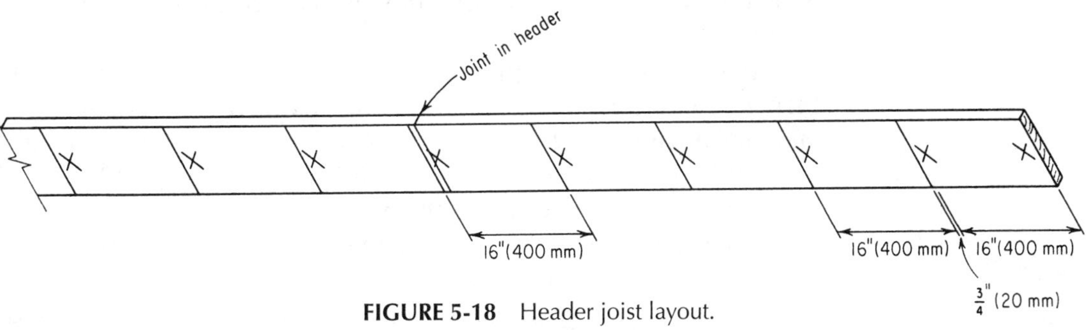

FIGURE 5-18 Header joist layout.

9. Mark these trimmer joists for header positions (see Fig. 5-16), cut headers to exact length and end nail in place.
10. Add the second trimmer if doubling is required.
11. Add the second header if doubling is required.
12. Cut tail joists to exact length and nail them in place *on regular centers*.
13. Locate the position of walls running parallel to floor joists and nail blocking at those locations (see Fig. 5-15).
14. Space the top edges of the joists properly over the beam using a 1 × 4(19 × 89) nailing strip to hold them in place, and then toenail to beam (see Fig. 5-9).
15. Mark the centerline of the bridging with a chalk line [not more than 7 ft (2.1 m) from end supports] and nail bridging to the line.

Manufactured Wood Joists and Truss Systems

As mentioned before, manufactured systems provide greater clear spans and are lighter in weight and straighter than conventional framing. This will provide a flatter floor and straighter ceilings below, and as the chord members are wider than standard joists, the need for strapping is eliminated. Wood prefabricated members are in the form of a wooden I-beam or a flat truss as shown in Figs. 5-10(a) and (b).

Heating ducts, plumbing pipes, and electrical wires are easily incorporated into the joist systems. Trusses utilizing metal webs have many large openings allowing room for services. Holes are easily cut into the webs of I-beams of plywood or waferboard. Holes $1\frac{1}{2}$ in. (38 mm) can be cut anywhere in the web, but larger holes can only be placed according to the manufacturer's specifications. In most cases the manufacturer will provide a chart to be posted on the job site to assist the framers or those workers installing services, as well as for building inspectors. Improperly positioned holes could seriously weaken the joists.

In a manufactured joist floor frame, the joist header can be $\frac{3}{8}$ in., $\frac{3}{4}$ in., or 1 in. (9.5, 19, or 25 mm) material, the same material as the joist web. Figure 5-19 illustrates a typical way in which the floor is assembled, but this information is usually available from the manufacturer.

Placement of these prefabricated joists is much easier and faster than standard joists since fewer are needed. They are much lighter, and they do not need to be supported until fastened to the joist header. Standard spacing for prefabricated I-beam joists are 12, 16, 19.2, and 24 in. (300, 400, 480, and 600 mm). Bridging also can be eliminated when using I-beam floor joists. Longer spans are available, reducing or eliminating the need for beams in the floor frame. The straightness of the joists and their lack of shrinkage also reduce

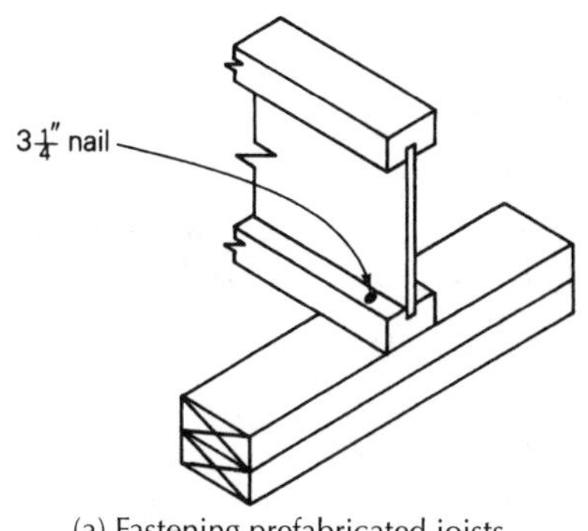

(a) Fastening prefabricated joists.

(b) Fastening joist header.

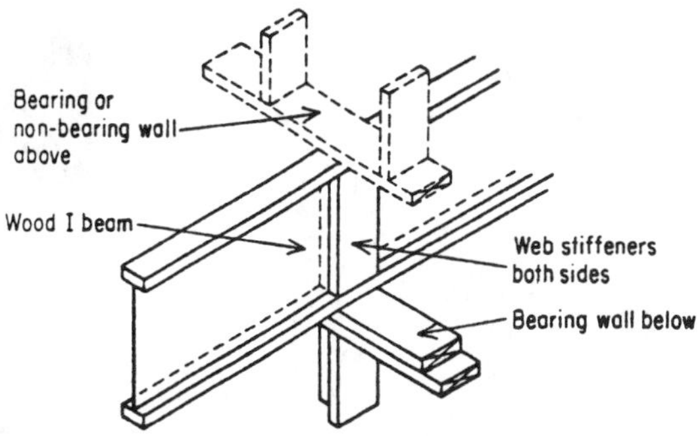

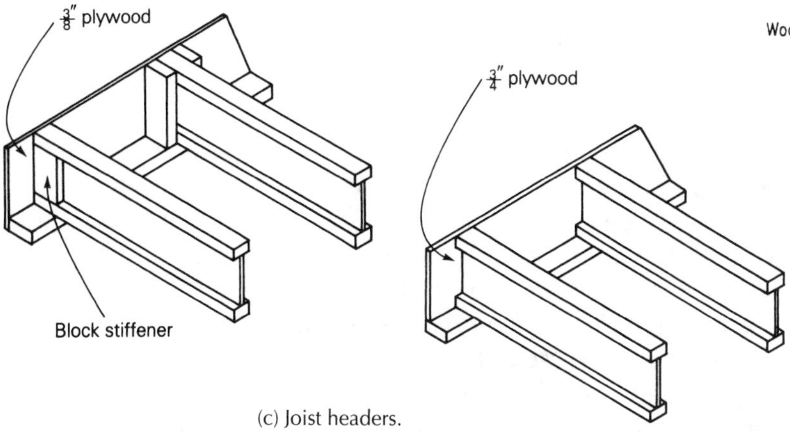

$\frac{3}{8}''$ plywood

Block stiffener

$\frac{3}{4}''$ plywood

(c) Joist headers.

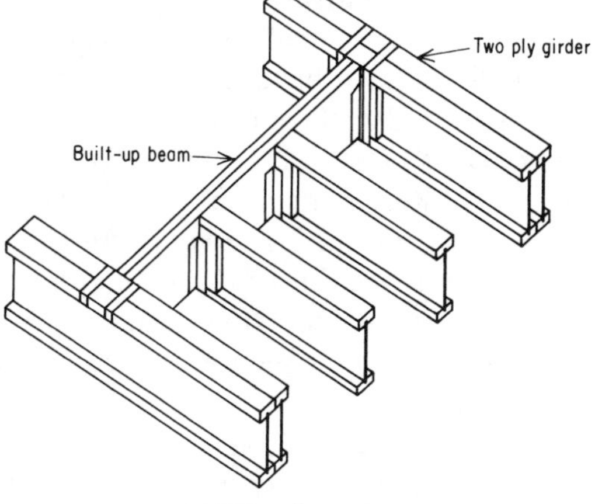

Bearing or non-bearing wall above

Wood I beam

Web stiffeners both sides

Bearing wall below

(d) Joist stiffeners.

Two ply girder

Built-up beam

(e) Stairwell opening.

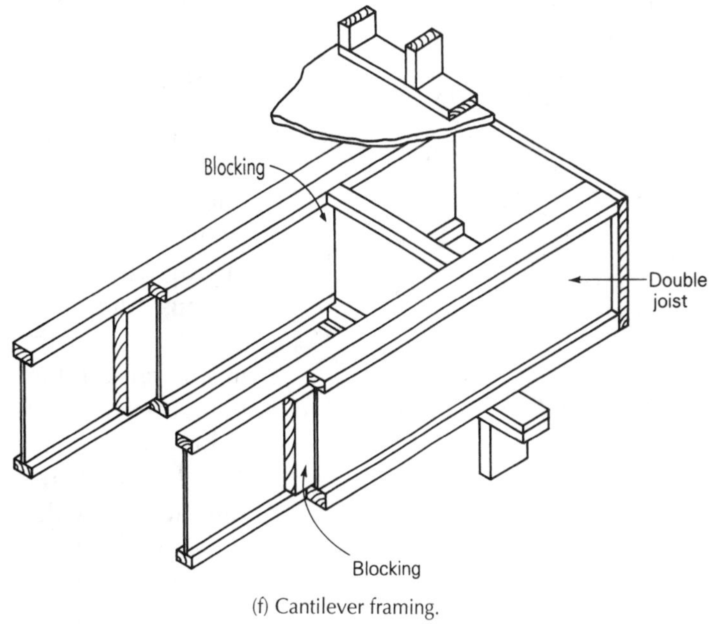

Blocking

Double joist

Blocking

(f) Cantilever framing.

FIGURE 5-19

FIGURE 5-20 Bridging open web joists.

the potential for squeaky floors. Care must be taken not to walk on the joists until they are adequately braced, as they are unstable.

Another type of prefabricated joist floor system uses a member known as a *steel web truss*. The trusses' upper and lower chords are 2 × 4s(38 × 89 mm), and the web members are made of tubular steel. Spans up to 38 ft (12.6 m) are possible, depending on the loading and spacing of trusses. The top chord supports these trusses and spacing is usually 24 in. o.c. (600 mm). Bridging is required with this type of truss to make the entire bay act as a single unit (see Fig. 5-20).

Steel Joists

Steel joists of various kinds are available for use in place of wood joists and are particularly useful where relatively long spans are required. They are all prefabricated units, some made in various depths to suit various span requirements. Steel joists have greater loadbearing capacity than equivalently sized wood joists, and can be used with various other materials as illustrated in Figs. 5-21(a) and 5-21(b).

One type, the cold-formed steel joist, is made from sheet steel in several standard depths as shown in Fig. 5-22. The *nested joist section* is used as a trimmer joist at floor openings, and the *perimeter closure section* is used as a rim joist in an all-steel floor frame.

In an all-steel floor frame, the perimeter section is secured to the sill plate with screws or staples, and the regular joists are normally secured to the perimeter section (see Fig. 5-23) at 16 in. (400 mm) o.c. with screws. The other ends of the joists rest on the center beam or bearing wall and are provided with *web stiffeners*, as shown in Fig. 5-23, in order to develop the required web strength.

(a) Steel joist with wood header. (Courtesy U.S. Steel Corp.)

(b) Steel joists with concrete floor.

FIGURE 5-21

Floor openings in steel frame construction are framed in much the same way as in wood frame construction. The *nested joist section* is used in place of double trimmers and headers around the opening, and the tail joists are supported by *hangers* (see Fig. 5-24) that are held in place by screws.

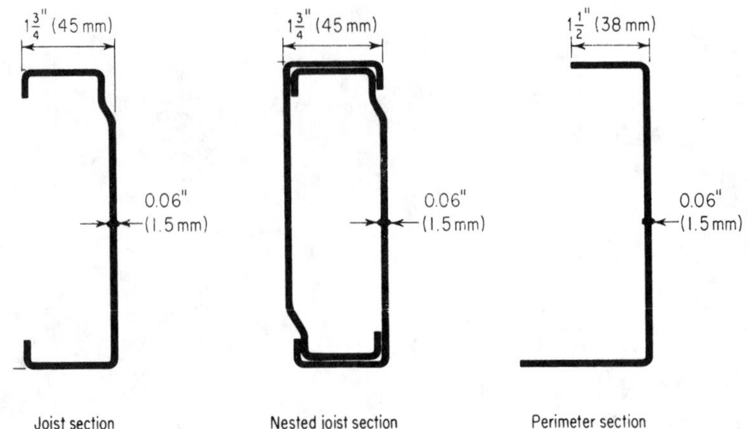

FIGURE 5-22 Cold-formed steel joist shapes.

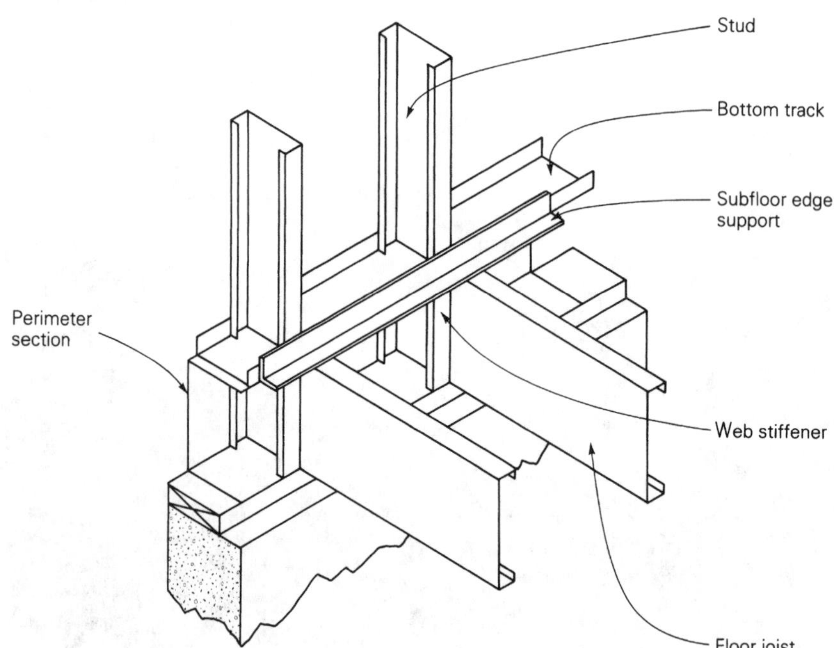

FIGURE 5-23 Steel floor framing.

Steel joists may be *recessed* into the top of the foundation to provide a *flush floor*. The recessing may be done by lowering the sill plate into the top, inner edge of the foundation wall, as illustrated in Fig. 5-25. This method leaves part of the upper surface of the foundation exposed as a base for brick veneer exterior finish.

When the lowered sill plate method is used, joists are provided with end clips or stiffeners and secured to the sill plate by screws through their bottom edge.

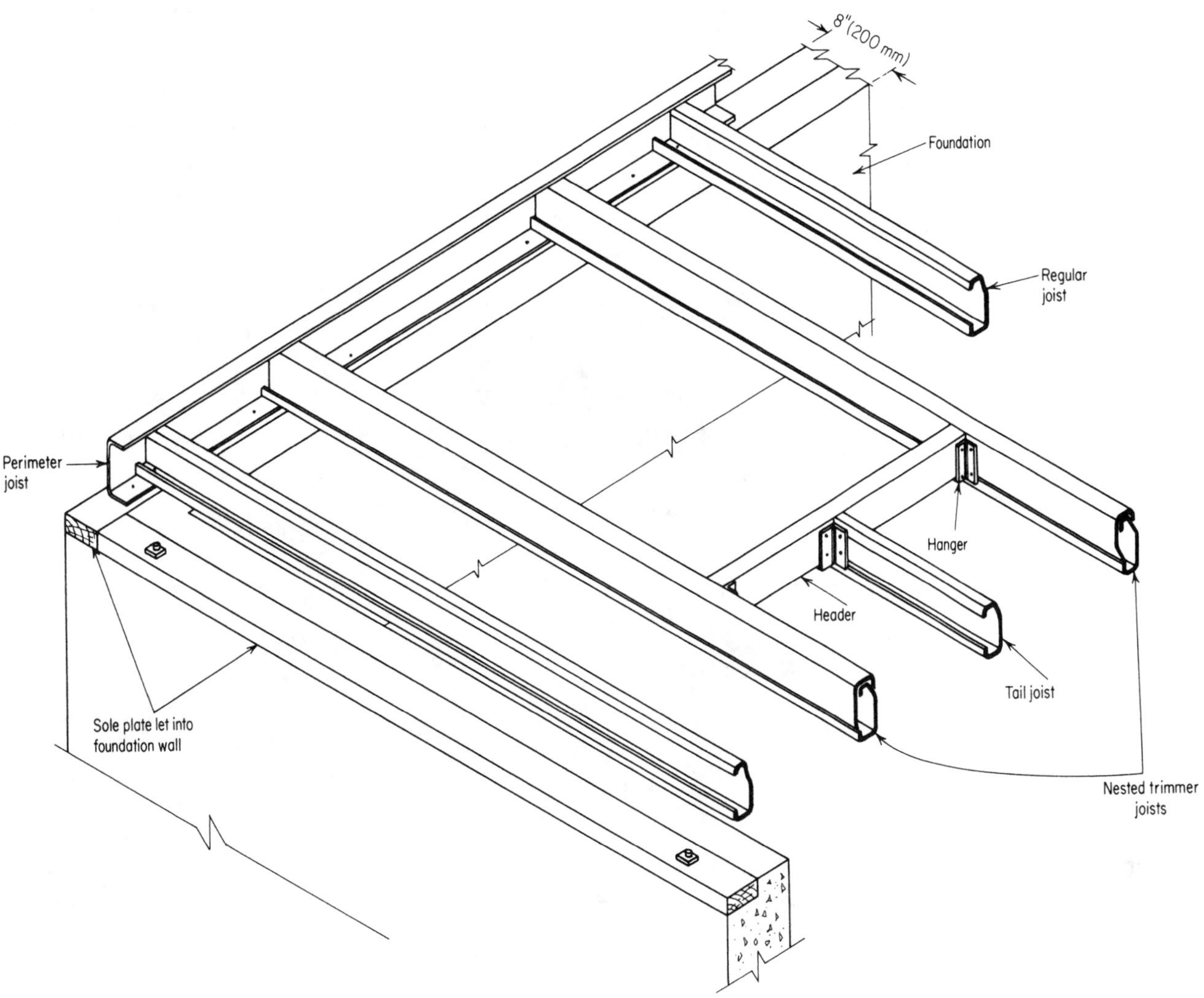

8"(200 mm)
Foundation
Regular joist
Perimeter joist
Hanger
Header
Tail joist
Sole plate let into foundation wall
Nested trimmer joists

FIGURE 5-24 Framed opening in steel floor frame.

Wall studs
Subfloor
Sole plate
Base for brick veneer
Joist end stiffener
2" x 4" (38 x 89 mm) sill plate
8"(200 mm)
Anchor bolt
Steel joists

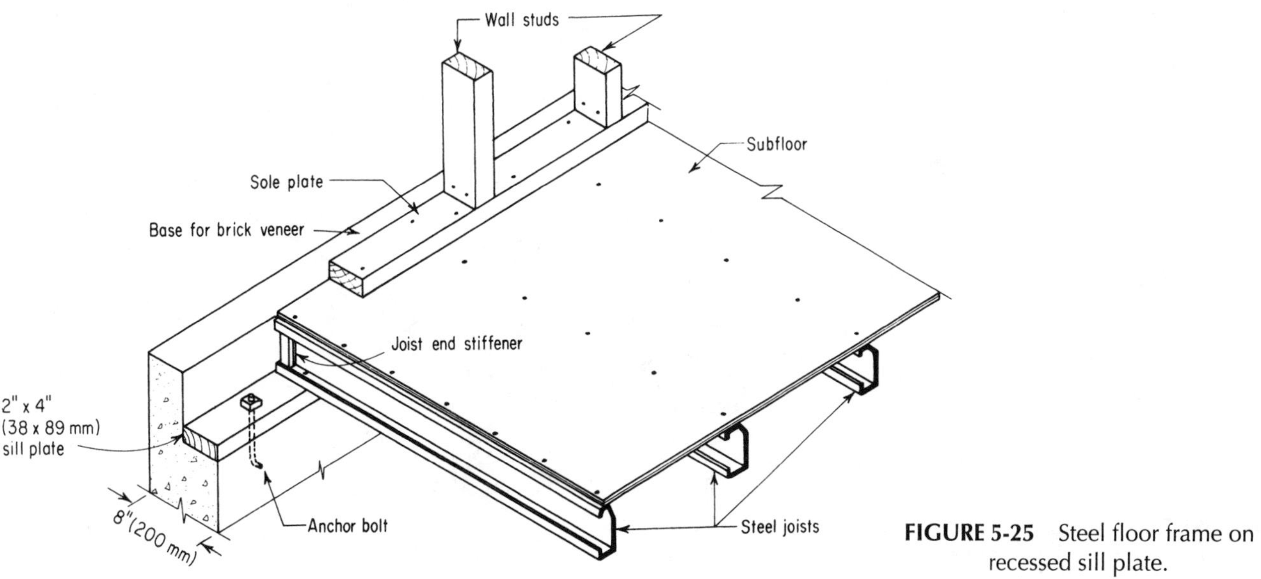

FIGURE 5-25 Steel floor frame on recessed sill plate.

Floor Framing at Projections

Floor joists occasionally project beyond the foundation wall to provide support for bay windows or additional floor space in upper rooms (see Fig. 5-26). The amount of cantilever projection is specified in building codes. The space between the floor joists should be left open to allow for circulation of warm air so even floor temperature occurs throughout the room (see Fig. 5-27). When the regular

FIGURE 5-26 Cantilever projection (extension of prefabricated joists).

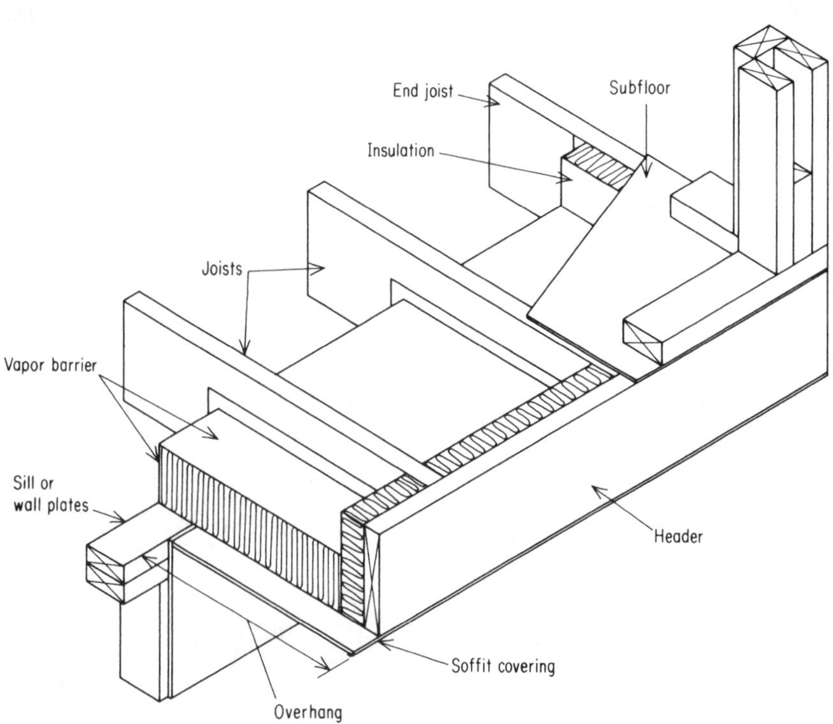

FIGURE 5-27 Cantilever projection insulation in cold climates.

FIGURE 5-28 Cantilever joists at right angles to main joists.

floor joists are perpendicular to the projection, the joists must be long enough to include the cantilever portion as illustrated in Fig. 5-26. However, if the floor joists are parallel to the projection, cantilevered joists must be at right angles to the regular joists (see Fig. 5-28). In this case the joists must extend inward at least six times the amount of projection and be joined to a double header. Again, local codes must be observed.

If the cantilever is to support floor loads above it, then design calculations are necessary to ensure the projection can safely carry the load (see Fig. 5-29).

FIGURE 5-29 Cantilever supporting wall above.

Framing for balconies can be the same method as for bay windows, but as less load is supported, the joists can project farther. Other methods of supporting balconies include an outer beam to provide support for the balcony framing. Bearing posts can also be installed, transferring the load of the balcony to lower floors or foundations (see Fig. 5-30). The top level is often trimmed 2 in. (50 mm) to compensate for decking, which still provides a break in the floor

FIGURE 5-30 Post and beam supporting a deck.

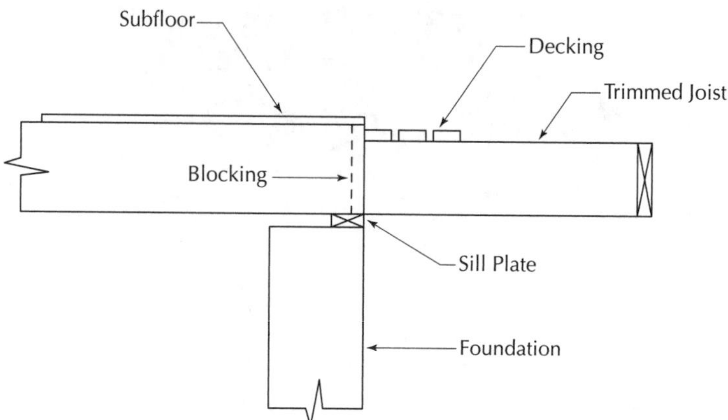

FIGURE 5-31 Cantilever joists trimmed for deck.

level and does not cause interference with the functioning of the balcony door (see Fig. 5-31).

SUBFLOOR

Laying the subfloor is the final step in completing the floor frame. If *center match* (tongue and groove), or *common boards* are used, then they should be laid at an angle of not less than 45° to the joists. If *plywood, oriented strand board* (OSB) or *waferboard* is used, the sheets are laid with the long dimension at right angles to the joists (see Figs. 5-32 and 5-33). *Particleboard* can only be used when it is applied in a factory setting where it cannot be exposed to the weather. Both OSB and waferboard are stamped with a "This Side Down" label along with applicable manufacturing and other required references such as standards and grade of product.

FIGURE 5-32 OSB subfloor.

FIGURE 5-33 Plywood subfloor installation.

The minimum thickness of subflooring must conform to local codes. The thickness required will depend on the spacing of the floor joists, but typically, if the joists are spaced at 16 in. (400 mm) on center then the thickness of boards will be $\frac{3}{4}$ in. (19 mm), and the thickness of panels will be $\frac{5}{8}$ in. (15.5 mm). However, much thicker panels are used in some cases and will provide a stiffer floor surface. If square-edge panels are used, blocking between the joists should support the long dimension of the panel. However, in most cases tongue and groove panels are used. The matching of the tongue with the groove in the panel is easier to achieve if the tongue is fed into the groove. This allows for hammering the joints together without damaging the tongue. A block of $2 \times 4 (38 \times 89$ mm) can be laid against the groove edge of the panel and then hammered with a sledgehammer without damaging the panel edge.

Nails for plywood, OSB, or waferboard subflooring must conform to local codes. In most cases, if common coated nails, spiral nails, or staples are used, they must be at least 2 in. (50 mm) long. If annular ring nails or screws are used, then the length need only be $1\frac{3}{4}$ in. (45 mm). The spacing of nails is required to be 6 in. (150 mm) o.c. along the ends of the sheet and 12 in. (300 mm) o.c. on intermediate supports. Annular ringed nails or screws will provide the superior holding power where future squeaking floors will be eliminated or at least minimized. To further provide a squeak-free floor, a subfloor adhesive is used to bond the panels to the joists (see Fig. 5-34).

Panel-type subflooring is attached to steel joists with steel joist nails or self-drilling tapping screws, using a power nailer for the nails or a power screw gun for the screws.

FIGURE 5-34 Applying subfloor adhesive.

REVIEW QUESTIONS

5–1. What is the advantage of using an adjustable steel bearing post to support the main beam in a floor frame?

5–2. Define the following terms:

a. Clear span.

b. Supported joist length.

5–3. At what locations in a built-up wood beam are butt joints allowed in the laminations?

5–4. Outline two primary reasons for using bridging.

5–5. What are three ways of connecting a wood floor frame to a concrete foundation wall?

5–6. What are the main advantages of using prefabricated wood joists in a floor frame?

Chapter 6

THE WALL FRAME

OBJECTIVES

Here is what you will be able to do when you complete each component of this chapter:

1. Identify the characteristics of a platform frame.
2. Analyze the purpose for frame components.
3. Describe how frame components are assembled.
4. Describe how to erect the frame.
5. Identify light steel framing.
6. Identify masonry wall framing options.

The most common system for framing walls is the *platform* frame as shown in Fig. 6-1. Occasionally you may encounter an older system called the *balloon* frame (see Fig. 6-2), particularly if you are involved in renovation work. The reason why the platform framing system is so popular is because shorter studs can be used and workers always have a platform or floor on which to work, particularly on buildings of two or more floor levels.

COMPONENT PARTS, PLATFORM FRAME

As illustrated in Fig. 6-1, a frame begins on top of the subfloor. The bottom member is the *sole plate* to which are attached *regular studs* one story in length, special arrangements of studs at corners, extra studs to which partitions are attached—*partition junctions*—and other shorter members. On top of these vertical members is a *top plate*, and on top of that there is a *cap plate*. Over door and window

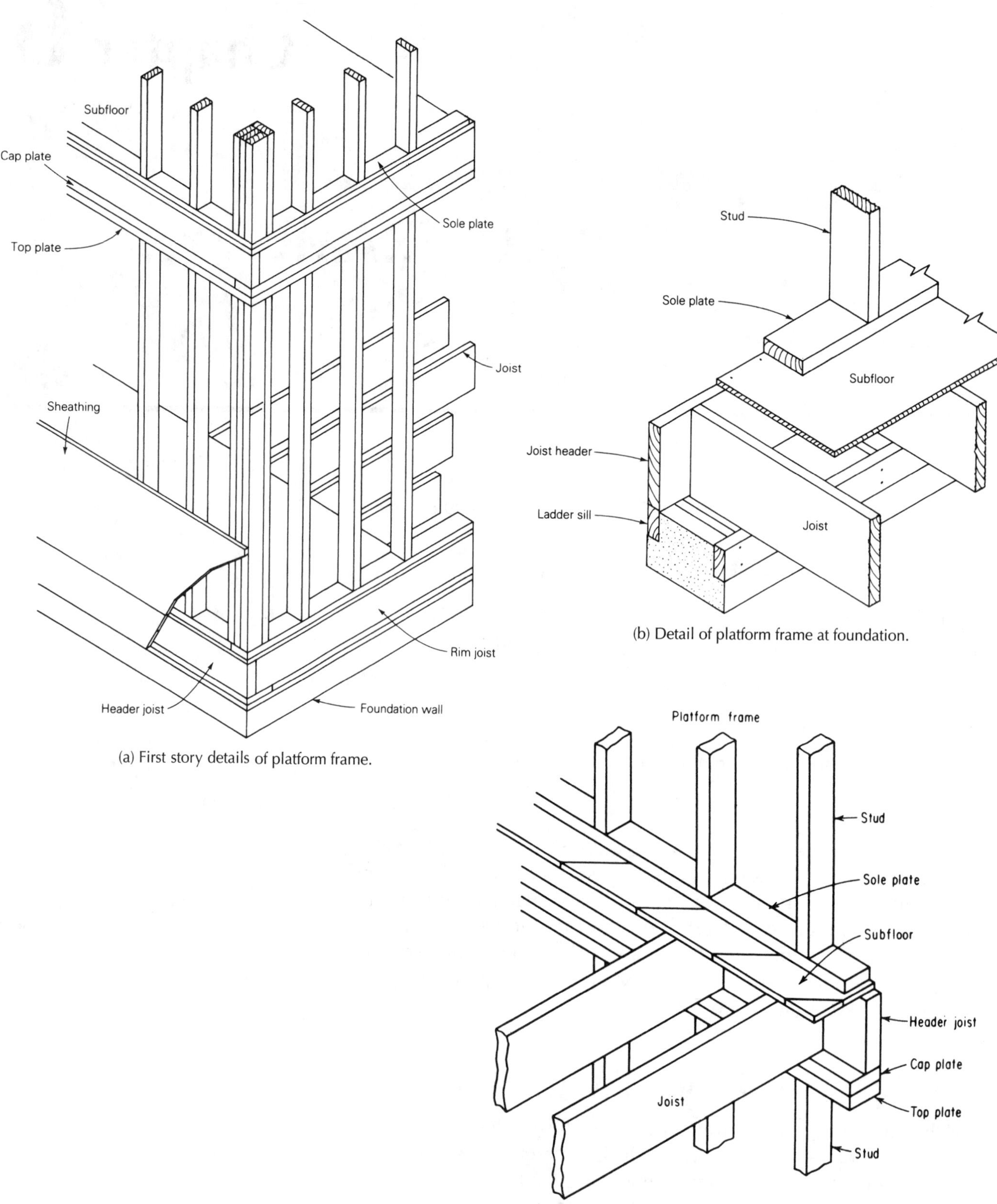

(a) First story details of platform frame.

(b) Detail of platform frame at foundation.

(c) Detail of platform frame at second floor.

FIGURE 6-1

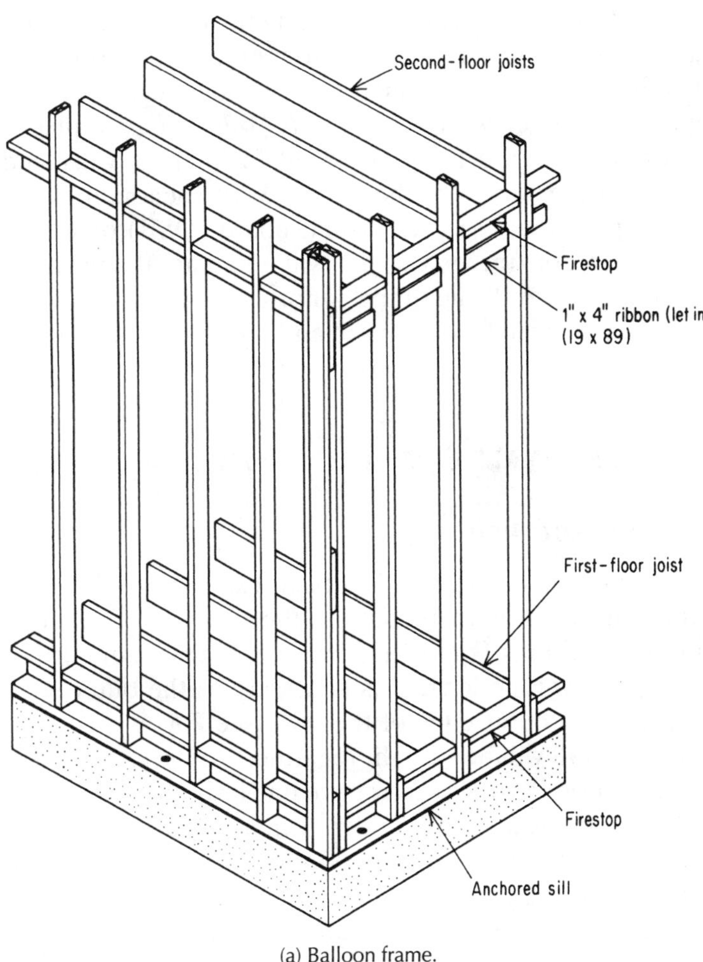

(a) Balloon frame.

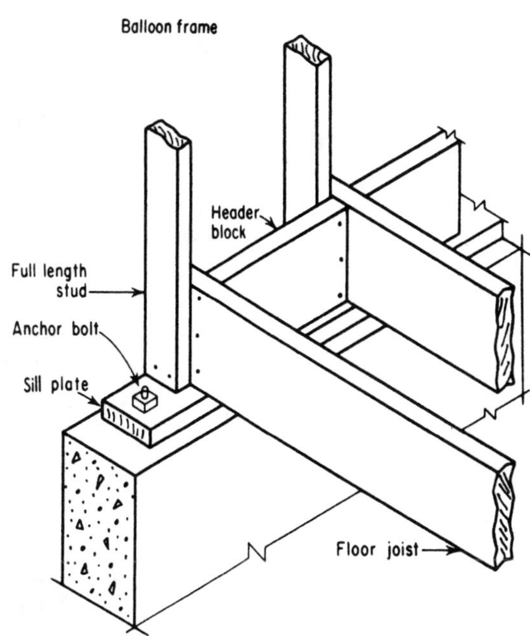

(b) Detail of balloon frame at foundation.

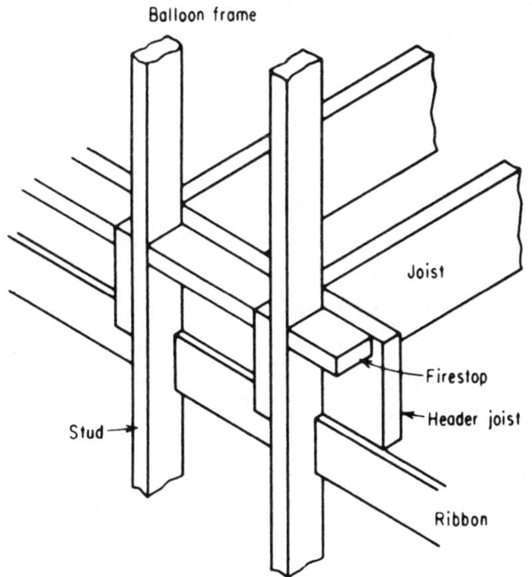

(c) Detail of balloon frame at second floor.

FIGURE 6-2

openings are *headers* or *lintels* and, supporting the ends of these are *trimmer studs.* A rough sill frames the bottom of a window opening, and the spaces between rough sill and sole plate and between header and top plate are framed with *cripple studs. Wall backing* is placed where sinks, drapes, etc. are to be attached to interior walls, and *sheathing* covers the exterior of the frame. Wall sheathing, when used, consists of plywood, Oriented strand board (OSB) or waferboard, gypsum board, or fiberboard that will eliminate the need for diagonal bracing. When wall sheathing is not used then some other method of keeping the wall frame square and rigid must be used.

PLATFORM FRAME WALL CONSTRUCTION

Wall and Partition Location

After the subfloor or concrete pad has been cleared of all debris, most builders snap chalk lines to outline the location of exterior walls and interior partitions. For exterior walls, only the inner edge of where the sole plate will be located is necessary as the outer edge will be in line with the outer edge of the wall [see Fig. 6-3(a)]. This line will ensure the wall will be straight regardless of the straightness of the edge of the floor. Partitions may have one or both edges of the sole plate outlined. In some cases builders will also mark with a felt pen the general location of windows and doors before the plates are laid out accurately [see Fig. 6-3(b)]. Where plumbing services penetrate the floor, such as in the case of a surface foundation, the exact location of the sole plate is laid out [see Figs. 6-3(c) and 6-3(d)] to ensure complete enclosure within the partition.

When a wood floor system is used, these plumbing and other services are usually installed later, after the walls and partitions have been erected.

Plate Layout

The first step in the construction of a wall is to *lay out* on the sole plate the exact location of each member required in that wall. They will include *corner posts, regular studs, opening trimmers, partition junctions*, and *cripple studs*. Since the location of the members on the top plate will be identical, the two plates are laid out together. One method is to proceed as follows:

1. Pick out straight stock for the plates; two or more pieces are probably required for each one. Set them out across the subfloor, side by side.
2. Square off one end of each plate and cut them to length. If more than one piece is needed, the end joints should be located in the center of a stud position.

(a) (b)

(c) (d)

FIGURE 6-3 (a) Chalk line for exterior wall location; (b) Chalk lines for interior partitions; (c) Chalk lines for partition inclusion of plumbing fixtures; (d) Chalk lines to place partitions for plumbing fixtures.

3. Check the plans for the locations of the centers of door and window openings. Mark these on the plates by a centerline, as illustrated in Fig. 6-4.
4. Measure on each side of the centerline one-half the width of the rough opening, and mark for trimmer studs outside these points (see Fig. 6-5). Use a "T" to indicate trimmer. Rough openings are determined by increasing the width of the door or

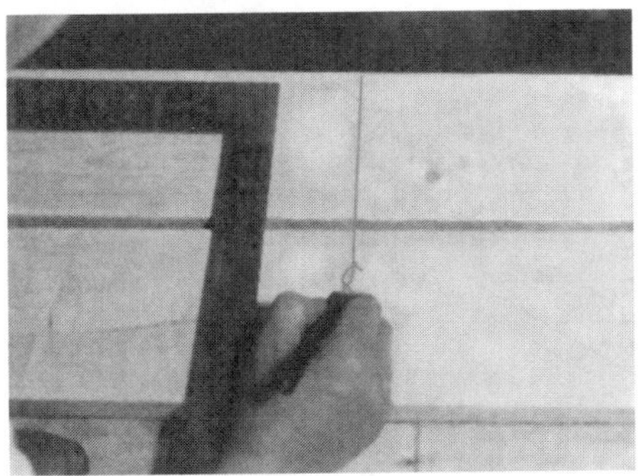

FIGURE 6-4 Centerline of opening.

FIGURE 6-5 Locating trimmer and regular stud.

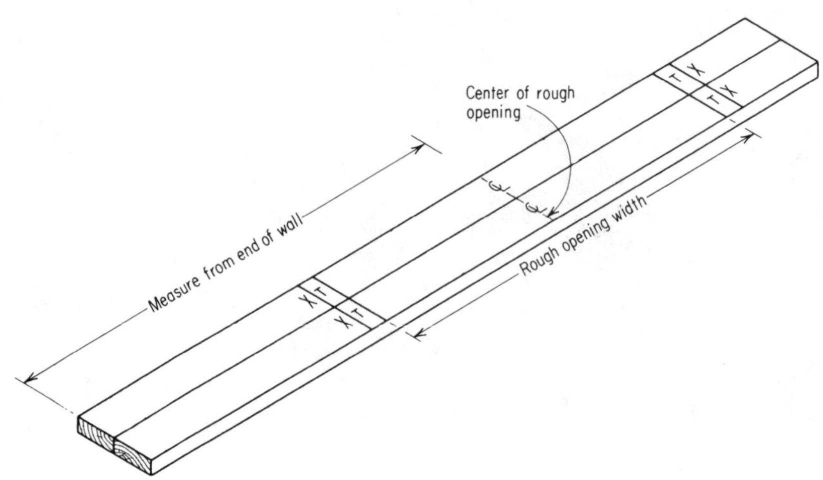

FIGURE 6-6 Layout for trimmer at rough opening.

window unit by the recommended clearances for fitting, usually $\frac{3}{4}$ in. (20 mm).

5. Outside the trimmer, use an "X" to indicate a full-length stud (see Fig. 6-6).
6. Check the plans for positions of partitions that intersect the wall and mark the position and framing needed (see Fig. 6-7). There are several ways to provide the necessary backing for partitions as discussed later.
7. Locate the positions of all the regular studs and mark with an "X," making sure the first space is $\frac{3}{4}$ in. (20 mm) smaller so panel sheathing joints will occur on studs [see Fig. 6-8(a)]; stud locations within an opening are marked with a "C" to indicate cripples.

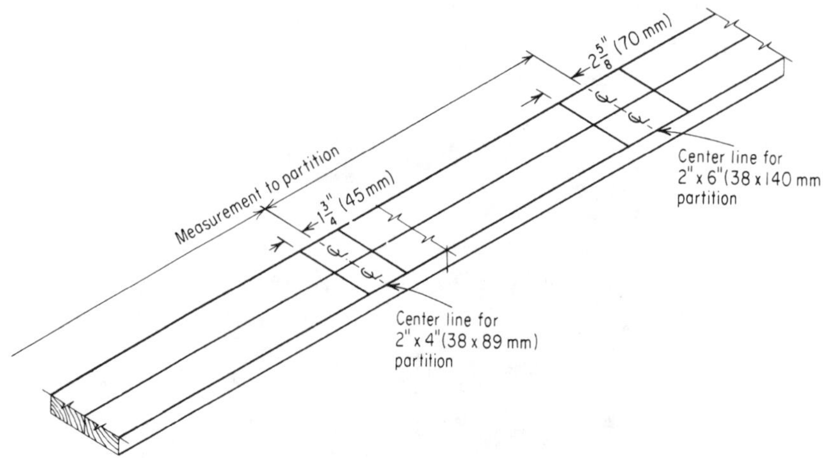

FIGURE 6-7 Layout for partition junctions.

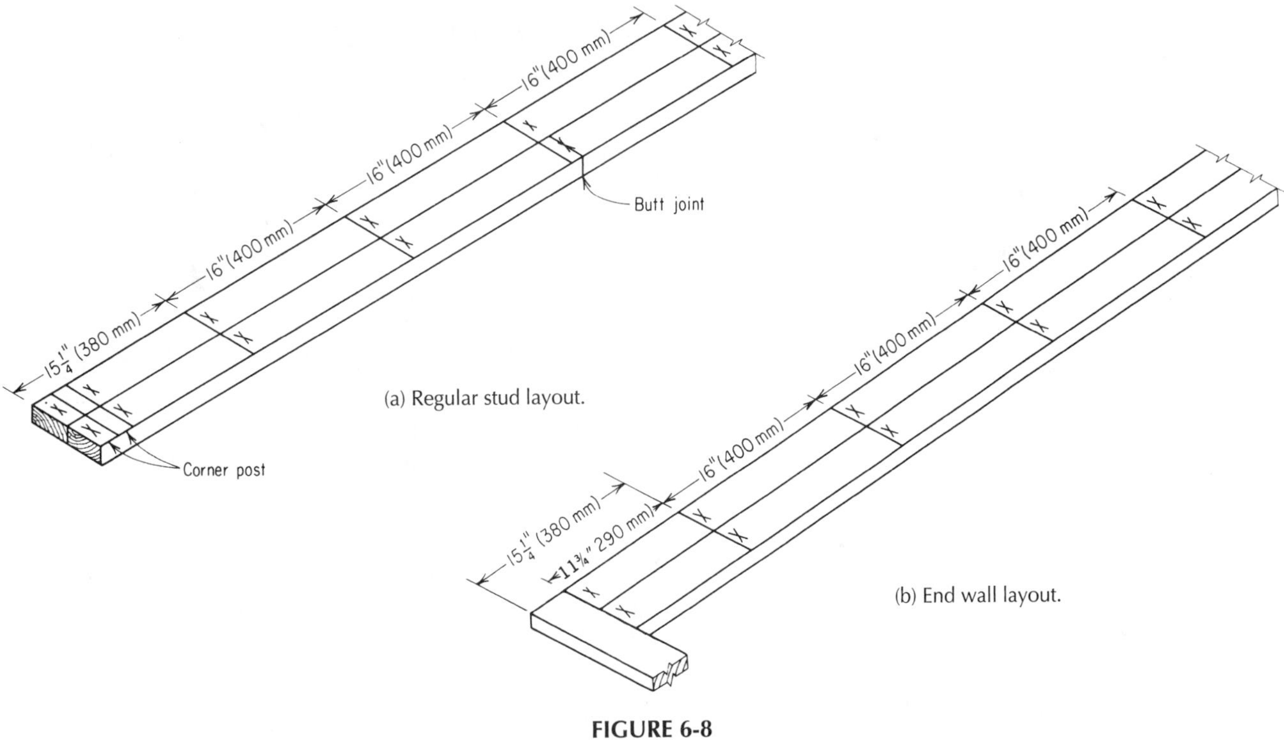

(a) Regular stud layout.

(b) End wall layout.

FIGURE 6-8

End walls must fit snugly between sidewalls when they are in place. Therefore the plates must be two plate widths shorter than the end wall length. The first stud space must be smaller by the plate width minus one-half the thickness of stud, as illustrated in Fig. 6-8(b) [Note: this illustration depicts a 2 × 4(38 × 89-mm) wall]. The rest of the studs will be on regular centers from that point.

These illustrations show the layout on the face of the plates while many framers only lay out the location of members on the edge of the plates.

Size and Spacing of Studs

The size and spacing of studs are determined by the *location* of the wall, its *height*, and the *load* that it will have to support. For example, a partition constructed with 2 × 2 (38 × 38 mm) studs cannot support any load and must not be higher than 8 ft (2.4 m). A wall or partition constructed with 2 × 4 (38 × 89-mm) studs may support a roof and up to one additional floor provided the studs are not longer than 12 ft (3.6 m) and are spaced not more than 16 in. (400 mm) center to center.

It is important that you consult local building codes to determine the maximum allowable size and spacing of studs in various load conditions.

CUTTING THE FRAME

The assembly of the frame will be made much simpler if all the pieces have been cut accurately first. For standard-height walls, studs are readily available pre-cut to the proper length. Read the drawings carefully and find the height of the walls and partitions. Check sole and top plate layouts for the number of full-length studs required, taking into account the extras needed at corners, partition junctions, wall openings, etc. Check the plans for the width and height of all exterior openings and for the height of the top of the openings above the subfloor. For standard wood-sash windows, the rough opening should be $\frac{3}{4}$ in. (20 mm) larger in height and width than the frame. Rough openings for wood door units should also be $\frac{3}{4}$ in. (20 mm) larger than the frame. Regardless, manufacturers of window and door units will provide recommendations for fitting clearances.

Count the number of trimmers, lintels, rough sills, and cripples required from the layout. With rough opening sizes and heights, it is not difficult to calculate the length and cut these ready for assembly.

Stud Lengths

Regular. The length of regular studs, corner post members, and partition junction studs will be the finished wall height plus clearance [usually 1 in. (25 mm)] less the thickness of *three* plates. For example, if the finished wall height is to be 96 in. (2400 mm), the regular stud length will be $96\text{ in.} + 1\text{ in.} - \left(1\frac{1}{2} \times 3\right) = 92\frac{1}{2}\text{ in.}$ $[2400 + 25 - (38 \times 3) = 2311\text{ mm}]$.

Trimmers (Jack Studs). The length of a trimmer stud will be the height of the top of the opening above the floor less the thickness of *one* plate.

Lower Cripple Studs. The length of the lower cripple stud will be the height of the bottom of the opening above the floor less the thickness of *two* plates.

Upper Cripple Studs. Although it is possible to calculate the length of the upper cripple studs, it is usually more satisfactory, from a practical standpoint, to measure the distance between the top of the lintel to the underside of the top plate after the wall has been assembled (see Fig. 6-9).

Rough Sill Length

The length of the rough sill (see Fig. 6-9) will be equal to the width of the rough opening.

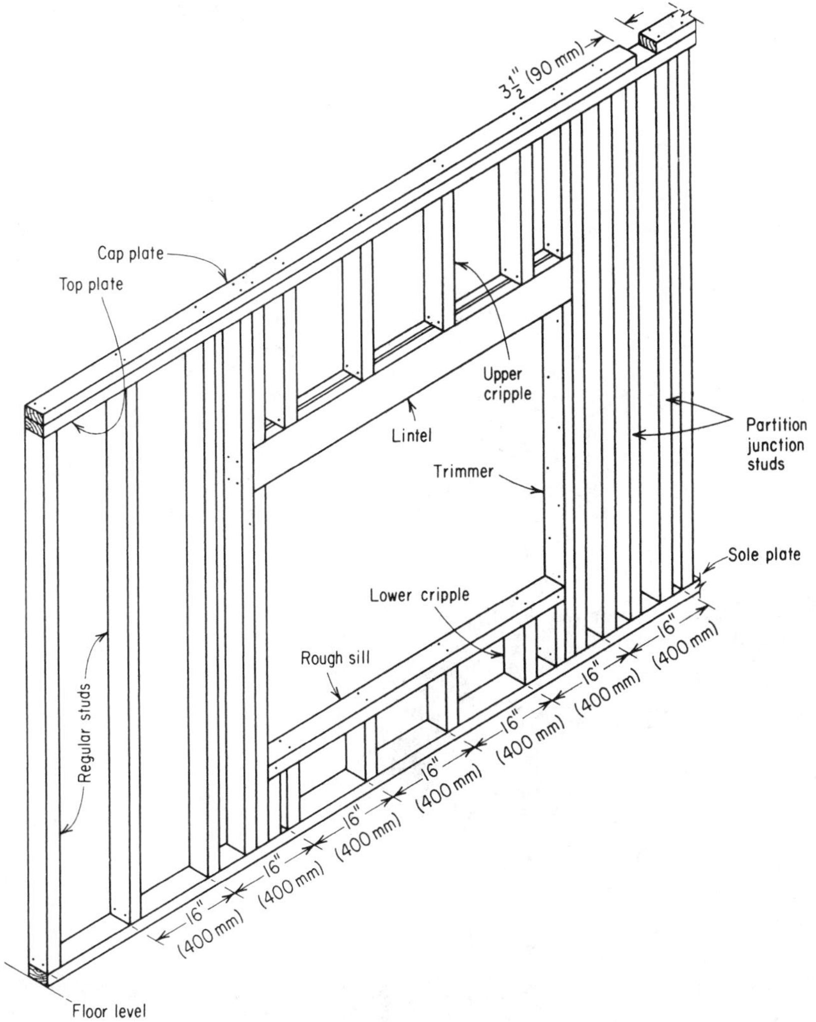

FIGURE 6-9 Wall framing members.

Lintel

The length of the lintel will be the width of the rough opening (see Fig. 6-9) plus the thickness of two trimmers [3 in. (76 mm)], while its depth will depend on the material being used and the load it must support. For example, the required depth of a lintel supporting a roof load only will generally be less than one supporting one or more floors plus a roof load. Again, you must consult local building codes for the allowable spans for lintels of various depths and loads.

The thickness of the lintel will be equal to the thickness of the wall frame and must be made up accordingly. For a 2 × 4-in.(38 × 89-mm) wall, it is usually made of two pieces of $1\frac{1}{2}$-in. (38-mm) material nailed together, with the proper thickness of spacer between them, as illustrated in Fig. 6-10(a). For a 2 × 6 (38 × 140-mm) wall, two pieces of material could be used, with a 2 × 6 nailed to the bottom edge [see Fig. 6-10(b)]. In some cases a solid wood member is used for a lintel, as shown in Fig. 6-10(c).

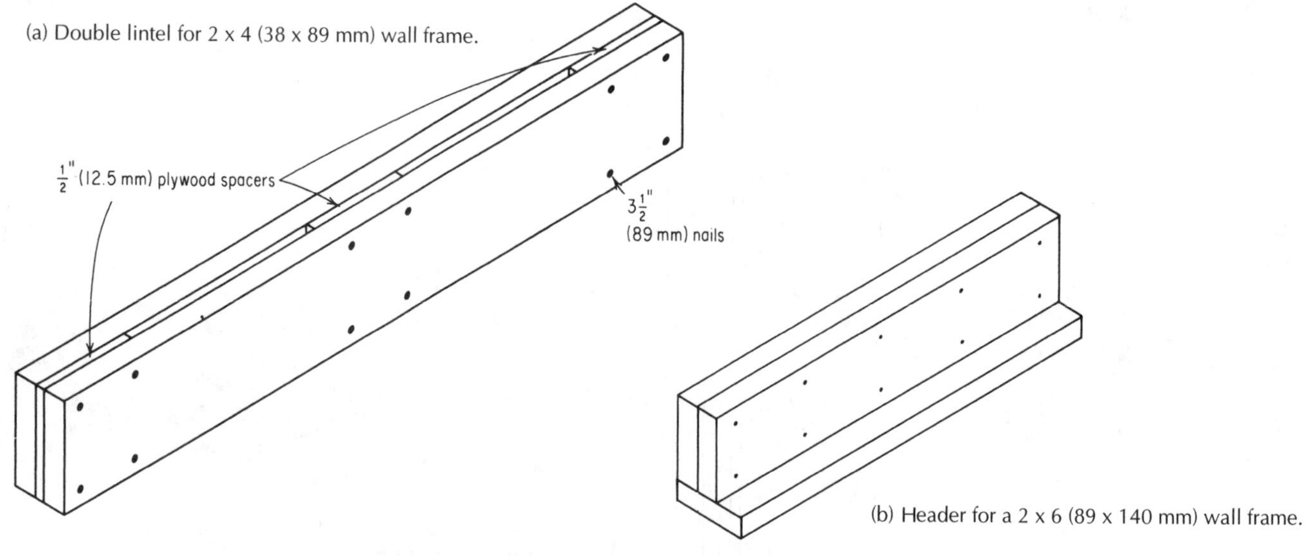

(c) Solid lumber lintel.

FIGURE 6-10

OSB assembled lintels are also used as illustrated in Fig. 6-11.

ASSEMBLING THE FRAME

When the pieces have all been cut, the process of assembly can begin. The first step is to assemble lintels for door and window openings, and in many cases it is advantageous to assemble corner and partition junction studs. Corners and partition junctions joining exterior walls must be assembled to provide interior finishing backing. A

(a)

(b)

FIGURE 6-11 (a) OSB lintel; (b) Using power nailers to assemble wall frame.

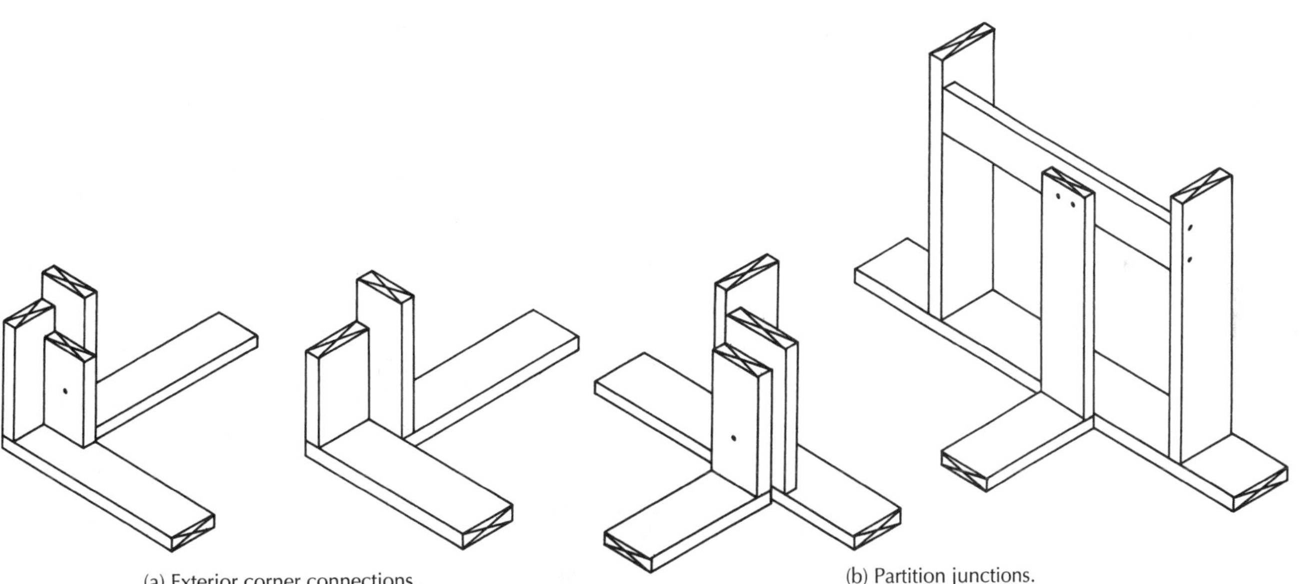

(a) Exterior corner connections.

(b) Partition junctions.

FIGURE 6-12

number of types of connections are used, as illustrated in Fig. 6-12. A multiple stud connection, made up of either two or three studs, is used at exterior corners or partition junctions to tie walls together and to provide nailing surfaces for wall finishes. Two stud arrangements may be used if metal plasterboard backup clips are used for support.

The assembly of the wall frames can now begin, starting with one of the sidewalls or longest walls. Generally, the wall will be assembled on the subfloor and raised into position in one or more units, depending on the length. Proceed as follows (refer to Fig. 6-13):

1. Once the sole and top plates have been marked for the correct position of the studs (Fig. 6-8), position them, on edge, so they are a stud length apart, with the laid-out faces toward each other. The sole plate should be near the edge of the floor frame on which it will rest.
2. Place a full-length stud at each position indicated on the layout.
3. Nail the sole and top plates to the ends of these with two $3\frac{1}{2}$-in. (89-mm) nails in each end.
4. Nail all the window and door trimmers to the full-length studs on each side of the openings.
5. Nail the end lower cripple studs to the inside of the trimmers.
6. Lay each rough sill on the ends of the two lower cripples and nail.
7. Set the lintels on the ends of the trimmers and end nail through the full-length studs.

(a) Order of wall member assembly.

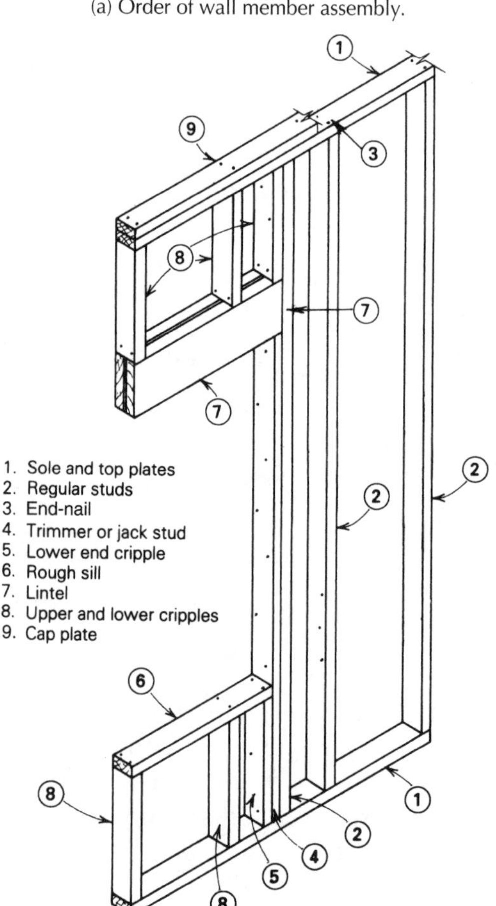

FIGURE 6-13 Order of wall member assembly.

8. Set the remainder of the cripple studs, upper and lower, in position and nail. The upper cripples must be toe nailed to the top edge of the lintel.
9. Nail on the cap plate. At each end it must be shortened the thickness of end walls and a gap left open at partition junctions to allow these joints to be tied together [see Figs. 6-14(a) and 6-14(b)]. Another reason for a cap plate is to bridge any joints in the top plates to provide rigidity to the wall.

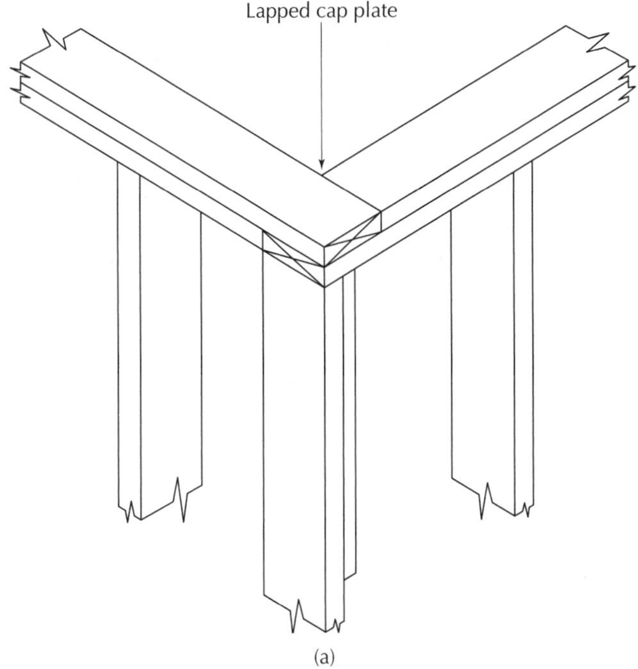

(a)

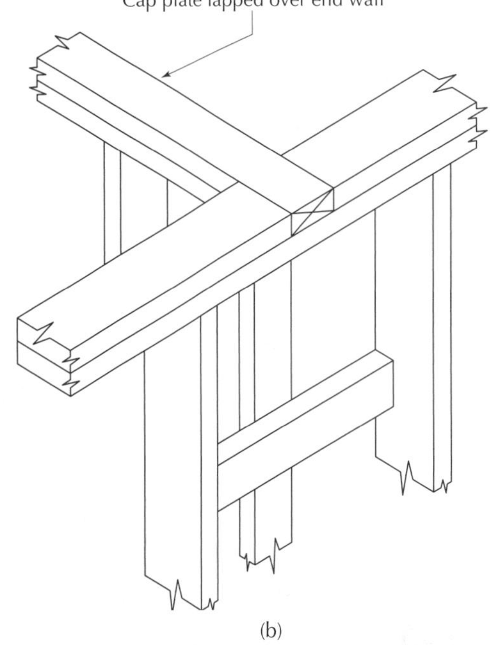

(b)

(c)

(d)

FIGURE 6-14 (a) Cap plate junction at corners; (b) Cap plate junction at partitions; (c) Corner framing; (d) Partition junction.

WALL SHEATHING

It is usually advantageous to sheathe the frame before standing it in place. First, align the sole plate with the snapped line located near the edge of the floor frame, as discussed above. If the subfloor is wood, tack the sole plate to the floor to keep it straight. Next, make sure that the frame is square by checking the diagonal distances from the bottom corners to the opposite top ones. These measurements should be exactly the same. Tack the wall frame to the subfloor to keep it square. If the walls are being assembled on a concrete pad, then more care has to be taken to ensure that the frame is straight and square as sheathing is being applied.

There are a number of materials available that may be used as sheathing. They include *plywood, exterior fiberboard, exterior gypsum board, OSB or waferboard,* and *insulating sheathing.* Sheathing-grade plywood or waferboard is probably the most widely used, but all the others do a satisfactory job, and, in an age of energy conservation, Styrofoam sheathing is particularly attractive because of its high insulation value.

When the entire wall is to be sheathed with plywood, it should be applied with the long dimension horizontal for greater rigidity. The required thickness must conform to local building codes, and will depend on the spacing of studs. The location of the end joints of the plywood should be offset two stud spaces if possible. Use 2-in. (50-mm) coated or spiral nails, spaced 6 in. (150 mm) along the edges of the panel and 12 in. (300 mm) on intermediate supports (see Fig. 6-15).

A space equal to the thickness of a 2-in. nail should be left between panels to allow for expansion (see Fig. 6-16).

Some framers let the sheathing overhang past the bottom of the wall to allow for alignment (see Fig. 6-17).

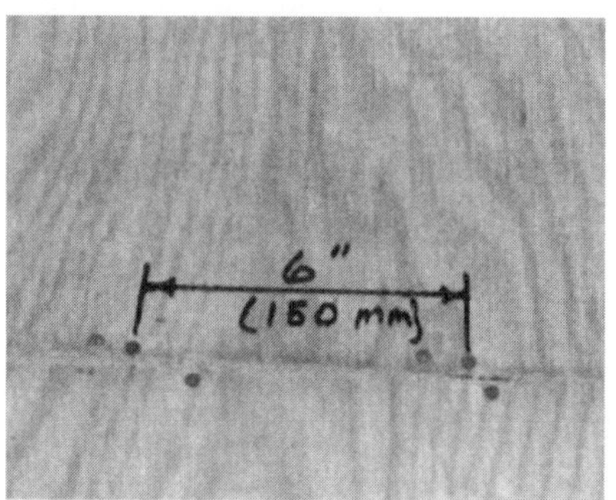

(a) Nail spacing at edge of sheet.

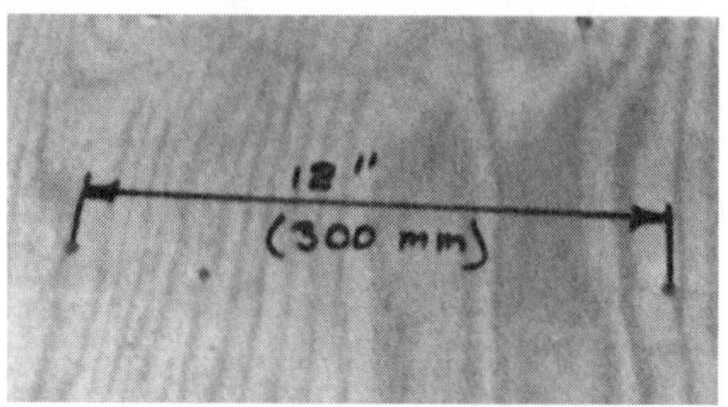

(b) Nail spacing along intermediate supports.

FIGURE 6-15

FIGURE 6-16 Space between sheets.

FIGURE 6-17 Overhang at bottom of wall.

FIGURE 6-18 Poly for sealing joint at wall and floor.

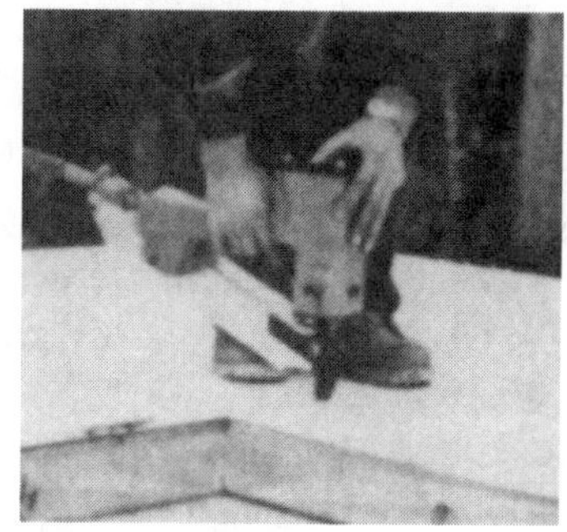

FIGURE 6-19 Using a power nailer on sheathing.

When the sheathing is flush with the bottom of the wall, polyethylene is used to seal the joint (see Fig. 6-18).

Power nailers are often used for assembly (see Fig. 6-19) and routers are often used to cut out window and door openings (see Fig. 6-20).

FIGURE 6-20 Using a router to cut openings.

Waferboard is applied by the same method as plywood sheathing. Panels can be placed horizontally or vertically, as they will not be affected by the difference in strength that occurs when plywood is placed with the grain parallel to studs as opposed to perpendicular. OSB panels have more strength if placed with the length of the panel perpendicular to the supports.

Exterior fiberboard, a material made from shredded wood fibers impregnated with asphalt, is commonly made in 4 × 8-ft (1200 × 2400-mm) sheets, $\frac{7}{16}$ in. (11 mm) thick. The panels are nailed with $1\frac{3}{4}$-in. (44-mm) broad-headed nails or $1\frac{1}{2}$-in. (38-mm) staples, spaced 6 in. (150 mm) along the edges and 8 in. (200 mm) along intermediate supports. Vertical joints should be offset, similar to plywood (see Fig. 6-21).

FIGURE 6-21 Fiberboard sheathing.

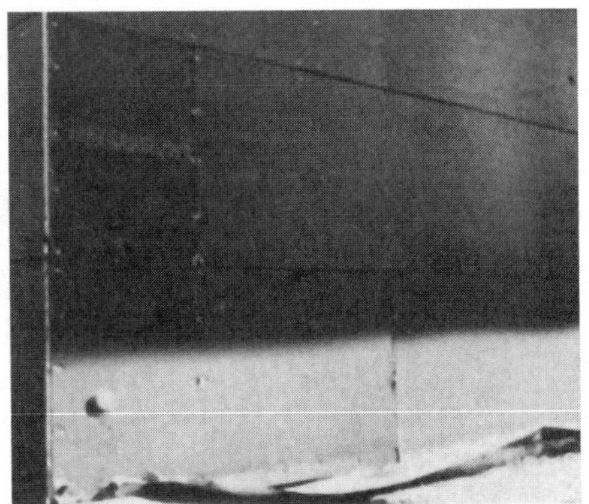

FIGURE 6-22 Gypsum board exterior sheathing.

Exterior gypsum board is made with a core of gypsum encased in asphalt-impregnated paper. The sheets are 2 × 8-ft × $\frac{1}{2}$-in. thick (600 × 1200 × 12.5 mm), with the long edges having a tongue and groove horizontal joint. The sheets are applied with the long dimension horizontal. Two-inch (50-mm) coated or spiral nails, spaced 6 in. (150 mm) apart on all studs, are used. All vertical joints must be staggered (see Fig. 6-22).

Insulating exterior sheathing board is applied to the outside of exterior wall studs much in the same manner as conventional sheathing. Insulating sheathing will increase the "R" values of the wall to meet today's energy-saving requirements. Insulating sheathing includes such materials as Styrofoam, fiberglass, and Thermax board.

Styrofoam insulating sheathing is a synthetic material made from expanded polystyrene in rigid sheets with a smooth, high-density skin. It has a thermal resistance ("R" value) of 5 per inch (25 mm). The sheets are available in 2 × 8-ft (600 × 2400-mm) or 4 × 8-ft (1200 × 2400-mm) panels, 1–2-in. (25–50-mm) thick with butt edges, and are applied like other panel sheathing. Panels that are under $1\frac{1}{2}$ in. (38 mm) thick must be placed over plywood or waferboard to ensure sufficient wall strength (see Fig. 6-23). Figure 6-24 illustrates Styrofoam applied directly to the wall studs, and in this case a metal mesh has been included ready for the application of a stucco finish.

Fasteners may be broad-headed (roofing) nails, staples, or screws, with a spacing of 6 in. (150 mm) for nails or staples. The length of the fasteners should be a minimum of $\frac{3}{4}$ in. (19 mm) longer than the thickness of the sheathing.

The Styrofoam should be covered with exterior building paper, over which any type of exterior finish, including wood or metal siding, stucco, or brick veneer may be applied.

Styrofoam will burn, and during shipping, storage, installation, and use it must not be exposed to open flame or other ignition source.

FIGURE 6-24 Unsupported Styrofoam sheathing.

FIGURE 6-23 Styrofoam sheathing.

Fiberglass sheathing boards are composed of resin-bonded glass fibers faced with a durable air barrier. They will not rot even after continuous wetting and drying cycles and are not affected by fungi or insects. The glass fiberboard is permeable to water vapor and will not trap moisture. The moisture-resistant facing has fair resistance to impact loads.

Glass fiber insulating board is attached to the studs with large head galvanized roofing nails. The nails should be $\frac{3}{4}$ in. (19 mm) longer than the thickness of the board. Fasteners must be placed 6 in. (150 mm) along edges and 12 in. (300 mm) along intermediate supports. If 1-in. (25-mm) head diameter nails or washers are used under the head, the spacing can be increased to 12 in. (300 mm) along the edges and 18 in. (450 mm) along intermediate supports.

Glass fiber sheathing is available in sheets 4 × 8 ft and 4 × 9 ft (1200 × 2400 and 1200 × 2700 mm). One-inch and $1\frac{1}{2}$-in. (25-mm and 38-mm) thickness sheets are available. Thermal resistance at 75° F (24° C) mean temperature is 4.4 (RSI 0.77) for 1-in. (25-mm) thickness and 6.7 (RSI 1.18) for $1\frac{1}{2}$-in. (38-mm) thickness (see Fig. 6-25).

FIGURE 6-25 Glass fiber sheathing.

Thermax sheathing consists of a glass-reinforced polyisocyanurate foam plastic core with aluminum foil faces. Since Thermax sheathing has a closed cell structure and aluminum faces that make an efficient barrier to moisture as well as heat flow, there is concern in colder climates for the potential of entrapped water vapor within stud spaces. A vent strip system is used for moisture relief along the top edge of the wall, allowing for the escape of water vapor (see Fig. 6-26).

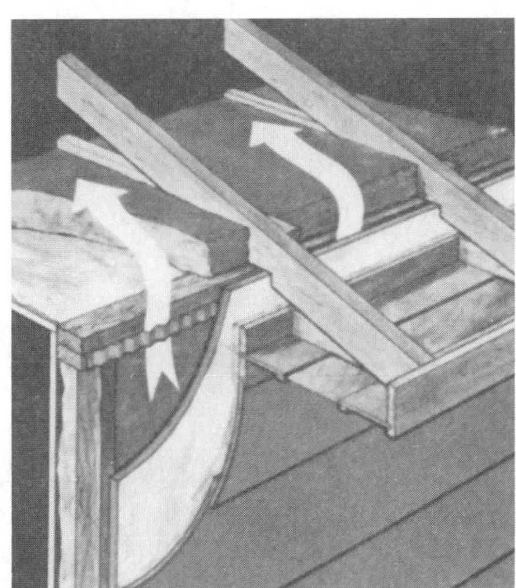

FIGURE 6-26 Corrugated plastic vent strip along top plate.

No special fastening is required. The boards are secured in place with galvanized roofing nails long enough to penetrate the framing by $\frac{3}{4}$ in. (19 mm). Thermax sheathing is not a structural panel, so wood let-ins or metal strap bracing is used for panels that are under $1\frac{1}{2}$ in. (38 mm) thick. The panels are available in standard insulation board sizes of 4 × 8 ft (1200 × 2400 mm) and 4 × 9 ft (1200 × 2700 mm) and are available from $\frac{1}{2}$ in. (12.7 mm) to $2\frac{1}{4}$ in. (57.2 mm) thick. Thermal resistance at 75° F (24° C) mean temperature ranges from 3.6 (RSI 0.63) for $\frac{1}{2}$-in. material to 16.2 (RSI 2.85) for $2\frac{1}{4}$-in. material (see Fig. 6-27).

FIGURE 6-27 Thermax sheathing.

FIGURE 6-28 OSB corner sheathing.

When walls are fully sheathed, they will provide sufficient strength to withstand wind or seismic forces. However, in many places in North America, this is not the practice. Instead, you will find only strategic corners will be sheathed with OSB or plywood panels (see Fig. 6-28).

In these situations a number of metal diagonal braces are used to provide lateral support to walls. One type is a ribbed metal strap (T-shaped) that is inserted into a saw cut in the edge of every stud and then nailed in place [see Figs. 6-29(a) and 6-29(b)].

In addition, diagonal braces are used around the tops of each window or door opening (see Fig. 6-30 and Fig. 6-11).

(a)

(b)

FIGURE 6-29 (a) Metal bracing; (b) Metal bracing at gable end.

To provide more resistance to uplift in high wind areas, metal clips are used to tie the ends of studs to the plates, and in the case of multistory buildings, metal straps are installed across each floor frame to tie all walls together [see Fig. 6-31(a), 6-31(b), and 6-31(c)]. In some areas metal anchors are cast into a concrete slab and are later attached to the framed walls [see Fig. 6-31(d)].

FIGURE 6-30 Metal bracing at window/door opening.

(a)

(b)

(c)

(d)

FIGURE 6-31 (a) Metal tie-down, stud to plate; (b) Metal straps across floor frames; (c) Metal bracing and straps across floor frame; (d) Metal tie-down anchored to concrete slab.

ERECTING THE FRAME

Usually wall frames can be raised by hand unless they are particularly long or heavy, in which case wall jacks may be used [see Figs. 6-32(a) and 6-32(b)]. Be sure that the bottom of the frame is close to the edge of the subfloor so that as the wall is raised the sheathing overhang does not catch on the floor. When the sole plate has been tacked to the subfloor the tacks act as a hinge as the wall is raised, keeping it straight.

(a) Raising a section of wall by hand.

(b) Raising a wall with wall jacks.

FIGURE 6-32

FIGURE 6-33 Sheathing overlap with floor system and corner.

When the wall is in a vertical position, it must be tied in at the bottom and straightened and braced at the top. Adjust at the bottom until the overhang of the wall sheathing is snug against the face of the floor frame (see Fig. 6-33). When the wall rests on a wood subfloor, nail the sole plate down with two $3\frac{1}{2}$-in. (89-mm) nails between each pair of studs. Be sure the nails reach a joist or the joist header. Walls that do not have the sheathing overhanging will be set flush with the edge of the floor frame.

If the wall is being positioned on a concrete pad, then it must be anchored to the concrete using anchor bolts that have been previously set as the concrete was placed. The sole plate will have to be pre-drilled for each anchor bolt prior to the assembly of the wall frame (see Fig. 6-34). Sometimes anchor bolts will occur at a stud location that should be avoided if possible (see Fig. 6-35).

You will also note in Fig. 6-34 that there is no exterior sheathing, only a black building paper. In this situation a polyethylene strip bridges the space across the lower part of the wall frame and the concrete pad to prevent an influx of moisture during rainy days. Also, in both Figs. 6-34 and 6-35 a treated sole plate has been used.

FIGURE 6-34 Treated sole plate and anchor bolts.

FIGURE 6-35 Anchor bolt and stud conflict.

Next, use a hand level to plumb the two ends of the wall and brace. To straighten the top, run a line very tightly along the top plate, tying it around the ends. Block the line out at the ends with a small piece of $\frac{3}{4}$-in. (19-mm) material (see Fig. 6-36). Take another piece of $\frac{3}{4}$-in. (19-mm) material and check at various points to see if the line is the correct distance from the plate. Push the top of the wall in or out, where necessary, to correct any points not in line and secure with braces by nailing one end to the face of a stud at the top and the other end to a block fastened to the subfloor. If the wall is erected on a concrete pad then other means of temporary bracing will have to be devised, such as bracing on the outside using stakes driven into the soil.

When one sidewall has been erected and plumbed, the opposite one may be assembled and erected in the same manner, followed by the end walls, one by one. If the entire wall is to be sheathed, it is impractical to sheathe the end wall frames completely on the subfloor because the end wall sheathing should extend over the corner posts (see Fig. 6-32), but the majority of it may be applied at this time. With

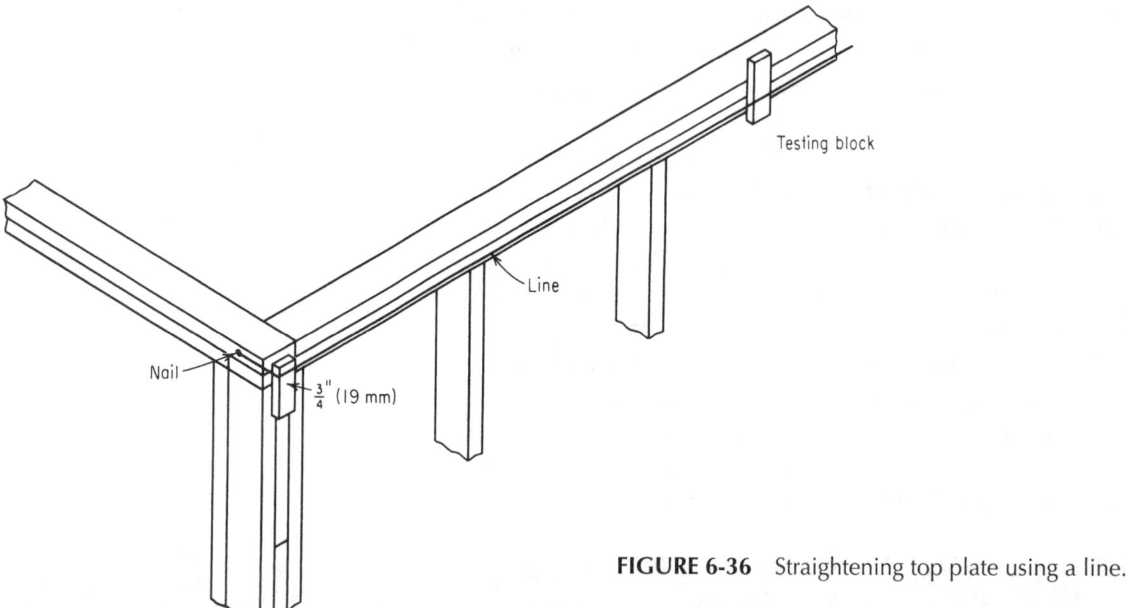

FIGURE 6-36 Straightening top plate using a line.

the end wall erect and the sole plate anchored in position, the end studs can be nailed to the sidewall partial corner posts to make the post complete.

The remainder of the sheathing can now be applied, the wall plumbed and braced, and the end wall cap plate nailed to overlap the sidewall top plate to tie sidewalls and end walls securely together.

PARTITIONS

Partitions may be *bearing* or *nonbearing.* Bearing partitions carry part of the roof load, one end of ceiling joists, or both, whereas nonbearing partitions simply enclose space and carry the finishing materials (see Fig. 6-37).

(a) Loadbearing wall.

(b) Non–loadbearing wall.

FIGURE 6-37

Partitions may be laid out, assembled, and erected in the same way as outside walls. As mentioned before, snapping a chalk line first marks the position of the sole plate on the subfloor.

Plates are laid out and studs and other members cut and assembled. As a final step, add a cap plate, with its ends overlapping the side-wall top plate as illustrated previously in Fig. 6-14(b). Erect the longest partition first, then the cross partitions, and, finally, the partitions forming clothes closets, hallways, etc. Two methods of providing interior finish backing at partition junctions are illustrated in Figs. 6-38(a) and 6-38(b). In cold climates where there is a danger of moisture condensing inside a wall cavity, a polyethylene vapor barrier is installed on the warm side of the wall. To ensure there is no interruption to the barrier narrow strips are placed between the partition ends and the exterior wall backing as shown in Fig. 6-38(b). Also, a strip is placed between the top and cap plate of partitions to seal ceiling spaces (see Fig. 6-39).

(a) Partition junction.

(b) Alternate partition junction.

FIGURE 6-38

FIGURE 6-39 Vapor barrier between top and plates.

FIGURE 6-40 Pocket door framing.

One partition requiring special attention will be the one for the bathroom in which the main plumbing vent stack (soil stack) is located. In some cases, this one will have to be made 6 in. (140 mm) wide to accommodate the size of the pipe.

Broom and clothes closet partitions may sometimes be framed with 2 × 2(38 × 38-mm) material in order to save space, but only if the partition is short or in a protected location.

Sliding Door Opening

Framing to provide for doors that slide into the wall also requires special consideration. The thickness of the door must first be determined. This portion of the partition frame must be wide enough to accommodate the thickness of the door plus clearance and at least $\frac{3}{4}$-in. (19-mm) framing on each side (see Fig. 6-40). The width of a pocket door opening must be twice the door width plus jamb thickness and clearance $\left[\frac{3}{4}\text{ in.} (20\text{ mm})\right]$. Height will vary depending on design of track assembly. These are usually purchased as a unit and can be set in place without any additional framing. However, if the door is located in a bearing wall, then a lintel of suitable size must span the entire opening.

Openings for Heating and Ventilating

Openings must be made in the frame to accommodate heating system stacks leading to registers, if the registers are of the wall type, as well as openings for air-conditioning and ventilating systems, where they are specified.

If the cold air return will fit between a pair of regular studs, all that is necessary is to cut the sole plate out between the studs, cut a hole in the subfloor, and put in a header between the studs at the required height [see Fig. 6-41(a)]. If a wider space is needed, a header is placed in adjacent spaces. The sole plate is cut out and a hole is made in the subfloor, as above [see Fig. 6-41(b)]. Placing a piece of screen over the opening during construction will keep debris out of the heating pipes [see Fig. 6-41(c)].

Wall Backing

Installations such as wall-type basins, cupboards, etc., which must be fastened to the wall, must be provided with some type of solid backing. Various examples are shown in Figs. 6-42(a), 6-42(b), and 6-42(c). You will need to consult the plans to determine the location where special backing is needed. In many cases, plumbers will provide their own backing.

(a) Partition openings for registers.

(b) Large partition opening for cold air return.

(c) Screen over register opening.

FIGURE 6-41

(a) Support for water lines.

(b) Backing for tissue holder.

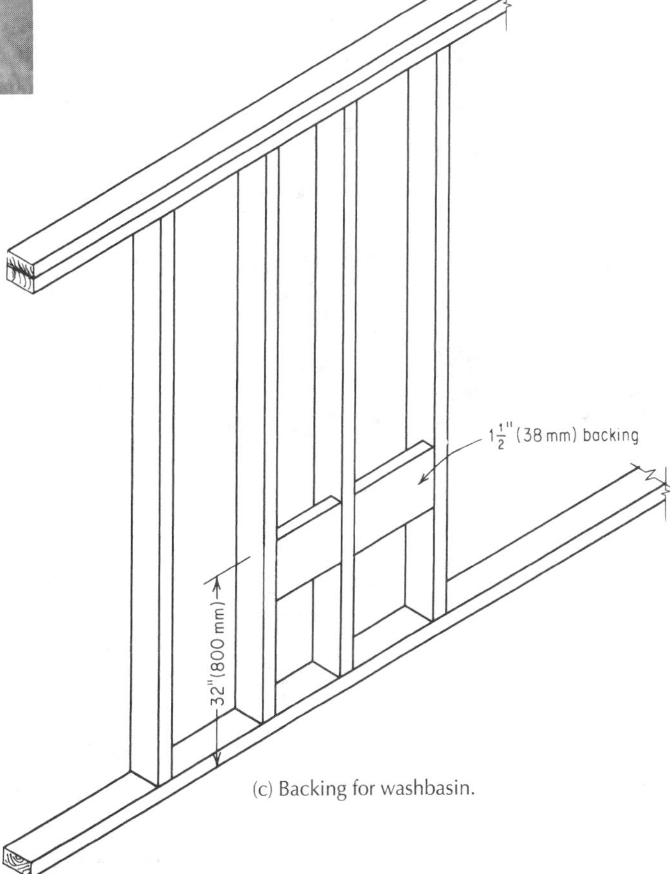

(c) Backing for washbasin.

FIGURE 6-42

LIGHT STEEL WALL FRAMING

Light steel wall framing members in several styles, depending on the manufacturer, are made from sheet steel, cold-formed, and consist basically of *studs* and *mounting channels* [see Fig. 6-43(a)].

Studs are made in the form of channels, in two types, *load-bearing* and *non–loadbearing.* The thickness of the metal used for load-bearing studs varies from 0.036 to 0.075 in. (0.91–1.9 mm), with web sizes from $3\frac{5}{8}$ to 8 in. (92–203 mm) and $1\frac{5}{8}$ to $1\frac{3}{4}$-in. flange. Non–load-bearing studs are made from lighter-gauge steel and in narrower widths.

Mounting channels are made slightly wider to receive the end of the studs [see Fig. 6-43(b)] and are used for top and bottom tracks as well as windowsill and head track. No cap plate is required as shown in Fig. 6-43(a), but horizontal bracing is installed between studs to provide lateral support.

(a) Prefabricated light steel wall frame. (Courtesy U.S. Steel Corp.)

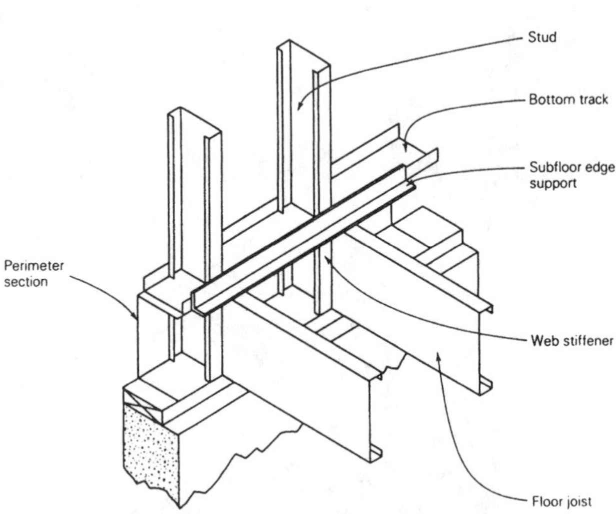

(b) Metal joists and stud framing detail.

FIGURE 6-43

Lintels are usually made of two wood members or metal channels or beams with their top and bottom edge enclosed by a length of mounting channel (see Fig. 6-44). Where openings do not reach to the bottom edge of the lintel, another length of mounting channel forms the top of the opening, with cripple studs between it and the lintel (see Fig. 6-44).

Wall frames may be prefabricated and brought to the site ready for erection (see Fig. 6-45), assembled on the subfloor, and raised into position. Before being raised the pre-assembled frames are usually sheathed with plywood, OSB, or gypsum board, fastened with steel nails driven by a pneumatic hammer or screws utilizing a screw gun.

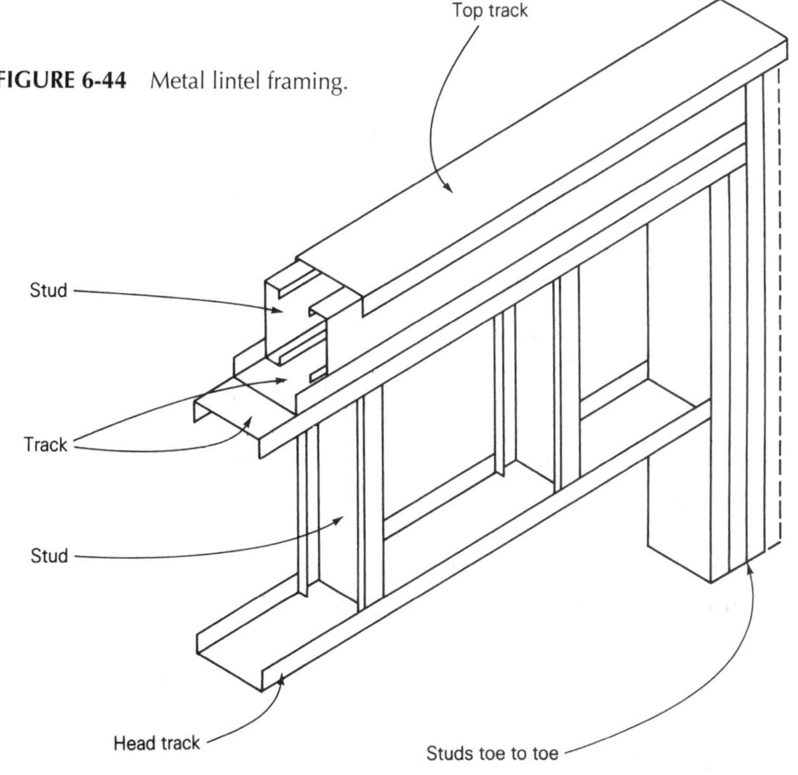

FIGURE 6-44 Metal lintel framing.

FIGURE 6-45 Raising wall.

Wall frames are anchored to concrete floors with power-actuated pins, placed 24 in. (600 mm) o.c. Screws are used when fastening to wooden floors. Rafters or trusses are anchored over supports to the top plate with *U-clips,* which are welded to the frame and bolted to the roof members.

The lighter, non–loadbearing framing material used for interior partitions provides a considerable saving of floor space (see Fig. 6-46). Non–loadbearing studs measure $1\frac{3}{16} \times 3\frac{5}{8}$ in. (30 × 91 mm) with a

FIGURE 6-46 Interior steel partitions.

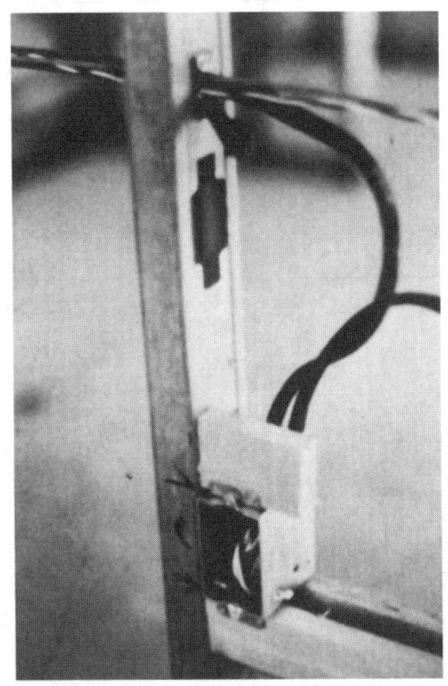

FIGURE 6-47 Placing electrical wires in metal studs.

metal thickness of 0.21 in. (0.53 mm). Studs are also available in $2\frac{1}{2}$- and $1\frac{5}{8}$-in. (64-and 40-mm) widths for further space saving. Holes that are pre-cut in the studs are at 24-in. (600-mm) centers for easy placement of electrical wires. Electrical clips are used to protect unarmored wires (see Fig. 6-47).

Mounting channels are tapered for better grip of the studs (see Fig. 6-48) and are fastened to concrete floors with power-actuated pins and with screws to wooden floors (see Fig. 6-49).

When wood trim or baseboard is to be fastened to metal framing during finishing operations, a wood runner is placed under the mounting channel. Studs are fastened to the channel with screws or a with a crimping tool [see Fig. 6-50(a)]. The studs are easily placed in the channel with a twisting action [see Fig. 6-50(b)]. Studs should be cut in lengths $\frac{1}{4}$ in. (6 mm) shorter than the wall height to allow for variations in height as illustrated in Fig. 6-51. Also shown in Fig. 6-51 is the recommended method of framing partition junctions. Mounting channels are fastened in the desired location first, and then the studs are placed individually into the channel [see Fig. 6-50(b)].

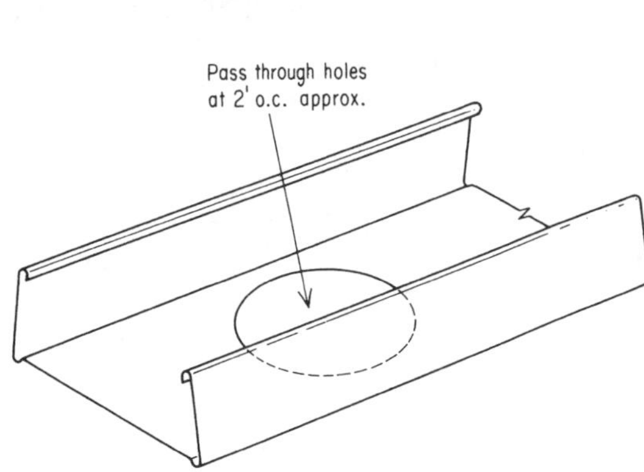

FIGURE 6-48 Mounting channel.

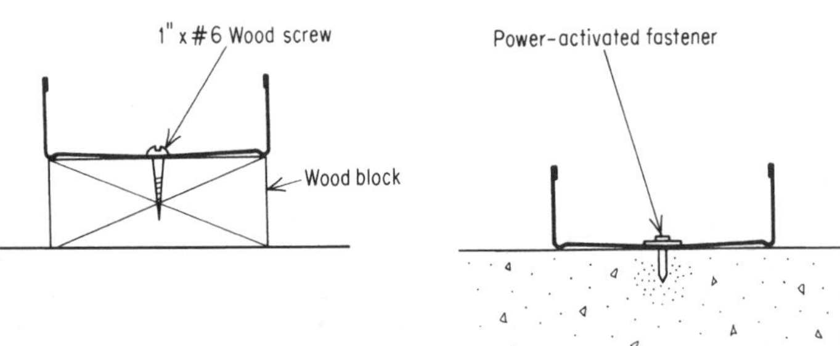

FIGURE 6-49 Fastening mounting channel.

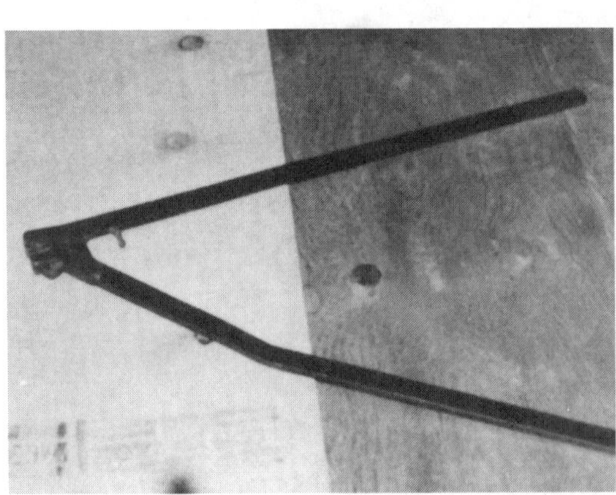

(a) Crimping tool.

(b) Erecting partition studs.

FIGURE 6-50

Wall corners are framed as illustrated in Fig. 6-52. Studs are sometimes placed 2 in. (50 mm) away from the junctions to allow for easy access of screw guns when attaching gypsum board facing. Headers for door openings are cut 12 in. (300 mm) longer than the rough opening to allow for easy attachment (see Fig. 6-53).

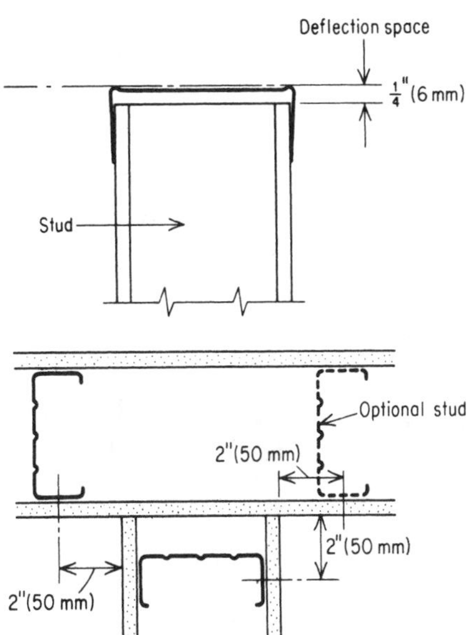

FIGURE 6-51 Allowance at top of wall.

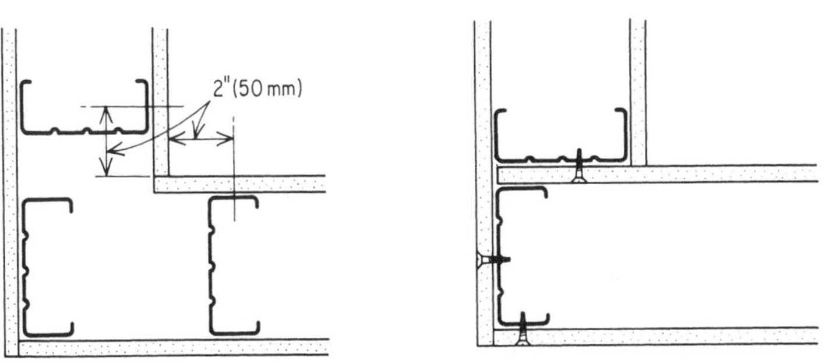

FIGURE 6-52 Partition connections.

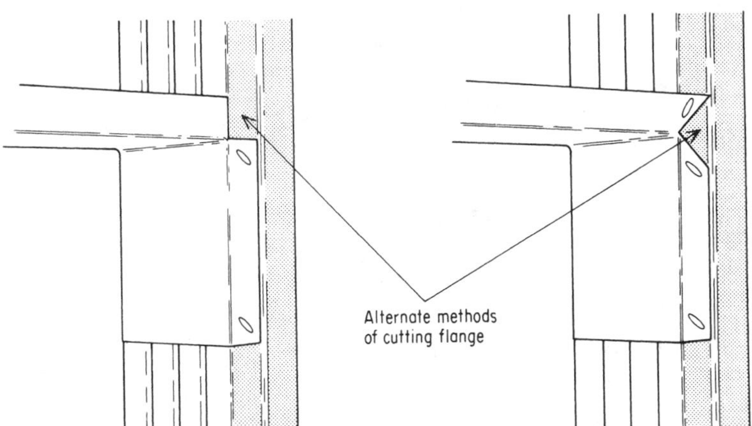

FIGURE 6-53 Header for door opening.

MASONRY WALL SYSTEMS

Masonry units may be used in walls in a number of ways in light construction. The most common one is to use brick, stone, or block units as a *veneer* over a wood frame or a concrete block backup wall. Another is to build a brick or block single wythe wall, with the masonry units as the exterior finish and in some occasions as the interior finish as well.

Brick Veneer

Over Wood Frame. A single wythe of brick, $3\frac{5}{8}$ in. (90 mm) thick, is often used to face a sheathed wall, framed in wood. Both the building

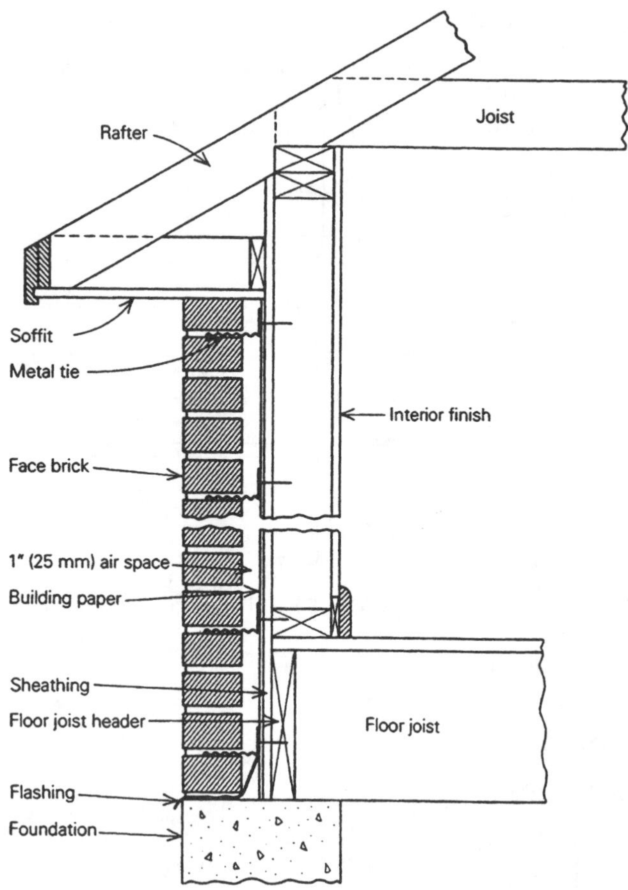

FIGURE 6-54 Typical wall section, brick veneer on frame construction.

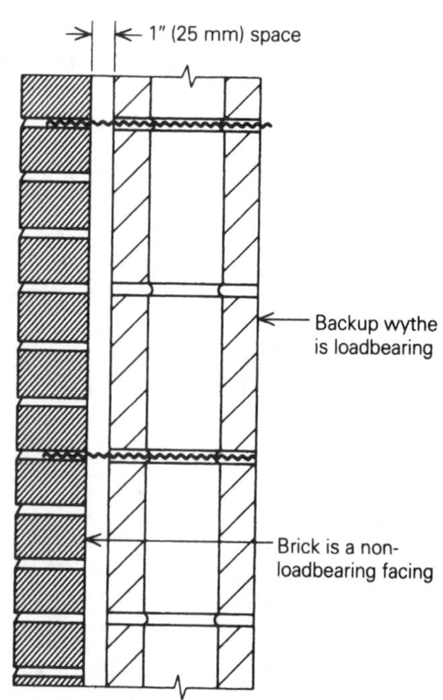

FIGURE 6-55 Brick veneer over masonry wall.

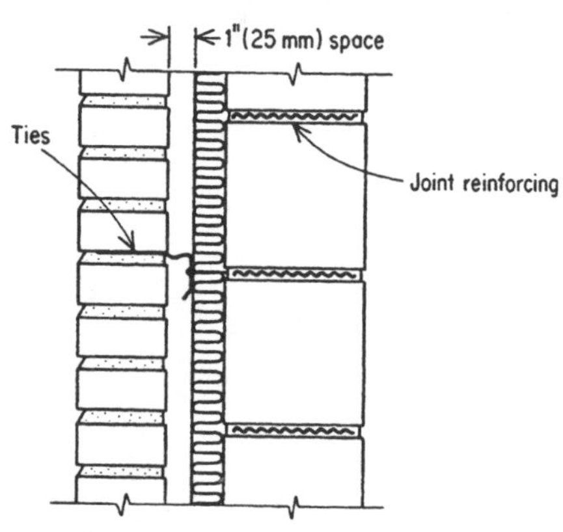

FIGURE 6-56 Brick veneer with cavity insulated.

frame and the brick wythe must be supported on the foundation wall (see Fig. 6-54), and a 1-in. (25-mm) space should be left between brick and sheathing.

The brick must be anchored to the frame by noncorrosive metal straps or ties, not less than 22 gauge (0.76 mm) and 1 in. (25 mm) wide, spaced in accordance with local codes. Generally, for studs spaced 16 in. (400 mm) o.c. the ties should be spaced vertically at 24 in. (600 mm) o.c.

Over Concrete Block. Four, six, or eight-inch (100, 150, or 200 mm) block may be used as a backup wall for a 4-in. (100-mm) brick veneer face, depending on the height of wall. This veneer should be separated from the backup by an unfilled space of at least 1 in. (25 mm) as illustrated in Fig. 6-55. When rigid insulation is used on the outside of the block backup, the space must be increased in size so the 1-in. (25-mm) space exists between the insulation and the facing (see Fig. 6-56). The facing wythe has to carry its own weight but otherwise is not considered to contribute to the vertical or lateral load resistance of the wall. The backup is designed to resist vertical or lateral loads. The space serves as a drainage gap between the ve-

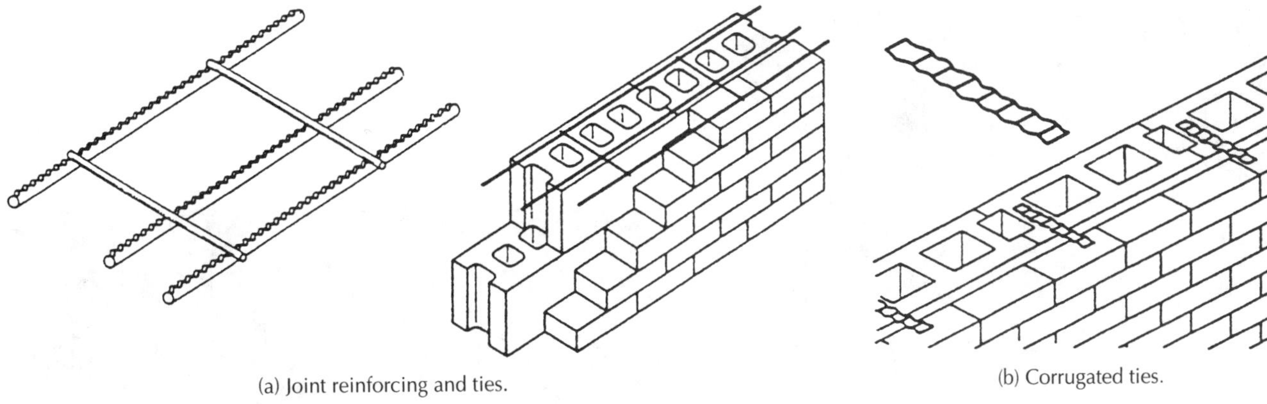
(a) Joint reinforcing and ties.

(b) Corrugated ties.

FIGURE 6-57

neer and the backup wall, and any forces on the facing are transmitted across the gap to the backup by ties.

Tying to the backup wall can be accomplished by using corrugated ties embedded in the mortar joints with the tie spacing regulated by local codes or by using continuous joint reinforcing in every second or third row of the block backup (see Fig. 6-57).

The brick veneer over openings in walls must be supported by a *lintel,* usually a steel angle with its ends supported on the brick on either side of the opening. The maximum allowable span for lintels depends on the size of lintel used, as prescribed by local building codes.

Single-Wythe Masonry Walls

Solid masonry walls in one-story buildings and in the top story of two-story buildings may be constructed $5\frac{1}{2}$ in. (140 mm) thick provided the walls are not over 9 ft, 2 in. (2.8 m) high at the eaves and 15 ft, 1 in. (4.6 m) at the peaks of the gable ends. The exterior walls of two- and three-story buildings should not be less than $7\frac{1}{2}$ in. (190 mm) thick. Solid or hollow units are normally used for this type of construction.

On the inside surface, the wall may be *furred out,* using either wood or metal, and the interior finish applied to this furring (see Fig. 6-58). Anchoring of metal studs to a masonry wall is illustrated in Fig. 6-59 that also shows the inclusion of a wood backup for electrical or plumbing fixtures.

Figure 6-60 illustrates the securing of an electrical box to metal stud furring.

This furring allows for the application of a vapor barrier, makes for easy installation of electrical services, and provides space for the inclusion of insulation. An 8-in. (200-mm) foundation wall is adequate, but the details of construction depend on the type of floor being used. Figure 6-61 illustrates one method of construction using a single-wythe brick wall. Single-wythe block walls were discussed in Chapter 4.

FIGURE 6-58 Metal stud furring over masonry wall.

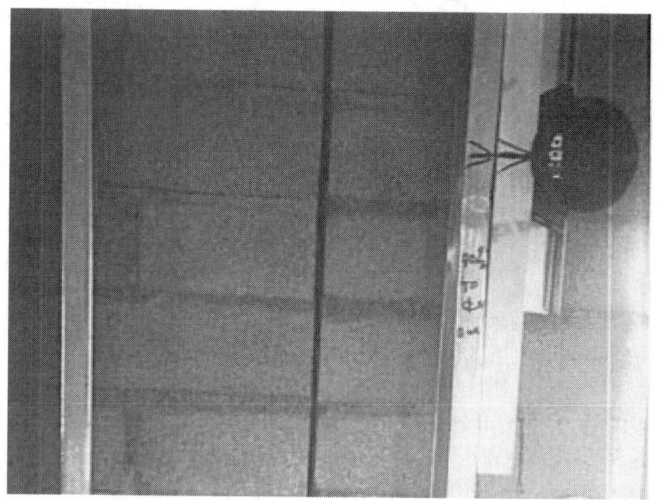

FIGURE 6-60 Securing electrical box to metal stud.

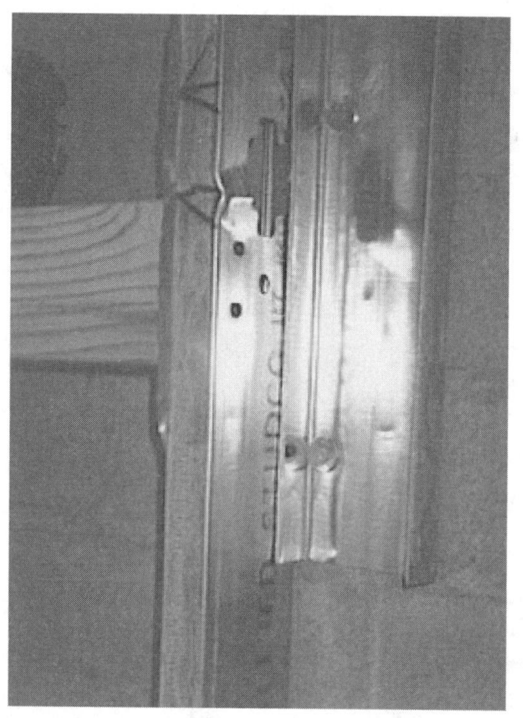

FIGURE 6-59 Anchoring metal furring.

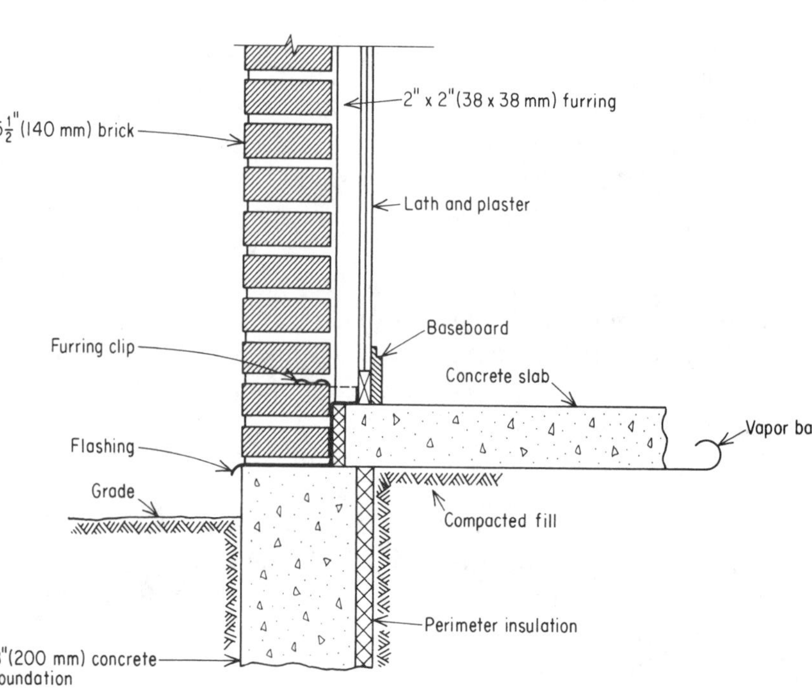

FIGURE 6-61 $5\frac{1}{2}$-in. (140-mm) brick wall.

REVIEW QUESTIONS

6–1. What is platform framing?

6–2. What is the difference between a wall and a partition?

6–3. Explain why it is important to have wall backing at some locations in the wall frame.

6–4. Give two reasons for the use of cap plates in wood wall frames.

6–5. Why are screens secured over heating vents during framing operations?

6–6. How are metal studs and tracks secured together?

6–7. What is the advantage of fully sheathing walls with either OSB or plywood?

6–8. Why are metal straps anchored to sill plates and studs in some areas?

6–9. Why are single-wythe masonry walls frequently furred out on the interior?

Chapter 7

THE CEILING AND ROOF FRAME

OBJECTIVES

Here is what you will be able to do when you complete each component of this chapter:

1. Describe how to install ceiling joists.
2. Identify eight different types of roofs.
3. Define roof terms.
4. Describe how to lay out ridges, common rafters, hip rafters, valley rafters, and jack rafters.
5. Describe how to use rafter tables.
6. Calculate line lengths of rafters.
7. Describe how to assemble a roof.
8. Define dormer.
9. Explain how truss roofs are erected.
10. Describe how roofs are sheathed.
11. Identify selected alternate roof shapes.

The final step in completing the skeleton of a building is the framing of the roof system. The methods used depend on the type of roof and whether the roof assembly is built on site or premanufactured in a truss plant. If all the work is completed on the construction site, it can include the assembly of a ceiling frame as well as the roof frame. When a trussed roof system is used, the ceiling and the roof-framing members are part of the same self-supporting structure.

CEILING JOIST SIZES

The size of members used for ceiling joists depends on the span and spacing of the members, the type of material used for the ceiling, and the species and grade of lumber used. Ceiling joists that are required to independently support part of the roof load must be at least 1 in. (25 mm) greater in depth than ceiling joists not providing support. Check your local building codes to determine specific joist sizes.

CUTTING CEILING JOISTS

The lengths of the joists depend on how they meet over the bearing partition. If two joists lap one another over the partition, exact lengths are not required [see Figs. 7-1(a) and 7-1(b)].

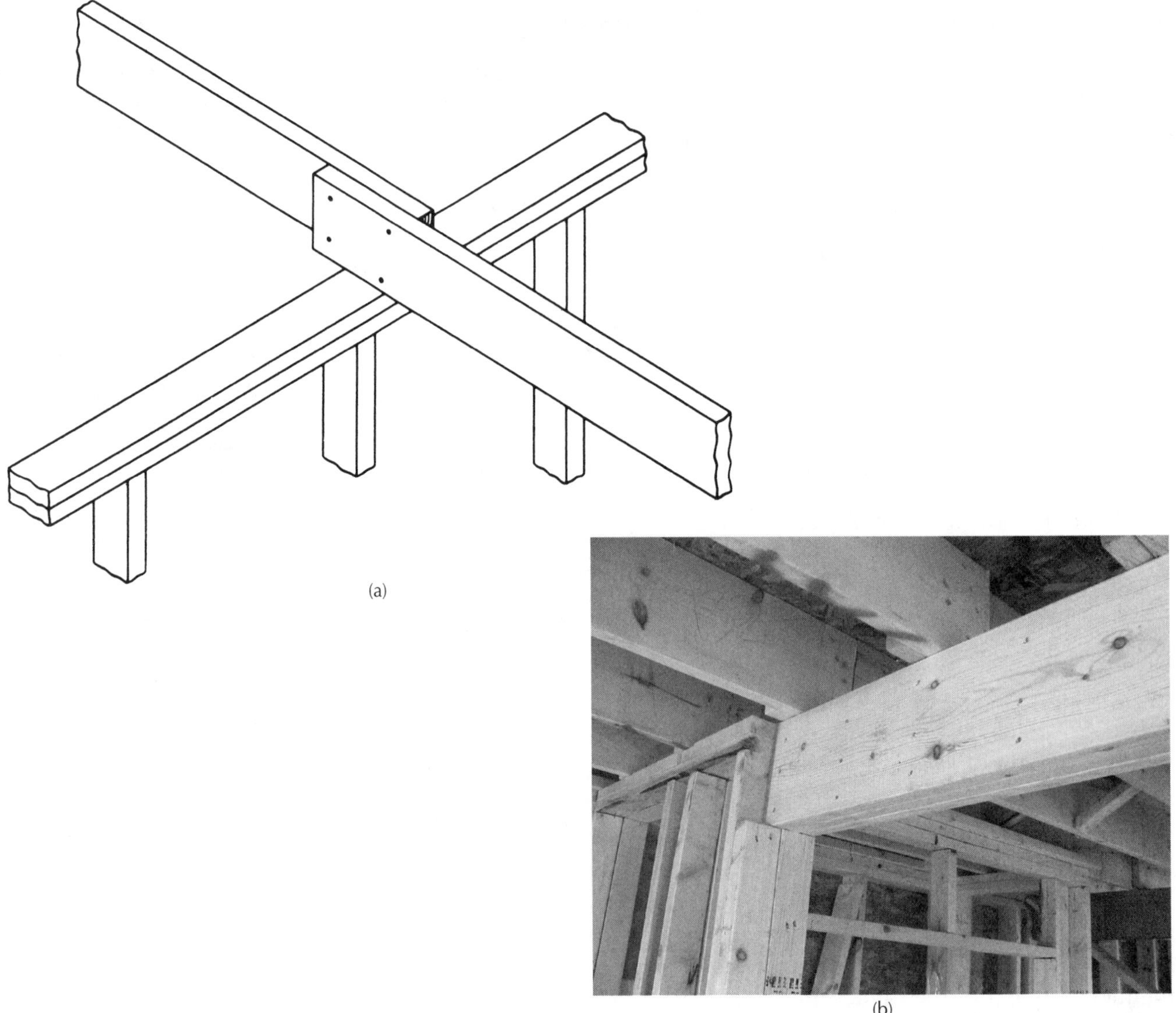

(a) (b)

FIGURE 7-1 (a) Ceiling joists lapped over bearing partition; (b) Ceiling Joists lapped over a beam.

In many cases ceiling joists may not always be supported on partitions; rather they may be supported on beams that provide more open space on a floor plan (see Fig. 7-2).

At the outer end, the joists may have to be cut to conform to the slope of the roof (see Fig. 7-3), but this depends on the depth of joists as well as the depth of rafters. To make this cut properly, two things must be known: (1) the slope of the rafter and (2) the height of the back of the rafter above the plate (see Fig. 7-4.).

FIGURE 7-2 Ceiling beam.

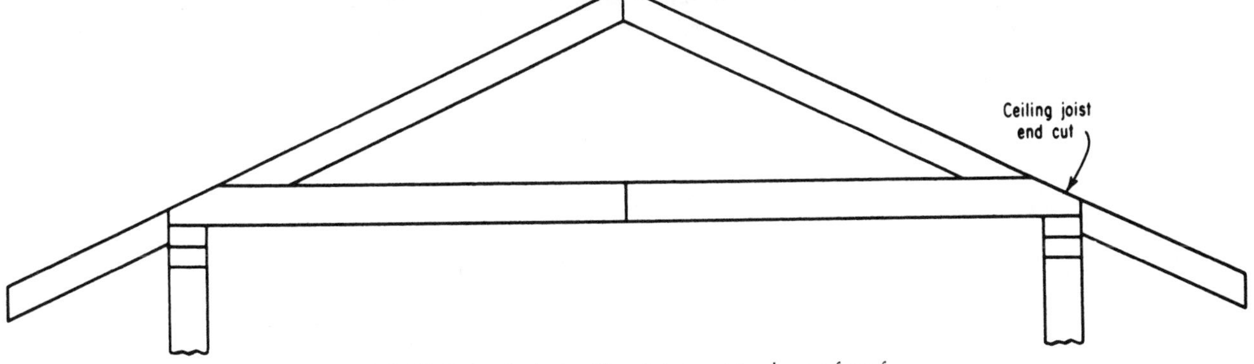

FIGURE 7-3 End of ceiling joists cut to slope of roof.

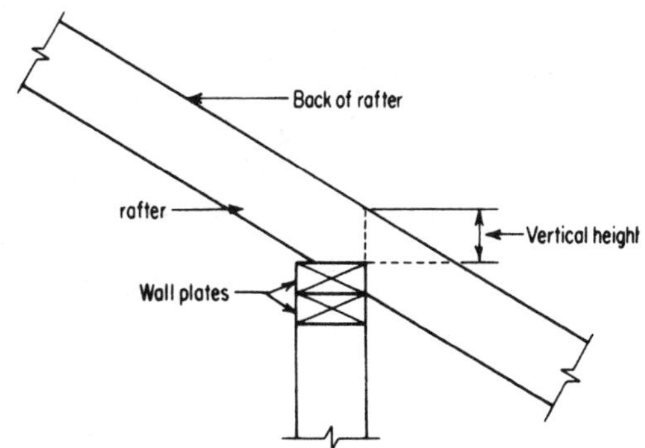

FIGURE 7-4 Height of back of rafter above plate.

Having determined these, proceed as follows:

1. Check to see which is the crown edge of the stock and make sure that it becomes the *upper* edge.
2. Measure up from the bottom edge of the joist, at the end, a distance equal to the height of the back of the rafter (see Fig. 7-5) and mark point A.

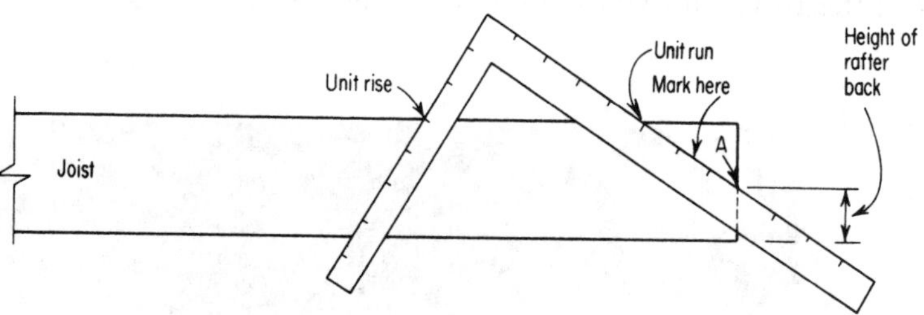

FIGURE 7-5 Layout for ceiling joist end cut.

3. Lay the square on the stock with the unit rise on the tongue and 12 in. (250) (unit run) on the blade touching the top edge and the edge of the blade passing through A. For an explanation regarding "unit rise" and "unit run," see Fig. 7-16(a).
4. Mark on the blade and cut the joist end to that line.

When a hip roof is involved, ceiling joists cannot be set close to the end walls, because they would interfere with the end wall rafters. In such a case, the regular ceiling joists must be stopped back far enough for the rafters to clear them (normally one or two joists spaces, depending on the slope of the roof), and *stub* joists are run at right angles to the end wall plate (see Fig. 7-6). In this case the joist

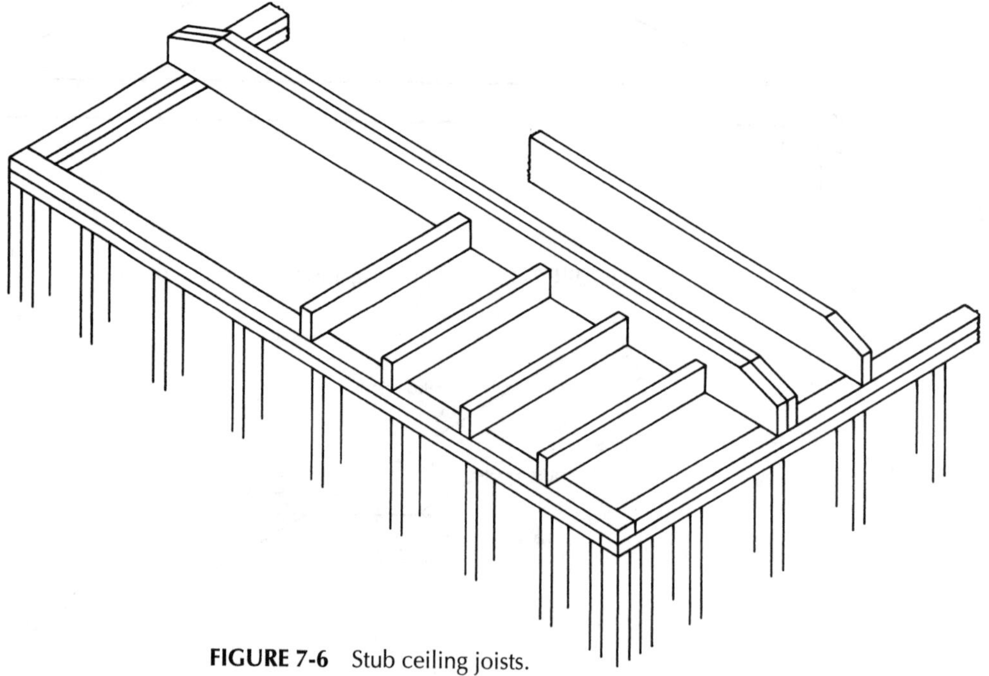

FIGURE 7-6 Stub ceiling joists.

supporting the stub joists is doubled and the stub joists are usually spaced the same as the regular ceiling joists.

ASSEMBLING THE CEILING FRAME

Normally, ceiling joists run across the narrow dimension of the building, but this is not always the case. Some joists may run in one direction and others at right angles to them. The main consideration is that there be adequate bearing and support at the ends (see Fig. 7-7).

Sometimes it is desired to have a *clear span ceiling* in some part of the building—a ceiling that runs unbroken from one outside wall to the other. Some means of supporting the inner ends of the joists is required, and this is done by means of a *flush beam*. A flush beam has its bottom edge flush with the bottom of the ceiling joists and is supported at its ends by a bearing wall or on a partition (see Fig. 7-8). Notice that these beams must be supported on built-in posts to absorb the concentrated load of the beam.

Ceiling joists that are carried by a flush beam must be supported on *joist hangers* fastened to the face of the beam as shown in Fig. 7-8.

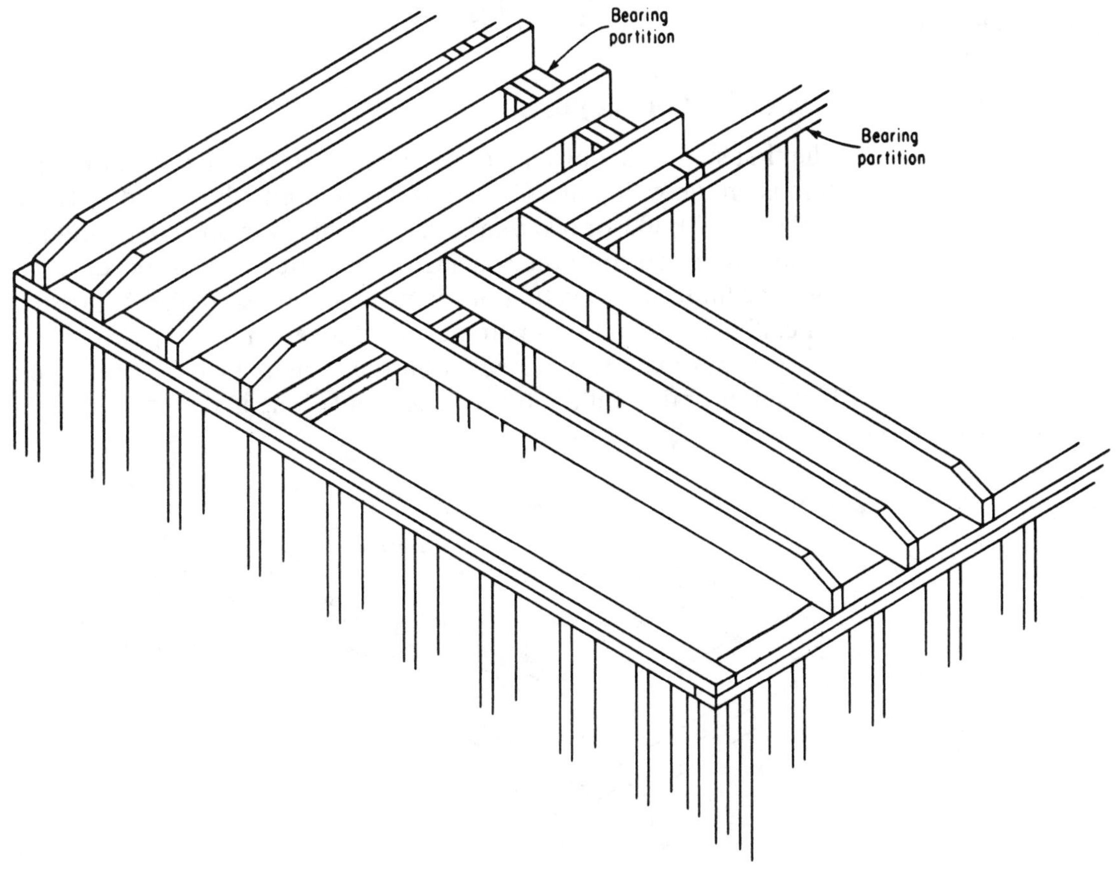

FIGURE 7-7 Joists running in two directions.

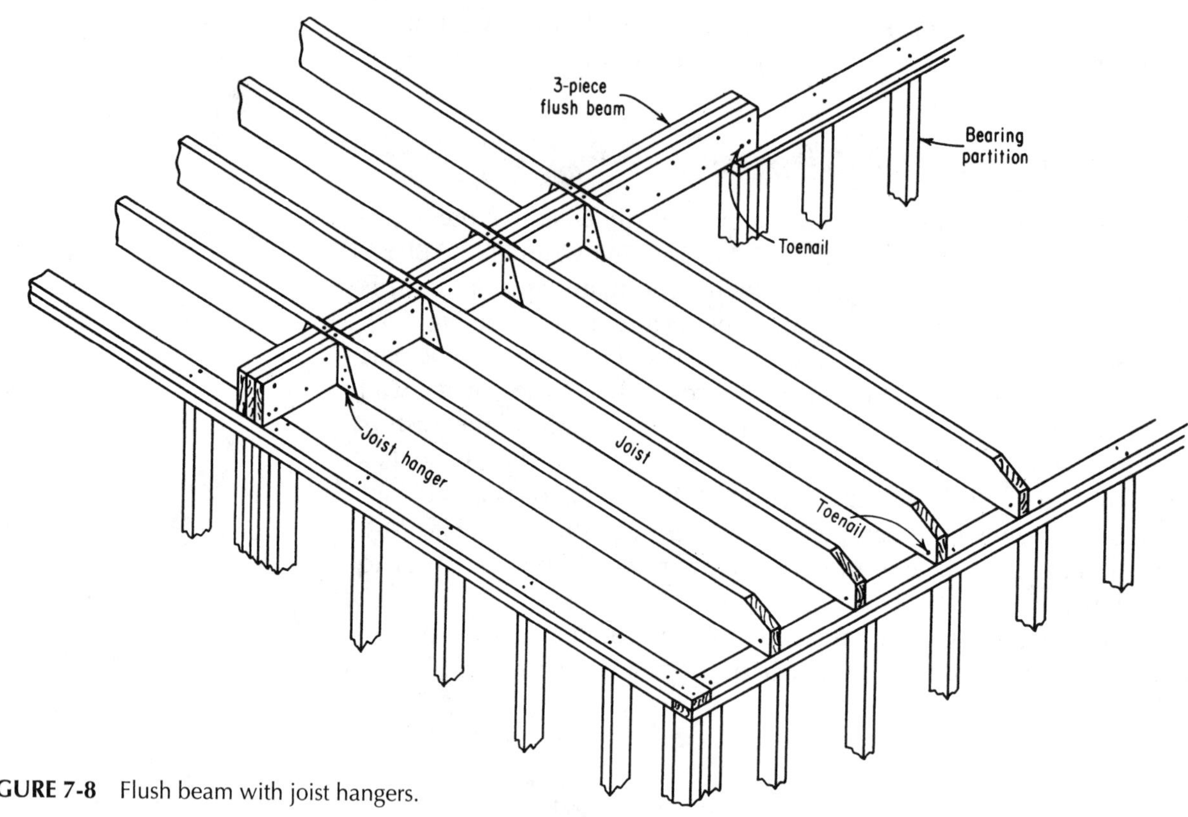

FIGURE 7-8 Flush beam with joist hangers.

Layout for Ceiling Joists

The first step in the placing of ceiling joists is the layout of their positions on the wall plate. Ceiling joists are normally spaced at 12, 16, or 24 in. (300, 400, or 600 mm) o.c. and, wherever possible, should be located to conform to the spacing of the rafters. This procedure not only facilitates the locating of the rafters but also makes it possible for ceiling joists and rafters to be nailed together.

Layout may begin either from the corners (see Fig. 7-9), from the center of the wall, or from some point along it, depending on the

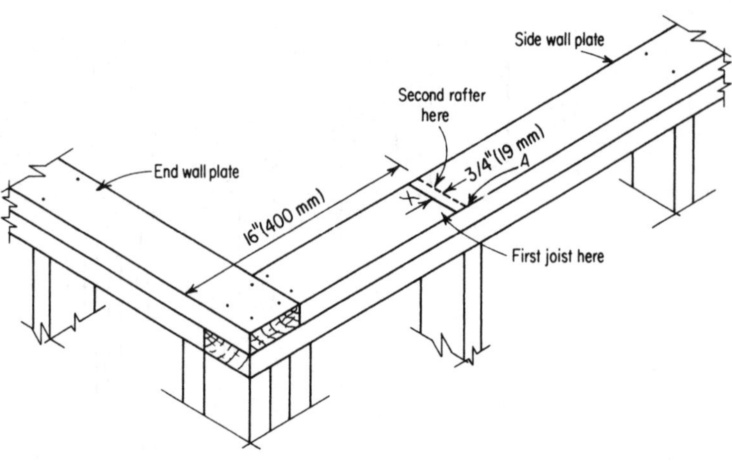

FIGURE 7-9 First joist position layout.

type of roof and the dimensions of the building. For a gable roof, the two sidewall plates must be laid out, while in the case of a hip roof, all four plates must be marked.

If the length is not evenly divisible by the joist spacing, it may be preferable to begin layout at the center of the wall and lay out both ways toward the corners. This will ensure that the ceiling joist spaces at both ends of the building will be the same, if that is desirable.

In a hip roof, there will normally be an end common rafter as shown in Fig. 7-14, which will be located in the center of the end wall. There should be a stub joist position next to it, and the remainder of the stub joist positions may be laid out from it.

Nailing of Joists

Ceiling joists must be toenailed to the wall or partition plates with a minimum of two $3\frac{1}{4}$-in. (82-mm) nails. In addition where the joists lap at the center they must be nailed with a minimum of two 3-in. (76-mm) nails at each end of the lap, as shown in Fig. 7-1(a).

Joist Restraint

Ceiling joists supporting a finished ceiling other than plywood, waferboard, or strandboard must be restrained from twisting by means of *cross bridging, blocking,* or *strapping* in a manner similar to that used for floor joists (see Chapter 5). If the ceiling is furred for application of ceiling material, the furring provides the necessary restraint.

Ceiling Backing

Partitions that run parallel to the direction of ceiling joists or trusses must be provided with some means of carrying the edges of the ceiling material that meet the partition. Therefore, *ceiling backing* is nailed to the cap plate as shown in Fig. 7-10. A piece of $1\frac{1}{2}$-in. (38-mm) material, at least 2 in. (50 mm) wider than the cap plate, is used, allowing it to project the same amount on both sides. Vapor barrier should be placed between the cap and top plates of the wall to provide a continuous barrier over the entire ceiling when adjacent to a roof cavity.

Attic Access

Building codes and fire regulations demand that there is access to the attic, and it is provided by a framed opening or *hatchway* as prescribed by local building codes, but is usually not less than 20 × 28 in.

(a) (b)

FIGURE 7-10 (a) Ceiling backing—main floor; (b) Ceiling backing—roof cavity.

(500 × 700 mm) for single dwelling units, or 22 × 36 in. (550 × 900 mm) for a building containing more than one dwelling unit (see Fig. 7-11). For appearance sake, it is usually placed in a relatively inconspicuous location, such as in a hallway, and provided with a tight fitting trapdoor or other type of cover that opens upward.

FIGURE 7-11 Attic access.

ROOF SHAPES

The shape of the roof may be one of several common designs, which include *shed* roof, *gable* roof, *hip* roof, *gambrel* roof, *dutch hip* roof, *mansard* roof, *flat* roof and *intersecting* roof [see Fig. 7-12(a–i)].

(a) Shed roof over entrance.

(b) Gable roof.

(c) Hip roof.

(d) Gambrel roof.

(e) Dutch hip roof.

(f) Modified Mansard roof.

FIGURE 7-12

(g) Flat roof.

(h) Intersecting roof.

(i) Unequal sloped gable.

FIGURE 7-12 (cont.)

The shed roof slopes in only one direction. The gable roof has two slopes, and the continuation of the end walls up to meet the roof is known as a *gable end.* The hip roof has four slopes, which terminate at a point if the building is square or in a ridge if it is rectangular [see Fig. 7-12(c)]. A gambrel roof is a modification of a gable, each side having two slopes instead of one. The Dutch hip roof is a combination of the gable and hip roof, with small gable ends and slopes on four sides. The mansard roof is a modification of the hip with two slopes on each side instead of one. The flat roof has no slope at all. The meeting of two sloped roofs of one type or another forms an intersecting roof as shown in Fig. 7-13.

RAFTER TERMS

To understand and solve the problems involved in laying out and cutting a set of rafters, it is necessary to know the terms used in discussing the subject. By examining a plan view of a roof frame, the different types of rafters involved in forming roofs can be easily distinguished. Figure 7-14 is a plan view of the frame of an intersecting hip roof where all types of rafters are involved.

FIGURE 7-13 Multiple intersecting roofs.

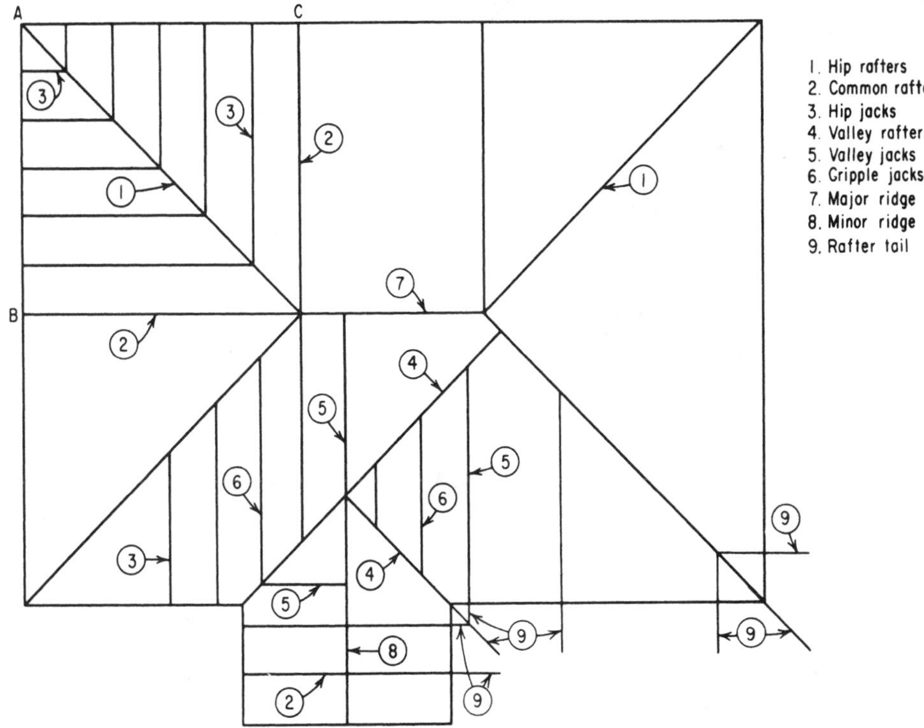

FIGURE 7-14 Roof plan.

The *common* rafters are those that run at right angles to the wall plate and meet the *ridge* at their top end. In a gable roof, all the rafters are *commons,* while in a hip roof, the two center end rafters and those side rafters, which meet the ridge, are *commons.* Hip rafters run from the corners of the wall plates to the ridge at an angle of 45° to the plates and form the intersection of two adjacent roof surfaces. *Valley* rafters occur where two roofs intersect. Jack rafters run parallel to the commons but are shorter and are named according to their position. *Hip jacks* run from plate to hip, usually meeting at the hip in pairs. *Valley jacks* run from the valley rafter to the ridge or plate. *Cripple jacks* run from hip to valley or from valley to valley, touching neither plate nor ridge. The part of any rafter that projects beyond the wall plate is known as the *rafter tail.*

Common Rafter

One of the basic terms, which applies to all rafters, is the *span,* the dimension of a building bridged by a pair of common rafters, while that part of the span traversed by one of the pair is called the *run* of the rafter. The length of the rafter, measured on a line from the center of the ridge to the outside edge of the building, is the *line length* of the rafter (see Fig. 7-15). The *total length* of the rafter is the sum of the line length and the *tail length* (see Fig. 7-15). The vertical distance from the level of the wall plates to the line length meeting point of a pair of rafters is the *total rise* of the rafter (see Fig. 7-15).

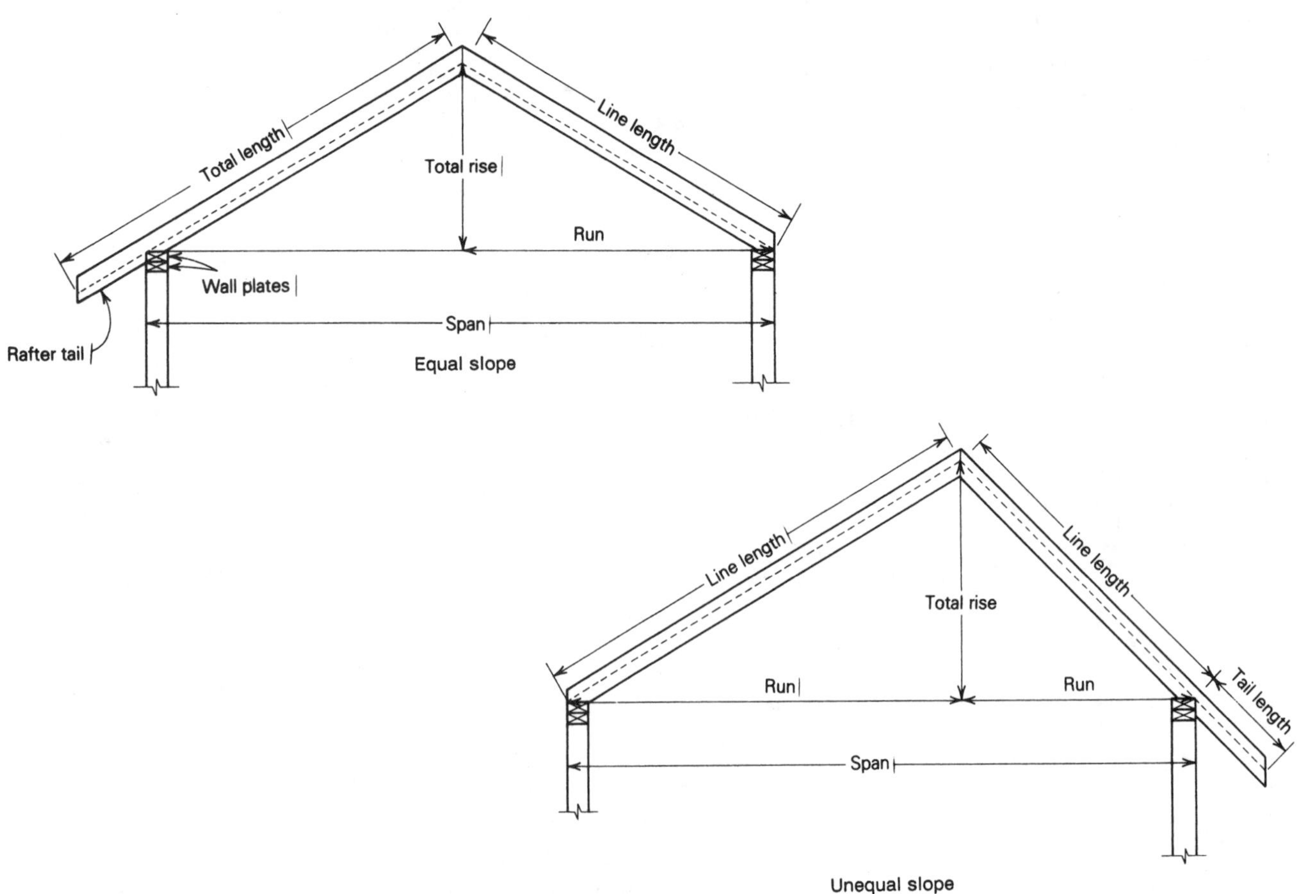

FIGURE 7-15 Span, run, rise, and line length of a rafter.

To make rafter layout simpler, run, rise, and line length are broken down into *units*. The basic one is the *unit run*—a standard length of 12 in. (300 mm) [Fig. 7-16(a)]. The *unit rise* is the vertical distance a rafter rises for one unit of run, while the slope length of a rafter resulting from one unit of run and one unit of rise is the *unit line length* [see Fig. 7-16(a)].

If a framing square is applied to a common rafter that is in position, as in Fig. 7-16(b), with the 12-in. (300-mm) mark on the blade coinciding with the outside edge of the wall plate, a figure on the tongue will indicate the *unit rise* of the rafter. In this case, the figure is 6 in. (100 mm) and the diagonal distance between 6 in. (100) on the tongue and 12 in. (200) on the blade is the *unit line length* which is 13.42 in. (223.6 mm) for that rafter [see Fig. 7-16(b)].

The inclination of a rafter is called the *slope* and can be expressed as a fraction or in degrees. The slope is most commonly expressed as the unit rise per unit run. For example, in Fig. 7-16(b), the slope is $\frac{6}{12}\left(\frac{1}{2}\right)$.

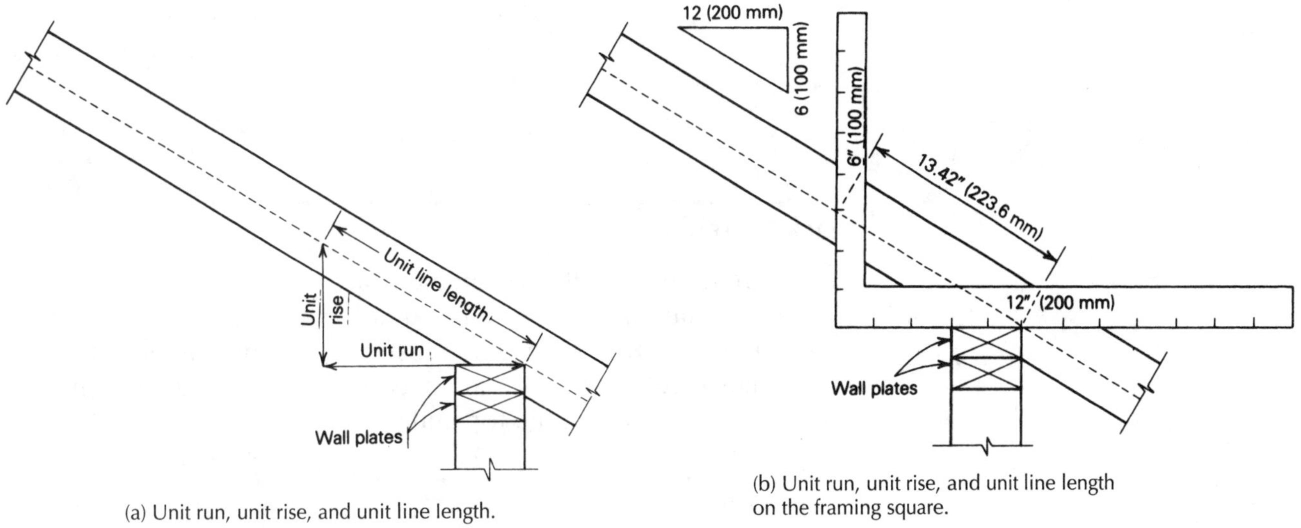

(a) Unit run, unit rise, and unit line length.

(b) Unit run, unit rise, and unit line length on the framing square.

FIGURE 7-16

In order that rafters may seat securely on the wall plate, it is common practice to cut a triangular section from the bottom edge, at the point at which it meets the wall plate, as shown in Fig. 7-17. This notch is called a *birdsmouth,* which is made by making a *seat cut*—cut horizontal when the rafter is in position—and a *plumb cut*—vertical when the rafter is in position (see Fig. 7-17). Common rafters are made to fit together at the top or fit against a ridge board (see Fig. 7-18) by making a *plumb cut* at the upper end of each, and the rafter tail may have a single *plumb cut* or a plumb cut and a *seat cut* at the bottom end (see Fig. 7-17). The horizontal distance from that bottom plumb cut to the rafter *tail plumb cut* is known as the *overhang* (see Fig. 7-17). In some cases the rafter tail cut may consist of both a tail plumb cut and a tail seat cut.

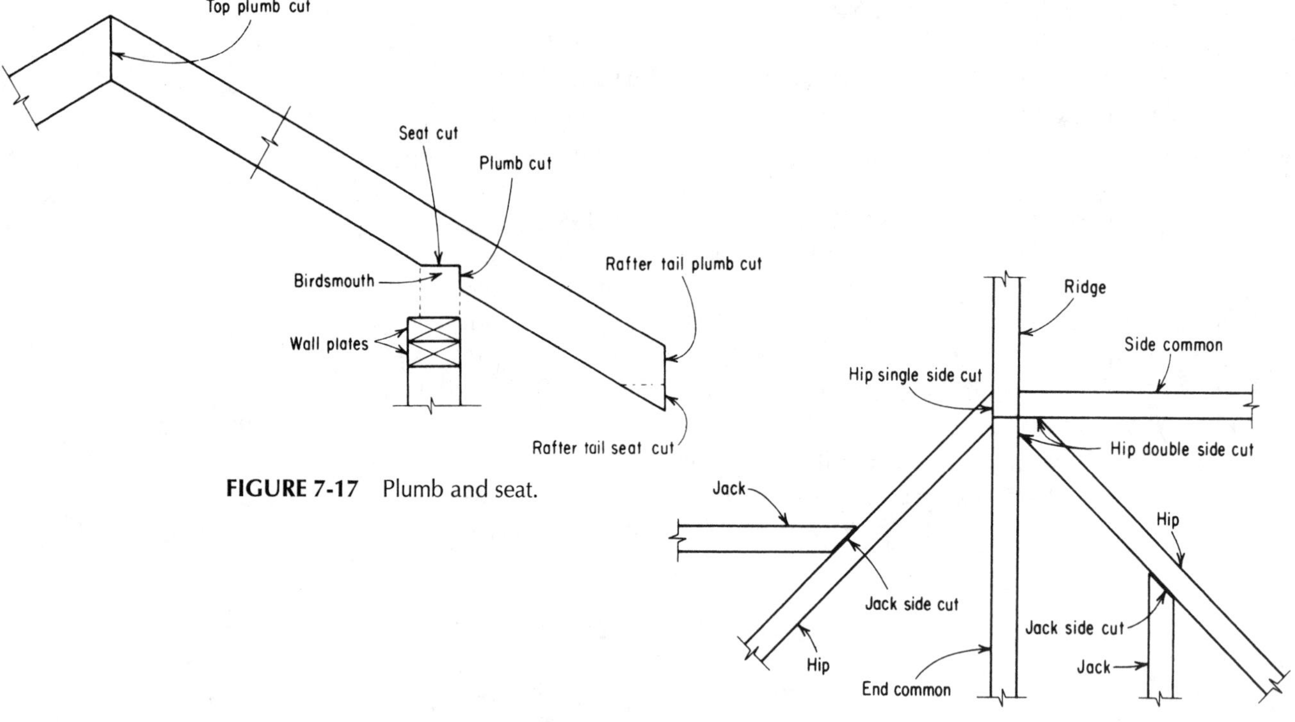

FIGURE 7-17 Plumb and seat.

FIGURE 7-18 Side cuts on hips and jacks.

Jack Rafter

Jack rafters run parallel to common rafters and therefore have the same unit run, unit rise, and unit line length. They have the same birdsmouth at the plate and must have a top plumb cut. But, since they meet a hip rafter at an angle, each one must also have a *side cut* or *cheek cut* at the top end.

Hip Rafter

Hip rafters also have a birdsmouth at the plate but, since they run at an angle to the plate and the ridge, they must also have a *side cut* at the top end as well as a plumb cut. That side cut may be *single* or *double* (see Fig. 7-18), depending on how the rafter meets the ridge.

Hip rafters run at an angle of 45° to the wall plate (see Fig. 7-14), and, as a result, their unit run is different from that of a common rafter. As illustrated in Fig. 7-19(a), a hip rafter must traverse the diagonal of a square in order to span one unit of common rafter run. Thus the unit run of a hip rafter will be the length of the diagonal of a square with sides of 12 in. (200 mm)—namely 17 in. (283 mm).

If the framing square is applied to a hip rafter in position, as shown in Fig. 7-19(b), the 17-in. (283-mm) mark on the blade must coincide with the outside edge of the wall plate to represent the *unit run,* and a figure on the tongue will indicate the *unit rise.* If the rafter has the same rise as the one shown in Fig. 7-16, then that fig-

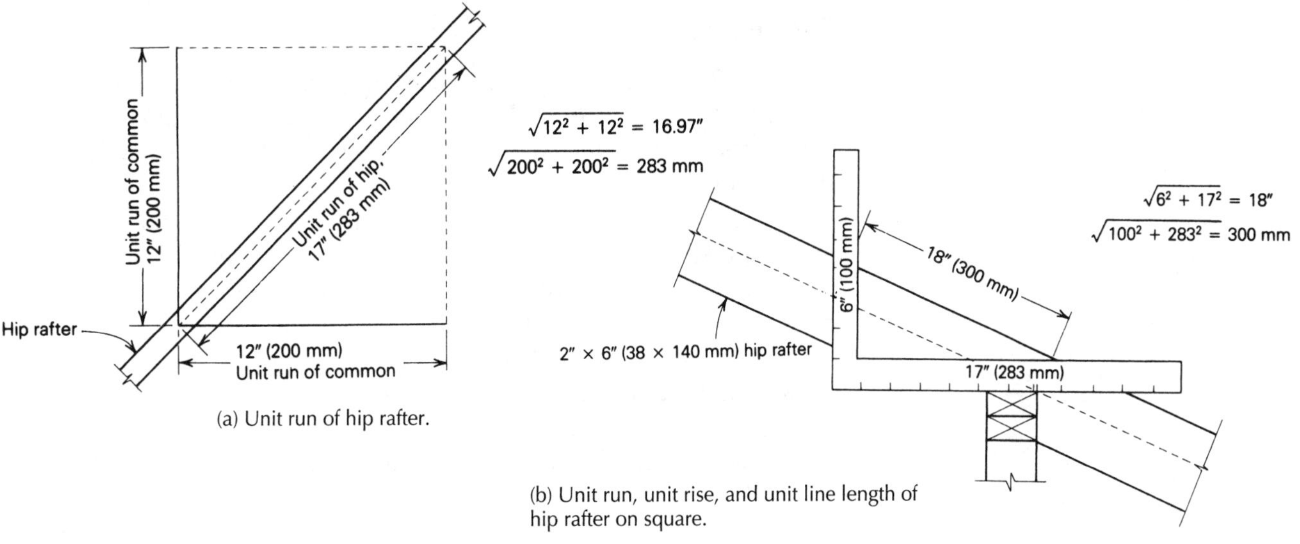

(a) Unit run of hip rafter.

(b) Unit run, unit rise, and unit line length of hip rafter on square.

FIGURE 7-19

ure will be 6 in. (100). Again, the diagonal distance between 6 in. (100) on the tongue and 17 in. (283) on the blade is the *unit line length* for the hip rafter.

Since hip rafters occur at the intersection of two surfaces of a hip roof, the *roof sheathing* on each surface must meet on a hip. To provide a flat surface on which the sheathing ends may rest, the birdsmouth must be adjusted to lower the hip rafter so that the outside edge is flush with the roof surface (see Fig. 7-20).

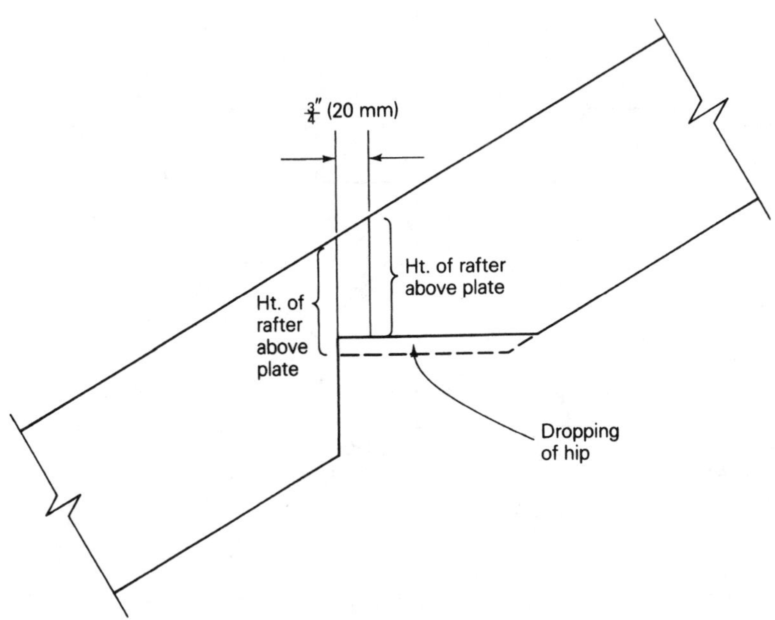

FIGURE 7-20 Dropping the hip.

Shortening

In Fig. 7-21(a), two lines *AC* and *BC* represent two common rafters such that these lines pass through the junction of the plumb and level cuts of the birdsmouth. In addition, a ridge board is inserted between the two upper rafter ends.

The two lines *AC* and *BC* meet in the center of the ridge at *C*, and the distance from *A* or *B* to *C* is the line length of the rafter as shown in Fig. 7-15. However, the rafter actually ends at *D*; the distance from *A* or *B* to *D* is the actual length of the rafter. It is *shortened* by the measurement *CD*, which can vary depending on the rise of the rafter. However, if the *shortening* is measured at *right angles to the plumb cut*, this measurement will remain constant—*one-half the thickness of the ridge*. For a $1\frac{1}{2}$-in. (38-mm) ridge, that distance will be $\frac{3}{4}$ in. (19 mm).

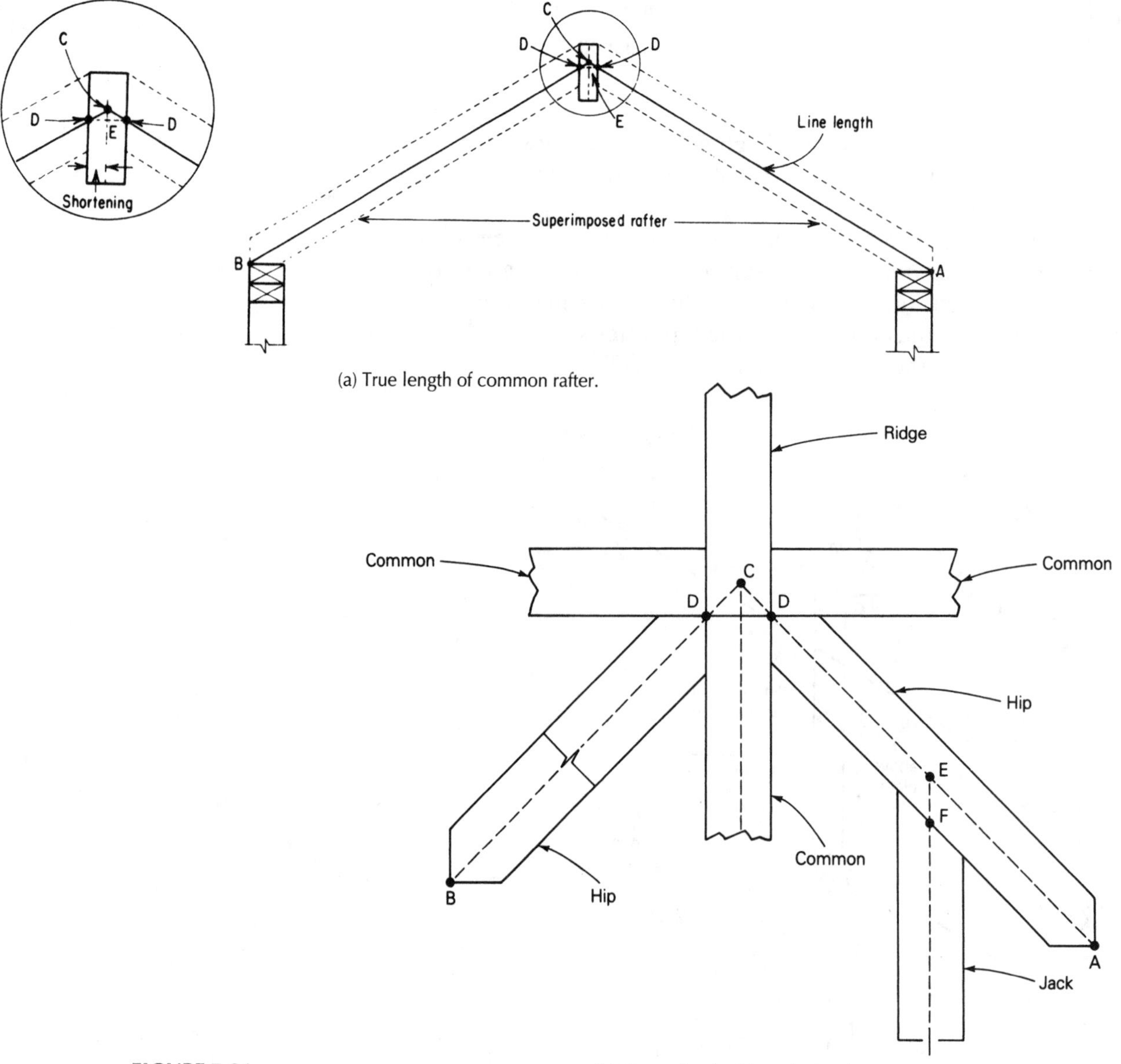

(a) True length of common rafter.

(b) Shortening for hip or jack rafter.

FIGURE 7-21

With regard to a hip rafter, it meets the ridge at an angle of 45° [see Fig. 7-21(b)] and therefore must be *shortened*, in a horizontal direction (at right angles to a plumb cut) by a distance *CD* [see Fig. 7-21(b)], *one-half the diagonal thickness of the rafter*. For a $1\frac{1}{2}$-in. (38-mm) rafter, that will amount to approximately $1\frac{1}{16}$ in. (27 mm).

A jack rafter meets the hip at an angle of 45° in plan [see Fig. 7-21(b)] and must be *shortened* by a distance equal to *EF*, taken at right angles to the plumb cut. For a $1\frac{1}{2}$-in. (38-mm) hip, that distance will also be $1\frac{1}{16}$ in. (27 mm).

Ridge

Rather than have a pair of rafters meet together at their top end, it is customary to introduce a ridge board between them. This ridge board makes it easier to keep the top line of the roof straight and provides support for the roof sheathing between rafters.

The ridge of a gable roof will have the same length as the length of the building plus roof overhang at the gable ends, if any. The length of a hip roof ridge, however, takes a little more consideration.

Turn back to Fig. 7-14 and study it a moment. The plan view of the hip rafter is the diagonal of a square, the sides of which are *AB* and *AC* where*AB* is equal to half the width of the building. The top end of the hip is at a point half the width of the building *along* the length. The hip at the opposite end covers a like distance. Therefore, the distance between the top ends of the two hips is equal to the length of the building minus the width. In other words, the line length of the ridge is the length of building minus the width.

When a ridge board is introduced into the frame, the common rafters are shortened by half the ridge thickness. Consequently, the end commons would not reach the ends of the ridge if they were cut to true length. So the ridge length is increased by half its own thickness at each end. In other words, the *true length of the hip roof ridge is the length of building minus the width plus the thickness of the ridge.*

An intersecting roof contains two ridges. The ridge of the main roof is called the *major* ridge, whereas the ridge in the projection is known as the *minor* ridge.

HOW TO USE THE RAFTER TABLE

Having considered rafter framing terminology, it is now necessary to examine the methods used to determine the lengths of various types of rafters and how to lay out and cut them.

Calculation of lengths may be done in several ways, including the use of the *rafter table and mathematics*, by *scaling on the framing square*, and by *scale drawings*. Or, the framing square may be used to *step-off* the length. For most situations, the combination of rafter table and math, followed with using a taped measurement of lengths, is the simplest and most accurate.

Rafter Table

Figure 7-22(a) illustrates a framing square, with a *rafter table* on the face of the blade. The numbers along the top edge of the blade represent *unit rises,* with calculations for 17 rises ranging from 2 to 18 in. Figure 7-22(b) illustrates a metric framing square, with calculations for 14 rises ranging from 200 to 1500 mm, in increments of 100 mm. The first step in using the rafter table, then, is to locate the number that corresponds to the unit rise of the roof in question.

To find the *unit line length* of a common rafter, look on the first line of the table under the unit rise concerned; the figure found there is the line length for 1 ft (1000 mm) of common run. Multiply that figure by the number of units of run for that rafter to obtain the line length of the common rafter in inches (mm). The number of units of run for the rafter may be calculated by dividing the *total run* of the rafter in inches by 12 (mm × 1000).

23	22	21	20	19	18	17	16
LENGTH COMMON RAFTERS PER FOOT RUN					21 63	20 81	20 00
LENGTH HIP OR VALLEY PER FOOT RUN					24 74	24 02	23 32
DIFFERENCE IN LENGTH OF JACKS 16" INCHES CENTRES					28 84	27 74	26 66
DIFFERENCE IN LENGTH OF JACKS 2' FEET CENTRES					43 27	41 62	40
SIDE CUT OF JACKS USE					6 11/16	6 15/16	7 3/16
SIDE CUT HIP OR VALLEY USE					8 1/4	8 1/2	8 3/4
22	21	20	19	18	17	16	15	14

15	14	13	12	11	10	9	8
19 21	18 44	17 69	16 97	16 28	15 62	15 00	14 42
22 65	22 00	21 38	20 78	20 22	19 70	19 21	18 76
25 61	24 585	23 588	22 625	21 704	20 83	20	19 23
38 42	36 08	35 38	33 94	32 56	31 24	30	28 84
7 1/2	7 13/16	8 1/8	8 1/2	8 7/8	9 1/4	9 5/8	10
9 1/16	9 3/8	9 5/8	9 7/8	10 1/8	10 3/8	10 5/8	10 7/8
14	13	12	11	10	9	8	7	6

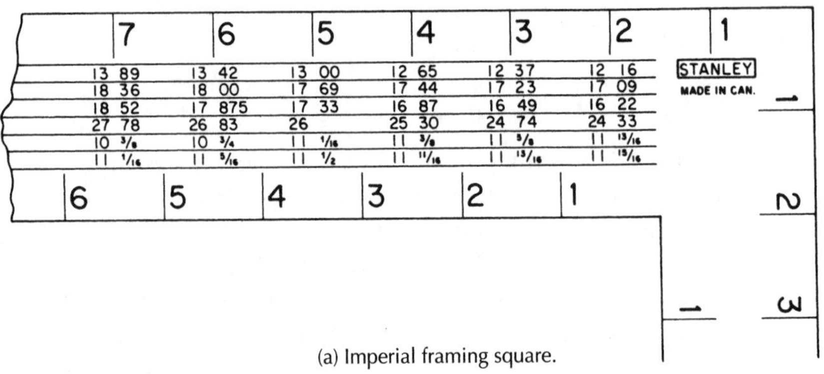

7	6	5	4	3	2	1
13 89	13 42	13 00	12 65	12 37	12 16	STANLEY
18 36	18 00	17 69	17 44	17 23	17 09	MADE IN CAN.
18 52	17 875	17 33	16 87	16 49	16 22	
27 78	26 83	26	25 30	24 74	24 33	
10 3/8	10 3/4	11 1/16	11 3/8	11 5/8	11 13/16	
11 1/16	11 5/16	11 1/2	11 11/16	11 13/16	11 15/16	
6	5	4	3	2	1	

(a) Imperial framing square.

FIGURE 7-22

MM RISE	PER METRE	OF RUN	250	300	400	500	600	700	750	HIP
MM LENGTH	COMMON RAFTERS PER METRE RUN		1031	1044	1077	1118	1166	1221	1250	VALLEY
"	HIP OR VALLEY	" " "	1436	1446	1470	1500	1536	1578	1601	RAFTER
MM DIFF. IN LENGTH OF JACKS 400 MM O.C.			412	418	431	447	466	488	500	SET
" " " " " "	600 MM	"	618	626	646	671	700	732	750	POINT
SIDE CUT OF	JACKS	USE OPP. 200MM LINE	206	209	215	224	233	244	250	
" " "	HIPS OR VALLEYS	" " " " "	203	204	208	212	217	223	226	

HIP	800	900	1000	1100	COMMON	1200	1300	1400	1500	2MM
VALLEY	1281	1345	1414	1487	RAFTER	1562	1640	1720	1803	GRADUATIONS
RAFTER	1625	1676	1732	1792	SET	1855	1921	1990	2061	
SET	512	538	566	595	POINT	625	656	688	721	
POINT	768	807	848	892		937	984	1032	1082	
	256	269	283	297		312	328	344	361	
	230	237	245	253		262	272	281	292	

(b) Metric framing square.

FIGURE 7-22

The second line gives the *unit line length* of a hip or valley rafter per unit of common run. The line length of the hip or valley rafter will be that figure, multiplied by the number of units of common run in the building.

The third line gives the difference in length of successive jack rafters spaced 16 in. (400 mm) o.c. and is also the line length of the first jack rafter from the corner, spaced 16 in. (400 mm) o.c. Thus, having found the *true* (shortened) length of the first jack rafter from the corner, the length of the next one is found by adding that "difference in length" figure to the shortened length.

The fourth line on the square gives the difference in length of jack rafters spaced 2 ft (600 mm) o.c. The fifth line indicates the figure to use on the tongue for the side cut of jack rafters. Again, 12 in. (200) is the blade figure, and the cut is marked along the blade. The sixth line on the square indicates the figure to use on the tongue of the square in laying out the side cuts for hip and valley rafters. The blade figure is always 12 in. (200 mm), and the cut is always marked along the blade.

Framing Calculations and Layout

Figure 7-23 is a plan view of a hip roof with an intersecting gable roof, with dimensions as indicated. On it are marked a number of typical roof framing members whose length and layout will be demonstrated.

Length of Major Ridge (A)

The length of the ridge for a hip roof is the length of the building minus the width plus the thickness of the rafter. In this example the length

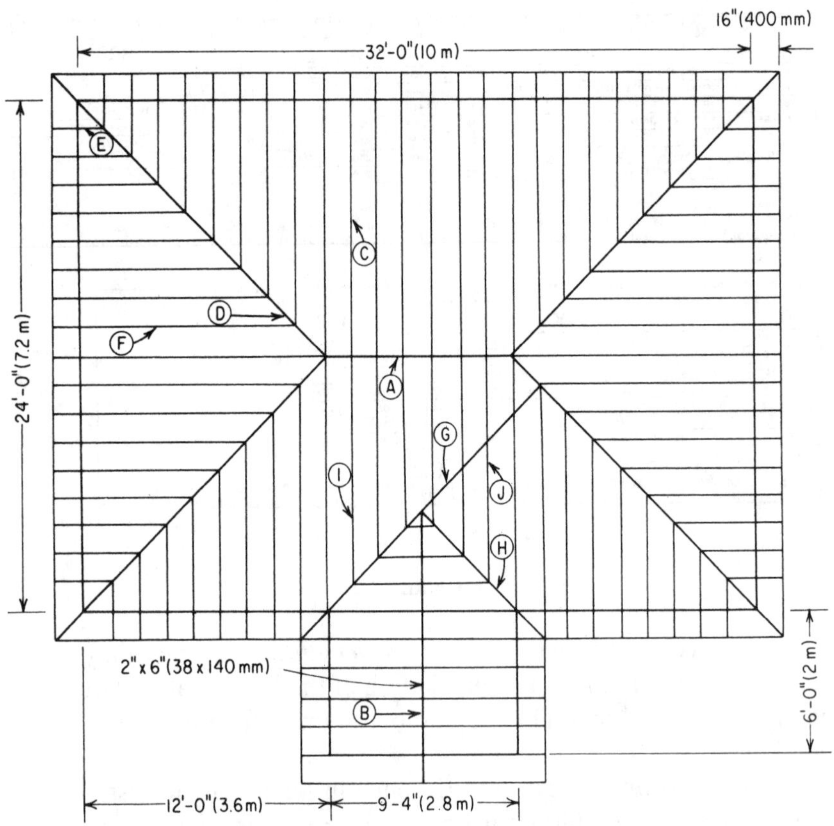

FIGURE 7-23 Plan view, intersecting roof.

is 32 ft − 24 ft + $1\frac{1}{2}$ in. = 8 ft, $1\frac{1}{2}$ in. (10,000 mm − 7200 mm + 38 mm = 2838 mm). The size of the material for the ridge will normally be 2 × 6 in. (38 × 140 mm).

Length of Minor Ridge (B)

The length of the minor ridge will be the length of the projection (see Fig. 7-23) plus one-half of its width plus the overhang minus one-half the diagonal thickness of the supporting valley rafter. In this case the length will be 6 ft + 4 ft − 7 in + 16 in. − $1\frac{1}{16}$ in. = 11 ft,9-$\frac{15}{16}$ in. (2000 mm + 1400 mm + 400 mm − 27 mm = 3773 mm).

Length and Layout of Common Rafter (C)

The unit line length for a common rafter with a slope of 6 to 12 as shown under 6 [see Fig. 7-22(a)] is 13.42. The line length of the rafter is equal to the number of units of run (feet) times the unit line length: 12 × 13.42 = 161.04 in. or 13 ft, $5\frac{1}{16}$ in. The corresponding metric slope of $\frac{1}{2}$ will result in a unit line length of 1118 as shown under 500 [see Fig. 7-22(b)]. The number of units of run for the common rafter with a run of 3600 mm will be 3600 ÷ 1000 = 3.6. The line length of the rafter will be 1118 × 3.6 = 4024.8 ≈ 4025 mm.

The line length of the rafter tail will be $\frac{16}{12} \times 13.42 = 17.89$ in. or 17-$\frac{7}{8}$ in. $\left(\frac{400}{1000} \times 1118 = 447.2 \approx 447 \text{ mm}\right)$.

A typical common rafter (C) may now be laid out, cut, and used as a pattern for all the common rafters. Proceed as follows:

1. Pick out a piece of straight 2 × 4(38 × 89 mm) stock of sufficient length and lay out a plumb cut at the top end. This is done by laying the square on the stock with the rise—6 in. (100 mm)—on the tongue and the unit run—12 in. (200 mm)—on the blade. Mark along the tongue, making sure the square is set so the crown is on the topside of the rafter [see Fig. 7-24(a)].
2. From the top plumb line, measure 13 ft 5$\frac{1}{16}$ in. (4025 mm) along the topside of the rafter to locate the plumb cut at the birdsmouth [see Fig. 7-24(b)].
3. Measure 2$\frac{1}{2}$ in. (64 mm) down from the back of the rafter along the birdsmouth plumb cut to locate the seat of the birdsmouth; draw a line perpendicular to the plumb cut at this point to establish the seat cut [see Fig. 7-24(c)].
4. From the birdsmouth plumb cut, measure 17-$\frac{7}{8}$ in. (447 mm) along the topside of the rafter to the tail plumb cut. Draw a plumb line through this point parallel to the other plumb lines [see Fig. 7-24(d)].

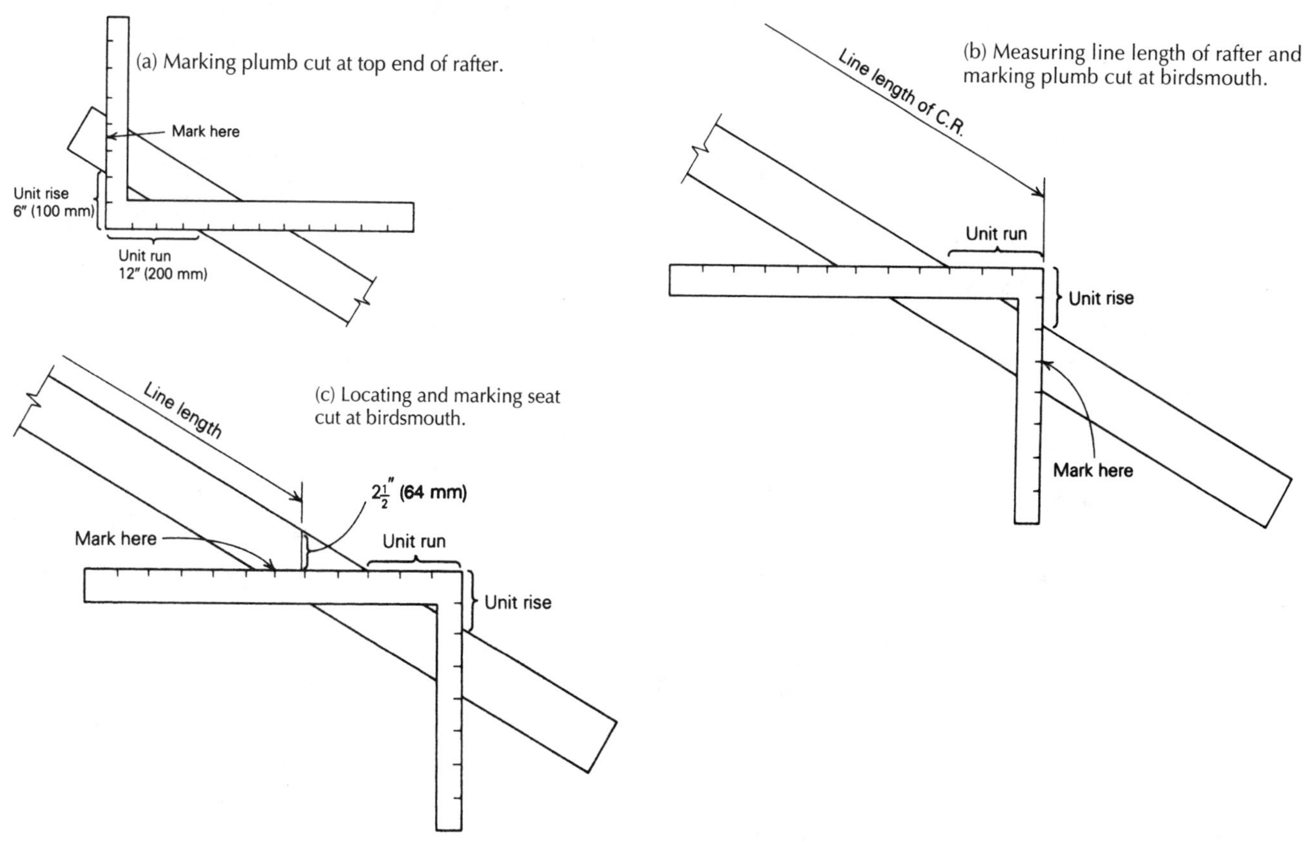

FIGURE 7-24

5. Measure a distance equal to the thickness of the rough fascia perpendicular to the tail plumb cut for the shortening at the tail end. Cut the tail end at this point [see Fig. 7-24(e)].
6. At the top end of the rafter, shorten the rafter a distance equal to half the thickness of the ridge. This measurement is made at right angles to the plumb line at the top end of the rafter. Cut the top end at this point [see Fig. 7-24(f)].
7. Use this cut rafter as the pattern for other rafters. Make sure that the crown (bow) is always placed on the top edge of the rafter [see Fig. 7-24(g)].

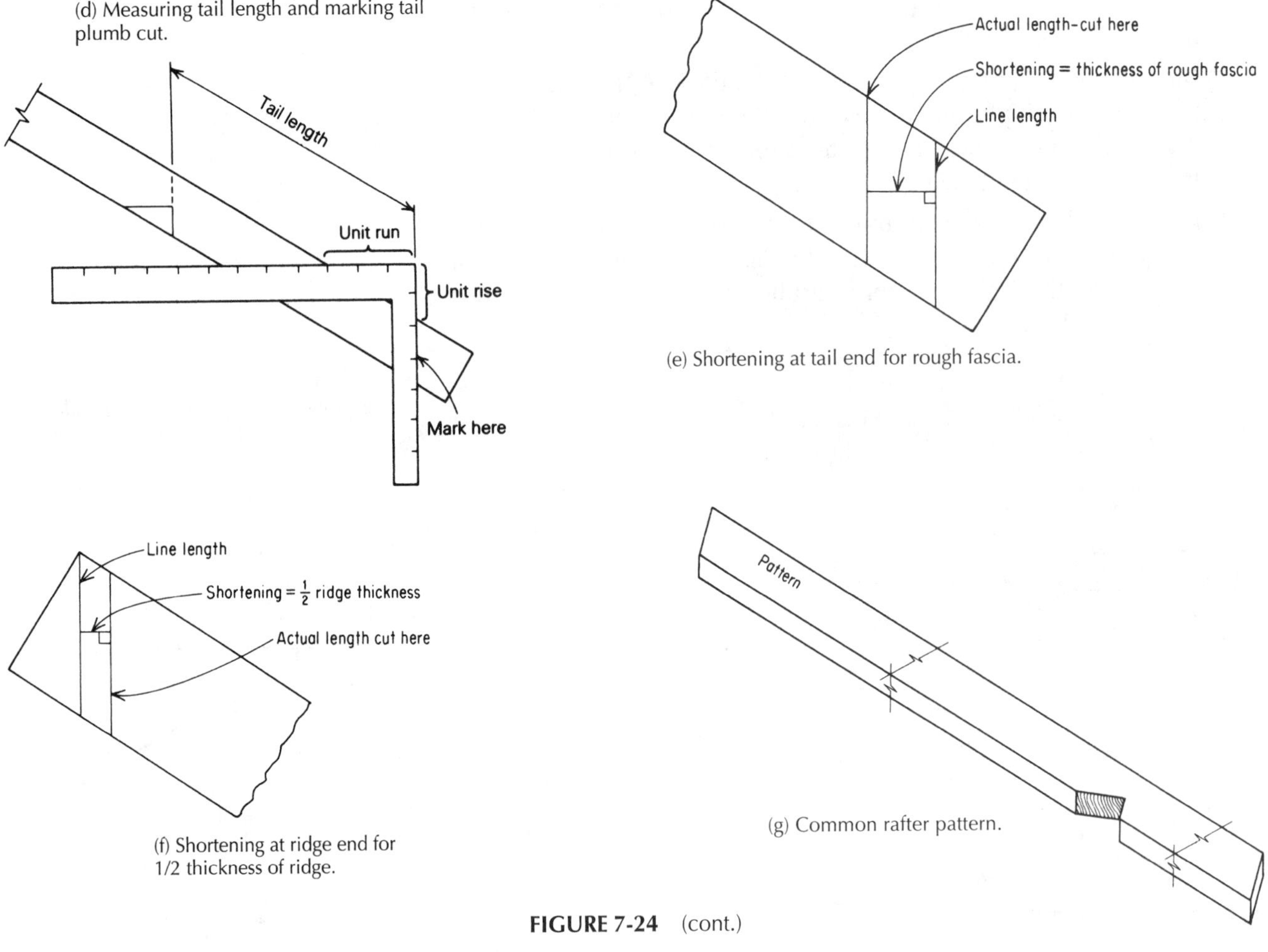

(d) Measuring tail length and marking tail plumb cut.

(e) Shortening at tail end for rough fascia.

(f) Shortening at ridge end for 1/2 thickness of ridge.

(g) Common rafter pattern.

FIGURE 7-24 (cont.)

Length and Layout of Hip Rafter (D)

The unit line length for a hip rafter with a unit rise of 6 in. is 18 in. [as shown under 6 on the second line of the rafter table in Fig. 7-22(a)]. Since the number of units of run is 12, the line length of the rafter will be $12 \times 18 = 216$ in. $=$ 18 ft. The line length of the rafter tail will be $\frac{16}{12} \times 18 = 24$ in.

The corresponding metric slope of 1 to 2 will result in a unit line length of 1500 mm [as shown under 500 on the second line of the rafter table in Fig. 7-22(b)]. The line length is equal to the number of units of run for the common rafter (3.6) times the unit line length ($3.6 \times 1500 = 5400$ mm). The line length of the rafter tail is $\frac{400}{1000} \times 1500 = 600$ mm.

A typical hip rafter (D) may now be laid out using the following procedure:

1. Pick out a straight piece of 2 × 6 (38 × 140-mm) stock of sufficient length and lay out the plumb line as near one end as possible. This is done by using the unit rise (6 in. or 100 mm) on the tongue and the unit run (17 in. or 283 mm) on the blade and marking the plumb line along the tongue. Make sure the crown of the 2 × 6 corresponds with the topside of the rafter [see Fig. 7-25(a)].
2. From the top end plumb line, measure 18 ft (5400 mm) along the back of the rafter to the plumb line at the birdsmouth [see Fig. 7-25(b)].
3. At right angles to this plumb line draw another plumb line $\frac{3}{4}$ in. (19 mm) closer to the top end plumb line. Measure $2\frac{1}{2}$ in. (64 mm) down from the back of the rafter to locate the seat of the birdsmouth. Draw a line perpendicular to the plumb line at this point to establish the seat cut [see Fig. 7-25(c)].
4. From the birdsmouth plumb line, measure 24 in. (600 mm) along the back of the rafter to establish the tail plumb line [see Fig. 7-25(d)].
5. Measure a distance equal to the diagonal thickness of the rough fascia perpendicular to the tail plumb cut for the shortening at the tail end. This would be $2\frac{1}{8}$ in. for a 2 × 6 (54 mm for a 38 × 140) fascia. The end of the rafter tail must fit into the apex of an external angle and therefore must have a *double cheek cut* at the end [see Fig. 7-25(e)]. Lay out the two side cuts by drawing a line parallel to the shortened plumb cut a perpendicular distance of one-half the thickness of the rafter from the plumb cut. Join this line to the midpoint of the top of the plumb cut squared across the edge [see Fig. 7-25(f)].
6. From the top end plumb line, measure back at right angles a distance equal to one-half the diagonal thickness of the ridge $\left(1\frac{1}{16}\text{ in. or 27 mm}\right)$ and through this point draw a second plumb line. The rafter is now properly *shortened* for the ridge. Square across the top edge of the rafter from this line and mark the center point. Single- or double-side cut lines will be drawn through this point to a point established by measuring back at right angles a distance equal to one-half the thickness of the rafter [see Fig. 7-25(f)].

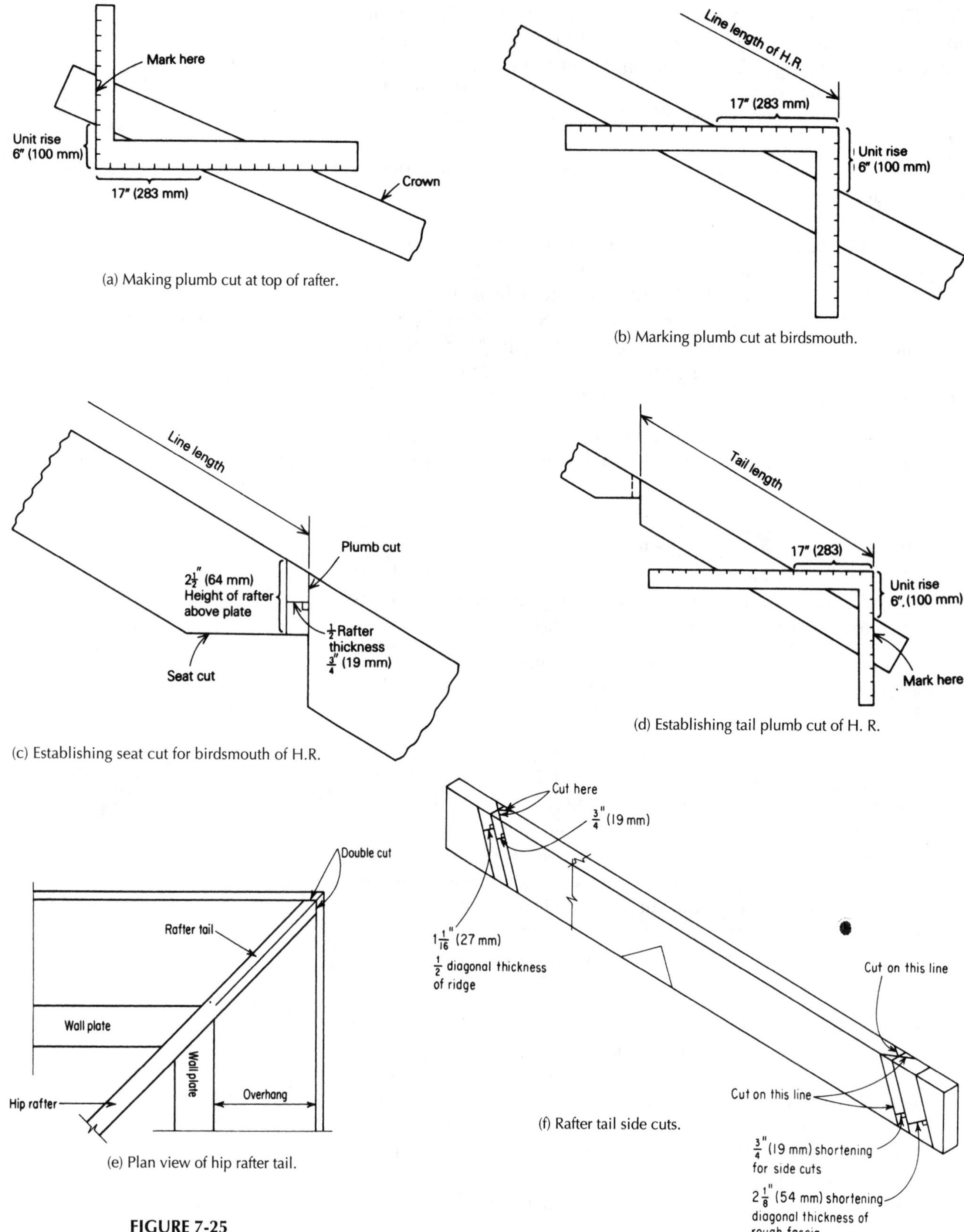

(a) Making plumb cut at top of rafter.

(b) Marking plumb cut at birdsmouth.

(c) Establishing seat cut for birdsmouth of H.R.

(d) Establishing tail plumb cut of H. R.

(e) Plan view of hip rafter tail.

(f) Rafter tail side cuts.

FIGURE 7-25

Length and Layout of Jack Rafter (F)

The rafter tail and the birdsmouth layout of this rafter are identical to the common rafter. The third line of the rafter table indicates that, for a 6-in. (500-mm) rise, the difference in length of jack rafters 16 in. (400) o.c. is 17.875 in. (447 mm). That is also the amount the longest jack rafter is shorter than the common rafter. To lay out this rafter, proceed as follows:

1. Pick out a piece of stock (2×4) and mark a plumb, cut as near the top end as possible. This is done by using the unit rise of 6 in. (100 mm) on the tongue and the unit run of 12 in. (200 mm) on the blade. Mark along the tongue, making sure the crown of the rafter is on the top edge [see Fig. 7-24(a)].
2. From the plumb cut, measure the jack rafter line length to locate the birdsmouth. The longest jack rafter line length is equal to the common rafter line length minus the difference in length of adjacent jack rafters: $161.04\text{ in.} - 17.875 = 143.164\text{ in.} = 11\text{ ft } 11\frac{3}{16}\text{ in.}$ ($4025 - 447\text{ mm} = 3578\text{ mm}$) [see Fig. 7-24(b)].
3. The layout of the birdsmouth and the rafter tail are exactly the same as for the common rafter.
4. From the top plumb cut line, measure back at right angles a distance equal to half the diagonal thickness of the hip rafter—$1\frac{1}{16}$ in. (27 mm)—and through it draw a second plumb line parallel to the first plumb line. With the electric handsaw set at 45°, cut along this line. Remember that these rafters are cut in pairs to be placed on opposite sides of the hip rafter (see Fig. 7-26).

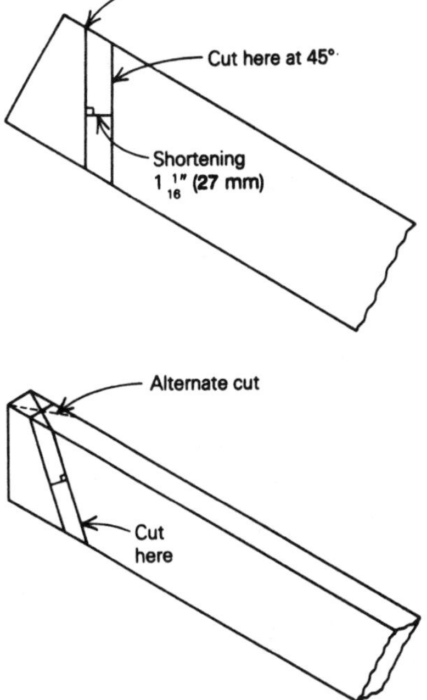

FIGURE 7-26 Shortening at top of jack rafter.

Line Length and Layout of Jack Rafter (E)

The jack rafter (E) is the eighth and shortest rafter in the series, and therefore its length will be eight times the difference in length of jack rafters shorter than the common rafter.

Length and Layout of Valley Rafter (G)

The total run of the valley rafter (G) is 16 in. (400 mm) less than that of a common rafter, namely 10 ft, 8 in. (3200 mm). Its line length will be $10.67 \times 18 = 192.06$ in. or 16 ft, $\left(\frac{3200}{1000} \times 1500 = 4800\text{ mm}\right)$.

The layout for the rafter tail plumb line and top plumb line is the same as for a hip rafter of the same rise. The layout for the birdsmouth differs, as the rafter must fit on an inside corner as opposed to the outside. Figure 7-27 illustrates the layout of the birdsmouth.

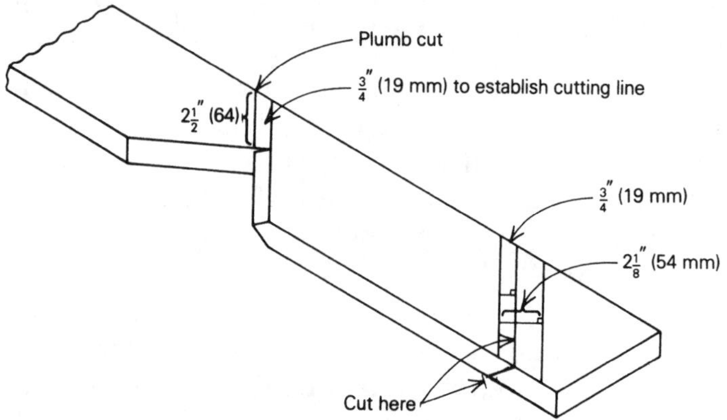

FIGURE 7-27 Layout of birdsmouth and cut at tail end of rafter.

The valley meets the hip at right angles in the plan view, and therefore the *shortening* will be one-half the thickness of the hip, $\frac{3}{4}$ in. (19 mm), measured at right angles to the plumb line (see Fig. 7-28).

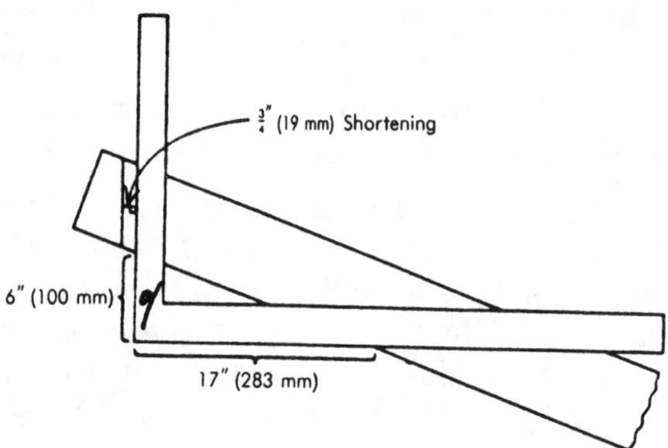

FIGURE 7-28 Shortening at top of valley rafter.

The end of the valley rafter tail must fit into an internal angle, as illustrated in Figs. 7-29(a) and 7-29(b). Figure 7-29 illustrates the layout of the double cut needed.

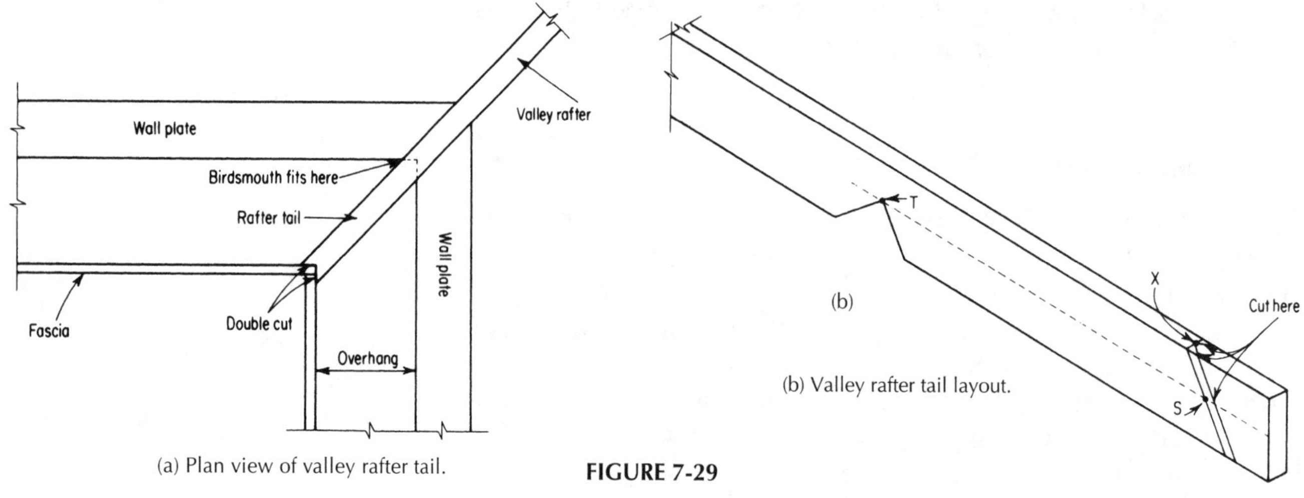

(a) Plan view of valley rafter tail.

(b) Valley rafter tail layout.

FIGURE 7-29

The layout of valley rafter (H) is exactly the same as valley rafter (G); the only difference is that the run is shorter so it will affect the line length.

Length and Layout of Valley Jack (I)

The run of valley jack (I) is 16 in. (400 mm) less than the run of the common rafter without a rafter tail. The line length of the rafter will be 161.04 in. − 17.875 = 143.165 in. = 11 ft, $11\frac{3}{16}$ in. (4025 − 447 = 3578 mm).

The plumb line and shortening at the top end are the same as for a common rafter, while at the other end the plumb line, shortening (one-half the diagonal thickness of the valley rafter), and the side cut at the bottom end are identical to the top end of a hip jack.

Line Length and Layout of Cripple Jack (J)

The run of cripple jack (J) is 3 ft, 4 in. (1000 mm). The line length of the rafter will be 3.33 × 13.42 = 44.49 in. or 3 ft, $8\frac{11}{16}$ in. (1000/1000 × 1118 = 1118 mm). Shortening and side cuts, top and bottom, are the same as for other jack rafters.

FIGURE 7-30 Gable studs.

ROOF FRAME ASSEMBLY

When all the rafters have been cut, they can then be assembled into a roof frame. In a gable roof, the end rafters are positioned first, at the ends of the wall plates (see Fig. 7-30) and nailed to the plate and to the ridge. The remainder of the rafters are then raised and positioned against the ceiling joists, properly spaced at the top and then nailed to the plate, ridge, and the ceiling joists.

In a hip roof, the common rafters at the ends of the ridge (see Fig. 7-14) will be erected first, with their bottom end against a ceiling joist and nailed, bottom and top, as above. The end commons are raised next, followed by the hip rafters and finally, the jacks, in pairs. End commons and all jacks will be located against a regular or stub joist (see Fig. 7-6) and nailed, top and bottom.

GABLE FRAME

In a building with a gable roof, that triangular portion of the end wall that extends from the top of the wall plate to the ridge is known as the *gable.*

The method used to frame the gables will depend on the type of framing system employed. If *platform framing* is used, the gable is framed separately; those short studs extending from top plate to rafters are *gable studs* (see Fig. 7-30). In either case, the cuts at the top ends of the studs will be the same.

Each gable stud will be laid out in exactly the same way and each will be longer than the preceding one by the line length of the first. Those on the opposite side of center will be marked and cut with the opposite slope. Openings for ventilating louvers are framed as illustrated in Fig. 7-31 and should be as near the ridge as possible.

FIGURE 7-31 Opening for a louver.

RAFTER BRACING

As is the case with other load-bearing members, the clear span of rafters is limited, depending on depth of rafter, spacing, and species of timber used. Local building codes give maximum clear spans for a number of species, with varying widths and spacing. The clear span is expressed in terms of the horizontal projection of the rafter.

When the clear span of rafters exceeds the maximum allowable, they must be provided with a support. The support is given, where possible, by braces resting on a bearing partition (see Fig. 7-32). First, a *purlin* is nailed to the underside of the rafters, as shown in Fig. 7-32, second a purlin plate to the ceiling joists directly over the partition. Purlin studs are cut to fit between these, preferably at right angles to the rafters. If they are so placed, the cut at the bottom of the stud will be the same as that on gable studs. If the purlin studs are vertical, this same cut will apply to the top end (see Fig. 7-33).

When no bearing partition is available to carry the load, a strongback must be used (see Fig. 7-34). A strongback is a straight timber, either solid or laminated, rigid enough to carry the imposed roof load. This member runs over the ceiling joists, blocked up so that it will clear the joists by $\frac{3}{4}$ in. (19 mm). Another method is to have a dwarf wall set on the ceiling joists. When this occurs, the size of the ceiling joists must be increased to carry the load.

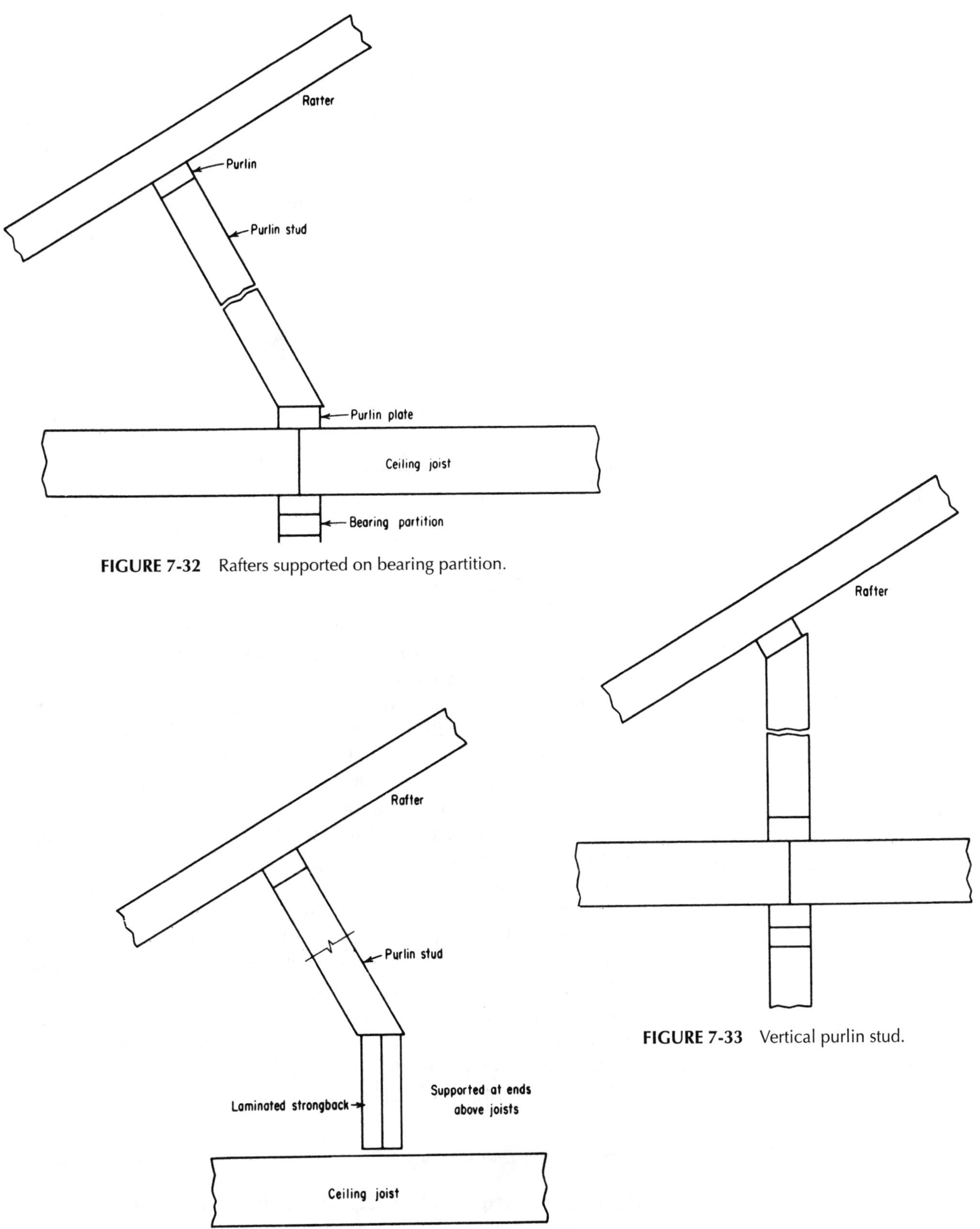

FIGURE 7-32 Rafters supported on bearing partition.

FIGURE 7-33 Vertical purlin stud.

FIGURE 7-34 Rafters supported by strongback.

Collar Ties

Rafters are tied together and stiffened by means of *collar ties.* These are horizontal supports nailed to the rafters, as illustrated in Fig. 7-35, and should be located in the middle third of the rafter length. For rafters on roof slopes of 4 in 12 (1 in 3) or more, intermediate support is generally provided by 2 × 4s (38 × 89 mm). When the length of the ties is over 8 ft (2400 mm), the ties are stiffened by nailing a 1 × 4- (19 × 89-mm) member across the center of their span, from end to end of the roof.

FIGURE 7-35 Rafters tied by collar tie.

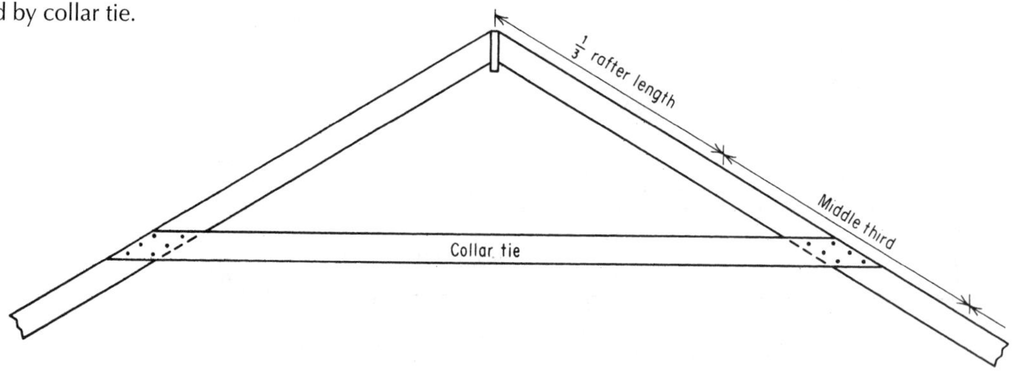

Gable End Projection

Construction of roof projections commonly used at gable ends is shown in Fig. 7-36. Roof overhang projections less than 16 in. (400 mm) over the gable end face will usually terminate with a framing member called a *rake rafter.* When plywood soffit is used, a ladder-type construction is nailed to the rafter located above the gable end wall. Blocking usually spaced 24 in. (600 mm) o.c. will act as backing for the plywood soffit. When metal or vinyl is used for soffit material, no special framing is needed for fastening of the soffit. The overhang is finished with a 2 × 6 (38 × 140-mm) rake rafter, supported at the top by the ridge and at the bottom by the rough fascia with the roof sheathing providing the intermediate support.

Roof overhang projections over 16 in. (400 mm) beyond the gable end wall are supported by members called *lookouts.* These will extend back into the roof system a distance equal to the overhang. When the lookouts are placed with their narrow dimension parallel to the roof sheathing, the gable end is built lower to allow room for the lookouts. When the lookouts are placed with the wider dimension parallel to the roof sheathing, the gable end rafter is notched to allow room for the lookouts (see Fig. 7-37).

DORMER FRAMING

Sometimes it is desirable to let light into the building through the roof, and this may be done by means of vertical windows. The house-like structure containing such windows is called *dormer* (see Fig. 7-38). In

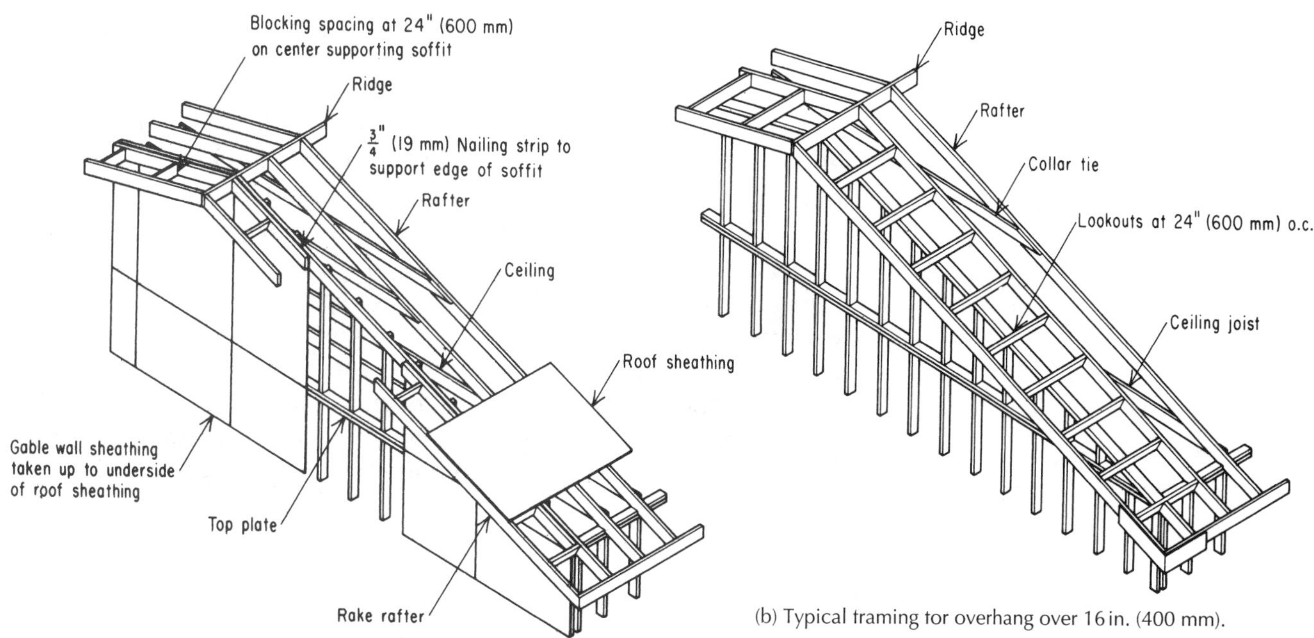

(a) Narrow overhang construction.

(b) Typical framing tor overhang over 16 in. (400 mm).

FIGURE 7-36

FIGURE 7-38 Dormers.

FIGURE 7-37 Overhang framing using lookouts on flat.

addition to letting in light, a dormer may increase the usable floor space in the attic.

The roof frame must be reinforced to support the dormer. This is done by doubling the rafters on which the sides of the dormer rest and by putting in double headers at the upper and lower ends of the opening. On this reinforced frame the dormer is built, as illustrated in Fig. 7-39. Framing procedure is the same as for any other wall and roof frame. Cuts on the bottom end of the dormer studs will be the same as for gable studs. If the studs are spaced 16 in. (400 mm) o.c., each will be longer or shorter than the preceding one by the amount of rise for 16 in. (400 mm) of common run.

The rough opening for the dormer window is framed in the same way as the opening for a window in a wall frame. Window headers usually need not be as large, since they carry very little load.

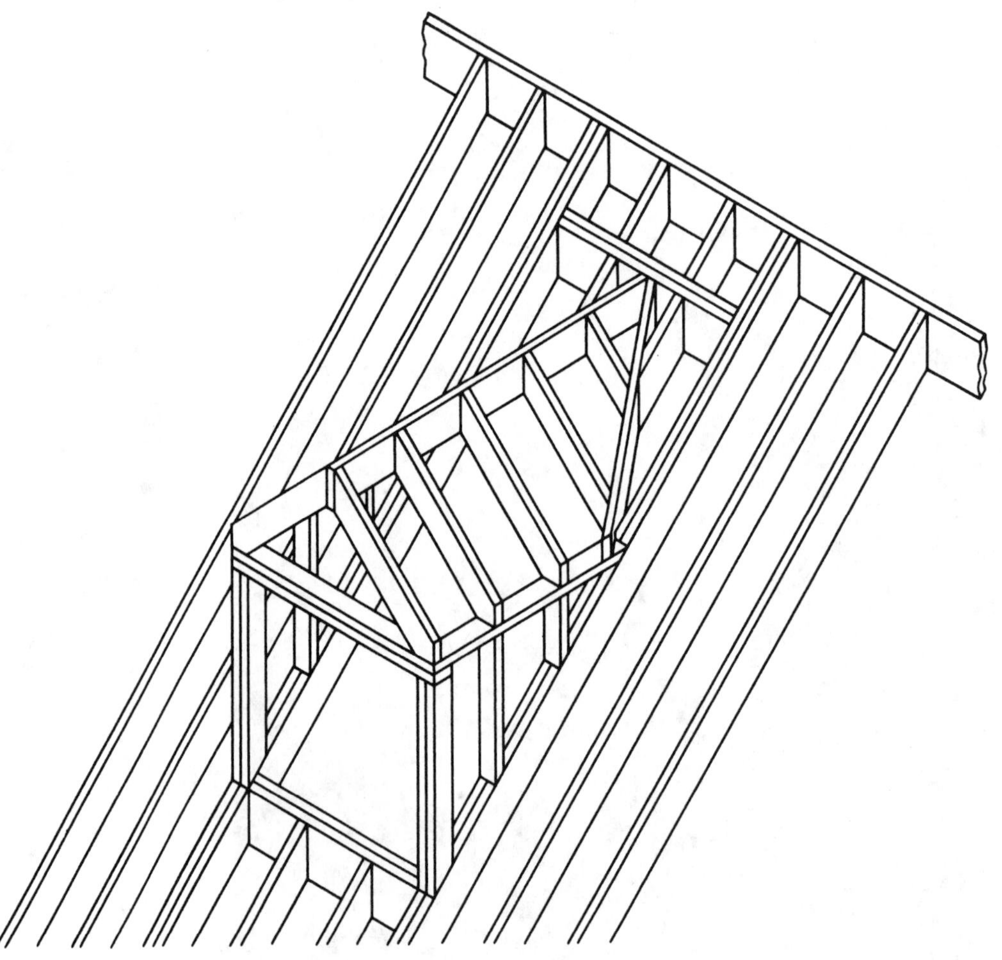

FIGURE 7-39 Dormer frame.

TRUSSED ROOF SYSTEMS

Trussed rafters are rafters that have been tied together in pairs, along with the bottom chord, to form an individual unit. In addition to the two rafters and the bottom chord, compression and tension webs are incorporated into the unit, making it a truss—a self-supporting structure. Roof trusses are now much more commonly used for roof framing than standard rafters and ceiling joists. They save material and can be put into place much quicker than standard framing. Trusses are usually designed to span from exterior wall to exterior wall, so a great deal of flexibility is available in size and shape of rooms. The entire living area can be designed as a single living area.

A wide variety of roof shapes and types can be framed with trusses. Numerous sloped truss types are available including King post, Fink, Howe, mono, and scissor, as illustrated in Fig. 7-40. Flat or parallel chord trusses are widely used for floor systems and flat roof systems, and are often more economical than open web steel joist systems. Some types of parallel chord (flat) trusses utilize

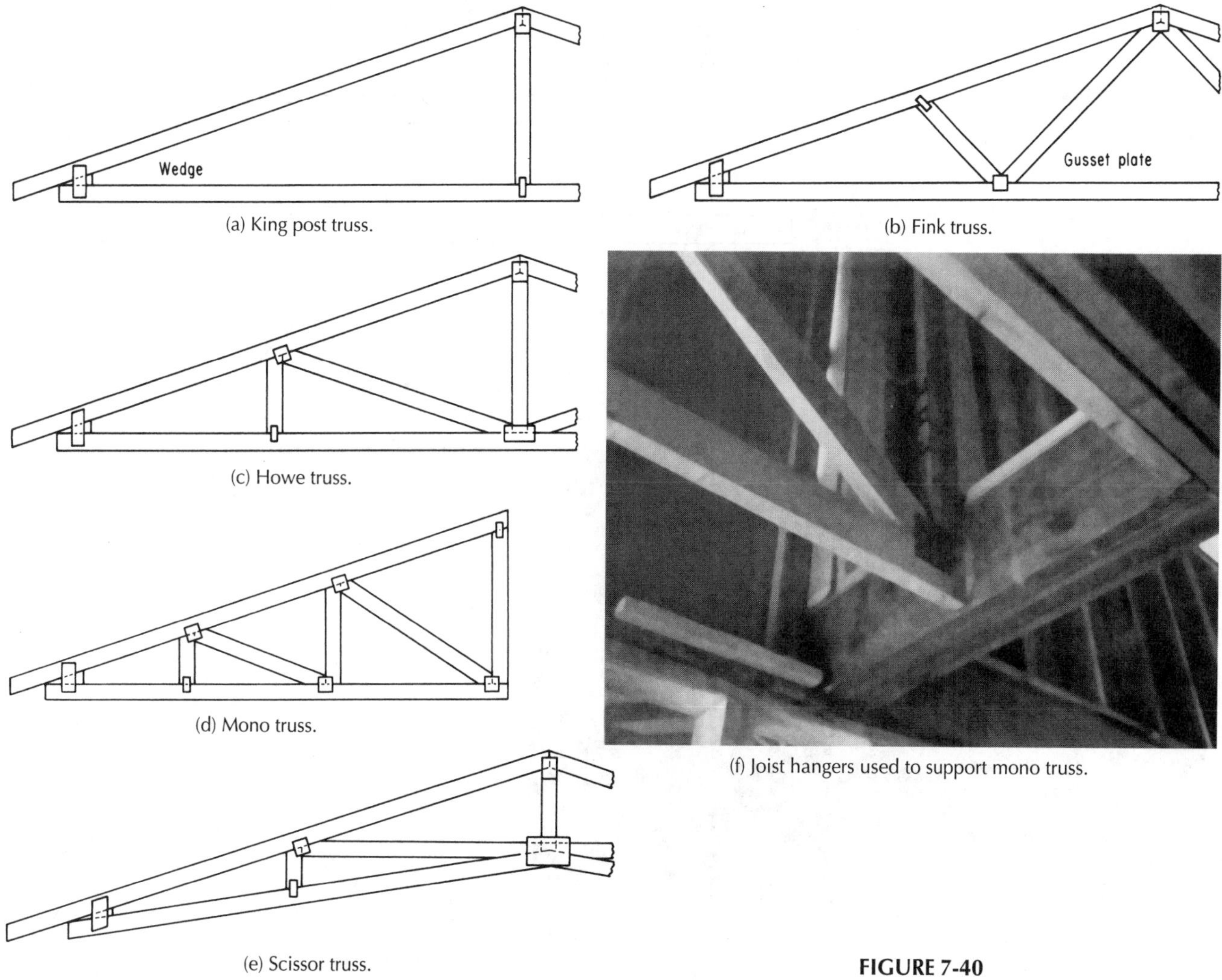

(a) King post truss.

(b) Fink truss.

(c) Howe truss.

(d) Mono truss.

(e) Scissor truss.

(f) Joist hangers used to support mono truss.

FIGURE 7-40

steel tension members and can be supported either by the top or bottom chord [see Figs. 7-41(a) and 7-41(b)]. Flat trusses may be ordered with built-in camber to offset deflection and to provide drainage when used as a flat roof system. Special trusses such as gable end trusses, hip trusses, and girder trusses are used to meet special needs [see Fig. 7-42(a), 7-42(b), and 7-42(c)].

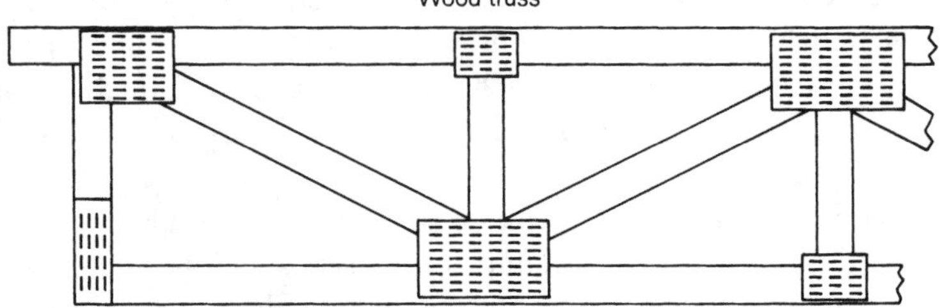

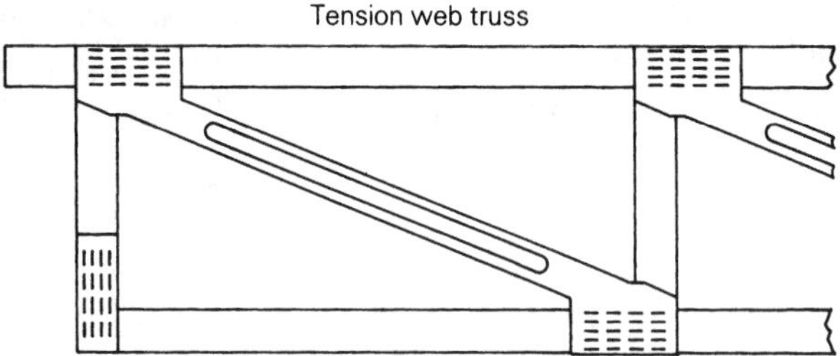

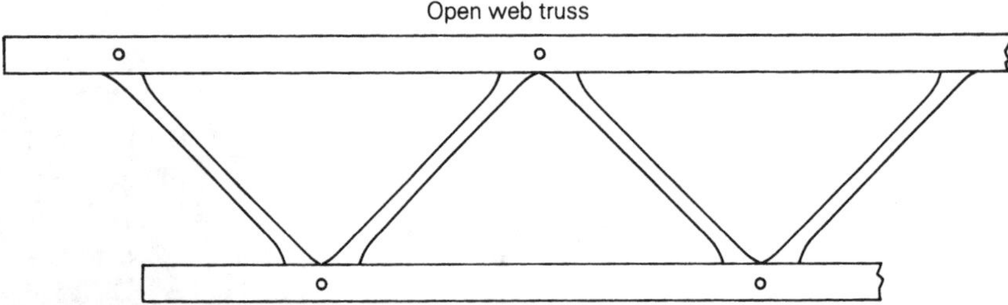

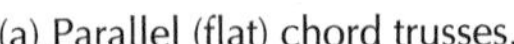

(a) Parallel (flat) chord trusses.

(b) Flat trusses used in sloped position.

FIGURE 7-41

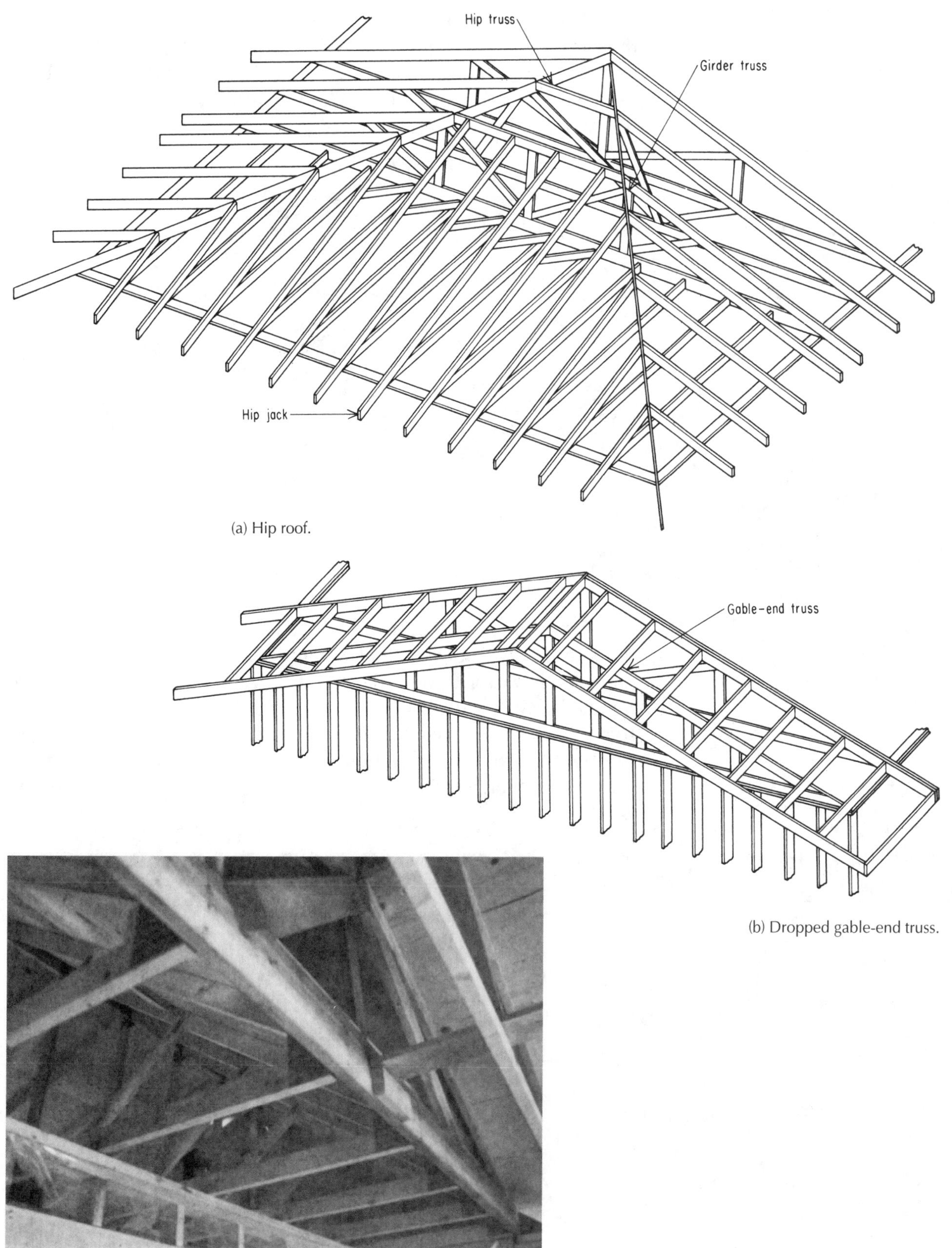

(a) Hip roof.

(b) Dropped gable-end truss.

(c) Girder truss used in L-shaped building.

FIGURE 7-42 Special trusses.

Trusses are most adaptable to rectangular houses because of the constant width requiring only one type of truss. This quick erection of the roof frame results in the fast enclosing of the house. Trusses can also be used for L-shaped houses with the use of some special trusses (see Fig. 7-43).

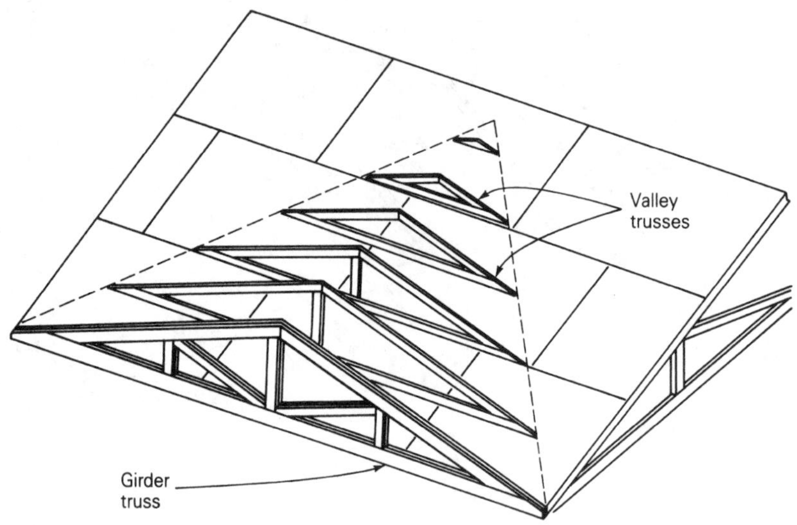

FIGURE 7-43 Framing for an intersecting roof.

Trusses are commonly spaced at 24 in. (600 mm) o.c., allowing efficient use of exterior sheathing or interior finish. Roof trusses must be designed, however, in accordance with accepted engineering practice for the particular details being used. Suppliers of pressed-on metal truss plates have developed an economical design service to fill this need. Trusses for smaller sections of roofs can be prefabricated on the ground and then lifted into place with a crane [(see Figs. 7-44(a), and 7-44(b)].

(a) Pre-assembled roof section with gable end.

(b) Pre-assembled roof with intersection.

FIGURE 7-44

One of the reasons for prefabricating sections of trusses on the ground is the ease in which workers can erect them without being on top of the wall frames. There is a certain degree of safety in this practice. In Fig. 7-45(a), a section of trusses have been pre-assembled ready for lifting, but notice that the hip rafter has been left out for insertion later.

In Fig. 7-45(b), a crane is in the process of lifting the section where workers position it on top of the walls (see Fig. 7-45(c).

Another section is shown being prepared for lifting in Fig. 7-45(d)where lifting cables have to be carefully position to ensure the section will be lifted safely. Crane operators should always be consulted regarding how best to do this.

(a) Pre-assembled roof section at hip.

(b) First section being lifted with a crane.

(c) First section being positioned.

(d) Second section being readied for lifting.

FIGURE 7-45

Figure 7-45(e) and 7-45(f) illustrate the section being lifted and positioned where workers anchor it to the cap plates. Allan Mah of A.M. Construction was kind enough to allow these photos to be taken.

(e) Second section being lifted.

(f) Second section being positioned.

FIGURE 7-45 (cont.)

Standard Gable Roof

A standard gable roof consists of a number of common trusses set at 24-in. (600-mm) intervals and finished at either end with gable-end trusses [see Fig. 7-44(a)]. Eave overhangs may be formed in two ways. One is with the type of truss illustrated in Fig. 7-46(a). Here the overhang will be exactly the same as that formed by an ordinary rafter with a rafter tail. The back of the rafter can be raised farther above the wall plate to allow extra room for insulation [see Fig. 7-46(b)]. If the truss is made so that its bottom chord extends to the ends of the rafters, then the truss overhang will be formed by part of the truss end extending beyond the plate line [see Fig. 7-46(c)]. Figure 7-47 illustrates supporting overhang over the gable end.

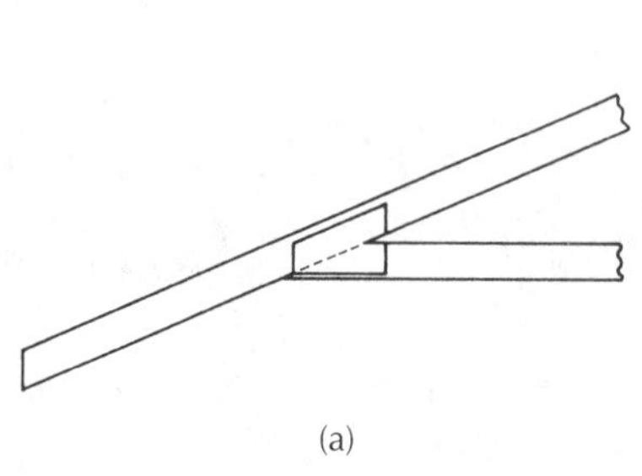

(a)

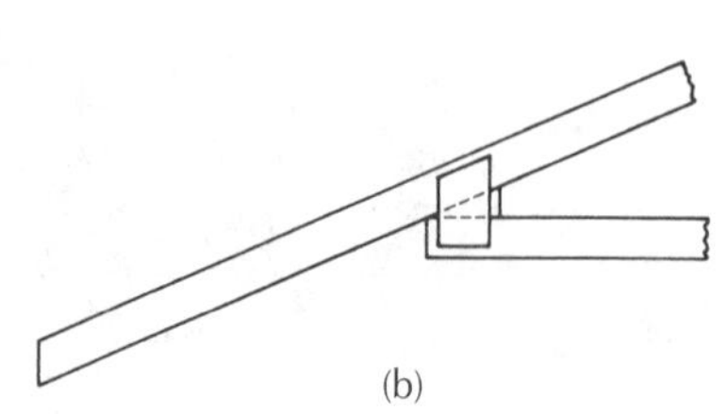

(b)

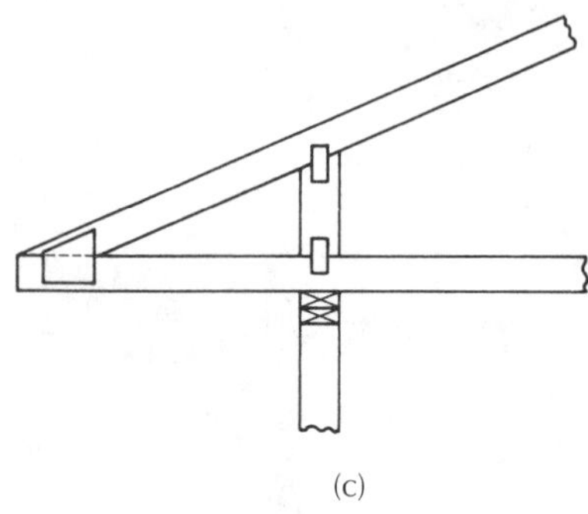

(c)

FIGURE 7-46 Framing eave overhangs.

FIGURE 7-47 Overhang support at gable-end.

Erection of trusses will usually begin at one end with the gable end and then continue by adding common trusses and nailing them at prescribed spacing. Bracing is added to keep the gable end plumb (see Fig. 7-48), as well as a strip nailed to chords or web members to keep members straight and at correct spacing (see Fig. 7-49). Trusses are delivered to the job site banded and ready for placement (see Fig. 7-50). These packages should be covered if left for more than five days.

FIGURE 7-48 Bracing gable-end.

FIGURE 7-49 Bracing web members.

The L-Shaped Roof

The L-shaped roof requires common trusses as well as some specialty trusses (see Fig. 7-43). The girder truss is placed first and braced in a plumb position. Truss hangers are fastened to the lower chord of

FIGURE 7-50 Trusses delivered to job site.

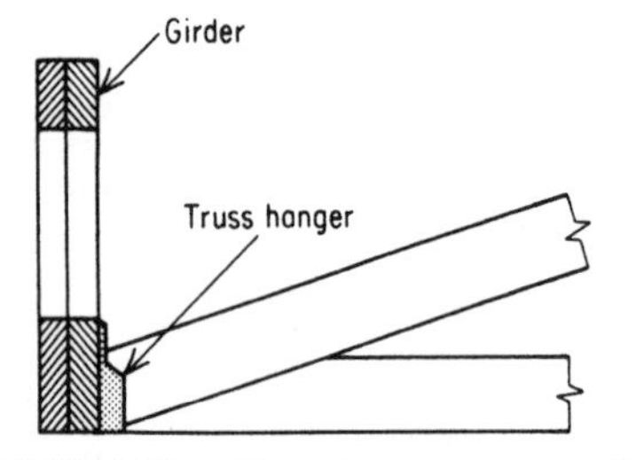

FIGURE 7-51 Truss hangers supporting trusses.

the girder to support the ends of the common trusses (see Fig. 7-51). If the overhangs of the trusses to be supported by the girder are still in place, cut them off prior to placement in hangers. After all common trusses are nailed into position, valley trusses are nailed in position on the sloped roof (see Fig. 7-52). Care must be taken to keep the peaks of the valley trusses in line with the common trusses. Blocking is nailed between the trusses at the peak to maintain spacing and provide support for sheathing (see Fig. 7-53).

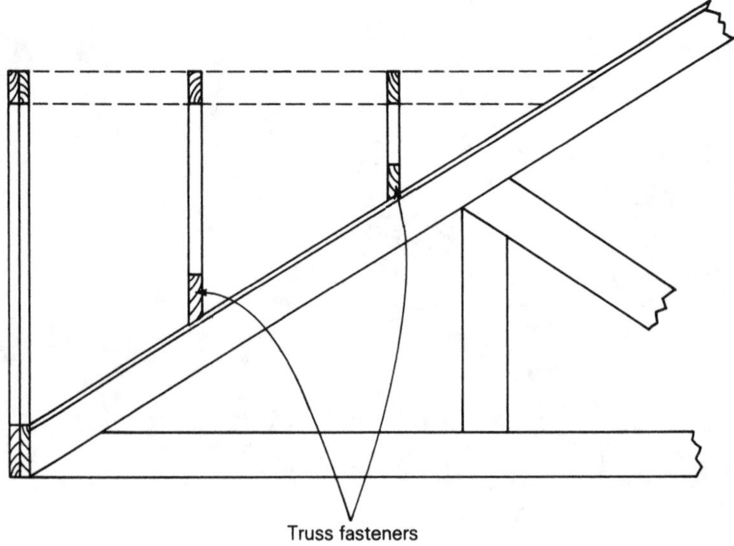

FIGURE 7-52 Valley trusses nailed in position.

Hip Roof

Hip roof construction starts with the placement of the hip girder in location as specified on the drawings. Hip jacks are then fastened to the girder and nailed to the end wall plate. Hip trusses are then posi-

FIGURE 7-53 Blocking at peak of roof.

tioned, followed by the common trusses [see Fig. 7-42(a)]. The other end of the roof is finished in the same way as the first end. Apply all permanent bracing as per the structural truss drawing, and the roof is ready for sheathing.

Roof Sheathing

Sheathing for the roof frame may be plywood, OSB, or in some cases spaced solid lumber (see Fig. 7-54). The minimum thicknesses for roof sheathing materials are based on the rafter spacing and are prescribed in local building codes. For example, rafters or trusses spaced 24 in. (600 mm) o.c. will generally require $\frac{1}{2}$ in. (12.5 mm) OSB or plywood.

FIGURE 7-54 Spaced roof sheathing.

Solid lumber may be spaced equal to wood shingle, wood shake, or tile roofing in areas not subjected to wind-driven snow (see Fig. 7-55).

FIGURE 7-55 Plywood at eaves with spaced roof sheathing.

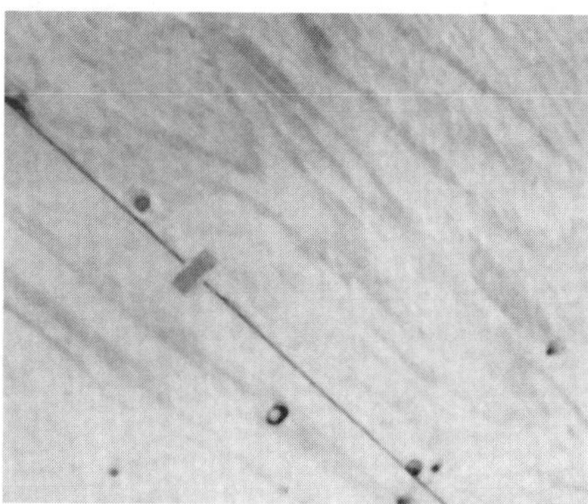

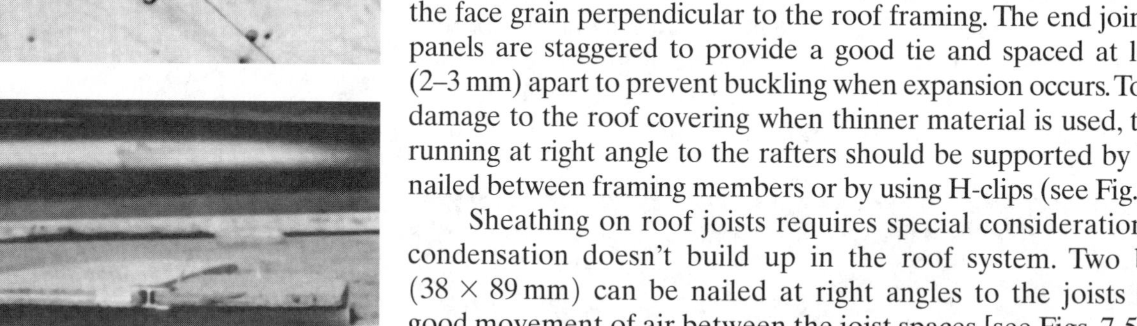

FIGURE 7-56 Using H-clips.

When plywood is used for roof sheathing, it should be placed with the face grain perpendicular to the roof framing. The end joints of the panels are staggered to provide a good tie and spaced at least $\frac{1}{8}$ in. (2–3 mm) apart to prevent buckling when expansion occurs. To prevent damage to the roof covering when thinner material is used, the joints running at right angle to the rafters should be supported by blocking nailed between framing members or by using H-clips (see Fig. 7-56).

Sheathing on roof joists requires special consideration so that condensation doesn't build up in the roof system. Two by fours (38 × 89 mm) can be nailed at right angles to the joists to allow good movement of air between the joist spaces [see Figs. 7-57(a) and 7-57(b)]. The sheathing can then be installed with the grain parallel to the roof joists and perpendicular to the boards.

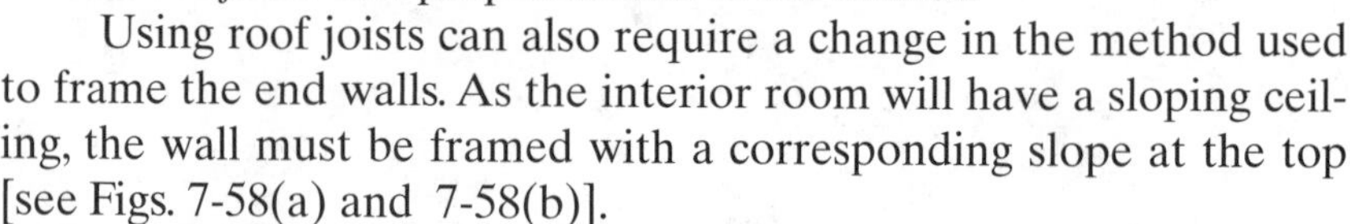

Using roof joists can also require a change in the method used to frame the end walls. As the interior room will have a sloping ceiling, the wall must be framed with a corresponding slope at the top [see Figs. 7-58(a) and 7-58(b)].

ALTERNATE ROOF SYSTEMS

When one thinks of a roof on a building in the category of light construction, particularly a house roof, the same picture usually appears. It is the picture of a sloped roof, either gable or hip, made with the conventional roof-framing materials. And, indeed, a great percentage of the roofs, on dwelling houses especially, are made in just that way.

(a) Spaced sheathing for ventilation.

(b) Spaced sheathing on roof joists for ventilation.

FIGURE 7-57

(a) Wall framing for roof joist system.

(b) Special trusses requiring special wall framing.

FIGURE 7-58

There are alternatives to this roof, and more and more in modern light construction one of these alternatives is being used. Among them are (1) a *flat roof* in which the ceiling joists are also the roof joists, (2) a flat roof carried by laminated beams resting on the top of the walls, (3) *a stressed-skin panel roof*, and (4) an *arched roof*.

The roof to be used in a particular situation is a matter of some architectural importance. A number of factors are involved in the choosing of a roof type, and they must all be weighed carefully before making the final choice.

One of the important factors is the overall appearance desired. If the long, low look is being sought, the flat or low-pitched roof will probably do most to enhance it. On the other hand, flat roofs may tend to be troublesome in wet climates or where the snowfall is heavy or wet.

Special effects are obtained by using roof beams with either a flat or a sloped roof, but the cost of the roof may be increased, because of the quality of roof decking usually required.

From the foregoing it is evident that there are a number of alternatives possible in the selection of a roof type. However, that choice should not be made lightly. Once the choice is made, every effort should be made to see that it is properly executed. The following pages outline the general appearance and steps in construction of each roof type mentioned above.

FLAT ROOF WITH REGULAR JOISTS

We have already seen the procedure for framing a ceiling when a regular sloped roof is to be used on the building. If a flat roof is to be used instead, the same general ceiling-framing scheme may be used with some important alterations.

In the first place, the size of the ceiling joists must be increased. In general, 2 × 6 (38 × 140mm) members are commonly used for ceiling joists. If the ceiling joists are also to be the roof joists, the size must be increased, because of the additional loads of roofing materials, snow, and live loads. Size 2 × 8-, 2 × 10-, and 2 × 12- (38 × 184-mm, 38 × 325-mm, and 38 × 286-mm) members are commonly used—the choice in a particular case depending on the above-mentioned factors and prescribed in local building codes.

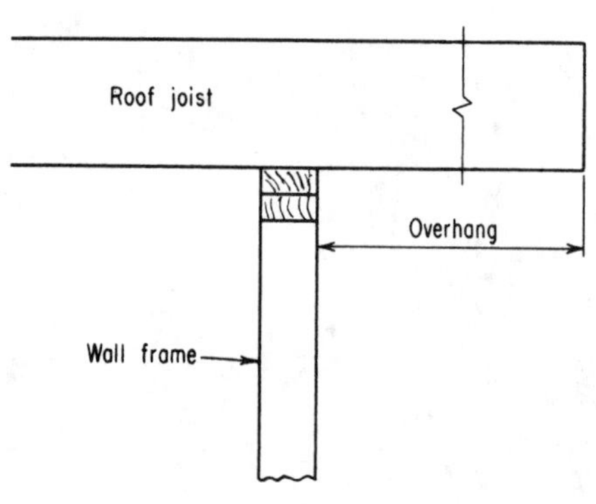

FIGURE 7-59 Roof joist overhang.

It was also noted in Fig. 7-3 that the outer ends of ceiling joists are cut off flush with the outside of the plate and that the top edge at the end is cut in the plane of the roof. If they are acting as roof joists, the ends will be cut off square, and the joist ends will extend beyond the wall plate if the building is to have a cornice (see Figs. 7-59 and 5-57).

The overhang on the end walls will be formed by stub joists extending over the end wall plates and anchored at their inner ends to a double regular joist. Remember that these stub joists should extend at least as far inside the wall plate as they project beyond it. For example, if the joists are on 16-in. (400-mm) centers, the last regular joist should be kept back two spaces or 32 in. (800 mm) wide (see Fig. 7-60).

Sloped Roof Joists

It is sometimes desirable to have enough slope to a flat roof so that the water will drain in one direction. It is generally considered that a slope of 1:25 is sufficient. This will allow the water to run but will not be noticeable as a slope on the roof. One method to provide for roof

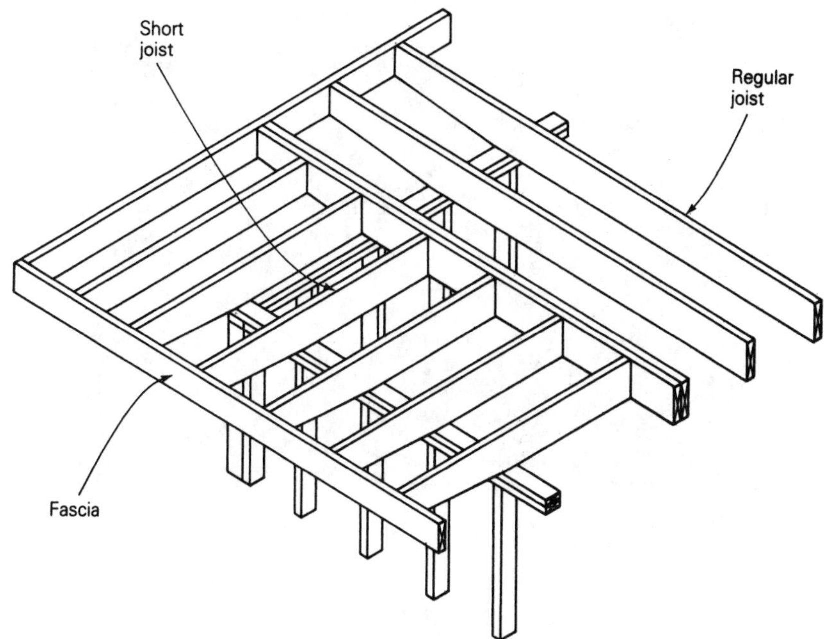

FIGURE 7-60 Framing a flat roof.

drainage is to slope each joist. This can be achieved by building the supporting walls of different heights or by tapering each joist or by adding a tapered strip to the top of each joist. Where insulation for the roof is placed between the roof joists, a ventilated space of at least $3\frac{1}{2}$ in. (89 mm) must be provided between the top of the joists and the underside of the roof sheathing. This can be achieved by placing 2 × 4 stringers on edge at right angles over the top of the joists (see Fig. 7-61).

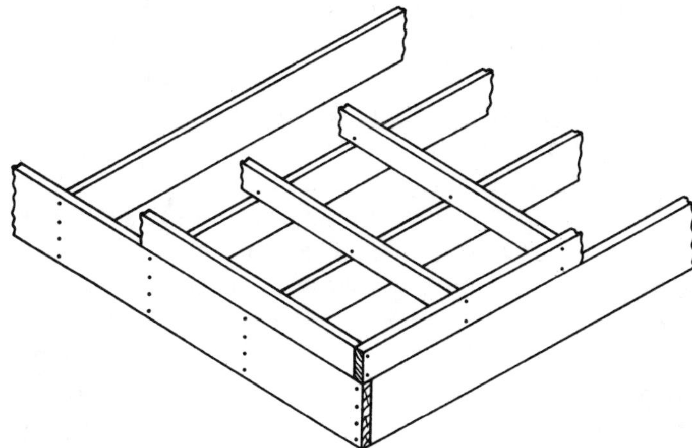

FIGURE 7-61 Providing roof ventilation for insulated joist spaces.

An easier way to build a roof that has good ventilation capability is to use flat trusses as the roof system. Cross ventilation is easily achieved through the web openings [see Fig. 7-62].

FIGURE 7-62 Flat trusses in sloped position supported on a beam.

FLAT ROOF WITH LAMINATED BEAMS

An *open style* ceiling may be produced in a flat roof by using heavy roof beams to carry the roof decking and leaving the underside of the decking and the beams exposed to view. It is necessary, therefore, that both decking and beams be of such a grade of material as to make that exposure practical.

The roof beams are normally laminated members—that is, they are made up of several pieces glued together to form a solid unit. The lamination may be of two or more pieces on edge or of several pieces laminated on the flat [see Figs. 7-63(a) and 7-63(b)]. Material to be used will usually have to be clear or nearly clear stock, since the finished beam will form part of the interior finish. In some cases, regular stock may be used and the two sides and the bottom of the beam covered with a thin veneer of the required type or texture. Laminated veneer lumber and parallel strand lumber is also available for this purpose [see Fig. 5-1(b)].

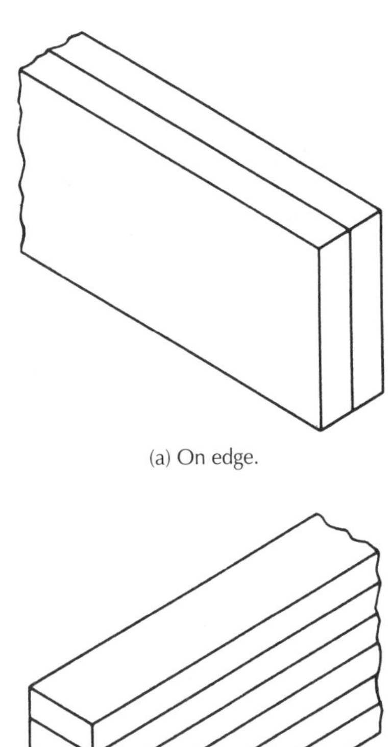

(a) On edge.

(b) On the flat.

FIGURE 7-63 Laminated roof beams.

The sizes of the beams to be used will depend on their span and their spacing. The size required for a particular job should never be decided arbitrarily. Consult an engineer or other building authority to determine the width and depth best suited to the case.

Laminated beams are made to order by manufacturers specializing in this type of construction. Facilities for applying great pressure are required, because the parts of the beam are glued together, no nails or other fasteners being used. In addition, suitable means of surfacing the beams must be available, since they represent a finished product.

The sizes of the beams required must be calculated for each job. Size will depend, as stated previously, on span and spacing as well as on the type of roofing used. The longer the span, of course, the greater the load imposed on the beam for any given type of roofing. And the farther apart the beams are spaced, more roof load must be carried on each. Nothing can be said, therefore, about the size of beam that should be used. Generally, however, they will be relatively narrow in width in comparison to their depth. Remember that the strength of a beam varies directly as its width. In other words, if you double the width of a beam, you double the strength. On the other hand, the strength of a beam varies as the square of its depth. That means that if you double the depth, you then increase the strength four times.

The number of beams used for the roof, or, in other words, the spacing of the beams, will depend on the span, the weight of the roofing material, the type of roof decking used, and live loads such as snow. Check the local building code for greater detail.

Roof Decking

Roof decking over roof beams usually consists of $1\frac{1}{2}$-in. (38-mm) single tongue-and-grooved or $2\frac{1}{2}$- and $3\frac{1}{2}$-in. (64- and 89-mm) double tongue-and-grooved (depending on load and span) cedar, Douglas fir, pine, or hemlock 5 or 7 in. (127 or 178 mm) wide. The underside of this decking may be exposed, so certain precautions must be taken in selecting and laying it.

First, the material must be dry so that shrinkage and cracking are eliminated or kept at a minimum. Second, the appearance of the decking must be such that it harmonizes the rest of the interior finish. Third, the pieces must be drawn tightly together by edge nailing through predrilled holes with 8-in. (200-mm) spiral nails, spaced about 30 in. (750 mm) o.c. and then face-nailed to the beams (see Fig. 7-64). In some cases, clear material may be required, while in others a knotty appearance may be specified.

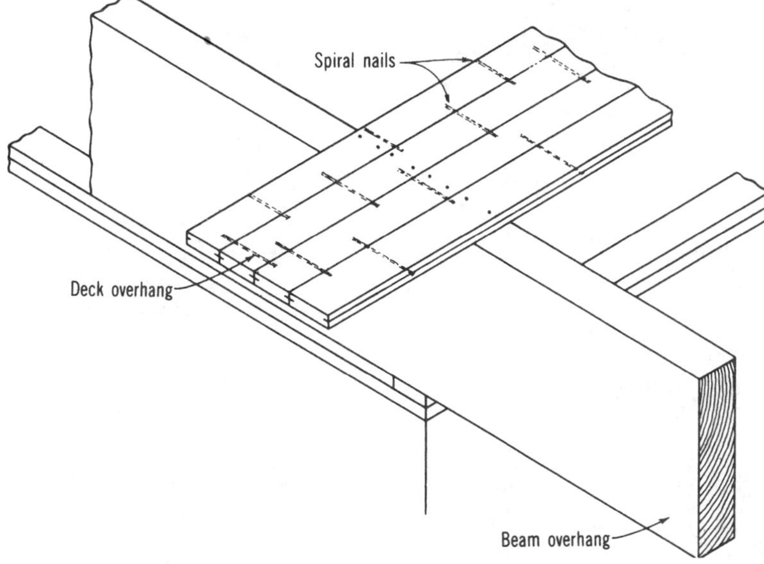

FIGURE 7-64 T & G roof decking.

Stressed-Skin Roof Panels

A *stressed-skin* panel consists of a frame of dimensional material covered on both sides with oriented strand board or plywood (see Fig. 7-65). The internal structure consists of spacer studs made of strand board or dimension lumber and, when insulation is required, injected with polyurethane insulation. The panel parts are glued and stapled together to form a structural panel of great strength and dimensional stability. To tie the panels together effectively, the skin projects over the frame at the edge to overlap the adjoining panel.

Panels may be of various shapes but are most often either *rectangular* or *triangular.* The spacing of framing members for stressed-skin panels depends on the thickness of the skin and the direction of the face grain in relation to the long dimension of the framing member. Sizes can range up to 8 × 24 ft (2.4 × 7.2 m) and 4 in. to 6 in. (100 mm to 150 mm) in thickness.

Large panels result in a saving on construction time. Even larger time savings are possible with factory-applied wall and ceiling coverings such as gypsum board. A variety of modern coatings can be applied directly to the panels ranging from spray-on fiber-reinforced acrylic stuccos to torch-on modified bitumen roof membranes.

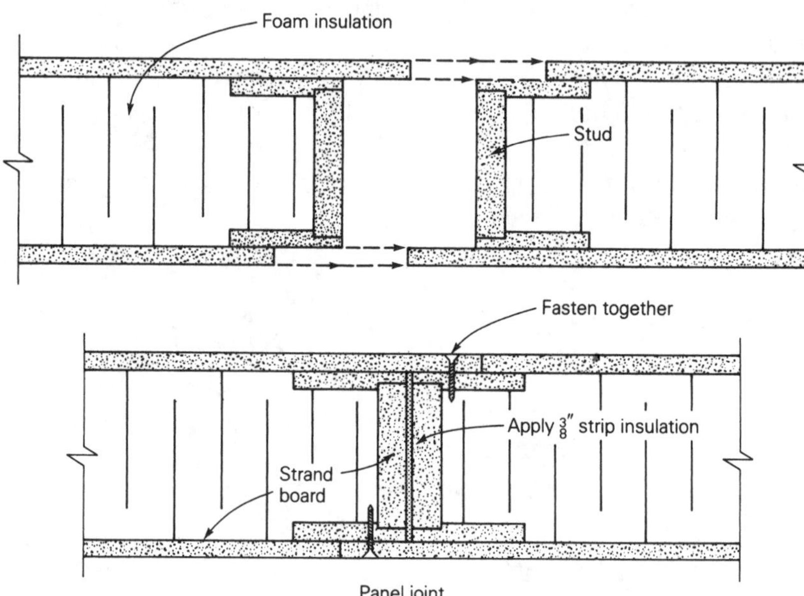

FIGURE 7-65 Stressed skin panels.

GLUE-LAMINATED ARCHES

Glue-laminated arches are structural components made by gluing together thin pieces of lumber of any required width. In this way a member of any desired thickness and shape may be produced. Because of the wide scope in shape, size, and span, buildings using laminated arches for their frames are very popular. A great many are made commercially, some very large, with spans of at least 180 ft (60 m). Great care is taken in the selection of lumber and the cutting of splices so that pieces fit perfectly, end to end, in the manufacture of these large arches. Large band saws and planers are used to cut and dress them to size. They are finally sanded, treated, and wrapped so that when they arrive on the job they are unmarked and, when in place, produce a finished appearance.

Smaller, lighter arches, in two or three standard shapes, with spans up to about 54 ft (18 m) are made with less sophisticated equipment for use in buildings such as that illustrated in Fig. 7-66.

FIGURE 7-66 Arched rafter building.

Although many shapes are possible, probably the most often-used are the semicircular arch, the parabolic arch and the gothic arch (see Fig. 7-67). The semicircular arch and sometimes the parabolic arch are made in one piece, but in most other cases two separate

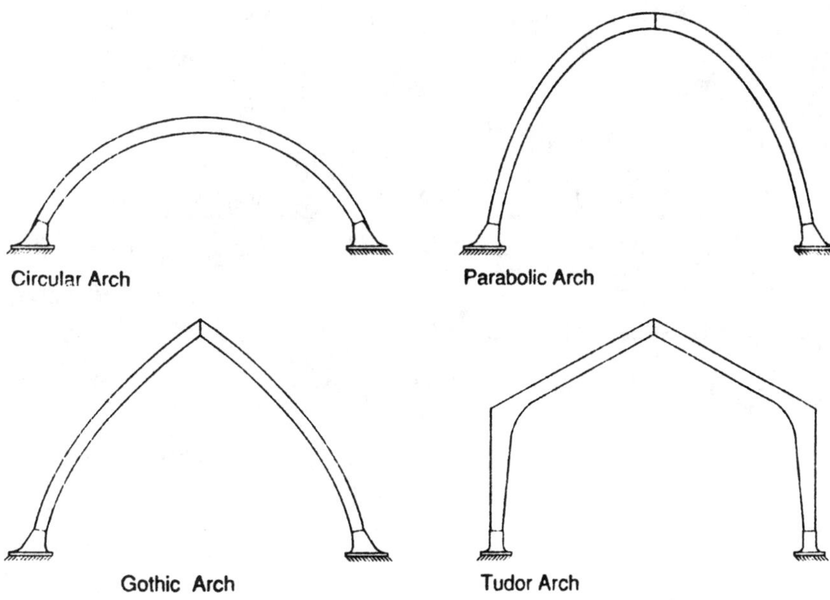

FIGURE 7-67 Arch shapes.

halves of the complete arch are formed. The two halves are put together on the site, being secured together at the top by bolts or with steel plates acting as gussets.

Spacing of the arches varies greatly, depending on the design, the span, and the type of roof deck to be applied. In some instances the roof decking will be carried on purlins running across the arches or hung in between them. With other designs, the decking will be $2\frac{1}{2}$- or $3\frac{1}{2}$-in. (64- or 89-mm) tongue-and-grooved material, usually cedar, spanning directly from arch to arch.

REVIEW QUESTIONS

7–1. List three main factors that influence the size of ceiling joists to be used in any particular situation.

7–2. What figures would you use on the framing square to lay out the cut on the outer end of ceiling joists used in conjunction with a 7-in. (600-mm) rise roof, and on which part of the square would you place the mark?

7–3. When is it necessary to use *stub* ceiling joists?

7–4. a. What is the purpose of ceiling backing?

b. What width of ceiling backing should be used on a 2 × 4 (38 × 89-mm) partition?

7–5. a. What is the main reason for providing access to the attic through the ceiling?

b. In what area of the ceiling would you suggest that the opening be placed?

7–6. What do you understand by "a rafter with a 12-in. (1000-mm) rise?"

7–7. What is the difference between line length and total length of a rafter?

7–8. Give the length of the ridge board in each of the following cases:

a. Hip roof, plan dimensions 22 ft (6600 mm) × (26 ft (7800 mm) $1\frac{1}{2}$-in. (38 × 89 mm) ridge board.

b. Hip roof, plan dimensions 26 ft, 10 in. (7850 mm) × (32 ft, 8 in. (9675 mm), $\frac{3}{4}$-in. (19 × 140 mm) ridge board.

7–9. Give the unit line length of common rafter with a unit rise of 8 in. (650 mm).

7–10. Explain the difference between a trussed rafter and a standard common rafter.

7–11. Where trusses cross an exterior wall, what is the advantage of having the upper chord of the truss elevated above the bottom chord?

7–12. Why would some builders pre-assemble trusses on the ground?

7–13. Why is it necessary to place blocking between trusses at the ridge?

Chapter 8

STAIR BUILDING

OBJECTIVES

Here is what you will be able to do when you complete each component of this chapter:

1. Identify the terms associated with stairs.
2. Recognize the different types and shapes of stairs.
3. Calculate stairwell openings.
4. Describe how to build common stairs.
5. Identify the requirements of handrails.

Stair building is virtually a trade in itself, and it would be impossible to cover the subject in all its facets in a single chapter. Nevertheless, a stair of one kind or another is still a necessity in many types of light construction, and we shall look into the basic elements of the subject to find out how to construct some of the most commonly required kinds of stairs.

Because most stairs are a finished component of most residential buildings, they are usually prefabricated in a shop and then transported to and installed at the job site. In many cases with multileveled buildings, stairs become an architectural feature (see Fig. 8-1) and become impractical for on-the-job manufacturing due to the specialized equipment facilities needed in their construction.

FIGURE 8-1 Architectural feature—circular stair.

TERMS USED IN STAIR BUILDING

There are many terms used in conjunction with stairs, and you should be familiar with them and to what they refer. Refer to Fig. 8-2 through 8-4 and 8-10 for the location of the following terms.

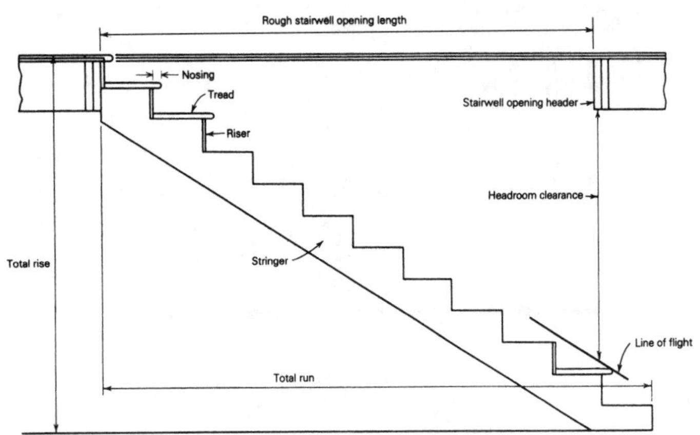

FIGURE 8-2 Stair elevation.

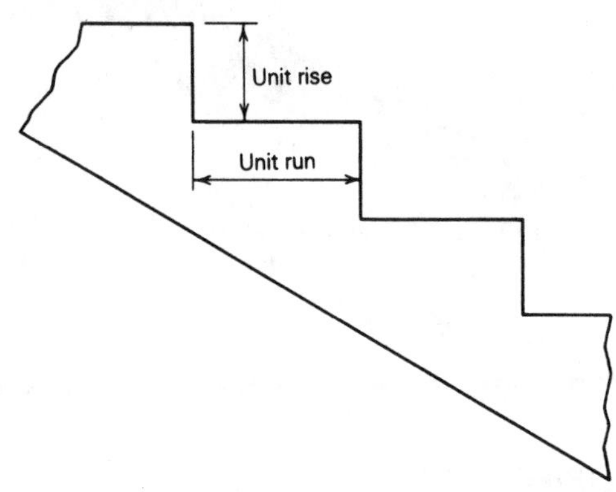

FIGURE 8-3 Stair unit rise and unit run.

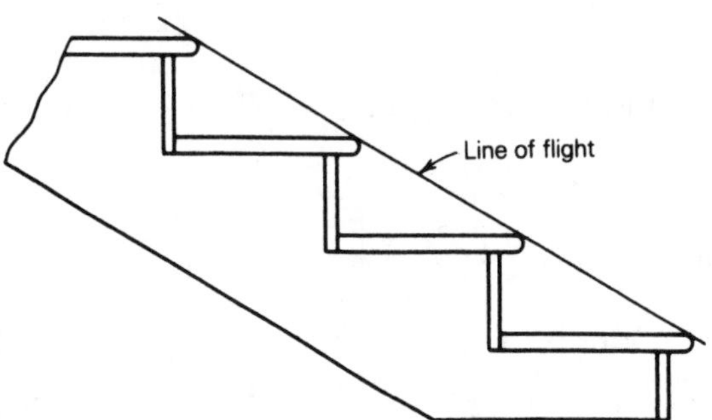

FIGURE 8-4 Line of flight.

Stairwell opening—refers to the framing in a floor frame to allow the installation of a stair. These stairwell openings must be framed during the floor-framing stage of construction, so the length and width of the opening must be known.

Rough stairwell opening—refers to the width and length of opening in the floor frame from framing member to framing member.

Stringer—a stringer (sometimes called a carriage or string) is the inclined structural member that supports the *risers* and *treads*. There are different types such as a *notched stringer* (sometimes called a cut-out stringer) where each *unit rise* and *unit run* is cut out of the top edge of the stringer. Another type is called a *housed stringer*, where each of the risers and treads are routed into dadoes on the surface of the stringer to conceal their ends. Housed stringers also make use of wedges to tighten each riser and tread in the dadoes. Another type is called a *built-up stringer* (sometimes called a semi-housed stringer) that consists of a notched stringer (or blocking) used to support risers and treads attached to an un-notched stringer.

Riser—refers to the vertical member attached to the stringer between treads.

Tread—refers to the horizontal member on which you place your foot.

Nosing—is the projection of a tread beyond the face of a riser. This may also be accomplished by back-sloping each riser (see Fig. 8-5).

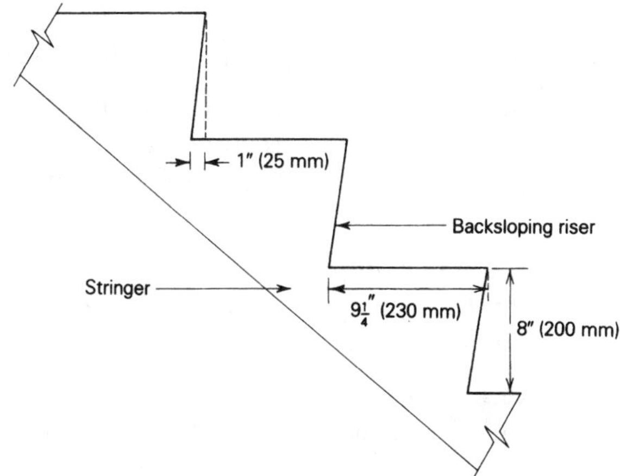

FIGURE 8-5 Back slope on risers.

Unit rise—this is the vertical distance between the surface of one tread to the surface of another tread.

Effective depth—is a measurement from the convergence of unit rise and unit run to the lower edge of the stringer. This minimum measurement is prescribed by building codes to ensure that the stringer is sufficiently strong to carry any anticipated load imposed on the stair.

Total rise—is the sum of all unit rises, which is also the vertical distance between finished floor to finished floor.

Total run—is the sum of all the unit runs.

Line of flight—refers to an imaginary line drawn along the outer extremities of the tread nosings.

Headroom clearance—is the vertical distance from the underside of a finished ceiling on the floor above the stair to the line of flight.

Handrail—is the upper member of a *balustrade* and is parallel to the line of flight. Handrails may also be supported against a wall rather than on a balustrade.

Newel post—are the vertical structural members that support a balustrade at each end, at turns, and at intermediate locations as needed. *Half-newel posts* are generally used adjacent to a wall, usually at the top of the stair.

Balusters—are the vertical spindles supporting the handrail and are positioned such that children cannot pass through between them (particularly a child's head).

Baluster shoe—(sometimes called a shoe rail) is a slotted member located at the bottom end of the balusters. Blocks are usually placed in the shoe slot between the balusters.

Landing—(or *platform)* is the horizontal space located at the top and bottom of a stair, or is located between two flights of stairs (see Fig. 8-9). Building codes prescribe the minimum size required.

Winder stair—consists of wedge-shaped treads that converge to a center point used to change the direction of a stair flight. Some building codes will allow no more than a 90° turn, and each tread must turn 30°.

Curved stair—as the name implies, is a stair built along a curve. Building codes generally prescribe the minimum size of tread to ensure the safety of the users.

Spiral stair—is like a curved stair but the treads rotate around a center post (or point). Generally, building codes require each tread to turn not less than 30°, and there are restrictions on the maximum unit rise as well as tread width and length.

STAIR DIMENSIONS

The design of stairs has evolved over many years, and through experience certain design criteria have been developed. The reason for these criteria is for the comfort and safety of those using the stair. Improperly designed stairs can be a hazard causing a person to stumble if there are irregular risers, or become difficult to use because of too high a riser. Likewise, if the treads are too narrow a person could stumble descending because of insufficient bearing for the foot.

Most building codes provide guidelines for dimensions for stairs. Most building codes, for example, allow the following for interior stairs in residences and exterior stairs serving residences:

Unit rise between 5 in. (125 mm) and 8 in. (200 mm);

Unit run between $8\frac{1}{4}$ in. (210 mm) and 14 in. (355 mm);

Minimum tread width of $9\frac{1}{4}$ in. (235 mm).

Stairs that are used by the public are generally restricted to:

Unit rise between 5 in. (125 mm) and 8 in. (200 mm);

Unit run between run 9 in. (230 mm) and 14 in. (355 mm);

Minimum tread width of 10 in. (250 mm).

In most building codes, stairs must have a minimum width of 2 ft, 10 in. (860 mm) between walls and a minimum headroom clearance of 6 ft, 4 in. (1.95 m) in residences (see Fig. 8-2). In public buildings, the minimum width must be 3 ft, 0 in. (900 mm) and the headroom clearance must be 6 ft, 8 in. (2.05 m). The stairwell opening length will depend on the steepness of the stair and must be calculated accordingly.

Handrails run parallel to the stairs and are designed to be grasped while ascending or descending the stairs. Building codes usually require that all interior stairways of more than two risers have a handrail, while exterior stairs serving a dwelling unit must have a handrail if there are more than three risers. It should be installed on both sides if the stair is over 43 in. (1.1 m) wide, but on only one side if less than this dimension. Handrail height is generally required to be between 36 in. and 38 in. (800 and 965 mm) above the line of flight. They must be continuous throughout the stair length except where interrupted by doorways, newel posts, at landings, and at changes of direction. Handrails on landings can be as high as 42 in. (1070 mm). To ensure that handrails do not project too far into a stairway while at the same time providing easy grasping, they are usually restricted to be between $1\frac{1}{2}$ in. and 4 in. (40 and 100 mm). Handrails must be anchored to structural members to ensure the safety of those using them.

Some regulations require that the spacing of spindles on stair railings be placed such that a spherical object having a diameter of 4 in. (100 mm) cannot pass between them, although there are exceptions as determined by local building codes.

TYPES OF STAIRS

Stairs are classified by the *kind of stringer* used in their construction, by the way the complete stair is fitted into the building, and by the shape of the complete stair.

Stringer Types

One type of stringer used is the open stringer or notched stringer (see Fig. 8-6), in which pieces are cut from the stringer and risers and treads attached so that their ends are exposed. Another type is the

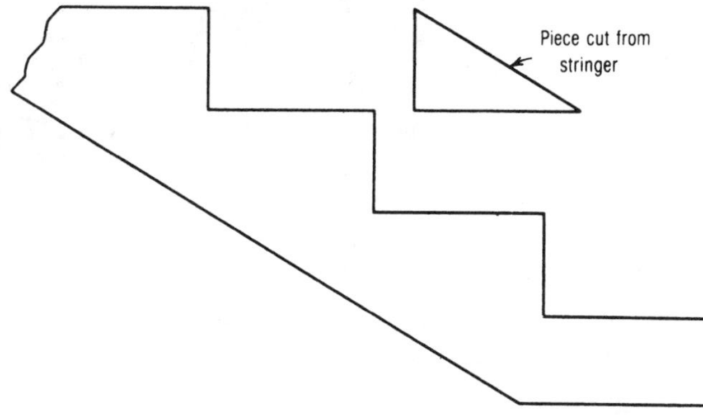

FIGURE 8-6 Open or cut-out stringer.

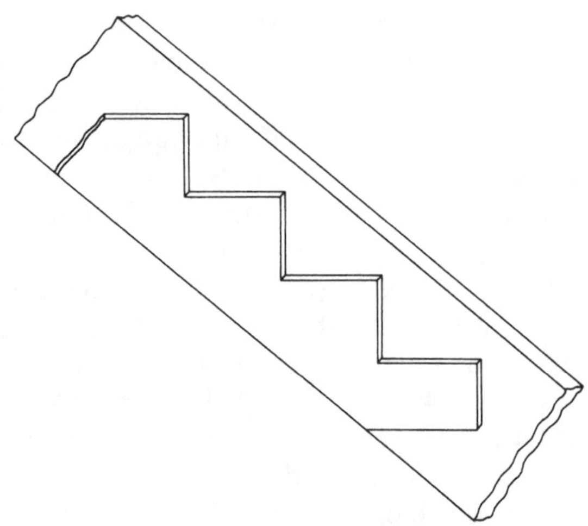

FIGURE 8-7 Semi-housed stringer.

semi-housed stringer, in which a piece of $\frac{3}{4}$-in. (19-mm) material is cut out, as in Fig. 8-7, and then fastened to the face of a solid $1\frac{1}{2}$-in. (38-mm) stringer. The ends of the risers and treads are thus concealed in the finished stair. A third type is the housed stringer, which has dadoes, $\frac{1}{2}$ in. (12 mm) deep, cut on its inner face to receive the ends of the risers and treads (see Fig. 8-8). The dadoes are tapered so that wedges can be driven below the tread and behind the riser to hold each tightly in place.

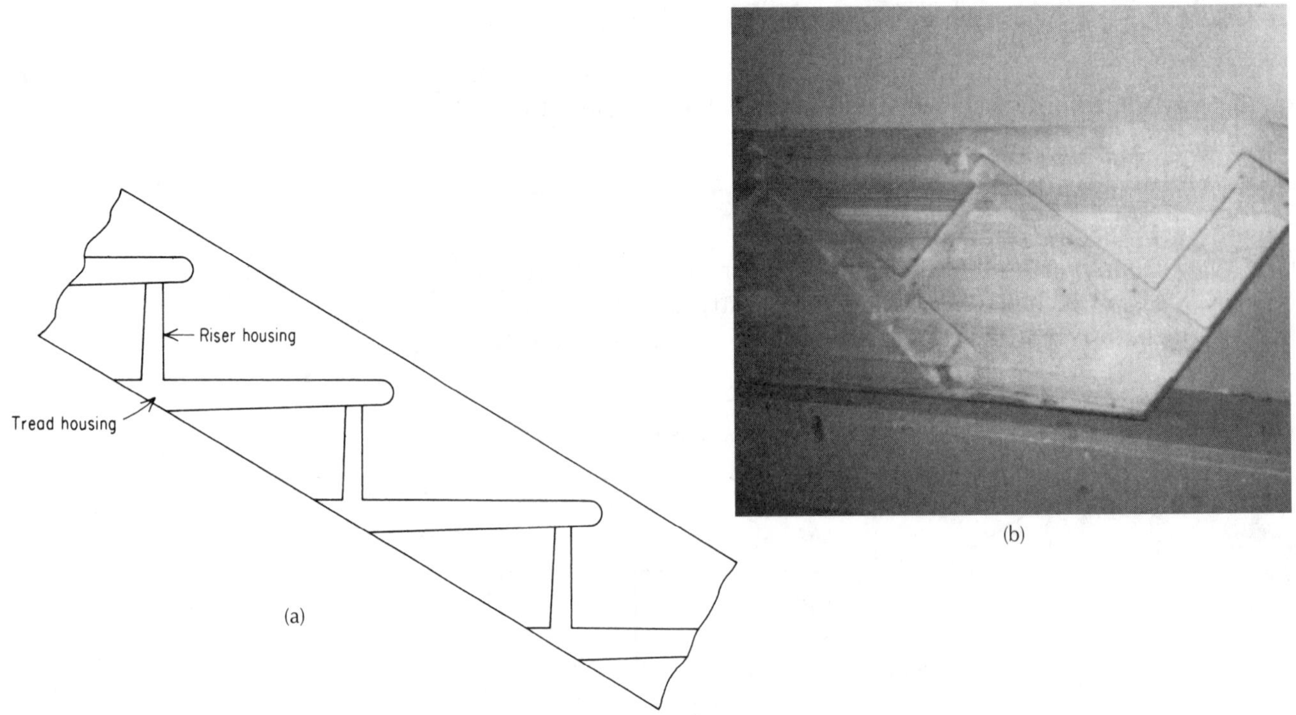

FIGURE 8-8 Housed stringer.

Stair Types

A complete stair that has no wall on either side is called an *open stair.* If it has a wall on one side only, it is a *semi-housed stair* (although in some areas this type is also called an open stair); if it is built between two walls, it is a *housed stair* or *closed stair.*

Stair Shapes

A stair that rises with uninterrupted steps from floor to floor is known as a *straight flight;* if it has a break between top and bottom, it is a *straight flight with landing.* A stair that makes a right-angle turn by means of a landing is called an *L stair,* and a stair that makes a right-angle turn step by step is called a *winder.* In some cases, rather than using a winder to change direction, a landing is installed between flights to change direction, other than 90°. A stair that makes a 180° turn is called a *U-stair* (see Fig. 8-9).

It should be noted here that a winder stair could be dangerous because of the wedge-shaped treads. The width of tread at the inner point is so narrow that a person cannot comfortably place a foot on the tread. The stair at this location is also very steep.

Circular stairs, on the other hand, are restricted as to the width of tread along the inner stringer, so they are not considered dangerous. They are usually intended to be an architectural feature in a building [see Figs. 8-1 and 8-9(f)].

An example of a stair complete with handrail is shown in Fig. 8-10.

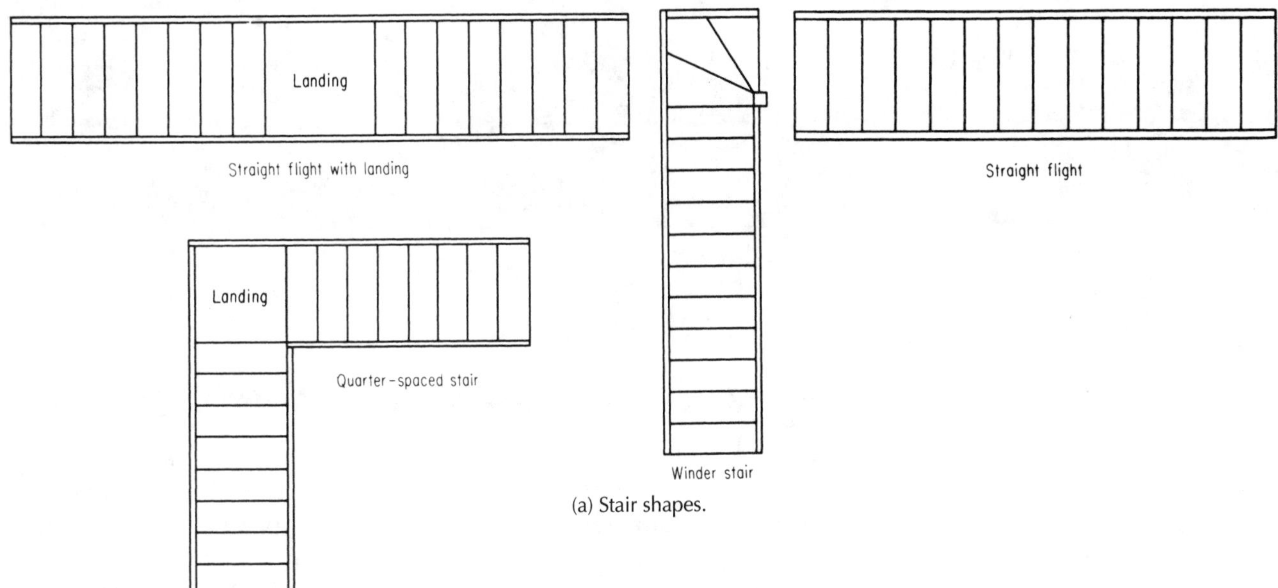

(a) Stair shapes.

FIGURE 8-9 Stair shapes.

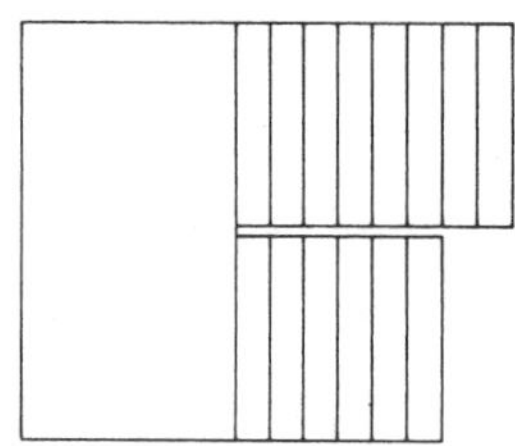

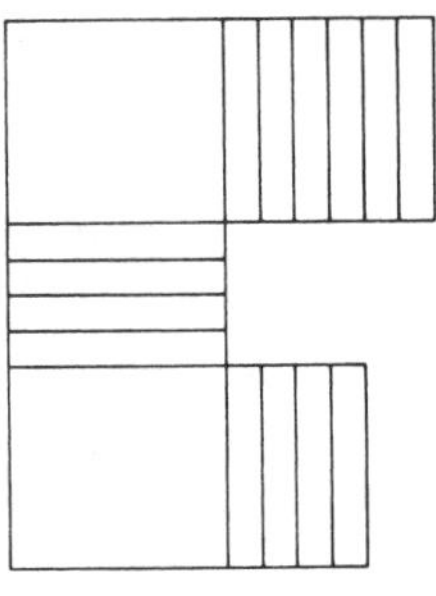

(b) U-stairs.

(c) Lower section winder stair.

(d) Looking down on winder stair.

(e) Polygon landing.

FIGURE 8-9 (cont.)

HOW TO BUILD AN OPEN STRINGER STAIR

The first calculation necessary in connection with a stair is that of finding the length of the stairwell opening. This actually must be done during the floor-framing stage, because the opening must be framed at that time. In order to do this the total rise of the stair must be known by either consulting the building plans or by taking the actual measurement after the floor system has been installed.

(f) Circular stair.

FIGURE 8-9 (cont.)

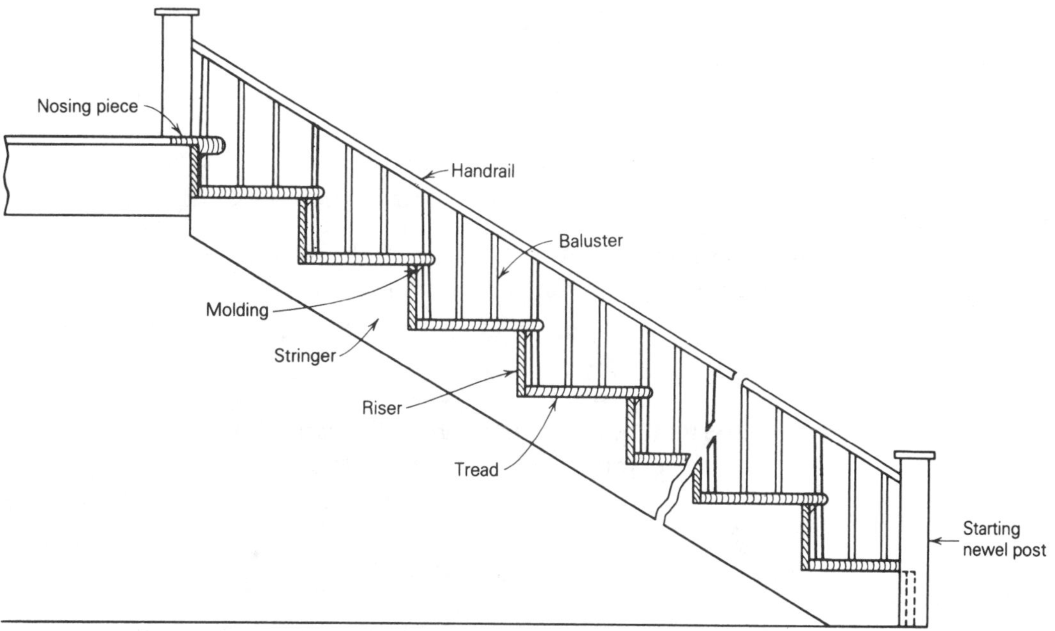

FIGURE 8-10 Parts of a stair.

Calculation of Stairwell Opening Length

A simple method of calculating the stairwell opening length is by comparison of two similar triangles involved in the stair layout. One contains unit rise and unit run as two sides of a triangle and the other the stairwell opening as one side and the headroom clearance plus thickness of ceiling finish, floor frame, subfloor, and finish floor as another. A portion of the line of flight is the third side of both.

As a specific example, suppose the finish floor to finish floor height is 108 in. (2700 mm), the headroom clearance required is 6 ft, 4 in. (1950 mm), and the floor assembly thickness is $11\frac{1}{2}$ in. (290 mm). The unit rise is to be between 7 and $7\frac{1}{2}$ in. (175 and 190 mm). It should be noted that some building plans will identify the unit rise and run, but if there is flexibility in this, the product of the unit rise and the unit run should be 70–75 (45,000–48,500) in order to have a flight that is comfortable to climb.

Using the above figures, what length of stairwell opening is required? Use the following procedure to determine stairwell opening length:

1. Determine the number of risers required by dividing the total rise by 7 (175):
   $108 \div 7 = 15.4$ use 15 risers ($2700 \div 175 = 15.4$ use 15 risers)
   (There must be an even number of risers, hence 15 has been chosen.)

2. Determine the height of each riser by dividing the rise by the number of risers:
   $108 \div 15 = 7.2$ in. ($2700 \div 15 = 180$ mm)

3. Determine the unit run by dividing 72 (45,000) by the individual riser size:
   $72 \div 7.2 = 10$ in. ($45{,}000 \div 180 = 250$ mm) [The reason for choosing 72 (45,000) is to achieve a comfortable angle for the stair]

4. Determine the drop to line of flight by adding the floor assembly thickness to the headroom (see Fig. 8-11):
   6 ft, 4 in. + $11\frac{1}{2}$ in. = 7 ft, $3\frac{1}{2}$ in. or 87.5 in.
   (1950 mm + 290 mm = 2240 mm)

5. Determine the finished stairwell opening by setting up a ratio with the common sides of the two triangles:
   unit rise is to unit run = total drop is to finish stairwell opening (F.S.O.)
   $\frac{7.2}{10} = \frac{87.5}{\text{F.S.O.}}$, F.S.O. $= 87.5 \times 10 \div 7.2 = 121.5$ in. or 10 ft, $1\frac{1}{2}$ in. $\left(\frac{180}{250} = \frac{2240}{\text{F.S.O.}}\right.$, F.S.O. $\left. = 2190 \times 250 \div 180 = 3111 \text{ mm}\right)$

6. The rough stairwell opening is equal to the stairwell opening plus the riser thickness plus the nosing and finish on the stairwell header. Usually adding $2\frac{1}{2}$ to 3 in. (65 to 75 mm) to the opening will allow for these items.
   rough stairwell opening = 10 ft, $1\frac{1}{2}$ in. + $\frac{3}{4}$ + $1\frac{1}{4}$ + $\frac{1}{2}$ in.
   = 10 ft, $4\frac{1}{2}$ in. riser thickness nosing
   = (3111 + 75 = 3186 mm)

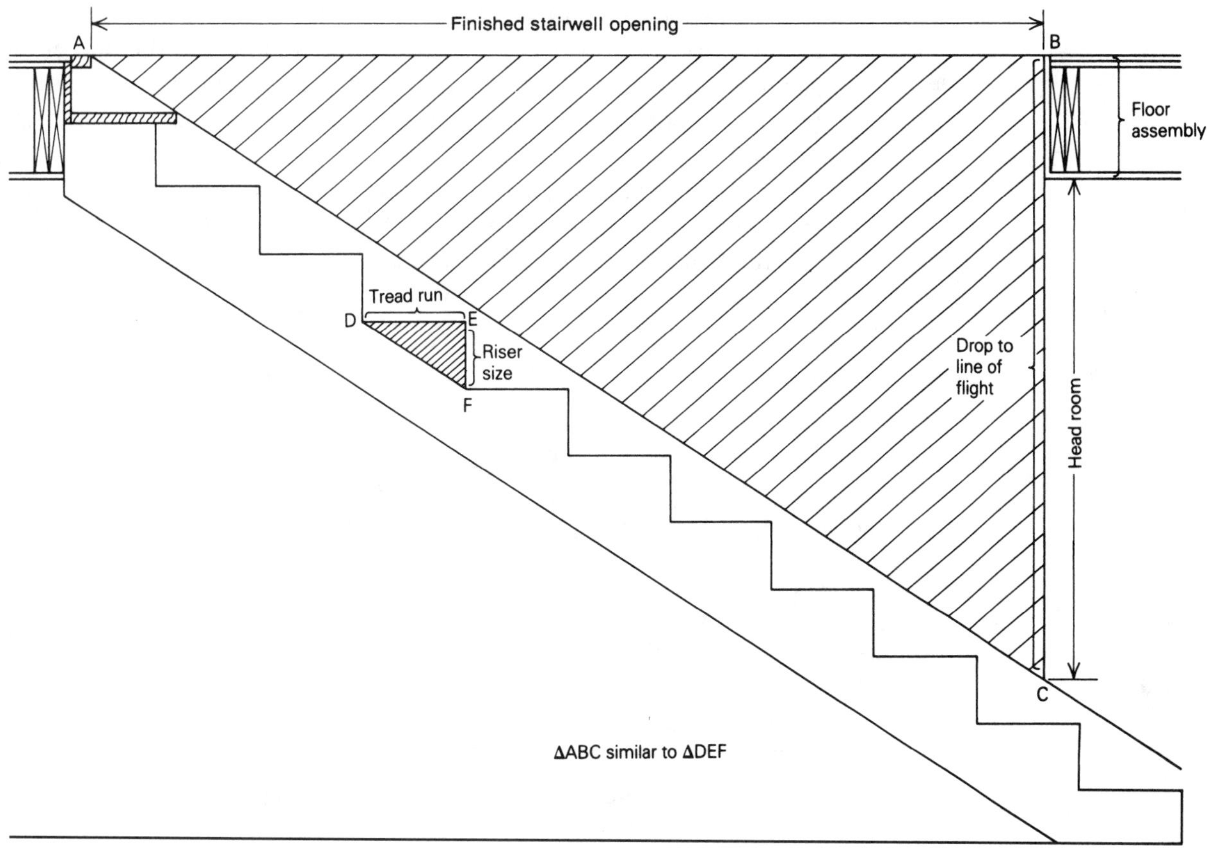

FIGURE 8-11 Similar triangles for setting up ratio.

Layout of Stair Stringer

Use the unit rise on the tongue of a framing square and the unit run on the blade to mark out the stair. Using a pair of stair gauges clamped to the square at these points will make the job easier and consistently accurate (see Fig. 8-12). Lay the square on the stringer

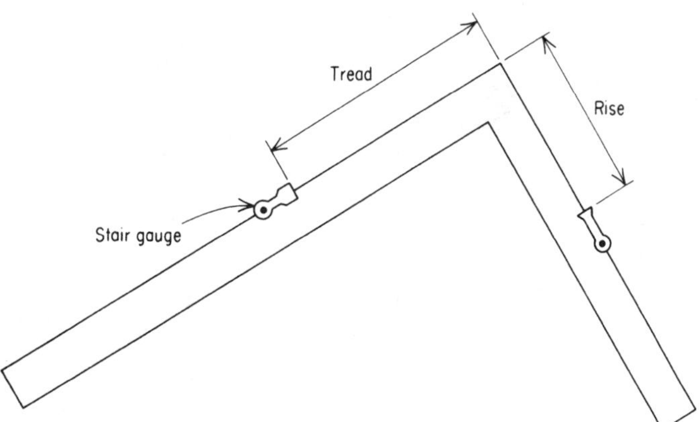

FIGURE 8-12 Square with stair gauges attached.

stock, close to one end, as illustrated in Fig. 8-13, and carefully draw on the stock the rise and run. Slide the square along to the end of the run line and repeat. Continue until the required number of risers and treads have been laid out. The stock will now look like the illustration in Fig. 8-14.

Since the stair begins with a riser at the bottom, extend the last riser and tread lines to the back edge of the stock, as shown in Fig. 8-15. Cut the stringer off along these lines.

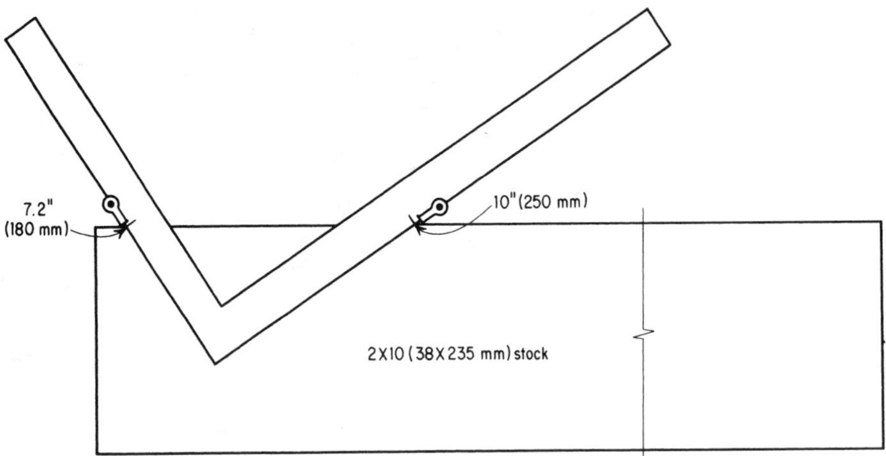

FIGURE 8-13 First step in stair layout.

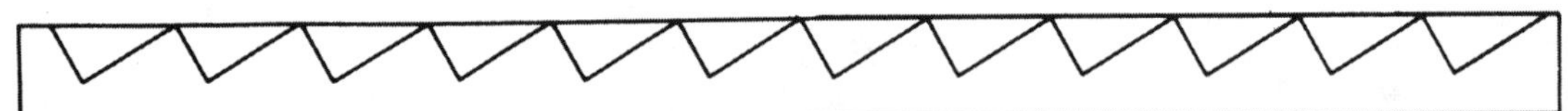

FIGURE 8-14 Stringer laid out.

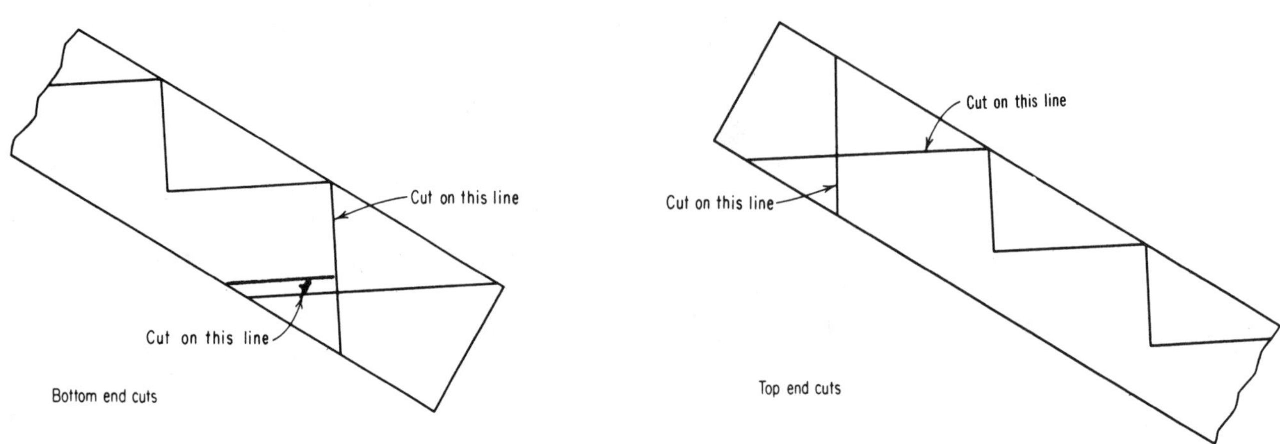

FIGURE 8-15 Cuts at ends of stringer.

At the top end, extend the last riser and tread lines to the back edge of the stock and cut as shown in Fig. 8-15. Cut very carefully along all the rise and tread lines to produce a cutout stringer (see Fig. 8-16).

When this stringer is set up in place (see Fig. 8-17), it is seen that the face of the header becomes the first riser. But when the treads are set in place (see Fig. 8-18), the bottom step becomes higher than the rest, and the top step becomes shorter than the others, each by the thickness of the tread. To remedy this discrepancy, cut off from the bottom an amount equal to the thickness of the tread (see Fig. 8-19). Now when the stringer is set in place, the bottom rise is less than the rest, and the top is greater, but when the treads are in place, all the rises will be equal.

FIGURE 8-16 Stringer cut out.

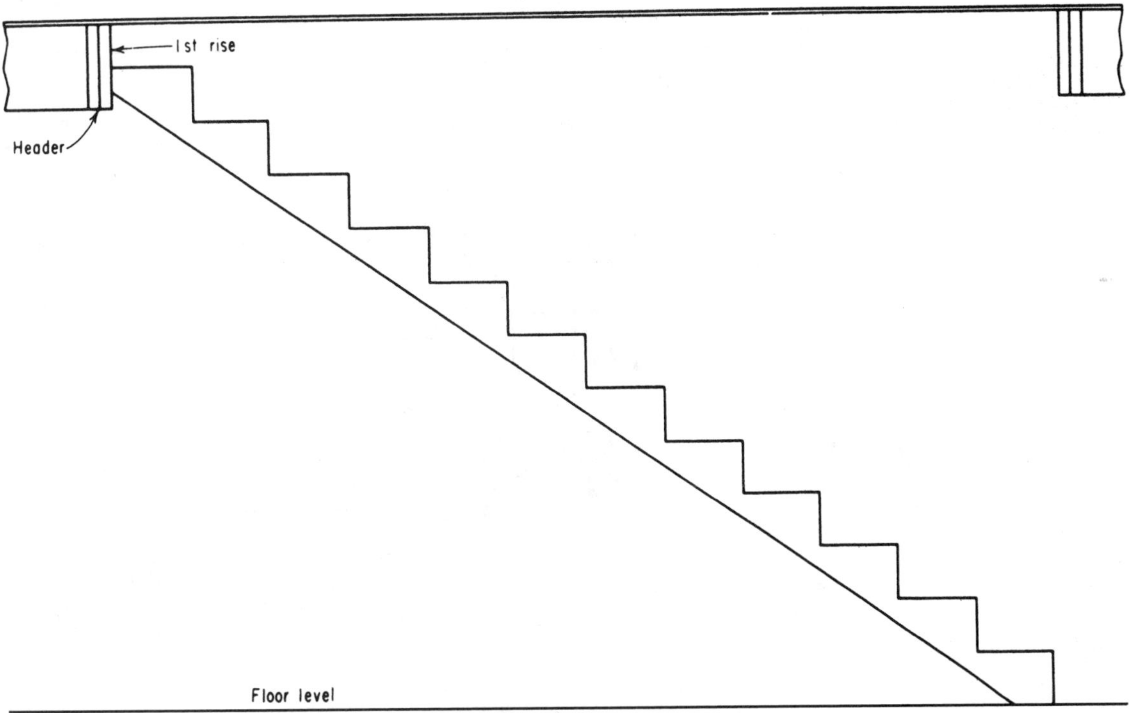

FIGURE 8-17 Stringer setup.

Stair Assembly

At the top of the stair, a nosing with the same projection as the rest of the steps should be provided. The method used will depend on the material used for the finish floor and stair finish [see Figs. 8-20(a) and 8-20(b)].

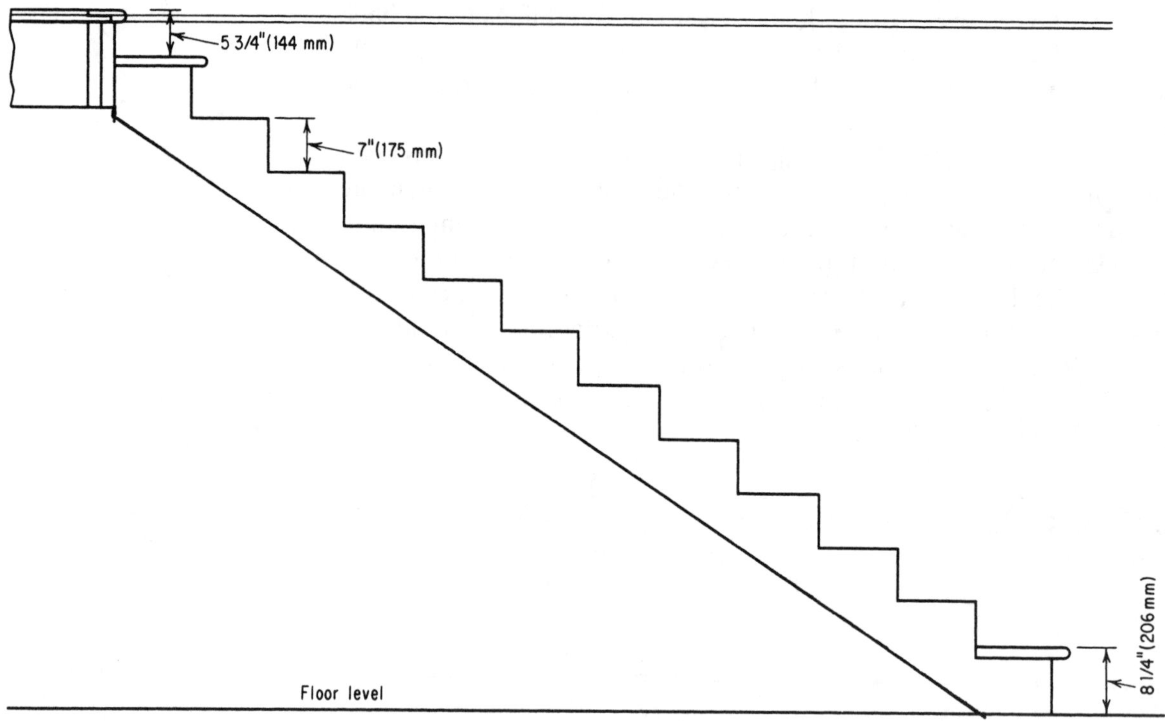

FIGURE 8-18 Unequal risers.

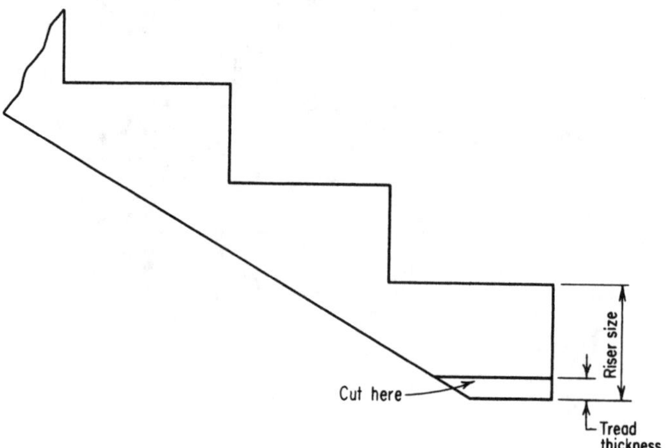

FIGURE 8-19 Bottom riser reduced.

Tread material should be clear, dry, edge grain (if treads are exposed), plywood or OSB (if covered) as illustrated in Figs. 8-20(a) and (b). The shape of the nosing may be round, beveled, or square. Some building codes restrict the amount of curvature or beveling, so it is important to check this out because the depth of the tread can be affected.

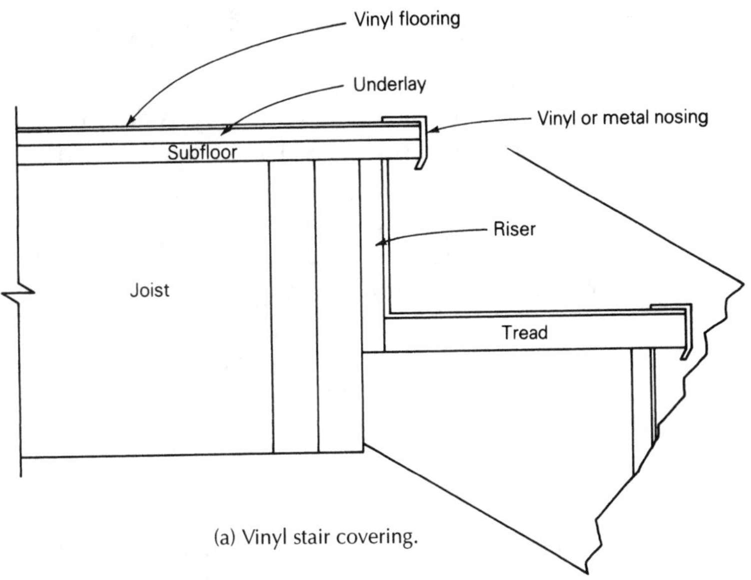

(a) Vinyl stair covering.

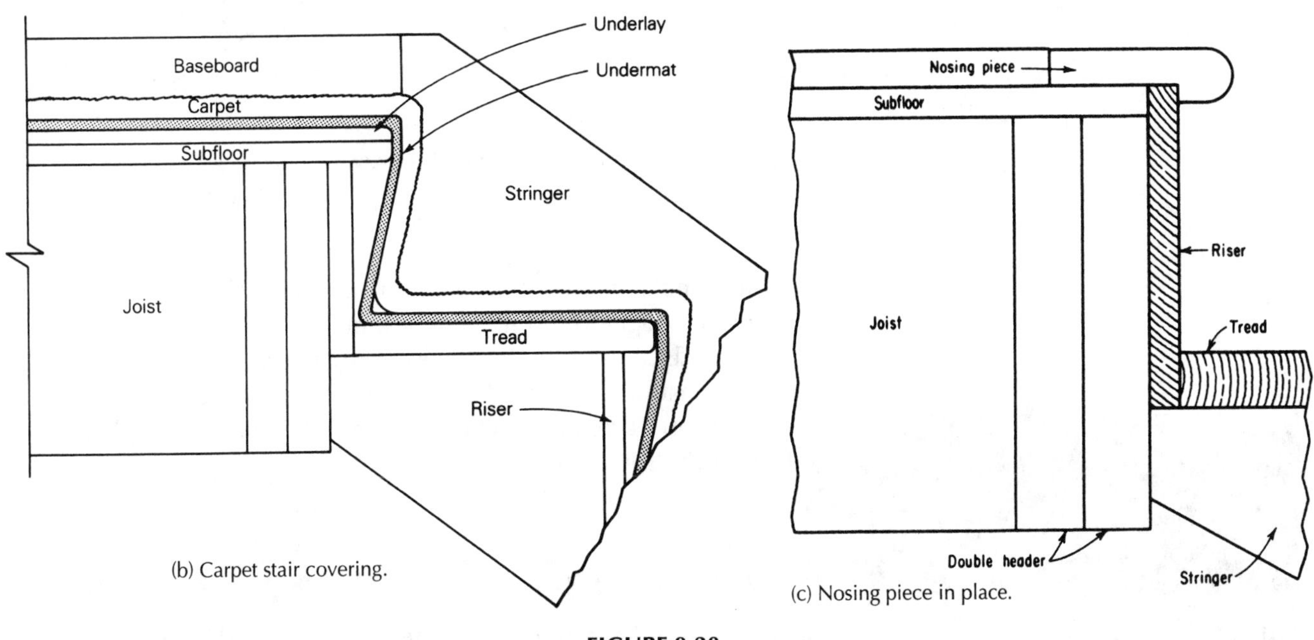

(b) Carpet stair covering.

(c) Nosing piece in place.

FIGURE 8-20

The risers are put in place first, nailed or stapled. If the risers are not to be covered, a finishing nail should be used and countersunk below the surface. The treads are then put on, nailed, stapled, or screwed in place, and from the back the bottom edges of the risers are nailed to the back edge of the treads. Glue or constructive adhesive is generally used to minimize squeaks.

HOW TO BUILD A SEMIHOUSED STRINGER STAIR

When this type of stair is to be built, the $\frac{3}{4}$-in. (19-mm) cutout stringers are made in exactly the same way as described above. The ends of the solid, backup stringers will, however, be cut differently. At the bottom, the stringer will be allowed to run past the riser until the vertical cut is equal to the height of the baseboard, if any (see Fig. 8-21). At the top end, it will be cut as illustrated in Fig. 8-21, again so that the vertical cut will be the same height as the baseboard.

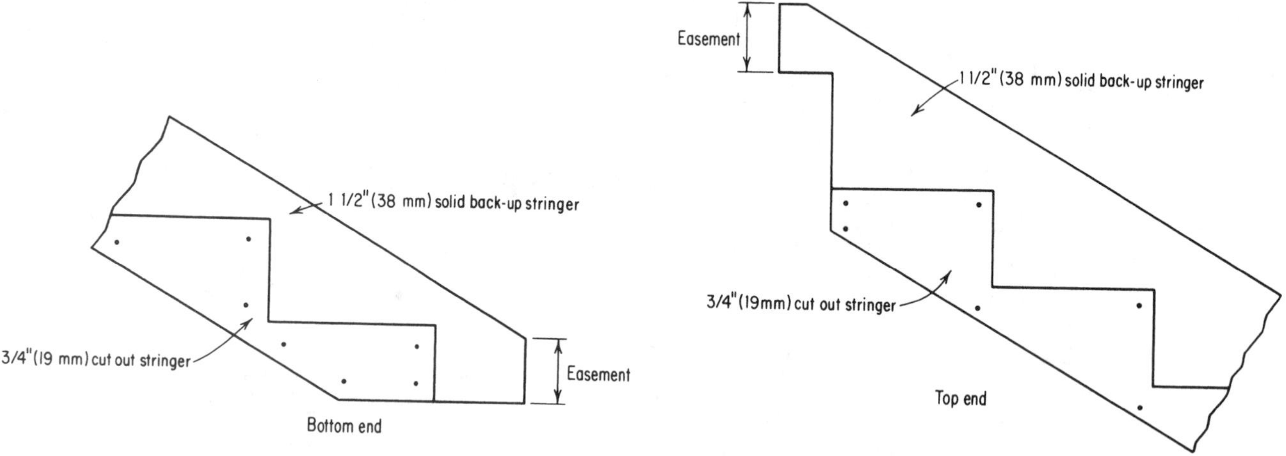

FIGURE 8-21 Top and bottom ends of semi-housed stringer.

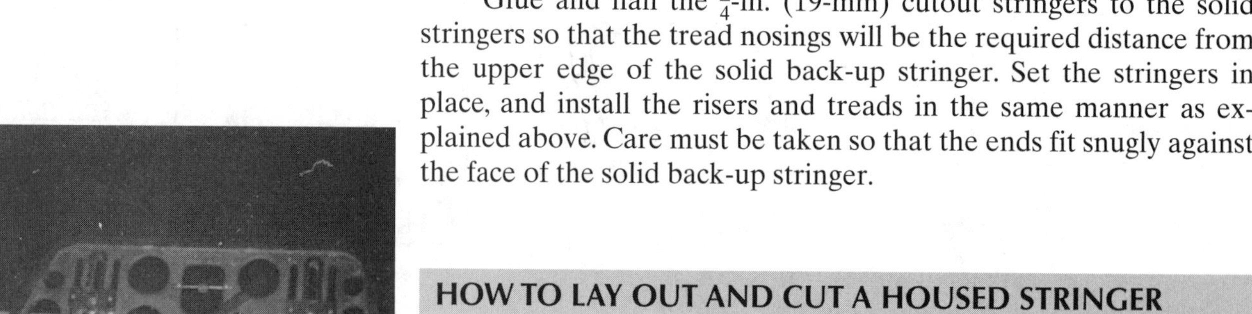

Glue and nail the $\frac{3}{4}$-in. (19-mm) cutout stringers to the solid stringers so that the tread nosings will be the required distance from the upper edge of the solid back-up stringer. Set the stringers in place, and install the risers and treads in the same manner as explained above. Care must be taken so that the ends fit snugly against the face of the solid back-up stringer.

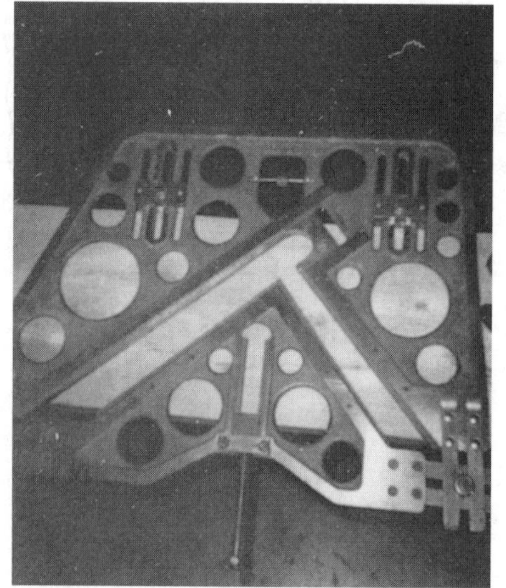

FIGURE 8-22 Adjustable metal template.

HOW TO LAY OUT AND CUT A HOUSED STRINGER

Calculations for riser heights are the same as for other types of stairs, but the method of layout is considerably different.

Tapered dadoes are cut in the stringer to receive the treads and risers; these can be drawn with a template but are more commonly cut out with the aid of a router. Adjustable templates are available that make the cutting of the dadoes a simple chore. These templates can be set to the required riser and tread size making a 1 in 16 taper to allow for installation of wedges to hold pieces in place (see Fig. 8-22). A simple template can be made from hardboard to be used with a router equipped with a collar [see Figs. 8-23(a) and 8-23(b)].

(a) Hardboard template.

(b) Router, collar, and bit.

FIGURE 8-23

To lay out and cut the stringer, proceed as follows:

1. Joint the top edge of the stringer so that it is perfectly straight.
2. Using the required run and rise figures, draw the slope of the tread across the face of the stringer (see Fig. 8-24).

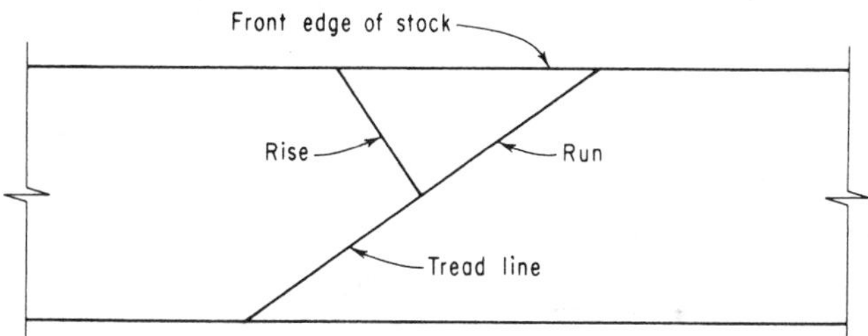

FIGURE 8-24 Tread line drawn on stringer.

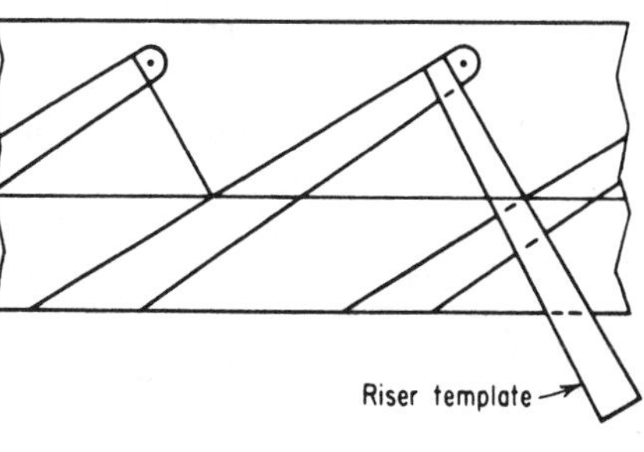

FIGURE 8-25 Nosing line.

3. Lay the template to this line, making sure the nosing is the required distance from the top edge of the stringer. Draw a line through this point parallel to the top edge. This distance is usually at least 1 in. (25 mm), as shown in Fig. 8-25.
4. Mark on the tread line the width of the tread, and through this point draw a line parallel to the front edge. This is the baseline from which the layout is made (see Fig. 8-26).

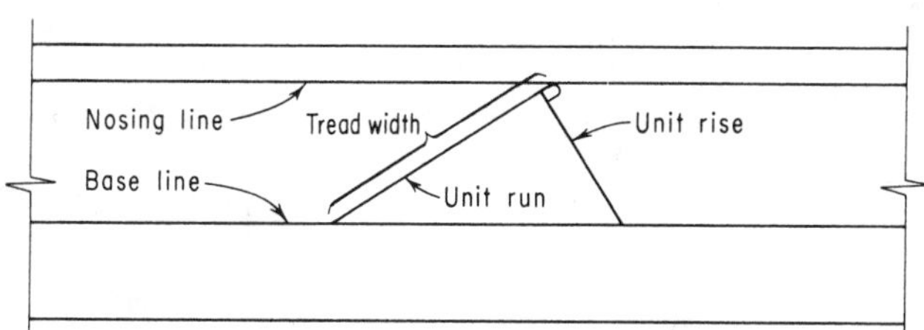

FIGURE 8-26 Base line drawn.

5. Secure the template to the stringer in the correct location and cut out the dadoes for each step using the router (see Fig. 8-27).

FIGURE 8-27 Template ready for routing.

6. At the bottom end, cut the stringer as illustrated in Fig. 8-28.

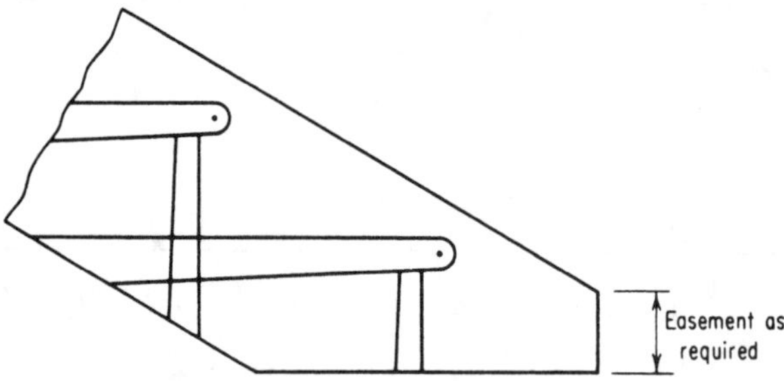

FIGURE 8-28 Bottom end cut.

7. At the top end, cut the stringer as shown in Fig. 8-29, making sure to cut the dado for the nosing piece.

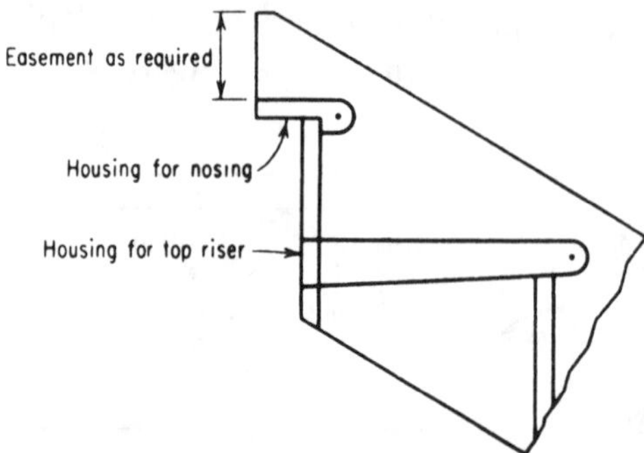

FIGURE 8-29 Top end cut.

8. Chamfer the top inner edge of the stringer as required and sand the surface clean.

ASSEMBLING A HOUSED STRINGER STAIR

Lay the stringers top edge down on the floor, far enough apart to take the treads and risers. Set all the treads in place first and hold the assembly together with pipe clamps placed to ensure that the stair is square. Check to see that the front edge of the groove in each tread lines up with the front edge of the riser dado. Set the nosing piece in place.

Now set all the risers in place. Check to see that the back edge of each tread fits snugly against the front face of its riser. The top riser cannot be wedged, since its dado is open at the back. Apply glue to the ends and nail it in place from the back.

The next step is to wedge the treads in place. Apply glue to the wedges and drive each firmly into place. The tread should thus be brought into a tight fit against the upper edge of the housing. Be sure that the wedges do not project beyond the back edge of the treads.

Now wedge the risers in place. Cut off the thin end of each wedge so that, when driven, it will not interfere with the tread above. Nail the bottom of each riser to the back edge of the tread, as illustrated in Fig. 8-30.

Nail and glue a cant strip into the junctions between risers and treads (see Fig. 8-31). The purpose of a cant strip is to limit or even eliminate squeaks in stairs by providing a positive connection between the top of the riser and the underside of the tread. The stair is now complete and ready to install.

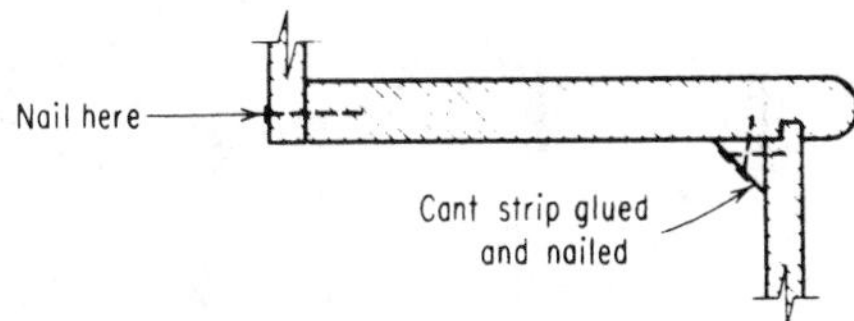

FIGURE 8-30 Riser and tread nailed or stapled.

FIGURE 8-31 Glued and nailed strip at junction of step.

When stairs are being installed between walls, a spacer board is first attached to the outside of the stringer to allow wall finishes to be applied later without having to fit precisely to the stringer [see Figs. 8-32(a) and 8-32(b)]. The wall finish can be placed between the stringer and the wall and there can be a molding applied to the top edge of the stringer to cover any space left.

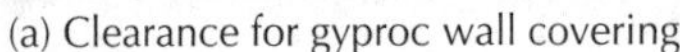

(a) Clearance for gyproc wall covering.

(b) 3/4 in. (19 mm) gyproc clearance.

FIGURE 8-32

ASSEMBLING THE HANDRAIL

There are several different shapes of handrails, and Fig. 8-33 illustrates some of the more common types. Some will have a recess cut into the bottom surface to receive balusters.

Once the stair assembly has been installed and fastened into place, the handrail must be assembled. For housed stairs, metal or wood brackets are easily secured to the studs in the walls to which handrails are fastened, as illustrated in Fig. 8-34. For semi-housed or

FIGURE 8-33 Typical handrail shapes.

FIGURE 8-34 Brackets supporting handrail.

open stairs that do not have walls nearby, newel posts at either end support the handrail along with balusters evenly placed along the length to support the handrail [see Fig. 8-35(a) and 8-35(b)].

(a) Wooden railing.

(b) Wood and metal railing.

FIGURE 8-35

The newel posts are generally placed first, with the bottom end extending into and fastened to the floor frame to provide lateral support or fastened directly to the top of the joists with double pointed lag screws where lateral support is provided by the handrail (see Fig. 8-36). If the handrail should run into a wall at either end, a $\frac{1}{2}$ newel post is fastened to the wall to provide support for the end of the handrail (see Fig. 8-37). The baluster shoe is placed next, fitted between the newel posts and fastened to the floor, top of a wall enclosing the lower part of the stair, or stringer with screws. Figure 8-38 illustrates a wall that has been erected along a stair stringer on which the baluster shoe will be placed. The handrail is usually placed

FIGURE 8-36 Newel post fastened to floor frame.

FIGURE 8-37 Railing fastened to wall.

FIGURE 8-38 Sloped wall adjoining stair.

FIGURE 8-39 Handrail fastened to newel post.

next, fastened with screws to the newel posts at either end, as shown in Fig. 8-39.

If wood balusters are used, they are inserted and held in place with blocks fitted and glued into the slot in the shoe and under the handrail (see Fig. 8-40). Recessed screws are used to hold the top of balusters to handrails with designs that do not have the slot to allow for the placement of blocks between the balusters. Wooden plugs are then used to cover the screws (see Fig. 8-41). Handrail parts are then finish sanded prior to painting or staining to match the decor of the room.

An example of a utility stair used for access between a residence and attached garage is shown in Fig. 8-42. In this case the support of the handrail is through the use of 2×4(38 $\times$ 89 mm) balustrade and the newel post also supports the landing.

FIGURE 8-40 Fastening balusters.

FIGURE 8-41 Camouflage plug.

FIGURE 8-42 Utility stair in garage.

Occasionally you may see a spiral stair where the treads radiate around a central post. This type of stair is usually restricted to a secondary access, as most building codes will not allow them to be the principle means of access or egress between floors (see Fig. 8-43).

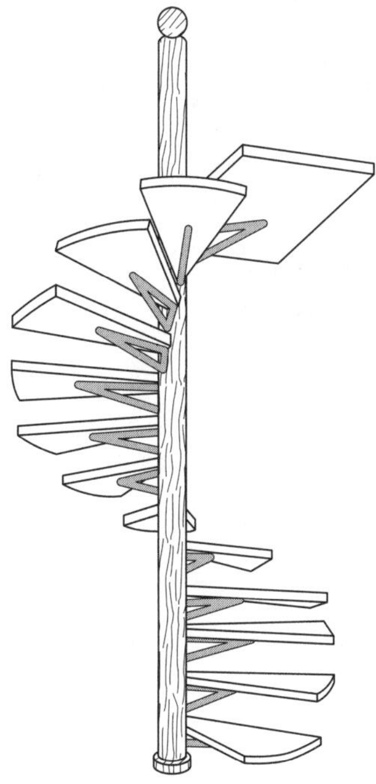

FIGURE 8-43 Spiral stair.

REVIEW QUESTIONS

8–1. Fill in the blank or blanks in each sentence with the correct word or phrase:

a. A stair begins at the bottom with a _________.

b. A stair leads to an upper floor through a _________.

c. A line drawn through the extremities of the nosings of stair treads is the _________.

d. Stair risers and treads are carried on _________.

e. The vertical distance from the underside of the stairwell opening header to the line of flight is the _________.

f. The vertical distance from one floor level to the next is the _________ of a stair.

8–2. Name three types of stringers used in stair building and indicate the differences between them.

8–3. Explain briefly the difference between an open, a semi-housed, and a housed stair.

8–4. What is the purpose of

a. Wedges in a stair?

b. A newel post?

c. A baluster?

8–5. If the total rise of a stair from finished floor to finished floor is 9 ft $1\frac{1}{2}$ in. (2800 mm), how many risers would be needed if they cannot exceed 7-$\frac{1}{4}$ in. (185 mm)? What will be the unit rise?

8–6. In the above question, if the headroom clearance is to be 6 ft, 4 in. (1.95 m), the unit run is 9 in. (230 mm), nosing projection is 1-$\frac{1}{4}$ in. (30 mm), the upper floor system including all finishes is 12-$\frac{1}{4}$ in. (310 mm), what will be the stairwell rough opening if the $\frac{3}{4}$-in. (20-mm) top riser is placed against the rough framing?

8–7. Explain why an amount equal to the thickness of a stair tread must be cut off the bottom of a notched (cut-out) stringer to reduce the unit rise at that point.

8–8. Why are winder stairs considered dangerous?

Chapter 9

EXTERIOR FINISHING

OBJECTIVES

When you complete each component of this chapter, you will be able to identify:

1. The different ways to complete the cornice.
2. Common types of roofing materials and how they are applied.
3. The different types of windows and how they are installed.
4. Exterior doors and how they are installed.
5. Common types of exterior cladding and how they are installed.

Once the frame of the building has been completed, the next step is to apply the exterior finish. This involves installing window and doorframes and outside casings, roofing, exterior paper, cornice work, and the application of whatever is to be used to cover the exterior.

The usual order in which these operations are carried out is as follows: (1) cornice work, (2) roofing, (3) fitting of door and window units, (4) application of exterior air barrier, and (5) application of exterior finish.

CORNICE WORK

The *cornice,* or eave, is formed by the overhang of the rafters and may be *open* or *boxed.* In either case, the work of finishing the eave should be done as soon as the rafters are in place.

Open Eaves

With open eaves, the rafter tails and the underside of the roof sheathing are exposed from below, and consequently the roof sheathing over that section of the roof may be replaced by a better quality of material [see Fig. 9-1(a) and 9-1(b)].

(a) Roof sheathing for open eaves. (b) Open eave exposed.

FIGURE 9-1

In addition, it is necessary to block off the openings between the rafters above the cap plate, and this is done by the use of *wind blocks*. One way is to use pieces of $1\frac{1}{2}$-in. (38-mm) material cut to fit snugly between each pair of rafters (see Fig. 9-2). It is sometimes necessary to provide air ventilation to the roof cavity by cutting

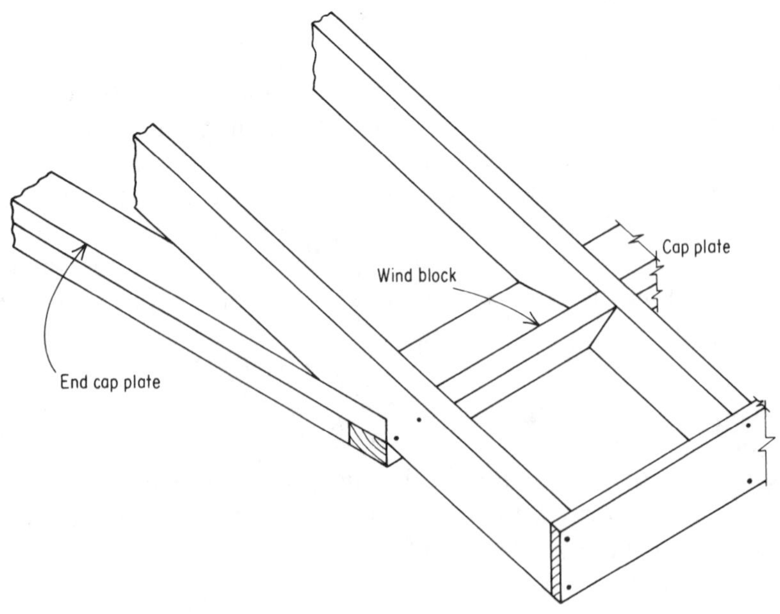

FIGURE 9-2 Open eave with wind block in place.

FIGURE 9-3 Wind block with ventilation holes.

openings in these wind blocks that must be covered with a screen to prevent the incursion of birds and insects (see Fig. 9-3).

With this type of eave, a single fascia may be used over the ends of the rafter tails, as shown in Fig. 9-2.

Boxed Eaves

With boxed eaves, the underside of the roof overhang is enclosed. This may be done by applying a *soffit* to the bottom edge of the rafter tails, as illustrated in Fig. 9-4 where finished plywood is used.

An alternative and more common method is to build a frame to which a horizontal soffit may be attached to enclose the eave (see Fig. 9-5). When a plywood soffit is to be used, the frame is made up of a *lookout ledger,* nailed to the wall, a *rough fascia* over the ends of the rafter tails, and *lookouts,* which span between the two and lie alongside each rafter tail (see Fig. 9-6). It may be fabricated on the ground and raised into place as a unit. Instead of a wind block, another, more popular way to restrict air flow into the

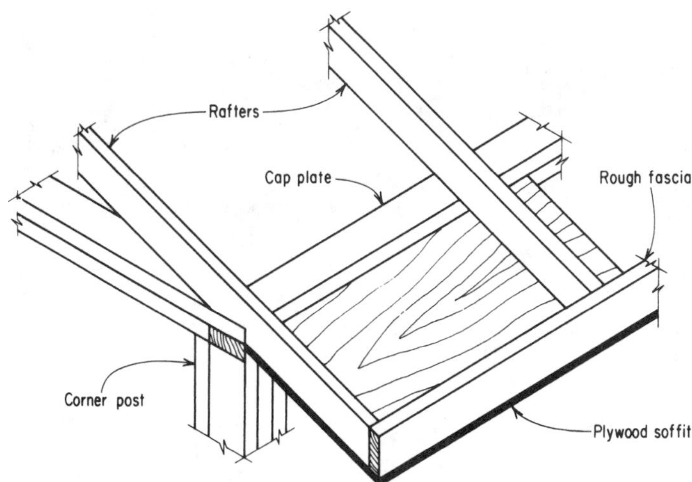

FIGURE 9-4 Eave boxed on slope of roof.

FIGURE 9-5 Boxed eave frame.

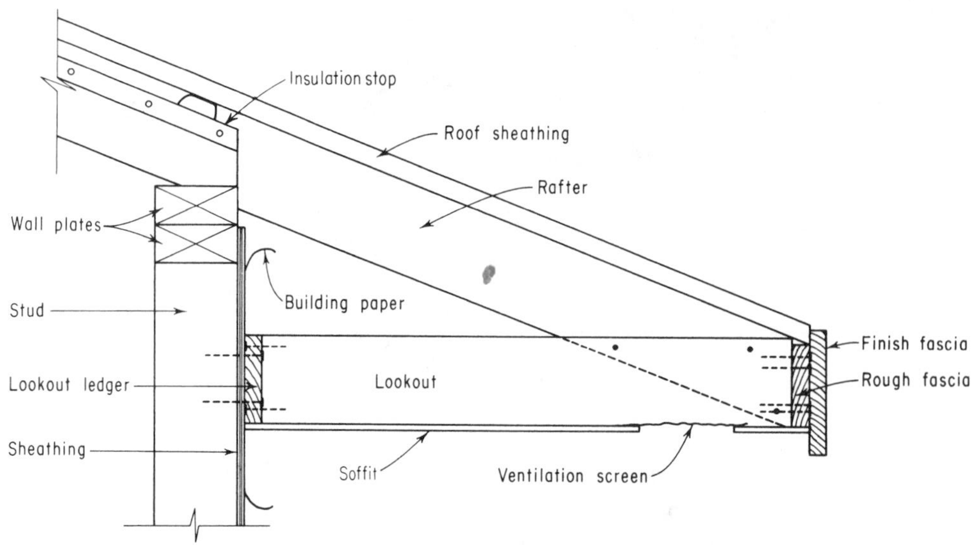

FIGURE 9-6 Boxed eave framing.

roof cavity is to staple ready-cut pieces of wax-coated cardboard in place as shown in Fig. 9-6.

As discussed in Chapter 7, at the gable-end additional framing is required to support the verge rafter. One method is to install lookouts that extended over the gable-end back to the next truss to give sufficient support (see Fig. 9-7). In a hip roof building, the horizontal soffit is framed the same way on all sides of the building.

Metal and vinyl soffit material has almost eliminated the use of wood finished soffits as the amount of labor to install the material is reduced and there is little or no maintenance required. The only framing required for a metal or vinyl soffit is a rough fascia at the edge of the roof overhang as a molding supports the soffit material where it meets the building (see Fig. 9-8). The outer end of the soffit

FIGURE 9-7 Overhang support.

FIGURE 9-8 Finished metal soffit.

is stapled to the underside of the rough fascia and is then covered with a pre-formed finish fascia.

With a gable roof, the horizontal eaves on the side walls can either stop at the corner of the building, as illustrated in Fig. 9-9(a), or it can extend flush with the edge of the roof, as shown in Fig. 9-9(b). The

(a) Eave stopped at corner of the building.

(b) Eave flush with the edge of the roof.

FIGURE 9-9

ends of the eave are then finished, as shown in Fig. 9-10. The gable-end soffit is finished the same way as the soffits on the sidewalls.

Another method of finishing the boxed eave at the gable end is illustrated in Fig. 9-11. This is known as *cornice return.* Sets of truss overhangs are nailed to the gable wall, producing the same overhang as the regular eave. The tops of the returns are shingled like the roof, and the soffit is carried around, finishing the underside.

If there is no gable overhang (see Fig. 9-12), a rough fascia is nailed to the outside of the gable-end, covering the edge of the roof sheathing. A pre-formed finish fascia is then nailed to the rough fascia with colored nails to finish the edge of the roof.

FIGURE 9-10 Finishing end of eave.

FIGURE 9-11 Cornice returns.

FIGURE 9-12 Gable-end with no roof overhang.

Also, before the roofing is applied, provision must be made at the lower edges of the roof for the proper direction of rainwater into the eaves trough. One method is to fasten eave flashing, like that illustrated in Fig. 9-13, to the edge of the roof, under the roofing material.

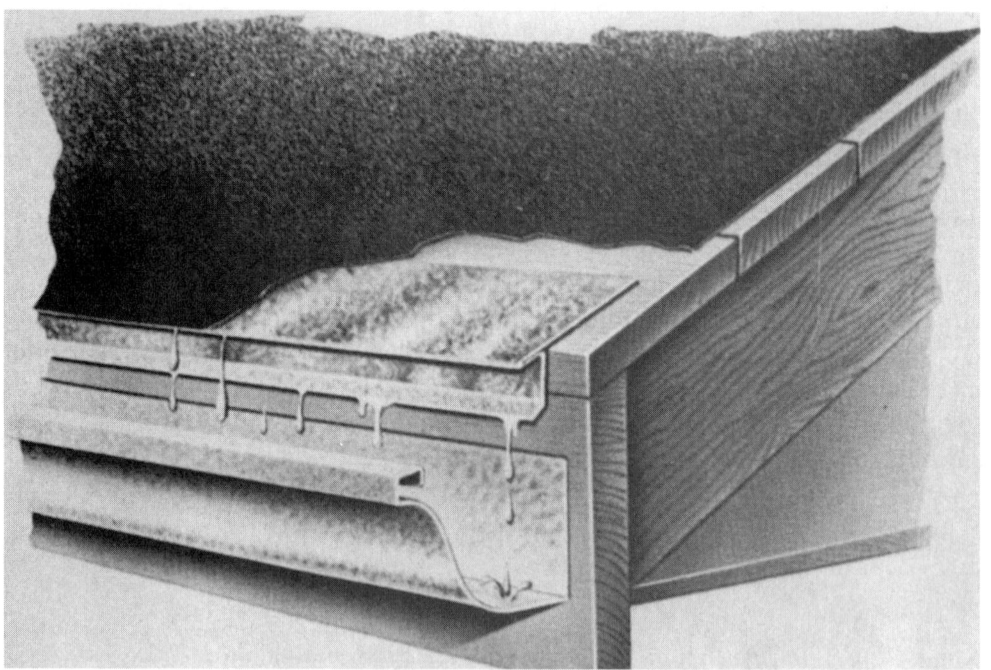

FIGURE 9-13 Eave flashing.

ROOF COVERINGS

Roof covering is installed as soon as the roof framing and sheathing have been completed. This will provide a weatherproof working space inside the building so that the other construction trades can begin. The most common type of roofing used on sloped roofs are shingles of one sort or another. These include wood (usually cedar or pine), asphalt, and hardboard. Roofing tile, sheet metal, and roll roofing are also used on sloped roofs. Roofing tile is commonly made of concrete, clay, or metal. Sheet metal roofing is made of galvanized steel or aluminum and is effective in areas subjected to heavy snowfall. Built-up roofing with a gravel topping or a cap sheet is commonly used on a flat or low slope roof.

Wood Shingles

Wood shingles are generally made from cedar, because it changes very little with atmospheric changes and withstands weathering better than most woods. Machine-cut wood shingles are made in a number of grades, but the commonly used grades for residential roofing are No. 1 and No. 2. The widths of these shingles vary from a minimum of 3 in. (75 mm) to a maximum of 14 in. (350 mm), and lengths vary from 16 to 24 in. (400–600 mm). It should be noted here that in some locations wood shingles are not allowed as they are not suitable as a fire suppresser.

The portion of shingle that should be exposed to the weather will depend on the steepness of the roof slope, the grade, and length of shingles used. Local building codes generally specify the amount of exposure, but the following is typical for No. 1 grade:

- With a slope of 1 in 3 or less, the maximum exposure for 16-in. (400-mm) long shingles is 4 in. (100 mm), while 18-in. (450-mm) shingles are allowed 4-$\frac{1}{2}$ in. (115 mm) exposure, and 24-in. (600-mm) shingles are allowed 6-$\frac{1}{2}$-in. (165-mm) exposure.
- With a slope of more than 1 in 3, the maximum exposure for 16-in. (400-mm) shingles is 5 in. (125 mm), for 18-in. (450-mm) shingles the maximum exposure is 5-$\frac{1}{2}$ in. (140 mm), and for 24-in. (600-mm) shingles the maximum exposure is 7-$\frac{1}{2}$ in. (190 mm).
- Note: make sure you check local codes for the allowable exposure.

The area of roof covered by one bundle of shingles will depend on the shingle exposure, and manufacturers will provide that data for you.

Decking for Cedar Shingles

Roof decking for wood shingles may be solid or spaced. If the deck is solid, it is usually made of OSB or plywood. The minimum recommended thickness is $\frac{3}{8}$ in. (9.5 mm) when trusses are spaced 24 in. (600 mm) o.c.

Spaced sheathing is usually 1 × 6 or 1 × 8(19 × 140 or 19 × 184) boards, spaced on centers equal to the exposure of the shingles (see Fig. 9-14). A row of OSB or plywood is usually installed along the eaves to provide better support for the eave protection membrane.

FIGURE 9-14 Spaced sheathing deck.

Paper for Cedar Shingles

Asphalt-impregnated paper is not usually used under cedar shingles. It prevents the completed roof from "breathing," that is, from allowing the moisture vapor under the roof to escape. If paper is required, plain or breather type paper is recommended, so check local codes for the requirements.

Application of Wood Shingles

Shingles should extend beyond the finish fascia about 1 in. (25 mm) to provide sufficient watershed (see Fig. 9-15). Tack a narrow piece of board 1 in. (25 mm) thick lightly to the fascia as a guide.

The first course of shingles at the eave must be doubled (see Fig. 9-16). Lay the first row with shingles $\frac{1}{4}$ in (6 mm) apart, butts to the guide strip. Use *two nails only* for each shingle, regardless of its width; nails should not be more than $\frac{3}{4}$ in. (20 mm) from the edge of the shingle. The second layer of the first course is laid directly over the first, shingles also spaced $\frac{1}{4}$ in. (6 mm) apart. Be sure that a joint

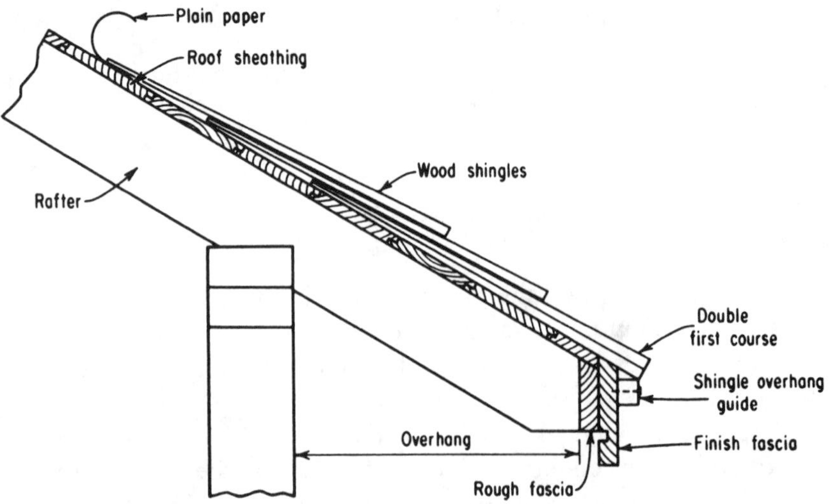

FIGURE 9-15 Shingle overhang for watershed.

FIGURE 9-16 Doubled first course.

between shingles does not come closer than $1\frac{1}{2}$ in. (38 mm) to a joint in the layer below (see Fig. 9-17). If a third layer is used, it too must have joints offset $1\frac{1}{2}$ in. (40 mm) from those underneath.

The second and succeeding courses are laid, with the specified exposure, measured from the butts of the course below. A strip of lumber may be used as a straight-edge against which to lay the shingles; a chalk line may also be used as a guide, or expert shinglers to

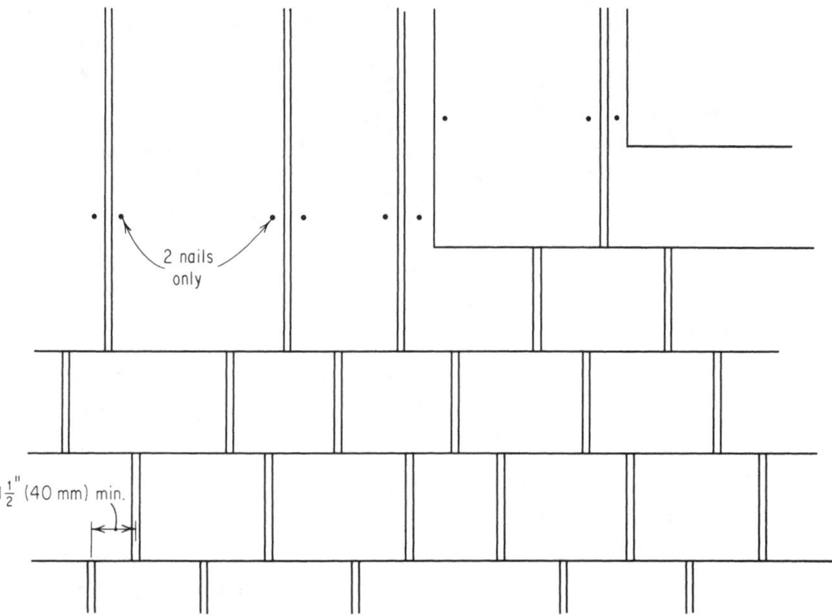

FIGURE 9-17 Side lap with wood shingles.

keep the shingles in a straight course sometimes use a shingling hatchet. Nails should be placed $\frac{3}{4}$ to $1\frac{1}{2}$ in. (19 to 38 mm) above the butt line of the next course.

Shingling Ridges and Hips

When ridges and hips are being shingled, the so-called modified *Boston lap* is used for best results. Use edge grain shingles at least 1 in. (25 mm) wider than the exposure used and select them all the same width. For hips, the butts may be cut on an angle so that they will be parallel to the butt lines of the regular courses (see Fig. 9-18). These ridge and hip caps are usually available pre-assembled.

Run a chalk line up the roof on each side of the hip centerline at a distance from the centerline equal to the exposure. Lay the first shingle to one of the chalk lines and bevel the top edge parallel to the plane of the adjacent roof surface. Now apply a shingle on the opposite side in the same way, beveling its top edge, as shown in Fig. 9-18(a). Place the nails so that they will be covered by the course above. The next pair of shingles is applied in *reverse order,* and each pair is alternated up the hip.

Ridges are done in much the same way. Start at both ends and work toward the center of the ridge, the last pair of shingles being cut to the exposure length.

(a) Shingling a hip.

(b) Pre-assembled ridge and hip caps.

FIGURE 9-18

Shingling Valleys

Valleys have to be *flashed* before they are shingled. The method of shingling the valley will determine if the valley is referred to as "open" or "closed."

Open valleys must be flashed with a strip of sheet metal at least 24 in. (600 mm) wide or with two layers of roll roofing [see Fig. 9-19(a)]. When two layers of roll roofing are used to flash the valley, the bottom layer must be an 18-in. (457-mm) strip of type S smooth surface roll roofing or type M mineral surface roll roofing applied with the mineral surface down. A 36-in. (914-mm) strip of type M roll roofing is placed over the first strip with the mineral side up. The top layer is applied over a 4-in. (100-mm) wide strip of cement along each edge of the bottom layer, and fastened with enough nails to hold the roofing in place until shingles are applied. The open part of the valley is usually 4 in. (100 mm) wide and will increase in size toward the lower end at a rate of 1:100 [see Fig. 9-19(b)].

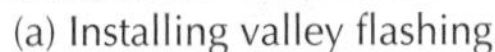

(a) Installing valley flashing.

(b) Open valley.

FIGURE 9-19

Closed valleys (or woven valleys) are flashed with one layer of sheet metal or type S roll roofing at least 24 in. (600 mm) wide. Each course of asphalt shingles is continued across the valley ensuring that shingle nails are not placed within 3 in. (75 mm) of the valley centerline (see Fig. 9-20). The courses are alternated to ensure a watertight valley. Another method of finishing the valley is to cut the shingles from the second roof slope along the valley centerline and set them in a strip of cement. Closed valleys should not be used with rigid shingles.

FIGURE 9-20 Closed valley.

Roof Flashing

To prevent infiltration of rainwater or melting snow, along any vertical surface that adjoins a roof surface flashing must be installed, such as around chimneys, dormers, or walls. Along the sides that are vertical to the shingle courses, individual flashings must be used, one for each course of shingles [see Fig. 9-21(a)]. Each leg is bent at a right angle, so that part of the flashing lies flat on the roof, between shingle rows, while the other half rests against the vertical surface and covered with the air barrier and exterior finish [see Fig. 9-21(b)].

(a) Step flashing installed.

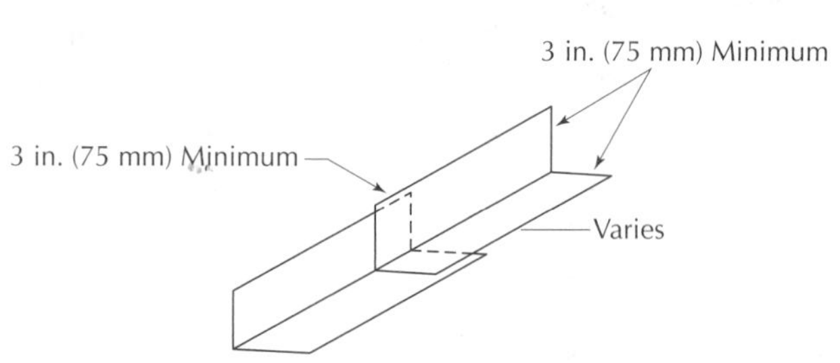

(b) Pre-bent step flashing.

FIGURE 9-21

Where a masonry chimney is installed, a *counter flashing* or *cap flashing* is embedded in the mortar joints (see Fig. 9-22). On the sloping sides step flashing will be required.

The lower sides of chimneys are flashed and counter flashed—one flashing running under the shingles and the other lying on top of them (see Fig. 9-23).

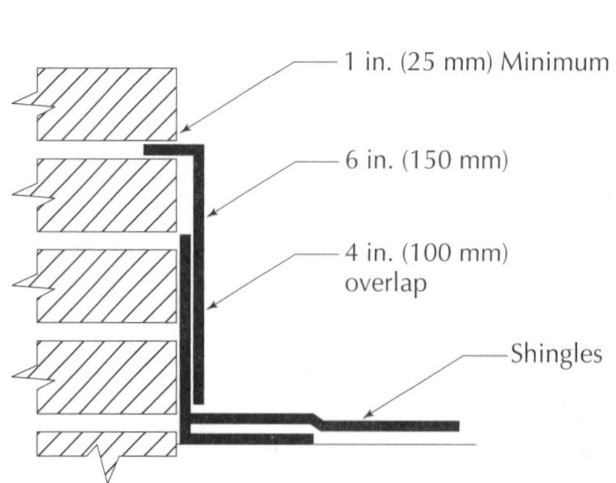

FIGURE 9-22 Counter (cap) flashing.

FIGURE 9-23 Counter (cap) flashing installed.

Framed chimneys are often used, as the cost of masonry chimneys is much higher. The same type of step and counter flashing is require as along any vertical surface [see Figs. 9-24(a), 9-24(b), and 9-24(c)].

Where a sloping roof butts against a vertical wall, flashing must be placed against the wall surface and along the tops of the shingles as shown in Fig. 9-25.

(a) Junction of step and counter (cap) flashing on framed chimney.

(b) Framed chimney step flashing.

(c) Exposed counter (cap) flashing.

FIGURE 9-24

FIGURE 9-25 Counter flashing against vertical wall.

Chimney Saddle

To prevent water from collecting on the *up-roof* side of a chimney which projects through the roof, a *saddle* should be built behind it to shed the water. It should be the same width as the chimney, built like a miniature gable roof [see Figs. 9-26(a) and 9-26(b)] with flashing at the chimney and in the valleys.

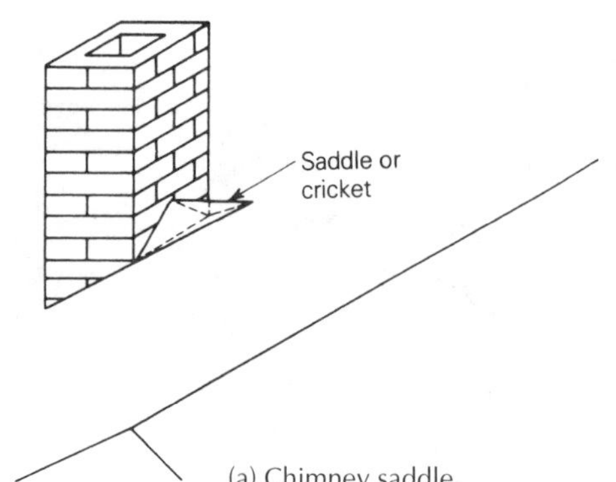

(a) Chimney saddle.

(b) Shakes installed on chimney saddle.

FIGURE 9-26

Wood Shakes

Wood shakes are commonly made of cedar and in some cases from treated pine (see Fig. 9-27). Shakes are longer and thicker than shingles, and they have a textured finish due to the splitting action used in their manufacture [see Figs. 9-28(a) and 9-28(b)].

FIGURE 9-27 Shake roof.

(a) Offset shake joints.

(b) Ridge cap on shake roof.

FIGURE 9-28

There are three types of wood shakes generally available: hand split and re-sawn, taper split, and straight split (see Fig. 9-29). Shakes are generally produced in 18- or 24-in. (450- or 600-mm) lengths with butt thickness varying from $\frac{3}{8}$ to $1\frac{1}{4}$ in. (9–32 mm). The maximum exposure recommended for double coverage on a roof is 10 in. (250 mm) for 24-in. (600-mm) shakes and $7\frac{1}{2}$ in. (190 mm) for 18-in. (450-mm) shakes. Shakes are recommended on slopes of 1 in 3 or steeper, and spacing should conform to limits set for wood shingles in areas where wind-driven snow conditions prevail, solid roof sheathing is recommended. Local building codes should be consulted.

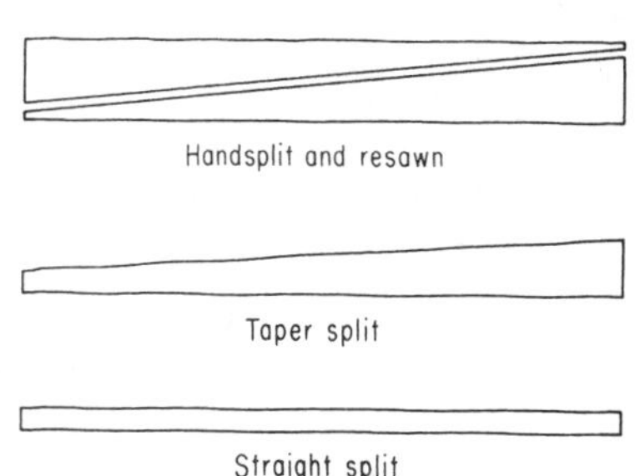

FIGURE 9-29 Types of wood shakes.

Application of Shakes

Apply a starter strip of No. 15 asphalt-saturated felt underlayment 36 in. (900 mm) wide along the eaves and 12 in. (300 mm) along hips and ridges. The first course is doubled, just like regular wood shingles. After each course of shakes is applied, an 18-in. (450-mm) strip of No. 15 asphalt-saturated felt is applied over the top portion of the shakes, extending onto the sheathing (see Fig. 9-30). The bottom edge of the underlayment should be positioned above the butt a distance equal to twice the exposure as shown in Fig. 9-30. Individual shakes should be spaced from $\frac{1}{4}$ to $\frac{3}{8}$ in. (6–10 mm) apart to allow for expansion. The joints in each row should be offset $1\frac{1}{2}$ in. (40 mm) from the joints in the previous row [see Fig. 9-28(a)].

Two nails or staples (see Fig. 9-31) are used in each shake, regardless of width. These must be rust resistant, normally 2 in. (50 mm) long placed approximately 1 in. (25 mm) from each edge and 1 to 2 in. (25–50 mm) above the butt line of the following course.

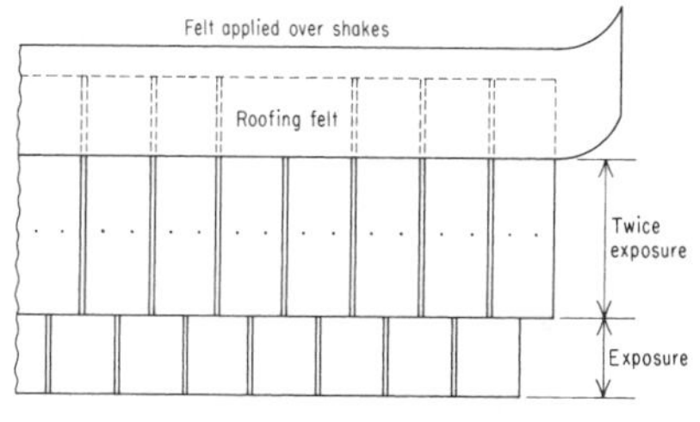

FIGURE 9-30 Positioning of felt.

FIGURE 9-31 Stapling shakes.

Eave Protection

Eave protection must be provided on all shingle and shake roofs, extending from the edge of the roof to a line up the roof slope not less than 12 in. (300 mm) measured horizontally inside the inner face of the wall (see Fig. 9-32). However, this protection is not necessary when the building is not likely to have ice forming along the eaves, causing a backup of water. Eave protection is not required over unheated garages, carports, and porches, or where the roof overhang exceeds 36 in. (900 mm) measured along the roof slope, or where low-slope shingles are used. A solid decking is typically used under the portion of the roof covered by the eave protection.

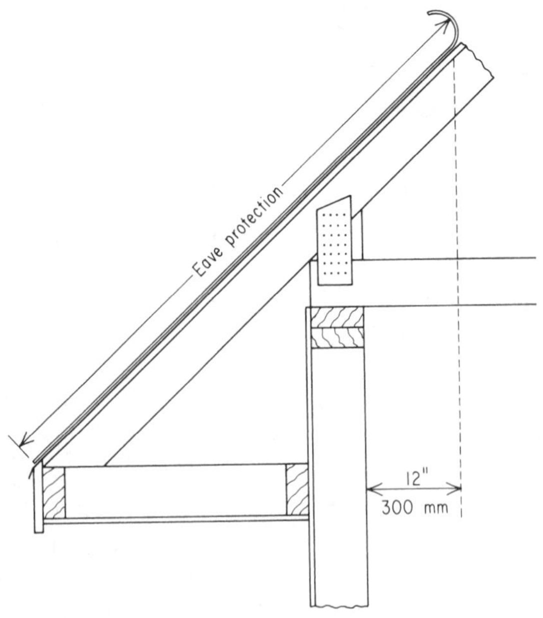

FIGURE 9-32 Eave protection.

Application of Asphalt Shingles

Asphalt shingles are made by impregnating heavy felt paper with hot asphalt and covering the upper surface with finely crushed, colored slate. Many types are available, one of the most common being a *triple-tab* shingle, actually three shingles in one (see Fig. 9-33). Interlocking asphalt shingles are also available, and they are very good for re-roofing jobs (Fig. 9-34).

FIGURE 9-33 Three-tab asphalt shingle.

FIGURE 9-34 Interlocking asphalt shingles.

Laying starts at the bottom edge of the roof, and on some occasions a chalk line is snapped down the center of the roof to act as a guide for vertical alignment. Eave flashing is usually placed before the eave protection to protect the edge of the roof sheathing from upward moisture migration (see Fig. 9-13).

The starter course along the lower edge of the roof is applied over the eave protection. The first course is doubled, with the first layer being placed with the tabs pointing up the roof slope [see Fig. 9-35(a)]. This row extends over the edge of the roof to provide a watershed. A strip of shingles may also be nailed up the rake to provide a straight edge and to divert moisture away from this edge [see Fig. 9-35(b)].

The first layer should be nailed near the eave edge, making sure the nails are not exposed in the slots in the next layer. The second layer of the first row is staggered so that the joints do not line up with the joints in the first layer, and each succeeding row is either offset one-half or one-third of a tab to provide a watertight roof (see Fig. 9-36). The shingles are fastened by nailing or stapling about $\frac{1}{2}$ in. (12 mm) above the top of the slot. To ensure straight vertical

(a) Starter strip.

(b) Strip along rake.

FIGURE 9-35

FIGURE 9-36 Staggering slots.

alignment of slots (see Fig. 9-37), some shinglers will build a pyramid up the roof slope rather than in horizontal rows. They will also use all of the shingles from one bundle before opening another, as shingle lengths between bundles can vary, causing crooked slot lines.

FIGURE 9-37 Alignment of slots.

Most triple-tab shingles have a strip of adhesive along the face of the shingle to cement the tabs down.

Interlocking shingles are manufactured so the bottom edge hooks into the shingle below and are very good in windy regions (see Fig. 9-34). A starter strip is needed on the bottom edge to provide a double layer over the entire roof slope. Individual shingles with the bottom portion cut off are commonly used to provide the starter strip as shown in Fig. 9-35. Open valleys are formed (see Fig. 9-38) using a double layer of roll roofing with a matching granular finish showing or a metal flashing, as discussed under wood shingles. A closed valley is also often used, as illustrated in Fig. 9-20. The shingles from one side are placed over a valley liner of roll roofing and up the opposite slope at least 12 in. (300 mm). The shingles on the other slope will be cut along the valley line and embedded in a continuous strip of roofing cement.

Individual shingles are used to cap hips and ridges (see Fig. 9-39). Fold the shingle over the ridge or the hip and nail so that the succeeding shingles will cover the nails. On the ridge they are placed in a direction so that the prevailing winds do not lift the edges of the tab.

Low-slope shingles are larger and are placed so that there are three layers over the entire roof surface. The shingles have two tabs instead of three. A continuous band of roofing cement is applied on each row equal to the width of the shingle exposure plus 2 in. (50 mm) located 2 in. (50 mm) above the butt line of the overlying shingle. Low-slope shingles can be used on a minimum slope of 1 in 6, while normal asphalt shingles can only be placed on a minimum slope of 1 in 3.

Architectural asphalt shingles are becoming increasingly popular in residential construction. These decorative shingles are a

FIGURE 9-38 Open valley—metal flashing.

FIGURE 9-39 Ridge cap.

particular kind of premium shingle with a decorative cut or finish, giving it a more upscale appearance and allowing it to compete aesthetically with wood shakes and roofing tiles at a more affordable rate. Laminating and texturing the tabs of the shingle achieve this architectural appeal.

Hardboard Shingles

Hardboard shingles are made of wood fibers, are resin treated, and are pressed into a dense mat. The mat has a cedar shake pattern embossed into the fibers (see Fig. 9-40). The individual shingles are 12 × 48 in. (300 × 1200 mm) and are manufactured with a self-aligning exposure line and a nailing line (see Fig. 9-41). On the job,

FIGURE 9-40 Hardboard shingled roof.

FIGURE 9-41 Hardboard shingle.

conventional tools are used in the application of this roofing material. Vertical joints are staggered to ensure a watertight roof. Pre-cut or field-cut hip and ridge caps are available, and valley treatment follows the conventional open valley practice.

Built-Up Roofing

There are two methods for preventing external water from entering a building through a roof. One is to use watershed units like various types of shingles, and the other is to use continuous membranes. Shingles rely on the principle of gravity and overcoming capillary action to prevent water entry through a roof, where the continuous membranes rely on the membrane preventing water penetration through it. A conventional built-up roof—so called because it is built up from several layers of material—is commonly used on flat or low-sloped decks. The materials consist of a primary membrane composed of several layers of #15 organic felts mopped, a separator sheet of two plies of #15 organic mechanically fastened to the deck. The primary membrane is covered with a flood coat of asphalt bitumen with sufficient gravel embedded to protect and hold down the roofing membrane.

The amount of material used determines the approximate life of the roof. The example in Fig. 9-42 illustrates a common procedure for laying a conventional flat roof system.

Here are the steps in this procedure:

1. Lay down two layers of #15 organic felt, starting with a half roll and then lapping each sheet 19 in. (480 mm) over the preceding one, and nailing or stapling it well enough to hold it in place.
2. Lay down three additional layers of the same felt as above, securing each by a layer of hot asphalt or tar bitumen [0.2 lb/ft (1 kg/m)], mopped full width. This step is begun by cutting a roll of felt into a 12-in. and a 24-in. (300-mm and a 600-mm) width. Lay down the 12-in. (300-mm) strip first, as illustrated in Fig. 9-42, then the 24-in. (600-mm) strip over it, and then the full width roll. Notice that these three layers all start from the same edge, resulting in three layers of mopped felt over the entire roof.
3. Flood the entire surface with a uniform coat of hot asphalt at the rate of 0.6 lb/ft (3 kg/m), with sufficient gravel embedded to allow minimal bitumen to show through. The weight of the gravel is approximately 3 lb/ft (15 kg/m) and should be rolled while the flood coat is hot to ensure that it is well embedded.
4. Check to make sure that the roofing is well up over any flashing and that there is a good seal where the flashing and roofing meet.

If the roof has insulation on top of the deck, the procedure must, of necessity, be somewhat different. A vapor retardant must be placed on the deck prior to the placement of the rigid insulation. If

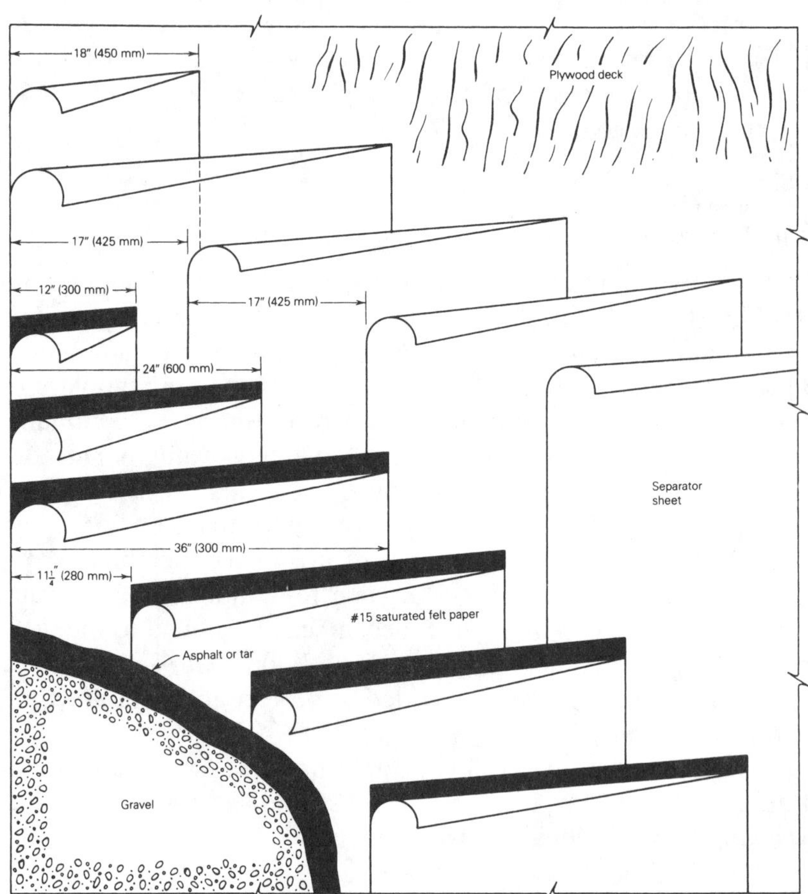

FIGURE 9-42 Built-up roof.

the insulation does not have a minimum compressive strength of 25 psi (172 kPa) a $\frac{1}{2}$ in. (12.5 mm), a layer of wood fiberboard or fiberboard sheathing is placed over the insulation prior to the placement of the primary membrane. If the roof has a slope of over 1:4, the primary membrane must be protected by two plies of wide selvage roofing with an inter-ply application of hot asphalt.

Roofing Tile

A number of types of tile are available as roof covering. They include concrete tile and metal roofing tile. Clay tile has been in use for a long time and is still used in some areas [see Fig. 9-43(a)]. Concrete tile is a more recent product, and for the most part, shapes resemble clay tiles [see Fig. 9-43(b)]. Concrete roof tiles have a nominal size of $16\frac{1}{2} \times 13$ in. (420×330 mm) with an interlocking side lap of $1\frac{3}{16}$ in. (30 mm). Metal roofing tiles are made of lightweight galvanized steel, shaped to resemble clay or concrete tiles. The surface has a coating of stone particles to give good protection from weather.

(a) Clay tile.

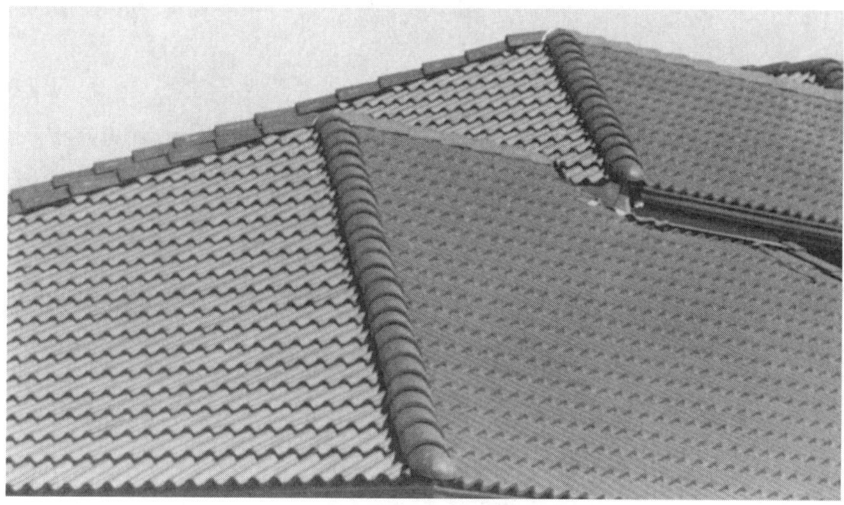

(b) Concrete roofing tiles.

FIGURE 9-43

Roofing Tile Application

Concrete and clay tiles are applied over solid sheathing such as plywood. Spaced sheathing may be used with thermo-ply underlayment. A series of counter battens are fastened through the deck into the supporting roof members. These counter battens run from the eave to the ridge elevating the horizontal tile battens, allowing a natural flow of air to pass beneath the tiles [see Fig. 9-44; also see Fig. 9-46(a)].

FIGURE 9-44 Installation of flat concrete tiles.

The raising of the batten eliminates the build-up of moisture absorbing debris, which could lead to rotting and premature failure of the support system. A heavy duty, quality underlayment is applied over the counter battens prior to the application of the tile battens. Standard roofing felt should not be used for this application, as the material will not provide the life expectancy required for tile applications. The size of batten will be determined by the spacing of roof trusses and whether or not a solid roof deck is used.

Tiles are predrilled to allow nailing near the top edge with corrosion-resistant roofing or shingle nails. Fascia is raised 1 in. (25 mm) above sheathing when rake tiles are used along a roof edge [see Figs. 9-45(a) and 9-45(b)].

(a) Roof ready for shingling—note raised barge boards.

(b) Rake tiles installed.

FIGURE 9-45

Strapping is built up under ridges and hips to provide support under caps [see Figs. 9-46(a) and 9-46(b)]. Joints should be sealed with caulking or putty made with masonry mortar. Open valleys are used and installed with metal flashing, using the method discussed under wood shingles [see Fig. 9-46(c)].

(a) Built-up hip for tile cap.

(b) Hip tile caps installed.

(c) Valleys flashing.

FIGURE 9-46

Metal roofing tiles are available in classic or Spanish roofing styles. The tiles are interlocking with a natural stone finish on the galvanized tiles [see Figs. 9-47(a) and 9-47(b)]. Strapping and asphalt-saturated paper are used under the tiles similar to the method used with concrete tiles. Strapping must also be built up under hips and ridges, as illustrated in Fig. 9-46(a). The main difference is that these tiles are started at the top of the roof working down the slope using rust-resistant screws along the bottom edge to fasten the tiles to the strapping [see Fig. 9-47(d)]. Open valleys are used, similar to the style used with wooden shingles [see Fig. 9-47(c)].

(a) Metal roofing tiles.

(b) Metal rake in place.

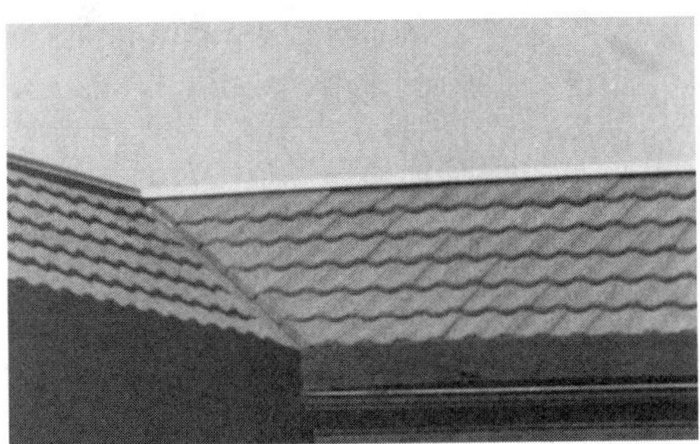

(c) Forming a valley.

(d) Applying metal roofing tiles.

FIGURE 9-47

Sheet metal roofing

Sheet metal roofing is more commonly used in areas that are subject to heavy snow loads. Many colors and profiles are available meeting a large range of aesthetic needs. Sheet metal roofing is manufactured in 30 to 45 in. (762–1143 mm) widths, depending on the profile of the corrugation and in any lengths specified by the designer. Panels are therefore available in full lengths, reaching from the eaves to the ridge. Accessories are available for hips, valleys, eave starter, and roof edges. Galvanized steel and aluminum are the most common metals used, and the minimum metal thickness [0.02 in. (0.5mm)] will vary depending on local snow loads.

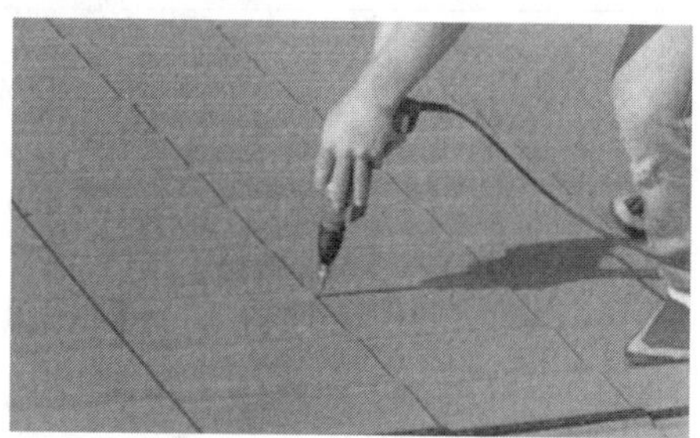

FIGURE 9-48 Sheet metal roofing application.

Sheet metal panels may be installed directly over continuous sheathing or over horizontal wooden battens (see Fig. 9-48). The profile and the metal thickness will determine the required spacing for the horizontal battens, usually around 16 in. (400 mm) o.c. Battens should be 1 × 3 in.(19 × 70 mm) for 16-in. o.c. truss spacing and 1 × 4 in.(19 × 89 mm) for 24-in. o.c. truss spacing; however, if better attachment and support are needed, 2 × 4 in.(38 × 89 mm) material is used. Local building codes should be consulted when applying sheet metal roofing.

WINDOWS

Windows form an important part of a building exterior, and a great variety of styles and sizes are manufactured to suit every conceivable purpose. Basically, they consist of one or more panes of *glass* surrounded by a *sash*, which is set into a *frame*. The sash may be wood, aluminum, PVC, or steel, and the frame also may be made of any one of these four materials.

Window Styles

Common window styles include *sliding* windows, in which the sash slide horizontally past one another [see Figs. 9-49(a) and 9-49(b), and *double hung*, in which the sash slide vertically [see Figs. 9-50(a) and 9-50(b)].

Another style is the *swinging* window, in which the sash is hinged at either top or bottom [see Figs. 9-51(a) and 9-51(b)]. If the sash swings inward, it is called a *hopper* type; if it swings outward, it is an *awning* type.

Casement windows have the sash hinged at the side [see Figs. 9-52(a) and 9-52(b)], and in *fixed* windows the sash does not move in the frame (see Fig. 9-53).

(a) Vinyl horizontal sliding window.

(b) Basement horizontal slider window.

FIGURE 9-49

(a) Tall vertical slider window.

(b) Upper floor vertical slider window.

FIGURE 9-50

(a) Awning window with fixed sash.

(b) Open awning window.

FIGURE 9-51

(a) One-and two-sash casement.

(b) Combination casement and fixed sash window.

FIGURE 9-52

FIGURE 9-53 Fixed sash picture window with openers.

FIGURE 9-54 Glass block windows.

Glass blocks are also becoming very popular (see Fig. 9-54) where privacy is desired without restricting light.

Many windows are made with no sash and consist of a single sheet of glass or two sheets sealed together, set directly into a window frame. Figure 9-55 illustrates fixed sash, sometimes called *clearstory* windows. When a large glass unit is fixed in a frame, it is commonly known as a *picture* window (see Fig. 9-56).

FIGURE 9-56 Feature picture window—fixed sash.

FIGURE 9-55 Fixed clearstory sash.

Windows that project out from the wall to create an extra interior space give a nice effect to the building exterior. These bay or curved bow windows are often found in residential living or bedrooms, but are effective in any room [see Fig. 9-57(a) and 9-57(b)].

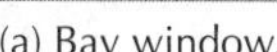
(a) Bay window.

(b) Bow window.

FIGURE 9-57

Window Manufacturer

Modern windows are made in a factory—a millwork plant—and shipped to the construction site, either ready for assembly or, in most cases, already assembled ready for installation in the openings. Windows will usually have the outside casing in place and may be provided with braces or battens to keep them square.

Windows may be made with a variety of combinations of panes in a sash. For example, Fig. 9-58 illustrates various combinations that can be made, including a combination of casement, fixed, and awning sash.

Considerable attention has been given to improving window design and performance because of their importance in the building envelope. The drive for energy conservation and comfort led to improvements in thermal performance, installation, operation, and maintenance. One way of improving the thermal performance is to control thermal radiation losses. The use of transparent low emissivity coatings provides a significant reduction in heat loss. Adding a low-E coating to the third surface of a clear insulating unit can increase insulating value by 50% [from R2 to R3 (RSI 0.35–0.53)]. Increasing the space between panes of glass and increasing the number of panes to three will also increase thermal performance. The introduction of argon gas into the space between panes in a sealed window also has a positive effect.

(a) Horizontal combination of casement and fixed sash units.

(b) Combination of vertical and horizontal units.

FIGURE 9-58

In sunny climates, where you want a dramatic view but do not want the heat gain and faded upholstery, the installation of low-E coating on the second surface of an insulating unit is especially effective in reducing heat gain and glare from the outside. Heat mirror, a transparent coated film that is suspended between the panes of glass, is often chosen since it is very effective in keeping solar heat out of the building. The installation of narrow slat blinds or pleated shades between the panes of double insulating glass or on the inside of the window will also help reduce heat gain.

As mentioned before, windows are manufactured in a variety of materials including wood, which can be left natural or clad with metal or vinyl, or solid PVC construction. Windows may be made with a wood sash set in a wood frame (see Fig. 9-59).

The application of a colored metal cladding or a vinyl coating to the outside reduces the need for frequent painting. Metal windows, in either wooden or metal frames, have been used for years, and solid PVC windows have made extensive inroads into the residential market (see Fig. 9-60). These windows are available in many colors and are not susceptible to decay, making them popular in humid climates.

Window Openings

The openings in the wall frame for the installation of windows must be large enough that the frame can be leveled and plumbed. It is therefore necessary to ascertain from the manufacturer either the size of rough opening that is required for the particular style, the size and combination of window chosen, or the dimensions of the frame

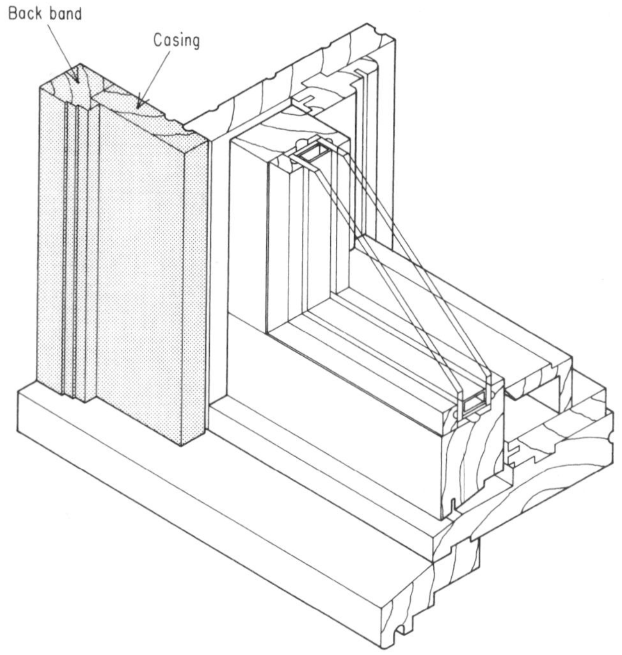

FIGURE 9-59 Sealed unit in wood sash.

FIGURE 9-60 Nailing or stapling through window flanges.

(see Fig. 9-61). If the frame dimensions are given, it is common practice to allow at least $\frac{3}{8}$ in. (10 mm) *on each side* of the frame and $\frac{3}{8}$ in. (10 mm) *above and below* the frame for this purpose.

In residential construction, it is standard practice to frame the top of the rough opening so that the height of window and door openings will normally be the same. The height of the bottom of the opening above the floor will depend on the location of the window. In a living room, for example, a distance of 12 to 24 in. (300–600 mm) above the floor is common, while in a dining room, it will normally be 30 to 36 in. (500 to 600 mm). Kitchen windows are usually over a counter, and the standard height for the bottom of the opening for such windows is 44 in. (1100 mm). In other rooms the height is optional and will depend on the size of windows to be used.

Window Installation

If the rough opening is the proper size and is level and plumb, it is a relatively easy matter to install windows. The first step is to tack a 12-in. (300-mm) wide strip of exterior sheathing paper (see Fig. 9-61), or house wrap [see Fig. 9-53 (b)] around the opening on the outside. Then place the window, with the outside casing attached, into the opening from the outside and secure it temporarily, after having closed the sash and locked them in place.

Wedge blocks are placed under the sill and can also be adjusted so that the sill is perfectly level. Long sills should have three or more wedges under them to prevent them from sagging in the middle. Nail

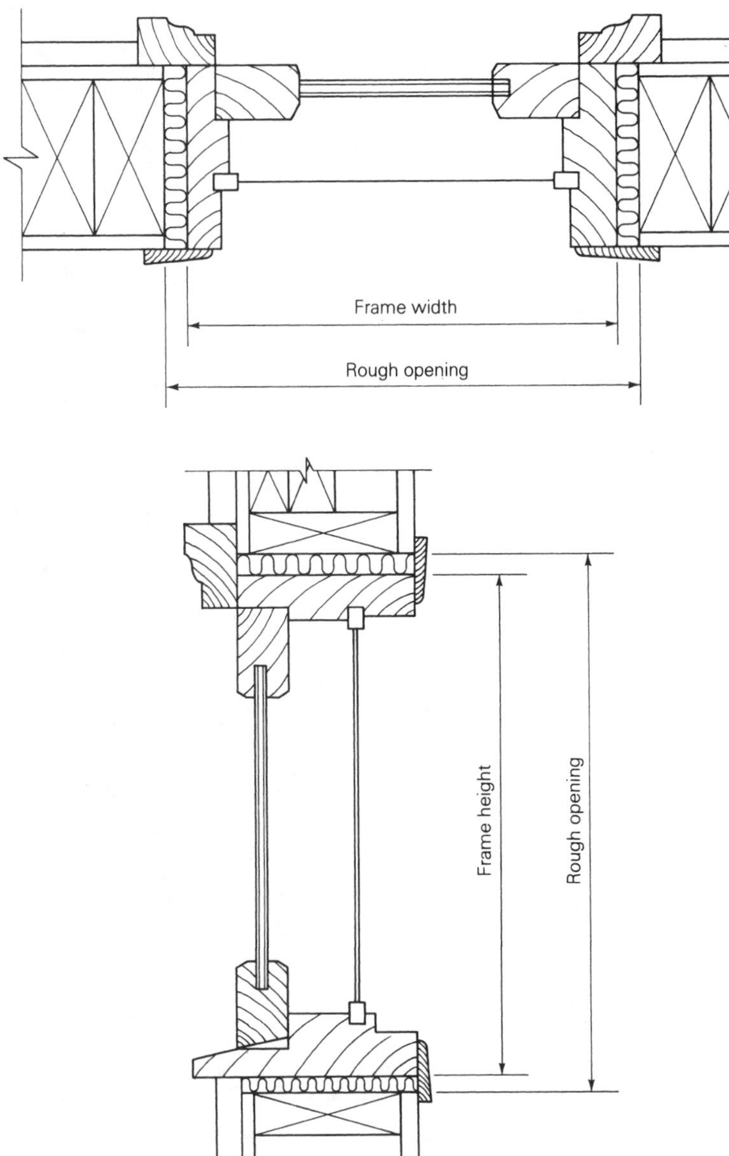

FIGURE 9-61 Rough opening size.

FIGURE 9-62 Fastening window in place.

the lower end of the side casings or flanges to secure the bottom of the frame in place (see Fig. 9-62).

Nail the top end of the side casings temporarily and check to see that the sash operates properly.

Finally, nail the window permanently in place with noncorrosive nails, long enough so that they will reach well into the building frame, as illustrated in Fig. 9-60.

It may be necessary to install flashing over windows. Generally, if the window is within $\frac{1}{4}$ of a soffit overhang no flashing is needed. However, if the window will be exposed to driving rain then flashing should be installed, or in some cases the top flange may be imbedded in a nonhardening caulking (see Fig. 9-63).

Skylights are sometimes incorporated in the roof structure. These come in a variety of sizes and shapes, some are with fixed glazing while others hinge open through either a hand-operated crank or a small electric motor. As they are located on a roof, special flashing that usually comes with the skylight unit must be used to ensure water does not penetrate into the building (see Fig. 9-64).

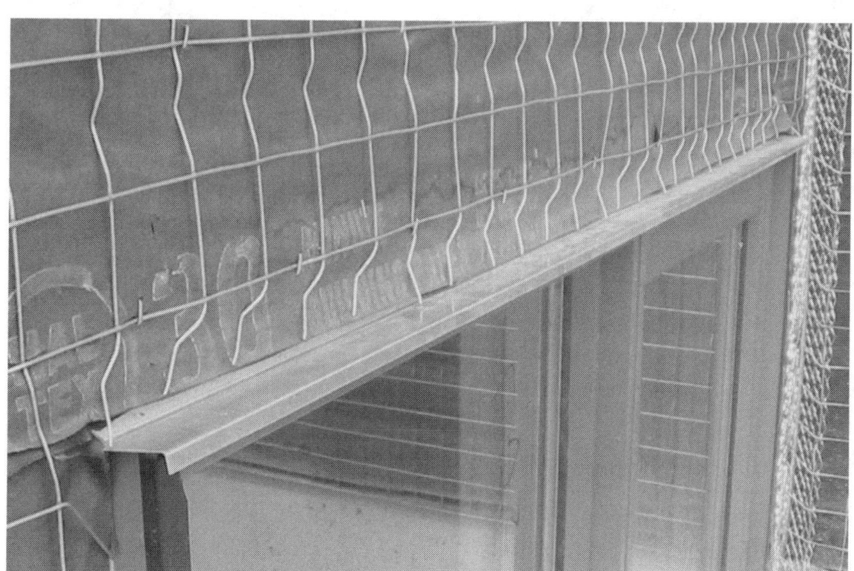

FIGURE 9-63 Window flashing.

FIGURE 9-64 Roof skylight.

EXTERIOR DOORS

Exterior doors may be made of wood, glass, metal, or combinations of these, such as wood and glass or metal and glass.

Wooden doors vary from a plain slab to ornate paneled doors, either of which may have glass inserts or a full glass panel. In some cases, *sidelights* may be introduced on one or both sides of the door [see Figs. 9-65(a) and 9-65(b)].

Wooden doors and their frames, or *jambs*, are made in a millwork plant and may come to the construction site as a complete unit, with the door hinged in the frame and the outside casing attached.

Glass doors are usually sliding doors, mounted in an aluminum track, top and bottom, and traveling on rollers. They are frequently used in a living or family room, as illustrated in Figs. 9-66(a), 9-66(b), and 9-66(c).

Metal doors have become very popular in residential construction. The door is made with two steel faces, separated by wooden stiles and a polyurethane foam core. This makes the door more

(a) Exterior door with sidelights.

(b) Oval-glazed door with sidelights.

FIGURE 9-65

(a) Patio door roller on track.

(b) Two-panel patio door.

(c) Three-panel patio door.

FIGURE 9-66

energy efficient and resistant to warping. The door surface is usually embossed with a series of patterns, and often glass panels are included in the design (see Fig. 9-67).

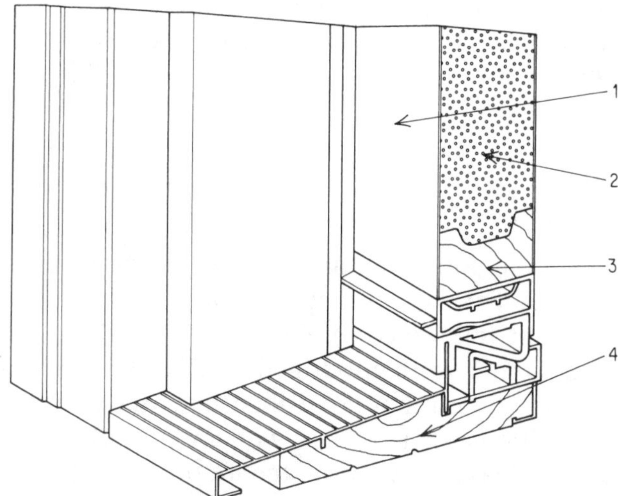

FIGURE 9-67 Insulated metal door detail: (1) Galvanized steel treated with rust inhibitive prime finish; (2) Polyurethane foam core; (3) Wood stiles and rails act as a thermal break; (4) Adjustable sill.

Door Sizes

The standard size of exterior doors used in residential construction is 2 ft, 8 in. (810 mm) wide by 6 ft, 8 in. (2030 mm) high by $1\frac{3}{4}$ in. (45 mm) thick. Door widths of 2 ft, 10 in. and 3 ft (860 and 910 mm) are used when larger openings are required.

Door Frame Installation

If the wall sole plate is still in the opening, it must be cut out, flush with the trimmers. A filler piece may be required under the doorsill to raise the top of the sill a sufficient distance above the finish floor to allow for a mat in wet weather.

If a pre-hung door unit is being used, the door is left in the frame during installation. Staple a strip of building paper around the outside of the opening, as was done with windows. Then apply two or three beads of caulking along the bottom of the opening to seal the crack under the sill. Place the frame into the opening from the outside, center it, and fasten it temporarily. Check the hinge side of the frame to ensure it is plumb. Shim it to hold it in the correct position, and then nail the bottom ends of the side casings or flanges to secure the bottom of the frame. Place additional wedges between the trimmer and the jamb at the hinge locations to make sure the jamb is straight. If the frame is wood, secure the wedges by driving a nail through the jamb and the wedges into the trimmer, as illustrated in

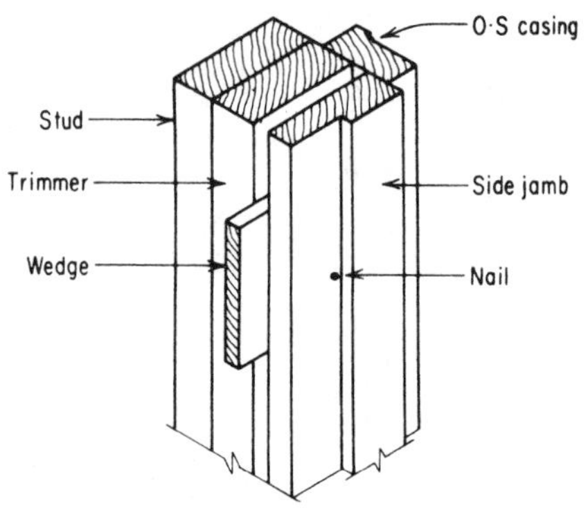

FIGURE 9-68 Nailing side jamb wedge.

Fig. 9-68. If the jamb is metal or PVC and there is a desire to eliminate a nail or screw from showing on the surface, the wedges will have to be toenailed to hold them in position. Check to ensure that the bottom of the door is parallel to the sill to allow proper swing of the door. Shim the lock-side of the jamb in the same manner. Finally, nail the rest of the casing or flange to secure the frame. A temporary cover should be placed over the sill during construction to protect it from damage.

Lock Installation

Locks for exterior doors are often more elaborate than interior locks, and the installation instructions, contained in the package with the lock, should be followed carefully.

Many doors come with pre-drilled holes for the latch, dead bolt, and lockset. If the door is not pre-drilled, open the door to any convenient ajar position and fix it there with a wedge placed between it and the floor. Measure up from the floor a distance of 36 in. (900 mm) (optional) and mark a horizontal line on both faces and across the edge of the door, which will be on a level with the center of the knob or thumb latch. Now, following the instructions and using the template provided, mark the centers of the holes required on the faces and edge of the door and drill holes of the proper size. Holes in the face of the door should be bored from both sides to prevent any splintering. In place of the template, a *boring jig* may be used to locate holes in the proper position. Drill holes in the jamb about $1\frac{1}{8}$ in. (29 mm) deep at the location of the mortise for the latch bolt and the dead bolt and square the holes out with a chisel.

Lay out the position of the rebates for the lock anchor plate and the striker plate, one on the edge of the door and the second on the jamb, over the mortise just completed and cut them out with a chisel. A *mortise marker* may be used to mark out the rebates. When drive-in latches are used, the latch is driven in using a block of wood between the latch and the hammer to avoid damaging the latch. (For details on lock installation, see Chapter 10.)

WALL SHEATHING PAPER

Wall sheathing paper is applied to the exterior of the walls of a frame building to provide an extra barrier for wind and rain that might penetrate the cladding. It must be permeable enough to allow the escape of any water vapor that might enter the wall from the interior. One layer of sheathing paper is usually used over wall sheathing and is usually applied horizontally with 4-in. (100-mm) lap at the joints. The upper sheets will overlap the lower sheets. At door and window frames a good lap should be provided over paper projecting from under the casings [see Fig. 9-57(a)].

When wall sheathing is not used, two layers of paper are used unless a panel-type siding, like plywood, is used. Both layers are applied vertically, with joints stapled and lapped 4 in. (100 mm) along the studs.

Another type of air barrier is made from a vinyl material and may be called a *house wrap*. This material comes in much larger widths, but the method of attachment is the same as for building paper [see Figs. 9-69(a) and 9-69(b)]. It is much more durable than the building paper and is more effective in restricting infiltration of moisture while at the same time allows the wall to "breath."

(a)

(b)

FIGURE 9-69 Vimyl house wrap.

TYPES OF EXTERIOR WALL FINISH

A great many exterior finishes are used today, particularly for a wood frame. They include *stucco, siding, shake and shingle siding, hardboard siding, metal siding, vinyl siding, vertical wood, wood panel, and masonry finishes.*

Stucco. Stucco finish can be applied directly over a masonry wall, but when a sheathed wood frame is to receive stucco, sheathing paper or house wrap material backing must be applied first. A wire mesh is applied over this material and should be of a type that has a relatively small mesh—about 2 in. (50 mm) or smaller is satisfactory—and is formed as illustrated in Figs. 9-69(a) and (b), and Fig. 9-70. When secured in place, the main body of the wire stands away from the wall surface, allowing the stucco material to form all around it.

The wire mesh should be stapled, with the curves to the wall, at least every 6 in. (150 mm) vertically and 16 in. (400 mm) horizontally, or 4 in. (100 mm) vertically and 24 in. (600 mm) horizontally. Side and end joints should be lapped at least 2 in. (50 mm) with end joints

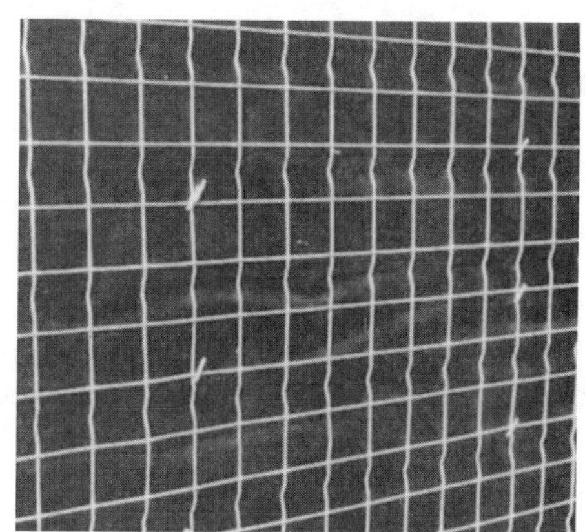

FIGURE 9-70 Stucco wire over building paper.

staggered. Local building codes should be consulted for requirements when sheathing is not installed on the framing. Figure 9-71 illustrates typical application of a stucco finish.

(a) First coat—wire only filled.

(b) Second coat—minimum thickness 1/4 in. (6mm).

(c) Finish coat—applied by trowel.

(d) Acrylic finish coat—sprayed on.

FIGURE 9-71

Typically a simple scaffolding system is used for workers applying stucco [see Figs. 9-72(a), 9-72(b), 9-72(c), and 9-72(d)].

Lumber Siding. Lumber siding is available in a variety of species with cedar being one of the more common types. In some areas pressure-treated lumber for siding is used, especially in areas prone to decay. In humid areas an air space is often formed behind the siding to prevent water penetration and to vent moisture away from the wall.

Horizontal Application. A number of styles of horizontal wood siding are manufactured, but probably the most popular is bevel siding, available in widths from $5\frac{1}{2}$ in. (140 mm) to $11\frac{1}{4}$ in. (286 mm). Each course should overlap the one below approximately 1 in.

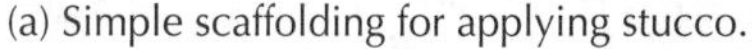

(a) Simple scaffolding for applying stucco.

(b) Tube-and-coupler scaffold system.

(c) Temporary securing method.

(d) Galvanized metal trim between stucco and brick combination.

FIGURE 9-72

(25 mm), the exact lap and exposure depending on the width of board being used and the space to be covered.

Under the bottom edge of the first course, nail a furring strip about 1 in. (25 mm) wide and the thickness of the siding at the point of overlap. This furring strip will allow the surface of the first course to have the same slope as that of succeeding courses (see Fig. 9-73).

There are two common methods of fitting bevel siding at external corners. One is to miter the two meeting ends. Another method is to butt the siding ends against corner boards [see Figs. 9-74(a) and 9-74(b)].

At internal corners, nail a $1 \times 1 (25 \times 25\,\text{mm})$ strip into the corner and butt the siding ends to it from both sides.

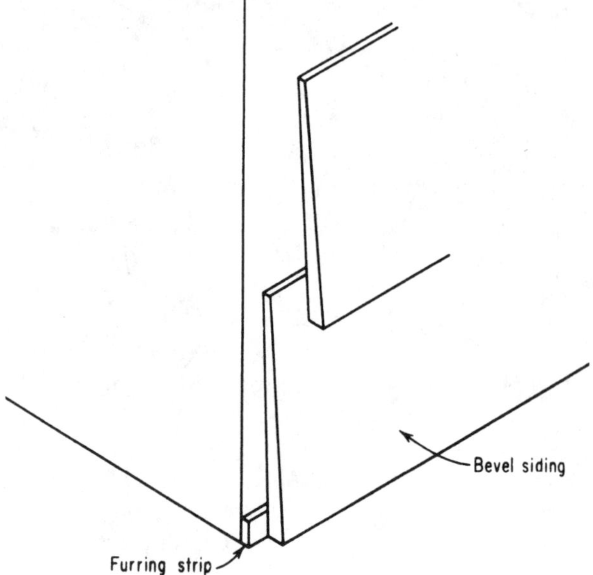

FIGURE 9-73 Bevel siding – first and second row.

(a) Mitered corner.

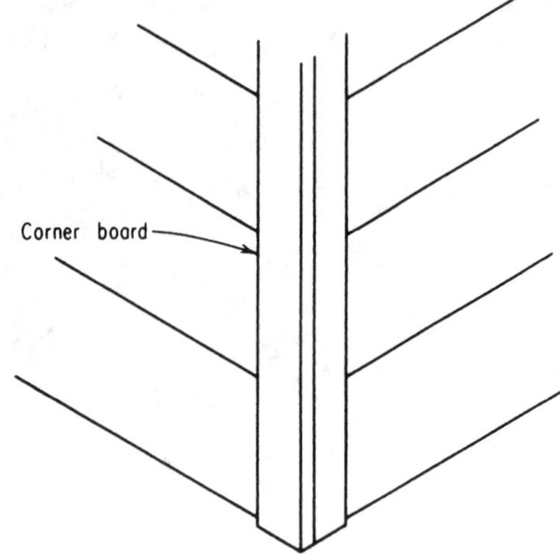

(b) Bevel siding at external corners.

FIGURE 9-74

Plan to have butt joints between boards in a course fall on a stud. Be very careful that the ends meet in a perfect joint [see Figs. 9-75(a) and 9-75(b)]. Use one $2\frac{1}{2}$-in. (65-mm) siding nail per board at each stud, just above the lap. This system of nailing will allow seasonal contraction and expansion without interference. Do not drive the nails so hard as to crack the siding.

Vertical Application. This type of exterior finish is similar in style to boards and battens. However, the materials have tongue-and-groove or shiplap edges so that battens are not needed to cover the joints [see

(a) Angle cut at butt joint.

(b) Applying bevel siding.

FIGURE 9-75

Figs. 9-76(a) and 9-76(b)]. Horizontal joints in vertical boards should be sloped to the outside to shed water [see Fig. 9-76(c)]. A light layer of caulking in these joints will ensure a weather tight joint. On some

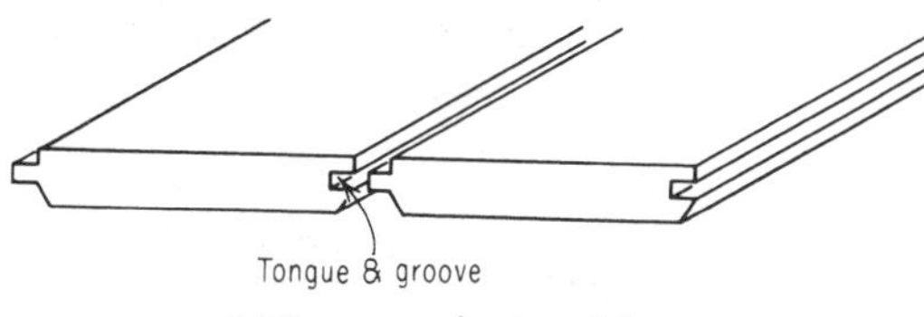

(a) Tongue and groove joint.

(b) Vertical wood siding.

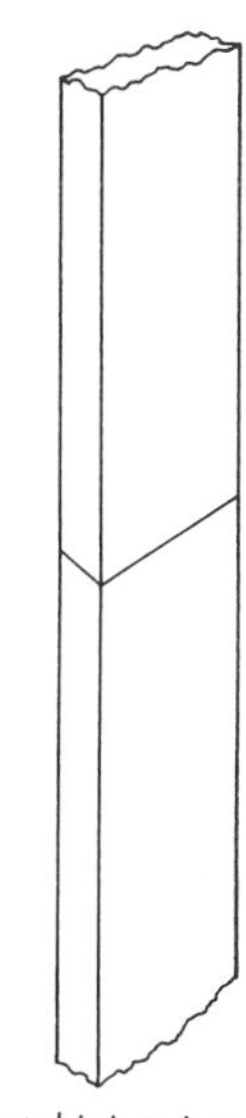

(c) Horizontal joints in vertical boards.

FIGURE 9-76

FIGURE 9-77 Angle application of tongue and groove siding.

occasions, to provide variety, this siding is placed at an angle, as illustrated in Fig. 9-77.

Vertical boards may be fastened to $\frac{9}{16}$ in. (14.3 mm) lumber sheathing, $\frac{1}{2}$ in. (12.5 mm) plywood, $\frac{1}{2}$ in. (12.5 mm) waferboard or strandboard. The use of 2 × 2(38 × 38 mm) blocking fitted between the studs 24 in. (600 mm) or 1 × 3(19 × 65 mm) o.c. strapping can be used for support of the vertical lumber siding.

Shake and Shingle Siding. Shakes and shingles are applied to sidewalls in either single or double course. They may be applied directly to walls with solid sheathing, but in other cases, furring strips must first be nailed to the wall, spaced the required amount of exposure [see Figs. 9-78(a) and 9-78(b), and 9-79).

Boards and Battens. This is the name given to a type of finish in which square-edged boards are placed vertically on the wall, and the joints between them are covered with narrow strips about $2\frac{1}{2}$ in. (64 mm) wide called battens. Boards may be all the same width, two different widths placed alternately, or random widths. Cedar is the best material to use, either dressed or rough-sawn.

For this type of finish, nail in two rows of blocking, evenly spaced, between the top and bottom plates. Boards can then be nailed at four points. Allow approximately $\frac{1}{8}$ in. (3 mm) between boards.

Hardboard Siding. This type of siding is made from wood fibers pressed into a hard, thin sheet, $\frac{1}{2}$ in. (12 mm) thick and used as a horizontal lap channel siding. They are impregnated with a baked-

(a) Shingle siding on gable end.

(b) Shingle siding with simulated beams and posts.

FIGURE 9-78

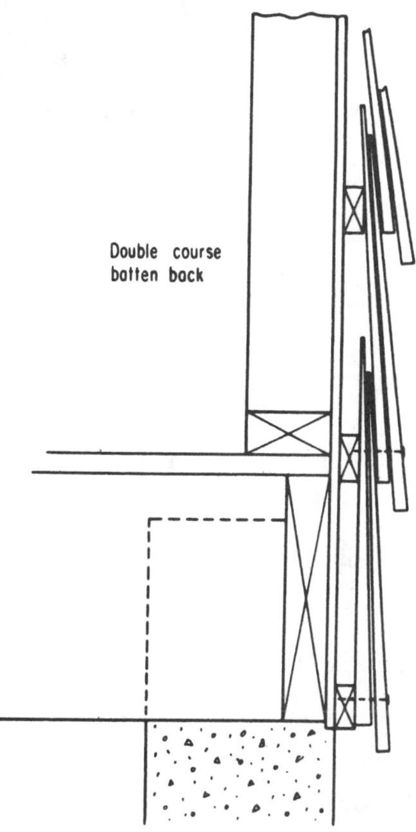

FIGURE 9-79 Double-thickness shingle siding installed over horizontal strapping.

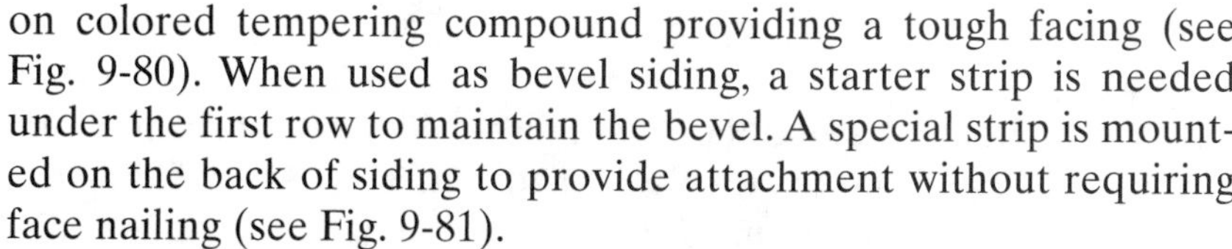

on colored tempering compound providing a tough facing (see Fig. 9-80). When used as bevel siding, a starter strip is needed under the first row to maintain the bevel. A special strip is mounted on the back of siding to provide attachment without requiring face nailing (see Fig. 9-81).

Special aluminum strips are used for butt joints (see Fig. 9-82), and exterior and interior corner pieces are used to finish ends of siding pieces.

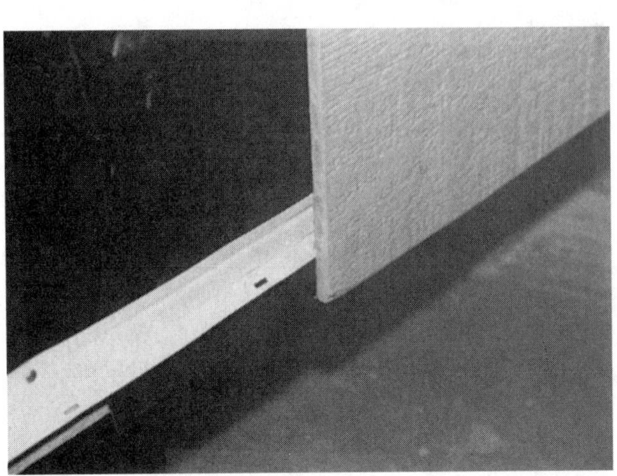

FIGURE 9-80 Hardboard siding.

FIGURE 9-81 Mounting strip.

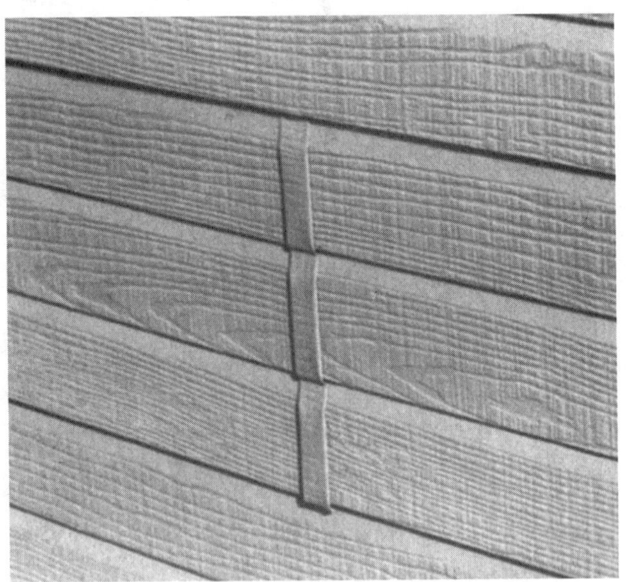

FIGURE 9-82 Butt-joint attachment.

Aluminum Siding. Aluminum siding is available in horizontal and vertical applications [see Figs. 9-83(a) and 9-83(b)]. Metal siding has a baked-on finish that requires little maintenance or care. Textures are applied to some surfaces to simulate wood siding, and insulation-backed siding manufactured by some companies provides greater insulation value to the building (see Fig. 9-84).

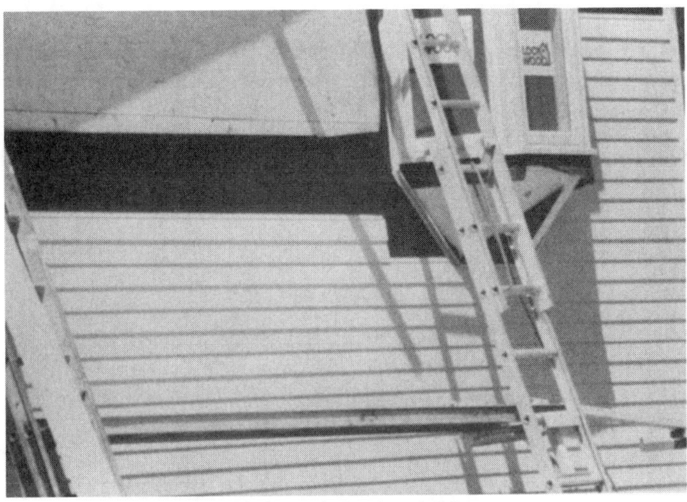
(a) Horizontal aluminum siding.

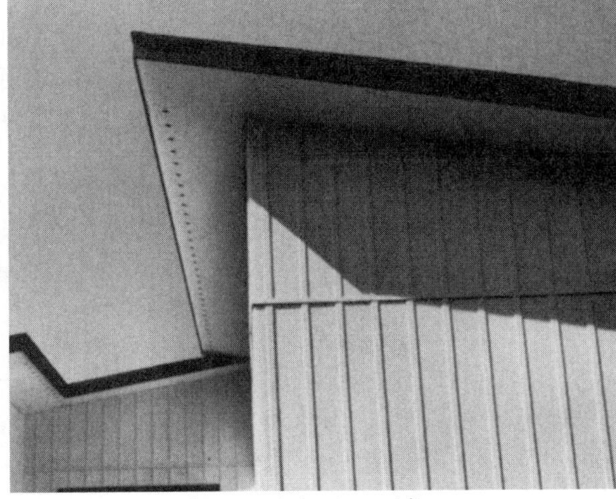
(b) Vertical aluminum siding.

FIGURE 9-83

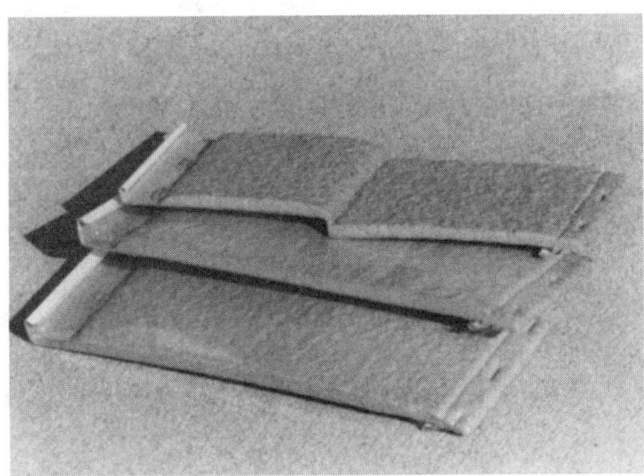
FIGURE 9-84 Insulation-backed aluminum siding.

Horizontal application starts with a starter strip at the bottom of the wall see Fig. 9-85(a). The pieces are interlocking along the bottom edge [see Fig. 9-85(b)] and are nailed in the slots at the top edge with rust-resistant nails. The nail should not be driven home so that movement is possible without buckling of the face. Special molding is used at window and doorframes [see Figs. 9-85(a) and (b)], and either individual or full-length corner pieces are used to finish exterior corners.

Vertical application siding has the interlocking feature on one side, and the strips are nailed or stapled along the other side (see Fig. 9-86). Similar moldings are used to finish edges and corners, though on some occasions the pieces are bent around a corner.

(a) Horizontal metal siding starter strip.

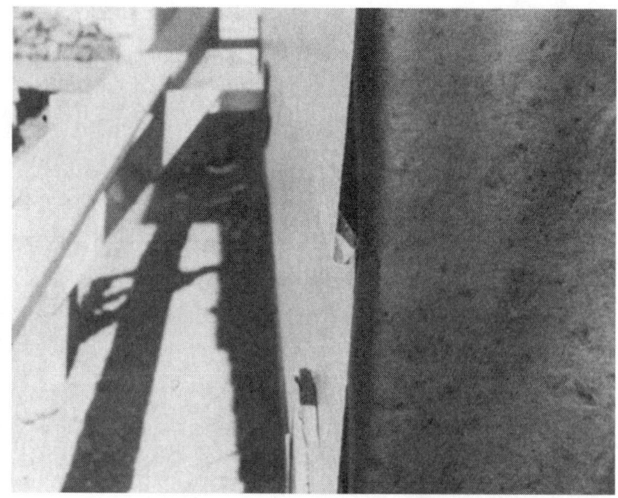

(b) Metal siding interlocking effect.

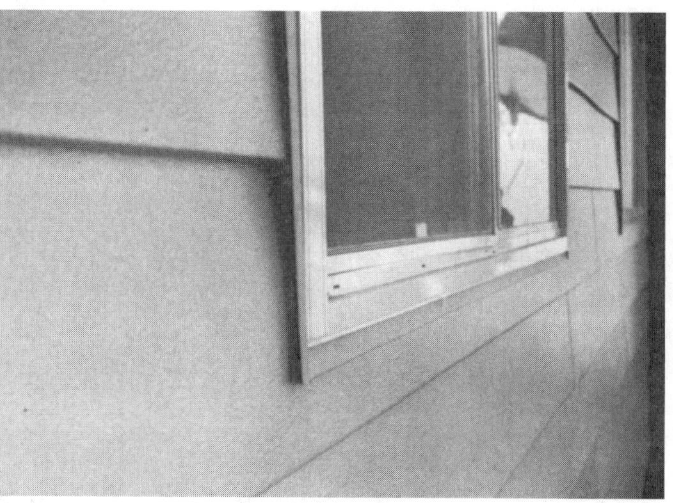

(c) Metal siding J-mold.

(d) Interior corner.

FIGURE 9-85

(a)

(b)

FIGURE 9-86 Application of vertical metel siding.

Vinyl Siding. Vinyl siding is a low-maintenance product and is the same color all the way through so scratches do not affect it, as is the case with metal siding. The application is similar to metal siding and is illustrated in (Fig. 9-87). Siding is available in single or double lap or cove patterns. Vinyl, the most economical of all sidings, is used extensively. It is, however, more susceptible to movement; so care must be taken during application, leaving space for expansion and contraction. The panels easily snap into the preceding rows, holding the strips in place until nailing is completed [see Fig. 9-87(d)]. A simple scaffolding system is often used to install vinyl siding as shown in Fig. 9-88.

Plywood Siding. Any exterior grade of plywood is suitable for siding purposes. Plywood panels are made with a smooth or decorative surface and are usually applied vertically. The joints are shiplap or butted, sometimes covered with a batten. Plywood is available with a resin-impregnated paper surface, providing a smooth, moisture-resistant surface that resists checking or splitting. The panel may be applied directly to the studs without sheathing (see Fig. 9-89).

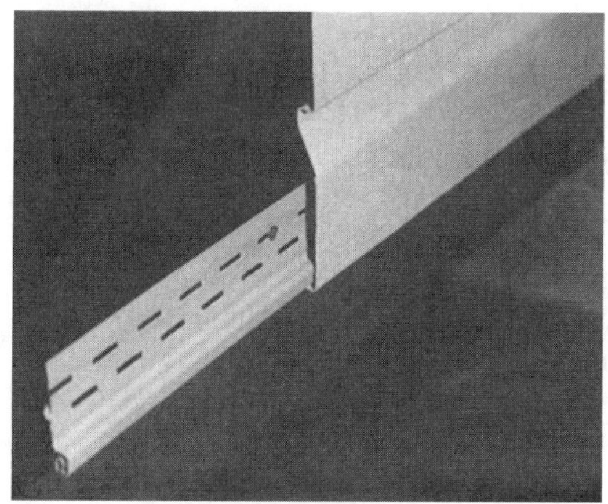

(a) Vinyl siding starter strip.

(b) J-mold around openings.

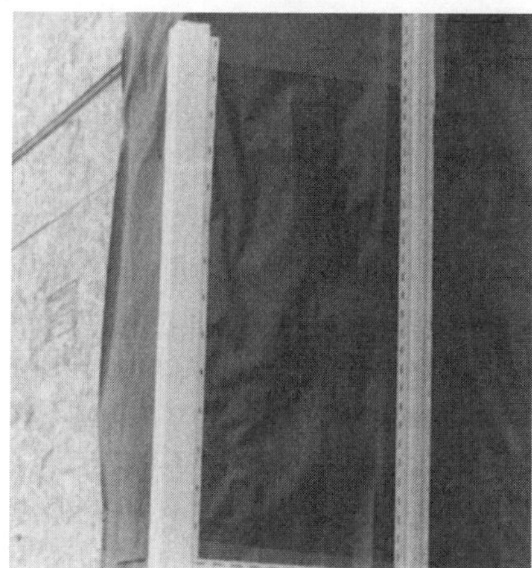

(c) Exterior and interior corner moldings.

(d) J-mold around openings.

FIGURE 9-87

FIGURE 9-88 Installing vinyl siding.

FIGURE 9-89 Plywood siding.

Masonry Finishes

Masonry finishes may be used in walls in a number of ways in light construction. One is to use it as a *veneer* over a wood frame, concrete block, or concrete backup wall. Veneering is done in two ways: (1) by facing a wall with a single wythe of brick or stone, nominally 4 in. (100 mm) in thickness, and (2) by facing it with a thin layer of brick or stone material approximately $\frac{1}{2}$ to $\frac{3}{4}$ in. (12–20 mm) in thickness. Another way is to build a wall using the masonry (usually brick) as the structural portion of the wall as well as the finish.

Brick Veneer

Over Wood Frame. A single wythe of brick, $3\frac{5}{8}$ in. (90 mm) thick, is often used to face a sheathed wall providing an exceptionally durable, maintenance-free finish. Both the building frame and the brick wythe must be supported by the building foundation. The brick facing can either rest on the concrete foundation (see Fig. 9-90) or it can be set on an angle iron that has been fastened to the wall (see Fig. 9-91).

A 1-in. (25-mm) space should be left between the brick and the sheathing paper to stop the migration of moisture from the facing to the framed wall. A base flashing should extend from the outside over the top of the supporting ledge and at least 6 in. (150 mm) up the wall behind the sheathing paper.

The brick must be anchored to the frame by noncorrosive metal straps nailed to the studs and embedded in the mortar joints between the masonry. The straps are not less than 22 gauge (0.76 mm)

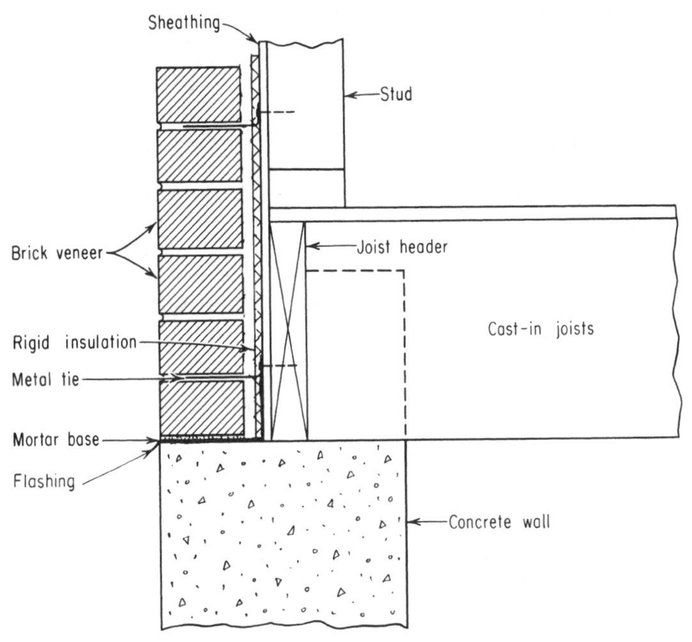

FIGURE 9-90 4″ (100 mm) brick veneer.

FIGURE 9-91 Angle iron support for veneer.

thick and 1 in. (25 mm) wide, and must be spaced in accordance with local building codes (see Fig. 9-92).

The brick pattern used will depend on the desired aesthetic effect. Several patterns are in use, some of the more common ones being running, Flemish, and stack (see Fig. 9-93).

Brick veneer and bevel siding may be used together. In this case, one material will be used to finish all or part of one wall from

FIGURE 9-92 Metal brick ties.

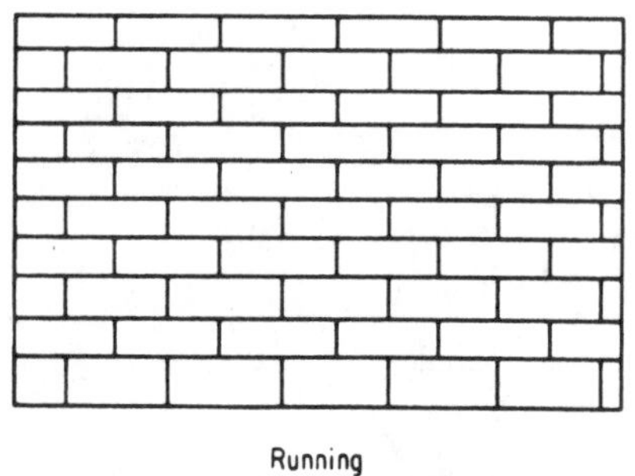

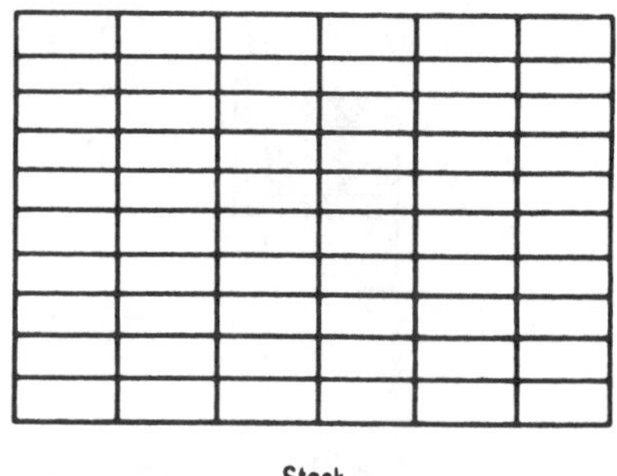

FIGURE 9-93 Typical patterns.

top to bottom. The other material then is used either on the remainder of that wall or on an adjoining one. The two materials should meet at an external corner or at a vertical dividing piece of the same size as the outside casing (see Fig. 9-94).

Another exterior feature utilizes a stone veneer with stucco as shown in Fig. 9-69(b).

The second type of brick facing is set into a mortar base. The wall is prepared as if a stucco finish were to be used. A base coat of

(a) Brick veneer and wood siding combination.

(b) Brick veneer junction with siding and casing.

FIGURE 9-94

plaster is applied over stucco wire and allowed to harden. As the second coat is applied, the brick facing pieces are set into it in the same positions as regular brick would be (see Fig. 9-95), and the joints are dressed after the mortar has partially hardened.

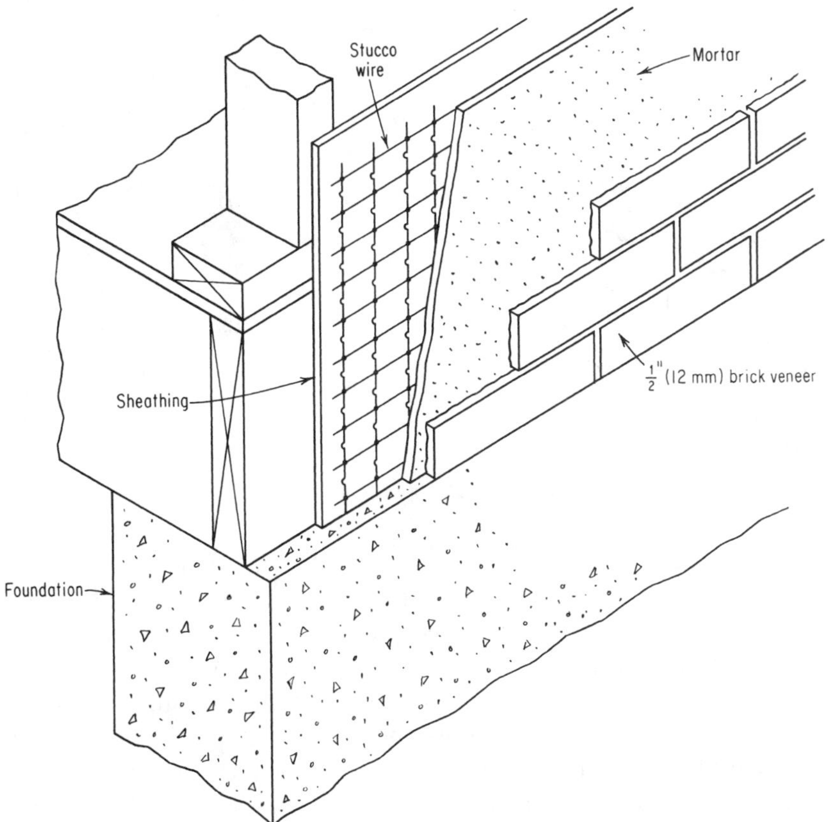

FIGURE 9-95 Thin brick veneer.

Over Concrete Block. Four-, six-, or eight-inch (100-, 150-, or 200-mm) block may be used as a backup wall for a 4-in. (100-mm) brick veneer face, depending on the height of wall. This veneer should be separated from the backup by an unfilled space of at least 1 in. (25 mm) (see Fig. 9-96). When rigid insulation is used on the outside of the block backup, the space must be increased in size so the 1-in. (25-mm) space exists between the insulation and the facing. The facing wythe has to carry its own weight but otherwise is not considered to contribute to the vertical or lateral load resistance of the wall. The backup is designed to resist vertical or lateral loads. The space serves as a drainage gap between the veneer and the backup wall, and any forces on the facing are transmitted across the gap to the backup by ties.

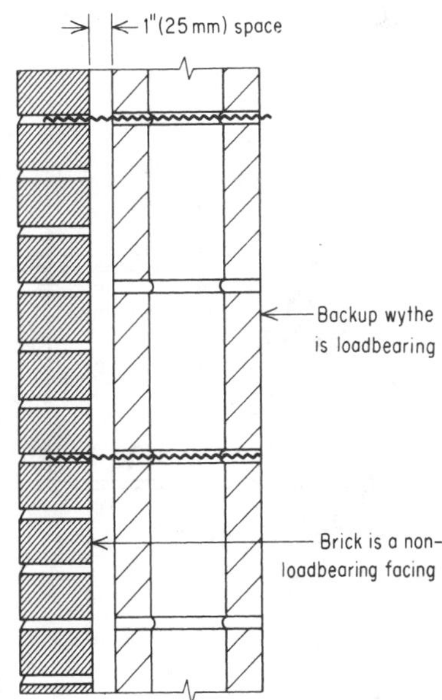

FIGURE 9-96 Brick veneer over masonry wall.

Tying to the backup wall can be accomplished by using corrugated ties embedded in the mortar joints with the tie spacing regulated by local building codes or by using continuous joint reinforcing in every second or third row of the block backup [see Figs. 9-97(a) and 9-97(b)].

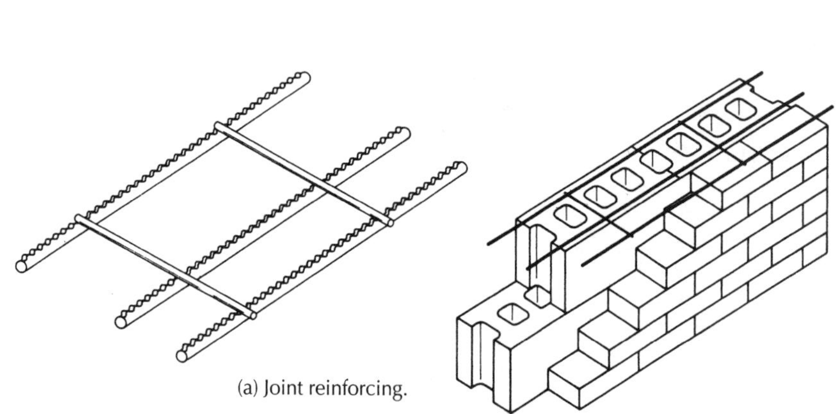

(a) Joint reinforcing.

(b) Corrugated ties.

FIGURE 9-97 Joint reinforcing and ties.

Flashing is provided at the bottom of the cavity between wythes to direct any moisture that collects within the wall toward the outside wythe (see Fig. 9-98), and *weep holes* in the outside wythe allow that moisture to drain to the outside (see Fig. 9-99).

The brick veneer over openings in walls must be supported by a *lintel,* usually a steel angle with its ends supported on the brick on either side of the opening. The maximum allowable opening span depends on the size of lintel used, as discussed in Chapter 4.

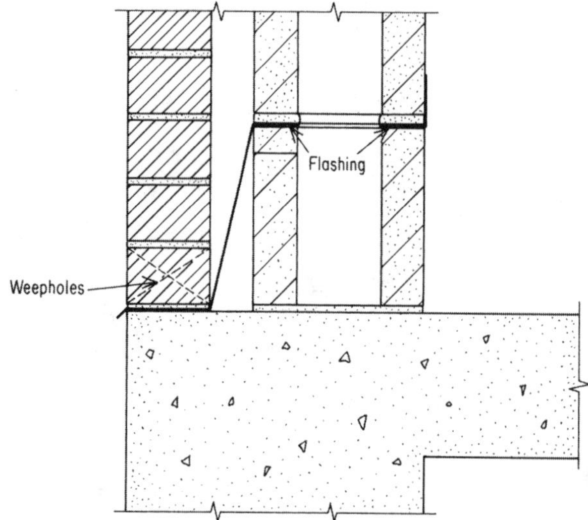

FIGURE 9-98 Flashing at base of brick veneer wall.

FIGURE 9-99 Weep hole in brick veneer wall.

Single-Wythe Brick Walls

Solid brick walls in one-story buildings and the top story of two-story buildings may be constructed of $5\frac{1}{2}$-in. (140-mm) solid units, provided that the wall is not over 9 ft, 2 in. (2.80 m) high at the eaves and not more than 15 ft, 1 in. (4.60 m) high at the peaks of the gable ends. Solid units or grouted hollow units are normally used for this type of construction.

On the inside surface, the wall may be *furred out,* and interior finish applied to this furring. This furring allows for application of a vapor barrier, makes for easy installation of electrical services, and provides space for the introduction of insulation. However, it is possible to plaster directly to the inside face of the brick, or face brick may be used, in which case no other finish is required.

An 8-in. (200-mm) foundation wall is adequate, but the details of construction will depend on the type of floor being used. Figure 9-100 illustrates a typical method of construction using a single-wythe wall.

Laying Brick

One of the primary requisites for a good brick structure is good mortar. To be able to fulfill its purpose, mortar must possess a number of important qualities, both in the *plastic* stage and after it has hardened.

In the plastic stage, the important qualities are *workability, water retention,* and a *consistent rate of hardening.* Hardened mortar must have *good bond, durability, good compressive strength,* and *good appearance.*

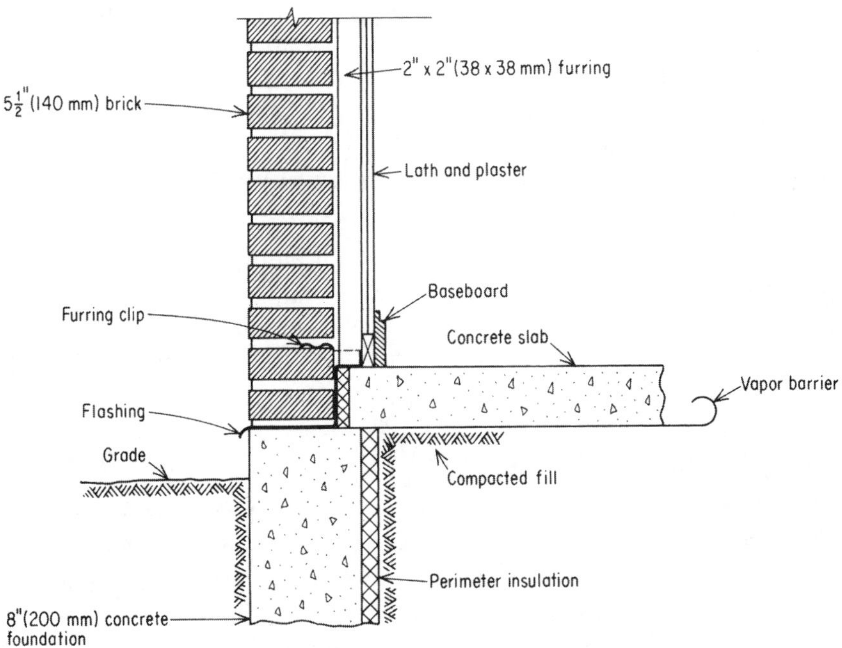

FIGURE 9-100 6-In. (150 mm) brick walls.

FIGURE 9-101 Furrowed bed joints.

FIGURE 9-102 Mortar with good adhesion.

FIGURE 9-103 Full head joint.

FIGURE 9-104 Setting closure brick.

Good workability is the result of a combination of factors, including the *quality of aggregate* used, the use of a small quantity of *hydrated lime or lime putty,* the use of *masonry cement,* the *amount of water* used, proper *mixing facilities,* and the ability of the mortar to *retain water.*

Mortar with good workability should *slip readily on the trowel, spread easily* on the masonry unit, *adhere to vertical surfaces,* and *extrude readily* from joints as the unit is being placed, without dropping. The consistency must be such that the unit can be properly bedded but its weight and the weight of following courses will not cause further extrusion of the mortar.

To obtain good masonry construction, it is essential that all mortar joints be completely filled as the bricks are being laid. Failure to do so will result in voids through which rain water can penetrate. Not only will water pass through the wall to mar the interior finish, but water in the wall may dissolve salts from the brick and then deposit them on the surface as *efflorescence* when it returns to the outside and evaporates. In addition, water in the wall may freeze and cause deterioration in the wall itself.

Mortar for the bed joint should be spread thickly, with a shallow furrow down the center of the bed (see Fig. 9-101). There will then be enough excess mortar in the bed to fill the furrow and allow some mortar to be extruded at the joint when the bricks are bedded to the line. The bed mortar should be spread over only a few bricks at a time so that water will not evaporate before the bricks are laid and thus result in poor adhesion. Figure 9-102 illustrates mortar that has good adhesion qualities.

Care must be taken that all vertical joints in both stretcher and header courses are completely filled with mortar. To obtain a full head joint in a stretcher course, apply plenty of mortar to the end of the brick being placed, so that when it is set, mortar will be extruded at the top of the head joint (see Fig. 9-103).

Closures in stretcher courses need careful attention. Mortar should be spotted in the ends of both bricks already in place, and both ends of the brick to be placed should be well buttered. Then set the closure brick without disturbing those already in place (see Fig. 9-104).

Tooling the mortar joint compacts the mortar, making it more dense, and helps to seal any fine cracks between brick and mortar [see Fig. 9-105(a)]. A number of styles of joint are used providing variety to the aesthetic effect of the brick [see 9-105(b) and 9-105(c)].

STONE CONSTRUCTION

In modern light construction, stone is used almost entirely as a veneer—an exterior facing over a wood frame or unit masonry structural wall or as an interior decorative material used for fireplaces, mantels, feature walls, and finish floors.

Stone for this purpose is available in two forms. One is a small stone block, commonly known as *ashlar,* usually 2, 3, or 4 in. (50, 75,

(a) Before and after tooling joint.

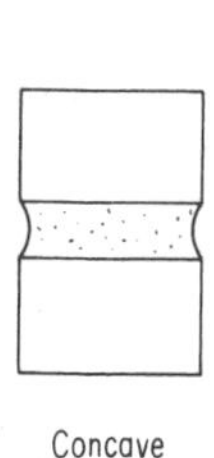

Concave

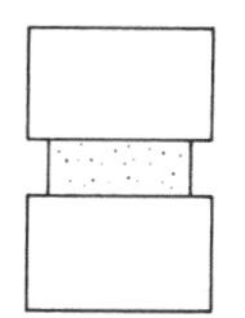

Raked

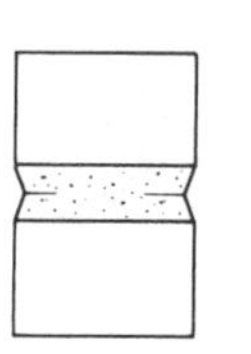

V–joint

(b) Tooled mortar joints.

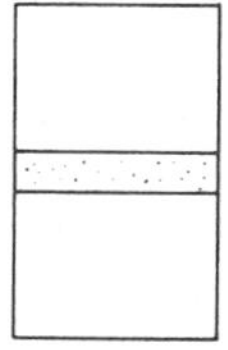

Flush

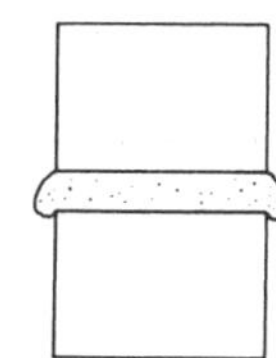

Extruded

(c) Non-tooled joints.

FIGURE 9-105

(a) Coursed stone ashlar.

(b) Stone set in mortar (random).

FIGURE 9-106

or 100 mm) thick, with regular or irregular face dimensions. Stones will usually not exceed 2 ft (600 mm) in length, while the height will vary from 4 to 12 in. (100–300 mm). The other is a thin, flat slab, from $\frac{1}{2}$ to 1 in. (12–25 mm) thick, with either the edge or the face set into mortar on the wall face [see Fig. 9-106(a)].

Ashlar veneer is applied in the same way as brick veneer. The stone must rest on the foundation and is bonded to the wall with metal ties, with one end nailed to a wood frame backup wall or laid in the mortar joints of a unit masonry wall. If the stones are cut to specific dimensions, they can be laid with regular course lines, and the result is known as *coursed ashlar.* But if the face dimensions are irregular, the result will be *random ashlar,* illustrated in Fig. 9-106(b).

Field stone is also used to create an architectural feature and is applied in the same way as other stone veneers. In this case the mortar joints will likely be much more pronounced, as illustrated in Fig. 9-107.

FIGURE 9-107 Field stone effect.

REVIEW QUESTIONS

9–1. List five building operations that may be classed under the general heading "exterior finishing."

9–2. a. What are *wind blocks?*
  b. Under what circumstances are they used?

9–3. Where is each of the following located?
  a. Lookouts
  b. Soffit
  c. Finish fascia

9–4. Name five different types of roofing that may be applied to light construction roofs.

9–5. Why should poly eave protection not be used under wood shingles?

9–6. Fill in the blanks in each statement below:
  a. Joints in successive rows of cedar shingles should be not less than __________ in. (mm) apart.
  b. Each shingle should be fastened with __________ nails only.
  c. Proper spacing of shingles in a course is __________ in. (mm).

9–7. Why would spaced battens be applied over counter battens when clay or concrete tiles are used for a roof finish?

9–8. What is a triple-tab asphalt shingle?

9–9. How are concrete tiles secured to the supporting members?

9–10. Describe briefly the chief distinguishing characteristic of each of the following window styles:
  a. Slider
  b. Casement
  c. Awning
  d. Hopper

9–11. How do patio doors operate?

9–12. What is the advantage of exterior metal doors?

9–13. What is "house wrap"?

9–14. What allows stucco to adhere to a vertical wood-framed surface?

9–15. What are two advantages of vinyl siding?

9–16. When securing vinyl siding, what is the main consideration?

9–17. a. What is meant by *brick veneer*?
  b. Explain how a brick course is tied to a wood sheathed wall.

Chapter 10

INTERIOR FINISHING

OBJECTIVES

Here is what you will be able to do when you complete each component of this chapter:

1. Describe how to install insulation and vapor barrier.
2. Identify seven types of interior wall and ceiling finishes and how they are installed.
3. Identify five types of floor covering and how they are installed.
4. Describe how to install interior doors.
5. Describe how to install interior trim.
6. Describe how to install cabinetry.

Upon completion of the exterior of the building, attention may then be given to the interior. Because this part of the job is not dependent on weather, it is wise to plan so that interior finishing can be done when the weather does not permit outside work.

First, arrangements must be made to have the wiring, plumbing, heating, and air conditioning installed. This is necessary for two reasons. One is that a considerable portion of these services will be situated in the walls and partitions and above the ceiling, and the work must be done while the space is open. The other is that heat and power particularly may be required during the finishing operation. Some examples are shown in Figs. 10-1, 10-2, and 10-3.

FIGURE 10-1 Built-in vent and electrical wiring.

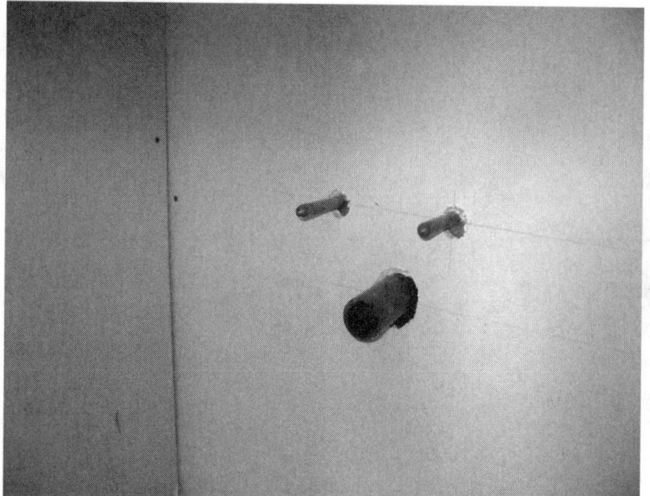

FIGURE 10-2 Plumbing rough in.

FIGURE 10-3 Clothes washer connections.

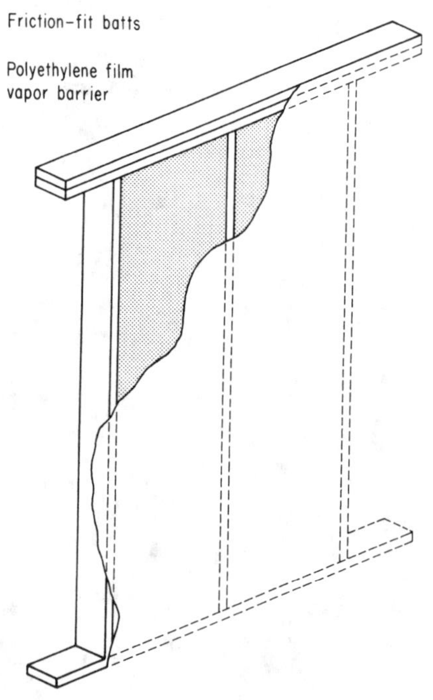

FIGURE 10-4 Vapor barrier over friction-fit batts.

INSULATION

Once these services have been installed, the next step is the placement of insulation in the outside walls, ceilings, and basement walls if applicable. The effectiveness of a building assembly in resisting the flow of heat is measured as its *thermal resistance* or *R value* (RSI). Most materials have some resistance to the flow of heat, but insulation effectively resists this loss or gain of heat in the building. Insulation is manufactured from a variety of materials and is available in several forms, such as batts, loose-fill, rigid, and foamed-in-place.

Batts are commonly used for insulating in framed walls. They are usually friction-fit batts that are stuffed into the stud space and held there by the friction of the batts on the studs. Batts are available in a variety of thicknesses, depending on local building codes or the needs of the client. The application of a polyethylene vapor barrier on the warm side of the insulation is recommended to achieve an effective seal (see Fig. 10-4).

A *loose-fill thermal* or *acoustical insulation* is appropriate for horizontal or moderately sloped attic areas up to a 1 : 3 slope. Insulation is placed by manual or pneumatic methods in open horizontal or moderately sloped locations with care taken to ensure full coverage. Minimum coverage will be determined by local code requirements.

Rigid insulation is best suited for application against flat surfaces, such as concrete or masonry foundation walls, as sheathing over wall studs (see Chapter 6), and over a roof deck. It can be cut to fit between studs, but it is not very cost effective or easy to place. Over concrete or masonry walls, rigid insulation can be applied with an adhesive or with mechanical fasteners. Insulation on walls to be backfilled is usually only nailed along the top and held in place by the backfill material. This type of insulation is secured to a wood surface or to studs with large-headed galvanized nails.

Foam insulation can be either sprayed or injected under pressure, using special applicators to adhere to surfaces or to fill wall cavities. The foam sets into a rigid mass quickly after application, as the foaming action is the last stage in the manufacture of the product. The installer must be highly skilled to provide a product of uniform quality and consistency.

Vapor and Air Barriers

A *vapor barrier* is an essential component of a building wherever there is a considerable difference between inside and outside temperatures and where the inside air has a high moisture content. The function of the vapor barrier is to stop or retard the passage of moisture as it diffuses through the wall or ceiling assembly. *Diffusion* is a process by which vapor migrates through materials. The rate at which it diffuses depends on two factors: the difference in vapor pressure between the inside and outside air, and the ability of the materials to resist moisture migration. If the temperature in the wall is low, the vapor will condense there to form water or ice. If the insulation in the wall becomes damp as a result of this condensation, its effectiveness is reduced. In addition, trapped moisture may cause the wood frame to deteriorate.

All materials have some resistance to moisture diffusion, but a vapor barrier offers a higher resistance than most other materials. A number of materials would be suitable as vapor barriers—materials such as aluminum foil, metal, or glass—but polyethylene film seems to be the most common. The vapor barrier must be placed on the warm side of the insulation for it to effectively control condensation. A vapor barrier need not be perfectly continuous to control moisture migration. Unsealed laps, pinholes, or minor cuts do not increase the overall rate of moisture diffusion, but it is worthwhile to keep these imperfections to a minimum.

Vapor barriers are applied in horizontal, room height strips, so that the number of joints can be kept to a minimum. Polyethylene joints are lapped and stapled over a framing member, as illustrated in Fig. 10-5. Where openings occur, the vapor barrier must be made to fit tightly around them.

The *air barrier* must be able to withstand the combined forces of wind, chimney effects, and fan pressures that are imposed on the wall assembly. The pressure it must resist is much greater than vapor diffusion, and failure to do so will result in a much greater volume of moist air in the wall cavity. The resulting condensation can create great amounts of damage to the materials within the wall. The barrier must be able to support the air pressure loads exerted from the inside or outside of the building. The material must be designed to support the pressure without rupturing, tearing, or coming loose from the surface to which it is attached. Materials chosen for air barriers must be as air impermeable as possible. They need not be vapor

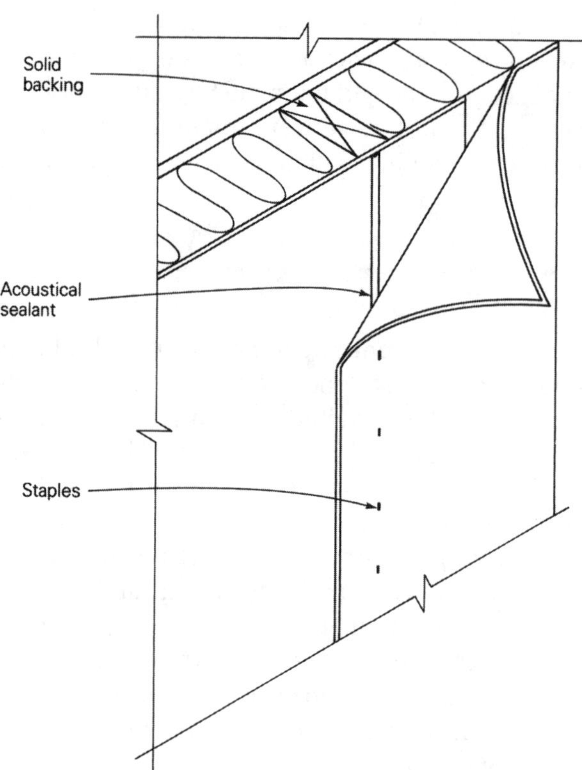

FIGURE 10-5 Installation of vapor barriers.

impermeable as long as a vapor barrier is also incorporated in the wall. Some examples of air barrier materials are gypsum board, plywood, concrete, or reinforced sheet membranes.

The air barrier may be placed at any point on the building envelope, not only on the warm side of the insulation, as is the case with a vapor barrier. Polyethylene placed on the inside can serve as a vapor and an air barrier, but more care must be taken to ensure a continuous surface. All joints must be sealed with an acoustical sealant to resist the movement of air through the material. Material used as an air barrier located near the outer surface of a wall assembly must allow the passage of water vapor from the inside of the wall assembly, or deterioration will occur. Several house wraps are available that will perform as an effective outer air barrier, as illustrated in Fig. 10-6. To be effective, all joints must be sealed with a pressure-sensitive polypropylene adhesive tape to ensure a continuous surface.

INTERIOR WALL AND CEILING FINISHES

Interior finish includes any material that is used to cover the interior wall and ceiling framing. Today, the principal type of interior finish is gypsum board (drywall); however, plywood, hardboard, lumber, tile, masonry finishes, and suspended ceilings are also used.

FIGURE 10-6 Exterior air barrier.

Gypsum Board Finish

Drywall is a term used to describe a finish produced by applying gypsum board to the inside of walls and ceilings. This material is made in sheets 4 ft (1.2 m) wide, from 8 to 16 ft (2.4–4.8 m) in length, and in thicknesses of $\frac{1}{2}$ or $\frac{5}{8}$ in. (12.7 or 15.9 mm). The $\frac{1}{2}$-in. (12.7-mm) thickness is the most commonly used for interior finishing, but the $\frac{5}{8}$-in. (15.9-mm) thickness is used in some applications and does offer some advantages. The board is usually applied in single thickness, but double thickness (*laminated drywall*) is used in some applications.

In a single application, the sheets may be applied horizontally or vertically. On ceilings, the board is generally applied with the long dimension at right angles to the joists or trusses. In many cases the horizontal application of long sheets reduces the number of fasteners, and fewer joints need to be filled than with vertical application (see Fig. 10-7). Horizontal joints at 4 ft (1.2 m) above the floor are below eye level, making them less conspicuous. The sheets are

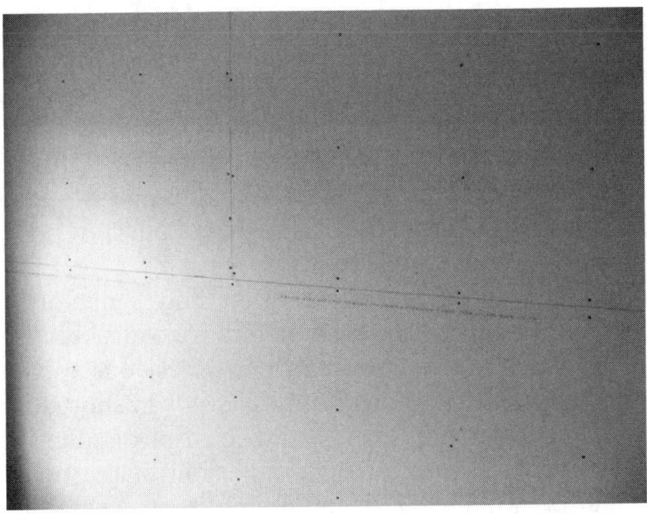

FIGURE 10-7 Gyproc (drywall) offset end joints.

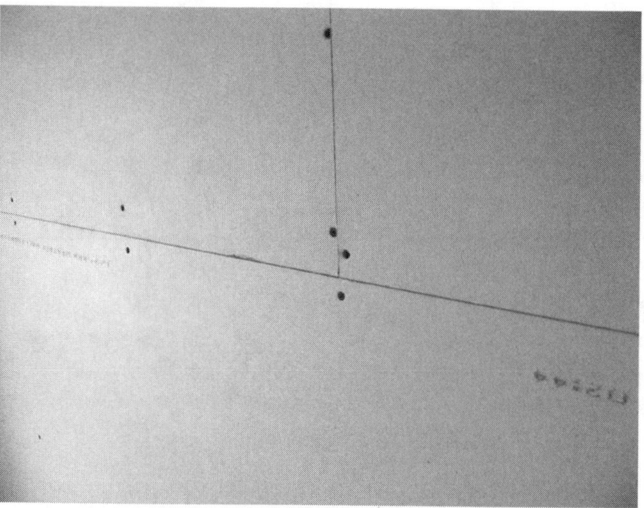

FIGURE 10-8 Gyproc (drywall) secured with screws.

FIGURE 10-9 Double nailing system.

usually ordered in a variety of lengths as needed in the building, so that vertical joints are minimal, and in some rooms will occur only in the corners.

Gypsum board is first fastened with supplementary nails to hold the sheets in place until final fastening can be completed. The gypsum board can be permanently attached with nails, adhesive and nails, or drywall screws (see Fig. 10-8). When nails are used, they should be nonrusting ringed nails long enough to penetrate into the support $\frac{3}{4}$ in. (20 mm). They should be spaced 6 to 8 in. (150 to 200 mm) o.c. along the edges of the board, and double nails 2 in. (50 mm) apart are set at 12 in. (300 mm) intervals along intermediate supports. The double nailing system draws the board tighter to the support and helps to prevent *nail popping* (see Fig. 10-9). Use enough force when driving the nails so that a slight depression is made in the surface when the nail is fully driven, but, at the same time, care should be taken not to break the surface of the paper.

When gypsum board is applied with drywall screws, the screws should be spaced not more than 12 in. (300 mm) o.c. along horizontal supports, or 16 in. (400 mm) o.c. along vertical supports no more than 16 in. (400 mm) o.c. The screws should be long enough to penetrate into the support at least $\frac{5}{8}$ in. (15 mm). Avoid using extra long screws or nails, as it will increase the possibility of nail or screw popping due to the shrinkage of framing members.

The adhesive and nail application method is common in some areas. This method can only be used on interior walls because the adhesive will not stick to the vapor barrier. Adhesive is applied with a caulking gun along the intermediate wall studs in short strips 16 in. (400 mm) o.c. or in a continuous bead. The strips of adhesive should be thick enough to ensure effective adhesion of the board to the stud. This method will reduce the number of spots where filling is required, and nail popping is eliminated. Exterior walls are still fastened with drywall screws because adhesive cannot be used where polyethylene is used as a vapor barrier.

The long edges of the board are depressed where two sheets meet so that a recess appears on the surface that must be filled to hide the joint and to produce a flat surface. To do this, gypsum joint filler and paper tape or fiber mesh are used. The joint tape is about 2 in. (50 mm) wide and has *feathered* edges. The joint filler is purchased pre-mixed and is applied with a mechanical applicator or with a drywall trowel or broad spatula. The first layer of joint cement is applied in a strip about 5 in. (125 mm) wide along the joint. The tape is pressed in the first coat of fresh filler with a wide putty knife or a trowel. Remove excess cement and ensure edges are feathered. After drying, a second coat is applied in a strip approximately 8 in. (200 mm) wide on recessed joints and even wider on butt joints as the ends of the gyproc sheets are not recessed. The final coat is applied at least 12 in. (300 mm) wide and is thinner than the second coat (see Fig. 10-10). Its purpose is to fill in spots missed with the second coat and to feather the edges of the joint. In no case should there be any evidence of the paper showing through the joint filler. Nail or screw indentations are filled with several layers of joint cement to ensure a flat surface. After a light sanding, the surface is ready for painting (see Fig. 10-11).

At internal corners, a strip of joint tape is folded at right angles and set into a bed of filler. The second and third coats are added and finished as with flat joints. At external corners metal corners are either nailed to the corner prior to filling, or a metal corner with a paper covering is pressed into fresh joint filler. The corner is then treated in the same way as other joints. At door or window openings, the gypsum board is stopped against the frame and the joint is covered with casing, as illustrated in Fig. 10-12.

FIGURE 10-10 Applying joint filler.

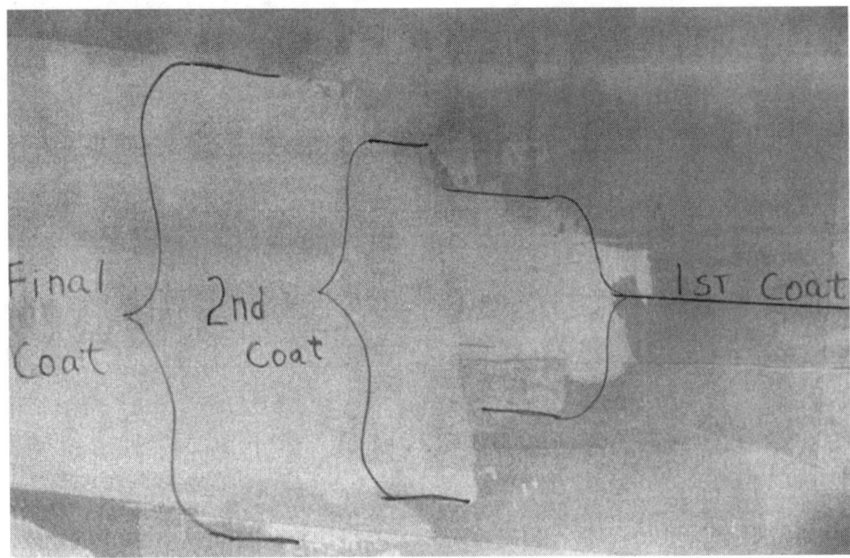

FIGURE 10-11 Three-coat joint filler application.

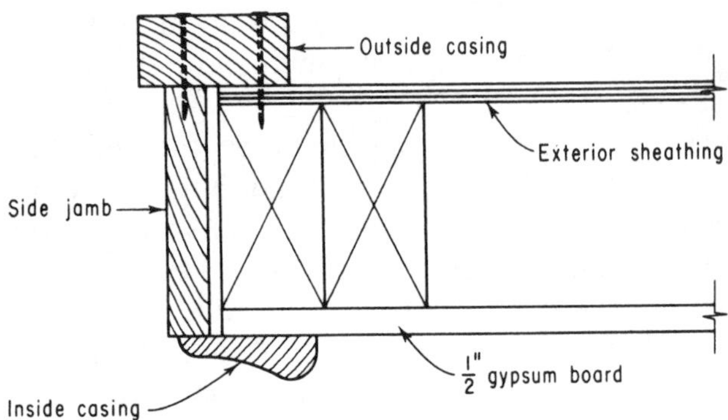

FIGURE 10-12 Opening trimmed with casing.

The board is usually applied to the ceilings first so that the board on the walls supports the edges of the ceiling board. A small space between sheets is recommended, but a large space will make taping and filling of the drywall joints more difficult. Decorative cove strips are available, made of gypsum board, wood, or polyurethane to provide an architectural effect at the ceiling wall joint (see Fig. 10-13).

Plywood Finishes

A great variety of plywood panels are available for interior finishing, both in hardwood and softwood. They may be obtained in plain sheets, in a number of decorative faces, such as simulated driftwood or pressed patterns, and in sheets that have been scored to imitate plank or tile. Plywood panels are also available in matched sequences of grain pattern and are numbered to aid in their installation.

FIGURE 10-13 Example of coved wall-to-ceiling finish.

Joints between sheets can be treated in several ways. One is to make the edges meet as tightly as possible in an attempt to hide the joint. This is relatively easy with patterned plywood, but it is difficult with plain sheets, particularly those in light colors. In such a case it is better to chamfer the meeting edges so as to accentuate the joint. Another method of finishing is to use battens over the joints.

Plywood panels are nailed with $1\frac{1}{4}$- to $1\frac{1}{2}$-in. (30- or 40-mm) finishing nails or glued in place with a panel adhesive. If the gluing process is being used, nailing is used at the top and bottom of the sheet to hold it in position while the adhesives dries.

Hardboards

Hardboards are produced in a great variety of face patterns for inside finishing. There are tile and plank effects, wood grain patterns, plastic-covered faces, and simulated boards with baked enamel surface, among others. A very important consideration in applying any of the hardboards, other than those with plastic or enameled face, is that of pre-expansion. Since these are wood fiber products, they will expand and contract with changes in humidity. Therefore, it is desirable that they be applied while at their maximum size. Otherwise, any expansion on the wall would cause buckling between studs. To pre-expand hardboard, wet the sheets on the backside and stack them flat, back to back, for 24 hours. Hardboard can be fastened in place with staples or nails colored to match the panel finish, or an adhesive can be used to support the panel. They can be fastened directly to the studs, provided that $\frac{1}{4}$-in. (6-mm) thick sheets are used for supports up to 16 in. (400 mm) o.c. Panels not meeting this minimum thickness require a gypsum board backing for support.

Tile

For interior finish, ceramic, plastic, or metal tiles are in common use, particularly in bathrooms and kitchens. The base used for ceramic tile must be suitable for the location; plywood or ordinary gypsum board is suitable in kitchens or laundry rooms. Moisture-resistant drywall or a cement board base is required for shower stalls or walls above bathtubs. The tiles are cemented to the surface, and joints are grouted after adhesive has set. A silicone sealer is applied to the surface after grouting has set. A caulking gun and a silicone tube is used to apply a corner bead in all corners to ensure they are water-tight.

Lumber

Lumber is sometimes used as a decorative finish for walls and ceilings. Solid wood boards are available in an attractive range of hardwoods and softwoods. Hardwood species include maple, birch, and cherry; softwoods include cedar, pine, and hemlock. In any of these species, the boards are easy to install. Special effects can be obtained by installing the boards horizontally or vertically, or in a combination of both. In some applications the boards are placed on an angle to give a special effect. Vertical application for boards that are approximately $\frac{3}{4}$ in. (19 mm) thick requires the placement of horizontal furring strips for backing (see Fig. 10-14). Boards are available in

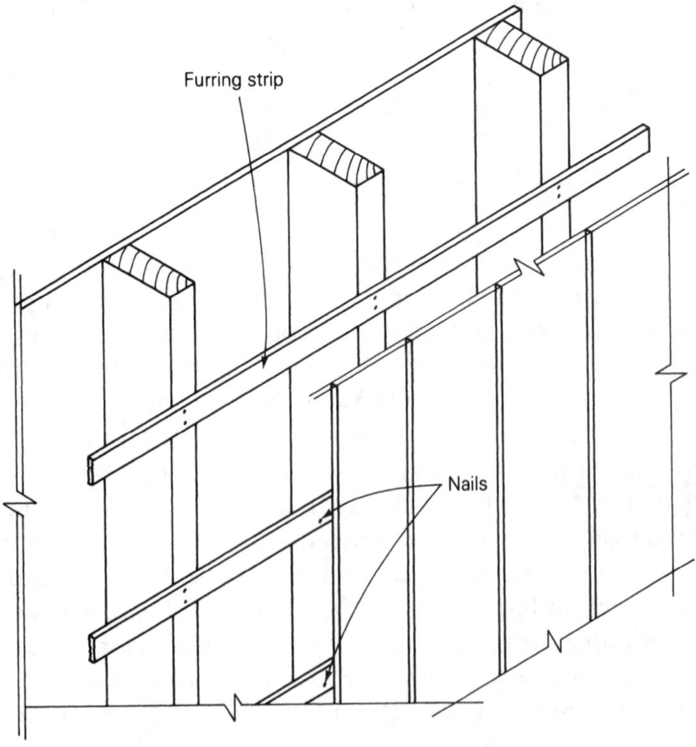

FIGURE 10-14 Vertical application.

butt or "V" joint tongue and groove, or in an offset shiplap joint producing a grooved pattern (see Fig. 10-15).

Thinner boards are also available but generally require a gypsum board backing to which the boards are installed using an adhesive and a minimum number of nails.

Some of these species are available in plywood form, usually available in random groove pattern, simulated board and batten, and tongue and groove joints. Installation of these panels is similar to standard plywood paneling.

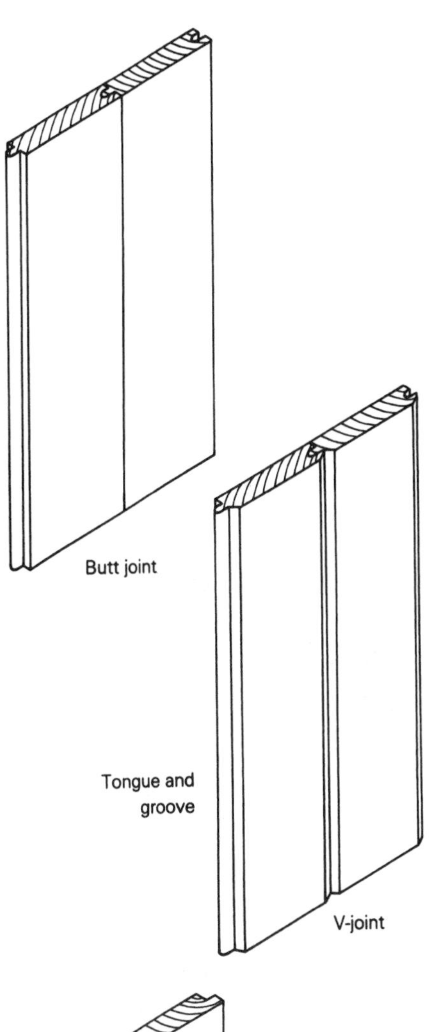

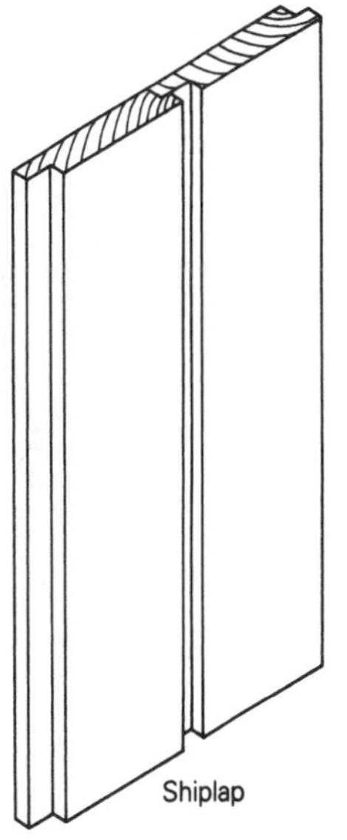

FIGURE 10-15 Joint patterns.

Masonry Finishes

Masonry products have an important place as interior finishes. In addition to brick, tile, concrete block, and stone of various types, thin veneers of brick, tile and stone, both real and artificial, are available. These may be fixed to a solid backing by adhesives; the joints being filled with grout after the units are in place.

Suspended Ceilings

Suspended ceiling tile is one of the fastest and least expensive ways to finish a ceiling and is often used to finish a basement ceiling or a dropped ceiling in a kitchen. The 2 × 4 ft (1200 mm) or 2 × 2 ft (600 mm) ceiling panels come in a variety of textures, colors and designs. Flexible vinyl-coated acoustical panels are very common because they are light and easy to install. Fluorescent light fixtures are available to fit into the suspended ceiling grid-work. The panels are supported by a grid-work made of wall angles, main and cross tees (see Fig. 10-16).

FIGURE 10-16 Suspended ceiling grid-work.

The installation procedures are:

1. Plan the layout of your ceiling panels, adjusting the layout to ensure that you do not end up with a narrow panel at either side or end. The edge panel should be more than half the panel width or length.
2. Locate the ceiling level, either by measuring up from the floor or down from the ceiling frame. Be sure to allow at least 3-in. (75-mm) clearance between the ceiling and the joists or trusses. Nail the wall angle around the perimeter of the ceiling at that level, as illustrated in Fig. 10-17.

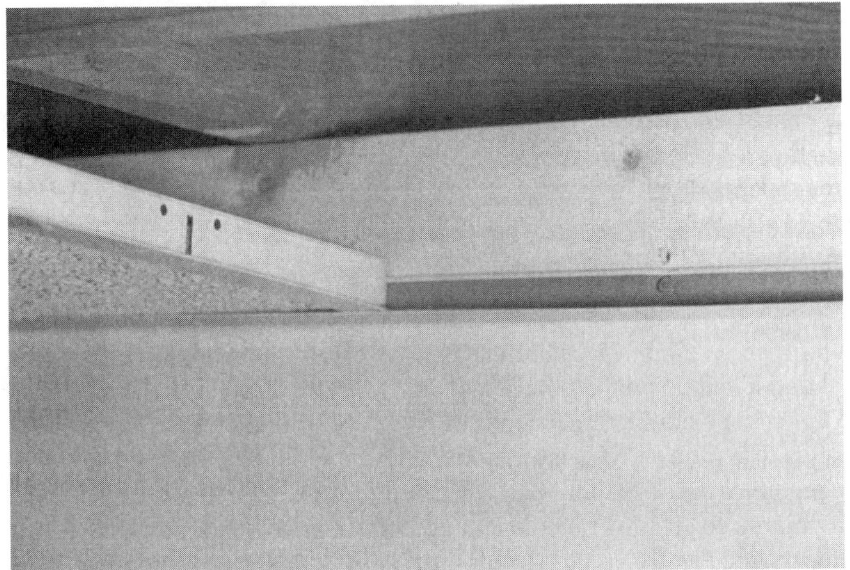

FIGURE 10-17 Wall angle.

3. Fasten screw eyes into joists or trusses at the appropriate locations and attach wires to support the main tees. Temporarily attach wires to main tees. If the main tees run at right angles to the joists, locating their position is relatively easy.
4. Insert cross tees into main tees to form the grid-work (see Fig. 10-18). Cut the pieces at the edge to fit into the remaining space. Level the grid-work and place light fixtures.
5. Insert ceiling panels, cutting the ones at the edges to size.

A suspended ceiling allows easy access to the area above the ceiling, making it possible to make future adjustments for hidden services without major renovations.

FLOORING

Flooring materials include *hardwood* in strip or parquet form, laminated flooring, *resilient flooring* in tile or sheet form, *ceramic tile*, and *carpet.* Each has some particular advantage, and many require some special preparation.

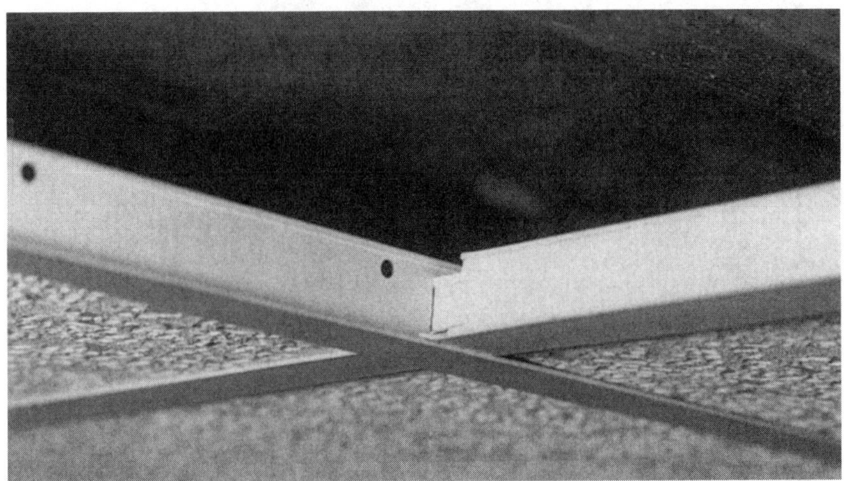

FIGURE 10-18 Cross T—Main T connection.

Hardwood Strip Flooring

Hardwood strip floors are a popular choice for many buildings, with *oak, birch, beech*, and *maple* all being used. They are available either pre-finished or unfinished. Flooring is milled in a number of widths and thicknesses with tongue-and-grooved edges and ends. The minimum thickness of wood strip flooring required for most interior applications is $\frac{5}{16}$ in. (7.9 mm) for floor joist spacing of 16–24 in. (400–600 mm) o.c.

The tongue and groove used to link the strips together is placed below the center of the piece to allow for more wear, and the bottom surface is hollowed for a tighter fit against the sub floor and for greater resilience (see Fig. 10-19). The top face of the strip is slightly wider than the bottom so that the joint is tight when the strips are driven together. The tongue must fit snugly, because a loose fit can cause squeaks in the floor.

Hardwood flooring should be laid only after the humidity caused by the placement of the basement floor and the gypsum board taping has been brought to the normal range. The material should be stored in the warmest and driest place in the building until it is installed.

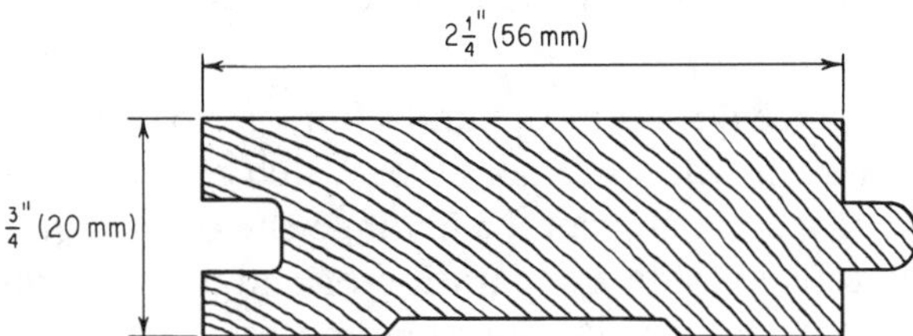

FIGURE 10-19 Section through hardwood flooring strip.

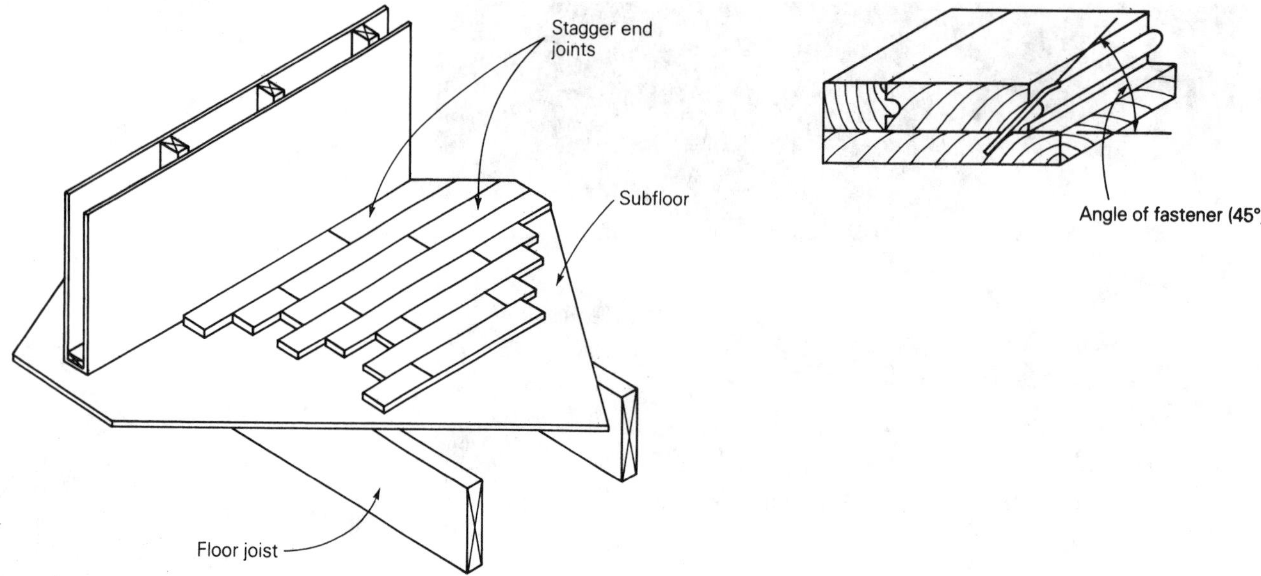

FIGURE 10-20 Hardwood strip application.

FIGURE 10-21 T & G end and side joints.

Following is the procedure for laying strip flooring over a wood subfloor:

1. Plan to lay the floor the long dimension of the room, and if possible lay it at right angles to the floor frame.
2. Start the first strip of flooring against the long wall. Place the grooved edge to the wall and leave a $\frac{1}{4}$-in. (6-mm) space between the floor and the wall to allow for expansion (see Fig. 10-20). The nails or staples driven through the face of the first strip should be driven close enough to the edge so that the base will cover the fasteners.
3. Succeeding strips are blind nailed or stapled (see Fig. 10-20) with flooring nails or staples. The length and the spacing of fasteners depend on the thickness of the flooring, and there should be no fewer than two fasteners per strip. Be sure that the strip is snug against the preceding one and that the end tongue-and-grooved joints are tight (see Fig. 10-21). Many applicators use a stapler or a mallet-driven nailing tool to drive the nails in the proper location. Nails should not be driven home with a hammer; a nail set should be used to avoid damage to the flooring. To avoid splitting, it is sometimes necessary to pre-drill nail holes through the tongue.
4. Use the piece cut off at the end of one strip of flooring to start the next strip wherever possible. Watch that end joints in successive strips are staggered. Arrange the pieces on the floor so that there is as wide a separation of end joints as possible, and such that there is a smooth blending of color and grain variation from piece to piece.

FIGURE 10-22 Offset end joints.

Qualified finishers using drum-type power sanders, preparing the surface for the final finish, usually do the sanding of unfinished hardwood floors. Several layers of a hardwearing acrylic coating are used to finish the floor.

Parquet Flooring

Parquet flooring is an easy way of having hardwood flooring without all the work and cost of hardwood strip flooring. The tiles come in a variety of special patterns and species of wood, and, because the tiles are pre-finished, the floor is complete as soon as installation is complete. Parquet flooring consists of small sections of hardwood laminated together, usually in three thin layers in the form of squares or rectangular strips (see Fig. 10-23). Parquet flooring usually has two adjacent tongued edges and two grooved edges, which fit together to make an integral unit.

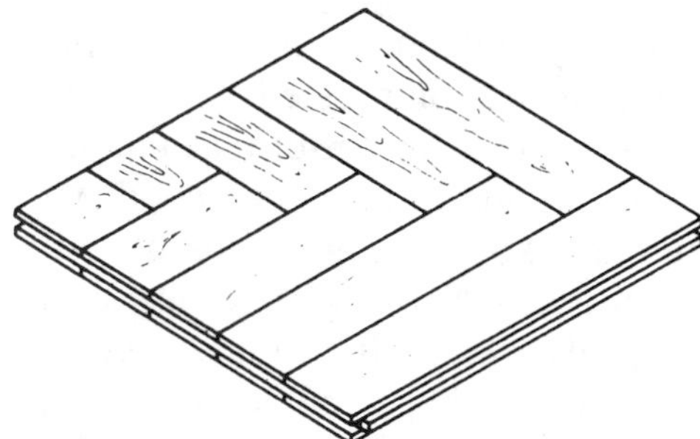

FIGURE 10-23 Parquet flooring.

Parquet flooring is laid much like vinyl tiles; the direction of the strips in squares are alternated to produce a checkerboard effect while the rectangular shapes are all laid in the same direction. An allowance of $\frac{1}{2}$ in. (6 mm) should be left adjacent to walls to allow for expansion. Both types of flooring are laid in adhesive and are not blind nailed like hardwood strip flooring.

With this method, prime the floor with a primer and after drying, apply the adhesive with a notched adhesive trowel. The tiles are started at the edge from a previously established line, and they are set in place and then tapped with a rubber mallet to ensure a good bond. Trim the bottom end of door casings and jambs to allow the tile to fit underneath, as illustrated in Fig. 10-24.

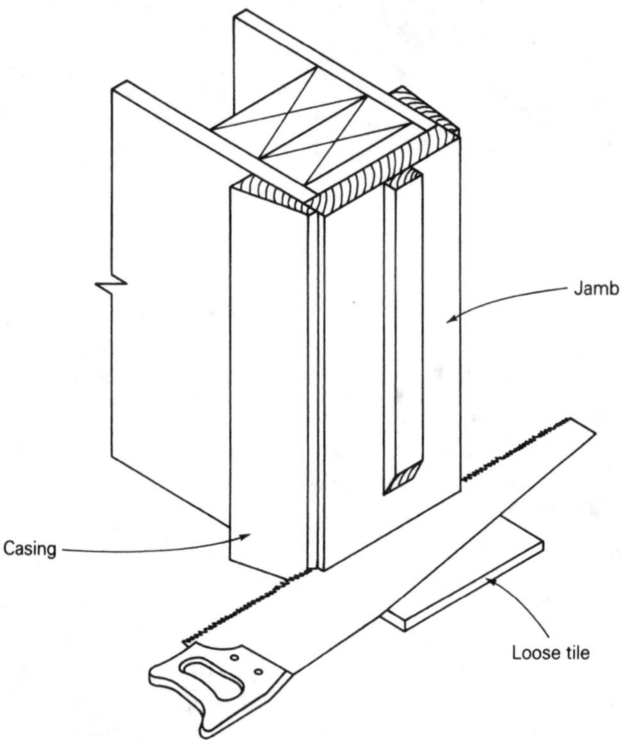

FIGURE 10-24 Trimming doorjamb and casing.

Laminate Flooring

Laminate flooring is manufactured using multiple layers of paper impregnated with resin and compressed using heat and pressure. The surface layer has a wood-grain pattern, available in various wood types. This material is made to resemble wood strip flooring and is about $\frac{1}{4}$ in. (5 mm) thick. Edges and ends of individual strips are manufactured to interlock with one another as they are installed without the use of nails or adhesive. In fact, they are referred to as a *floating* floor. Because of the manufacturing process, this type of flooring is extremely resistant to wearing or denting while at the same time providing the "warmth" of wood flooring.

Resilient Flooring (Individual Tiles)

Resilient floor tiles of all kinds require a smooth, regular surface in order to give satisfactory service and to maintain a good appearance. In most cases the conventional subfloor does not provide a surface that is smooth and even enough, and some type of *underlayment*, such as plywood, particleboard, or hardboard, must be applied over the subfloor.

Large defects in the subfloor, such as knotholes, should be patched before hardboard underlayment is installed, and the material should be allowed to stand unwrapped in the room for at least 24 hours to adjust to the prevailing humidity conditions. A space of approximately $\frac{1}{16}$ in. (1 mm) should be left between sheets when they are laid to allow for expansion. The end joints in the panels should be staggered, and the continuous joints should be at right angles to those in the subfloor.

Plywood and particleboard are dimensionally stable products, and sheets may be butted against one another when they are laid. They are also rigid enough that they will bridge most defects in the subfloor. Joints should be staggered in the same manner as with hardboard.

Annular grooved or *spiral* nails or *divergent* staples are used as fasteners for all these underlayment materials, with spacing not over 6 in. (150 mm) around the edges of the panels and 8 in. (200 mm) for the rest of the panel. The joints between panels and any defects in the surface should be filled with a nonshrink filler compound that will bond to the underlay. The filler should be sanded prior to application of the flooring.

Once the underlayment has been prepared for the resilient flooring, the following procedure outlines the method for laying the tile:

1. Clean the surface thoroughly and check to see that it is smooth and the joints are level. Remove any rough edges with sandpaper or plane.
2. Snap a chalk line down the center of the room in the direction of the long dimension.
3. Lay out another centerline at right angles to the main one, using a framing square or the 3–4–5 triangle to get the chalk line in its proper alignment.
4. Spread adhesive over one-quarter of the total area, carrying it up to, but not over, the chalk lines. Use the type of spreader recommended by the manufacturer of the adhesive.
5. Allow the adhesive to acquire an initial set. It should be slightly tacky but not sticky, and the length of time required to achieve this condition will depend on the type of adhesive.
6. Lay the first tile at the center of the room, with two edges to the chalk lines (see Fig. 10-25).

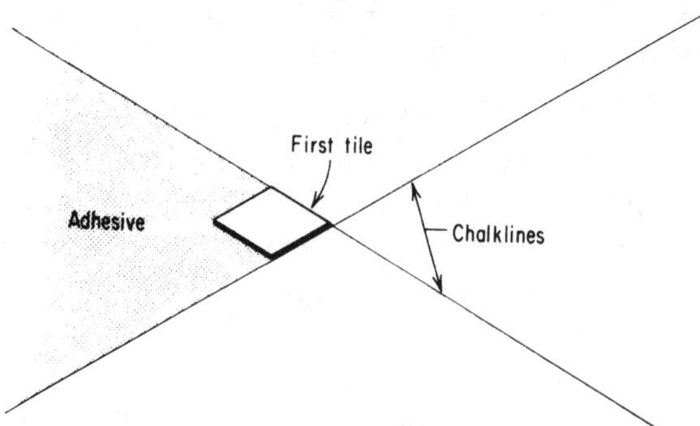

FIGURE 10-25 First tile positioned to center lines.

7. Lay a row of tiles to both chalk lines, being careful to keep the butt joints tight and the corners in line. Lay each tile in position–do not slide it into place.
8. Cut the last tile in each row to fit against the wall, with the cut edge to the wall.
9. Complete the installation of the tile over that quadrant of the floor and repeat the procedure for the rest of the floor.
10. Finally, roll the floor with a heavy roller to ensure effective bonding of the tiles.
11. It may be necessary to remove any adhesive from the tile surface by using the solution recommended by the adhesive manufacturer.

Resilient Flooring (Sheet Flooring)

Resilient sheet flooring is usually installed after most other trades have finished their work. Solid vinyl is the most common type of sheet flooring used; however, rubber flooring is used in some cases. It is produced in rolls from 6 to 12 ft (1.8 to 3.6 m) wide, in various thicknesses and with plain or patterned surfaces.

The following is the procedure for laying sheet flooring:

1. Cut the bottom ends of door casings and jambs shorter to allow room for the flooring to fit underneath. Then clean the surface to be covered to ensure that no particles are left under the flooring. Carefully roll out the sheet and cut it about 3 in. (75 mm) oversize.
2. Position the entire piece so that the edge curls up each wall. Make sure that patterned pieces line up precisely with the wall and then trim the flooring so it fits the room, leaving a $\frac{1}{8}$-in. (3-mm) gap at the walls for expansion and contraction.
3. Roll back half of the sheet and apply adhesive to the underlay with a notched trowel and return the flooring to its original location. Repeat the operation for the other half of the floor.

4. Clean the surface and roll the floor with a heavy roller to remove any air pockets. Start from the middle of the floor and work to the edge.
5. If the floor includes a seam, fasten one of the pieces to the floor leaving the adhesive 10 in. (250 mm) back from the seam. Position the second piece so that it overlaps the seam at least 2 in. (50 mm). If the flooring is patterned, make sure the patterns from both pieces will match. Cement the second piece to the underlay, again leaving the adhesive back from the seam. Overlap the two pieces at the seam and cut through both pieces with a linoleum knife or a sharp utility knife (see Fig. 10-26). Lift both pieces and apply the adhesive, reset the pieces, and roll the surface of the seam. Clean the seam and use a seam sealer to complete the application.

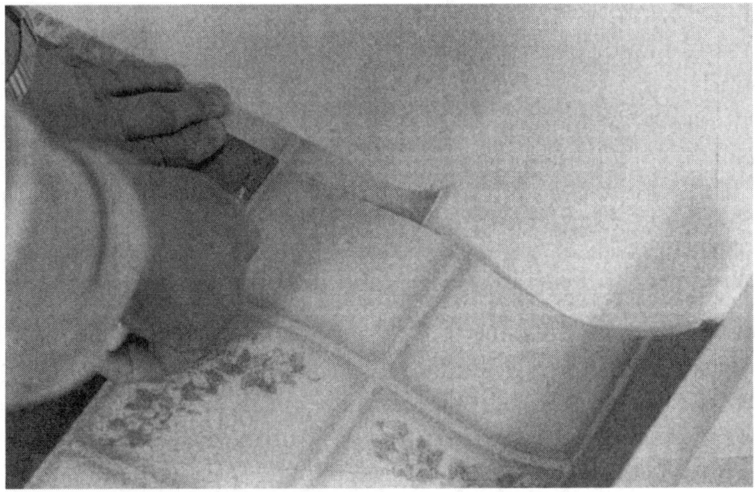

FIGURE 10-26 Cutting a seam.

Ceramic Tile

Ceramic tile is often used as a floor covering for bathrooms, front halls, kitchens, and fireplace hearths. Ceramic tile may be laid over a concrete base or attached with a special adhesive to particleboard or plywood underlay. A mortar base adhesive is used when laying ceramic tile on a concrete base. When laying tile over a wood floor, the underlay over the subfloor should be at least $\frac{1}{2}$ in. (13 mm) thick to ensure a good rigid base for the tile. Floors that allow movement will result in the tiles breaking up and coming loose from the floor. The procedure for the installation of the tile is similar to the procedure used on walls; the type of grout, however, is different since it contains sand.

Carpets

Carpets do not usually require underlayment because normally a rubberized underpad is first laid over the subfloor. However, the subfloor should be flat and even and cracks and knotholes filled with reliable crack filler. A carpet layer, using specialized equipment for stretching the carpet and holding it in place, normally does actual carpet installation.

INSIDE DOOR FRAMES

Interior door frames will include standard hinged doors, either pre-built at a shop or totally built on the construction site, folding doors, pocket, and sliding doors. *Folding doors* are available in either accordion or bi-fold type in a variety of sizes to meet most situations. *Pocket door* and *sliding door* kits are available to allow for easy installation.

Interior *hinged doors* come in a variety of sizes ranging from 24 to 36 in. (610 to 914 mm) in width, $1\frac{3}{8}$ and $1\frac{3}{4}$ in. (35 and 45 mm) in thickness and usually 80 in. (2032 mm) in height. Pre-built door frames can be manufactured either with the casing attached to a split doorjamb, reducing onsite work, or more commonly without casing, which is installed onsite.

The two most common styles of doorjambs used to make inside door frames are indicated in Fig. 10-27. The economical flat jamb, $\frac{3}{4}$ in. (19 mm) thick cut to a width equal to the thickness of the wall is most often used. A doorstop is fastened to the face of the jamb after the doorframe is installed in the rough door opening, and after the door has been hung, providing a good fit to the face of the door. Rabbeted jambs are used in better grade finishing, and they have one edge rabbeted out $\frac{1}{2}$ in. (13 mm) deep by $1\frac{3}{8}$ or $1\frac{3}{4}$ in. (35 or 45 mm) wide, depending on the thickness of the door used, as illustrated in Fig. 10-27(b).

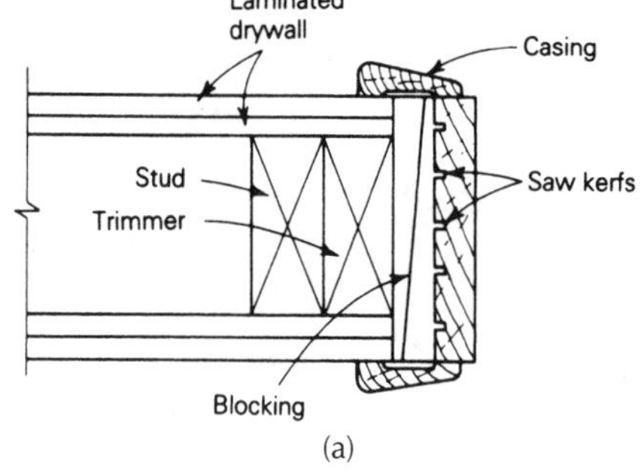

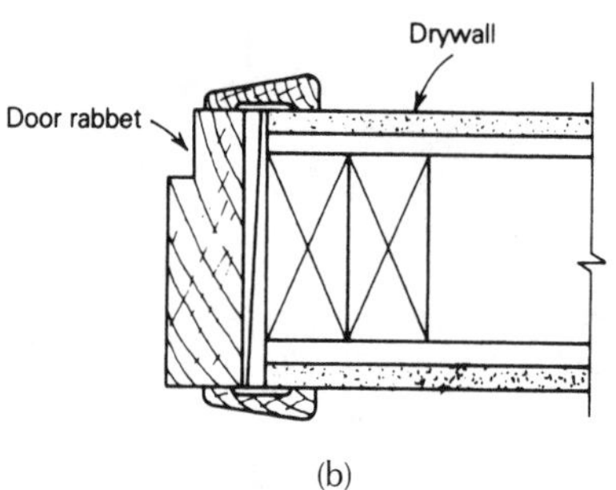

FIGURE 10-27 Inside door frames.

Installing Inside Door Frames

Once the door frame has been sanded and assembled and the door hung, it is ready for installation into the rough door opening. Pre-built doorframes are built with a head jamb at either end with the doorknob hole in the middle of the door height allowing it to be installed with either end up (see Fig. 10-28). The advantage of this allows the installer to have the door swing in either direction. The hinges are also set at an equal distance [11 in. (280 mm)] from the top and the bottom of the door to allow this universal use. The jamb at the bottom end is then removed and the frame is ready for installation.

Typically, pre-built door frames have the doors installed with approximately $\frac{1}{8}$-in. (3-mm) clearances at the top and both sides to allow the door to freely swing without binding against the doorjamb. When the jamb at the bottom is removed, there will be a clearance of approximately $\frac{3}{4}$–$\frac{7}{8}$ in. (19–22 mm).

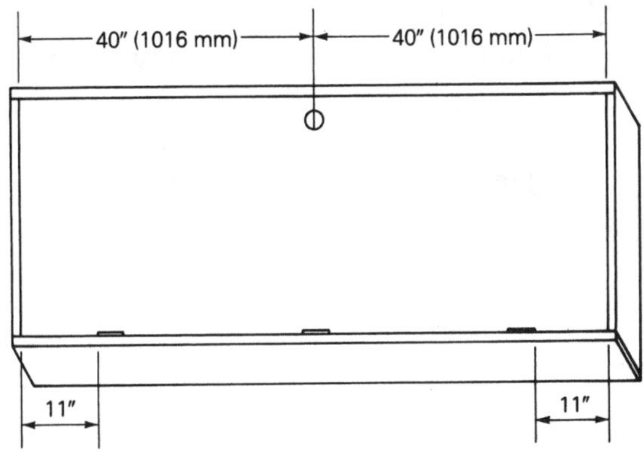

FIGURE 10-28 Pre-built door frame.

The procedure for the installation of inside door frames is as follows:

1. Check to ensure the rough opening is the correct size for the door frame. An opening width equal to the outside door frame width plus a clearance of $\frac{1}{2}$ to $\frac{3}{4}$ in. (13 to 19 mm) allows for proper plumbing of the frame. The rough opening height should have a $\frac{3}{8}$-in. (9.5-mm) space above the head jamb, and at least a $\frac{3}{4}$-in. (19-mm) space under the door plus allowance for the thickness of the carpet, under-mat, and underlay if applicable, as illustrated in Fig. 10-29. This space under the door will ensure air can circulate throughout the building.

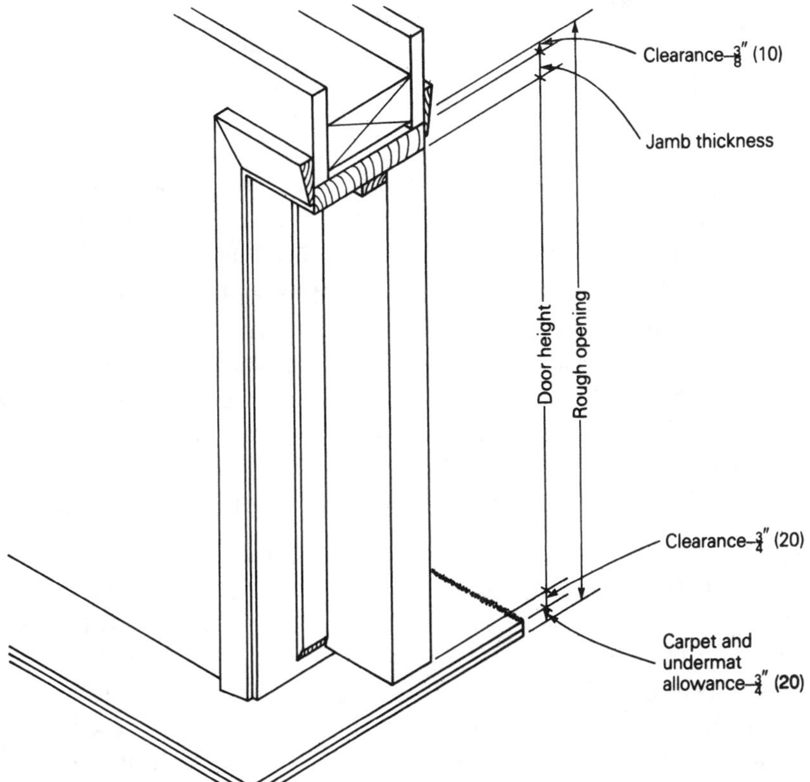

FIGURE 10-29 Rough opening height.

2. Set the frame in the opening and wedge it into position ensuring that the door is approximately centered. Plumb the door frame both ways, especially the hinged jamb. Secure the wedges by nailing or stapling through the frame into the trimmer, as shown in Fig. 10-30. Hide the nails or staples behind the doorstop in a flat jamb or in the corner of the rabbet. Pre-cut wedges are readily available and are approximately 1-$\frac{1}{2}$ in. (38 mm) wide.

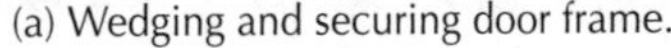
(a) Wedging and securing door frame.

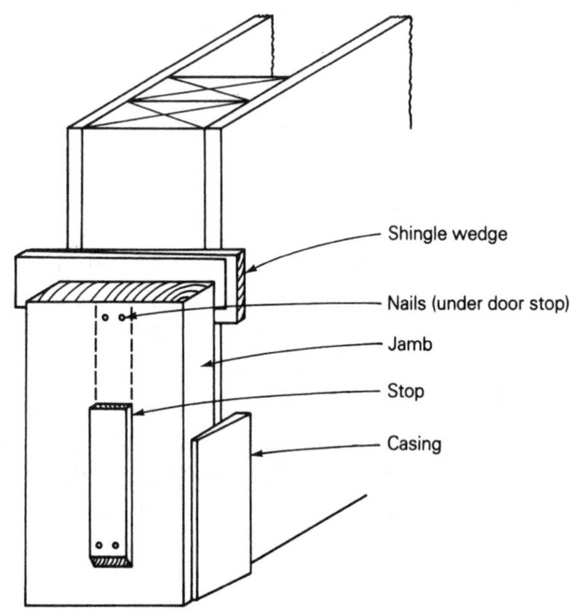

(b) Shingles used as wedges.

FIGURE 10-30 Shingles used as wedges.

3. Adjust the wedges until the jambs are straight, using the edge of the door as a straight edge. A space of $\frac{1}{8}$ in. (3 mm) between the jamb and the door should eliminate binding.
4. Wood screws are used to hold the frames for heavier doors in place. The support is especially important on the hinge side of the frame. The screws are concealed by placing them behind the doorstop or by replacing standard length screws in the hinges with ones long enough to fasten the frame firmly to the trimmer. Screws that are visible can be recessed and covered with wooden plugs, and sanded down flush with the jamb surface.

Door frames that are site built will involve additional work prior to the installation of the frame into the opening. Jambs will require cutting a dado at the top of the side jambs to accommodate the head jamb, and the hinge gains will have to be cut into the door and the side jamb so that the door can be set into the frame prior to installation in the opening. The lock side of the door should have a 5° bevel toward the closing side (see Fig. 10-31). Doors that are not pre-drilled will require drilling for installation of latch bolt and knob assembly.

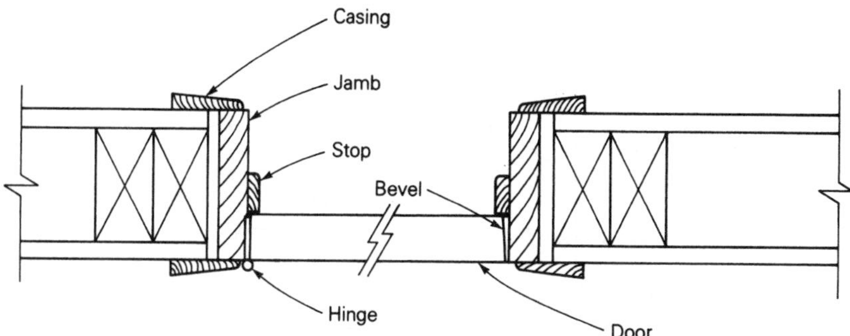

FIGURE 10-31 Door edge bevel.

A hinge jig can be used with an electric router to cut gains, or a hammer and chisel can be used if a jig is not available. Care should be taken to ensure that the gain is not cut too deeply or hinge bind will occur. The proper depth of the gain should be equal to the thickness of the hinges used (see Fig. 10-32), and the edge should be set $\frac{1}{4}$ in. (6 mm) back from the face of the door.

The hinges must be set to allow $\frac{1}{8}$-in. (3-mm) space between the door and the top and side jambs of the frame. Hinges are typically placed 7 in. (175 mm) from the top and 11 in. (275 mm) from the bottom, but these distances may vary slightly—especially in panel doors. Two 3-in. (76-mm) hinges are used on smaller lightweight doors; larger and heavier doors require additional and larger hinges. Some large doors will require as many as four 5-to 6-in. (127- to 152-mm) hinges. Additional hinges have an advantage in that they resist warpage and hold doors straighter. During the operation it is necessary to support the door firmly on edge, and this may be done with the aid of a woodworker's vise clamped to a sawhorse or a jig, as illustrated in Figs. 10-33 and 10-34.

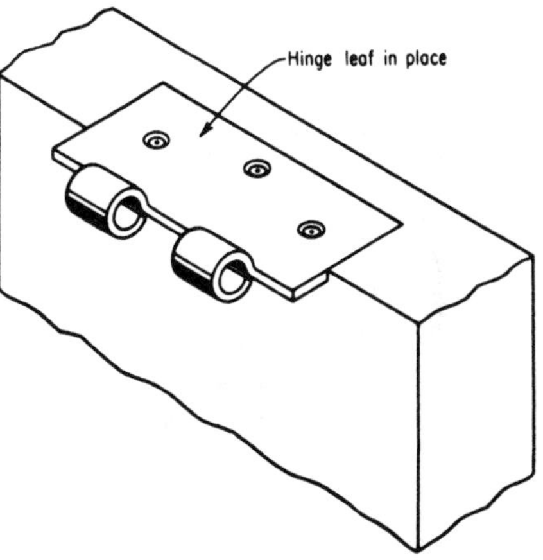

FIGURE 10-32 Proper depth of gain.

FIGURE 10-33 Sawhorse vise.

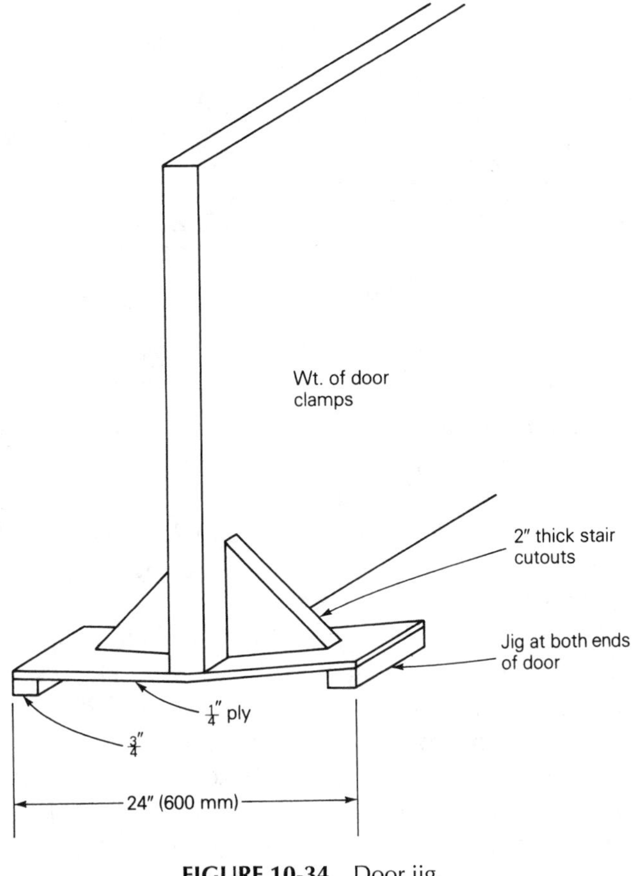

FIGURE 10-34 Door jig.

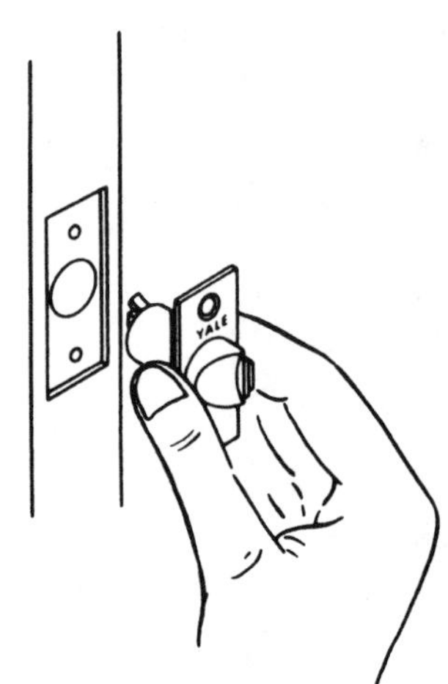

FIGURE 10-35 Installing latch unit.

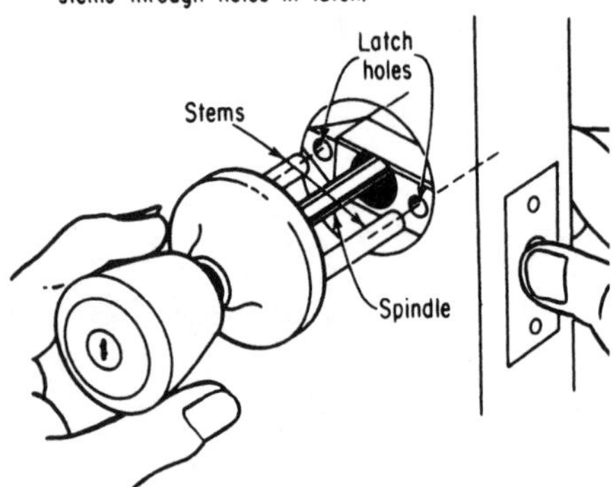

FIGURE 10-36 Installing exterior knob.

Installing a Lockset

When the door is hanging properly, it is ready for the lockset. Two types are in common use: *cylinder locks* and *mortise locks.* The first is mounted through the face of the door, and the latter through the edge and face.

Installing a Cylinder Lock

The procedure for installing a cylinder lock (or passage set) is as follows:

1. The lockset is mounted in the pre-drilled holes in the face and the edge of the door.
2. The latch bolt is placed first, fastened with screws through the latch bolt strike and set into a gain in the edge of the door (see Fig. 10-35) or the friction fit type is driven in.
3. The exterior knob is installed into the hole in the face of the door (see Fig. 10-36).
4. Next, install the interior knob as described in Fig. 10-37.

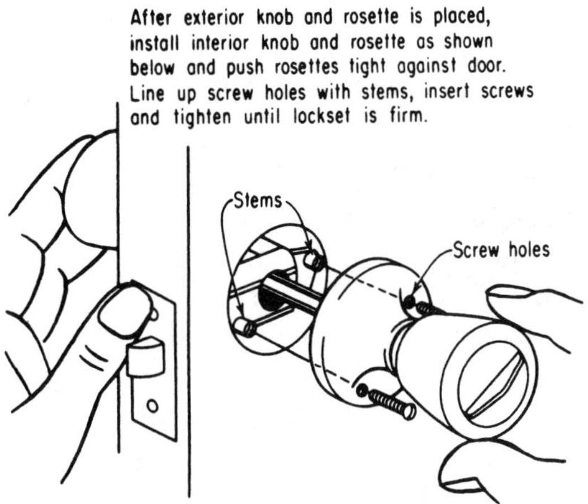

FIGURE 10-37 Installing interior knob.

5. Find the location of the strike plate and install it into a gain in the jamb (see Fig. 10-38). Use the template supplied with the lockset to locate and mark the location of the holes for doors that are not pre-drilled. The standard knob height is 36 in. (900 mm) from the floor, and locks should be installed accordingly.

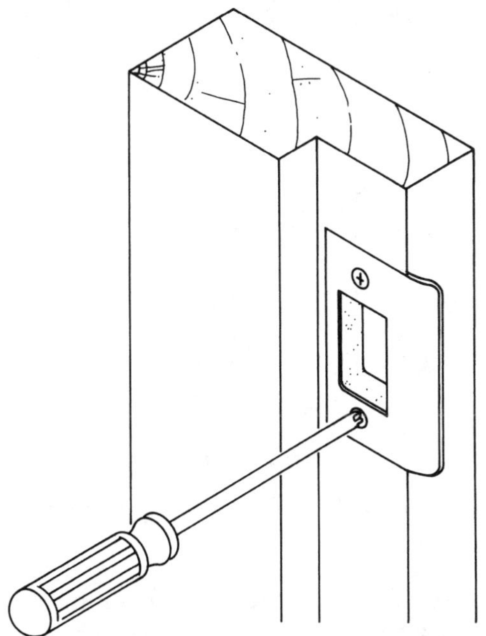

FIGURE 10-38 Installing a strike plate.

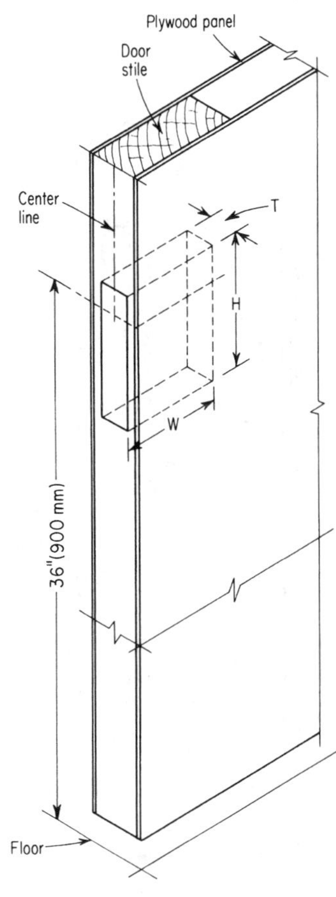

FIGURE 10-39 Door layout for mortise lock.

Installing a Mortise Lock

The procedure for installing a mortise lock is as follows:

1. Measure up 36 in. (900 mm) from the floor and mark that *height above floor* line on the face and edge of the door (see Fig. 10-39).

2. Measure the thickness and height of the *lock case* and lay out a mortise on the edge of the door with dimensions slightly larger than the height and thickness. Make sure that the layout is centered on the edge of the door and is located so that the center of the knob will fall on the height above floor line.
3. Select a wood bit with the same diameter as the thickness of the mortise layout and, from the centerline, drill a series of holes into the edge of the door $\frac{1}{4}$ in. (6 mm) deeper than the width of the lock case (see Fig. 10-40).

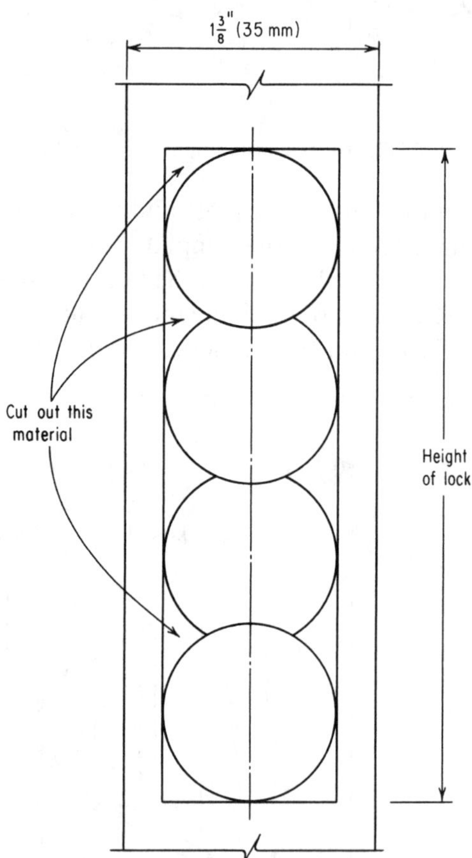

FIGURE 10-40 Holes drilled for lock mortise.

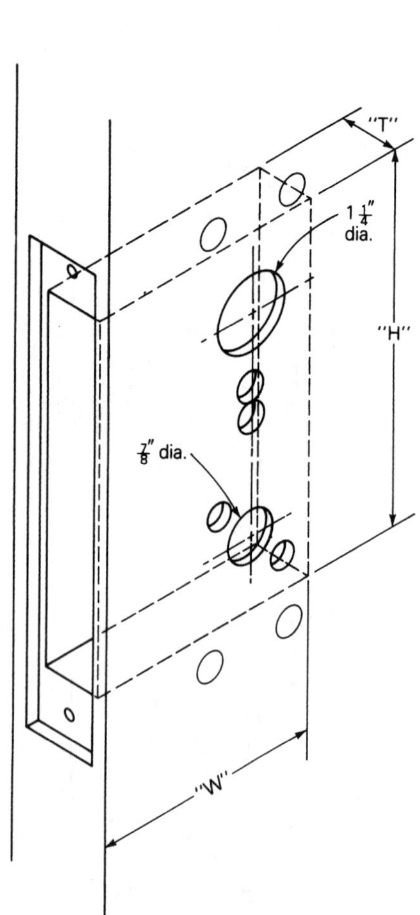

FIGURE 10-41 Lock mortise installed.

4. With a sharp chisel, remove the remaining wood around the holes to form a rectangular mortise. Check to see that the lock case will fit in the space.
5. Slip the lock into the mortise, and with a marking knife, lay out the outline of the lock-mounting plate on the door edge. Cut a gain for the plate as shown in Fig. 10-41.
6. Measure the distance from the face of the mounting plate to the center of the knob shank hole and the keyhole. Lay out these points on the face of the door and then drill holes of the size required.

7. Fit the lock into the mortise, drill pilot holes for the lock-mounting screws, and fasten the lock in place.
8. Install knob shank and knobs according to instructions included with the lockset.
9. Mark the location of the center of the latch bolt pocket on the jamb and fit the strike plate accordingly. A gain must be cut into which the strike plate fits and pockets for the latch bolt and dead bolt drilled and squared out (see Fig. 10-42). The strike plate must be positioned laterally so that the latch bolt will just engage when the door is closed and hold the door snugly in the closed position.

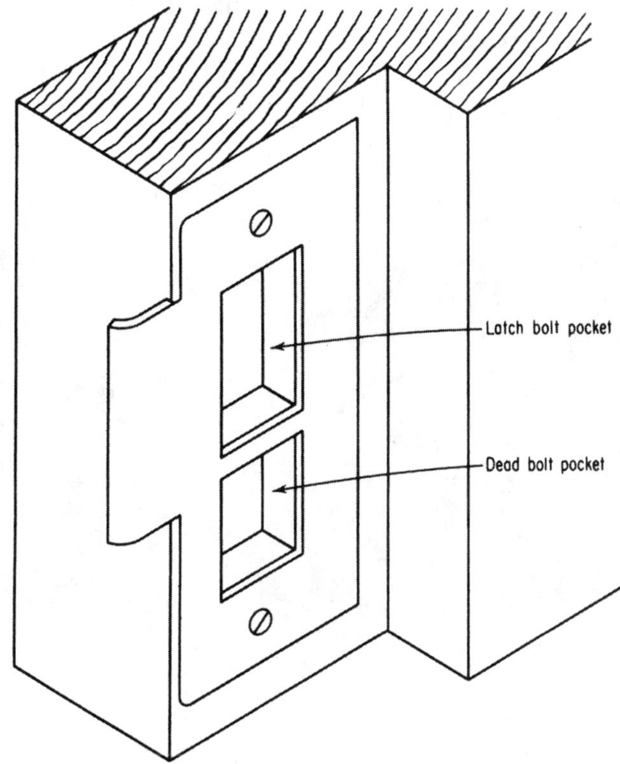

FIGURE 10-42 Strike plate in place.

The Hand of Doors

The term to describe the direction in which a door is to swing and the side from which it is to be hung is the *hand* of the door. The hand is determined from the outside.

The outside is the street side for entrance doors; it is the corridor side for doors leading from corridors to rooms; it is the room side for doors from rooms to closets; and it is the stop side—the side from which the butts cannot be seen—for doors between rooms.

Stand outside the door. If the hinges are on your right, it is a right-hand door, and if they are on your left, a left-hand door. If the door swings away from you, it is a regular, and if toward you, a reverse (see Fig. 10-43).

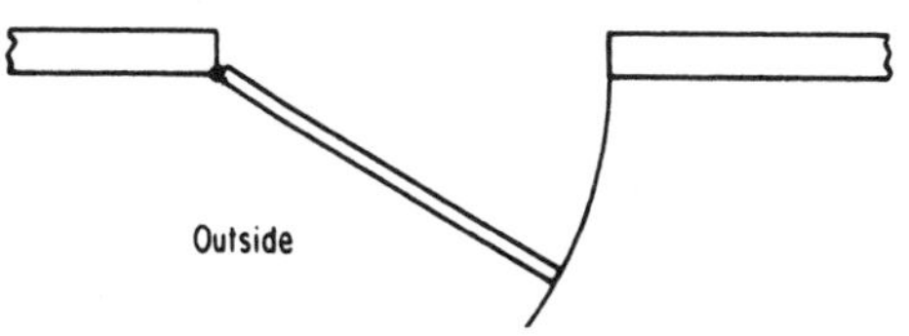

FIGURE 10-43 Left-hand reverse door.

Sliding and Folding Doors

In addition to conventional hinged doors, a number of other types are commonly used in modern construction. They include *pocket-type sliding* doors, *bypass sliding* doors, and *folding* doors.

Pocket-type Sliding Door. This type of door is considered to be a space saver, because it opens by sliding into an opening in the partition. During the framing stage an opening is framed twice the door width with allowance for jamb plus clearance—$1\frac{1}{2}$ in. (38 mm). The height of the opening will be equal to the door height plus room for the track at the top—2 in. (50 mm) and finish floor plus underlay and clearance at the bottom. The size of the opening can vary depending on the type of hardware used and is usually included in the installation instructions (see Figs. 10-44 and 10-45).

FIGURE 10-44 Pocket door rough opening.

FIGURE 10-45 Pocket door recess using metal reinforced framing.

The door frame consists of one solid and one split side jamb and a split head jamb. The track is an extruded aluminum product, and the rollers are usually nylon for longer wear and silent operation (see Fig. 10-46). The rollers are secured to the top of the door, mounted such that they are in the center of the door, and can be adjusted to ensure the door properly fits the opening. A recessed pull is installed on the face of the door.

Bypass-type Sliding Doors. Two doors sliding past one another in an opening are used in this case, so that only half the width of the opening can be utilized at a time. A standard type of doorframe may be used, with a head jamb long enough to accommodate two doors. The track may be mounted on the underside of the head jamb (see Fig. 10-47), or a split head jamb may be used to recess the track to permit the door to ride flush with the underside of the jamb (see Fig. 10-48).

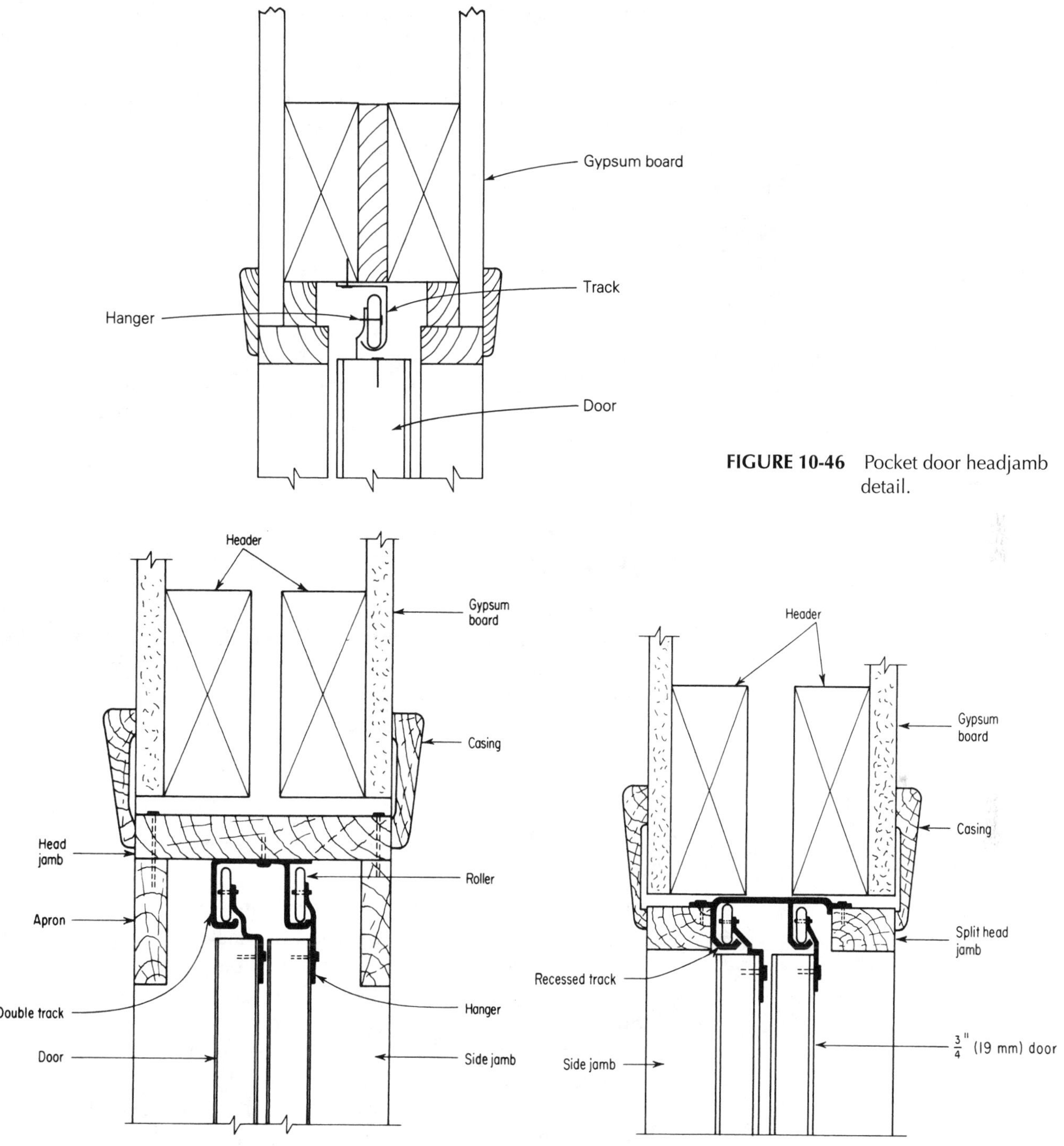

FIGURE 10-46 Pocket door headjamb detail.

FIGURE 10-47 Track mounted on underside of jamb.

FIGURE 10-48 Recessed track for sliding doors.

Nylon rollers are secured to the back of the doors, and offset, so the brackets are not visible from the front, as shown in Figs. 10-47 and 10-48. Recessed pulls are installed on opposite sides of the doors.

Folding Doors. A folding door unit (*bi-fold door*) consists of a pair of doors hinged together at the center with one door pivoted top and bottom at the outer edge. A track is mounted at the top of the open-

FIGURE 10-49 Folding door pivot bracket in track.

ing, and the second door is guided along the track with a special pivot bracket (see Fig. 10-49). One set of two doors or two sets of two doors each is a common enclosure for closets. The pivots fit into *pivot brackets*, which are adjustable to provide the proper clearance between the edge of the door and the finish opening. The pivot is also adjustable to raise or lower the door to set clearance at the top. The doors are manufactured to provide the required clearance, such as a 48-in. (1220-mm) wide door will fit into a 48-in. (1220-mm) finished opening, and the doors will fit in a standard finished opening height of 80 in. (2032 mm). The hinges joining pairs of doors together and the track guiding the pivot bracket as the door is opened or closed provide the folding action.

Accordion-type folding doors consisting of metal, vinyl, or wooden slats joined with vinyl hinges finished to simulate various wood or fabric finishes are also used and are available in a variety of door widths.

INTERIOR TRIM

Most windows and exterior doors used in construction come to the job as a complete unit—frames with outside casing attached and sash, glass, or doors already installed. All that is normally required is that the frames be *trimmed* on the inside. Interior finish between walls and floors, and the joints between walls and ceilings are placed as required.

Window Trim

Windows are usually cased on all four sides with natural wood or pre-finished moldings made of wood or plastic. *Casing* is the edging trim used around window and door openings. Many standard patterns in various widths and thicknesses are obtainable. When window casing is used, apply the bottom casing first, mitered on both ends, then proceed with the side casings and the top. The casing should be set back from the inside edge of the frame a distance of $\frac{1}{8}$ in. (3 mm), and all mitered connections should be glued because a glued joint is less likely to open when slight shrinkage occurs. Wood casings are stapled or nailed to both the framing studs and the jambs with staples or finishing nails. Fasteners should be spaced about 16 in. (400 mm) apart and should be countersunk and filled. A good job of fastening plastic moldings is not possible unless they are glued. Some windows are trimmed without the use of casing, where a paper-backed metal angle is set into a pre-cut saw kerf in the jamb (see Fig. 10-50) when a drywall finish is applied.

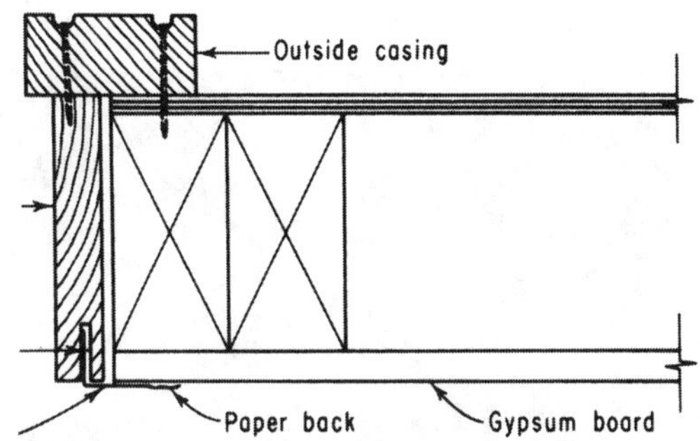

FIGURE 10-50 Opening trimmed with metal angle.

Door Trim

Casings are applied to both sides of interior doors to cover the space between the frame and the wall, to secure the frames to the wall, and to hold the jambs in a rigid position. They must therefore be nailed, stapled, or glued to both the jambs and the wall frame. The procedure is as follows:

1. Set the side casings in place, with its inner edge set $\frac{1}{8}$ in. (3 mm) back from the inside edge of the jamb. Raise the casing up enough to allow the finish floor to fit under the end of the casing [$\frac{1}{8}$ in. (3 mm)]. Mark the top and then cut to the desired length using a miter saw.
2. Nail, staple, or glue the side casings into the proper location.
3. Fit the headpiece into place, using a small block plane to ensure a tight fit at the miter joints. Glue the corner miter joints prior to fastening the casing into place. Wood trim blocks are sometimes used at the corners to provide an alternate finish (see Fig. 10-51).
4. Sand the exterior corners where side and head casings meet, and set and fill fastener holes.

FIGURE 10-51 Trim blocks.

Base Trim

When the vinyl or wood floors have been laid and the doors trimmed, the base trim can be installed. For interior corners, rather than making a mitered joint, a better fit can be accomplished by coping one base trim to another one. To get a coping line, cut the base at a 45° angle and then cut the base along the corner of the cut as shown in Fig. 10-52(a). Once the cut has been made using a coping saw, the corner becomes a butt joint, as shown in Fig. 10-52(b).

Outside corners are mitered and glued together. In some cases, because the corners may not be perfectly framed at 90°, the joint may have to be adjusted using a block plane.

The base is raised $\frac{1}{2}$ in. (13 mm) above the floor in areas where carpet is to be placed. This allows the edge of the carpet to be pushed

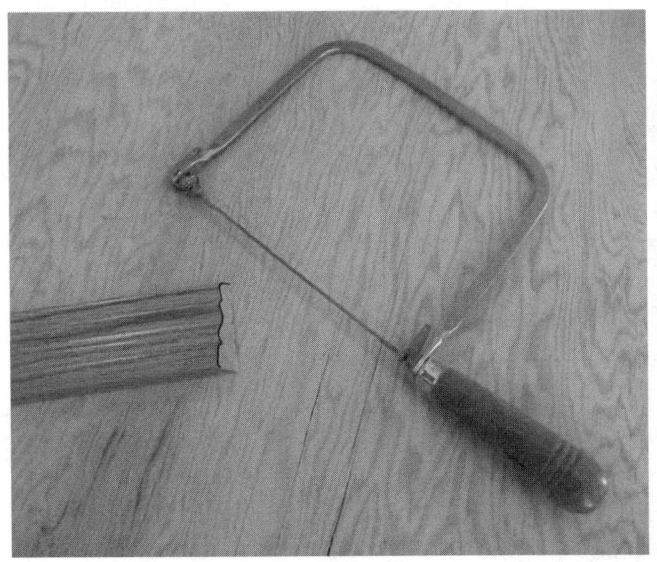

(a) Cutting a coped joint.

(b) Coped joint.

FIGURE 10-52

under the base and makes it much easier to remove the carpet when it must be replaced.

Sometimes, the base is further trimmed using a $\frac{1}{4}$-round as illustrated in Fig. 10-53.

FIGURE 10-53 Base with $\frac{1}{4}$-round.

CABINETWORK

Kitchen and bathroom cabinets, desks, shelving, mantels, and other millwork items are installed at the same time as the interior trim (see Fig. 10-54). Such items may be *custom-built* in a cabinet shop for specific installation, *mass-produced* in components in a millwork factory, or *built on the job*.

FIGURE 10-54 Kitchen cabinets.

Installing Mill or Factory-Built Cabinets

Most kitchen cabinets are built in a mill cabinet shop or in kitchen-cabinet manufacturing plants, and then installed by a skilled tradesperson following plans supplied by an architect or a kitchen-planning specialist. Most cupboards are built in modules varying from 12 to 36 in. (300–900 mm) in a variety of units. Base units vary from door to drawer units or a combination of both. Corner units are available with a rotating lazy susan, providing a good solution to the corner problem. Upper wall cabinets come in standard, over-appliance, and corner units. When modular cupboard units are installed, there are several basic procedures to be followed.

1. The base for all of the lower units is built first $3\frac{1}{2}$ to 4 in. (89–100 mm) high, usually out of $\frac{3}{4}$-in. (19-mm) material (see Fig. 10-55). Make sure the base is level by using shims as needed so as to eliminate future problems in fitting the cabinets together and against walls. The base is secured to both the floor and walls where available.

FIGURE 10-55 Base for cupboards.

2. To install base cabinets, first place the cabinets in their approximate locations as close as possible to the wall on the leveled base.
3. Start with the corner units fitting the units properly in place, finishing with a filler piece as needed to fit against the wall or against another corner unit in "U" shaped cupboards (see Fig. 10-56).

FIGURE 10-56 Installing base cabinets.
(Courtesy Merit Kitchens Ltd.)

FIGURE 10-57 Installing countertop.
(Courtesy Merit Kitchens Ltd.)

4. Once the base cabinets are properly fitted, they are bolted together and fastened to the wall with screws through the nailing strips into the studs. Shims are placed between the cupboard and the stud wherever spaces occur due to irregularities in the wall.
5. Some cupboards come with countertops already covered with plastic laminate, but this is not usually part of the cabinetry. The usual procedure is to fit a $\frac{3}{4}$-in. (19-mm) particleboard or plywood top on the base cabinets (see Fig. 10-57).
6. Prior to starting the installation of upper cabinets, first build supports on which cabinets can rest while being installed (see Fig. 10-58).
7. Place the cabinets in position, starting with the corner ones and fitting the units in place. Check to ensure that units are level and plumb. If the wall is uneven or out of plumb, put wood shims behind the cabinets and then fasten the units together and to the wall studs.
8. Finally finish the upper units with a filler piece, as needed, cut and fitted against a wall or other corner unit (see Fig. 10-59).

If plastic laminate is to be used as the countertop, it can be cut in many ways, either with a table saw or a handsaw. A small scoring tool, as illustrated in Fig. 10-60, is very useful because the surface need only be scored and then it is snapped upward with the face up. This method is especially good for irregular cuts, but the scoring must be deeper to ensure proper breakage. Special support of the laminate is not necessary because scoring works very effectively on a flat surface like the floor.

(a) Supporting upper cabinets. (Courtesy Merit Kitchens Ltd.)

(b) Wall support beveled to support cabinet.

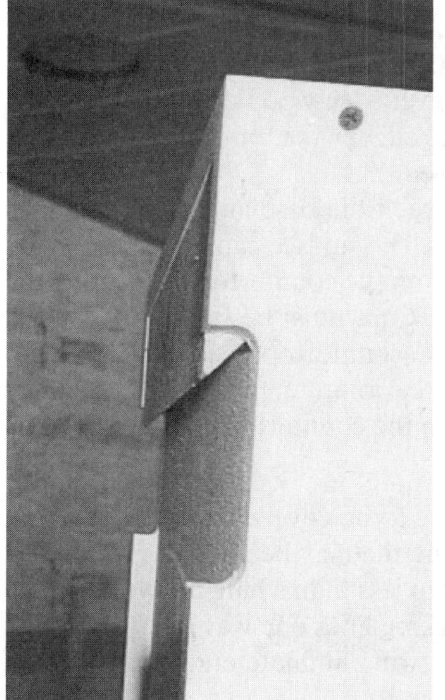

(c) Upper cabinet shaped to hang on support.

(d) Upper cabinet in position.

FIGURE 10-58

FIGURE 10-59 Filler piece.

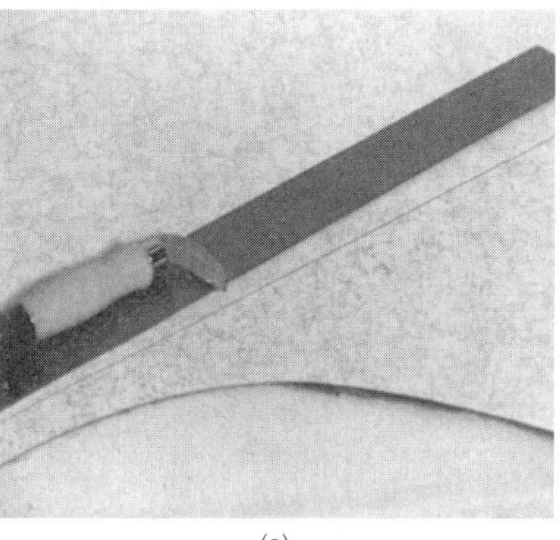

(a)

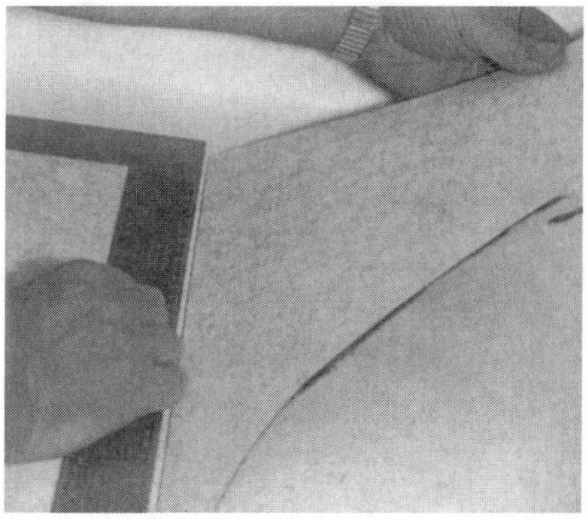

(b)

FIGURE 10-60 Cutting plastic linate.

Once the plastic laminate has been cut, it has to be fitted against the wall, or where necessary against a second section. Files and block planes can be used for this fitting. When ready, contact cement is used to bond the plastic laminate to the wood countertop, following the manufacturer's instructions. When the plastic laminate is to be placed, care must be taken to avoid contact before it has been properly positioned. Thin strips of wood or a wax-coated paper placed on the countertop will provide this separation, and can be slowly removed to allow full contact. Using a rubber roller on the surface or tapping a wood block on the surface with a hammer should ensure proper contact. The overhang can be removed with a laminate trimmer, or a router with a special cutter can be used (see Fig. 10-61). A flat file can also be used to trim the edge, always filing with a downward stroke at an angle to avoid damaging the top surface. Bevel edge wood or plastic laminate moldings are sometimes used on the edge of the top to provide a more decorative finish to the countertop edge.

FIGURE 10-61 Laminate trimmer.

The vertical wall surface between the base and upper cabinets can be finished in a variety of ways. The surface can be covered with the same plastic laminate as is used on the countertop, cementing the laminate directly to the wallboard. Care must be taken to ensure a tight joint at the connection with the countertop; a small bead of silicone is an effective way of sealing this joint.

Ceramic tile is often placed on the countertop and the wall surface and is set in the following way:

1. Lay out the tile on the surface to be covered, marking vertical and horizontal lines so that the tile may be aligned precisely. If the end tiles should work out to less than a half-tile width, move the vertical or horizontal working lines one way or the other by half the width of the tile. This will eliminate ending up with an unattractive narrow tile.
2. Most ceramic tile has tiny lug spacers along the four edges that automatically space the tile for grout lines. If the tile you use does not have this feature, you should use the small plastic spacers to establish the grout lines. (see Fig. 10-62).
3. Spread the tile mastic over the surface with a V-notched adhesive trowel. Usually for standard wall tile the notches are $\frac{3}{16}$ in.

FIGURE 10-62 Tile spacers.

deep. Work in small areas at a time, so you don't lose track of your guidelines on the wall.

4. Starting at the countertop set the tiles in place, avoiding sliding because that will cause the mastic to come up in the spaces to be grouted. Every few tiles, tap the tiles with a hammer and a block of plywood to ensure tiles are well set. As you work, add spacers (if the tiles are not pre-spaced as previously mentioned). The partial tiles in corners or at the edge are cut with a tile cutter prior to placement. Clean off any adhesive from the tile surface.
5. Once the mastic has set, the surface is ready for grouting. The grout is spread with a rubber float or grout spreader over the tiles in a diagonal direction, preventing the grout from being drawn out of the joints and forcing it well into the joints. Once the joints are full, smooth the joints with a grout-smoothing tool. When the grout has set (as per the manufacturer's instructions), clean the haze from the surface with a cleaner as recommended by the grout manufacturer.
6. Apply a grout sealer to the grout once it is fully set and apply a bead of silicone along the joint between the countertop and wall tiles.

Sinks

One important item in cabinet building is the installation of a sink. It is common practice to wait until the finished countertop surface has been installed before installing the sink. Kitchen sinks are available in several materials, ranging from stainless and porcelainized steel to cultured marble and to acrylic sinks.

If a plastic laminate countertop is used, the first step in the installation is to trace the shape of the sink using the template supplied with most sinks and cut the appropriate hole for the sink. Most sinks sit on top of the countertop; so the hole must be at least $\frac{1}{4}$ in. (6 mm) smaller on all sides than the sink lip to provide adequate support. A bead of caulking compound should run all around the edge of the hole under the lip of the sink to ensure a water-tight fit. The sink is then placed in the opening and secured to the countertop from the underside, as illustrated in Fig. 10-63.

If ceramic tile is to be used on the countertop, the hole for the sink must first be cut and the tile fitted around the hole.

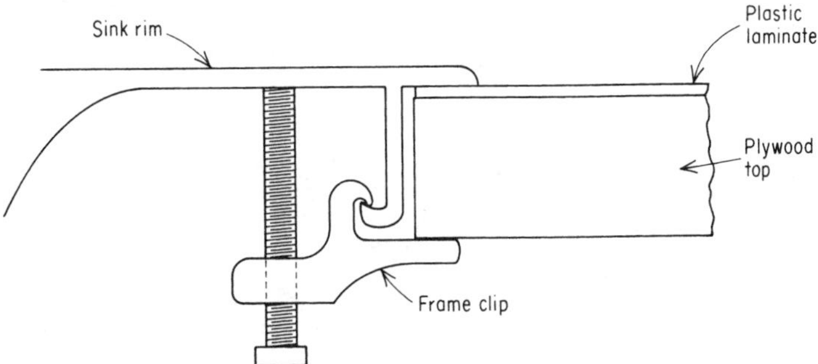

FIGURE 10-63 Securing sink with brackets.

REVIEW QUESTIONS

10–1. a. Where in a frame wall is an *air barrier* located?

b. What are three materials that can be used as an air barrier?

10–2. a. What are three ways to fasten gypsum board to a frame wall?

b. Why is drywall applied to the ceiling before the walls?

c. Why are the joints between the long edges of drywall easier to fill with joint filler than the end-joints?

10–3. List four forms of insulation used to prevent heat loss or gain.

10–4. What material is suitable for a backer board in a shower stall?

10–5. What is the difference between an air barrier and a vapor barrier?

10–6. Why is a silicone bead installed between the vertical and horizontal corners of a tiled shower tall?

10–7. How are $\frac{3}{4}$-in. (19-mm) vertical wood boards secured to a wall as an interior finish?

10–8. Explain what is meant by a *laminated drywall finish.*

10–9. Illustrate three methods of treating joints between sheets of plywood used as interior finish.

10–10. Explain how the pre-expanding of hardboards is carried out.

10–11. a. List four species of hardwood flooring in common use.

b. Why is the bottom surface of hardwood flooring strips concave?

c. Why is a $\frac{1}{4}$-in. (6-mm) space left between hardwood flooring and the wall?

d. What is "blind" nailing?

10–12. What is the basic difference between a mortise lock and a cylindrical lock?

10–13. a. Where is the strike plate located?

b. What is the normal height of a doorknob from the floor?

c. What is a hinge *gain?*

10–14. a. How is the hand of a door determined?

b. If a door from the outside swings toward you, with the hinges on the left-hand side, it is a __________ door.

10–15. When a flat doorjamb is installed, when should you install the doorstop?

10–16. Approximately how much space should be allowed between a door and the jamb?

10–17. What is a pocket door?

10–18. What is a bi-fold door?

10–19. What is a *coped* joint in base trim?

10–20. What is the recommended height of the base of a kitchen cabinet?

10–21. Why is it important that the base for cabinets is installed level?

10–22. When should you cut the hole for a sink to be mounted on a plastic laminate countertop?

Chapter 11

ENERGY-EFFICIENT HOUSING

OBJECTIVES

Here is what you will be able to do when you complete each component of this chapter:

1. Identify reasons for energy-efficient housing.
2. Describe special considerations for foundations.
3. Describe special considerations for floors, walls, ceilings, and roofs.
4. Identify the principles of solar gain options.
5. Identify how buildings are evaluated for heat loss.

Housing in cooler regions has undergone a significant change due to the ever-increasing concern with saving energy. The cost of fuel continues to rise dramatically and this results in additional cost to homeowners to keep dwellings comfortable. Clearly the construction of houses that are as energy-efficient as possible makes good long-term common sense. These houses are likely to be here for many years, and as costs will likely rise in the future, efficient construction is going to be continually more important.

Increasing the thickness of the insulation and being more careful with the placement of the vapor barrier was used to upgrade typical construction. Insulation of the foundation and the outside of the wall frame followed, resulting in more efficient housing. However, better design and construction technology has brought forth a new breed of highly efficient houses. These houses are described by such terms as "super-energy-efficient" or "super-insulated." Energy-efficient housing does not dwell exclusively on cutting heat losses. Heat gains are augmented where possible through an effort to increase *passive solar gain.*

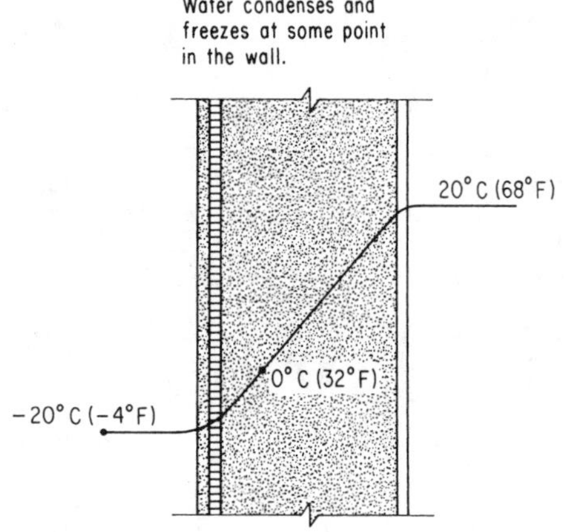

FIGURE 11-1 Condensation in walls.

The increase of methods used to reduce heat loss should not take place without an understanding of the possible problems associated with moisture in buildings. In a typical house airborn moisture generated through normal activity escapes to the outside through flues and chimneys and by seeping out through cracks and holes. Water vapor also escapes by diffusing through building materials. Moisture escaping through cracks and holes and by diffusing through materials does not disappear without a trace. As air and moisture pass through the structure from the heated interior, air is cooled, thus reducing its ability to hold moisture. This cooling may result in condensation within the walls or the attic of the house (see Fig. 11-1). Water condensation in the wall can cause a loss in insulation effectiveness and increase degradation of materials.

In older houses, a vapor barrier was normally installed to prevent moisture damage. Vapor barriers do reduce the moisture loss through materials but do very little to control condensation associated with air leakage. Conventional houses are so leaky that the inside air tends to be dry, and less condensation will take place. Energy-efficient housing is more vulnerable to condensation problems as it does not benefit from this air movement. Careful control is necessary to effectively seal moisture inside the house. The installation of an air barrier will prevent air leakage into the shell.

Since energy-efficient houses are built to be as airtight as possible, it is critical that the indoor air quality is regulated. A fresh air supply must be provided to maintain good-quality air. Also, the provision of controlled ventilation is needed to replace stale air. Stale air must be exhausted through one vent, and fresh air must be drawn through another vent. Heat loss must be minimized by maintaining the minimum acceptable rate and by incorporating a heat exchanger to recover heat from the exhaust air (see Fig. 11-2).

FOUNDATIONS

Foundations to be considered in this section will include *slabs-on-grade, crawl spaces,* and *basements.* These foundation types can be insulated from the interior of the building or the exterior, each requiring special considerations.

Slabs-on-Grade

In this type of foundation, the concrete slab can be the combined foundation and finish floor (see Fig. 11-3), or the slab can be isolated from the load-bearing foundation wall (see Fig. 11-4).

Rigid polystyrene insulation is used below the slab to lower floor heat loss. Perimeter insulation is also used at the edge of the floor slab to reduce heat loss. Polyethylene is placed under the floor slab and is sealed to the wall air-vapor barrier (see Fig. 11-3). Protection in the form of parging or preserved plywood (if allowed) should

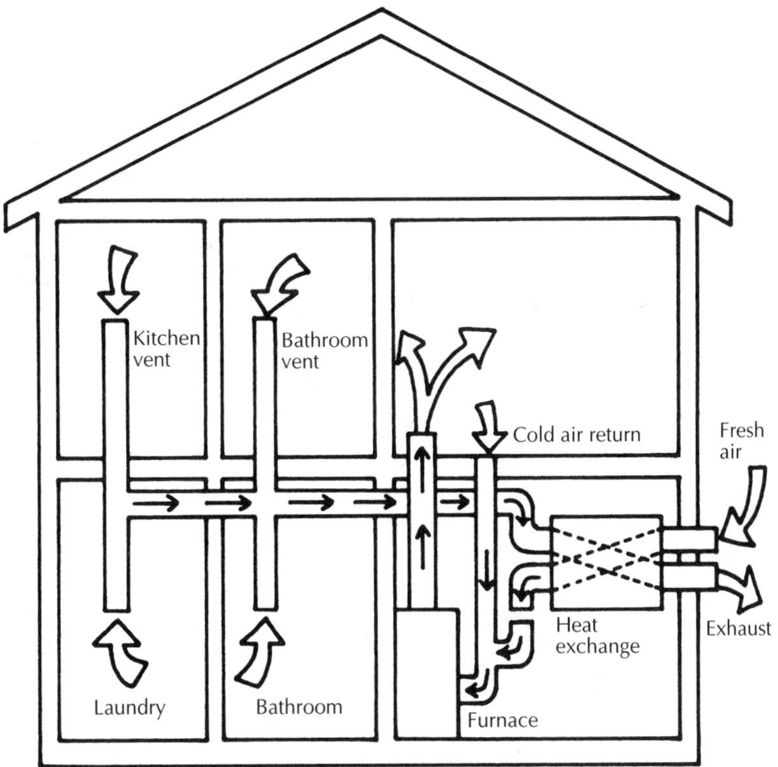

FIGURE 11-2 Air-to-air heat exchanger.

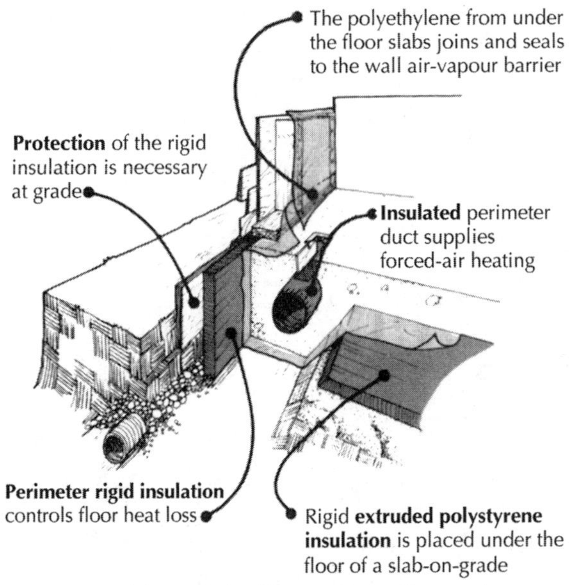

(a) Slab-on-grade. (Courtesy Home Community Design Branch, Alberta Agriculture)

(b) Perimeter insulation at edge of floor slab.

FIGURE 11-3

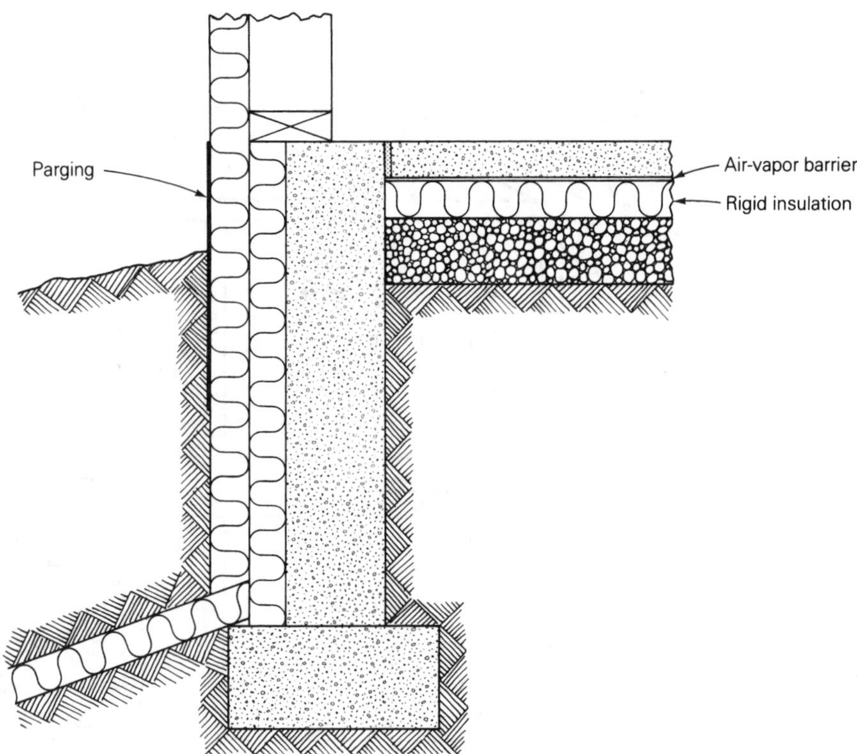

FIGURE 11-4 Independent slab and perimeter foundation.

be placed over the insulation around the perimeter. Even foundation walls that are separated from the slab on grade allow for extra load-bearing capacity because the footing under the wall carries the load. This system is also less susceptible to frost action because the foundation can be extended to the frost line. Even though slabs-on-grade are usually insulated on the outside of the foundation, insulation is placed on the inside in some cases (see Fig. 11-5).

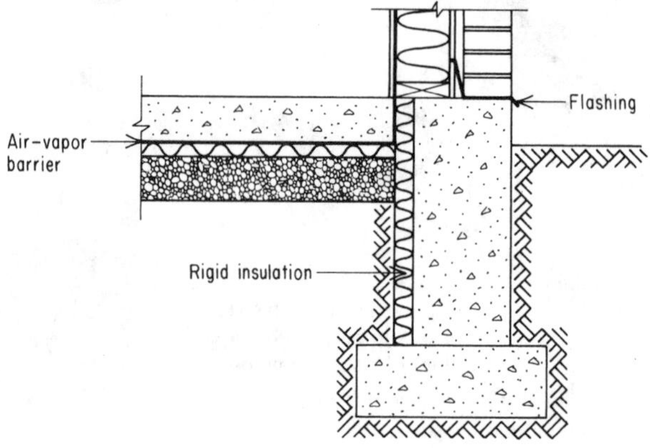

FIGURE 11-5 Slab-on-grade (interior insulation).

Crawl Spaces

In a crawl space foundation, the main concerns are to provide insulation in the right places and to protect the crawl space from moisture build-up. This space is often used for mechanical services; so insulation is needed to keep the temperature above freezing. If this space is heated, insulation is needed on the exterior walls and under the floor slab. The walls may be insulated on the inside or the outside. A moisture barrier is placed between the floor slab and the under-slab insulation. Unheated crawl spaces must be ventilated by openings with a cumulative area of at least 1 ft^2 for every 500 ft^2 (0.1 m^2 for every 50 m^2) of floor area with the main insulation provided between the floor joists. R (RSI) values should equal or exceed those indicated in Table 11-1. When batt insulation is used, it should be supported from underneath with particleboard or with wire mesh of small enough size to prevent the entry of rodents. All ductwork and plumbing in an unheated space is wrapped with insulation of the same R (RSI) value as used between the floor joists. A moisture barrier, usually covered by a layer of sand, is placed over the ground surface to keep the space dry (see Fig. 11-6).

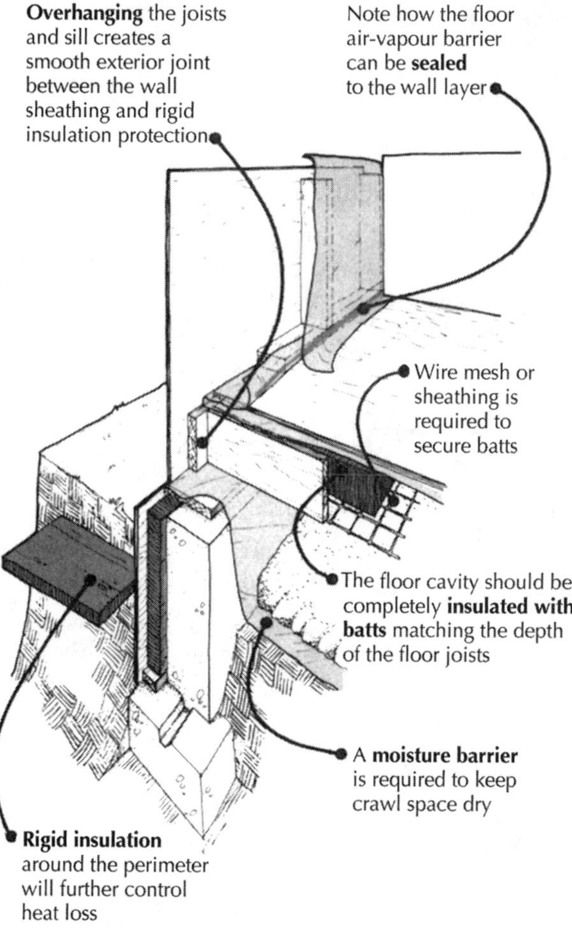

FIGURE 11-6 Crawl space construction.
(Courtesy Alberta Agriculture)

TABLE 11-1: Appropriate energy—efficient insulation levels

	R value	*R SI (metric)*
Ceilings	40–60	7–11
Walls	20–40	3.5–7
Foundation walls (50% or more below grade)	12–20	2–3.5
Floors over crawl spaces	30–40	5–7
Slabs-on-grade	10	1.8
Basement floors	10	1.8

Basements

Preserved wood and concrete are the two main types of basements used, although concrete block is popular in some areas. Wood foundation walls can be economical and easy to insulate but are not allowed in some areas. The spaces between the studs provide an ideal place for friction-fit batt insulation. An air-vapor barrier covers the insulation on the inside (see Fig. 11-7). The polyethylene from under the floor is sealed to the wall vapor barrier (see Fig. 11-8). Two types of basement floors used in wood basements are illustrated in Fig. 11-8.

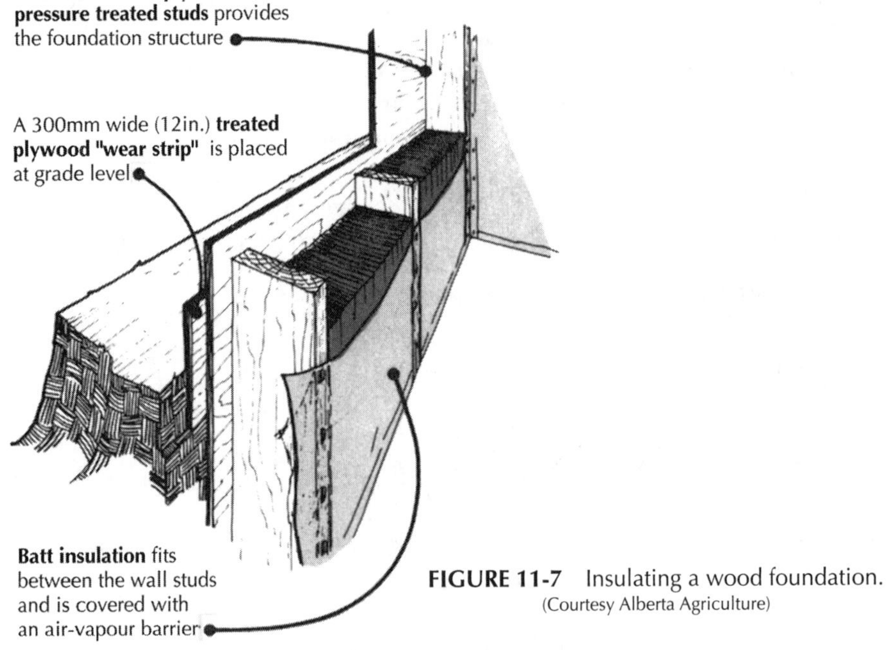

FIGURE 11-7 Insulating a wood foundation. (Courtesy Alberta Agriculture)

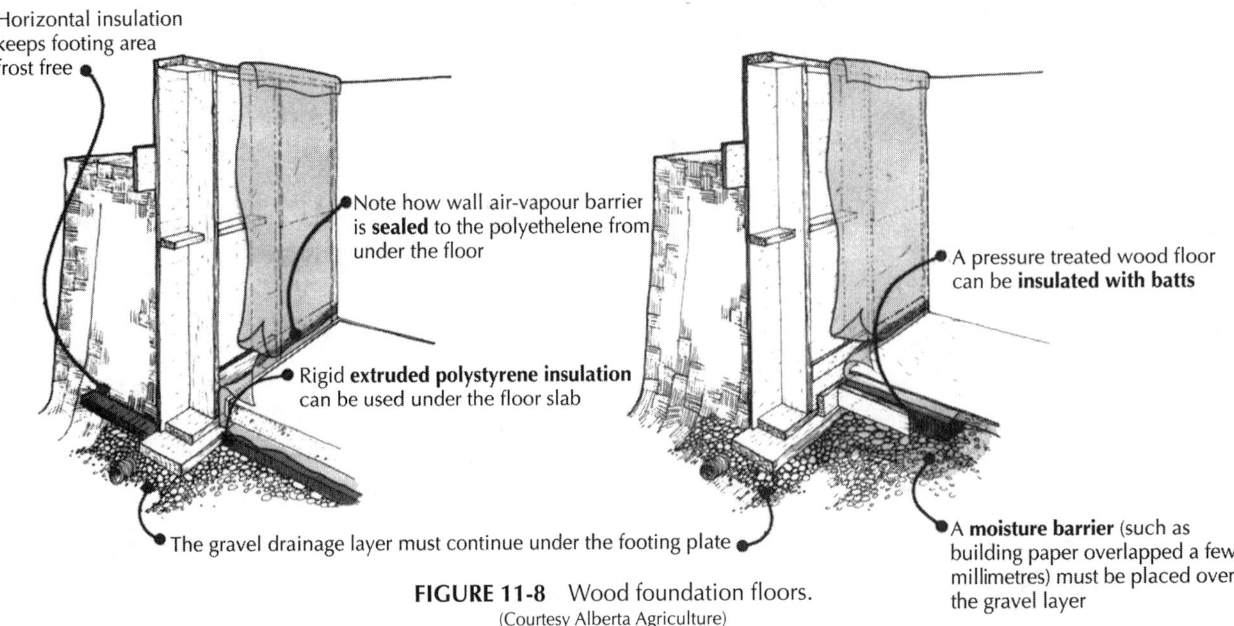

FIGURE 11-8 Wood foundation floors. (Courtesy Alberta Agriculture)

The best place for insulation in a concrete basement is on the outside. The foundation is then less susceptible to frost damage and leaking. The foundation wall is inside the insulation, and so its large thermal mass acts as a vehicle for heat storage. The exterior insulation can be continued up the wall, making an effective blanket. The polyethylene is placed on the inside of the concrete wall and sealed at the bottom to the poly from under the floor and at the top to the polyethylene around the header. Insulation and a vapor barrier are placed under the floor to provide a warm dry floor (see Fig. 11-9).

Most masonry and many concrete walls will be insulated from the inside, as illustrated in Fig. 11-10. A moisture barrier must be placed against the concrete wall from floor level up to the grade (see Fig. 11-10). This will protect the building materials from moisture migration.

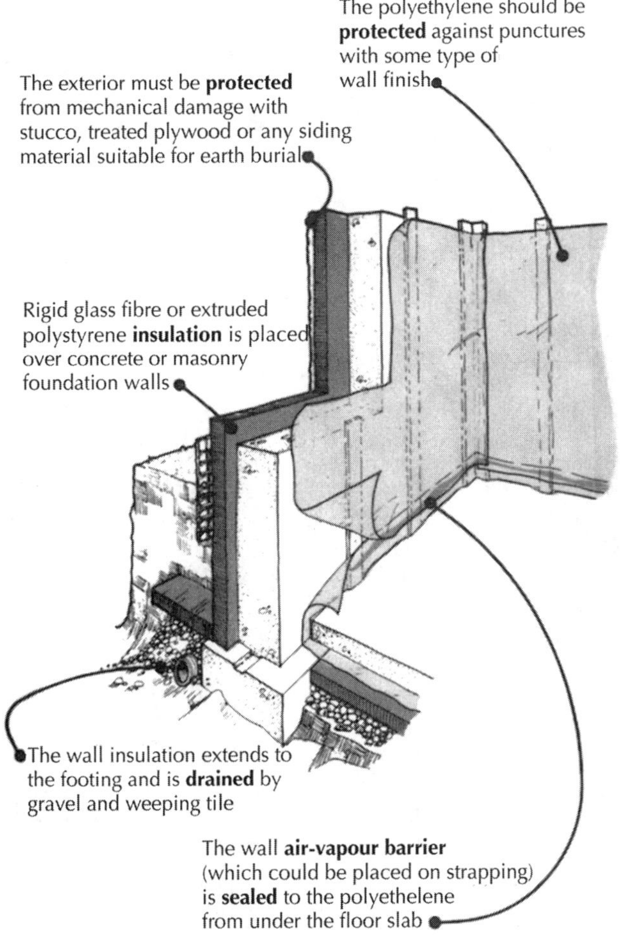

FIGURE 11-9 Foundation wall insulated on outside. (Courtesy Alberta Agriculture)

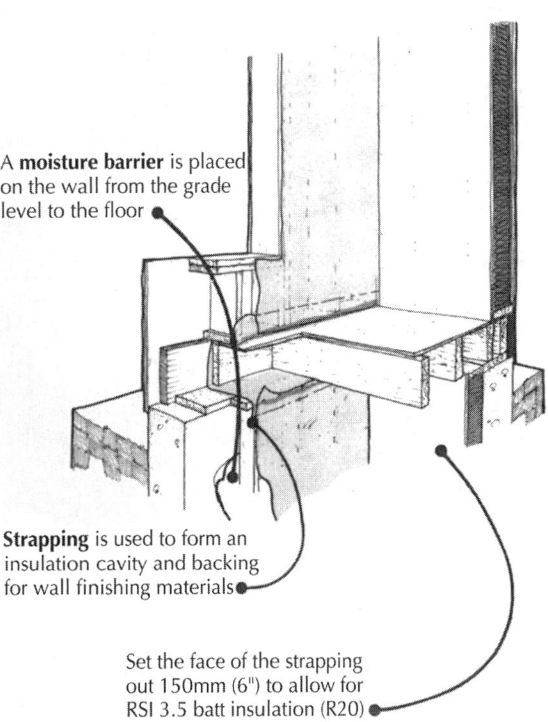

FIGURE 11-10 Foundation wall insulated on inside.

FLOOR FRAME

The floor frame is a major point of heat loss, as it is more difficult to insulate and still have a continuous air-vapor barrier at this point (see Fig. 11-11). A strip of polyethylene must be installed around the joist header during framing. The polyethylene must be under the floor frame and over the foundation wall sealed to the basement wall polyethylene. The upper edge will extend under the wall plate and be sealed to the wall vapor barrier. Two layers of insulation are placed outside the header to give it sufficient *"R" value.* To make a better connection, the bottom wall plate should be narrower to allow room for the insulation to cover the outside (see Fig. 11-12).

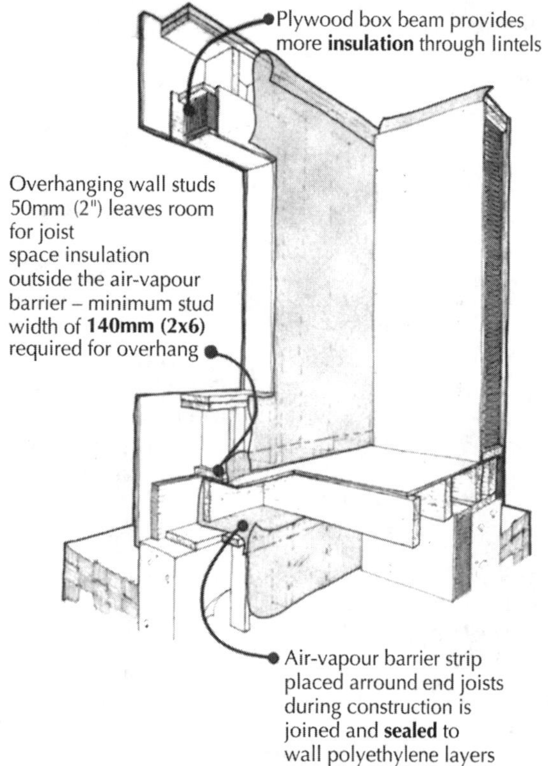

FIGURE 11-11 Placement of vapor barrier around header.
(Courtesy Alberta Agriculture)

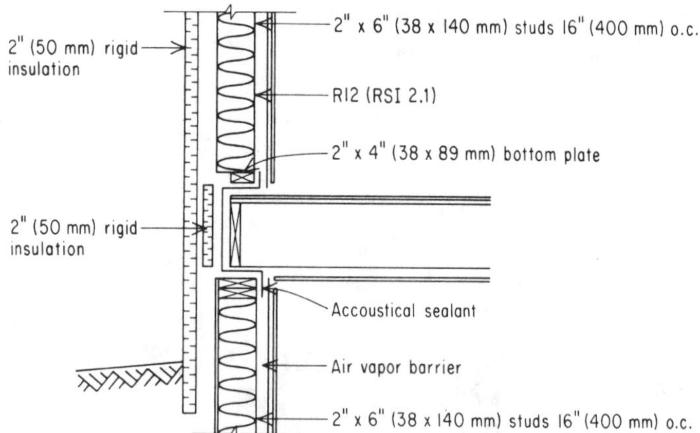

FIGURE 11-12 Insulating floor system header.

Cantilevered floor projections create a special problem. Although they provide for additional floor space, they create problems in providing a continuous vapor barrier. Figure 11-13 illustrates a method using polystyrene insulation between the floor joists as a vapor barrier. Even with sealing around these pieces, the floor joists still pierce the vapor barrier.

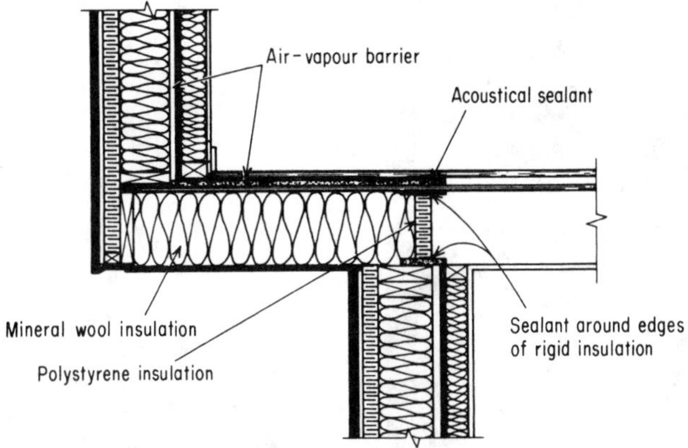

FIGURE 11-13 Cantilevered floor.

WALL FRAME

Traditional wall construction seriously restricts the level of energy efficiency that can be achieved. A number of variations in design have been developed to increase the efficiency of walls. The typical single-stud walls have been increased in thickness to accommodate additional insulation by using larger studs and more effectively by strapping the inside of the studs. This strapping allows a place for the installation of electrical wires without interfering with the vapor barrier, as the barrier is placed between the strapping and the studs (see Fig. 11-15). Double-stud walls are very effective in increasing the energy efficiency of walls (see Fig. 11-16).

Single-Stud Walls

The use of single-stud walls is the most common form of construction. The size of the stud has been commonly increased to 2 × 6 (38 × 140 mm) to be able to increase "R" values (RSI values) in the cavity (see Fig. 11-11). The walls are often offset over the edge of the floor frame to allow for a layer of insulation on the outside of the joist header. In an effort to provide additional insulation and to cut down on the thermal bridges (studs) in the wall, a rigid insulation is added to the outside of the sheathing (see Fig. 11-14).

Probably the most effective way of increasing the efficiency of this wall is to strap the inside of the wall with 2 × 3's (38 × 64 mm) at right angles to the wall studs after the insulation and air-vapor barrier have been applied to the exterior wall (see Fig. 11-15). This provides a convenient space for electrical wires and some plumbing vents so the barrier is not punctured. Two-thirds of the insulation value should be outside the vapor barrier.

(a) Rigid insulation over plywood sheathing.

(b) Single-stud wall with exterior application of rigid insulation.

FIGURE 11-14

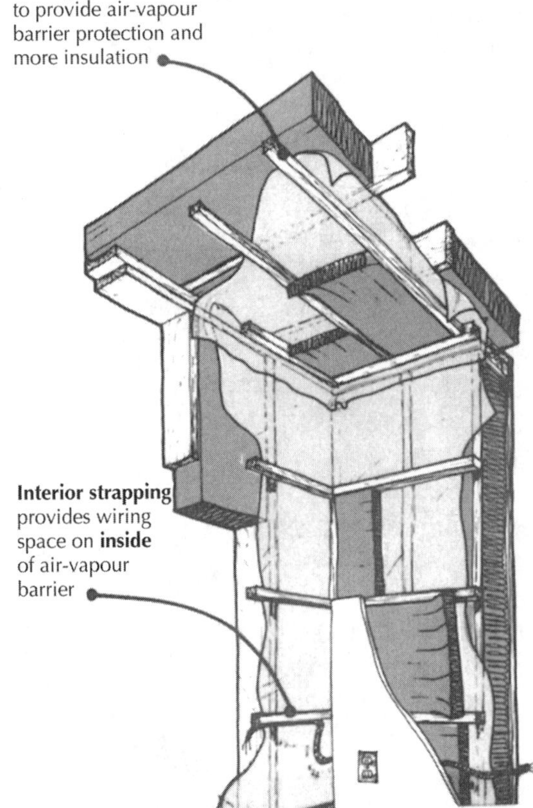

FIGURE 11-15 Interior wall strapping on single-stud wall. (Courtesy Alberta Agriculture)

Double-Stud Walls

Double-stud walls include two frame walls with a space between them. These walls can be built to almost any thickness to achieve very high insulation values. The air-vapor barrier can be easily isolated in a protected position in the wall assembly (see Fig. 11-16).

The inside wall is the structural wall and includes lintels, double plates, and sheathing. The vapor barrier is placed under the outside sheathing on the outside of this wall. The outside wall is placed out

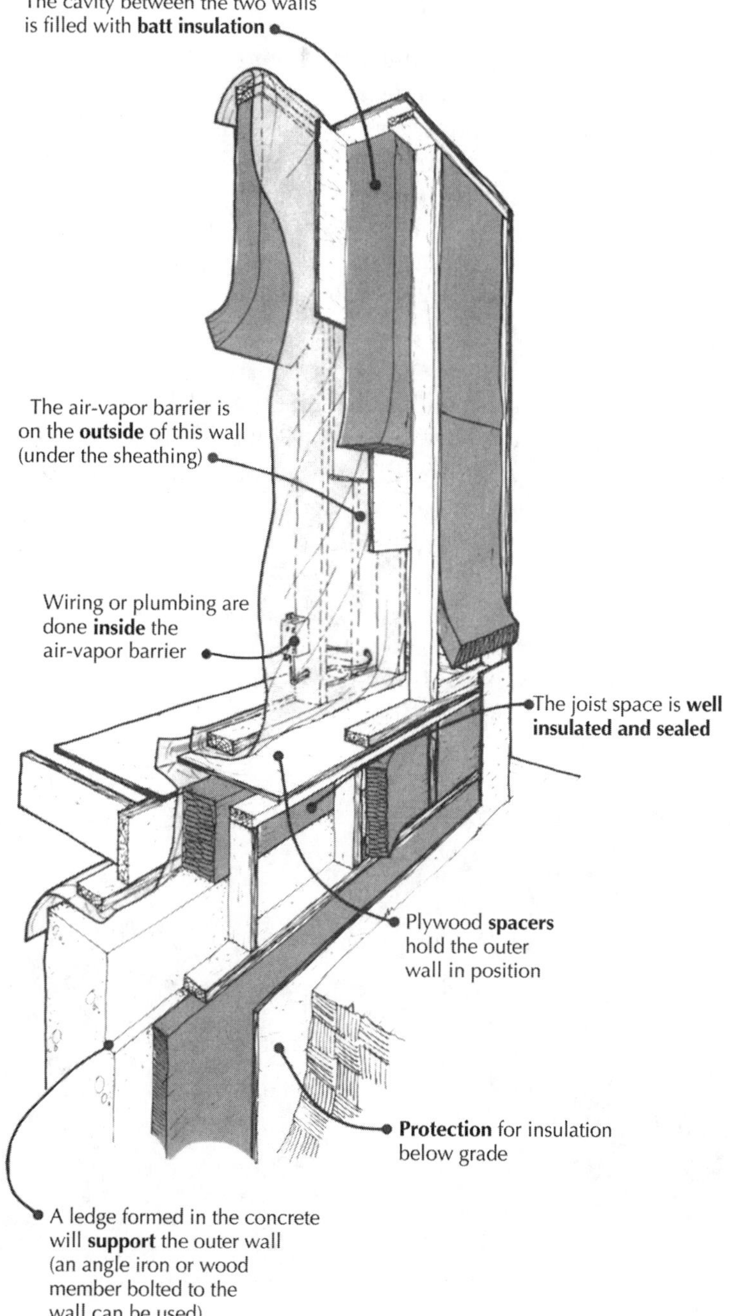

FIGURE 11-16 Double wall. (Courtesy Alberta Agriculture)

from the structural wall, and it provides support for the exterior finishing material. Plywood spacers [$\frac{1}{2}$ in. (12.5 mm) thick], top and bottom, can be used to position the exterior wall (see Fig. 11-16). The vapor barrier flaps at the top and bottom of the structural wall are stapled to the inside of the plates to limit damage and to provide for easy sealing with polyethylene from the floor frame and the attic. This air-vapor barrier is usually 6 mil (150μm) and is sealed with an acoustical sealant.

FIGURE 11-17 Polystyrene lintels and panels.

Modular Wall System

Some manufacturers produce modular energy-efficient systems. One on the market is a system using solid polystyrene panels. Chemically bonded within the panel are wood studs or structural steel tubing (see Fig. 11-17). The panels are lightweight and easy to handle, allowing for speedy assembly. Special lintels are provided over window and door openings (see Fig. 11-17). Figure 11-18 illustrates the use of polystyrene panels in residential construction.

Air-Vapor Barrier

The air-vapor barrier in an energy-efficient house must be installed in such a way as to provide a nearly completely sealed building envelope. It must be sealed with an acoustical sealant to provide a long-lasting seal. An acoustical sealant does not harden or form a skin and is used for sealing polyethylene. The air-vapor barrier controls air leakage and prevents vapor movement. To ensure an effective seal, all joints between the polyethylene must be made on a wood backing. The first layer is stapled to the framing member, a continuous bead of sealant is placed, and the second sheet is placed over the first and stapled (see Fig. 11-19).

(a) Panels in place.

(b) Sealing edge of panel.

FIGURE 11-18

(c) Completed modular system.

FIGURE 11-18 (cont.)

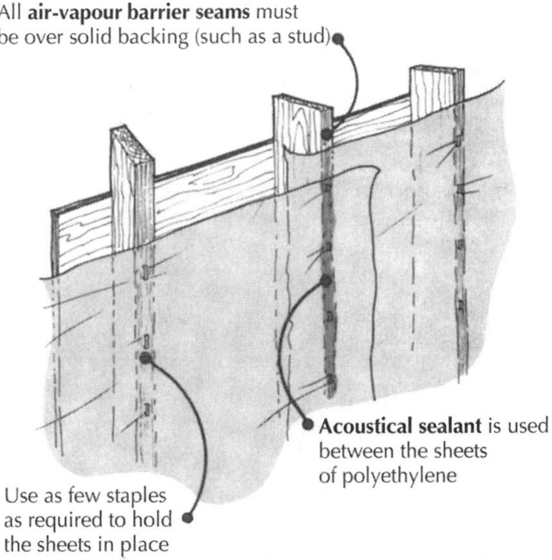

FIGURE 11-19 Joining air-vapor barrier layers.

Special consideration is needed to seal the air-vapor barrier at obstructions. To achieve a continuous envelope at partition walls in single-stud walls, a piece of polyethylene is placed behind the end stud and then sealed to the vapor barrier (see Fig. 11-20). At plumbing pipe openings plywood backing is installed and sealed to the vapor barrier (see Fig. 11-21). Around electrical outlets a *vapor barrier pan*

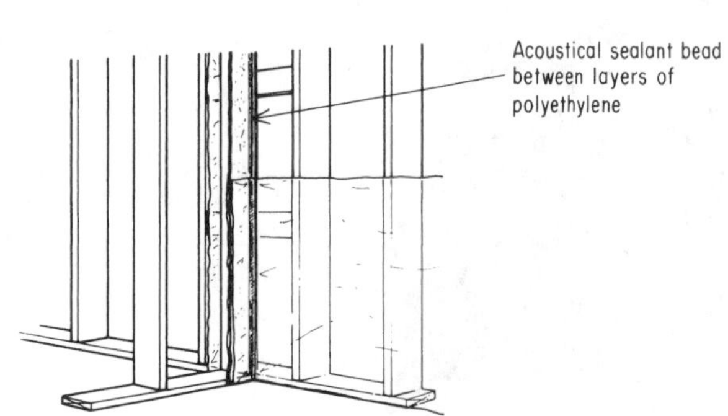

FIGURE 11-20 Sealing air-vapor barrier at partition.

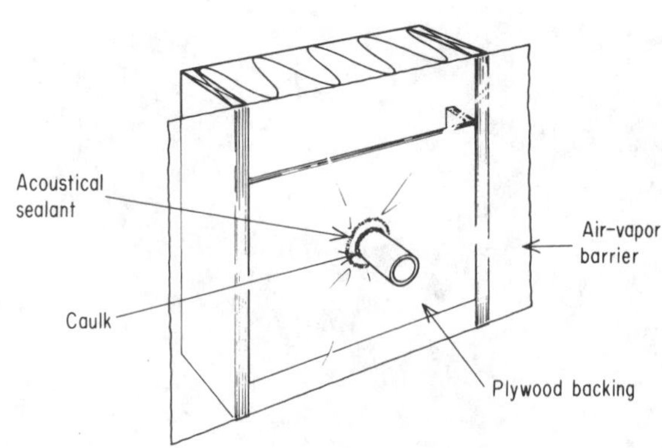

FIGURE 11-21 Sealing plumbing pipe.

can be used to achieve a seal (see Fig. 11-22). Placing a piece of polyethylene around the box before installation and then sealing to the vapor barrier can be quite effective (see Fig. 11-23).

Windows and doors also need special consideration. To achieve an energy-efficient building, energy-efficient windows and doors must be used. Casement, awning, and hopper windows are good performers. Metal insulated doors are good as they do not warp easily, and so a good seal is maintained. Figure 11-24 illustrates an effective method of achieving a good vapor barrier seal around openings. Double or triple glazing provides some resistance to heat loss, increasing R (RSI) values from 0.85 to 2.16 (0.15–0.38). Increasing the spacing between panes can also have a positive effect. The use of low-emissivity coatings to the glass will reduce radiant heat loss. Thermal shades are added to the outside to cut heat loss (see Fig. 11-25).

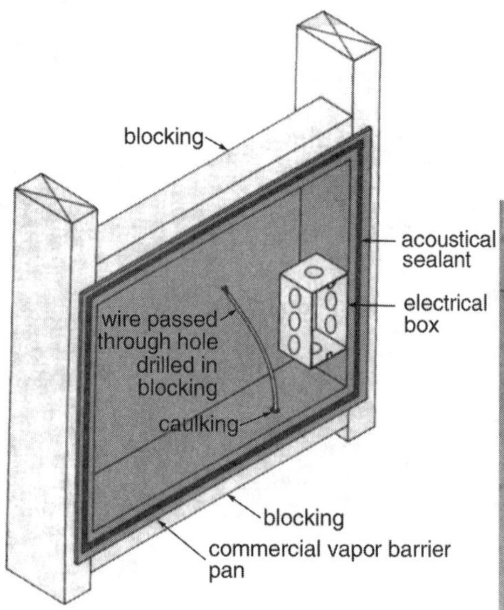

(a) Vapor barrier around electrical box.

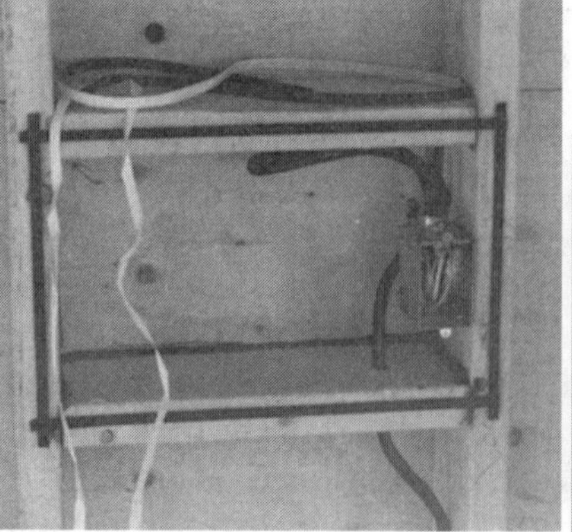

(b) Sealing around an electrical box.

(c) Commercial vapor-barrier pan.

FIGURE 11-22

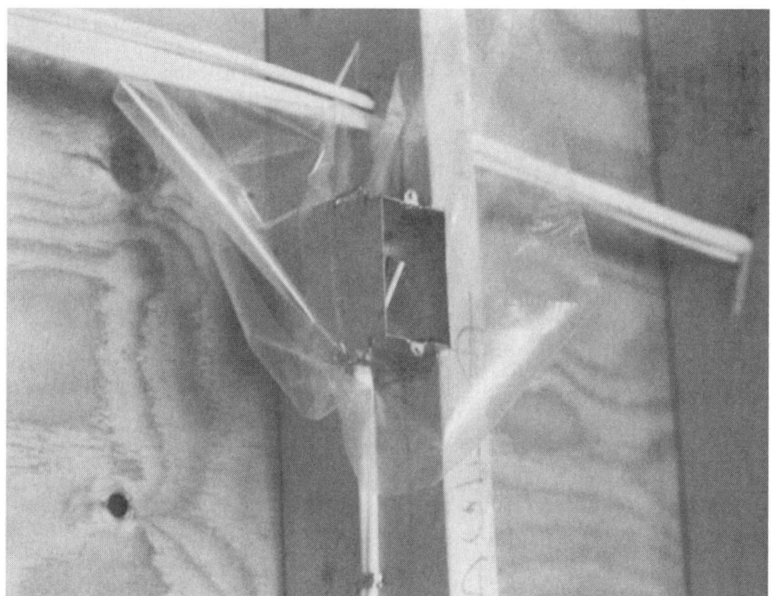

FIGURE 11-23 Vapor barrier behind box.

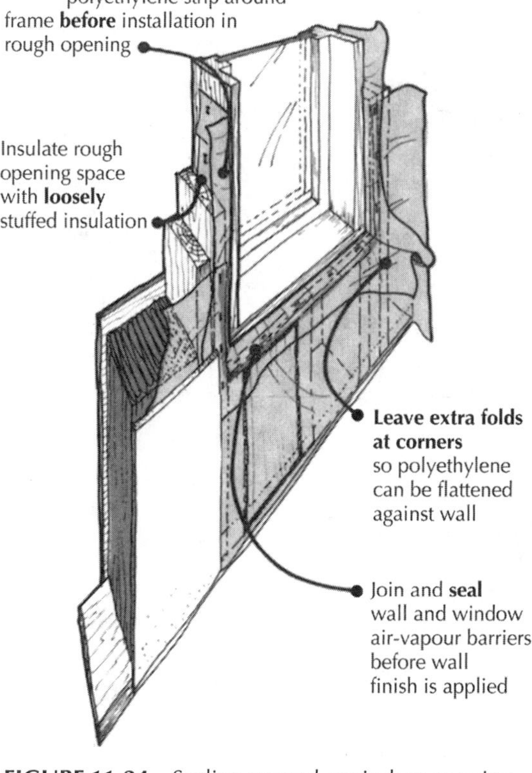

FIGURE 11-24 Sealing around a window opening.

FIGURE 11-25 Window shades.

CEILINGS AND ROOFS

Most houses have sloped roofs with interior ceilings either flat or sloped. A complete, well-sealed air-vapor barrier is essential but, because of light fixtures, chimneys, plumbing vents, and attic access, is difficult to install. Strapping the ceiling in a manner similar to walls, allowing room for wires, as illustrated in Fig. 11-26, can help.

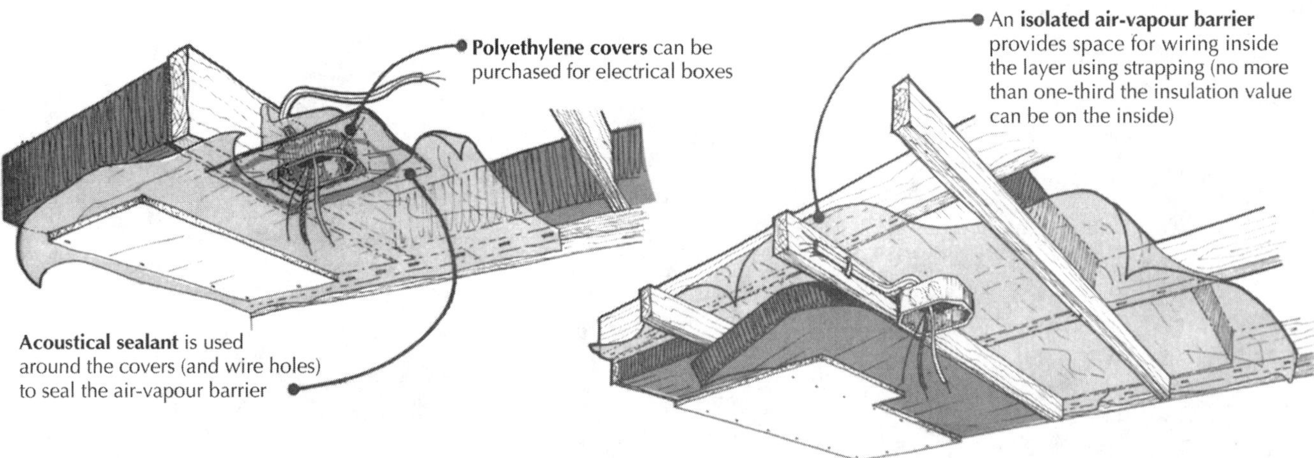

FIGURE 11-26 Sealing vapor barrier and strapping ceiling.
(Courtesy Alberta Agriculture)

Light fixtures such as pot lights need special boxes built over the fixture so that an effective seal can be maintained (see Fig. 11-27).

Polyethylene can be placed above electrical boxes and sealed to the vapor barrier to provide a continuous membrane. Metal fire stops around chimneys should be sealed at the ceiling level to impede the upward flow of heat and air-vapor (see Fig. 11-28).

Vent stacks can be sealed around the opening they pass through at the wall plate line (see Fig. 11-29).

FIGURE 11-27 Sealing around an electrical light.

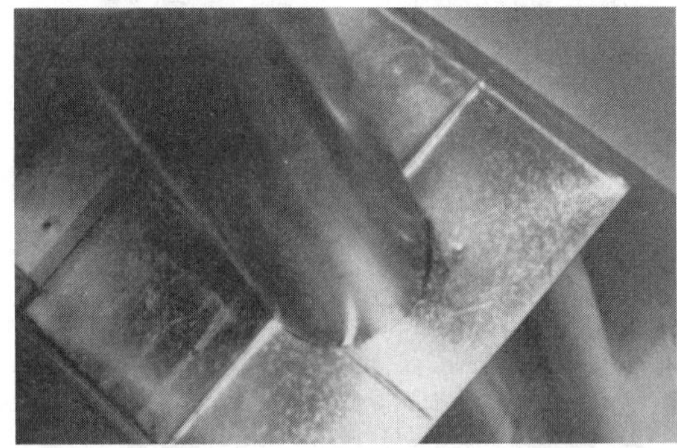

FIGURE 11-28 Fire stop around chimney.

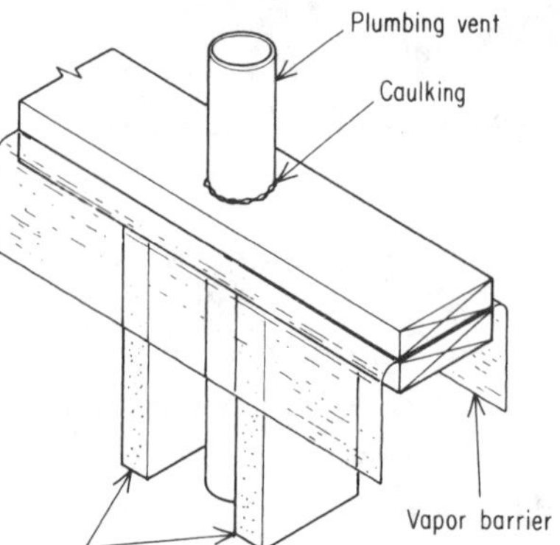

FIGURE 11-29 Sealing around vent stack.

Attic access probably provides the greatest loss of heat and vapor leakage. If the access cannot be eliminated from the ceiling, seal and insulate the hatch as illustrated in Fig. 11-30.

To provide a continuous seal over partitions, a piece of polyethylene is placed between the top plates and then sealed to the ceiling vapor barrier (see Fig. 11-31).

Attic ventilation can be maintained by installing insulation stops between the trusses above the plate line (see Fig. 11-32).

Ventilation can be provided in a sloped ceiling by using a wide truss with openings for ventilation (see Fig. 11-33).

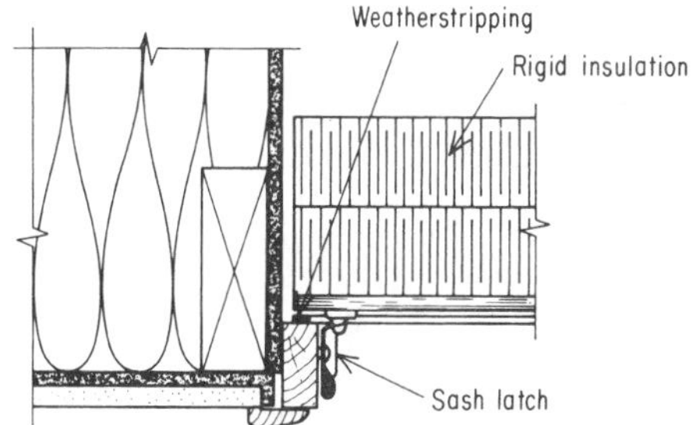

FIGURE 11-30 Sealing and insulating attic access.

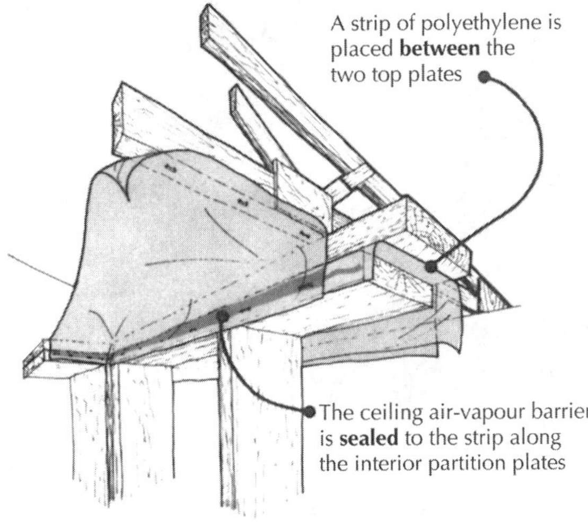

FIGURE 11-31 Seal over partition.
(Courtesy Alberta Agriculture)

FIGURE 11-32 Insulation stops.

FIGURE 11-33 Sloped truss ceiling.

PASSIVE SOLAR GAIN

A building designed for passive solar gain catches heat from the sun, stores it, and then releases it slowly to reduce energy costs. Passive systems are designed as part of the building; as such they have little cost and operate independently. Active systems, on the other hand, utilize collectors to collect and store energy and can be expensive to operate (see Fig. 11-34).

FIGURE 11-34 Solar collector panels.

Passive systems utilize south-facing windows and patio doors to collect energy. In northern climates, windows on the north side lose heat in the winter due to cold north winds, so these should be as small as possible, and large windows should face south. The opposite is recommended for southern climates.

On sunny days, rooms with a sunny exposure may become overheated while other areas are still cool. To maintain a more uniform temperature, the heat gained must be stored and released when the temperature drops. This heat gain can be stored in a large thermal mass such as concrete or masonry walls and floors or in a rock bin or water storage compartment (see Fig. 11-35).

Care must be taken that windows do not take up too much wall area, making temperature difficult to manage. Sunny spaces can be effective, as they are directly heated and will provide indirect heating (see Fig. 11-36). However, ventilation must be provided for these spaces so excess heat can be released in hot seasons.

The roof overhang of the building should be designed to allow full sun into the house during the cold season and provide shade during the hot season (see Fig. 11-37). An adjustable overhang is ideal. A large awning or movable overhang will do this quite effectively. Window shutters or shades can be used to prevent overheating during warmer weather (see Fig. 11-25).

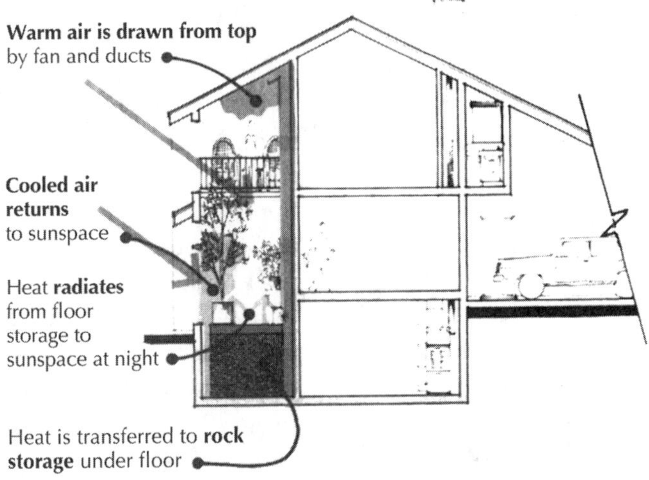

FIGURE 11-35 Passive heat storage.
(Courtesy Alberta Agriculture)

FIGURE 11-36 Sun space.

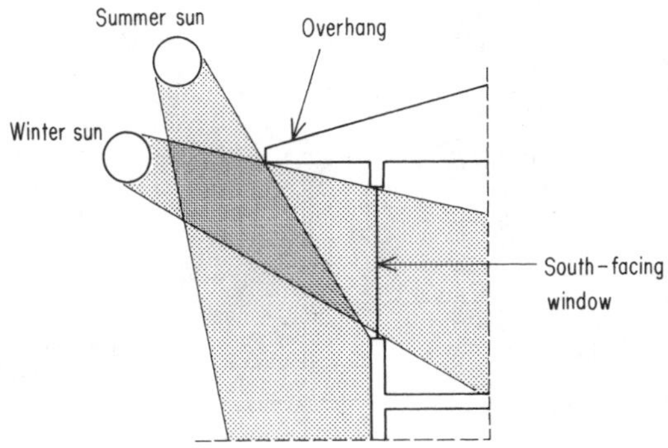

FIGURE 11-37 Use of overhang to regulate heat gain.

BUILDING EVALUATION

The special demand of cold climates, coupled with the growing requirement for energy efficiency, provides an opportunity to develop building enclosures appropriate to the environment. To do this we must assess the actual performance of existing buildings and develop a greater ability to predict the performance of new buildings.

All objects radiate energy to their surroundings. This infrared energy is a function of the objects' surface temperature and emissivity. The process of utilizing an infrared scanning system to produce a thermal image is called *thermography*. The technique of utilizing infrared scanning procedures on both new and existing buildings is a primary diagnostic tool for determining the thermal performance of a building envelope.

FIGURE 11-38 Infrared scanning equipment.

Thermography can identify surface temperature variations of the building that relate to problems in the structure. The surface temperature is also influenced by air-flow within or through the building envelope. Surface temperature irregularities can indicate defects in the structure such as insulation defects, thermal bridging, moisture content, or air leakage. Thermography can play an important role in identifying design, construction, and material problems as well as deterioration of components within the envelope. These defects can be detected throughout the structure, including roof, walls, and foundations.

The two primary mechanisms for heat loss in buildings are *conduction* and *air leakage*. Both can be detected from the surface of a building with an infrared scanning device, as illustrated in Fig. 11-38. Figure 11-39 illustrates an example of a picture of the scan showing the differences in temperature that are evident. Bright white color on the scan indicates higher temperature and level of heat loss. The flaring effect of the image usually indicates an area of air leakage.

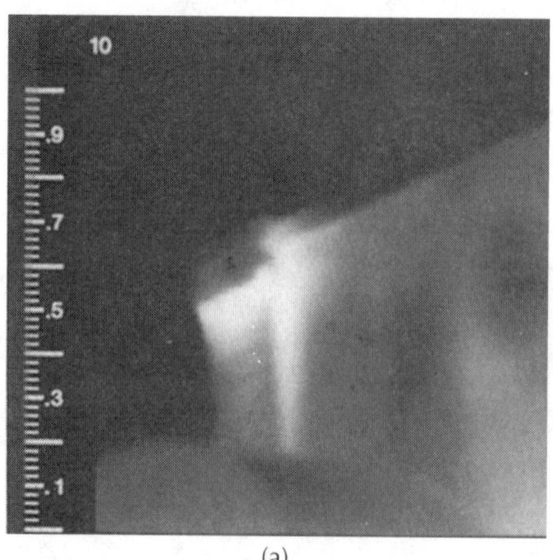

(a)

(b)

FIGURE 11-39 Thermal image.

Another method to determine air leakage is to have an air leakage test performed on the house to determine the integrity of the air barrier. The fan depressurization door illustrated in Fig. 11-40 can be used to determine the air leakage rate of houses. The target for some energy-efficient houses is 1.5 air changes per hour at a pressure difference of 0.00725 PSI (50 Pascals). This means that at a pressure of 0.00725 PSI (50 Pascals), a volume of air equivalent to 1.5 times the house volume will be drawn into the house every hour through leaks in the building envelope.

FIGURE 11-40 Fan depressurizing door.

REVIEW QUESTIONS

11–1. Why is it difficult to achieve an effective air-vapor barrier in typical single-stud wall construction?

11–2. Explain how an air-to-air heat exchanger works.

11–3. What should be done with spaces in walls and ceilings that are too small to insulate or to eliminate condensation associated with air leakage?

11–4. What problems can occur with buildings that are sealed so tight that air exchanges are minimal?

11–5. Why is it better to insulate concrete foundations on the outside as opposed to the inside?

11–6. What properties do acoustical sealants have that make them suitable for sealing air-vapor barriers?

11–7. How can the thermal bridges in a single-stud wall be eliminated?

11–8. What percentage of the insulation thickness must be outside the air-vapor barrier to achieve an effective barrier against moisture condensation?

11–9. Explain the principle of passive solar systems.

11–10. What building defects can an infrared scanning device detect?

11–11. What are the two primary mechanisms for heat loss in buildings?

GLOSSARY

TECHNICAL TERMS

Acoustical insulation: Insulation material that has the ability to reduce sound transmission.

Admixtures: A substance that is added to concrete or mortar to change the characteristics for a particular purpose.

Aerial platforms: Any type of scaffold that can be raised or lowered while occupied. Usually attached to a boom or scissor-like lifting equipment.

Aggregate: Granular materials such as gravel, crushed rock, or sand that are used in the making of concrete.

Air barrier: An element or assembly designed to provide a continuous barrier to the movement of air.

Air leakage: Air that escapes from an enclosure or penetrates a surface outside the enclosure.

Aligned: Brought into a straight line, as in placing masonry units.

Anchor bolts: Bolts that are embedded in concrete that are intended to tie a frame structure to the foundation.

Anchor straps: Metal straps that are embedded in concrete to tie a frame structure to the foundation.

Annular grooved nails: A type of nail that has been formed with rings around the stem for better holding power.

Annular rings: The growth layers of wood. One ring as shown on a cross section of a tree represents the amount of growth in one year.

Armored wires: Refers to electrical cables that have a metal covering.

Asphalt bitumen: Brown or black tar-like substance made by evaporating petroleum.

Asphalt shingles: Paper layers impregnated with asphalt and formed into various styles of shingles. The upper surface is coated with finely ground slate of various colors.

Attic: The area located immediately below the roof and above the ceiling of a building.

Awning window: A top-hinged window.

Backfilling: The process of replacing soil in an excavation, such as around a foundation.

Balloon frame: An older style of building in which the wall studs extend from a sill plate to the rafter plate. First floor joists are attached to the side of the studs and the second floor joists are supported on a ribbon that is notched into the stud faces.

Baluster shoe: A slotted member located at the bottom end of the balusters (sometimes called a shoe rail).

Balusters: The vertical spindles supporting a handrail.

Balustrade: Consists of a handrail supported on posts with balusters inserted between the handrail and the base such as a shoe.

Base trim: Often called baseboard, it is a type of trim used between a floor and a wall or other vertical surface.

Basement: A story below the first floor.

Batten: A narrow strip of wood placed over another surface such as over a joint between panels to hide it.

Batter board: A temporary framework consisting of posts driven into the ground with a horizontal member to which strings can be attached between opposite ones. Used to establish building lines and elevations.

Batts: Refers to pre-cut insulation blankets that are installed between framing members and held in place by friction.

Bay window: A type of window that extends beyond a wall consisting of three independent windows.

Beam: A horizontal structural member spanning between posts or walls that supports a load above it.

Beam pocket: A recess cast in a concrete foundation wall into which a beam will be placed.

Bearing posts: Posts that support elements above it such as a beam.

Bearing wall: A wall that supports itself as well as a load above it.

Bedding joints: Refers to the mortar joint on which a masonry unit is placed.

Beech: A type of hardwood that closely resembles birch or maple but is generally considered inferior to these species. It is used for flooring or furniture, but has a high shrinkage quality.

Benchmark: A particular known point of reference at which the exact level above sea is known. Locations of benchmarks are generally available from municipalities and are used for laying out a building and other services.

Birch: A type of hardwood with the sapwood having a yellowish color and the heartwood having a reddish color. It is used for flooring, cabinets, furniture, interior finishing, and trim, and is quite durable but not as strong as oak.

Birdsmouth: A notch made in a rafter where it rests on a plate, consisting of a plumb and level cuts.

Blade: It is the longer of the two sections on a framing square.

Blocking: The solid members placed between joists or studs to maintain their spacing and prevent excessive warping or deflection. A type of bridging.

Board: Lumber that is less than 2 in. (38 mm) thick with square edges.

Bond: To adhere or bind together, as with mortar bonding with masonry.

Box sill: A floor frame system where floor joists span between headers, all of which rest on a perimeter foundation and beams or bearing walls. The completed frame forms a "box" with four sides.

Boxed eave: The underside of the roof projection is enclosed with a soffit material.

Brick ties: Metal corrugated straps used to anchor a brick veneer wall to a structural wall such as wood or masonry.

Brick veneer: A nonstructural finish of bricks bonded together with mortar. Usually attached to a wood or masonry structure.

Built-up beam: A beam assembled from several pieces of lumber, usually $1\text{-}\frac{1}{2}$ inches (38 mm) thick. Three or more are placed side by side and are nailed or bolted together to form the beam.

Built-up stringer: A notched stair stringer (or blocking) used to support risers and treads attached to an un-notched stringer (sometimes called a semi-housed stringer).

Bullfloat: A large flat trowel attached to a long handle used to float or smooth the surface of fresh concrete.

Butt joints: Formed when the ends of two pieces are cut square and joined end to end, as in a built-up beam.

Buttered: Refers to the act of placing mortar on the ends of masonry units before positioning the unit.

By-pass door: A type of sliding door in which two or more doors are guided along top tracks, typically used for closets.

Cant strip: A piece of wood used to reinforce a joint such as between a stair riser and tread as seen on the underside. It may be rectangular or triangular in shape.

Cantilever: An extension beyond a support, as in cantilevered floor.

Cap flashing: Counter flashing.

Cap plate: The horizontal member attached to the top of the top plate.

Carpenter bracket: A triangular structure that can be attached to wall studs to support a narrow platform on which workers can perform various activities.

Carpet: A thick heavy fabric floor covering, usually made of wool or synthetic materials woven together.

Carport: A roofed structure usually open on all or some of the sides to provide weather protection for vehicles.

Casement window: A side-hinged window.

Casing: A type of trim used around an opening such as a door or window.

Cast-in joist system: Floor joists and header are embedded into the concrete foundation by casting the concrete around them. The floor members are placed on top of the forms before concrete is cast.

Cast-in-place: Refers to concrete that is placed in a form at a job site, where the concrete will remain in position (as opposed to pre-cast concrete).

Caulk: The process of applying flexible material to seal or waterproof a joint, such as around windows and doors. Caulking tubes are generally used.

Ceiling backing: Refers to framing material that is provided to attach ceiling finishes. When partitions run parallel to ceiling joists or trusses, ceiling backing must be attached to the partition.

Center match: Lumber machined with a groove along one edge and a tongue along the other edge.

Chamfer: The edge of material beveled at an angle of 45°.

Cheek cut: (see Side cut).

Chimney Saddle: A small gable roof framed on the upper slope of a roof where a chimney penetrates the roof. Its purpose is to shed water away from the chimney. Sometimes called a cricket.

Chord: The upper or lower member of a truss.

Clear span: A measurement taken from the face of one support to the face of another support.

Closed valley: Roof shingles are woven together to completely cover the valley flashing.

Cold air return: Consists of ductwork that leads directly to a furnace for the purpose of recirculating interior air. The exposed end is usually located in a partition and covered with a register.

Collar ties: Horizontal members spanning between opposite-sloped common rafters, above ceiling joists and below the ridge.

Combined slab and foundation: A monolithic concrete foundation consisting of a reinforced concrete slab with a thickened perimeter cast in such a way that the finished floor is at or slightly above the finished grade line.

Common boards: Lumber, usually $\frac{3}{4}$ in. (19 mm) thick with square edges.

Common rafter: A structural roof member that extends from a wall plate to the ridge at right angles to the wall, as seen in a plan view.

Compacted gravel: Granular material that has been consolidated using a mechanical compactor.

Compression web: A member located on a truss that transfers a load from the top chord to the bottom chord.

Concentrated loads: A load that is located at a specific point as opposed to spread out over a larger area or length. A bearing post positioned on a floor frame is an example.

Concrete block: A rectangular masonry unit made from concrete, usually pre-cast in a factory setting.

Conduction: Transmission of heat (or other forms of energy) through a substance.

Construction joint: A separation between sections of a concrete slab or wall that controls cracks due to shrinkage or other causes of differential movement. Commonly used where large sections of concrete are cast.

Continuous footings: Foundation footings that are monolithic and not separated in any way.

Control joints: A depressed line in a concrete slab to weaken the concrete at that point to minimize indiscriminate cracking due to shrinkage or settlement.

Coping a joint: The act of using a coping saw to shape a butt joint on an irregular surface, such as in base trim.

Corner post: The assembly of two or three studs to form a corner in a wall or partition frame. Also refers to a solid wood post located at a corner of a wall frame.

Cornice: Trim located at the junction of a roof and wall.

Corrugation: Any series of parallel folds, ridges, wrinkles, or furrows as in sheet metal roofing.

Counter battens: Narrow strips of wood placed at right angles to the surface to which they are attached, such as at right angles to the slope of a roof to which roofing tiles are attached.

Counterflashing: Flashing material placed over a base flashing such as around chimneys.

Crawl Space: The space between a floor and soil or concrete not used as a basement. May or may not contain storage or mechanical equipment.

Cribbing: Refers to wood, concrete, or steel that is driven into the ground before excavating to prevent soil sliding into the excavation (see Shoring).

Cricket: (see Saddle).

Cripple jack rafter: A shortened common rafter that extends from a valley rafter to a hip rafter.

Cripple stud: A short stud located between the sole plate and the underside of a rough sill in an opening, or from the top of a lintel to the underside of the top plate.

Cross bridging: Angled pieces that run from the top of one joist to the bottom of an adjacent joist, placed in opposite pairs (see Bridging).

Crown: Refers to the curved edge of a member. For example, if you sight lengthwise along the edge of a member the curved edge is called the crown, as in joists.

Curing: The process of hydration in concrete as it hardens.

Curved stair: A stair built along a curve.

Custom-built cabinets: Typically refers to cabinets that are designed to fit a particular location, as opposed to factory built.

Cylinder lock: A type of lock that is cylindrical in shape requiring a round hole to be drilled in a door surface for installation.

Damp-proofing: A material used to prevent the infiltration of moisture into another material, such as concrete. It may be a membrane or an asphalt substance.

Datum point: A temporary reference point used in laying out a building, including elevations, where the exact elevation is known as taken from a benchmark.

Dead load: Refers to the fixed or constant load of all the members. For a roof, it refers to the framing members and all finishes including roof coverings. For a floor, it refers to all framing and finishing members as well as all stationary fixtures.

Deformed rods: (see Reinforcing).

Depth of penetration: Refers to the average depth to which ground moisture will freeze in a particular area.

Diagonal bracing: Blocking or strapping that is notched into the edges of studs placed on an angle of about 45° to provide rigidity to a wall. Used if structural wall sheathing is not used.

Diffusion: The act of gases such as air-laden vapor being spread out or dispersed.

Divergent staples: Power-driven staples where the leg ends are shaped such that they go in opposite directions as they are driven.

Dormer: A relatively small intersecting roof with gable end that joins a roof slope and usually has a vertical window.

Double hung: Vertical sliding window where two sashes are used.

Double side cut: (Double cheek cut) The angle cuts as laid out on the top edge of a hip rafter that joins two common rafters.

Drywall: (Gyproc) Gypsum panels covered with a paper membrane used for interior (or exterior) covering of surfaces.

Ductwork: Sheet metal rectangular or round pipes used in heating and air conditioning systems.

Dutch hip roof: A type of gable roof where a relatively small section of the gable is framed with a hip roof.

Dwelling unit: Term used to mean suite operated as a housekeeping unit, such as a house, apartment, or condominium.

Eave protection: A membrane placed around the perimeter of a roof, particularly at the lower ends, to prevent rainwater seeping under the roof covering. It is particularly important in locations where ice can form along the lower roof surfaces.

Eave: Underside of the roof projection beyond the face of a wall.

Edge grain: Lumber cut such that the annular growth rings are between 45° and 90° to the surface as seen on the ends.

Effective depth: A measurement from the convergence of unit rise and unit run to the lower edge of the stringer.

Efflorescence: In masonry, it is a whitish powder formed on the surface.

End nail: Driving a nail through a plate or header into a joist or stud.

Entrained air: In concrete or mortar mixes a chemical is added to create tiny bubbles of air. Commonly used in concrete that is exposed to freezing and thawing to prevent the surface from flaking. It also makes the concrete more easily shaped into a form.

Expansion joints: A separation between independent concrete sections, such as between a foundation wall and a floor, to allow differential movement without undue stress on either.

Extrude: In masonry terms, means to have the mortar extend outward from the masonry units irregularly.

Face grain: Refers to fiber direction of the outermost layer of plywood veneer.

Feathered: A gradual thinning of a material, as along the edges of gyproc panels.

Fiberglass sheathing: Panels made from glass fibers bonded together with a resin and covered with an air-barrier membrane.

Fill: Material that is used to make full. For example, in foundation work fill refers to soil that is placed to take up a space or cavity on which a concrete floor is to be cast.

Finish fascia: The exposed horizontal member that is located at the ends of rafters or trusses and forms part of the eave.

Fixed window: An un-openable window.

Flashing: A material used to shed water to prevent it from penetrating behind an exterior finish on a roof or wall.

Flat grain: Lumber cut such that the annular growth rings are between 45° and parallel to the surface as seen on the ends.

Flat roof: A roof that is relatively flat, although most have a very little slope to drain rainwater.

Floating: The process of smoothing the surface of fresh concrete. This compresses the concrete by pressing the larger aggregate below the surface.

Floating floor: A system of interlocking strips of flooring that is unsecured to a sub-floor.

Flush beam: Means a beam supporting joists that butt into it and the lower surface is continuous. For example, when a ceiling finish is applied the beam is hidden.

Foam insulation: Insulation that is applied under pressure and expands as it dries.

Folding doors: A type of door in which two or more panels are hinged together (as in bi-fold doors), typically used for closets.

Footing plates: The term used for a preserved wood member that acts as a footing for a preserved wood foundation wall. Typically these plates are supported on granular fill.

Footing: That part of a foundation that is wide enough to distribute the weight (mass) of a structure over a wide area. Footings are typically found at the base of foundation walls, piers, or posts and are wider than the supported element.

Foundation: The element that rests on soil or rock to provide support to a structure.

Frame scaffolds: Tubular metal welded together to form a standard-sized frame, consisting of horizontal, vertical, and angular tubes to support a platform.

Furred out: A type of strapping used to create a space between a subsurface and a finish surface.

Gable: The triangular wall contained between a double-sloped roof, or in the case of a single-sloped roof, the triangular wall formed between the lowest point of the slope and the opposite wall supporting the highest point of the roof, sometimes called a gable end.

Gable roof: A roof that has a slope on two sides of a rectangular building.

Gable studs: Vertical structural members that extend from the cap plate to the underside of gable rafters.

Gambrel roof: A roof that has two different slopes on two sides only (sometimes called a "barn" roof).

Gliding windows: Windows that can be opened by a sliding action.

Grade: Refers to the surface of the soil around a building or part of a building. For example, the finished grade is the final surface of the soil around a building after all backfilling and topsoil has been placed.

Grade of lumber: A labeling system of identifying certain qualities in lumber that refers to the use to which it can be put. For example, No. 1, No. 2, Common, Clear, Construction, Utility.

Green concrete: Concrete that has not cured sufficiently to resist being damaged.

Gypsum board: A panel consisting of a gypsum core covered with a paper membrane. Used to cover interior walls and partitions or as an exterior sheathing if it has a waterproof surface.

Hand split shakes: Shakes formed from blocks of wood by driving a knife into the end of the block to cause it to split to form a shingle.

Handrail: The upper member of a balustrade, parallel to the line of flight. Handrails may also be supported against a wall rather than on a balustrade.

Hardboard: Material made from wood fibers and resin and compressed into a very dense, heavy panel.

Hardwood: A term to denote the wood from broad-leaved trees belonging to the botanical class *Angiosperms*.

Hatchway: An access, as in attic or crawl space access.

Header: A framing member placed at right angles to other members used to maintain their spacing and tie them all together. A header joist is the same size as the joists in a floor or ceiling frame and is located at their ends.

Headroom: The space between a floor and a ceiling that allows a person access without bumping their head. Codes generally prescribe the minimum allowed.

Headroom clearance: The vertical distance from the underside of a finished ceiling on the floor above the stair to the line of flight.

Hip rafter: Extends from a corner of a rectangular building to the ridge at an angle to common rafters. It sits on top of the wall plates and butts against two common rafters or the ridge board.

Hip roof: A roof that has a slope on all four sides of a rectangular building.

Hopper window: A bottom-hinged window.

House wrap: Plastic sheets used to enclose a structure on the exterior to prevent the infiltration of air.

Housed stair: A stairway that has walls on both sides (sometimes called a closed stair).

Housed stringer: Risers and treads are routed into dadoes on the surface of stair stringer to conceal their ends. Housed stringers also make use of wedges to tighten each riser and tread in the dadoes.

Hydration: The chemical reaction between cement and water that produces heat as a by-product.

Hydrostatic pressure: Refers to the ability of water to exert pressure on a structure, as it cannot be compressed. A high water table can exert pressure on a foundation.

Ice lenses: The formation of thin flakes of ice in soils due to cold temperatures. When there is an accumulation of ice lenses the effect causes the soil to expand in an upward or sideways direction.

Impermeable: Preventing the passage of water.

Independent slab-on-ground foundation: Consists of a perimeter foundation wall/footing that extends below the topsoil or frost level where required, and a reinforced concrete slab cast on granular fill at or slightly above the finished grade line.

Insulating sheathing: Sheathing material that has insulating qualities, such as Styrofoam. Another type is made with fibers saturated with asphalt and compressed together to form a panel.

Intermediate supports: Any supporting member found between end supports. For example, the studs or joists found between the ones to which the ends of panels are attached.

Intersecting roof: A roof formed when rooflines join one another at an angle. For example, an "L"-shaped building will have an intersecting roof.

Jack rafter: (Hip jack rafter) A shortened common rafter that extends from the wall plate to a hip rafter.

Jack stud: (see Trimmer).

Joint filler: A pasty material used to fill the joints between drywall panels.

Joist hanger: A u-shaped metal device that provides bearing support to a joist where the joist butts against another joist or beam. They are nailed to the supported joist as well as the supporting member.

Joist: A framing member, when a series are placed parallel to one another, is used to support floor, ceiling, or roof loads. Joists are supported on foundation walls, beams, or bearing walls.

Keying: The process of providing a way in which two components are joined together to prevent movement, such as between a footing and a foundation wall. For example, a keyway or groove is made in a footing before the concrete foundation is cast.

L stair: A stair that makes a 90° turn at a landing.

Ladder jack scaffold: A platform bracket that can be attached to a ladder. Requires at least two ladders and platform brackets with a plank spanning between them.

Laminate: To build up in several layers.

Laminated drywall: A process where two or more layers of drywall panels are applied to a surface using an adhesive to bond the panels together.

Laminations: Several pieces or the surfaces of large panels are placed face to face to form a thicker member.

Land developers: Businesses or organizations that prepare tracts of land for various land uses such as residential and related structures. Often the area is stripped of topsoil and then roads, sidewalks, and services such as electricity, water, and sewer are installed before parcels (lots) are sold to individuals or contractors.

Landing: A relatively small intermediary floor situated between main floor levels, such as a stair or entrance "landing."

Lateral loads: Pressure exerted in a sideways direction. For example, it is the resulting pressure of soil on a full basement foundation.

Layout: Refers to the marking of the location of wall studs, usually on the sole and top plates. Also applies to the marking of the location of joists on a header, beam, or bearing wall.

Lazy Susan: The name that refers to a type of circular shelving often used in corner cabinets.

Level cut: The angle cut on a rafter that is horizontal when the rafter is in position. A level cut is located at the birdsmouth and may be located at the tail of the rafter.

Leveling instruments: Equipment that is used in laying out a building that includes establishing elevations and location on a building site.

Line length of a rafter: The theoretical sloped length of a rafter from the center of the ridge to the outside face of the wall on which it is supported.

Line of flight: An imaginary line drawn along the outer extremities of the tread nosings.

Lintel: A structural horizontal member over a window or door that supports a load from above.

Lintel blocks: Specially formed concrete blocks that allow reinforced concrete to be cast into them to form a beam or lintel over a door or window.

Live load: Refers to the non-fixed or variable load. For a roof, it refers to the pressure of wind, rain, or snow. For a floor it includes all moveable fixtures and occupants.

Loadbearing partitions: Interior walls that support a load, such as another floor, ceiling, or roof.

Loam: The uppermost layer of soil that contains organic matter.

Local building authority: Refers to those people charged with the responsibility to issue building permits and do inspections for compliance to codes and regulations within a certain boundary, such as a municipality.

Lock case: The housing for a mortise lock.

Lookout ledger: A horizontal framing member located along an exterior wall level with a rough fascia to which lookouts are fastened.

Lookouts: Horizontal framing members fastened between the rough fascia and the lookout ledger to which soffit material is secured.

Loose-fill insulation: Insulation particles or beads that can be used in a horizontal, or near-horizontal position.

Low emissive coatings: A special transparent coating that can be applied to glass to reflect radiant heat.

Major ridge: The largest of two or more intersecting roof ridges.

Mansard roof: A roof with two different slopes on all four sides of a rectangular building. The upper slope is usually less steep than the lower slope, and the lower slope usually has dormers.

Maple: A type of hardwood that is a light creamy color with very little difference between sapwood and heartwood. It is a hard wood that wears well and is used for flooring, furniture, interior finishing, and trim.

Masonry: Brick, concrete block, stone, tile, slate, or similar materials that are bonded together with a cement mortar.

Mass-produced cabinets: Factory-built standard cabinet units of different sizes and styles.

Metal strap bracing: Narrow steel straps placed diagonally along the edges of wall studs to provide rigidity to a wall. Used when structural wall sheathing is not applied to a wall.

Millwork: Refers to a factory setting where a wide variety of products are manufactured, such as moldings, stairs and stair parts, cabinets, shelving, door units, and window units.

Minor ridge: A shorter ridge of an intersecting roof.

Monolithic: Solid, single, and uniform.

Mortar: Cement, sand, and water mixed for the purpose of bonding masonry units.

Mortise lock: A type of rectangular-shaped lock requiring a rectangular recess to be cut into the edge of a door for installation.

Mortise: A recess cut into wood such as to encase a mortise lock. Also refers to a type of wood to wood joint where one piece is shaped with a tongue that fits into a recess.

Mounting channels: The top or bottom metal member to which metal studs are attached. They are U-shaped.

Nail popping: The result of wood structural members shrinking and the nails used to secure panels, such as drywall being exposed.

Newel post: The vertical structural members that support a balustrade at each end, at turns, and at intermediate locations as needed.

Noncorrosive nails: Nails made from a material that will not rust, or nails with a protective coating to prevent rusting.

Non–loadbearing partitions: Interior walls that are positioned parallel to the joists above that do not carry any load other than themselves.

Nosing: The projection of a tread beyond the face of a riser.

Notched stringer: Each unit rise and unit run is cut out of the top edge of a stair stringer (sometimes called a cut-out stringer).

O.C.: On center.

Oak: A type of hardwood with open grain often used for flooring and for other uses such as cabinets, furniture, interior finishing, and trim. The most common type is Red Oak, which has a reddish-brown color and is hard and strong.

OHS: Occupational Health and Safety Act (Canadian).

Open eave: The underside of the roof sheathing and the rafters or truss ends are exposed.

Open stair: A stairway that does not have a wall on either side.

Open valley: Roof shingles are cut parallel to the valley to expose the valley flashing.

Organic felts: Fibers of organic origin bonded together with asphalt and formed into continuous sheets approximately 36 in. (1 m) wide and made into rolls.

OSB: (oriented strand board) A panel manufactured with strands or chips of wood arranged at right angles to one another.

OSHA: Occupational Safety and Health Act (United States of America).

Overhang: Refers to the roof extension outside the exterior walls.

Parging: A type of mortar made with mortar cement, sand, and water. Parging is typically found on the exposed face of a concrete or concrete block foundation.

Parquet flooring: Relatively short pieces of hardwood flooring pre-assembled in a herringbone design that is installed like ceramic tile.

Particleboard: Panels manufactured with small particles or chips of wood, bonded together with a resin through heat and pressure.

Partition junction: The position where a partition joins a wall or other partition.

Partitions: Interior walls. They may or may not support loads above them.

Passive solar gain: Utilizing the sun's energy to absorb heat for later distribution without the use of any mechanical means.

Paving stones: A type of precast concrete used for a sidewalk, patio, or driveway.

Perpendicular: At right angles.

Picture window: A relatively large unobstructed window.

Pier foundation: A column or large post of concrete or masonry used to support a structure.

Pilaster: A column incorporated into a wall to add strength to the wall.

Pivot brackets: Special floor-mounted bracket into which the pin located on the bottom of a folding door panel is inserted.

Plan view: Refers to looking down from above on a set of architectural plans for a structure. Sometimes called a "birds eye" view.

Plastic laminate: Refers to pressure-formed laminates of paper with the top surface having a pattern (or color) used for countertops.

Plate: A structural horizontal member found at either end of wall studs. It may also be called a sill or sill plate.

Plumb: Vertical as opposed to horizontal.

Plumb cut: The angle cut on a rafter that is vertical when the rafter is in position. Plumb cuts are located at the ridge, the birdsmouth, and the tail of a rafter.

Pocket door: A type of sliding door that is guided along a top track into a cavity in a wall or partition.

Porch: A roofed deck attached to a building (sometimes called veranda).

Post footing: (See Footing) A footing that supports a post often used to support a beam.

Posts and beams: In a floor frame, this refers to the use of one or more bearing posts supporting a beam or beams that in turn support floor joists. Post and beam framing refers to a framing system that uses posts supporting beams rather than bearing walls.

Pre-cast concrete: Refers to concrete that is cast in a factory setting and is moved to a construction site once the concrete has cured.

Preservative: A substance that will prevent or slow down the process of decay or the infiltration of various insects in wood.

Professional engineer: A recognized licensed and practicing professional who has been trained in engineering principles.

Pump jack scaffold: A type of climbing scaffold using a horizontal platform structure attached to a post of wood or metal. A jacking system raises or lowers the platform.

Purlin plate: A horizontal roof member located above the top edges of ceiling joists and supported on bearing walls. Purlin studs are supported on the purlin plate.

Purlin studs: Structural members located between purlin plate and purlin. They transfer roof loads to bearing supports.

Purlin: A horizontal roof member that is located on the underside of common rafters at a point between the ridge and the wall plate. Purlins help to distribute roof loads across several rafters.

PVC: (Polyvinyl chloride.) A type of plastic material formed into various shapes, such as window sash and frames, or plumbing pipes.

Quarter point: A location $\frac{1}{4}$ of a span between supports, such as in a beam.

Rafter table: Measurements that have been precalculated for rafters, such as line length, often included on the blade of framing squares.

Rafter tail: The lowest end of a rafter.

Rafter: A sloping structural member that extends from the cap plate of a wall to a ridge. It is the structural member of a roof frame.

Rake rafter: A common rafter located at the end of a gable projection and supported by the ridge board at the top and the rough fascia at the bottom. Lookouts may or may not be used for intermediate support.

Ready-mix: Concrete that has been dispatched from a central mixing plant and transported to a job site. Mixer trucks continue to mix the concrete until it has been discharged.

Register: A grilled fixture that is located at the ends of heat or air conditioning ducts to direct the flow of air.

Registered architect: A recognized licensed and practicing professional who has been trained in design work, particularly in relation to buildings, although there are many other specialists.

Reinforced concrete: Concrete in which reinforcing bars and/or steel mesh is enclosed to resist forces.

Reinforcing bar: A round steel bar that is deformed such that there are ridges along its length; used in concrete.

Renovation: To repair, replace, or make new. Commonly applies to an existing building in which changes are made.

Re-sawn shakes: Split shakes that are taper-sawn in half to form two shingles.

Resilient flooring: A flooring material that is elastic in nature.

Retempered: The mixing in of a small amount of water to a mortar mix to prolong its use.

Ridge: The highest horizontal line of a roof frame.

Ridge board: A horizontal roof member that joins rafters at their highest point (peak).

Rigid insulation: Insulation materials that are rigid as opposed to being flexible.

Rim joists: The joists that are located at the ends of a floor or ceiling and are parallel to the main joists.

Rise: A vertical measurement.

Riser: The vertical stair member between adjacent treads.

Roof cavity: (Attic) Any space located between ceiling joists and rafters, or that located between lower and upper truss members.

Roof decking: A type of roof sheathing that is much thicker, such as $1\frac{1}{2}$ in. (38 mm) or thicker. Roof decking is used to span greater distances than roof sheathing and is often left exposed on the underside that forms a ceiling finish.

Roof flashing: The material used to shed water to prevent it from penetrating under the roof covering.

Roof joist: A combination of roof framing member and ceiling framing member as one usually finds on flat roofs or a roof with a vaulted ceiling.

Roof load: The total load that is supported by a roof, such as the dead and live loads.

Roofing cement: An asphalt material used between layers of roofing felt.

Roofing tile: Individual shingle-like pieces of metal, concrete, or slate.

Rough buck: Frame that is placed in a concrete wall form or concrete block wall to create a cavity into which a window or door will be placed.

Rough fascia: Framing material fastened to the ends of rafters or trusses to form part of the eave.

Rough stairwell opening: The width and length of opening in the floor frame from framing member to framing member.

Run of a rafter: The horizontal distance a rafter covers.

Run: A horizontal measurement.

R-Value: A measurement used to identify thermal resistance.

Sash: A frame to hold a glass pane.

Scale drawings: Drawings (plans) that are proportionately smaller (or larger) than actual sizes. For example, building plans are drawn to a scale to represent a full-size building.

Screed: A horizontal guide used to aid in the leveling of fresh concrete. Sometimes refers to a concrete float or the process of leveling fresh concrete.

Sealant: A type of mastic that bonds to other materials to from a "seal" to prevent the infiltration of water, moisture, or air.

Segregation: Refers to larger particles being separated from smaller ones, as in concrete.

Semi-housed stair: A stairway that has a wall on one side.

Shake: A thick wood shingle.

Sheathing: The covering of a form, wall, or roof, usually in the form of a panel although boards are sometimes used.

Shed roof: A roof that slopes in one direction only.

Shoring: (see Cribbing) A temporary brace. In excavations, a temporary wall is erected to prevent the soil from sliding into the excavation.

Side cut: The angle cut on a jack rafter, hip rafter, or valley rafter as marked out on the top edge. For example, the angle cut on a jack rafter where it joins a hip rafter, or the angle cut on a hip rafter where it joins the ridge board. Also called a cheek cut.

Sidelights: Window sash located beside a door.

Sill gasket: A flexible, gap-filling material placed between a sill and concrete or concrete block to prevent the infiltration of air through the joint.

Sill: The bottom member of a door or window frame. Also refers to the horizontal member located on top of a foundation wall to which a floor frame or wall is attached and called a sill plate.

Single dwelling unit: Term used to mean a dwelling unit designed for one family.

Site investigation: The act of investigating all aspects of a proposed building site to determine any and all factors that could have an effect on the structure or might affect options for location and orientation.

Site plan: That part of a set of building plans that describes, in a top view, the location of a building on a site and all contributing factors that influence the building. Such things as property boundaries, setback measurements, building floor area, location of services, and surrounding elevations are commonly shown.

Slab-on-grade: Concrete surface foundation as opposed to a slab below grade.

Sliding door: Any door that is guided along a top track. One type is called a bypass door.

Slope of a roof: The inclination of a roof surface, usually expressed as a ratio of unit rise to unit run.

Soffit: Horizontal material located on the underside of eaves.

Soil investigation: The process of determining types and characteristics of soil found on a particular site for the purpose of determining how that soil might affect a building under various situations.

Soil stack: The vent pipe for plumbing fixtures that extends through the roof to vent gases to the outside.

Soil-bearing capacity: The ability of soil to support a load. This ability is dependent on the characteristics of the soil.

Sole plate: The horizontal member on which studs are supported.

Span: The horizontal distance between supports, as in joists, beams, or rafters.

Species: A distinct kind of plant (or animal) having certain distinguishing characteristics. Refers to a particular type of tree from which lumber is cut.

Spiral nails: A type of nail shaped by twisting the stem for better holding power.

Spiral stair: A curved stair where the treads rotate around a center post (or point).

Split-level entrance: The entrance to a building that is located vertically between the first floor and the basement. Usually includes an entrance landing with stairs leading up and down.

Spreaders: Wood or metal pieces placed between concrete forms to maintain a uniform thickness for a foundation wall.

Stair gauges: Small clamps that attach to a framing square to assist in the laying out of stair unit rise and unit run, or for laying out rafter angles.

Stairwell opening: The framing in a floor frame to allow the installation of a stair.

Station: Refers to a specific point at which a leveling instrument is set up.

Step flashing: Relatively short flashing material bent at right angles, located between a vertical surface and a roof to shed water. Each piece of flashing is installed to overlap the lower flashing similar to shingles.

Stepped footings: Footings that are cast with sections at different elevations to accommodate a sloping site or where there are different elevations in the foundation. They look like a stair.

Storey: That portion of a building that is situated between the top of any floor and the top of the floor, or ceiling, next above it.

Straight flight stair: A stair that rises from one floor to another without any landing or change in direction.

Strapping: (Furring) Spaced narrow strips of wood used as a nailing base for another material. Often used to form a flat surface over an irregular surface, or to form an air space between materials. Also refers to horizontal wood strip secured to the underside of joists to maintain spacing and restrain warping.

Stressed skin panel: A panel consisting of an upper and lower panel separated with an inner framework all glued together for rigidity. Insulation is usually included on the inside of the panel.

Stringer: The inclined structural member that supports the risers and treads of a stair (sometimes called a carriage or string).

Strongbacks: Vertical structural members placed on the outside of walers to provide additional support to a concrete form.

Stub joists: Short ceiling joists that typically are placed at right angles to the main joists, as required in hip roofs.

Stucco: A fine plaster-like material made with a fine sand, cement, and water to be applied to a surface as a finish.

Subfloor: The flooring material placed directly over floor joists over which the finished flooring will be placed.

Sump: A round or rectangular pit into which unwanted water is drained and then pumped out using a sump pump. They are common in areas where there is a high water table or in most preserved wood foundations that contain a basement.

Supported joist length: A term used to determine the load that will be imposed on a wall or beam. For example, it refers to half the joist span on either side of a beam.

Surface foundation: A foundation placed on the surface of the surrounding soil, extending to a point below the topsoil or the lowest penetration of frost. They usually contain a crawl space.

Suspended wood floor: A type of basement floor used in preserved wood foundations where the floor frame is supported on short bearing walls that are in turn supported on granular fill.

System scaffolds: Manufactured metal tubes with regularly spaced anchor points to which horizontal and angular tubes can be attached to form a structure that supports a platform.

Tail joists: Joists that span between a floor or ceiling opening header joist and a support, parallel to the main joists.

Tail length: Refers to the theoretical sloped length of a rafter tail that forms the overhang.

Taper split shakes: Hand split shakes that are split in such a way to produce a shingle that is thinner at one end.

Tension web: A member located on a truss that transfers a load from the bottom chord to the top chord (opposite to compression).

T-Footing: A continuous footing on which a raised center portion has been cast to support a framed bearing wall. The footing looks like an inverted "T."

Thermal resistance: Ability to resist the conductance of heat through a substance, measured in "R" units (RSI units).

Thermography: A process using infrared scanning instruments to reveal temperature variations around the exterior of a building to detect energy loss.

Ties: As in concrete ties—metal rods of various shapes and sizes used between an inner and outer concrete form to maintain their position during the placing of concrete.

Toenailing: Driving nails at an angle near the end of one member that is to be joined to another right-angle member, as opposed to end nailing. For example, studs can be toenailed to a plate.

Tongue: It is the shorter of the two sections on a framing square.

Tooled: Refers to the use of a metal jointing tool used to compress and shape a mortar joint.

Top plate: The horizontal member attached to the top of studs.

Total length of a rafter: A combination of line length and tail line length.

Total rise: The sum of all unit rises, which is also the vertical distance between finished floor to finished floor.

Total rise of a rafter: The vertical distance a rafter rises above the wall plate on which it rests.

Total run: The sum of all the unit runs.

Tread: The horizontal stair member on which you place your foot.

Treated: Coating placed on a material to prevent decay or corrosion.

Trimmed: The process of fitting an element by sawing, planning, or both.

Trimmer joists: Joists that run parallel to main joists and are located on either side of an opening, such as a stairway opening in a floor frame. They are usually doubled.

Trimmer stud: A stud located on either side of an opening and extending from the sole plate to the under side of the lintel or header. It is attached to a full-length stud. Its purpose is to transfer loads imposed on the lintel directly to the sole plate.

Troweling: The process of using a hand or machine trowel to produce a very smooth surface to partially set concrete.

Truss: A manufactured structural unit consisting of upper and lower members joined with angled members forming triangles. A truss utilizes a minimum amount of material while allowing long unsupported spans.

Truss joist: A prefabricated joist consisting of an upper and lower member joined together with a plywood, OSB, or waferboard web. Truss joists allow long unsupported spans and are not subject to warpage.

Tube and coupler scaffolds: A system of independent metal tubes that are attached using couplers or clamps to form a structure that supports a platform.

Unarmored wires: Refers to electrical cables with a flexible plastic or vinyl covering.

Underlayment: A smooth-surfaced panel product used under a finished flooring material. Also refers to felt sheets in a roll saturated with asphalt and placed on top of the roof sheathing before installing shingles or shakes.

Undisturbed soil: Soil as it appears in its natural state, as opposed to disturbed soil.

Unit line length: A diagonal measurement between the unit rise and unit run of a rafter.

Unit rise: A unit of vertical distance a rafter covers as a ratio to the unit run. Also refers to the height of a riser in a stair as determined by dividing the total rise of a stair by the number of risers.

Unit run: Refers to a unit of horizontal distance a rafter covers, usually based on 12 in. (300 mm). Also refers to a single stair tread width, excluding a nosing.

U-stair: A stair that makes a 180° turn by way of a landing.

Valley jack rafter: A shortened common rafter that extends from a valley rafter to the ridge.

Valley rafter: Located at the intersection of roofs that forms a valley. For example, a valley rafter extends from the junction of two walls to the ridge and is parallel to a hip rafter.

Vapor barrier pan: A manufactured three-sided box in which to install an electrical device to minimize the passage of air or vapor.

Vapor barrier: An element that controls the diffusion of water vapor.

Waferboard: Panels manufactured with thin chips of wood and bonded together with a waterproof resin through heat and pressure. Also see OSB.

Walers: Horizontal structural member used to brace or distribute a load, such as along the outside of wood studs on a concrete form. Also called a whaler.

Wall backing: Blocks placed between studs to provide an anchor point for such things as plumbing fixtures, electrical fixtures, or drapery rods. Sometimes ribbons are notched into the edges of studs for this purpose.

Wall jack: A type of jacking clamp that is attached to wood members to assist in lifting a framed wall into a vertical position.

Water retentivety: The ability of a material, such as mortar or stucco, to retain water as opposed to water "bleeding" out of the material.

Water/cement ratios: The amount of water mixed with a specific unit of cement. The strength of concrete is greatly controlled by this ratio.

Waterproofing: A material or process of preventing water under hydrostatic pressure from penetrating a material, such as concrete or wood foundations.

Web: The member(s) in a truss that join an upper and lower member.

Weep holes: Passages between masonry units such as brick to allow any accumulation of moisture behind the units to drain to the outside.

Wind blocks: Framing material placed between rafters or trusses at the junction with an exterior wall to protect insulation from being disturbed due to wind action.

Winder stair: Consists of wedge-shaped treads that converge to a center point used to change the direction of a stair flight.

Windowpanes: Glass panel held in a sash.

Wood sleeper floor: A type of basement floor used in preserved wood foundations where the wood floor frame is supported on parallel strips of treated wood resting on a granular fill.

Workability: Refers to concrete, mortar, or stucco where the mixture has a consistency conducive to being formed or shaped, or will readily adhere to a surface.

Wythe: Stacking masonry units in a single wall, as in brick veneer.

Zoning laws: Regulations passed by municipalities regulating what can and cannot be done in a particular area. In residential construction some zoning restrictions might apply to minimum or maximum floor area, height, setback from property lines, and type of occupancy to name but a few examples.

INDEX

R

S